Jörg Maler's Kunstbuch

Writings of the Pilgram Marpeck Circle

Das Kunstbüch bin ich genant · d' fleyschlichen welt unbekant,
wer aber den geist christi hat, der sucht darinnen frue und spat,
was sein hertz und gmüet thut fergen, bis got allain kombt zu ehren,
es ist weit über silber und gold, darum sammle dir sie von hertzen
hold, vil götlich geheimnüst send darinn, welcher es erlangt
der hertz müth und sinn, darum laß dies sein dein
hertzen liebt, in gotesforcht dich allzeit üb, was du
nit kanst vernemen, bit got das er dies geb zu erkennen,
vor gähem urtel dich wol hüt, das geb uns got durch
seine güeth, durch Jesum Christum seinen Sun, der
helff uns zum sein genaden. Amen

Geschriben und geendet, den sechsundzwaintzigsten
Septembris, im ains und sechtzigisten jar, nach
dem hab ich es tragen lassen, wo es dann hingehör
et hat, got verleich uns allen sein genad. Amen

Jörg vom Augspurg
[illegible] · den man nennth Maler · [illegible]

Nalm sein mit dir und gmach. so
schreib verantwort mit all sach, [illegible] und [illegible]
[illegible], dem obern · [illegible] hüt dich vor, [illegible]
· [illegible] ·

Jörg Maler's Kunstbuch

Writings of the Pilgram Marpeck Circle

Edited by John D. Rempel

PLOUGH PUBLISHING HOUSE

Published by Plough Publishing House
Walden, New York
Robertsbridge, England
Elsmore, Australia
www.plough.com

Plough produces books, a quarterly magazine, and Plough.com to encourage people and help them put their faith into action. We believe Jesus can transform the world and that his teachings and example apply to all aspects of life. At the same time, we seek common ground with all people regardless of their creed.

Plough is the publishing house of the Bruderhof, an international community of families and singles seeking to follow Jesus together. Members of the Bruderhof are committed to a way of radical discipleship in the spirit of the Sermon on the Mount. Inspired by the first church in Jerusalem (Acts 2 and 4), they renounce private property and share everything in common in a life of nonviolence, justice, and service to neighbors near and far. To learn more about the Bruderhof's faith, history, and daily life, see Bruderhof.com. (Views expressed by Plough authors are their own and do not necessarily reflect the position of the Bruderhof.)

ISBN: 978-0-874-86279-9

Map: Area and Places of Marpeck's Life and Work, by Kerry Jean Handel, reprinted from Klaassen, Walter, and William Klassen, *Marpeck: A Life of Dissent and Conformity* (Herald Press, 2008). Used with permission.

Library of Congress Cataloging-in-Publication Data

Names: Rempel, John D., editor. | Maler, Jorg, compiler. | Marpeck, Pilgram, approximately 1495-1556.
Title: Jorg Maler's Kunstbuch : writings of the Pilgram Marpeck Circle / edited by John D. Rempel.
Other titles: Briefe und Schriften oberdeutscher Taufer, 1527-1555. English.
Description: Walden, New York : Plough Publishing House, 2019. | Series:
Classics of the radical Reformation ; 12 | Translation of the "Kunstbuch" (Burgerbibliothek Bern cod. 464), a ms. compilation made in 1561 by Jorg Maler of several writings by the Anabaptist leader Pilgram Marpeck and his followers. Based on the critical ed. of the ms. published as: Briefe und Schriften oberdeutscher Taufer, 1527-1555 ([Gutersloh] : Gutersloher Verlagshaus, c2007). | Includes bibliographical references and index. | Summary: "Writings compiled in the sixteenth century provide a glimpse into the spiritual life of one fellowship during the Radical Reformation"-- Provided by publisher.
Identifiers: LCCN 2019044933 (print) | LCCN 2019044934 (ebook) | ISBN 9780874862799 (paperback) | ISBN 9780874862805 (ebook)
Subjects: LCSH: Anabaptists--Germany--History--16th century--Sources. | Anabaptists--Doctrines--Early works to 1800. | Theology, Doctrinal--Early works to 1800. | Church and state--Germany--History--16th century--Sources. |
Reformation--Germany--Sources. | Germany--Church history--16th century--Sources. | Maler, Jorg. | Marpeck, Pilgram, approximately 1495-1556.
Classification: LCC BX4933.G3 B7313 2019 (print) | LCC BX4933.G3 (ebook) | DDC 284/.3--dc23
LC record available at https://lccn.loc.gov/2019044933
LC ebook record available at https://lccn.loc.gov/2019044934

Dedication

To my brother Henry Rempel, voice of justice for ordinary people
and my sister Rita Brown, source of hospitality and companionship

Classics of the Radical Reformation

Classics of the Radical Reformation is an English-language series of Anabaptist and Free Church documents translated and annotated under the direction of the Institute of Mennonite Studies, which is the research agency of the Anabaptist Mennonite Biblical Seminaries, and published by Plough Publishing House.

1. *The Legacy of Michael Sattler.* Trans., ed. John Howard Yoder.
2. *The Writings of Pilgram Marpeck.* Trans., ed. William Klassen and Walter Klaassen.
3. *Anabaptism in Outline: Selected Primary Sources.* Trans., ed. Walter Klaassen.
4. *The Sources of Swiss Anabaptism: The Grebel Letters and Related Documents.* Ed. Leland Harder.
5. *Balthasar Hubmaier: Theologian of Anabaptism.* Ed. H. Wayne Pipkin and John Howard Yoder.
6. *The Writings of Dirk Philips.* Ed. Cornelius J. Dyck, William E. Keeney, and Alvin J. Beachy.
7. *The Anabaptist Writings of David Joris: 1535–1543.* Ed. Gary K. Waite.
8. *The Essential Carlstadt: Fifteen Tracts by Andreas Bodenstein.* Trans., ed. E. J. Furcha.
9. *Peter Riedemann's Hutterite Confession of Faith.* Ed. John J. Friesen.
10. Sources of South German/Austrian Anabaptism. Ed. C. Arnold Snyder, trans. Walter Klaassen, Frank Friesen, and Werner O. Packull.
11. *Confessions of Faith in the Anabaptist Tradition: 1527–1660.* Ed. Karl Koop.
12. *Jörg Maler's Kunstbuch: Writings of the Pilgram Marpeck Circle.* Ed. John D. Rempel.
13. *Later Writings of the Swiss Anabaptists: 1529–1592.* Ed. C. Arnold Snyder.

Table of contents

Table of contents

Series preface

The modern publication of sixteenth-century Anabaptist source documents has been under way since the beginning of the twentieth century. Scholars working with German-language texts, both treatises and court records, continue to publish meticulously annotated editions of seminal texts from the Radical Reformation. Most of these have appeared in the series *Quellen und Forschungen zur Reformationsgeschichte* and its sub-series *Quellen zur Geschichte der Täufer.* Early in the twentieth century (*Bibliotheca Reformatoria Neerlandica)* and again more recently (*Commissie tot de Uitgave van de Documenta Anabaptistica Neerlandica)*, the similarly impressive publication of Dutch-language sources has gained momentum.

The series Classics of the Radical Reformation (CRR) was inaugurated to make major selections from this literature, in and beyond the above series, available in translation with interpretive introductions for a broad English-language readership.

Jörg Maler's Kunstbuch: Writings of the Pilgram Marpeck Circle is the twelfth volume in the CRR series. Its distinction is that it gathers together a broad range of writings that could be called the core library of the farflung Marpeckite congregations across German-speaking Europe. In reading it we encounter theological and spiritual currents that gave sustenance and unity to these scattered communities. The diversity of its contents strikes the reader immediately. Of course Pilgram Marpeck, Leupold Scharnschlager, and their fellow ministers figure prominently in this anthology. But so does the editor, Maler, until now a shadowy figure in Anabaptist historiography. Anabaptists from other streams of the movement as well as figures from the Reformation at large also have a place in this collection. It portrays one Anabaptist approach to the elusive goal of theological and communal unity in which patience and tolerance were also seen as part of the Holy Spirit's work.

The publication of *Jörg Maler's Kunstbuch: Writings of the Pilgram Marpeck Circle* follows volume eleven, *Confessions of Faith in the Anabaptist Tradition,* by three years. We hope that another volume of primary sources will be forthcoming within a similar length of time.

On the occasion of his retirement as general editor of Herald Press, a word of gratitude to Levi Miller is in order. Throughout his tenure Miller has been a consistent proponent of Herald Press's publishing of academic works in Anabaptist history and theology, and of CRR volumes in particular. When it seemed wise to all parties to co-publish the series with Pandora Press, with distribution by Herald Press, Miller helped to put that arrangement on a stable footing.

I am thankful for the shared vision among the staff of the Institute of Mennonite Studies that makes possible the ongoing publication of Mennonite-related research, including Classics of the Radical Reformation. For the fruitful partnership IMS has with its co-publishers, all of us are grateful.

John D. Rempel, Editor, Classics of the Radical Reformation
Institute of Mennonite Studies, Elkhart, Indiana

Editor's preface

Scholars have been fascinated by Pilgram Marpeck and his circle since the rediscovery of the long-lost legacy of their writings, and that interest has not abated. This volume offers another part of that legacy to English-speaking readers, not only scholars, but also inquiring general readers who might find theological insight and spiritual depth in the conviction and diversity of the authors who make up this anthology. It is a remarkable amalgam of pastoral letters, meditations, tracts, and poems.

Awareness of the distinctive significance of Marpeckian Anabaptism did not extend beyond specialists in North America until Marpeck's ideas began to appear in English. J. C. Wenger translated short pieces of Marpeck texts that appeared in the *Mennonite Quarterly Review* in the late 1930s. But it was William Klassen's 1968 doctoral dissertation, *Covenant and Community: The Life and Writings of Pilgram Marpeck*, that set the course of Marpeck studies on this continent. A decade later William Klassen and Walter Klaassen translated core texts by Marpeck, including his letters in the Kunstbuch, in the *Writings of Pilgram Marpeck* (1978). This splendid collection first made the study of the primary texts possible for English speakers. Klassen and Klaassen's comprehensive biography, *Marpeck: A Life of Dissent and Conformity* (2008), will be the door into Marpeck studies for the next generation.

Jörg Maler's manuscript of the Kunstbuch has been in the Burgerbibliothek in Bern, Switzerland, for about three centuries. I am grateful to Patrick Andritt, curator, for providing access to the manuscript as well as for sending a high quality copy of its title page (which serves as the frontispiece for this English edition). This translation of the Kunstbuch is based on the critical German edition of the original text, the 2007 *Briefe und Schriften oberdeutscher Täufer 1527–1555: Das "Kunstbuch" des Jörg Probst Rotenfelder gen. Maler,* edited by Heinold Fast, an independent scholar and Mennonite minister in Emden, Germany. It was Fast who first brought the manuscript to the attention of the scholarly world. Martin Rothkegel, a historian of sixteenth-century radical reform movements in Moravia, and assistant professor of church history at the Baptist seminary in Elstal near Berlin, completed the task that ill health had compelled Fast to lay down. Rothkegel worked in consultation with Gottfried Seebaß, chair of the series *Quellen und Forschungen zur Reformationsgeschichte.* The Kunstbuch was published as volume 17 in its subseries *Quellen zur Geschichte der Täufer.* The annotated edition pays meticulous attention to all the aspects of concern to scholarship, among them literary and social context, textual variations, linguistic archaisms, implicit scripture references. Without their enormous achievement in bringing the original manuscript to life and comprehension, an English translation would have remained out of reach.

Both the scholarly achievement of the modern critical edition and the translation project fired the imagination of the Institute of Mennonite Studies, especially the Reference Council of IMS's Classics of the Radical Reformation. That group quickly arrived at agreement to publish an English translation of the Kunstbuch. Since the modern critical German edition would be the authoritative text for scholars, it was agreed that the English translation should be carried out in a format that would bring these letters to a less specialized readership. The translation was to be faithful to the original text, of course. But, given the complexity of German syntax, it was to be a dynamic equivalent rather than a strictly literal rendering. We were confident that the Kunstbuch merited the attention of church leaders, students, those seeking guidance on the spiritual path, and those looking for another kind of Anabaptist model for the church's relationship to society.

The goal of accessability led to two decisions. One was that there should be a carefully but significantly reduced critical apparatus. The other decision was that the commentaries on the individual pieces and the volume as a whole should highlight their pastoral and spiritual, as well as historical, relevance. For the sake of its intended audience, the English version should supply theological comments on the major themes of each document and offer concise explanations of European historical and geographic references unfamiliar to people from other continents.

To the Anglophone ear the long lists of nouns and verbs and the Germanic word order found in these writings are hard to follow. This linguistic difference is a challenge to translator and editor alike. How much do we translate verbatim in order to remain faithful to text and context? How much do we edit to make the text (and perhaps even the context) come alive for readers in another language and culture?

It is the task of a translator to concentrate on exact equivalents in concepts and turns of phrase. It is the task of an editor to make a piece of literature come alive in another time and tongue. My maxim was: the translator's chief responsibility is to the author, while the editor's chief responsibility is to the audience. I tried to honour both callings as I edited the translations I received. My heartfelt thanks go to the translators—C. J. Dyck, Leonard Gross, Linda Huebert Hecht, Daniel Liechty, Walter Klaassen, William Klassen, Gerhard Reimer, John D. Roth, C. Arnold Snyder, Jonathan Seiling, and Victor Thiessen—for their labour of love, for their high level of competence (sometimes under the pressure of deadlines), and for the affection they lavished on the words and thoughts they conveyed into another language. I am grateful for a research grant from William Klassen and Walter Klaassen that allowed Victor Thiessen to devote himself to translating several of the most challenging texts. Late in the process, when there seemed to be no acceptable way of accommodating all the original and modern annotations in a readable text, a generous grant from William Klassen and Dona Harvey allowed us to hire Andrea Dalton to undertake that arduous and exacting task. In consultation with Barbara Nelson Gingerich, Dalton devoted her scholarly and technical skills not only to the accurate placement of annotations but to the indices and the refinement of other details of the manuscript. My thanks also to Jonathan Gingerich for his careful work in completing the scripture index, and to Sarah Thompson and Jonny Gerig Meyer for their heroic efforts in proofreading the indices under pressure of a deadline.

In addition to the translators there have been other significant partners in this project. Let me begin by thanking the Reference Council of the Institute of Mennonite Studies series, Classics of the Radical Reformation—Karl Koop, Gerald Mast, John D. Roth, and C. Arnold Snyder—for helping me arrive at an adequate conceptual framework for the unusual challenge of translating a sixteenth-century collection of forty-two texts by a dozen authors for a scholarly as well as a general audience. They have counselled and encouraged me at each step of the way. In addition, John Roth has been a patient conversation partner on a number of puzzling issues arising from my research. I am equally grateful to the Institute of Mennonite Studies at Associated Mennonite Biblical Seminary, in the persons of director Mary H. Schertz and managing editor Barbara Nelson Gingerich, for sustained moral and financial support. With the encouragement of Marlin Jeschke I applied for and received a generous research grant from the Mennonite Historical Society. It allowed me to take my sabbatical in Germany, where I had access to specialized libraries and the counsel of specialists in the field. During my sabbatical I lived with long-time friends, Goetz and Katharina Doyé in Bergholtz, near Berlin. They offered me not only space and seclusion but also conversation and companionship that sustained me in my toil. In Hamburg I benefited from many hours of probing conversation with Hans-Jürgen Goertz and Martin Rothkegel about the significance of the Kunstbuch and the ephemeral Marpeck Circle. Their insights and academic camaraderie gave my work a depth it would not otherwise have achieved.

I have three debts to pay to colleagues who helped create the book. The first one I owe to Barbara Nelson Gingerich for the wisdom, competence, and steadiness with which she prepared the texts for publication. The second debt I owe to James Nelson Gingerich for undertaking the formatting process from start to finish with an aesthetic sensibility that both pleases the modern eye and conveys original illustrations in elegantly stylized form. The third debt I owe to Brent Graber, our director of information technology. He kept his patience and good cheer on a thousand different occasions when computer problems stumped me.

Andy Alexis-Baker freely offered his skill in solving stylistic, formatting, and other computer problems at a time when I had almost given up on the project.

Finally, I am indebted to Jonathan Seiling for his insightful critique of the introduction to this volume. My thanks go to Jan Gleysteen for his kind permission to reproduce the historic photos in this volume. I am grateful to Elinor Neufeld and Hedy Rempel for volunteer work in incorporating documentation of scripture references. I applaud Pandora Press for its commitment to scholarly and popular publication of all things Anabaptist, and I am grateful for the flexible and cooperative spirit of Christian Snyder, publisher.

The writings of the Kunstbuch are both a handbook and a cautionary tale. They are a handbook for radical Christians in search of models for being in but not of the world. At the same time these writings are a cautionary tale about the vulnerability and precariousness of such a stance.

John D. Rempel

List of Illustrations

List of abbreviations

AB — Armour, Rollin Stely. *Anabaptist Baptism: A Representative Study.* Studies in Anabaptist and Mennonite history, no. 11. Scottdale, PA: Herald Press, 1966.

AD — Rott, Jean-Georges, and Simon Leendert Verheus, eds. *Anabaptistes et dissidents au XVIe siècle: actes du Colloque international d'histoire anabaptiste du XVIe siècle tenu à l'occasion de la XIe Conférence Mennonite mondiale à Strasbourg, Juillet 1984.* Bibliotheca dissidentium; Scripta et studia, no. 3. Baden-Baden : Éditions Valentin Koerner, 1987.

ARG — *Archiv für Reformationsgeschichte*

BCSB — Snyder, C. Arnold, ed.; Gilbert Fast and Galen A. Peters, trans; *Biblical Concordance of the Swiss Brethren, 1540.* Kitchener, ON: Pandora Press, 2001.

BD — Séguenny, André, ed. *Bibliotheca dissidentium: répertoire des non-conformistes religieux des seizième et dix-septième siècles.* Bibliotheca bibliographica Aureliana Baden-Baden: Éditions Valentin Koerner, 1980.

BH — Pipkin, H. Wayne, and John H. Yoder, trans. and ed., *Balthasar Hubmaier: Theologian of Anabaptism.* Classics of the Radical

Reformation, vol. 5. Kitchener, ON, and Scottdale, PA: Herald Press, 1989.

Bern MS Heinold Fast. Transcription and commentary on Das "Kunstbuch" des Jörg Probst Rotenfelder gen. Maler (Burgerbibliothek Bern, Cod. 464). Unpublished manuscript. Electronic copy sent by Fast to John Rempel, 1998.

BSOT Fast, Heinold, and Martin Rothkegel, comp. *Briefe und Schriften Oberdeutscher Täufer 1527–1555: Das "Kunstbuch" des Jörg Probst Rotenfelder gen. Maler (Burgerbibliothek Bern, Cod. 464).* Quellen zur Geschichte der Täufer, vol. 17. Edited by Heinold Fast and Gottfried Seebaß. Gütersloh: Gütersloher Verlagshaus, 2007.

CC Klassen, William. *Covenant and Community: The Life, Writings, and Hermeneutics of Pilgram Marpeck.* Grand Rapids: Eerdmans, 1968.

EAS Liechty, Daniel. *Early Anabaptist Spirituality.* Mahwah, NJ: Paulist Press, 1994.

GOT Müller, Lydia, ed. *Glaubenszeugnisse oberdeutscher Taufgesinnter.* Quellen und Forschungen zur Reformationsgeschichte, vol. 20. Gütersloher Verlagshaus: G. Mohn. Reprinted New York: Johnson Reprint, 1971.

HB Packull, Werner O. *Hutterite Beginnings*: Communitarian Experiments during the Reformation. Baltimore: Johns Hopkins University Press, 1995.

KB Kunstbuch

LWPM Klaassen, Walter, Werner O. Packull, and John D. Rempel, trans. *Later Writings by Pilgram Marpeck and His Circle.* Kitchener, ON: Pandora Press, 1999.

ME *The Mennonite Encyclopedia,* 5 vols. Scottdale, PA: Mennonite Publishing House, 1955–1959, 1990. This material is available in the Global Anabaptist Mennonite Encyclopedia Online <http://www.gameo.org/>

MESG Packull, Werner O. *Mysticism and the Early South German-Austrian Anabaptist Movement, 1525–1531.* Studies in Anabaptist and Mennonite History, no. 19. Kitchener, ON, and Scottdale, PA: Herald Press, 1977.

MEWLT Seebaß, Gottfried. *Müntzers Erbe: Werk, Leben und Theologie des Hans Hut.* Quellen und Forschungen zur Reformationsgeschichte, vol. 73. Göttingen: Gütersloher Verlagshaus, 2002.

MGB *Mennonitische Geschichtsblätter.*

MLDC Klaassen, Walter, and William Klassen. *Marpeck: A Life of Dissent and Conformity.* Waterloo, ON: Herald Press, 2008.

MQR *Mennonite Quarterly Review.*

PAW Snyder, Arnold C., and Linda A. Huebert Hecht, eds. *Profiles of Anabaptist Women: Sixteenth-Century Reforming Pioneers.* Studies in Women and Religion. Waterloo, ON: Published for the Canadian Corporation for Studies in Religion by Wilfrid Laurier University Press, 1996.

PMA Loserth, Johann, ed. *Pilgram Marbecks Antwort auf Kaspar Schwenckfelds Beurteilung des Buches der Bundesbezeugung von 1542.* Quellen und Forschungen zur Geschichte der oberdeutschen Taufgesinnten im 16. Jahrhundert. Vienna: Carl Fromme, 1929.

PMLST Boyd, Stephen B. *Pilgram Marpeck: His Life and Social Theology.* Durham: Duke University Press, 1992.

PRR Goertz, Hans-Jürgen, ed., and Walter Klaassen, English edition ed. *Profiles of the Radical Reformers: Biographical Sketches from Thomas Müntzer to Paracelsus.* Eugene, OR: Wipf and Stock Publishers, 1982.

WPM Klassen, William, and Walter Klaassen, trans. and ed. *The Writings of Pilgram Marpeck.* Classics of the Radical Reformation, vol. 2. Kitchener, ON, and Scottdale, PA: Herald Press, 1978.

Introduction

On 26 September 1561, Jörg Maler, a painter, minister, and author from Augsburg, Germany, deposited a treasure at Gregor Mangold's bookbinding shop in Zurich, Switzerland. Half of that treasure has been lost without a trace. The half that remains is the book before you, now in English translation. These writings by a wide range of authors were collected into one volume because scattered congregations living a precarious existence—as a result of their dissent from the theological and political commitments of the realm—had found them life giving.

The manuscript Maler brought to Zurich consists of fifty-six eclectic writings: pastoral letters, theological treatises, tracts, devotions, poems, and sayings. It includes twenty-seven letters, sixteen of them by Pilgram Marpeck, an engineer, minister, and theologian, also from Augsburg. Marpeck was the outstanding leader of these scattered congregations. In addition to his letters there are eleven by other ministers of what has come to be called the Marpeck Circle. Six were written by Leupold Scharnschlager, Marpeck's closest co-worker. Many of these are open letters,[1] usually addressed to a particular party but intended for a wider readership. This form of writing was common in the age of the Reformation. In addition, there are five tracts by formative figures

[1] *Sendschreiben.*

in South German–Austrian Anabaptism, one each by Hans Hut and Hans Schlaffer and three by Leonhard Schiemer. All three men died a martyr's death in the early years of the Reformation.

Jörg Probst Rothenfelder, called Maler ("painter") because of his profession, was editor of the Kunstbuch and the author of three of its treatises: an evangelistic letter, a digest of the community's convictions, and a confession of faith. The remaining seven writings have in common only that they were known and prized by members of the Marpeck Circle; they include meditations on God's faithfulness, a member's confession of sin, and a poem warning against false belief.

The book begins with four prefaces, and ten interludes are scattered throughout the volume. The second preface is an epic poem by Spiritualist Valentin Ickelsamer on the dangers of misusing academic training. The other three prefaces contain short meditative thoughts that fit into spaces left vacant when a text did not completely fill a given quire of the manuscript. At the same time extra leaves have been inserted into the codex.[2] The interludes are also short; they contain devotional and prophetic writings, including two statements by Maler. Most of the interludes seem to have been added at the last minute to make use of vacant space.

The arrangement of the original table of contents[3] is different from the one used in the critical German edition[4] and in this translation. It reveals the first of several surprises connected with the Kunstbuch. The original table lists thirteen dated epistles by Marpeck. Then come four "Epistles of Pilgram, Written at Unknown Times." One of them is "Concerning True Godliness" (no. 41), which scholars now know was actually written by Christian Entfelder, a Spiritualist with whom Marpeck debated! In the next section are three notes by Maler. Five writings by Scharnschlager follow. Then come six texts by "Anabaptist brothers." One is actually Marpeck's "Concerning Hasty Judgments and Verdicts" (no. 7). It is remarkable that Marpeck's colleague Maler would not have

2 Perhaps when the compiler had selected a piece to fill the blank, he couldn't relinquish its place in the volume even when it more than filled the available space.

3 BSOT, 94–96.

4 BSOT.

known who had penned this signature writing. The remaining texts, including the Athanasian Creed, make up the final category. The original table of contents also includes two treatises that have gone missing and must have been taken over into the second half of the codex: "Questions concerning Word and Sacrament" and "Questions and Answers Having to Do with Magistrates."

Most of the manuscript was copied by Maler.[5] On the left side of each page a blank column was reserved for marginalia, consisting of biblical citations, glosses, and corrections. Besides Maler's handwriting, two other distinct writing styles are evident. One of these copyists penned the title page and the table of contents. The other one corrected spelling errors on a few pages of the codex.[6]

Because of the many layers of editing of which this edition of the Kunstbuch is a product, an explanation is in order regarding how scripture references, glosses, and other notes, penned by various hands, appear in this edition. Scripture references included in the text of the original appear here in parentheses in the form (Heb 10 [37]) (with verses in brackets supplied by the editors of the German critical edition, BSOT). Presumably these references were included by the original author of the article. When a reference appears in the text in brackets, in the form [Heb 10 (37)], that reference was written in the margins of the original text, presumably by a sixteenth-century editorial hand (Jörg Maler?). Other marginal notes in the Kunstbuch are included as footnotes in this edition, with an asterisk next to the footnote number. Bracketed footnotes were written by the editor or translator of the article in the present edition. Plain footnotes—with no asterisks or brackets—are English translations of footnotes taken from the German critical edition.

It is noteworthy, given Maler's precarious circumstances, that he did not merely copy in the simplest possible fashion the documents he had assembled. The first page of the text is copiously illuminated,

---

5 BSOT, 83–87.

6 A third hand wrote a family chronicle in 1579 and added it to the codex after "Concerning the Two Golden Calves (1 Kgs 12) and the Two Beasts (Rv 13)" (no. 42). This chronicle is not included in the English translation, because it was not originally part of the anthology.

and the first letter of the opening and closing paragraphs of each text is illuminated. The creator of the Kunstbuch cared not only about truth but also about the beauty of the truth.

We do not know how long the codex remained in Anabaptist hands. It was listed for the first time in a 1697 catalogue of the Burgerbibliothek in Bern, Switzerland, where it was discovered in the 1950s; with that event the reclaiming of the Marpeck literary legacy reached its culmination.

The first recovery of a Marpeck Circle text took place in the 1860s as part of church historian T. W. Roehrich's innovative research on Anabaptism in Strasbourg.[7] He found a copy of "A Clear and Useful Instruction," not yet attributed to Marpeck but known to date from Reformation-era Strasbourg. Fortunately, Roehrich copied excerpts from it; the printed version perished in an 1870 fire that consumed the Strasbourg city archive.

A scholarly sensation of Radical Reformation studies in the 1920s was the discovery of three substantive writings of Marpeck and his circle: the admonition of 1542 (*Vermannung;* also called the *Bundesbezeugung* or baptism booklet of 1542),[8] Marpeck's response (*Verantwortung*) to Caspar Schwenckfeld's judgment (*Judicium*),[9] and the explanation of the Testaments (*Testamentserläuterung*).[10] Discoveries of other writings in European archives continued through the following decades. In 1950 Delbert Gratz, an American Mennonite historian of Swiss Anabaptism, discovered the Kunstbuch codex in Bern and had it microfilmed, but never determined its identity.[11] Then in 1956 a Ger-

---

7 Jan J. Kiwiet, *Pilgram Marbeck: Ein Führer der Täuferbewegung im Süddeutschen Raum* (Kassel: J. G. Oncken, 1958), 9, 50.

8 It was discovered in the British Museum by American Mennonite church historian John Horsch in 1923. See J. C. Wenger, "The Life and Work of Pilgram Marpeck," MQR 12 (July 1938): 158.

9 Johann Loserth, Austrian Catholic church historian, meticulously studied the three extant copies (Zurich, Munich, Olmütz [Olomouc]) and published the text with commentary in 1929 (PMA, 48–53).

10 German Mennonite minister Christian Hege discovered it in the Zurich central library in the mid-1920s. See Wenger, "The Life and Work of Pilgram Marpeck," 161.

11 Delbert Gratz, "Research Note," MQR 31 (October 1957): 294–95.

man doctoral student, Heinold Fast, and fellow student J. F. G. Goeters discovered this codex for a second time and identified it as a Marpeck Circle collection. The significance of their discovery is attested by the fact that *Archiv für Reformationsgeschichte,* the most prominent journal in the field, immediately published Fast's article about it.[12] For thirty-five years Fast devoted himself to the study of the Kunstbuch and its literary and geographical context, especially in eastern Switzerland.[13] When ill health prevented him from completing his task, Gottfried Seebaß, chair of the Anabaptist documentation commission,[14] entrusted Martin Rothkegel, a German church historian, with completing this massive project. In 2007 a meticulously researched critical edition of the Kunstbuch was published. As is noted in the preface, the critical edition is the basis of this translation into English. Without it, the present project would have taken many more years to publish.

The title *Kunstbuch* can be translated in a number of ways, because the term was widely and variously used in the sixteenth century. Some books bearing that title would most accurately be translated into English as "book of understanding." The term also suggests skill or artistry, hence the possible translation "book of artistry." In other instances, Kunstbuch was used in the sense of "handbook," an introduction or guide to a certain subject. Preface 1, by the editor, tells us what he had in mind for his anthology. He calls it "a divine mystery" that can "illuminate your heart, courage, and understanding."

In addition to being the most diverse collection of Marpeck Circle writings, the Kunstbuch is also the most provocative document to emerge in that network of congregations: it includes authors whose understanding of faith and of the church were sharply critical of Pilgramite ones. As a foretaste of more detailed discussion in the commentaries that accompany each document, let us look at one example. Already in the late 1520s, as radical groups in Strasbourg further de-

12 Heinold Fast, "Pilgram Marbeck und das oberdeutsche Täufertum: Ein neuer Handschriftenfund," ARG 47 (1956), 212–42. It is reprinted in BSOT, 13–41.

13 Heinold Fast, ed., *Quellen zur Geschichte der Täufer in der Schweiz* 2: *Ostschweiz* (Zurich: Theologischer Verlag Zürich, 1973).

14 The Täuferakten Kommission has published more than thirty volumes of sixteenth-century documents.

fined themselves, Entfelder and Marpeck went in contrary directions. The former preached that the Spirit's working is purely inward, while the latter argued that a visible church and its ceremonies are also essential aspects of the Spirit's activity.

The reader should bear in mind three things, in order to get a fair picture of the Kunstbuch's editor and his purposes. First, the Marpeck Circle was a type of Anabaptism that placed great weight on Christ as a living presence in each believer. Marpeck never tired of reciting Galatians 2:20: "It is no longer I who live, but it is Christ who lives in me. And the life I now live in the flesh I live by faith in the Son of God, who loved me and gave himself for me." At the same time Marpeck placed great weight on the theological exposition of belief. Thus the unity of the church lay equally in a shared subjective experience and an objective articulation of foundational beliefs. It was not that discipleship was of secondary value, but the form it took was not as uniform as in other types of Anabaptism.[15] Because of where the weight fell, Pilgramite Anabaptism had the capacity to accept diversity of conduct and theology. One expression of this approach was plural leadership. Even though Marpeck was a charismatic leader, neither he nor any other single individual determined the life of the congregations who shared a covenant.

Second, if we consider the striking diversity of the Kunstbuch's writings, the selection process, culminating in Maler's work, seems to have been based on the meaning a particular text held for some grouping within the Marpeck-related congregations and not on whether it conformed to Marpeck's theological position. Judging by the number of writings in the Kunstbuch offering comfort, guidance, and warning to Christians under persecution, we conclude that inspiration to remain

---

15 Marpeck has a clear place for separation from worldly habits and people. The difference between Marpeckites and the Swiss is not on nonconformity as such but in understandings of the nature of nonconformity. Marpeck's approach can be seen in embryo in "Concerning Hasty Judgments and Verdicts" (no. 7). There he first urges separation from the body of Christ for persistent evildoers, but then he warns against banning such people and making irrevocable judgments about them. Finally he warns against reducing to our own rules a Pauline understanding of good and evil.

faithful in suffering was a chief criterion for their inclusion; the collection contains such works by authors with whom Marpeck and others had had disputes. Marpeck is given pride of place in the Kunstbuch, but his writings are not presented as a canon within the canon. We will look in more detail below at factors at work in the shaping of the codex.

The third criterion for inclusion in Maler's collection is geographic breadth. Documents representing the life and thought of the circle—from the Alsace, in present-day France, to Moravia, in the present-day Czech Republic—are preserved.

The didactic poems, passionate meditations, pastoral letters, and searing confessions that are part of the Kunstbuch open a door into the intimate life of a now lost community. Maler's collection is like an album of photographs taken over a period of thirty years, documenting the life of a family and its friends. In rare detail it records the existence of one kind of Anabaptism, preserving for posterity the personalities and issues, the brilliance and the tragedy that made it what it was. Many of these "photographs" were probably already in the family's possession years before they were pasted into the album we have before us. But there are late additions, some of them written by the compiler or gathered by him from other collections. It was five years after Marpeck's death in 1556 that Maler copied these writings into the handwritten manuscript.

Mid-twentieth-century readers of the Kunstbuch brought to their reading a particular set of concerns. Then scholars were seeking to legitimate the Radical Reformation as a third form of sixteenth-century church renewal. It was of urgent importance for its defenders within and beyond Mennonitism to see Anabaptism as parallel to the official forms of Reformation—Lutheran, Reformed, and Anglican. To meet that standard, scholars and church leaders (in that generation, the same people often served in both roles) identified with some parts of the radical reform movement[16] and distanced themselves from

---

16 Hans-Jürgen Goertz distinguishes social movements from organizations or institutions. A movement involves a collective actor, continuity on the basis of a strong collective "we" sense, with many fluid forms of participation. See *Pfaffenhass und gross Geschrei: Die reformatorischen Bewegungen in Deutsch-*

others. Those who used this approach were a generation of scholars now known as the "Bender school," so named for Harold S. Bender, an American Mennonite scholar and churchman.[17] Thus, there came to be an "evangelical Anabaptism," made up of leaders and writings that were theologically orthodox, pacifist in principle, and remote from apocalyptic fervour.[18] Moreover, scholars of this school assumed that evangelical Anabaptism had a single source, in Zurich, and that it had spread from there.

Much has changed in scholarship since then.[19] In every discipline concerned with examining history, scholars know vastly more about religion and culture in central Europe than their counterparts half a century ago knew. This expanded knowledge has affected the study of radical reform movements such as Anabaptism. Most students of the subject now assume that Anabaptism was a charismatic, barely institutionalized movement—or movements—shaped by various backgrounds and taking many forms. This understanding of Anabaptism

---

land 1517–1529 (Munich: C. H. Beck, 1987), 246. In personal conversation (in Hamburg, 6 December 2006) Goertz claimed that some expressions of Anabaptism, including the network (his word) of which Marpeck was a key figure, do not meet the criteria of a movement.

17 Bender's emphasis was spelled out in his presidential address to the American Society of Church History and published as "The Anabaptist Vision," MQR 18 (April 1944): 67–88.

18 For instance, Hans Denck, an Anabaptist writer with a mystical orientation, was on the edge of orthodoxy. Balthasar Hubmaier, who made a case for defensive warfare, did not quite belong. The Münster Anabaptists, who legitimated violence and transgressed moral norms on the basis of apocalyptic visions, clearly did not belong.

19 The seminal essay that inaugurated a new historiography of Anabaptism is James M. Stayer, Werner O. Packull, and Klaus Deppermann, "From Monogenesis to Polygenesis: The Historical Discussion of Anabaptist Sources," MQR 49 (April 1975): 83–121. For new syntheses of the subject, see Hans-Jürgen Goertz, *The Anabaptists* (New York: Routledge, 1996), esp. 6–35; C. Arnold Snyder, *Anabaptist History and Theology* (Kitchener, ON: Pandora Press, 2002), esp. 379–404; and J. Denny Weaver, *Becoming Anabaptist* (Scottdale, PA: Herald Press, 2005), esp. 161–222. For a survey of scholarship on Marpeck, see William Klassen, "The Legacy of the Marpeck Community in Anabaptist Scholarship," MQR 78 (January 2004): 7–28.

makes it irresistible to ask, what kind of Anabaptism—or what kinds of Anabaptism—are represented in the Kunstbuch? In what follows, I hope to shed light on that question, and on the surprises, puzzles, and ambiguities that accompany it.

Pilgram Marpeck: The man and the movement[20]

Pilgram Marpeck was born about 1495 to a devout Catholic patrician family in Rattenberg, Tyrol (40 kilometres east of Innsbruck, in western Austria). He learned the skills of a mining engineer and entered public life as a mining magistrate, also serving one term as mayor of Rattenberg. Sometime before 1520 he married Sophia Harrer. By 1528 she had died, and he had married a woman named Anna, whose maiden name we do not know. She became his companion for life.

During the early 1520s Marpeck was drawn to the cause of reform, first through his parish priest, Stephan Castenbaur, then through Lutheran reformers, and finally through radical reformers such as Leonhard Schiemer and Hans Schlaffer, whose legacy is preserved in the Kunstbuch. He was attracted to their primitivist vision of a church like the one portrayed in the New Testament, but he is not known to have been involved in the fledgling Anabaptist congregation that emerged in the area. In late 1527 the imperial government ordered local officials, including Marpeck, to arrest leaders of the radicals and execute them. This provoked a crisis of conscience for Marpeck. He resigned, and he and Anna were banished in early 1528.

They made their way to Moravia, a region of historic religious tolerance near the present Czech, Slovak, and Austrian borders, where Anabaptist groups were in the process of formation. The Marpecks first stopped in Krumau (now Ćeský Krumlov in the Czech Republic), a mining town to which other radicals from the Tyrol had fled. They settled in Austerlitz (now Slavkov u Brna in the Czech Republic), where a community based on voluntary communalism was in the process of forming. They were probably baptized there. We know they were com-

20 Immediately upon its publication, the comprehensive and probing biography of Marpeck by Walter Klaassen and William Klassen, *Marpeck: A Life of Dissent and Conformity* (Scottdale, PA: Herald Press, 2008), became the standard reference.

missioned to lead a similar group establishing itself in another haven of relative tolerance, the free city of Strasbourg, on the present French-German border.

From the mid-1520s to the early 1530s, Strasbourg was a crossroads for many kinds of reformation. Even though the city had officially embraced reforms championed by Martin Bucer and Wolfgang Capito (along the lines of the Swiss reformers Ulrich Zwingli and Johannes Oecolampadius), Catholic, Anabaptist, and Spiritualist dissenters also had limited religious freedom. Marpeck secured a position as forestry engineer for the city, which gave him personal stability and allowed him to develop a vision of a church that remained more engaged with political institutions, a posture most groups of Anabaptists were unwilling to venture. Remaining in such a public position was rarely possible for the radicals, most of whom sought refuge in transient or menial labour. It was in Strasbourg that Marpeck began his lifelong pastoral and theological partnership with Leupold Scharnschlager. Both men came from prosperous Tyrolean families. Each had left behind a secure life. They must have been kindred spirits, because they soon collaborated in fostering a nonconformed yet not withdrawn form of church life. This partnership continued when both moved to eastern Switzerland, where they undertook writing projects together.

It was in the midst of Strasbourg's religious and social ferment that Marpeck's theology crystallized. He shared general Anabaptist convictions that belief cannot be coerced and the church cannot be one with the state. In debate with the city's leading reformers, Bucer and Capito, he ably articulated the Anabaptist interpretation of the New Testament on believer's baptism and nonresistance. Yet his more original contribution to Anabaptist identity came out of his confrontation with Spiritualism, a diverse movement that saw the spiritual and the material, the inward and the outward, in opposition.[21] Protestant and

---

21 Much controversy surrounds Spiritualism. Some students of the phenomenon argue from its inwardness that it was not a movement, as other types of radical reform were. Scholars who rose to prominence in the field in the 1960s, such as George H. Williams and Rollin Stely Armour, refer to Spiritualism as a loosely definable type of Christian faith. This approach is continued in recent writing by R. Emmet McLaughlin, "Reformation Spiritualism: Typology, Sources,

Catholic reform during the sixteenth century was inspired by the Spiritualist impulse, as a corrective to the externalism of much late medieval religion. But in keeping with much Catholic and Lutheran thought, Marpeck argued that to take the inward impulse as the norm for the Christian life is to deny belief in the incarnation. To make his case, Marpeck authored two treatises[22] that set the course of his theological identity. His argument at its most basic is that "Christ became a natural man for natural man"; the Word became flesh to bring humanity salvation on its own terms. In the power of the Holy Spirit the outward and material becomes the medium of the inward and spiritual. The visible church is the prolongation of the incarnation of Christ, the extension of his humanity in time and space.

By late 1531 Strasbourg had greatly restricted freedom of dissent. When Marpeck refused to recant his criticism of infant baptism, he and Anna were banished once again. They moved to the Grisons (Graubünden) in eastern Switzerland, where Swiss Anabaptists, simply called "Brethren," were trying to establish stable congregations. Because of the threat of persecution, which kept them outside the towns, these believers were more withdrawn from civic life than Marpeck, Scharnschlager, and others in their congregations had been. Yet it was not their separatism but their legalism that Marpeck criticized. Apart from fragments, we know little about the twelve years that followed. Marpeck had work as a water engineer for part of that time. He became acquainted with the local Brethren, but we have no information on the nature of their relationship. All we know about it comes from Marpeck's pastoral letters written to the Swiss a decade later and pre-

---

Significance," in *Radikalität und Dissent im 16. Jahrhundert,* ed. Hans-Jürgen Goertz and James M. Stayer (Berlin: Duncker & Humblot, 2002), 123–40. Geoffrey Dipple argues that there were "Spiritualist Anabaptists" who tried to reconcile the two radical impulses; see "The Spiritualist Anabaptists," in *A Companion to Anabaptism and Spiritualism, 1521–1700,* ed. John D. Roth and James M. Stayer, (Boston: Brill, 2007), esp. 293. In his response (*Verantwortung*) to Schwenckfeld's judgment (*Judicium*) (LWPM, 67–157), Marpeck honours the Spiritualist impulse as a corrective to an overly externalized Christian identity but rejects it as the norm of that identity.

22 "A Clear Refutation" (WPM, 43–67), and "A Clear and Useful Instruction" (WPM, 69–106).

served in the Kunstbuch; in these epistles he accused the Swiss of having a narrow view of the Christian life.

The unguarded intensity of his reaction against certain Swiss practices sounds like theirs was a quarrel if not between lovers at least among siblings. Taking this relationship into account is essential to fairly appraising their debate. Marpeck was incensed because so much was at stake. The Marpeck Circle and the Swiss Brethren had both been stung by the Hutterite judgment that only those who hold all things in common are faithful Christians. These two groups considered the Hutterite model coercive. They argued that the free sharing of one's worldly goods belongs to the call to discipleship. Their point was that giving needs to happen voluntarily. Marpeck concluded that the Swiss were discrediting the voluntary model by rushing to premature and coercive judgment.

During this period Marpeck became active as an itinerant elder (overseer) for a different grouping of congregations who looked to him for leadership; this network stretched from the Alsace across southern Germany to Moravia. With reference to this time in Marpeck's life the term *circle* begins to be used to describe the unusual dynamic of a religious community characterized by a variety of articulate voices, a collegial leadership group of elders, and one individual whose thinking was especially relied upon and whose person was highly esteemed.

In their attempts to piece together a description of Marpeckian Anabaptism, scholars have emphasized different aspects. Jan Kiwiet, a Dutch church historian who first suggested the term *circle,* gives a concise summary of the ferment within the Radical Reformation in the South German realm in the late 1530s and early 1540s. Alignments were solidifying: the Hutterites were taking the vision of renewal in a communitarian direction and the Spiritualists in an individualistic one.[23] Werner Packull, a more recent historian of sixteenth-century radicalism in South Germany, Austria, and Moravia, also sees Marpeck as the pivotal figure in an unstable mediating path. His case focuses on Marpeck's decisive role in the debates with Spiritualists in Moravia.[24]

---

23 Kiwiet, *Pilgram Marbeck,* 54–64.

24 HB, 135–58.

On the other hand, Martin Rothkegel, co-editor of the critical edition of the Kunstbuch, describes Marpeck as one who deliberately remained a largely anonymous partner in a collective leadership. This is suggested by the fact that no author is named in any of the major writings—the admonition (*Vermannung*) of 1542,[25] the response (*Verantwortung*) to Caspar Schwenckfeld's judgment (*Judicium*),[26] and the explanation of the Testaments (*Testamentserläuterung*). Rothkegel argues that it is only the writing of twentieth-century theologians that has constructed Marpeck as an original personality and pulled him out of the literary anonymity in which he and his colleagues chose to work.[27] Rothkegel's graciously contrarian argument stands as a warning against tendencies in certain Mennonite and Baptist settings to remake Marpeck in our image, to see our own pastoral and theological commitments in his.[28] But it is unclear what Rothkegel makes of Marpeck's extensive pastoral correspondence, which bears the stamp of a strong personality with deep convictions.

Toward the end of his time in Switzerland and at the beginning of his time in Germany, Marpeck became a prolific author, often writing collaboratively with Scharnschlager and others. In addition to the letters collected in this volume, he and his closest comrades in the tribulation of Christ[29] expanded an existing treatise by a fellow Anabaptist[30]

---

25 WPM, 159–302.

26 LWPM, 114–19.

27 Personal conversation in Hamburg, Germany, on 11 December 2006.

28 It is instructive to see Marpeck portrayed in North America, on the one hand, as an ally of progressive Mennonites (John D. Rempel, "Ambiguous Legacy: The Peace Teaching, Speaking Truth to Power, and Mennonite Assimilation through the Centuries," in *At Peace and Unafraid*, ed. Duane Friesen and Gerald Schlabach [Scottdale, PA: Herald Press, 2005], 349–63); and, on the other hand, of traditional Baptists (Malcolm B. Yarnell, *The Formation of Christian Doctrine* [Nashville: B & H Academic, 2007], 73–106).

29 Typically the closing lines of his letters identify him as *mitgnoß am truebsal Christi* ("comrade in the tribulation of Christ").

30 Bernard Rothmann, *Bekentnisse van beyden Sacramenten, Doepe unde Nachtmaele der predicanten tho Münster* (Münster, November 1533); see Frank Wray, "The Vermanung of 1542 and Rothmann's Bekenntnis," ARG 47 (1956): 243–51.

on the meaning of baptism and the Lord's Supper; they called it "the admonition" (*Vermannung*). When Marpeck's most formidable Spiritualist critic, Caspar Schwenckfeld, read the book, he bitterly accused Marpeck of abandoning the inward experience of Christ for lifeless outward forms. Marpeck and his comrades responded, no less adamantly, with the *Verantwortung*, a 586-page synthesis of the Spiritualist and sacramentalist impulses in the gospel, grounded in a Trinitarian understanding of the incarnation.

In 1544 the Marpecks moved to Augsburg—a surprising choice, given that the official church of the city had suppressed religious pluralism and was caught up in political and military alliances that created a situation in which authorities perceived all dissent as seditious. An Anabaptist conventicle in the city survived by making itself almost invisible.[31] Once again Marpeck found some provisional stability for his ministry by working as a forestry engineer. Since the authorities in Augsburg did not tolerate visible acts of dissent, Marpeck shifted from public proclamation to pastoral and theological writing as the most fruitful way to nurture Anabaptist church life and foster unity. It is difficult not to see in this shift a retreat from Marpeck's breakthrough insight that the humanity of Christ is prolonged in the visible church and its visible acts of preaching, baptizing, communing, and loving our neighbours. At the same time, it is hard to imagine that stable relationships and rituals could develop in a setting such as Augsburg in the 1540s and 1550s. In Augsburg, at least, the evidence suggests that the Pilgramite presence was more a matter of the occasional gathering than of covenanted congregational life.

Congregations from the Marpeck Circle in the Alsace and Moravia also struggled to remain true to themselves in settings without freedom of expression, yet the literature suggests that they were more able to strive toward Marpeck's vision of nonconformed but not withdrawn church life. It is a disconcerting irony that Marpeck's belief about the visible church as a continuation of Christ's incarnation applied more readily to the Swiss Brethren—and more fully to the Hutterites—than

---

31 For a succinct portrayal of the effect in Augsburg of the Schmalkaldian War and the imperial rule that followed it, see MLDC, 287–96.

to the Pilgramite congregations, including his own congregation in Augsburg. Even though the Augsburg congregation was unable to sustain itself on Marpeck's ecclesiology of patience and freedom, he remained sharply critical of the separatist congregations in the Grisons. They were almost as hemmed in as the one in Augsburg, but their severe discipline enabled them to survive long after the Pilgramites in Augsburg had dispersed.

Marpeck continued to write until just before his death late in 1556. In 1561 his colleague Jörg Maler gathered together sixteen of Marpeck's pastoral epistles and assorted other materials—twenty-five tracts, devotionals, poems, and pastoral letters by his co-workers and others—that had acquired enduring significance for the circle of congregations Marpeck led, to form the collection of writings now before us. Some of the congregations in Moravia continued to build church life in Marpeck's spirit, until they and all dissenters were suppressed in the 1620s.[32] Elsewhere they gave up their separate existence soon after Marpeck's death. Marpeck's legacy lived on most tangibly among the Swiss Brethren, in southern Germany and Moravia as well as in Switzerland. In another irony, the Swiss took to heart his approach to discipline as well as the rudiments of his incarnational theology in vindicating their way of life to their critics, but they did so without mentioning Marpeck's name.[33] Thus Marpeck was forgotten; his writings were lost to posterity for three centuries. He was like those described in Sirach:

> But of others there is no memory;
> they have perished as though they had never existed;
> they have become as though they had never been born,
> they and their children after them.

---

32 The last pastoral correspondence on record is in 1579. But other sources mention Pilgramite congregations as late at 1632; see Jerold Zeman, *The Anabaptists and the Czech Brethren in Moravia* 1526–1628 (The Hague: Mouton, 1969), 256–58, 301.

33 C. Arnold Snyder, "The (Not-so) 'Simple Confession' of the Later Swiss Brethren," MQR 73 (1999): 677–722; and "The Evolution of Separatist Anabaptism," MQR 74 (2000): 87–122. John D. Roth, "Marpeck and the Later Swiss Brethren 1540–1700," in *A Companion to Anabaptism and Spiritualism*, ed. Roth and Stayer, 347–88.

But these also were godly men. . . .
Their descendents stand by the covenants.[34]

Of Marpeck it can be said, "This also was a godly man." In the course of the twentieth century the rediscovery of Marpeck as someone who stood by the covenants has allowed us to probe, test, and (at least for some) confirm Marpeck's vision, to an extent that never happened during his lifetime.

Pilgram Marpeck: The theologian

Pilgram Marpeck is an original and eclectic theologian whom history forgot. In the past two generations he has come to the attention of students of the sixteenth century because he, and the short-lived movement whose deepest thinker he was, holds a mediating position within the spectrum of Anabaptist experiments. The model of church life he advocated attracted believers who were looking for a via media—a mediating path, an alternative to trends that took hold in early Anabaptism.[35] One of these trends believed that reform inspired by the New Testament would lead to an inward life in the Spirit that went beyond outward doctrinal or ecclesial forms. The opposing trend was based on a strictly literal reading of the New Testament and a code of discipleship set down in doctrinal and ecclesial forms.

Marpeck affirmed both an inward life in the Spirit and an outward life of discipleship but placed them within a more complex and developed frame of reference. First, he put great weight on letter, Spirit, and community as inseparable in finding the truth of the Bible.[36] This dynamic kept the movement both from extreme literalism and from private paths to the spiritual life. Second, Marpeck sided with the majority conviction in Anabaptism, which held that the Sermon on the Mount, especially its teaching of noncoercion in matters of faith, nonresis-

---

34 Sir 44:9–12.

35 A via media is not a middle ground or centre. The Marpeck Circle was not the centre of Anabaptism but an attempt to combine antitheses into a new synthesis. For instance, Marpeck was not primarily focused on compromise, as we see from his blunt criticism of the Appenzell Brethren and Schwenckfeld.

36 "A Clear and Useful Instruction" (WPM, 76–82); "Marpeck's *Response* to Caspar Schwenckfeld's *Judgement*" (LWPM, 120–24).

tance to evil, and love of enemies, is central to the meaning of Jesus' ministry and death.[37] But third, he taught that conformity to Christ is not brought about simply by conversion or by ethical rigour. The life of obedience—to cite one of Marpeck's cherished themes—calls for a holy patience that waits for the blossoms, then the flowers, and finally the fruits of faith.[38] His fourth trait was a commitment to nonconformity to the world but not withdrawal from it.[39]

The outworking of this cluster of convictions is the dynamic that animates Marpeck and Scharnschlager's writings in the Kunstbuch. Their vision of the church was distinctively Anabaptist but sought to overcome two of the movement's weaknesses. One was the factionalism this vision had generated among those who pursued its perfect realization. The second tendency was the inverse of the first: it overcame such factionalism by the internalization of all things spiritual. The distinctive convictions of Marpeck and his circle emerged in their competition with other radical groups for adherents.[40] The Pilgramite mediating path stressed sets of complementary differences: visible community as well as individual gifts, rigorous but not legalistic ethics, ability to bear with different stages of spiritual development without making hasty judgments, and the capacity to discern what is essential for unity and what is not.

The writings in the Kunstbuch by Marpeck and his fellow ministers dealt, for the most part, with two areas of church life. One was spiritual guidance for everyday conduct. This included the tendency toward legalism (and its opposite) as a pastoral problem that could be addressed through practical counsel and a deeper grasp of the Spirit's work. Helena von Freyberg's "Confession of Guilt" (no. 28) belongs to this category. The other area was the path of self-surrender and the accompanying riddle of innocent suffering for Christ's sake. This too the ministers' letters addressed pastorally in terms of the believer's

---

37 See "Concerning the Love of God" (no. 13).

38 "Concerning Hasty Judgments and Verdicts" (no. 7).

39 "Exposé of the Babylonian Whore" (LWPM, 31–37).

40 Werner Packull (HB, 133–46), and Martin Rothkegel ("Anabaptism in Moravia and Silesia," in *A Companion to Anabaptism and Spiritualism*, ed. Roth and Stayer, 177–89), describe how this struggle unfolded in Moravia.

experience and the promises of God. In their writing on the spiritual life, Hartmut von Cronberg, Hans Has von Halstatt, and Christian Entfelder's meditations are cut from similar cloth.

While these letters empathetically engage the issues before the congregations and lift up the promises of the Bible, they do not attain the profound grasp of the spiritual life and its existential intensity found in the treatises of Hans Hut, Leonhard Schiemer, and Hans Schlaffer. These writers achieved a rare understanding of the stages of spiritual growth[41] and identified the illusions and temptations the believer needs to come to terms with in order to die and rise with Christ. The fusion in these letters of lament, pain, and joy gives them a depth and insightfulness that comes only to those who live in the shadow of death. These treatises were included because in them "heart speaks to heart."[42] On that primal level Marpeck and his colleagues would have welcomed their inclusion.[43] More will be said of this in the next section.

At the same time, the enormous theological creativity that arose from the minds of Marpeck and his comrades shows their ongoing concern with Spiritualism—when it became an autonomous approach rather than a corrective—as the foremost doctrinal threat to their understanding of the gospel. Their scholarly writing in the 1540s shows that they viewed Spiritualism as a theological challenge that could ultimately be addressed only by appeal to the doctrines of the Trinity and the incarnation. Thus legalism and suffering were dealt with in the elders' epistles in the Kunstbuch, while Spiritualism was addressed in two lengthy books, the admonition (*Vermannung*) of 1542, and the response (*Verantwortung*) to Caspar Schwenckfeld. Both books were in circulation when Maler gathered writings for a collection, whereas the elders' pastoral epistles were not readily available.[44] They and

41 In late medieval mysticism these stages were renunciation, illumination, and unity. This threefold path is not laid out step-by-step in these texts, but it is implicit in them.

42 From Augustine (*Cor ad cor loquitur*).

43 MESG, 182, describes a similar dynamic among the Hutterities of this era, which led to the inclusion of Spiritualistic texts in their chronicles.

44 Was Maler's criterion for inclusion length or availability? Likely it was not availability, because there were multiple copies or printings of works such as Hans

the prophetic and meditative writings of other authors seem to have been included because of their pastoral relevance, not their affinity for Marpeck's theology.[45]

We need to understand the Marpeckian theology that informed pastoral practice, in order to make sense of the tensions and complementarities in the writings of this anthology as a whole. The great and abiding achievement of Marpeck and his co-workers was their thoroughgoing critique of Spiritualism. The nature of Spiritualism had changed over time. It began as a tendency in much of the late medieval church to overcome the externality and corruption of religious life by seeking the inner reality behind the outward form. At that point, it developed within—and was based on—Catholic institutions. In the chaos of the Reformation, Spiritualism burst this framework and became a new type of religiosity, unconstrained by ritual or dogma, a state of affairs that would have been unimaginable to a medieval Christian.

In some settings of radical reform, the movement toward inner religiosity was as much a tactic as a conviction: in the face of relentless persecution, believers did what they had to do in order to survive. This sometimes included abandoning outward forms by which believers could be identified and controlled. So, as much for practical as for theological reasons, the turn toward Spiritualism remained an abiding challenge for Anabaptism.

Hut's "A Beginning of a True Christian Life" (no. 6) and Christian Entfelder's "Concerning True Godliness" (no. 41). Did Maler then exclude excerpts from the admonition (*Vermannung*) of 1542 (WPM, 152–302), or his response (*Verantwortung*) to Caspar Schwenckfeld's *Judicium* (LWPM 67–157), on his own pastoral or theological grounds?

45 Werner Packull offers a nuanced examination of the mystical Spiritualism of Hans Hut, Leonhard Schiemer, and Hans Schlaffer, and its "devolution" and "evolution" in the South German–Austrian realm (MESG, 118–54). On the one hand, he notes the affinity of the *Aufdeckung der babylonischen hürn* ("Exposé of the Babylonian Whore") (MESG, 150–51), now attributed to Marpeck, for the early phase of Spiritualism. This impulse and the Christology out of which it arose were carried forward by figures such as Entfelder (MESG, 163–75). Marpeck was an "unlikely progeny" (MESG, 180) who countered that tendency by "systematizing the theological doctrines of the movement" (MESG, 183).

Marpeckite Christology and ecclesiology constituted the most sophisticated Radical Reformation rebuttal of Spiritualism. It made the case for a believers church on the grounds of the incarnation. A summary of its convictions follows. Behind the New Testament practice of a visible church of believers lay the principle of the incarnation: just as the Word had become flesh, so God prolonged the humanity of Christ in his body on earth, the church. As Marpeck liked to say, God continues to use the outward to reveal the inward.

The context for this defining belief was the doctrine of the Trinity, whose formulation was the most profound doctrinal achievement of the fathers of the fourth and fifth centuries, especially Augustine and the Cappadocian Fathers (Gregory Nazianzus, Gregory of Nyssa, and Basil of Caesarea). It safeguarded the primal claim of the New Testament, that Jesus and the Spirit are part of the identity of God. In other words, had the Son not been one with the Father, there would have been no incarnation—merely the appearance of the greatest among the prophets. From the vantage point of dissident Christian movements across the ages, the official church gravely compromised its teaching of God as Trinity by becoming the religion of the empire and legitimating violence as the basis of order. In so doing, the church abstracted dogma from discipleship. In the thinking of some radical movements in the sixteenth century (and the twenty-first), Trinitarianism and a state church ecclesiology cannot be disentangled.[46]

It is the surpassing merit of Pilgramite Anabaptism that it attempted the daunting task of reuniting dogma and discipleship. However lacking in philosophical precision certain of its formulations may have been, Marpeckian thought went on the offensive to defend its ecclesiology with Trinitarian thinking.[47] Marpeck's genius was that he under-

---

46 A summary of J. Denny Weaver's approach may be found in "Nicaea, Womanist Theology, and Anabaptist Particularity," in *Anabaptists and Postmodernity*, ed. Susan Biesecker-Mast and Gerald Biesecker-Mast (Telford PA: Pandora Press US, 2000), 251–79.

47 It was perhaps the great virtue of an "amateur" theology that it couldn't and didn't engage in speculative philosophizing about the inner nature of God. Theological systemization remained marginal to Anabaptism in general and to its Marpeckian form. See Preface 2 in this volume, "The Learned Ones, the

stood the classical doctrines well enough to apply them in a novel way: he used the incarnation to provide a theological defence for a believers church ecclesiology and believers baptism.[48] His insight was that that the very notion of a pure church as the visible embodiment of the converted life was under siege as much by Spiritualism as by the magisterial churches.

There is at the same time an irony in the development of Marpeck's position. Both outward circumstance (suppression of dissent in Augsburg) and inner disposition (a lack of raw courage to persistently defy authority) combined to make theological writing Marpeck's foremost expression of his calling. It was more and more by means of his writing, and less and less by means of a visible, disciplined church, that he sought to vindicate Anabaptist belief. The contrast between Marpeck and Menno Simons is instructive at this point. For Menno a disciplined, visible community was the lifeblood of the church's mission and the measure of its integrity; theology was a necessary evil. For Marpeck it was the other way around. Hans-Jürgen Goertz reinforces this characterization when he notes Marpeck's defence of diversity in the church's composition. He points to Marpeck's principle of patience with each believer's stages of growth—from blossoms and leaves to fruit. He goes on to say that there is no evidence of a call for common outward forms of holiness in Marpeck's pursuit of unity with the Swiss Brethren and the Hutterites. In both cases outward diversity was held together by inward theological principles and commonly held spiritual experience.[49]

Wrongheaded Ones," for a protest against arid abstractions used in defence of the status quo.

48 In his practical orientation, Marpeck was not unlike most of his contemporaries. In their introduction to *The Cambridge Companion to Reformation Theology* (Cambridge: Cambridge University Press, 2004), editors David Bagchi and David Steinmetz write, "A point which can never be made too often is that the theologians of the Reformation were not ivory tower academics. Their principal tasks were in most cases pastoral, and we derive their theologies from utterances from the pulpit, from spiritual advice given in letters, from rushed polemical outbursts, in the midst of persecution" (4).

49 Conversation with Hans-Jürgen Goertz in Hamburg on 6 December 2006. In Goertz's mind the debate about the presence of texts in the Kunsbuch that are at variance with Marpeck's views omits the fact that South German–Austrian

Looked at from that perspective, the pluriformity of the Kunstbuch is largely in keeping with the development of Marpeck's convictions in his Augsburg years.

Jörg Maler: Keeper or maker of the legacy?

The editor of the Kunstbuch, Jörg Maler, was born in Augsburg about 1500. We first hear of him as an apprentice in the studio of an established Augsburg artist, and then in 1526, when he was charged with molesting a woman. In 1532 Maler was baptized, at a time of growing repression, into the Anabaptist congregation in Augsburg. In the same year in which he was baptized, however, he was well known to pastors of the official church and considered for ordination—until his ties to the radicals became known.[50]

Maler's story illustrates how fluid individual religious loyalties were in the first three decades of sixteenth-century reform, even though confessional identities quickly hardened. In the magisterial Reformation there was a steady movement toward confessionalization beginning in the late 1520s. Confessionalization was the fusion of political and religious identity in a particular territory.[51] In mid-century this dynamic was especially at work in cities such as Augsburg, where the reigning religions toppled each other. In this turbulent and repressive setting, the Anabaptist presence was reduced to clusters of believers who met sporadically so as not to arouse public attention. Even so there were periodic arrests and deportations.

Maler himself was arrested in the year of his baptism. To the authorities he described his relationship to the Anabaptists as "nothing other

---

Anabaptism arose out of the Spiritualism of Hans Hut, whose influence continued to shape the movement. Even in the Marpeck Circle it was believers' mystical experience of God more than their outward disciplines that created church unity.

50 Heinold Fast, "Vom Amt des 'Lesers' zum Kompilator des sogenannten Kunstbuches; auf den Spuren Jörg Malers," in *Aussenseiter zwischen Mittelalter und Neuzeit: Festschrift für Hans-Jürgen Goertz zum 60. Geburtstag,* ed. Norbert Fischer and Marion Kobelt-Groch (Leiden: Brill, 1997), 191; MLDC, 262.

51 Wolfgang Reinhard, "Pressures towards Confessionalization? Prolegomena to a Theory of the Confessional Age," in *The German Reformation: The Essential Readings,* ed. C. Scott Dixon (Malden MA: Blackwell, 1999), 169–92.

than the pursuit of truth."[52] Before long he recanted of his dissident faith. This "recantation" was not so much a repudiation of all things Anabaptist as it was a relativizing of certain of the movement's postulates. Maler asserted, with regard to "the Word" (with reference to Romans 10) that inner and outer can not be separated. Here Marpeckites agreed with Lutherans against the Spiritualists. Yet, he went on, salvation does not depend on externals such as baptism and Communion. He allowed that a Christian can be a magistrate and that some oaths can be taken.[53] It is difficult to say whether the spiritualistic tone of his statement on the sacraments left a permanent mark on his thinking (see no. 40: "Confession of Faith according to Holy Scripture"); at least it offered him theological formulations that would lessen his conflict with the authorities. Later he made a second disavowal of his Anabaptist belief. Later still he fled Augsburg because he could not abide by his renunciations. He made contact with Anabaptists in the Grisons and Moravia, then settled in the Grisons for six years as a weaver and a leader in a Swiss Brethren congregation. On Easter Sunday of 1537 Maler was ordained as an elder in St. Gall and spent eight years in that role in nearby Appenzell.[54] By working in shops outside city walls Maler and his fellow Anabaptists in the area managed to maintain a precarious participation in the commercial life of the towns.

Maler was truly a man in pursuit of a Christ-like life. Even though he endured a two-year prison sentence for his faith, he seems to have been ambivalent about how his pursuit of Christ could best be carried out. His ambivalence concerned the same issues Marpeck faced in Strasbourg: is spiritual reality ultimately inward, and are the outward forms of the church ultimately of secondary significance? It was an ingrained ambivalence. On the one hand, Maler defended believers baptism[55] and church discipline.[56] He astutely corrected the treatise on baptism of Spiritualist Anabaptist Hans Hut, moving it in a sacra-

---

52 Fast, "Vom Amt des 'Lesers' zum Kompilator des sogenannten Kunstbuches," 193.

53 ME 4:365.

54 Ibid., 200.

55 "An Attempt to Win Him for Christendom" (no. 14).

56 "Confession of Faith according to Holy Scripture" (no. 40).

mental direction.[57] He seems to have spared no effort in his role as the compiler of the communal legacy preserved in the Kunstbuch.

On the other hand, in talking about himself late in his life, Maler minimized the contact he had had with Marpeck while they were both leaders in Appenzell. He was careful not to call himself an elder but instead referred to himself as a reader, a role assigned to literate members who could read the Bible to illiterate ones. At the same time Maler was willing to carry mail for Marpeck to distant places, documents the authorities would have considered seditious. He speaks gratefully of Marpeck's care for him during sickness, but there is only one fragment of recorded evidence for the nature of their relationship. Maler writes that his view on the oath had changed to one very like that of Marpeck.[58] To complicate matters, apparently Maler was not thoroughly familiar with Marpeck's writings. Two of his editorial decisions stand out as illustrations. In the original table of contents to the Kunstbuch,[59] Maler ascribed authorship of one of Marpeck's seminal treatises, "Concerning Hasty Judgments and Verdicts" (no. 7) to an unknown Anabaptist. At the same time, he ascribed to Marpeck "Concerning True Godliness" (no. 41), when it was actually the work of Spiritualist Christian Entfelder.

Contradictory evidence abounds about Maler's convictions and the nature of his role in the Marpeck Circle. In his meticulous compiling of the seminal texts of the movement gathered around Pilgram, was Maler simply paying homage to Marpeck and his collaborators in leadership, such as Leupold Scharnschlager and Cornelius Veh? Did he, as Walter Klaassen and William Klassen have stressed, "emphatically . . . not abandon Marpeck's theological accomplishments as out-of-date and unworkable"?[60] Other scholars wonder whether Maler was one of the "homeless minds" of his age, who could not find a place in any community.[61] Heinold Fast, Maler's biographer, concludes that Maler

---

57 "A Beginning of a True Christian Life" (no. 6).

58 "Why He Changed His Position on the Oath," Interlude 4.

59 BSOT, 94–96.

60 MLDC, 354.

61 The term is Packull's, and he does not apply it explicitly to Maler (MESG, 155).

remade what was originally a literature of dissent and struggle into one of edification.[62] Examining the evidence from yet another perspective, Martin Rothkegel asserts that Marpeck's vision of a bourgeois urban Anabaptism was no longer viable by the time of his death.[63]

And why did the editor of the codex take it to Zurich to be bound? Was it merely that it was less dangerous to approach a bookbinder in a strange place than in one where he was known and watched? Or was the book intended for a likeminded but more tenacious community than his own Augsburg one? Does Maler's journey to Switzerland suggest that he believed the legacy he had compiled would be more faithfully preserved by the very Swiss Brethren congregations against whose biblicism and separatism he had once chafed?

These are overarching questions that can guide readers as they make their way through an ambiguous and fascinating treasure.

Historical and theological considerations

Thus far this introduction has sought to place Marpeck and Maler within their personal, intellectual, and social backgrounds in order to illuminate their role in the formation of the Kunstbuch. The task before us now is to turn our focus to the codex itself and what it can teach us about the distinctive stream of Anabaptist church life we associate with Pilgram Marpeck.

The first question is, how did the Kunstbuch come to be? Three possibilities suggest themselves. First, is its content the final stage of a long process? In other words, had this collection already been circulating—and growing as it incorporated local favourites? Second, is the content of the anthology largely an embodiment of the movement's communal leadership, combined with the respect it accorded individual inspiration? In other words, is the Kunstbuch's diversity a faithful expression of the communities it documents? If either of these is the case, Maler would be primarily a copyist, someone who wrote out familiar writings for a new generation of believers. Or, third, is Maler's role that of an editor: are the contents of the collection a reflection of his com-

---

62 Fast, "Vom Amt des 'Lesers' zum Kompilator des sogenannten Kunstbuches," 217.

63 Martin Rothkegel, "Randglossen zum Kunstbuch," MG 61 (2004): 62.

mitments? If that is the case, then Maler is engaging in an act of theological creativity and dissent—going against the communal grain and rehabilitating figures such as Hut and even Entfelder.

Scholarship has long been divided in its judgment about whether the codex preserves Marpeckite tradition. This first question needs to be asked in two ways. First, are its authors and subjects of one mind with Marpeck and his closest co-workers? The second approach is to ask if the Kunstbuch's authors and subjects are in keeping with the ethos of the broader movement around Marpeck. Most often the question is phrased only in the first way.

In his probing examination of the ever-growing polarization between Anabaptists such as Entfelder, who had turned toward Spiritualism, and Marpeck, Packull finds it "inexplicable" that Entfelder was given a place in the Kunstbuch; he goes so far as to question whether it is truly a Pilgramite document.[64] Rothkegel continues this line of thought. He asks whether Maler was conscious of the theological heterogeneity—indeed, the contradictory character—of his collection of texts, in which Marpeck texts stand next to those of his theological opponents Christian Entfelder and Valentin Ickelsamer.[65] Later in his portrayal of the community behind the Kunstbuch, Rothkegel describes it as urban through and through, bearing the literary and intellectual traditions of artisan guilds, as well as their limitations.[66]

The confessionalization of the German cities and territories exacted such comprehensive conformity from citizens that this remarkable experiment in fusing urban sensibility with radical religion, a bourgeois way of life with costly discipleship, appeared to be doomed.[67] Therefore, Rothkegel concludes, the Kunstbuch represents Maler's departure from Marpeckite Anabaptism. Marpeck's most recent biographers vigorously contest this conclusion. On the basis of Marpeck's own pastoral writing, Klaassen and Klassen acknowledge that a middle ground between legalism and its opposite could not be stabilized. But they

---

64 MESG, 163.

65 Rothkegel, "Randglossen zum Kunstbuch," 55.

66 Ibid, 62.

67 Klaassen and Klassen describe the harsh effect of the Schmalkaldian Wars on this process (MLDC, 287–96).

draw a conclusion different from Rothkegel's. "The Kunstbuch was the last, herculean effort of an aging follower to give the Marpeck legacy new life in a radically different setting."[68]

For all his mastery of the subject, Rothkegel's assertion that Marpeckian Anabaptism was an urban phenomenon seems too unguarded a claim, at least without further defining of what is meant by urban. For instance, was Nikolsburg, with a few thousand inhabitants, considered to be an urban center in sixteenth-century central Europe? Were the congregations in the Leber Valley, south of Strasbourg, urban because of their association with Strasbourg? Could it be that Maler's taking of the Kunstbuch codex to Zurich to be bound (and by implication, to the Swiss Brethren) was a last, faithful attempt to give the Marpeck Circle legacy a home outside the confessionalized cities, in the unstable but durable Swiss Brethren settings outside town walls and on remote mountainsides?

The Kunstbuch is remarkable in the range of its writings. The more closely one looks, the more this breadth seems to mirror the diversity of influences on Pilgramite congregations, as seen in the codex's pastoral writings. This diversity should not surprise us, because Marpeck himself was an eclectic thinker and imaginative compiler. His world of ideas stands behind the borrowing and editing of Bernard Rothmann's *Bekentnisse van beyden Sacramenten* and its refashioning into the admonition (*Vermannung*) of 1542. He willingly employed a text that had been useful in reaching a notorious outcome that went totally against his grain, namely, the takeover of Münster in an Anabaptist holy war.[69] In addition, Marpeck's personality should be taken into account. What we know of him suggests that unlike many people, his ego needs were modest. In contrast to other early South German–Austrian radicals, such as Schiemer and Schlaffer, Marpeck relied on the model not of a self-appointed prophet but of a minister commissioned by the church. He had an unusual talent for collaborative work, as is evident in his collective writing projects.

---

68 MLDC, 353–54.

69 Conversation with Hans-Jürgen Goertz in Hamburg on 6 December 2006.

Because a pluralism of positions had characterized the Marpeck Circle from the beginning, and because Marpeck's personality and habits nowhere suggest that he thought himself the only authority in the circle, there was never the assumption that the community's canon would reflect only Marpeck's theology. Therefore it is improbable that Marpeck would have been threatened to find that his words alone were not enough, in the age of confessionalization, to sustain these beleaguered communities. If not in all its particulars, then in the principle of borrowing texts that speak to the need at hand, the Kunstbuch may be seen to be compatible with Marpeck's approach to ministry. His explicitly stated goal when he revised Rothmann's work on the sacraments was the unity of the fractured body of Christ.[70] The evidence suggests that this was also Maler's goal in his compilation of the codex.

This claim still leaves unanswered the question of who first made the editorial decision to preserve writings beyond those of the Pilgramite elders, documents that had become life giving for congregations whose existence was precarious. The presence of many glosses within and beside the columns of text can be read in two different ways. They could be Maler's personal stamp on writings already canonized by the community. Yet they could also be taken as evidence of Maler's active style of editing: he aspired not to be a mere copyist but to shape the collection from start to finish. Maler's lack of reluctance to edit Hut's mystical contribution ("A Beginning of a True Christian Life," no. 6) or Marpeck's own epistles may be taken as evidence for seeing the Kunstbuch as much as Maler's creation as it was of the congregations in whose life these writings already had a place.

Let us turn to the texts themselves for clues. What light do they shed on these questions and assertions? Preface 1 sets forth Maler's intention[71] in verse.

Many a divine mystery lies in this book;
if you so desire,

---

70 WPM, 164–67.

71 At this stage of research we cannot say to what extent Maler's selections represent communal choices that have grown up over the years and to what extent the contents of the codex reflect Maler's personal judgment. Hence, the use of "Maler" in this discussion includes both possibilities.

it will illuminate your heart, courage, and understanding.
Therefore make room for it with heart's devotion.
Constantly practise the fear of God.
When you can't grasp something,
ask God to grant you understanding.
That will protect you completely from violent judgment!

Maler is offering his readers help along the path of spiritual comprehension. This purpose is reinforced in Preface 2, in which Ickelsamer warns with wit and passion against the pretensions of scholarship and its too-ready alliance with hierarchy and violence. The author (and the editor) makes bold political judgments in an attempt to be faithful to the gospel. Ickelsamer debunks the pretensions of the official churches as well as the divisive sects. It is Ickelsamer's prophetic utterances and his iconoclasm, much more than his Spiritualist frame of reference, that seem to make him appealing to Maler.

As we prepare ourselves to examine the texts—particularly those that seem furthest from the core—it is important to remind ourselves that modern categories are inadequate to grasp the nature of the communities of thought represented by the Kunstbuch. To take the example of the Spiritualists: to insist that the Bible is not primarily a book of commandments does not necessarily mean that one is rejecting its authority. To seek a mystical experience of grace rather than a code of behaviour does not mean that one is thereby necessarily trying to reduce the cost of discipleship. In fact, the Spiritualist goal was to free oneself from the lesser forms of the spiritual life for the greater ones. It was crystal clear to the writers and the hearers of the Kunstbuch that "When Christ calls a man, he bids him come and die," as Dietrich Bonhoeffer wrote in *The Cost of Discipleship.* One senses from the opening passages of the Kunstbuch onward that the criterion for inclusion in this canon is less theological, in the sense of doctrinal formulations, than spiritual, in the sense of learning the art of surrender.

This is clearly the case for the presence in the collection of writings by three brilliant martyrs who shaped South German Anabaptism before it split into factions: Hans Hut (no. 6: "A Beginning of a True Christian Life"), Leonhard Schiemer (no. 9: Concerning the Grace of God"; no. 10: "The Twelve Articles of the Christian Faith"; and no. 11:

"A True, Short Gospel to Be Preached Today to the World"), and Hans Schlaffer (no. 12: "A Simple Prayer"). It was they, more than any others, who married an apocalyptic strand of late medieval mysticism to a believers church ecclesiology, including its biblical literacy and missionary fervour. Apocalyptic mysticism was not Marpeck's stance, but he does share with his three forerunners a commitment to a life of surrender.[72] Here again Marpeck's character traits need to be taken into account. From what we know, Marpeck did what he could to avoid martyrdom. Models for faithfulness to death had to come from elsewhere. When the writings of this cloud of three martyr witnesses are read with a critical theological eye, their spiritualist and mystical bent stands out. But they were cherished primarily for reasons other than their theological orthodoxy; they were models of prayerful nonresistant faithfulness in the face of death.

The Kunstbuch gives Marpeck ample space to make his theology and spirituality clear. In no. 7 ("Concerning Hasty Judgments and Verdicts") he extols patience as the surpassing gift of the Spirit. In no. 18 ("Concerning Five Fruits of True Repentance") his piety is laid out with remarkable conciseness. In no. 33 ("Concerning the Christian and Hagarite Churches") he warns against false manifestations of church. And in no. 35 ("Concerning the Lowliness of Christ") he rises to lyrical bursts of praise for the lowliness of Christ. His own writing in the codex (no. 14, "An Attempt to Win Him for Christendom"; no. 25, "An Account of Faith"; and no. 40, "Confession of Faith according to Holy Scripture") provides evidence that Maler shared many of these convictions. In no. 14 he concludes his conversation with a seeker by appealing for faith sealed in believers baptism in a believers church. Texts included from the popular Lutheran Hartmut von Cronberg (no. 21, "War Ordinance of the Heavenly Emperor for His Captains") and the even more popular Spiritualist Christian Entfelder (no. 41, "Concerning True Godliness") take their place in this anthology because of their

72 With Walter Klaassen's ascription of the authorship of "Exposé of the Babylonian Whore" to Marpeck (LWPM, 22–23), common assumptions about Marpeck's theological stance need to be reviewed.

burning conviction that God leads his suffering church. This was the word of God the church craved to keep it on the path of faithfulness.

The publication of the Kunstbuch in a German critical edition and an English popular edition moves us a mighty step closer to a true perception of the Marpeck Circle—Marpeck himself and his fellow leaders, especially Maler, as well as the circumstances, habits of mind, and spiritual pursuits of the congregations they led. As we read we can begin to imagine the world the Kunstbuch reflected and what it meant to the original writers and readers. Yet the full logic of the editor's choices still eludes the modern reader.

The modern editions of the Kunstbuch measurably expand our knowledge of one largely urban expression of Anabaptism that flourished between 1530 and 1560. As noted above, it records the life of one kind of Anabaptism in rare detail, preserving for posterity the personalities and issues, the brilliance and the tragedy, that made it what it was. If it is akin to an album of photographs taken of a family and its friends over a period of thirty years, we cannot say with certainty who started assembling the album. But we know who completed it. The fact that there are many photos of a few people tells us they were the immediate family. But the album had space for pictures of others, some of them estranged relatives and even strangers. In the mind of the album maker, all of them belonged. To move from metaphorical to literal speech, the Kunstbuch is Maler's record of Marpeck's legacy.

In the writings it puts between two covers, the Kunstbuch cuts its own swath and at the same time demonstrates Marpeck's principle of synthesis: biblicist principles and Spiritualist ones, dogma and discipleship, inwardness and outwardness. This outwardness is the implicit, pastoral form of Marpeck's sacramentalism, which is worked out explicitly in other volumes of the Marpeck Circle, whose concern was theology.

The writing and compiling of the Kunstbuch arose from impassioned attempts to be the body of Christ faithfully and to trust God utterly in the midst of terrifying insecurity. In their faithfulness and trust, Marpeck's people are a cloud of witnesses who have a claim on us today.

Preface 1 [title page]

"The Book of Understanding is my name"

Jörg Maler
26 September 1561

A straightforwardly composed piece of verse serves as the foreword to the Kunstbuch. It is the first of several introductions or prefaces to portions of the text, written in rhyming quatrains (in the original) and concluded with a proverb. Jörg Maler promises the reader that his volume contains "many a divine mystery," perceived only by practising the fear of God. This preface makes clear that the book's contents are not primarily intellectual but spiritual, not accessible to reason but to the inspiration of God's Spirit. Maler repeatedly quotes from a late medieval tradition of pious sayings and writes in the same style.

The preface to the Kunstbuch was added after Maler had "transported it to where it then belonged." Is this comment coded, in order to protect the authors, editor, and binder, or is it a flourish intended to add a touch of mystery to the text? We know that the Kunstbuch was bound in Zurich, so it likely was intended for the use of the Swiss Brethren. In addition, Maler's appeal to read it with humility so as to avoid harsh judgment evokes Pilgram Marpeck's arguments with the Swiss.[1] This does not preclude Maler's more fraternal concern to pro-

---

Vorspann 1: Jörg Maler, "Das Kunstbuch bin ich genannt" (Titelseite); 26. September 1561. Translation by Leonard Gross.

1 See KB, no. 7: "Concerning Hasty Judgments and Verdicts."

vide persecuted fellow believers with a collection laying out the struggles and insights of other communities of Anabaptists.

The Book of Understanding is my name;
I am unknown to the fleshly minded.
Yet whoever has the Spirit of Christ
will find in me, throughout life,
whatever frees heart and soul.
What we do flourishes solely through God;
it is far above silver and gold.
Therefore, devout one, be pleasing to him from the heart.
Many a divine mystery lies in this book;
if you so desire,
it will illuminate your heart, courage, and understanding.
Therefore make room for it with heart's devotion.
Constantly practise the fear of God.
When you can't grasp something,
ask God to grant you understanding.
That will protect you completely from violent judgment!
May God grant this to us through his goodness,
through Jesus Christ, his Son.
May he help us from his throne of grace. Amen.

Written and completed
the twenty sixth of September,
in the sixty-first year,
after which I transported it
to where it then belonged.
May God bestow his grace on all of us. Amen.

Jörg of Augsburg, called Painter[2]

"If you desire peace and tranquility,
remain silent, not responding to every concern.
Make allowances, and meet obligations
to the magistracy. Avoid evil society. . . ."

Freidank[3]

2 [Original: *Maler.*—Ed.]

3 [See BSOT, 98.—Ed.]

Preface 2

"The learned ones, the wrongheaded ones"

Valentin Ickelsamer

The poem that dominates the introductory section of the Kunstbuch is part of a long tradition of devotional literature that can now be traced back to the fifteenth century. Decrying academics as those who pervert the truth, as people who use intellectual refinement to get around the truth, is an ancient theme. Recent scholarship has discovered a lineage of texts, of widely varying lengths, that elaborate on the dangers of learning and the wrongness of compulsion in matters of faith.[1] The bulk of the poem is an expansion of these ideas into a biting commentary on the "perversion" of the Reformation.

Valentin Ickelsamer was born around 1500 in the area of Rothenburg on the Tauber River in south-central Germany (80 kilometres due west of Nuremberg). He studied in Erfurt (170 kilometres due north of Nuremberg) from 1518 to 1520, and afterward—during the culmina-

---

Vorspann 2: Valentin Ickelsamer, "Die Gelehrten, die Verkehrten." Translation by Gerhard Reimer.

1 Heiko A. Oberman, "Die Gelehrten, die Verkehrten: Popular Response to Learned Culture in the Renaissance and Reformation," in *Religion and Culture in the Renaissance and Reformation*, Sixteenth Century Studies and Essays, vol. 11, ed. Steven E. Ozment, 43–62 (Kirksville, MO: Sixteenth Century Journal Publishers, 1989).

tion of Andreas Karlstadt's radical reform—in Wittenberg (80 kilometres south of Berlin).[2] He sided with Karlstadt and gave him refuge in Rothenburg when Karlstadt had been banished by Martin Luther. Then Ickelsamer—who participated in a citizens' group that was in contact with the rebellious peasants—fled Rothenburg after the suppression of the Peasants Revolt in 1525. Beginning in 1530 he seems to have lived in Augsburg, where he probably wrote his famous German grammar, *Ein Teütsche Grammatica,* and perhaps crossed paths with Jörg Maler.

Ickelsamer was acquainted with Caspar Schwenckfeld, who was also in Augsburg in 1534–35. Schwenckfeld dedicated a letter to Ickelsamer, in which he comforted him during an illness.[3] In the summer of 1542 Ickelsamer directed a small tract (*Tractettlin*) to Schwenckfeld, in which he opposed Pilgram Marpeck's supposed teaching that Christ incarnate was capable of sinning. In a circular letter dated New Year's Eve, 1544, Marpeck responded angrily to Schwenckfeld and Ickelsamer's attacks. Again in an undated second part of his response opposing Schwenckfeld, Marpeck polemicized against Ickelsamer's tract of 1542.[4] To the best of our knowledge, Ickelsamer died in Augsburg in 1546.

We do not know whether Maler knew Ickelsamer and Schwenckfeld. In any case, he was attracted to the thinking of these fierce opponents of Marpeck, enough to open a collection of Marpeck Circle writings with an epic poem by one of them. This fact in turn fuels debate about whether Maler edited the Kunstbuch as a faithful perpetuator of the Marpeck tradition or as someone trying to take it in a different direction.

Ickelsamer's religious-didactic poem "The Learned Ones, the Wrongheaded Ones" is written in rhymed couplets with four accented syllables per line. It extensively interprets and makes contemporary the

---

2 Karlstadt was one of Luther's professors and was won to Luther's cause. Karlstadt became more radical than Luther and a source of teaching for Swiss Anabaptists.

3 This anonymous tract, possibly written by Schwenckfeld or Ickelsamer, had already been printed twice by the year 1533. It is included in the Kunstbuch (no. 39): "An Epistle of Comfort Compiled from Holy Scripture."

4 PMA, 426.

proverb "The educated ones, the false ones," a proverb documented in Sebastian Franck's collection of proverbs (*Sprichwörtersammlung*), among other sources. We do not know why Ickelsamer's poem is included twice in the Kunstbuch, once in the introduction and again as no. 22.[5]

Scholars are the villains of this story. The term *Gelehrten* ("scholars" or "learned ones") applies here to everyone who uses intellectual savvy to deceive and dominate, beginning with the scribes of the New Testament, going on to the architects of the imperial church, and culminating in the self-serving and polemical rhetoricians of the sixteenth century. The author shows no mercy! Part of the Spiritualist protest against academic dogmatism was its futility: it could not lead people to the simplicity of faith. We don't know whether the author's target is only the educated clergy of the magisterial churches or also Anabaptist theologians, perhaps even including Marpeck.

The polemic has an egalitarian tinge, insisting that all Christians are taught of God, on the model of 1 Corinthians 14. Their only ruler is Christ. It castigates imposed faith that forces uniformity on people of different beliefs. This accusation is clearly directed against the official churches. But the accusation that "each one interprets it as he jolly well likes" fits better as a criticism of the many Anabaptist groups. At the same time, Ickelsamer's indictment of contemporary attempts to bring the kingdom of God (or at least the church) by force—the Peasants' War, the slaughter at Zurich, the Münster revolution, and the Schmalkaldian War—and his counsel of patience against enemies are cut from the same cloth as Marpeck's views.

5 In this edition and in BSOT this poem appears only once, here. In other recensions of this poem, parts of the text appear in varying order. A number of the variants in this version come from Maler's hand (BSOT, 100).

Foreword to the reader

It's about the old proverb concerning the learned ones,
telling us why they were called
the wrongheaded ones by those of yore—
that's what you're going to find out in this text.

What I've simply tried to do here is to collect
what the learned ones have said about this,
those who have written recently or a long time ago.
I've left it at that
and have not added anything new to it.
However, I've put it into rhymes
that are brief and a pleasure to read,
as was the custom even of the ancients,
for they accomplished great things, albeit not in overabundance,
with few words.
So read this with modesty. Pay attention!
Note who we're talking about and what is being said,
with nothing uttered to hurt or praise anyone,
as God in heaven above knows,
but to test the teachings
as well as the teachers
to see if they are just and of God.
This is a test that Christ has commanded,
and for this reason it is really important
for those in the church and for individual Christians
who wish to preserve themselves from errors
and continue firmly in their faith.
Such a one shall form his own verdict
and not depend on some scholar.
If the ancients had done this
they would have proceeded differently.
May God protect us
so that we might note the difference
about which Christ himself says Mt 13 (52)
that some are learned about things of the kingdom of God, 1 Tm 5 (17)

and these are worth twice their value.
You should listen to them and accept them
but let the wicked ones go.
This is the way you should understand the proverb
if you do not want to be led astray.
Take note of this, dear reader,
I want to give you my opinion;
if you don't like it, you can disregard it.
To this end, may God protect us. Amen.

All of my days I've heard
a lot said about experience. People justly say
that she's the mistress of all understanding.[6]
So it's not for nothing
that experience is called the mother
of all proverbs, as is well known.
And we're also told
that those of old said:
The more learned you are,
the prouder and the more senseless you will be.
For that's the way they experienced it
with the learned ones who dwelt among them
shortly after the time of the apostles.
They confused everyone
when they tried to rule all of Christendom
with their philosophy
and with Moses' law,
using their power and tyranny.
That resulted in murder and great sorrow,
as one finds it amply told
in chronicles and ancient history.
Then came the Sophists,
Ockamists and Scotists,
Albertists and Thomists,

---

6 [*Kunst* could also be translated "art," "artistry," "savvy," or even "knowledge."—Ed.]

not to mention Alexander of Hales,
Nominalists and Realists,[7]
and the whole lot,
as they are well known
to the institutes of higher learning, all of whom
have ruined Christendom
with their questions,
arguments, and opinions,
with their inquisitiveness and their worldly wisdom—
although I have no doubts
that among them also was many a pious scholar
who did not know any better
and behaved this way because he thought he did right.
I want to excuse all these
and talk only about those
about whom all the prophets complain,
those who have always misled the people,
and with whom Christ himself argued.
As we read in Matthew, Mt 15 (1–20); 23
there have always been these scribes,
who, with their idle talk, forever
demeaned Holy Scripture of
its reverence and true intent.
Even during Paul's time
there were learned people like this,
concerned especially about circumcision, Gal 5 (11); 6 (12)
who, without sense and without the Spirit of God,
simply clung doggedly to the letter of the law,
with which they played around in all the churches,
muscled their way in,
and also claimed to be apostles, Acts 15 (1)
advancing their cause with good appearances.
So that they might live in peace,

7 [These names refer to late medieval philosophers and schools of philosophy.—Ed.]

they preached Moses and in addition
introduced circumcision,
confusing everybody
and stirring up great discord
in all of early Christendom.
Paul argued against them
with the power of God and with miracles,
not solely with scriptures,
for they had those in common with him,
they studied it day and night,
and with scripture they carried on pompously.
Otherwise they had neither power nor might
with which to give value to their teaching.
They were nothing but scribes
who perverted all Paul's teachings,
rebelling against Paul,
and indeed, frequently persecuting him,
even calling on secular powers,
the same as the Pharisees did to Christ.
These people had the same spirit.
Everywhere, above all,
they resisted the Holy Spirit,
as Stephen said they did Acts 7 (51)
and as all the prophets lamented.
People like the ones mentioned
from antiquity into our time
stand by the proverb that is true
and you will find much written about it
in books both new and old.
They interpret it in the same way
that I'm telling you here.

Now listen and be very quiet;
I'm pointing you to the true goal.
Note with all modesty
about what and whom we're talking here.
For I wouldn't want

to blame any pious scholar.
For whoever is pious and well learned,
such a person is worthy of all honour. Mt 13 (52)
But so that I get on track here,
let me begin with the first case:
Who was it that cast Susanna into such grief,[8] Dn 1; Susanna
condemned her falsely to death,
but the old priests and the false learned ones,
who got judgment and justice turned around?[9]
Who was it that brought pious Daniel
into such fear and suffering,
but the deceitful learned ones,
as it is clearly revealed
in the book of Daniel?[10] Dn
Hear this, in truth, what Christ himself says,
about this mob of false learned ones.
Who was it that persecuted the prophets of God,
stoned them and had them killed,
but the scribes alone
who flaunt their arrogance,
who fulfilled the measure of their ancestors
by the incessant spilling of blood?[11]
Who was it that killed Christ
and brought Jerusalem into such dire straits
so that the city and its walls were turned upside down?
(Such lamentation never was heard!)
It was none other than the learned council,
who were blinded by jealousy and envy.
As it is written,
they opposed Christ Jesus, our Lord,

---

8 [The reference here is to Dn 13, which is found only in the Apocrypha.—Ed.]

9 [The whole of the apocryphal book of Susanna is concerned with this story.—Ed.]

10 Dn 6:13ff. [Dn 6:1–18; in this case, the learned ones are politicians.—Ed.]

11 Mt 23:29–34.

perverting his Word and teachings
until they finally killed him.

Now continue to listen and take note:
Who was it that destroyed the city of Rome
and brought its empire to an end?[12*]
Who was it that always fought with emperors
and subjugated their empire to foreign domination?
Who was it that made the emperors into their subjects
and made them servants of the church,
so that they were subject to the pope
and had to receive their crown from him,
to believe in him, honour and swear
and recognize him as their lord,
so that they themselves were in control
of the empire as well as the kingdom of heaven?
He gives to whom he will,
and withholds from whom he will: that person is simply
out of luck.
Who betrayed Christianity
with such finesse and swiftness
but the perverse ones learned in Holy Scripture?
They caused all this wickedness;
they brought this false doctrine into the world
to achieve honour and money.
Outwardly they appeared pious,
but the world wants to be fooled.
They took good note of this
and really worked and wormed their way
into worldly society
so that very soon
they got power, their own subjects, and land,
that their power and wealth
made them obey
and bow down before them,

12* Rome the city.

the rulers of this world.
That's what their deceit brought about.

Now keep listening and paying attention:
Who collected the treasures of this world,
with indulgences and Turkish money?
Indeed, none other than the scribes,
the ones who also perverted the kingdom of Christ
and turned it into a worldly kingdom,
living off the fat of the land,
idling away all day long,
as they keep doing until this very day?
Who was it that split up the churches so badly
from Greece up to the Occident[13]
with false glosses and commentaries?
Who was it that desecrated the simplicity of faith,
breaking up your covenant in many a way?
It was the scribes with their tricks and savvy!
Who brought about this disfavour
between Christians and those called Turks,
in the process ruining people and land?
None others than the scholars of Rome
with their bulls and indulgence crap,
which they used to go to war with the Turks!

Now take note, each one of you, whether I'm lying
and not sticking to the facts.
The learned ones never have remorse,
which is the way we see it today;
their manner and malice do them no service.
This is true of the books
written by scholars on both sides,
What useless words they write,

---

13 [A chief criticism made by the Spiritualists about all visible structures of church life, including those of the Anabaptists, was that they divide the church. It is evident here that their understanding of the body of Christ included the Eastern Churches.—Ed.]

ripping each other apart
like boys competing to sell hotcakes in front of your house!
Even if there were something good in it,
it does not appear that way
because of all the berating and malice of every kind.
With spite, boasting, and a lot of noise
each one of them tries to get the upper hand,
forcing their understanding on everyone else.
In the name of faith, both new and old, Rv 13
each side hangs on to its spitefulness;
they call each other liars in public.
In the pulpit they do nothing but make war.
Where they should teach salvation of the soul,
they offer nothing but jealousy and envy for sale.
And especially in their writings,
whatever one knows about the other one,
all this has to be brought up
and exposed like some great calamity.
What earlier was considered a scandal even among the pagans
is now an honour in a Christian country.
For whoever can carry on the most
thinks he's caught the prize and claims to have done no wrong,
trying to twist things around
so that it is all for the glory of God.
The Word of God, the teachings of Christ,
the councils of old, the advice of the elders,
the customs of the church and old habits,
these are the things with which the scoundrels adorn themselves,
until each of them finds support
that protects him in his teachings.
Then they go on boasting,
sparing no effort to write yet more books.
The devil himself must get a kick out of that.
You're not supposed to do anything in God's congregation
but what they formulate and teach.
There is no more fear and trembling

before God's congregation and Paul's teaching.
The discipline[14]
Paul gave to the Corinthians is despised, 1 Cor 14 (26–33)
about how the people in the church should behave,
not to mention the teachers,
that when they prophesy,
only two or three are testing it,
when such evaluation should be open
to the whole congregation in attendance,
so that they all benefit from the teaching.
And when God reveals something
to someone else at the same time,
then he should first listen to that person,
fraternally disciplining and teaching each other, Mt 18 (15–17); Lk 17 (3)
as Paul did to Peter. Gal 2 (11)
We're a long way from this now:
no one wants to be disciplined anymore,
and if you question this you'll be hated.
So you depend on power and trickery
and on the favours of the princes and lords.
If someone speaks up against it,
yes, even if it were Christ himself
in an attempt to discipline them for an error,
then they all scream bloody murder
that such heresy,
mob spirit, and fanaticism
should be quickly uprooted and expelled,
stabbed, snarled at, and killed,
so that none will remain.[15*]
Yes, even if it was quite obvious
that they themselves had
publicly written and taught

[14] [Original: *ordnung*.—Ed.]

[15*] Gloss: In 1532 in the Synod of Bern they fell from their primary teachings again and set secular law into the kingdom of Christ and began to tyrannize.

this as Holy Scripture,
it must not be considered valid anymore,
and they're justifying this with boasting and abusing words,
or they're emphasizing and continuing to persist
that they did it with the best of intentions,
and that earlier they simply did not understand them,
even though you can still check it out in their books.
Thus they gloss it over nicely
and lead us around by the nose.
They even think they can make us blind
while we see clearly with our eyes!
No matter what a mess they've created,
they claim to be quite innocent:
"The devil must have done it!"
They don't know anything about it
and blame others for it.
They notice about others
what is true of their own hearts:
they're heretics, wretches, fanatics, sectarians,
which really proceeds from their very own teaching,
from their writings, both new and old.
Solely those things are valid that please them
and serve their cause at every turn;
everything else does not count.
Even what is spiritually valid,
what we call "the decree,"
and which is found in scripture,
yes, and in the Gospels,
if any of this opposes the way they behave,
they quickly explain it away,
deriding and laughing at it.
They're instigators and defenders of their own cause,
which wasn't even considered right by pagan peoples,
and for these scholars of Christendom
it's supposed to be considered completely in order.
Oh, will they be sorry some day!

With the help of the government
they wanted to lord it over faith,
rob Christians of their freedom,
likewise be masters of God's congregation,
thinking they are the only ones that know anything.
Because they have the proper title,
they are called master and doctor,
even though it is written
that all Christians are taught of God.[16]
Among them no one should be called master; Mt 23 (8)
they should confess Christ alone as their head,
for he is the only one that guides and directs them
and adorns them through his Spirit with gifts.
Whoever simply believes and teaches this,
such a one is shabby and of no worth, 1 Cor 4 (13)
perverted in the extreme.
They accuse him of jealousy and hate:
he simply wants to mislead others
and cancel everything that's true.
That's how they explain away Christ's teachings,
turning everything upside down.
They praise or desecrate
to arouse enmity or favour
by using rhetoric or self-invented arts.
These are all things they use to achieve their ends,
causing great troubles
throughout all of Christianity,
because without any differentiation
they mix up
worldly power with the kingdom of Christ,
wanting to make matters of faith
common among all people,
bringing about unity of faith
with the force of the government.

---

16 Is 54:13; Jn 6:45; 1 Thes 4:9.

That's never the way
it's been since the beginning of time!
For belief is a gift of God,
not something over which humans have control,
and it's not everyone's thing either.[17]
They, however, don't pay any attention to this.
By doing that, they destroy the natural right
of those on top and those below, of the lords as well as the servants.
They cause avoidance between the classes
and say they do it for faith's sake; secretly they're jealous
and claim to serve God doing this,
which is something he never commanded.
Everyone claims to have the best belief
and they're probably still far from it—
you already sense that
when you consider their fruits.[18]
That's what the scholars are always up to:
with their writings and their carrying on
they inflame people against one another
so that the people in the whole country
turn against one another in anger,
and piously they cover up this dangerous poison
with the letters of Holy Scripture.
They just turn up their nose:
today they say one thing, tomorrow another;
now it's a stone, and then it's bread.[19]
Scripture is nothing but a bag of tricks
with which they perform their monkey games.
Each one interprets it as he jolly well likes;
once they go this way, then again the other way.
They can pull a text in any direction,
doing their best to make it look good,

---

17 2 Thes 3:2.

18 Mt 7:16, 20.

19 [Lk 11:11.—Ed.]

giving the impression this is God's Word and will.
Indeed, no one dare interrupt them!
They confuse ordinary people,
so they don't know if they're coming or going.
This is a problem especially concerning the sacrament,
as they call it,[20*]
even though it is clearly stated
how the apostles and Christ himself celebrated it.
As a result the common people turn against the learned ones—
papists, Lutherans, whatever they are.
This is all because of the scholars' wanton spirit.
Thinking so highly of oneself has never been a good thing,
and no good ever came out of it.
People understood this
long ago and do so in our day.
I don't want to talk more about it now,
for that's the way it is,
even if people can't see it or put it into words.
I'm going to leave it at that,
for in this text I meant
to refer only to the bad guys.

You can probably still find
someone who is both pious and learned,
as was the case when Nicodemus was with the Jews Jn 3 (1)
and Paul a part of the group of the apostles.
God can use even learned people!
Whoever makes proper use of an art is not hurt by it,
for art is measured by
what its possessor does with it.
All knowledge and all good gifts of God
that scholars use for God's kingdom must be praised,
for from their goodly treasure, Mt 13 (52)
from both the old and the new laws,

[20*] Gloss: The bread of Christ is fat [as in the fat of a sacrifice]. He [or it] provides the royal pleasures.

they present good teaching
for our salvation and God's glory.
What Christ says of the wealthy
also applies to the learned ones and their ilk,
that they can enter the kingdom of heaven
only with much difficulty and grief. Mk 10 (23–25)
That, then, is why few of them
are chosen and called to be children of God.
As it is repeatedly written
at many places in Holy Scripture:
knowledge without love is vain poison. Mt 22 (14); 1 Cor 1 (26)
Love without knowledge would probably be enough,
for whoever puts his hand to the plow Lk 9 (62)
and looks for peace and rest in Christ
may still by accompanied by troubles
wherever he is, Mt 10 (17ff.)
for others may try to hurt him.[21]
If such a person persists and does not look back,
he would surely enter the kingdom of heaven,
even though he couldn't read or write.
There have been many pious people
who were dear to God and treasured by him
before reading and writing were taught,
since reading and writing were only known a thousand
years after the creation of the world,
when human memory was of service.
For God commanded Moses
to write down his miracles
so that they would not be forgotten.
The apostles also wrote
and commanded that the scriptures be read,
to help them evaluate and preserve Jn 5 (39); 2 Tm 3 (16)
the teachers and their teachings,
in order to judge and reinforce them,

21 Mt 7:12; Lk 6:31.

as well as learning to understand and take note
of God's judgments and works,
which are revealed to us in Holy Scripture.
Would to God that everyone knew
how to read and understand!
I'm not embarrassed to express this wish,
for it would improve our life.
After all, that's why God gave it to us!
Not that one should show off with one's knowledge of scripture,
everyone saying what he jolly well pleases,
vexing one another without end.
Doing this breeds
envy, hate, and lack of unity within Christianity,
as you have seen above.

Listen to what more I've got to say!
The Peasants' War and the slaughter at Zurich[22*]
have brought about a great transformation with regard
to preaching, writing, and teaching.
Oh God, what will become of this!
They're not striving for the right goal anymore,
and that's why we have all these sects.
In the first place, the ones called Münsterites,[23*]
who are well known to many a pious person;
according to their own interpretation,
they tried to raise up the kingdom of Israel again
by using the physical sword. Something like that is bound to fail,
and all of them perished.
It was clearly against the gospel.
That is revealed to us in Holy Scripture.
With pain and grief they realized this.

22* Peasants' War of 1525 and the Zurich slaughter of 7 October 1531.

23* Münsterites, 1533. [The reference is to violent Anabaptists' conquest of the city of Münster in northwest Germany.—Ed.]

The same thing happened to the Schmalkaldic League,[24*, 25]
who were hypocritical in their use of the gospel
when they revolted against Charles V,
which didn't do them much good.
Therefore, my dear reader, please understand
how it has been revealed to me through grace,
how Christ teaches us to fight
patiently against our enemies,
the way he did it himself
and left us with an example of this.
That's what the apostles taught,
not like those who twist scripture
as a cover-up for their malice.[26]
The time is going to come when they'll be sorry,
as will all those who have followed them.
According to the words of Christ the Lord,
eternal damnation will be their wage. Mk 9 (45–48)
Let everybody turn to him,
for without guile he directs us and teaches us.
Look into Holy Scripture for an example of this:
"Whoever takes the sword will perish!"[27]
Your own cleverness and reason won't count in this case;
Paul himself calls it foolishness. 1 Cor 1 (20)
In Ephesians 5 it tells us
how Christians should fight Eph 6 (16f.)
and how they will be judged,
but the world rejects this insight.
They continue foolishly;
resisting impatiently is what they like to do.
They demonstrate that with their behaviour—
their preachers feed them falsehoods.

24* Schmalkaldic League.

25 [In the 1540s a number of South German territories formed an alliance to impose religious and political uniformity.—Ed.]

26 1 Pt 2:16.

27 Mt 26:52.

But what does Christ say
to those who do not pursue his teachings,
who want to enter in by another way?
Whoever does so must be a thief and a murderer.[28] Jn 10 (1)
Whoever does not want to believe that
will find the Day of Judgment coming too soon.
Pay attention to what you do!
for that [violence] is not what Christ taught us.
Whoever wants a different way belongs to the riotous band
which will take him directly to hell. Nm 16 (31f.)
This is true, no matter what you say.
Christ is not going to offer us any other way.
Take note of where you're going!
Whoever will not take warning here
will suffer nothing but derision
and endure the severe judgment of God over there. Prv 1 (26); Mt 25
Whoever struggles differently loses God's grace.
Fleeing into the mountains and valleys will be of no avail[29]
when the trumpet is heard.[30]

Therefore, mortal, take this to heart!
Many a one who just goes according to his own opinion
has come to grief.
Those who still do it face utter ruin.
For what you don't like to experience here,
don't do it to your neighbour, either early or late;
remember what love has to teach you,
and do to others
what you would wish to happen to you. Mt 7 (12); Tb 4 (16)
That's what the law and the prophets are all about.
Pray for your enemy when he is in need.[31]
Repay evil with good. Rom 12 (17)

---

28 [Jn 10:7–10.—Ed.]
29 Mt 24:16; Mk 13:14.
30 Mt 24:31; 1 Cor 15:52; 1 Thes 4:16.
31 Mt 5:44.

That's what it says in Romans 5.
And you'll find the same thing in Luke 6.[32]
Take note of this, both poor and rich!
Let no one depend on his own delusion;
if you've done that, then quit it!
Confess it with remorse and sorrow,
and take up the cross with patience. Lk 9 (23)
With Christ you'll find grace; Acts 2 (38)
that's what the apostles clearly teach.
Christ led the way
so that we should follow him.
Patiently he spent his time here
and remained constant through all his suffering,
not like those pretending to be Christians,
who confuse law and gospel,
with the present as well as the former teachers,
trying to maintain their power with the sword.
In eternity that will not stand the test,
and it is truth I claim as my witness.
Oh God, come quickly; rescue us!
The godless ones are taking over,[33]
and because of that the godly suffer.
As you yourself have said,
it is clearly revealed to many
that the final hour is at hand. 1 Jn 2 (18)
Let us not be put to shame;[34] Lk 17 (5)
help us grow in faith and love;
take us up into your eternal rest,
which we anticipate in Christ.
Let us die in peace.
Do not let the world terrify us,
that we might continue on your path until death

32 Lk 6:27.
33 Mt 24:12.
34 [Ps 25.—Ed.]

and comport ourselves nobly
by the power of the Holy Spirit.
Lord, make us victorious in our faith. Amen.

Conclusion of this preface

My faithful advice therefore is
that we all look to God alone.
In things that pertain to faith,
we should not depend on any person,
neither on the highly learned, priests, laity,
neither clerical nor secular; whoever they are,
they can err and lead you astray.
We should glory in God alone.
However, those who want to become famous,

let them do it in Christ, the right goal,[35]
and let them quietly pray to God
that the will of our heavenly Father be done.
He alone can give faith,
which is what everyone should strive for.
May he grant that everything turn out well,
according to his pure Word and teaching.
He is the true way to live.
If you look for another way, you'll go astray!
Therefore all shame to us and all glory to him!
He'll not abandon us; what more do we want?
Truth is stronger than anything else;
it keeps the prize throughout eternity!
Whoever opposes truth and won't accept it literally
places his body and soul in grave danger 3 (1) Esd 4 (38)[36]

---

35 [This line begins the conclusion unique to Preface 2.—Ed.]

36 [In the NRSV, 4 Esdras/Ezra constitutes chapters 3–14 of 2 Esdras. It is considered canonical in the Slavic Bible but not the Septuagint. See Bruce M. Metzler and Roland E. Murphy, eds., *The New Oxford Annotated Bible with the Apocryphal/Deuterocanonical Books* (New York: Oxford, 1994), Apocrypha, 301.—Ed.]

and exposes himself
to great misery and danger,
as it has happened to many already.
May God look down on us in grace
so that our conscience will not get hurt,
for then the devil will give you a hard time,
trying to lead your conscience astray.
Lord, stand by us in our faith,
so that we might hold fast to the truth!
May your beloved Son help us
through your Holy Spirit of freedom,
that he himself may be our teacher
and that through him we might be able to differentiate all things
and come to eternal bliss,
which Christ has gained for us
through the bitter death he died,
becoming the expiation for our sins.
He stilled the Father's anger,
so that henceforth we would live as is pleasing to him,
so be it, in truth. May God help us all. Amen.

Blessed be the God of truth![37]

Valentin Ickelsamer,
who was a poet and died in Augsburg

Pray to God quietly.[38]
He alone can give faith,
which is the true understanding that leads to eternal life.
Let everyone strive for it,
so that God might bring everything to the best outcome.
Ours the shame and his the honour,

[37] [Original: *Benedictus Deus veritatis.*—Ed.] 3 (1) Esd 4:40.

[38] [This line begins the conclusion unique to no. 22 in the Kunstbuch collection (see fn. 5 above).—Ed.]

that we might be pleasing to God through Christ.
So be it in truth. God help us. Amen.

Interlude following no. 22: Mottoes

The remaining space on this page contains the following anonymous mottoes directly following the conclusion of no. 22:[39]

The world continues forever
and is ruled by vain insanity.
The world wants to be deceived;
it hates the truth and loves appearances.
It has high regard for the letter of the law, 2 Cor 3 (6)
and laughs at the intelligence of the Spirit.
Therefore the world also has its Christ,
whom it protects with its own actions.
It cannot stand the true Christ;
that's why he does not intercede for it. (Jn 17 [9]).

The devil isn't as ugly
as they draw him on the walls.
He wears a beautiful mask.
With that he deceives both women and men,
so that they offer him divine honour. 2 Cor 11 (14)
He is the world's god, sovereign, and lord. Mt 4 (9)
An important title and lots of money
are god and sovereign in this world.
Whoever does not worship and honour them Rv 13 (15); 14 (19)
is but dregs and worthless (1 Cor 4 [13]).

Blessed be the God of truth![40]

39 See fn. 5 above.

40 [Original: *Benedictus Deus veritatis.*—Ed.] 3 (1) Esd 4:40.

Preface 3

Admonition and warning: It is not what but that

Jörg Maler
4 March 1561

This piece of rhyming verse documents the beginning of Jörg Maler's editorial work on the Kunstbuch. He worries that his readers might rush to judgment; he urges them to let God be the judge. Readers face the danger that they may overrate their insight into spiritual matters, so their initial task in engaging thoughts that might seem strange to them is to be open to the work of the Spirit.

The theme of this piece, taken from 1 Thessalonians 5:19–21, is a favourite of Anabaptists and Spiritualists: "Do not quench the Spirit. Do not despise the words of prophets, but test everything; hold fast to what is good." The enigmatic motto "It is not what but that" can be traced back to a dispute between Marpeck and some Spiritualists in Strasbourg in 1531.[1] It is obviously intended as a response to another motto, "Not who but what," found on the title page of a Spiritualist polemic by Christian Entfelder in 1530.[2] The former—"Not what but that"—places the emphasis on the "that" of God's commandments in

---

Vorspann 3: Jörg Maler, Vermahnung und Warnung: Es ist nicht was, sonder das; 4. Marz 1561. Translation by Leonard Gross.

1 The motto is found on the title page of Marpeck's "A Clear and Useful Instruction," in WPM, 69–106. Its probable provenance is described in CC, 36–38.

2 BD, 42.

the Bible. For instance, in "A Clear and Useful Instruction," Marpeck argues with the Spiritualists that "I have been baptized precisely because it is written that one should do so."[3] Marpeck is not a simple literalist, but when he meets an argument for the autonomy of individual experience, he insists that it must be measured against an authoritative source. Against his view, the latter motto—"Not who but what"—discounts authoritative texts and individuals (the "who") and places the weight on the "what," the competence of the individual's Spirit-led private interpretation on any issue.

Maler's citation of one of Marpeck's signature phrases, "It is not what but that," as part of his introduction to the Kunstbuch clearly identifies his project with Marpeck's legacy. The dispute goes back to Schwenckfeld's derisive comments on a part of Marpeck's "A Clear and Useful Instruction" in the office of the censor in Strasbourg in 1531.[4] Schwenckfeld lumps all Christians other than Spiritualists into the same category: those who base their salvation in external forms. Thus the conflict between Schwenckfelder Spiritualists and Marpeckite Anabaptists goes back at least as far as 1531.[5]

---

3 WPM, 94.

4 These comments were copied out from the Strasbourg manuscript before it was destroyed in the fire of 1870 (Thesaurus Baumianus, MS 662, fol. 388 verso, Bibliotheque Nationale et Universitaire, Strasbourg): "After these last words, 'Not what but that,' by a certain hand which I think to be Schwenckfeld's are added as follows: 'I say that one should and must believe this, if you want to be saved.' Thus all are customed to doing so—sects, pope, Luther, Anabaptists—everyone has something external on which they base their salvation and which in its external form they require. They believe that in their procedures they are laying down requirements, but it is the devil's work even though they think it belongs to being pleasing to God from wherever he might get his power. Accordingly, the author of this booklet also follows this path. I consider it to be by Pilgram. He does not allow that any sect would be sufficient and would meet the fear of God, who would surely be satisfied with the simple fear of God. All of them attach something external to it. Everybody wants to add something to simple faith and damns or condemns all those who do not accept their position."

5 See Heinold Fast's historical and theological analysis in "Nicht was sondern das: Marpeck's Motto wider den Spiritualismus," in *Evangelischer Glaube und Geschichte*, ed. A. Raddatz and K. Lüthi (Vienna: Peter Karner, 1984), 66–74.

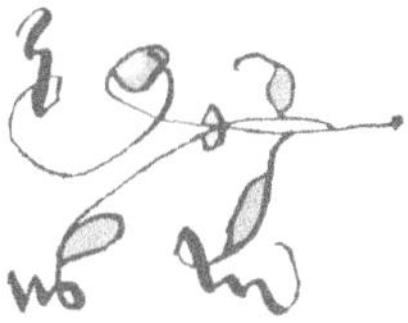

An admonition and warning not to judge maliciously so as not to violate the working of the Holy Spirit,[6] who works in us, according to our weakness, in incomprehensible ways through our reason and wisdom.[7*] In many undertakings we are too weak, even if we think we've achieved a certain spirituality.[8]

It is not what but that

This book has been written; now listen well:
from it you may receive good teaching.
In the year fifteen-hundred and sixty-one
it was begun, namely,
in the month of March on the fourth day.
Note well, godly reader, what I am saying:
don't let it become too difficult for you
if parts might not be composed to your liking,
concerning what is conceived in this book.
Then pay attention, O godly Christian,
to what the good Paul does to those
in Thessalonians; you can examine this
in the first [epistle], there in the fifth [chapter][9]
—also elsewhere in Ephesians. Eph 4 (7)
For the gifts of God are sundry,[10]
often seeming to be at odds with one another.

---

6 1 Thes 4:8; 5:19.

7* Gloss: As a common proverb states, it's easier to talk too much than eat too much.

8 1 Cor 14:37.

9 1 Thes 5:19–21.

10 Rom 12:6; 1 Cor 12:4.

If you desire that God stand at your side,
then judge nothing ahead of time. 1 Cor 4 (5)
Judgment belongs to God in this time of strife.
Rather, read all things with diligence and understanding,
asking God that it might become known to you.
Keep what is good; let go of the rest.[11]
And control your tongue,
so that blasphemers do not repudiate it,
as we are warned by Peter. 2 Pt 2 (12)
Just as you can examine everything in a chronicle
concerning what is happening in these times,
even though it is nothing new,
so you can also read Paul,
in 1 Corinthians, in the first chapter,[12]
how people there were also divided,
extolling humans more than God, 1 Cor 3 (21)
as also found in Corinthians 11.[13]
We should much more take to heart
how we are to stand before God,
holding solely to his truth,
asking for the spirit of discernment.[14]
Be mindful of the dangerous times,
and in faith, of the many kinds of strife
and tumult throughout the land.
The apostles—above all
Christ the Lord—had spoken
about the great division
in every land and kingdom,
as Matthew, Mark, Luke each describe.[15]
In each of their books, you are to understand
how things will emerge in the last days.

---

11 1 Thes 5:21.
12 1 Cor 1:12f.
13 1 Cor 11:19.
14 1 Cor 12:10.
15 Mt 24:7; Mk 13:8; Lk 21:10.

May God reward us with his grace,
that we might depart the world;
for it is going down the broad road[16]
that leads downward to perdition,
where there is only howling and the gnashing of teeth
of which Christ has spoken abundantly.[17]
I am concerned; the day is no longer distant:[18]
injustice is even taking the upper hand
within the upper and lower classes.
Love is growing cold.[19]

May God[20] rule over us!
Indeed, may he not turn his grace from us,[21]
through Christ, helping us to a blessed end.
May he grant this, the One who knows all hearts.[22]
Amen.

Jörg of Augsburg

---

16 Mt 7:13.

17 Mt 8:12; 13:42, 50; 22:13; 24:51; 25:30; Lk 13:28.

18 Rom 13:12; Heb 10:25.

19 Mt 24:12.

20 [Here the author uses *der liebe Gott,* a term of familiarity and affection not conveyed by the literal translation "the dear God."—Ed.]

21 Ps 89:34.

22 1 Kgs 8:39; 2 Chr 6:30; Ps 44:21; Acts 15:8.

Preface 4

Some lovely sayings

Jörg Maler took the following pieces of verse out of collections with writings going back to the Middle Ages and even classical sources, sometimes to identifiable books and manuscripts.[1] Preface 4 is the most perplexing entry in Maler's collection. It is a sampling of well-known wisdom sayings, but in contrast to the other prefaces, it lacks explicit reference to issues of concern to his community. Perhaps the way the book was bound left open pages at the beginning and end. The author apparently had no reservations about commending to his beleaguered fellow believers the insights of church fathers and even the pagan philosopher Seneca.

Vorspann 4: Etliche schöne Sprüche. Translation by Leonard Gross.

1 See the extensive footnotes in BSOT, 133–38.

There now follow a few lovely sayings.
O mortal, consider them carefully.
They are placed in rhyme,
striking the reader as he chooses.

Death, ghastly death, is my name,[2*]
fearfully known to the whole world.[3*]
Your proud, haughty disposition does not help;
therefore rid yourself of sins!
I will certainly spare no one
until I have in my grasp both rich and poor.
And so, if I have strangled you,
it's all the same to me, whether up or down is in the offing—
let me be clear: to hell, or to the throne of heaven.
Down one of these two paths you must travel.
If then you have lived well in luxury,
the more will you experience merciless dread.
Therefore do good deeds in your life;
then you will not fear me, or suffer torment.
If you, however, do not heed these things,
not considering your final end,
no one will be sorry apart from you yourself.
I will not be accommodating, believe you me.
And how you have conducted your life here
will determine how God will rule in your case.
If, however, you do not want to follow me,
tear yourself—which may not be your intention—away from me.
Of this I want to have warned you.

If you desire to live eternally with God,[4*]
then fear him and hold to his commandments.
If you desire to win out over evil temptation,
then be not idle in achieving good.

2* Death.

3* Today me; tomorrow you.

4* Bonaventure.

Whatever you do, begin it wisely;[5*]
consider the end, what will continue thereafter.[6]
Be quiet, careful; maintain simplicity.
You have this from a wise servant.

Consider each person for what he is;[7*]
speak evil of no one at any time.
Also, do not take unknown hardship on yourself.
If you heed this, you are a wise person.

Many a person mocks, despising another person appallingly,[8*]
who himself may be of great value.
Whoever belittles his neighbour, holding him in mockery,
will ultimately experience the same.
Envy and hate is widespread in the world,
even among those who count themselves Christian.
A true Christian does not do such things,
as I find noted in Holy Scripture.
For what he does not like,
he spares his neighbour from morning to night,
which is also Christ's counsel.[9]

Take this to heart, O mortal:[10*]
for each unnecessary word you utter Mt 12 (36)
you are accountable.
Christ states this clearly in Matthew.
If you, however, do not take heed,
you'll experience the anguish yourself,
for Christ will not lie to you.
Be sure you do not deceive yourself.

5* Solomon.

6 Sir 7:40.

7* Cato.

8* Egkennberger.

9 Mt 7:12.

10* Christ.

God's Word remains eternally;[11]
everything else comes to an end.
O mortal, take heed.
Look at how you conduct your life.
You are here for a mere moment,
after which comes the eternal: prepare yourself!
I counsel you about this in total devotion;
follow me—you will not be sorry.

Remaining silent is an art;
much talk brings disfavour.
To those not able to speak wisely,
remaining silent is becoming.
For talk can bring with it either disgrace or honour.[12]
All this is wise teaching.

Avarice, you terrible weed;[13*]
you evil root: Who has made you,
that you give a mortal so much anguish
that mammon loves him alone,
forsaking therewith his Creator and Lord,
and turning his heart solely to you?
He sleeps, he awakens, doing what he desires,
and you see to it that he surrenders to you.
He gathers and scratches forever, from morning to night,
and when he encounters you, he utterly locks you up.
His heart finds no peace, day or night.
"Only more, still more," his heart cries out within.
Through you he enters into great distress,
since avarice (says Paul) makes one blind.[14]
It is the root of all sin.[15]
And Christ manifestly says:

---

11 Ps 119:89; Is 40:8; 1 Pt 1:25.

12 Prv 11:12; Sir 20:5–7, 32:12.

13* It grows according to its own manner and attribute.

14 Eph 4:18f.

15 1 Tm 6:10.

No one can serve two lords; Mt 6 (24); 2 Cor 6 (15)
if one holds to mammon as God,
truly, God stands far distant.
Avarice has the practice of boring in,
to force someone to such a degree,
as if he is sat in a sharp hedge of thorns:
not knowing grace, as he otherwise could,
and closing his heart to poverty.
God measures according to his own measure:[16]
here, temporal punishment; there, eternal anguish.
O Lord, make us your own,
that we stand apart from all
that displeases you, until we go to our grave. Amen.

If you hold yourself in high regard, and not me,
you will certainly forget me.
If you, however, do not remember me,
you will need to bear a heavy judgment.
Talking behind one's back, maligning, is opposed to God,
and brings people into hellish adversity.[17]

Solely yours, O God;
Jesus Christ, may you be mine:
that is my desire.

O mortal, if you wanted to be spiritual,[18*]
I would be dearer to you than I am,
and were you to consider what I have done for you,
you would hold me most dearly.
Reflect well on all this.
And your heart should not flirt with any strange worship,
but rather, by doing what I have taught you,
you are proved worthy.

---

16 Mt 7:2.

17 Lv 19:16; Ps 15:3; 101:5; Jas 3:6; 4:11.

18* Christ.

My name is Heaven's Street.
If you desire, then walk along me.[19*]
I am raw, bloody, and untrodden, Lk 9 (23)
yet I lead you into the fatherland.

Before you undertake anything,[20*]
first seek God's kingdom daily.[21]
Do not disdain to hear his Word.[22]
When you pray, do it with reverence.

Do not sin, in order that God's compassion may abound.[23*, 24]
Bear your neighbour's burdens.[25]
Reflect on the misery of this disdainful world.
Do not scrimp on good works,[26] all the way to the end.

There was never a sinner so great[27*]
that if he sorrows and repents of sin in this life,
out of grace God will forgive him,
if—note well—he does it in time.

Nothing is more shocking[28*]
than that a mortal ventures out so light-heartedly
that he does not relinquish his sins,
and yet stands in danger of his life.

The way the world sees meaning and purpose,[29*]
it puts violence first, then reputation, knowledge, and wealth.

19* Gernolt.
20* Gregory.
21 Mt 6:33; Lk 12:31.
22 Jn 12:48.
23* Jerome.
24 Rom 6:1, 15.
25 Gal 6:2.
26 Eccl 5:3; Sir 5:8; 18:22.
27* Ambrose.
28* Augustine.
29* Athanasius.

And when they have acquired it all,
they then lay themselves down and die.

Violence is considered lawful.[30*, 31]
Of this, I lament to God,
poor servant that I am.
The regard in which someone is held
takes on ever greater significance;
this is what town and country boast about.

If we did what we ought to do, Dt 26 (16–19)
then God would do what we desired.

If someone's mind[32*]
is shaped by the lust of the world,
and one takes pleasure in one's sins,
without a doubt he can be assured
that he is a child of damnation.

A mortal lives here but for a short time,[33*]
with much worry and anxiety, not knowing what to do.
He suffers great danger in everything.
He begins something and it becomes loathsome to him.
If he lives long, he lays himself to rest.
In this manner grim death slinks in,
warning him about those things in which his heart rejoices.
Therefore mortals have no hour, no time in their power.
The young child, the old man
must go the way of heaven and earth.
Everything that has come into being through him
will again come to naught, rest assured.
Your heart should cleave solely to God;
then he will grant you eternal life.

30* Rothenfelder.

31 [These lines may come from the hand of Maler, whose legal surname was Rothenfelder.—Ed.]

32* Seneca, the wise man.

33* Tertullian.

Whoever has ears to hear, let him hear,[34]
turning from injustice to truth.
This is the divine teaching and will.
If you discover your salvation, be still in it.

Overcoming oneself: the greatest strength;
Understanding oneself: the highest wisdom;
Judging oneself: the most beautiful justice; 1 Cor 11 (31)
Controlling oneself: the best temperance.

O mortal, you have been created by God; Sir 15 (14)
based on this, hold to his commands.
He has given you the choice.
Do what you want, but take careful note:
fire and water has been placed before you.
Reach now for what you are lacking.
If you hold to his command,
then you are living peaceably; Dt 11 (26); 30 (15)
where not, you will have eternal death. 4 (2) Esd 7 (129); Jer 21 (8)
Therefore, if you want to avoid damage,
do not bathe yourself in sins.

34 Mk 4:9.

1

Concerning the end-time

To the congregation in Austerlitz
Sigmund Bosch
[Near Strasbourg?] 17 July 1548

We know little about Sigmund Bosch's early life. He came from Friesenheim near Strasbourg, then a German free city, now in France. By 1529 he was part of an Anabaptist congregation in Strasbourg. When he was arrested, he told the authorities that he had already been imprisoned twice for his faith.[1] The first of three hymns by Bosch was published in 1552. In 1583 it and two others were included in the expanded edition of the Ausbund.[2] In the letter from Moravia,[3] he is described as "the old and beloved brother and father." He wrote "Concerning the Office of Peace"[4] to Jörg Maler, editor of the Kunstbuch. A note written by Walpurga von Pappenheim in 1571 refers to Bosch as one of three leaders of the Marpeck Circle, after Pilgram Marpeck and Leupold

---

Sigmund Bosch an die Gemeinde in Austerlitz: Von der letzten Zeit; [Umgebung von Straßburg,] 17. Juli 1548. Translation by Victor Thiessen.

1 BSOT, 139.

2 "Gott Vater, Sohn, Heiliger Geist, in deinem höchsten Throne" (no. 68); "So will ichs aber heben an, Singen in Gottes Ehr" (no. 69); "Fröhlich so will ich singen" (no. 70); the Ausbund, the earliest Anabaptist hymnal in German, was first published in 1564.

3 KB, no. 17: "Gratitude for Letter We Received."

4 KB, no. 26.

Scharnschlager.[5] His senior status is underscored by the fact that he writes "Concerning the End-Time" on behalf of the elders and congregations in one region of the Alsace. He addresses the epistle to a congregation in Austerlitz, Moravia (now Slavkov u Brna in the Czech Republic), with which Marpeck also had a correspondence.[6] Records until the early seventeenth century mention this congregation. Those who followed Marpeck in Moravia were known as Pilgramites or Cornelites (after Cornelius Veh, overseer of an Anabaptist congregation in Austerlitz).

Many of Bosch's contemporaries across the spectrum of Christian movements shared a belief that the return of Christ was at hand. Writers and preachers used passages and images from all parts of the Bible—in both literal and allegorical fashion—to interpret the end-time. Although writers in the Marpeck Circle held this conviction, the letter to the Austerlitz congregation is one of the few writings in which end-time exegesis is the purpose for writing rather than a reminder attached to another theme. Other texts in the Kunstbuch illustrate the latter approach. Perhaps Bosch, in writing to his original audience, and Maler, in including the piece in the Kunstbuch, were moved to make the return of Christ more central to their congregations' beliefs. Noteworthy is the author's restraint in not speculating about the exact time of Christ's return.

Already persecuted and fleeing the world, Bosch's readers had an immediate affinity with the texts he cites. This fact may have been the reason Maler gave this letter pride of place in his collection.

In his salutation the author makes his main point: Christians are those who have persevered from death to life. Now they must persevere to the end in obedience to the faith. They prepare themselves for Christ not by violently participating in God's defeat of his enemies—as Anabaptists such as Hans Hut believed—but by persisting in faith and love. Marpeck's "Exposé of the Babylonian Whore" displays parallels to this train of thought.[7] Bosch's core text is Matthew 24:15–20. Children

---

5 BSOT, 139.

6 See KB, no. 16 ("Concerning the Service and Servants of the Church"), 17 ("Gratitude for the Letter We Received"), and 37 ("On the Inner Church").

7 LWPM, 33–38.

of God are prepared for what is to come because they have fled up onto the roof from the house already in flames. On no account may they return to what they have left behind.

To the elders together with the congregation in Austerlitz and all who are one with us in Moravia who might be reached with [this letter].

Proclamation and interpretation of Christ's discourse concerning the end-time, Mt 24, Lk 21, Mk 13.

To all those obedient in the faith, which counts for salvation in Jesus Christ, wherever they are scattered near and far because of persecution in the land of Moravia, but united in spirit and in truth—indeed, awakened from the dead and born again to a living hope[8] through faith in Jesus Christ. Truly they have persevered from death into life[9] through the blood of Jesus. Likewise, we persevere to the end in the obedience of faith.[10] For all those who are of such a spirit and desire, we pray and wish for grace, peace, and mercy from God our heavenly Father and the Lord Jesus Christ. Amen.

To you, most beloved in the Lord Jesus Christ:

First of all, we thank God, the Father of lights[11] and of all comfort [2 Cor 1 (3)], that we also continue to be encouraged by you through the witness of your faith. We hope to receive and to possess from you a similar witness and comfort, as long as we and you continue to live in

---

8 1 Pt 1:3.

9 Jn 5:24.

10 Mt 24:13.

11 Jas 1:17.

this present day.[12] And that by means of this comfort and witness we may happily appear together with you and with the glorious nobility[13] of all the elect on that great day in the future of our great king and Saviour Jesus Christ [1 Pt 4 (13)].

For soon, soon he will come! [Heb 10 (37)].[14] Look on the field of the great harvest, how very ripe it is, so white and mature![15] We see how the words of the Lord and all the prophets have been powerfully fulfilled. We have heard of war and rumours of war [Mt 24 (6f.)]. We see uprisings of one people against another [Rv 9 (2–5)]. We see the smoke rising from the well of the abyss, from which the locusts came that have plagued the peoples who live on the earth.[16] We see how Jerusalem will be placed under siege [Lk 21 (20)], fear arising in all places. We see the temptation that will spread over the whole world.[17] We see the desolating sacrilege of which Christ, Daniel, and all the prophets spoke.[18] Paul also spoke of the horrible events that will take place in the last days [2 Tm 3 (1ff.)], which have come on us today and break forth on the earth.

And since we observe the desolating sacrilege, it is time that we flee to the mountain in the land of the Jews.[19] These are all those who are in faith and have grasped who Jesus Christ is, he who is the right and true Jew, born of the line of Judah indeed, according to the flesh.[20] Thus all true believers in Christ will become true Jews and will receive the right, true knowledge of God and Christ; eternal life is found in this knowledge [Jn 17 (3)]. Those who have come to Judah flee to the mountain; that is, they look to their forebears who remained steadfast in such a faith, immoveable as mountains. These forebears have faith-

---

12 Heb 3:13.

13 [*Hörrlichen riterschaft* (BSOT, 140) could also be translated "spiritual knighthood."—Trans.]

14 Rv 3:11; 22:7, 12, 20.

15 Jn 4:35.

16 Lk 21:5–36 (Bern MS).

17 Rv 3:10.

18 Dn 9:27; 11:31; 12:11; Mt 24:15; Mk 13:14[–29.—Ed.].

19 Mt 24:16.

20 Rom 9:6–8.

fully sown among us [Jn 4 (35–38)]; that is, they have prophesied of the harvest which we have now come into, that we may now faithfully reap just as they have faithfully sown, so that we could rejoice with them, cut sheaves, gather the fruit, and receive the wages of eternal life.[21]

Therefore, beloved children of God, just as we have come up to that roof—that is, to the knowledge of truth about the whole world—let no one descend to retain something from the burning house.[22] For the house of the whole world is full of hellish flames,[23*] which is obviously sin and vice that oozes out of all the holes. Thus our hearts should all desire to be lifted up [Col 3 (2)] and pray without ceasing that no one might descend for any reason and thereby come to ruin in the house. For we have come out of the fire to the broad field.[24] That is, we now stand before God with a good, free conscience [Acts 24 (16)]. Let no one turn back in order to get his clothes, the evil, bloody cloak of sinful flesh, together with all evil lusts and desires. Let him leave behind our natural body and life, just as Joseph forsook his cloak so that he could flee from the Egyptian woman.[25*, 26] Now we pursue the right way, truth, and life;[27] we forget what is behind us and walk from one virtue to another,[28] striving toward what is before us [Phil 3 (13)].

But woe to pregnant women and infants in that day [Mt 24 (19)].[29] Yes, woe to those who—against their conscience informed by the preaching of the gospel—continue to be pregnant with sins they know; by their own evil lusts and desires they bear within themselves eternal death[30] with which they suckle themselves, as does a mother with a child whom she will not wean even if it means losing herself. But those who have been taken from the breast and weaned from the milk [Is 28

---

21 [Ps 126.—Ed.]

22 Mt 24:17.

23* Note.

24 Mt 24:18; also Lk 9:59–62 (Bern MS).

25* Parable.

26 Gn 39:12.

27 Jn 14:6.

28 2 Cor. 3:18.

29 Mt 24:24 (Bern MS).

30 Jas 1:15.

(9)], who have first tasted the sweet, pure milk, the foretaste of eternal life,[31] do not delay their flight until winter, or till the Sabbath.[32] For in the winter the earth is closed up hard, so that one cannot gather sheaves or fruit. On the Sabbath, work is prohibited; thus the door of the bridegroom will be closed [Lk 13 (25)]. The time of grace will be gone for those who have not laboured in the present,[33] while it was still summer [Mt 13, 25]. It will soon be the Sabbath, when hands and feet will be bound, and the fruit of life[34] can no longer be gathered. But the stern justice and wrath of God will be pronounced on all godless beings and human injustice,[35] on those who have neglected the summer, that is, the time of grace.

We pray to the God of lights,[36] however, that he might prepare our lamps with the true light and pour on us the healing oil of his grace, that our lights not be extinguished but shine without darkness before everyone, so that people can see our good ways and that they might praise him, the Father in heaven [Mt 5 (14–16)]. May God the Father grant us these things through Jesus Christ. Amen.

Beloved brothers, I write this not assuming that you should learn such things first of all from us. But we hope that you are ready in all things, so that you may have joy and comfort with us, just as we do with you. We also admonish you to pray diligently for us, as we also do for you, so that we can fight fearlessly and undaunted through this short evil time of our pilgrimage [1 Pt 1 (6)]. For we certainly know that our salvation is now nearer than when it was first proclaimed to us and when we believed it.[37] Upon such faith we have been baptized according to the order of Christ and the apostles, as is certainly correct; the world can get as annoyed as it wishes.

The elders together with the congregation at Strasbourg in the Alsace, in the Kinzig Valley and in the Leber Valley, send you greetings. I

31 1 Pt 2:2.
32 Mt 24:20.
33 Heb 3:13.
34 Jn 4:36.
35 Rom 1:18.
36 Jas 1:17.
37 Rom 13:11.

will say no more than this: the peace that is in Jesus Christ be with you and increase among you and all people. Amen. Written in haste on the Tuesday before Magdalene, 1548.[38]

Sigmund Bosch,
your most unworthy servant and
comrade in tribulation,[39]
which is in Christ

---

38 17 July 1548. [The feast day of Mary Magdalene is July 22.—Ed.]

39 Rv 1:9.

2

Concerning those dead in sin

To Magdalena von Pappenheim and others
Pilgram Marpeck
Augsburg, 1545

"Concerning Those Dead in Sin" is one of two pastoral letters in the Kunstbuch collection[1] from Pilgram Marpeck to Magdalena von Pappenheim,[2] "a noble lady, and others who are not identified"[3] by name. They might have been members of a house church that met in von Pappenheim's house. This pastoral letter "is a response to a letter, presumably from Magdalena, who had joined a Marpeckite congregation a few years earlier. She was a member of a noble family that maintained a longstanding connection with Anabaptism. A former nun of the Benedictine order, Magdalena was much concerned for her spiritual state. For several years she served as [an intermediary] for Marpeck,"[4] even as Helena Streicher fulfilled a similar role for Caspar Schwenck-

---

Pilgram Marpeck an Magdalena von Pappenheim und andere: Von den Verstorbenen in Sünden; Augsburg, 1545. Translation by Walter Klaassen. Previously published as "Those Dead in Sin" in WPM, 407–11. Reprinted, with editorial changes, by permission of the publisher.

1 The other pastoral letter is "Concerning Three Kinds of People in the Judgment and Kingdom of Christ: Concerning the Peasant Nobility" (KB, no. 38).

2 Christian Hege, Robert Friedmann, and William Klassen, "Pappenheim, Marschalk von," in ME 4:115–16; BO, 104–6; PAW, 111–17.

3 WPM, 407.

4 Ibid.

feld. Both women participated in ongoing theological correspondence between Anabaptists and Spiritualists between 1542 and 1544, in one of a few instances in the sixteenth century in which women were treated more or less as equals and partners by men. Von Pappenheim died in 1571.[5]

The occasion for this letter is Magdalena's doubt about whether she has been raised up in Christ. Marpeck responds: "According to the command of Christ, we release you with joy from the fear of death in which you were imprisoned." Von Pappenheim's struggle becomes an opportunity for her minister to exposit a favourite theme, that of participating in Christ's resurrection already in this life. It illustrates the pervasive influence of John's Gospel on Marpeck. From John he borrows the account of the raising of Lazarus, using it as a detailed parable of spiritual resurrection.[6]

The author wishes that his troubled colleague might discern the distinction (but not separation) between God's activity in Christ and in the church. As the parable unfolds, it becomes clear that Christ orders the deceased to come out of the grave, and his "friends and servants" take off the shroud. This is an attempt at a via media between the Roman Catholic approach, in which the church assumes the role of Christ, and the Spiritualist approach, in which Christ is the sole actor in the drama of salvation. Thus the role of the church is to release someone Christ has raised from the fear of death. The *act* of giving life is clearly Christ's alone, but the *mediation* of its power is the work of the church.

The letter bears Marpeck's trademark signature: "your servant and comrade in the tribulation of Christ."

5 PMA, 49–51.

6 Although this biblical text does not speak of Mary Magdalene, later tradition identified her with the sister of Lazarus.

The following letter concerns those who are dead in sin, God's work and the church's actions with respect to such people, together with a fine parable of the dead Lazarus [Jn 11].

The grace of our Lord Jesus Christ be with all[7] who fervently desire it.[8] Amen. My deeply beloved ones in Christ, first of all, in faith, confidence, and hope in Christ Jesus, our healer, which is the true work of God, we thank God our heavenly Father for you. Through Jesus Christ our Lord, he continues his work with us and you. We have confidence and faith in him whom the Father has sent,[9] the Lord Jesus Christ, who alone is the physician and healer [Lk 5 (31)]. He can call into being what is not;[10] he can raise up the dead in spirit, soul, and conscience from eternal death [Jn 11 (39–44)].[11]

Even today Christ raises up the dead Lazarus, who was buried for four days, stinking and bound with a head cloth and shroud, and calls him to come forth! Yes, even today he commands that Lazarus be unbound and released from the bonds and cords of eternal death. He commands that the head cloths of anxiety and distress, which are wound around his head and in which the deceased, in spite of all his reason, is entangled, be loosed from his head. He calls those whom God makes alive to be released from their shroud, from the cords and

---

7 Rom 16:20; etc.

8 Is 26:9; Dn 10:12.

9 Jn 6:29.

10 Rom 4:17 [in which God as Father, not as Son, is the actor.—Ed.]

11 Rom 4:17.

bonds of death, and to let them go. God, through Christ, yes, Christ himself, has brought them back to life.[12*, 13]

Thus, even today all the true friends of God in Christ rejoice over those who have been raised from the death of sin, for they witness the wonderful goodness and glory of God in their brother and friend, and can say with Martha and Mary Magdalene: "If the Lord had been with him, he would not have died" [Jas 1 (15)].[14] Sin, which brings forth death, has no power where Christ is, for Christ is life.[15] Now since Christ is the life that remains eternally, death and life cannot be one. Death, however, is the wage of sin, which also remains eternally [Rom 6 (23)]. Therefore, even though she referred to physical death, Martha spoke the truth. It is indisputable that one does not die in sin where Christ is, for he is life; he is the physician and healer, who can say even today: "Rise, take your bed and walk; your sins are forgiven" [Lk 5 (23f.)]. He can restore sight and light to all blindness. Of what use is the light to one who cannot see, or of what use is sight when there is no light? Where the light shines, sight and eyes become useful, and light exercises its blessed power wherever there are eyes and sight.

All this we write to you in order that you may receive perfect comfort in the knowledge of Christ, and may be able to discern the difference between the working of God the Father in Christ, yes, the working of Christ himself in and with his spouse[16] as the communion of saints.[17] Like the Father, Christ works in his congregation here, even today. It is this way: whoever is found to be dying and dead, because

---

12* Gloss: Sin kills. People bury their dead in grave clothes. The Lord can revive and raise them up; he can command them to release the head cloths and shrouds in which they have bound the dead. Yes, the Lord can command those who live for God, and he can allow the dead to go forth and walk before God. He removes the stone from the grave, which is the hardness of sin that encrusts the heart. Thus what God raises up and restores to life may come forth. That is the work of the church. Coming to life through faith is God's work alone.

13 Eph 2:5; Rom 5:12, 17; 6:23.

14 Jn 11:21, 32.

15 Jn 11:25; Phil 1:21.

16 The congregation as the bride of Christ (Eph 5:32; Rv 19:7; 21:2, 9; 22:17).

17 [In various of his writings, especially "The Admonition of 1542" (see especially WPM, 194–97), Marpeck emphasizes God's outer work through the Son and

of the deceitfulness of sin, is dead to God, and his face is covered with the head cloths of anxiety, distress, and affliction, for the light is of no use to these. It would be a mockery of light if one were to give light to a dead person. Therefore the deceased alone has the head cloth, which is anxiety and mourning, for his deluded, dead eyes. Beautiful clothing does not belong to the deceased, who is dead, for such beautifying clothing will rot together with him.

Similarly, if one adorns the dead in spirit with the virtues of faith, which are the true garments of the Holy Spirit, it will be of no use; all will rot and spoil in the death of sin and be a stench before God. Therefore such a one gets only a shroud. That is the law of the curse; in sorrow he is bound to the decay and destruction of the flesh, until God, who alone has the power, raises him up from the death of sin through Christ. The friends of God wait in mourning. When therefore the deceased is awakened and when Christ orders him to come out of the grave of death and he again comes to life, then the friends and servants properly take the head cloth from the face and remove the grave clothes in which, as a dead man, they had bound him. Thus you may easily understand the work God does only through and with Christ, as well as the service and work of the congregation and friends of Christ.

Thus, my deeply beloved, since you have been raised up in the call and act of Christ, and since Christ calls you to go forth from your mourning and suffering, from death and grave clothes, according to the command of Christ, we release you with joy from the fear of death in which you were imprisoned![18*]

---

his inner work through the Spirit. Christ "in and with" the church is God's concrete presence.—Ed.]

18* Gloss: When the lost son, who had fled abroad and wasted his inheritance, who was dead and who came to life again through Christ, recognized his misery and poverty in great lowliness and humility, the father rejoiced and received his lost child. So too did the woman, that is, the church, rejoice when she found one of the ten coins she had lost. Like the father and the woman, even as it is done in heaven (Lk 15 [11–24, 8f., 7]). Likewise, all true believers on earth rejoice over the one, even as in heaven they rejoice over the ninety-nine who need no repentance.

The only authority we have is to bury the dead with sorrow and to release the living from the bonds and cords of death. That is the service of the church and the saints.[19]

This is a hurried reply to all your writing. We fervently greet and comfort you in the peace of Christ, in order that we may be comforted with all who have true faith. The grace of our Lord Jesus Christ be with all of you and us. Amen.[20] Pray fervently to God for us, and we will be indebted to do the same for you. Dated at Augsburg, in the year 1545.

In the Lord Jesus Christ
your servant and comrade
in the tribulation of Christ,[21]
Pilgram Marpeck

Written to Magdalena von Pappenheim and others with her.

---

19 Mt 18:18.

20 Rom 16:20.

21 Rv 1:9.

3

Concerning the libertarians

To Cornelius Veh and Paul N. in Austerlitz
Pilgram Marpeck
Augsburg, 1544

"Concerning the Libertarians" is the first extant Pilgram Marpeck letter dated after his move to Augsburg. The city archive first mentions his presence there on 16 February 1544; he was employed by the municipality to work in forest management.[1] In part because of his privileged status as a mining engineer, Marpeck was able to function as the leader of the Anabaptist congregation in Augsburg, as he had in Strasbourg. He continued to travel to the Alsace and Moravia, as well as to his former home in Chur, near Switzerland's northeastern border with Germany.

This epistle is addressed to Cornelius Veh, overseer of an Anabaptist congregation at Austerlitz in Moravia (now Slavkov u Brna in the Czech Republic). A convert and co-worker of Marpeck, Veh was for years the leading minister of the moderate Anabaptist congregation in Austerlitz. Its members were called Pilgramites or Cornelites, names

---

Pilgram Marpeck an Cornelius Veh und Paul N. in Austerlitz: Von den Fleischfreien; Augsburg, 1544. Translation by Walter Klaassen. Previously published in WPM, 402–6. Reprinted, with editorial changes, by permission of the publisher.

1 PMLST, 134.

suggesting the prominence of both men.[2] They were kindred spirits; at the conclusion of this epistle Marpeck addresses Veh as "beloved Cornelius, given to me as a son in the faith,"[3] a tender designation that occurs nowhere else in Marpeck's writing. The Hutterite Chronicle records that Veh (and subsequently Marpeck) visited the community at Schäkowitz (or Tscheikowitz; now Čejkovice in the Czech Republic) in 1541 to mock its members' ways and seek to persuade them to unite with other Anabaptists. All that came of these encounters, tragically, was more disputes.[4]

Veh is the author of a letter that appears in the Kunstbuch.[5] Paul,[6] the other direct recipient of this missive, is likely the Paul referred to elsewhere as a minister among the Austerlitzers who was fluent in Italian. That detail reminds us that radical church groups in the sixteenth century were mobile and heterogeneous. Marpeck's letter to Veh was also sent as a general epistle to congregations in Moravia and the Alsace, for reasons that are not clear. Was it sent to let these congregations know that Marpeck had addressed a problem in one congregation, or was the threat of libertarianism present in the Pilgramite movement at large? A contemporary description of the range of Anabaptist groups calls one of them "*libertini.*"[7] So Marpeck's concern, as was often the case, might have been for the wider Anabaptist community.

As the text makes clear, some believers in Austerlitz, and perhaps beyond, had a more liberal interpretation than Marpeck's of the freedom of Christ. He had defended Christian freedom so strongly against the arguments of the Swiss Brethren. As we will see in some of his

---

2 Jerold K. Zeman, "Historical Topography of Moravian Anabaptism," MQR 41 (1967): 46; BSOT, 148.

3 For more information, see A. J. F. Zieglschmid, *Die älteste Chronik der Hutterischen Brűder* ([Philadelphia]: Carl Schurz Memorial Foundation, 1943), 224; Heinold Fast, "Pilgram Marpeck und das oberdeutsche Täufertum," ARG 47 (1956): 231–32; and William Klassen, "Veh, Cornelius," in ME 4:803.

4 See HB, 138.

5 KB, no. 24: "To the Whole Brotherhood."

6 Paul was the leader of the Austerlitz congregation after Cornelius Veh. See Henry A. DeWind, "A Sixteenth-Century Description of Religious Sects in Austerlitz, Moravia," MQR 29 (1955): 45.

7 BSOT, 149.

other writings, he argued for patience and trust in the exercise of discipline, opposed mandatory communalism, and believed that Christians could be in but not of the world. Related to the latter point was his acceptance of intermarriage with Christians of other communities.

But in the circumstances Marpeck addresses in this letter, the shoe is on the other foot. The author accuses some members of relying on collective and individual discernment rather than a fixed church order, and of using that discernment as license for self-indulgence. Some Hutterites and a member of the local nobility had accused the Austerlitzer Pilgramites of being libertines.[8] Marpeck's problem here parallels Luther's, when opponents frequently misinterpreted his teaching of *sola fide* as license for self-indulgence. This extreme situation does not lead Marpeck to abandon his via media approach to discipleship but instead leads him to reinforce it to both the legalists and the libertarians: where love is absent, people are slaves to sin, however pious their words are.

Marpeck reiterates his view that disciples are formed "according to the true liberty of the Holy Spirit and to the true rule and teaching of Christ." He contrasts the teaching of Christ with "human invention," using an argument Paul made in his letter to the Colossians. Both the Spirit and the Son act out of love. The chief mark of love is self-surrender to God and others. The difficulty, Marpeck argues, is that libertarians confuse self-surrender with loss of freedom.

8 BSOT, 149. See Peter Erb, "Schwenckfeld, the Anabaptists, and the Sixteenth-Century Crisis of Knowing," in AD, 141–42.

This is a copy of a letter concerning the libertarians who want to be free to do everything without any conscience. It is written to all in Moravia and Alsace who have true faith.

Dearly beloved in God our Father, and beloved in Jesus Christ, my fervent sighing, prayer, wish, and desire is that the Lord might open my way to you one of these days. I firmly believe that, through the grace of our Lord Jesus Christ, you too desire the same. May God so ordain, to his praise and our salvation, and our comfort, peace, and joy in the Holy Spirit. Amen.

My dearly beloved in God the Father through Jesus Christ, I also thank my God for you and for all who live not according to the flesh but according to the true liberty of the Holy Spirit and the true rule and teaching of Christ.[9] I am referring to those who have shed all false judgments and verdicts, who have extricated and freed themselves from all human invention, statutes, bonds, cords, and imprisonment of conscience, and who have become free through the Son of God.[10*] For whom the Son sets free is free indeed! [Jn 8 (36)]. I say it and witness before God and all creatures that this freedom is turned over and given alone to that love which is in Jesus Christ our Lord.

Whoever does not have that love may not boast about his liberty. Rather, he is and remains a slave, sold to serve the law and sin, and always a debtor to the law. Yet they are the ones who do not want to be in debt to anyone for the sake of the love that is in Christ. They boast about their freedom yet remain servants of destruction. In their invented liberty—which, according to the lust of the flesh, they imagine they possess—they live in open offence and scandal to those who have tender consciences [Rom 14 (20f.); 1 Cor 8 (7–13)]. Thus true liberty, and true love itself, is completely missing. About this kind of liberty we know of no instance in Christ's teaching, even as, on the other hand, we know nothing about self-invented human statutes, bonds, and cords of the conscience. The free commandment of the love we have in Christ is

9 Phil 3:6.

10* Note.

a single commandment. Liberty in Christ[11] is one unified liberty. Outside the love of Christ there is no liberty.

Therefore, my dearly beloved, it is my fervent prayer, supplication, reminder, and admonition that you take careful note to discern what I am writing to you here. Of what value would it be to escape the verdicts, bonds, cords—yes, the imprisonment—of conscience and human rules, only to run into the devil's hands because you falsely boast of new insight and indulge in the self-will of carnal liberty?[12*] For it is surely true and certain that neither flesh nor blood nor any creature in heaven or on earth has such power over a free conscience that it can command or forbid those of the true nature and character of God. Those who do possess the true Spirit of God are one nature, born again as they are by the Word and Holy Spirit.

Those who are driven by God's Spirit are children of God [Rom 8 (14)]. One can no more order or forbid the children of God than one can order or forbid the Holy Spirit of God.[13] Only the Holy Spirit is the commander and prohibitor in those to whom he has given birth.[14] Certainly and truly, all such freely born children do not seek their own advancement but the growth of all [1 Cor 10 (24); 13 (5)].[15] Like Christ Jesus, who was born like them, they do not seek only what is theirs. Similarly, the apostle Paul and other children of God did not seek what was their own. Rather, everything that already was and could have become theirs—yes, even themselves—they surrendered, sacrificed, and let go to God our Father, through Jesus Christ our Lord. What they surrendered they considered as dirt and garbage compared to the overwhelming riches[16] of Christ, who is the salvation of those who are to be preserved [Phil 3 (8)].

In short, the true liberty of Christ, and the love that belongs to it, is a free surrender, denial, and self-forgetfulness. The true liberty of

---

11 Gal 2:4.

12* Note.

13 Jn 3:8.

14 Gal 5:18.

15 [The original is unintelligible here: *sonnderr allein in dem geschennkt zůr pesserung.* The context suggests the translation.—Trans.] 1 Cor 10:23; Rom 8:34.

16 Eph 2:7.

Christ fervently desires to serve everyone in what is good, to the praise of God and the salvation of humankind. Yes, even though something is legitimate for them, they surrender it all for the sake of love and growth [1 Cor 10 (23)].

The true liberty of Christ may, according to such love, give evidence of no other spirit, nature, or characteristic. Whoever uses it differently misses the way of truth[17] and falls beside the rock on which all truth rests eternally.

Specifically, I write to you in the hope that I might hold the true liberty of Christ before your eyes as a mirror in which you may learn how Christ is formed in you.[18]

Again, I also put before your eyes the real anti-Christian, false, blown-up, disobedient, carnal liberty that serves, seeks, inflates, and raises up only the self. This liberty can in no way deny itself, nor can it ever forgive itself; it breaks, defies, and criticizes everything. It praises only what gives room to the lust and greed of the flesh, and yet defends and covers all wantonness and selfishness of the flesh with the liberty of Christ. Briefly, it desires to be unfettered, unbound, and unrestricted only according to its own pleasure. In its own wantonness and pride it fights and quarrels incessantly about those things in which the heart is imprisoned and entangled. It seeks redemption and liberty where there are only eternal imprisonment, bondage, and cords of the devil.

And still such libertarians say they have no qualms of conscience about it. They do not want to be under anyone's rule or authority. They use Paul's words[19] to verify that everything is legitimate for them. But-they read what Paul says with perverted eyes. They have no intention of being as beholden to others as Christ and St. Paul were.[20]

Dear friend, whoever you are who speak in this manner and use the words of Paul as a cover-up for your own invented liberty, examine your heart to determine whether you, like Christ and Paul, are yielded to everyone in all good things. If you are, then you may also say with a

---

17 2 Pt 2:2.

18 Gal 4:19.

19 1 Cor 10:23.

20 [Original: *und wellen doch mit Christo und dem h[eilige]n Paulo niemants geschennckt sein.*—Trans.] Rom 8:32.

true heart firm in the truth of Christ: "Although everything is permitted, not everything leads to improvement" [1 Cor 10 (23)].

My dearly beloved in Christ Jesus, especially you, beloved Cornelius, given to me as a son[21] in the faith, and you, my dear brother Paul, together with all the others elect of God, receive this, my admonition in the Lord. I have been afraid on your behalf. I had to write in order that we may help one another save our souls from all the cunning deceit of the devil. My dear brother Cornelius, and all the chosen of God, watch diligently over the flock of God. And with respect to liberty, first know your own minds, and then work with the congregation in order that it may be taught and led by the true rule of Christ. This is what God will demand of me and others.

May God grant that with St. Paul we may be able to boast about the Day of the Lord,[22] that we may have kept faith, and that we may be found not to have been a stumbling block to pious consciences. Amen.

Dated at Augsburg in the year 1544.

Pilgram Marpeck

---

[21] 1 Cor 4:17; 1 Tm 1:18; 1 Pt 5:13.

[22] 2 Cor 1:14.

Strasbourg, bridge and prison towers, where Melchior Hoffman and other radicals were imprisoned.

4

Concerning love

Pilgram Marpeck

"Concerning Love" is undated and lacks a specific address.[1] Heinold Fast conjectures that it was a sermon sent as a "round letter," circulating to one or more of the Marpeck groups.[2] Martin Rothkegel suggests that Jörg Maler, as editor of the collection, put this letter into its present form.[3] The allegorical use of the Song of Solomon, in which the lovers are understood to be Christ and the church, goes back to the patristic era; it remained popular into the Reformation period.[4] One element of Marpeck's treatment is noteworthy: his unqualified statement that love is God, a theme repeated in his writings.

Pilgram Marpeck, Von der Liebe. Translation by William Klassen. Previously published in WPM, 516–20. Reprinted, with editorial changes, by permission of the publisher.

1 WPM, 516.

2 See Fast's commentary on "Von der Liebe" (Bern MS, no. 4, 1).

3 BSOT, 95.

4 Bernard of Clairvaux's early twelfth-century commentary is among the most profound (see Bernard of Clairvaux, *Talks on the Song of Songs,* ed. Bernard Bangley [Brewster, MA: Paraclete Press, 2002]), yet his deep understanding of the Song of Songs did not prevent him from inaugurating the Fourth Crusade with an explicit charge to the crusaders to kill those who are not Christian.

"Marpeck returns in this little treatise to the theme of love as the sine qua non of Christian life. He resorts to the allegory of love in the Song of Songs. The treatment here is more pronouncedly allegorical than in the next letter in the Kunstbuch (no. 5); here he addresses individual details (for example, he identifies the little foxes as the cunning people of this world)."[5] The allegory focuses largely on the embodiment of love as a woman who without compulsion fulfils the works of grace, who is both the church's servant and its protector. Knowledge of God "is her mother, faith her brother, hope her sister." With the image of the fig tree comes the image of Christ as the gardener and then as "the rock in whose clefts true love dwells." The author "ends by announcing that the victory over these and all others who resist the gospel will be won by 'love through patience, by overcoming them with the truth even as Christ overcame the world.'"[6]

---

5 WPM, 516.

6 Ibid.

Concerning love, to serve one another in it[7] *according to the gift*[8] *of faith, all of which follows from true love. Otherwise everything is in vain [1 Cor 13].*

My dearest ones, let us faithfully serve one another for improvement in service according to the spirit of love and the measure and gift of faith[9] given to each one. Then for certain no useless member will be found on the true body, and truly, every member exercises his gift according to the measure of love in rendering service to the body.[10]

In this concern, deeply beloved, remember us, for I desire it fervently for the sake of the whole body. Through its members, that is, the word of grace[11] and the gifts of the Holy Spirit through love, which was prepared in Christ,[12] it is fused together for mutual service in love. Love is a true servant and fulfiller[13] of all the works of grace without urging, compulsion, force, or worry. Yes, love is never commanded, for she is the commandment herself.[14] She is God himself,[15] sole holder of sovereignty in all things, a monarch and ruler, yet still a free servant in all. She fulfils everything in all things for him with whom she dwells;[16] wherever she is absent, there is weakness, tribulation, mourning, and want. She cannot live with him who does not know her. She is always ready for him who longs fervently for her and makes herself known to him. Also, to him who truly learns to know her, she in turn makes herself known. She lives with her whole heart with him who embraces her, and surrenders enthusiastically[17] to him with everything she is and has. She gives herself to him who has been

---

7 Gal 5:13.
8 Eph 3:7.
9 Rom 12:3.
10 Eph 4:6.
11 Acts 14:3; 20:32.
12 Eph 2:10.
13 Rom 13:10.
14 Jn 15:12; 13:34; 15:5; Rom 13:9; 1 Jn 3:23; 4:21; 2 Jn 5f.
15 1 Jn 4:8, 16.
16 Gal 5:14; Eph 1:23.
17 [Original: *gar uber eigen.*—Trans.]

given to her. She is the honoured daughter of God. God lives in him to whom she is promised, and he lives in God.

Knowledge [of God] is her mother, faith her brother, hope her sister,[18] for through knowledge [of God], love is born. If a thing is not known, it is impossible to receive love from it, and if no love is received, one can't give birth to it. Therefore knowledge is the mother of love. Faith is the brother of love. For where there is no faith, love can have no brother.[19*] And where there is no hope, love has no sister. For love and faith cannot exist in this age without hope. Experience is the mother of hope, for experience gives birth to hope, and hope lets no one be put to shame [Rom 5 (4f.)]. Everything comes from one Father,[20] who is God. Faith, love, and hope will also be born with him who is born of God,[21] to live with him in this world. Beyond this age, faith and hope cease, but love remains eternally[22] in the knowledge of God and of his Christ, for she remains in God and God in her.[23]

Deeply beloved brothers and sisters, I write to you out of a foretaste of love to the extent to which God inclines his love to us. Nevertheless, our knowledge of what the love of God is, is only fragmentary, one knowing it more completely than another [1 Cor 13 (9)].

Deeply beloved sisters and brothers in God, the desire of my heart, my prayer, and my sighing to God for you and us is for that self-same love that fulfils everything in all.[24] Yes, we may well say and pray with the Spirit in the Canticle, "Draw me after you, and we will follow."[25] For truly, deeply beloved, where love does not draw, our path is dangerous and hard. If love has not been placed over the vineyard of God to protect it,[26] and if the vineyard does not bear the fruit of love, she does not protect it and allows it to be devastated. However, where love is the

---

18 1 Cor 13:13.
19* Note.
20 1 Cor 8:6; Eph 4:6.
21 1 Jn 3:9.
22 1 Cor 13:8.
23 1 Jn 4:15f.
24 Eph 1:23.
25 Sg 1:4.
26 Sg 1:6.

protector of God's vineyard and brings fruit, and the friend lives behind us constantly, stands behind all our actions,[27*] and looks for the fruit in the vineyard under the care of the keeper,[28*] the friend "looks through the lattice,"[29] our flesh and blood, in which we are now enclosed, into the heart. He replies to us and says to love who is our protector: "Arise, my friend, my fair one, and come to me. For behold, the winter is past, the rain is over and gone."[30] That is, the previous destruction has been removed from us, so that "now the flowers appear in the land." They appear in his congregation through the protector, which is love. "Spring[31] has arrived," the time to bring fruit to our God. "The turtledove," that is, the Holy Spirit acting through his Word and work in the hearts of the believers, "is heard in our land."[32] "The fig tree has developed buds," that is, the sweetness of God's graciousness—most lovely—breaks out in his own. "The vines have sprouted blossoms[33] and exude fragrance," that is, the planting of the heavenly Father, which he has planted[34] as the true vintner, in Christ Jesus, the true vine.[35] The shoots from the vine which are planted are the true believers in Christ Jesus. Through the sap of grace from Christ the vine, they develop blossoms, that they may see God's working in them through his plantings in Christ and give God praise,[36] in Christ Jesus. As the Spirit says: "They give forth fragrance."[37]

And again the Spirit says in another passage: "Arise, my friend, my fair one, and come to me."[38] Only that love is commanded which is the protector of the vineyard and which brings the fruit of the vineyard of

---

27* Note.

28* Exposition of Canticles.

29 Sg 2:9

30 Sg 2:10f.

31 [Original: *glänntz*. The conjecture is that this should be *länntz* = *Lentz* (spring). This is confirmed by Luther's rendering of Sg 2:12.—Trans.]

32 Sg 2:12.

33 [Original: *ougen* = *Augen* ("eyes").—Trans.]

34 Mt 15:13.

35 Jn 15:1ff.

36 Mt 5:6.

37 [Sg 2:13.—Trans.]

38 Sg 2:13.

God with her as a sweet aroma.[39] The Spirit speaks further: "My dove, in the clefts of the rock."[40] This is only that love which is in Christ Jesus; he is the rock[41] in whose clefts true love dwells. These clefts are his suffering, wounds, bloodshed, and dying, in which the believers in love have total safety and rest from birds of prey, that is, the devil and his seed, which are enemies of love. Again the Spirit continues: "Let me hear your voice, for your voice is sweet and your form is lovely."[42] Here God demands the fruit as well as the voice of love, so that word and work agree. This voice is lovely to God; its form is beautiful and pleasing.

Moreover, he commands the Spirit to catch the little foxes that spoil the vineyard.[43] He means the cunning people of this world, the small ones, who have no worth in God's eyes. For Christ also called Herod a fox when he said: "Go, and tell that fox . . ." [Lk 13 (32)]. These foxes are caught only in love through patience, by overcoming them with the truth even as Christ overcame the world [Jn 16 (33)]. He has promised us the same comfort of victory. As Paul says: "Our preaching of faith takes all reason and all fortresses captive, to destroy everything that opposes the knowledge of God" [2 Cor 10 (5)]. It is this kind of capture of which the Holy Spirit of God speaks here in the Canticle.

All this I have written to you in order to bring it to our mutual and heartfelt remembrance and that we may partake of the same gifts. Is the gift a costly one? If so, praise God as the giver and love him more than the gift. For the gift is given only in order that it may be used for the honour of the giver. No one should steal this honour for himself, lest he incur the displeasure of the giver, who is God. He alone merits all honour; may it be given to him from now on into eternity. Amen.

---

39 Eph 5:2.
40 Sg 2:14.
41 1 Cor 10:4.
42 Sg 2:14.
43 Sg 2:15.

In the Lord Jesus Christ,
your servant and brother in the kingdom
and the tribulation which is in Christ,
P. M.

Kinzig River dam. One of Pilgram Marpeck's work sites as timber master for Strasbourg

5

Concerning unity and the bride of Christ

To the congregations[1] in Strasbourg, in the Alsace, and in the Kinzig and Leber Valleys

Pilgram Marpeck

21 December 1540

"Concerning Unity and the Bride of Christ" is the earliest of Pilgram Marpeck's extant letters, written in response to an unknown letter from a congregation in the Alsace, concerning the unity of the church. It was written during his "obscure years,"[2] the time between his and his wife Anna's departure from Strasbourg (1532) and their arrival in Augsburg (1544). The theme of unity is not a surprise, because during this time he was living in Probin in the Grisons (Graubünden) in eastern Switzerland,[3] in an ambivalent relationship with the Swiss Brethren. Marpeck ministered among them, and both parties accepted each other as members of the true church, yet each was sharply critical of

Pilgram Marpeck an die Gemeinden in Straßburg, im Elsaß und im Kinzig- und Lebertal: Von der Einigkeit und der Braut Christi; Probin, 21. Dezember 1540. Translation by William Klassen. Previously published as "The Unity of the Bride of Christ" in WPM, 521–27. Reprinted, with editorial changes, by permission of the publisher.

1 According to Heinold Fast (Bern MS, no. 5, 1), this letter is addressed to the "elect" (*Auserwählten*); our translation follows BSOT (158: "congregations" (*Gemeinden*).

2 J. C. Wenger, "The Life and Work of Pilgram Marpeck," MQR 12 (1938): 155.

3 Torsten Bergsten, *Pilgram Marbeck und seine Auseinandersetzung mit Caspar Schwenckfeld* (Uppsala: Almqvist & Wiksell, 1958): 46; CC, 33.

the other. The letter is written in response to one from the congregations in and around Strasbourg, in whose creation Marpeck had had a formative role during and after his time of residence there. Perhaps his Swiss neighbours were also on his mind as he wrote.

The author starts his treatise with a digest of his theology of the Lord's Supper. He begins with a revealing reference to Communion practice in an unelaborated way that suggests that the terms he is using are familiar to his audience.[4] He includes thanksgiving—or Eucharistic—prayer, which the Spirit prays in us and in our behalf.[5] The Spirit blesses "the bread of his body" and "the cup in his blood." The clause "through it he has united us in his body . . . to become one body" is crucial: it clearly refers to Christ's body on the cross, but it also seems to refer to the bread and cup. Here Marpeck makes use of Paul's double meaning: with the sacrifice of his body of flesh, Christ makes believers into a body of flesh. Here we have the germ of a sacramental argument for a visible church of believers. Our oneness with the triune God is accomplished by the Holy Spirit, as is our sacrifice for one another in imitation of Christ's sacrifice for us. Marpeck's final thought on the breaking of bread is that it is a memorial of the "pure love" of Christ, which we know through the shedding of his blood.[6]

The author goes on to describe the dynamic that brings about the unity of the body of Christ, "the highest adornment of love." The emphasis on the divine initiative in the unity of the church is striking. Christ prays to the Father for this "treasure of love"; it brings with it the gifts of the Spirit.

"[Marpeck] employs the analogy of marriage from the Song of Solomon, as he does in many other letters, including the previous one. In his writing the bride is both love itself and the church. The latter allego-

---

4 A parallel situation is Rom 6. In formulating his argument about walking in the resurrection, Paul reminds his audience of the meaning of baptism, as if they already know exactly what he is referring to.

5 Rom 8:26–27. See Ernst Käseman, "The Cry for Liberty in the Worship of the Church," in *Perspectives on Paul* (Philadelphia: Fortress Press, 1971), 122–37.

6 These concepts are woven into the borrowed text of "The Admonition of 1542" (WPM, 159–302) and greatly elaborated on in Marpeck's reply to Caspar Schwenckfeld's *Judicium* (LWPM, 114–19).

ry has a long history going back through the mystic tradition to Jewish and Christian interpretations in the Hellenistic era. Jerome, Augustine, Bernard of Clairvaux, and Martin Luther all interpreted the Canticle as an allegory of Christ and the church."[7] In the spirit of this tradition are Marpeck's lovely description of the winter of our sin, Christ as the true summer, and the church as those blossoms—of the many that God has sown—that burst into flower.

At the same time, "Marpeck gives [the allegory] his own peculiar cast. He emphasizes the unique qualities of love as humility, endurance, patience, and longsuffering. These are the wedding gifts without which the unity of the church cannot continue. Thus he does not simply borrow but integrates an ancient interpretation into his own concrete flesh-and-blood Christianity."[8]

Although unity is a gift, the church must preserve it. Echoing the challenge of Hebrews 12, our author urges perseverance and purification in the race of faith.

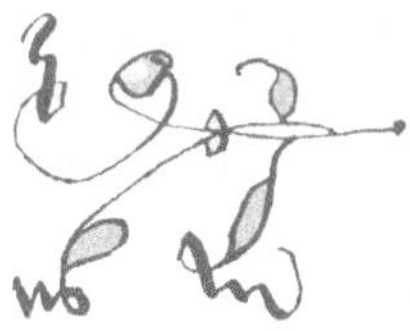

---

7 WPM, 521. On the history of the interpretation of the Song of Songs, see Gillis Gerlemann, *Ruth: Das Hohelied* Biblischer Kommentar, Altes Testament, vol. 18 (Neukirchen: Neukirchener Verlag, 1965), 43–51. For Marpeck's use of it and further literature, see CC, 120–21 (WPM, 585, n. 1).

8 WPM, 521.

This epistle concerns the unity of the bride of Christ, her adornment, and fruit. It is taken from the Canticle. It also tells how winter[9*] with its rain and storm is past, and how summer[10*] has come.[11]

To the chosen, God's saints in Jesus Christ, our beloved ones around Strasbourg, Alsace, the Kinzig and Leber Valleys[12] scattered here and there.

Grace and peace from God our heavenly Father, through Jesus Christ our Lord, be and remain among us and all[13] who seek and love Christ sincerely. Amen. Deeply beloved, loved in God the Father and in his Jesus Christ,[14] we have received and accepted the epistle you sent by the dear brother Ludwig Hafner,[15] together with the oral report of your well-being in our most holy faith, with affectionate love, peace, and joy, as well as with comfort of the Holy Spirit and your supporting comfort.[16]

We therefore thank God on your behalf, as you do on ours, for the redemption from sins through his blood,[17] our first cleansing, which we should never forget [2 Pt 1 (9)], with unceasing thanksgiving to our Father God through his Jesus Christ. Amen.

For the Holy Spirit also gives thanks in us on our behalf in the act of thanksgiving, the blessing of the bread of his body and the cup in his blood [1 Cor 11 (24f.)]. Through it he has united us in his body (with the sacrifice of his body) to become one body [1 Cor 10 (16f.)], and

---

9* Law: winter.

10* Gospel: summer.

11 Sg 2:11f.

12 [Two river valleys, in the Black Forest and Alsace respectively, both near Strasbourg. The Leber is now known as the Lièpvrette.—Trans.]

13 Rom 1:7; etc.

14 ["His Jesus Christ" is an unusual turn of phrase that occurs only rarely in Marpeck's writing.—Ed.]

15 [About the identity of this man nothing further is known.—Trans.]

16 [Literally, "co-comfort." The term parallels "co-witness," which means an outer witness corroborating and united with an inner witness.—Ed.]

17 Eph 1:7; Col 1:14.

has reconciled us with God the Father and himself,[18] that we should be one in him, as he is one in the Father and the Father is one in him [Jn 17 (21)]. Such unity of the Holy Spirit Christ begged of the Father for his own, to be one in him, as he is one in the Father, the Father in him, and he in us, provided we keep the unity we have in him with one another in the Holy Spirit [Eph 4 (3)]. Thus we may also be a sacrifice for one another before God the Father, as Christ was for us, for such a sacrifice of unity and reconciliation pleases the Father. That is the true worship of God[19] by which we may repay God for everything; it is the true blessing,[20] laud, praise, and honour of our Father in his Jesus Christ. Amen.

What's more, it is the proper and true remembrance of his death, by means of which we do not forget the cleansing from our first sin,[21] which has come to us through the blood of Christ out of the Father's pure love in his Jesus Christ. For in Christ, God is one and not divided or separated. How then can those who are born of him[22] in his manner and nature be separated? For unity is the bond of love[23] according to the manner of the Father and the Son. No one can live in Jesus Christ without this unity of love, nor can anyone find, see, or recognize the Father in Jesus Christ without it. Even the human being Jesus Christ cannot reveal the Father in himself to anyone outside this reconciliation and unity in the Holy Spirit.[24]

I write this to you that you may truly awaken and that you may not lose the glorious jewel, the true necklace, bracelet, wreath, and crown.[25] For the Father has decorated his Son and the Son's bride, love, the dearest of all. This is the communion of Christ, which the Father himself has

---

18 2 Cor 5:18.

19 Rom 12:1.

20 [The same word, blessing *(benedyung)*, is used for both Christ's self-giving and ours.—Ed.]

21 2 Pt 1:9.

22 1 Jn 3:9; 5:18.

23 Eph 4:3; Col 3:14.

24 [This train of thought expresses the traditional Trinitarian notion that the Spirit is the medium of the unity of Father and Son.—Ed.]

25 1 Cor 9:24; Phlm 3:14; Rv 3:11.

given in marriage to Christ his Son, with this jewel of unity. For Christ prayed to the Father for this jewel (and the treasure of love), in order to beautify his bride with it, which is love, the most beautiful of all. For unity is the highest adornment of love. This treasure, unity, brings with it all other virtues and treasures, namely, peace, joy, comfort in the Holy Spirit, as well as humility, meekness, temperance, modesty, knowledge, friendliness, endurance, patience, wisdom, perseverance, courage, and much else [2 Pt 1 (5–7); Gal 5 (22f.)],[26*] in order that the bride of Christ be clothed, adorned, and beautified.

Because of this adornment, even the angels desire and long to see[27] the bridegroom in his glory, together with his bride. Love appears and shows herself in this same adornment and beautification, with a happy countenance and in fair form, to the pleasure of her bridegroom. He invites his bride in her adornment and glory and says: "Arise, my love, my fair one, come here and see; the winter has passed, the rain is gone, the flowers have come forth in the land, the fig tree is in bud; the vines have developed blossoms and give forth fragrance. Arise, my love, my fair one, come here and show me yourself, and let me hear your voice. For your voice is sweet, and your appearance is lovely" [Sg 2 (10–14)].

My dearest ones, observe this text carefully with spiritual eyes. Although the words are brief, their understanding and meaning in the Holy Spirit are great. Flesh and blood can and will never attain it.[28] For the Lord will call his bride in no other form than in the adornment of the virtue of Christ,[29*] since the storm, winter, and rain—that is, the time of sin and sleeping—are past and gone; their affliction and tribulation is over. For we had nowhere to flee in the storm of our sin until Christ came down, the true summer,[30*] in which alone all the flowers can bloom.

These flowers are the people who before the advent of Christ remained stuck with their root in the earth through sin, without blossom or fruit. Indeed, although they were sweet, friendly, and happy people,

---

26* Fruit of the Spirit.

27 1 Pt 1:12.

28 Mt 16:17.

29* Interpretation.

30* Christ the true summer.

like the fig tree and the vine they had neither buds nor blossoms before the summer; that is, before the advent of the human being Jesus Christ, who is the true day, light, and summer of the world.[31*] Not until this true sun had left the lowliness of the winter of our sin, and again appeared in the presence of the Father in the heights in glory and power, did summer fully come. Before that, the sun of the Father shone on humanity as on arid ground, with the righteousness of the law through wrath, but no fruit was found in people because of the heat of the Father's wrath. But when the sun Christ Jesus[32*] appeared on earth in the weakness of his true humanity, from the seed of the woman[33] and the human race, only then did people begin to bloom. The fig tree and vine developed buds and blossoms, but without fruit, before the setting of this sun, Jesus Christ. Through this setting, the heat of the day, that is, the Father's wrath, has cooled. Until the time of the resurrection and ascension of Christ, the bridegroom revelled with his bride under flowers, buds, blossoms, and roses, as a foretaste and shadow until spring came.

When the turtledove, that is the Holy Spirit,[34*] was heard,[35] only then were the first and earliest fruits borne. The blossoms ceased with the appearance of the fruit; the shadow shrank away through the sun of union and reconciliation, to bring fruits to God through the lovely dawn.[36] This is also the sealing of the Holy Spirit[37] in the forgiveness of sins with the cool dew[38] of grace. My dearest ones, the highest ornament and adornment of love is therefore the preserving of unity in the Holy Spirit,[39] for without this unity there is no sincere love.[40]

31* Note.
32* Christ the summer.
33 Gn 3:15.
34* The Holy Spirit, the turtledove.
35 Sg 2:12.
36 Sg 6:10.
37 Sg 8:6; 2 Cor 1:22; Eph 1:13; 4:30.
38 Sg 5:2.
39 Eph 4:3.
40 2 Cor 6:6; 1 Pt 1:22.

My dearest ones, sisters and brothers in the Lord, behold humanity created in its natural state! A virgin, married or promised to a man, will eagerly seek and desire such carnal, temporal, earthy treasures and attire.[41*] She will receive from her bridegroom and parents such adornment for her marriage as gold, silver, pearls, and other precious stones, as well as silk, velvet, embroidered dresses with gold thread. But these treasures are only a picture of the treasures of the Holy Spirit, and according to their nature, an image of the supernatural and eternal. Human bridegrooms, according to their means, commonly give their brides coronets, lockets, necklaces, bracelets, dresses, and other things for their pleasure.

Suppose the bride were careless and inattentive, and a thief stole her best coronet in the presence of all her maidens, who were given to the bride for her honour, to serve her and take good care of her. Would not the bridegroom punish the bride, with her maidens, for such folly? And how would the bride and the maidens be able to excuse themselves? Would they not rather be sorrowful, weep, and mourn because of the loss, and confess their folly?[42*] And if the bridegroom recovered the treasure from the thief and through grace presented it again to the bride and her maidens, would she not rejoice with them and be much more careful and diligent to protect her treasures from thieves?

I do not write this to accuse you but to entice you to emulate the true and proper humility of Christ, that the innocent may not rise up against the guilty to insist on their rights,[43*] but rather act like the Lord who in his innocence gave himself for us, the guilty, accepted our guilt, and suffered, the just one for us, the unjust.

Still less should we become conceited, since none of us can excuse ourselves before God or people. If you truly contemplate these things, you will honour this great treasure of the bride (love) [2 Pt 1 (8)], which is unity in the Holy Spirit, and preserve it in your midst without laziness and carelessness.[44] For this treasure alone the bridegroom prayed to the Father on behalf of the bride [Jn 17 (21)], that is, to keep the unity

---

41* Parable.

42* Note.

43* Note.

44 Eph 4:3.

with one another as the Father and Son are one in spirit and truth. This is the true and chief treasure of our most holy bridegroom, Christ. This calls for us to be watchful, to pray, to act wisely, and to guard it from dogs and foxes that destroy the vineyard of God,[45] that the thief and robber[46] may not dig under our house. For we know that our enemy and antagonist never closes his eyes toward us [1 Pt 5 (8)].

My dearest ones, for your own improvement read Hebrews, chapter 12, diligently. This is the true admonition of Paul that you tolerate nothing unclean among you.[47] For the whole world would have to be judged and destroyed before God would tolerate evil in his congregation. For this we have ample analogies in Exodus. Pay diligent attention, so that the tempter does not catch you through human temptation, since we have been rescued and kept from all powerful errors through the grace of Christ. May the Lord rescue and redeem us, together with you, from all temptations, as he has done until now.

The grace of our Lord Jesus Christ be and remain with you and us all. Amen.

All the saints of God with us salute you with a greeting and unity in Christ. Pray fervently to God for us, and we as debtors will do the same for you in the love of Christ.

Given on St. Thomas Day[48] in the year 1540 at Probin in the Grisons (Graubünden).[49]

In the Lord Jesus Christ, servant to you and all true believers, members of the body of Christ, gathered and united in the alliance and the confederacy of the tribulation of Christ, which according to the flesh destroys, and in his Spirit.
Pilgram Marpeck

45 Sg 2:15.

46 Jn 10:8.

47 Heb 12:15.

48 December 21 [new reckoning.—Trans.]

49 [Heinold Fast in "Pilgram Marpeck und das oberdeutsche Täufertum," ARG 47 (1956): 223, n. 44, identifies Probin as a local place-name near Ilanz.—Trans.]

6

A beginning of a true Christian life (The mystery of baptism)

Hans Hut

[1527][1]

Hans Hut was born about 1490 and died in 1527, perhaps of smoke inhalation in an attempt to escape from prison. We first meet him as a colporteur travelling between Nuremberg and Wittenberg in south-central Germany, hotbeds of Radical Reformation ferment. There he took up contact with Thomas Müntzer. He refused to have his last three children baptized and as a consequence was forced into exile from his hometown, Bibra. In Nuremberg he encountered Hans Denck and introduced him to Müntzer and also to Andreas Karlstadt's thought.

Denck took their radical mysticism in a pacifist direction, but Hut took it in an apocalyptic and revolutionary direction. His personal connection to Müntzer is vouched for by the fact that Müntzer entrusted the manuscript of his "Express Exposee" to Hut for publication.[2] Not only that, Hut shared Müntzer's conviction that the battle of Frankenhausen[3]—the final battle of the Peasants' War, in which thousands of

---

Hans Hut, Ein Anfang eines rechten christlichen Lebens (Vom Geheimnis der Taufe); [1527]. Translation by Daniel Liechty and John Rempel.

1 The traditional date given for this treatise is 1526. Recent scholarship has favoured 1527. See MEWLT, 77, for the argument.

2 PRR, 55.

3 15 May 1525.

peasants were slaughtered—was the decisive conflict before the return of Christ, and he participated in it.

In the aftermath of the chaos, Denck baptized Hut on Pentecost in 1526. In Hut's recalculation of the end-time, he accepted an interim pacifism: until the time of the final battle of the godly against the ungodly, the saints are called to suffer in patient nonviolence. This message and his charisma won him many followers in rural areas. He escaped persecution by fleeing to Moravia, a haven of tolerance, where radicals of all kinds had gathered. His radical mysticism—and to a lesser extent his apocalypticism—shaped the Anabaptism emerging there, leaving its mark on people who were soon to become Pilgramites and Hutterites. Hut returned to Germany and under his influence gathered Anabaptists as a missionary force. He was soon arrested in Augsburg and tried but died before he could be executed.[4]

The inclusion in the Kunstbuch of Hut's signature text, as well as writings of his most prolific followers (nos. 9–12), is evidence that the Marpeck Circle was indebted to this earliest stratum (1526–28) of Anabaptist ferment in South Germany and Moravia. For the Pilgramite and Hutterite communities, the depth and passion of Hut's insight on the foundational subject of believers baptism outweighed the fact that his association with the revolutionary apocalyptic movement of the 1520s might have alarmed the authorities.

"A Beginning of a True Christian Life" is the form into which the inspiration of a prophet is poured. Its urgent message is addressed to two audiences. The explicit audience is "the congregation of God," believers who have undergone the baptism of water and the baptism of affliction in anticipation of the return of Christ. The implicit audience is the "debauched" preachers and scholars of the official churches, who say all the right words but don't act on them. The text gives the sense that Hut's readers are recent converts whom he warns to separate themselves from the religious influences under which they were reared. He urges them to listen directly to the Holy Spirit, the Bible, and the "poor in spirit."

---

4 For more on the life and teaching of Hut, see AB, 58–96; PRR, 54-61; MESG; MEWLT.

According to Hut, Mark 16:15–20 is the interpretive key to the Christian life. There Jesus commands his disciples to preach the "gospel of all creatures." Using Romans 1, Hut argues that all God's creatures reveal the truths found in the Bible; the submission of these creatures to human beings is a model for our submission to God. The Mark 16 passage also calls for believers baptism in water and then in affliction: the justification of the sinner comes by grace through faith. But faith is not simply *about* something; faith is *in* something—a process of surrender to God that makes us partakers of the saving affliction of Christ. This surrender has radical social consequences, such as leaving one's occupation and giving away one's wealth. When Christians do this, they become the body of Christ in the world today.

"A Beginning of a True Christian Life" was reprinted several times, usually without the author's name. After their 1527 arrest in Freistadt, Austria, followers of Hut submitted to the court a handwritten copy of the piece. It appears in two Hutterite manuscripts with minor editorial changes in 1573 (Nuremberg) and 1576 (Budapest). It was copied into a third Hutterite manuscript in 1615 (Alba Iulia, Romania) with major additions and deletions. The Kunstbuch version differs from other versions both editorially and substantively. Sometimes the changes seem to be deliberate, in keeping with Marpeckian sacramental teaching.[5] At other times we may account for the divergences by postulating a process in which someone who had memorized the text dictated it to a scribe.

5 BSOT, 164–66.

I wish all brothers and sisters in the Lord the pure fear of God, which is the beginning of divine wisdom.[6] You are the pure Christendom, the congregation of God, the bride and the spouse of Christ,[7] unified in the bonds of love[8] through the movement of the Holy Spirit. All who with contrite hearts and broken spirits[9] earnestly desire the righteousness of the crucified Son of God, and all who desire to be fed by this righteousness, to these I wish grace and peace through the Holy Spirit. Amen.

The final and most terrible times of this world are upon us.[2] With alert eyes we see and acknowledge that all that was prophesied and preached from the beginning through the prophets, patriarchs, and apostles will take place. It is happening even now! This is as Peter prophesied beforehand [Acts 3 (21)]. But the world (God have mercy) has absolutely no understanding of this, especially those who teach others but actually understand less than the apes, although they present themselves as scriptural authorities [1 Tm 1 (7)]. In fact, the truth is closed to them sevenfold [Rv 5 (1)], for they will not suffer it to be opened up to them by a work of God. Actually they are God's enemies, as Paul said [Phil 3 (18)]. Therefore all that they teach and read is in reverse order and based on false judgment. For them truth is concealed and covered over in the extreme [2 Cor 4 (3)]. The poor, ordinary man is being led astray, betrayed to all that is destructive and foul. No one believes this, even though it is spoken and proclaimed.

There is no worldly and debauched scholar alive (living in worldly honours and temporal splendour) who knows the judgments of the Lord [Hb 1 (4f.)]. Because they are perverted, they see everything as backward and thus they seduce both rich and poor with their bejewelled tongues. Well then, those who will be misled will always be misled.[10]

---

6 Ps 111:10; Prv 1:7; 9:10.

7 Rv 21:9; 22:17.

8 Col 3:14.

9 Ps 51:19; 143:4.

10 2 Tm 3:13.

Therefore I admonish all godly people who seek and love righteousness to earnestly safeguard themselves from all soft, usurious,[11*] debauched, haughty, and hypocritical scholars who preach for money. They do not look out for your good but only for their own bellies [Rom 16 (18); Phil 3 (19)]. We see that their lives are no better than other worldly people; anyone who trusts them will be betrayed. Word has it that they preach nothing but "Believe! Believe!" But they never say how this faith is to come about. The very thought makes me shudder. For where the order of divine mystery is not properly handled, there is only frivolous error and nothing lasting. This can be seen in all things.

Therefore, my deeply beloved brothers and sisters in the Lord, you must learn the judgments of God concerning his commandments and his Word for yourselves and be given understanding from God alone. Otherwise you will be led astray right along with the rest of the world. For they do not know the judgments of God or even what is meant by a judgment. So they say simply that it is impossible to know or grasp the judgments of God [Rom 11 (33)]. They arm themselves with the words of St. Paul, but forget what he said in 1 Corinthians 2 [9f.] or what is found in the Wisdom of Solomon 9 [13–19]. They also forget that David pled with the Lord to learn his judgments [Ps 119 (12, 26, 64, 68)]. And God earnestly commanded them to learn, keep, and accomplish his judgments [Dt 10 (13); 26 (16f.); 11 (1); Ez 20 (19)]. If we are to do them, we have to know what they are! Oh, how wretchedly they seduce the whole world under the guise of Holy Scripture with their false and fictitious faith, a faith that brings no betterment of life. Anyone can judge this for himself. Note that whenever two or three of them preach on the same scriptural passage, none of them agree in their interpretation.

Therefore, my beloved brothers and sisters in the Lord, if you truly desire to learn the judgments of God and the witness of Holy Scripture, do not listen to the cries of those who preach for money. Rather, seek the poor in spirit,[12] those forsaken by the world and called fanatics and devils [Mt 12 (24); Jn 8 (48, 52); 12 (48); 1 Cor 4 (9–13)], following the

---

11* Note.

12 Mt 5:3.

example of Christ and the apostles. Listen to them! For no one may obtain the truth except he follow in the footsteps of Christ[13] and his elect in the school of all affliction [Lk 9 (23)], or have the least part in following the will of God in the vindication of the cross of Christ. For the mysteries of divine wisdom cannot be learned in the rogues' galleries and dens of thieves of Wittenberg or Paris![14*] Neither can they be learned living on a comfortable stipend in the lords' courts. For the wisdom of God does not dwell among those living in ease.

So our new evangelicals, these soft scholars, have pushed the pope, monks, and priests from their stools. Now that they have succeeded, they begin once again whoring with the villainous Babylonians[15*, 16] in all lust, pomp, honour, greed, envy, and hatred, to the dismay of the whole world. They are building (God have mercy) an even more wicked popery than before. They will not listen to a poor man and cannot bear being convinced by Holy Scriptures, for they do not want to be found lacking knowledge or unlearned [2 Tm 4 (3)].

Therefore they conclude that all those who do not believe the way they do must be false prophets—just as happened to Christ.[17] Well then, leave them in their pits with their idols and rulers tickling their ears, so long as God allows. But their time is short, and everyone will witness their shameful end.[18]

I am moved by Christian love and brotherly concern to record the judgments necessary to the beginning of the Christian life, to the degree that God gives me grace, as a witness to all brothers and sisters in the Lord, to those who hunger and thirst for righteousness that counts before God, and not worldly, debauched people. For such judgments are incomprehensible to them; they consider them sarcastic and perverse, heretical and damned! Therefore all brothers and sisters who love and desire the truth, when you begin to read such a written judgment, I admonish you not to despise it because there are parts you do

---

13 1 Pt 2:21.

14* Note.

15* The whores and their Babylon.

16 Rv 17:1ff.

17 Jn 7:12.

18 2 Tm 3:9.

not understand. For everybody who has not been born anew [Jn 3 (4)], understanding has been made impossible because of the perverse understanding by scholars, even among themselves, in order to deceive the world.

Therefore, if we are to come to a true understanding of such judgments, from the start we must become as children and fools [1 Cor 3 (18)]. It is a lofty—indeed impossible—thing for a carnal person to grasp the judgments of God in truth, when they are not in all parts placed into a proper order.

Therefore we want to begin first of all with the judgment of baptism,[19*] the beginning of the Christian life. We want earnestly to note and see how it was instituted and mandated by Christ and practised by the apostles, with proofs from the divine witness of Holy Scripture, and not according to the good opinions of human wisdom, as it has been up until now, even among those who most celebrate the gospel. May God have mercy on all people but especially the poor. To that end may the cross of Christ help us. Amen.

If we want to arrive at a correct understanding and judgment concerning baptism, we must not rely on human opinion and cast aside the form and practice of Christ and his apostles. For God has forbidden us to do whatever seems right to us [Dt 12 (8); 4 (2); 13 (1); 17 (11, 20); Prv 30 (6)]. Rather, we should do only what God has commanded us to do and not waver to the right or to the left.[20] So if baptism is to be practised in the right order, as it was commanded by Christ and practised by the apostles, we must take the command of Christ as truth with all diligence and earnestness [Gal 6 (16)]. For he has instituted an order and a rule or measure that lays the proper foundation for the Christian life. Who has ears, let him hear![21] If someone is offended, so be it.

First of all,[22*] Christ said, "Go into all the world and preach the gospel of all creatures."[23] Second, he said, "Whoever believes." Third, "Who-

---

19* The first judgment of baptism.

20 Dt 5:32; 28:14; Jo 23:6; Prv 4:27; Is 30:21.

21 Mt 11:15; 13:9, 43; Mk 4:9, 23; Lk 8:8; 14:35.

22* 1. The order of Christ.

23 [Mk 16:15. Most English translations say "gospel to all creatures," and Hans Hut's term is *das Evangelium aller Kreaturen* ("gospel of all creatures"). The

ever is baptized will be saved" [Mk 16 (15)]. This order must be kept if we want to achieve a true Christendom, even if the whole world goes to pieces.[24*] Where this order is not kept, there is no Christendom as the congregation of God but only of the devil. We defy the whole world and all false Christians. Let them change their perverted order and the false things they champion.

First of all,[25*] Christ says, "Go into all the world and preach the gospel of all creatures." Here the Lord tells us how someone comes to knowledge of God and of himself—that is, through the gospel of all creatures. So our first task is to learn and understand just what is meant by this gospel of all creatures.

But (God have mercy) the entire world knows nothing of it, and neither is it preached in our time. It has been preached and declared by the poor in spirit and the simple, as it should be.[26*] But to the soft and lascivious people, especially those who preach for money and boast about their preaching of the gospel, it is seen as the worst kind of foolishness and fanaticism. They call those who preach it complete rogues and scold them as false prophets. Well, their day is coming! That's why Paul said the word of the cross is "foolishness to those who will be lost." But for those who "will be saved it is the power of God" [1 Cor 1 (18)].

In the "gospel of all creatures," nothing is signified and preached other than Christ the crucified one alone, not only Christ the head but the whole Christ with all his members. Preaching this Christ is what all creatures teach. The whole Christ must suffer in all members. It is not as these scholarly Christians preach (who would be seen as the best, as we constantly hear from them). They say that as the head, Christ carried out and fulfilled everything. But then what of the members and the whole body in which the suffering of Christ must be fulfilled [1 Cor 12 (12ff.); Rom 12 (4f.)]?

---

most recent revision of Luther (1984) retains the genitive "of"; the NRSV (1989) has "good news to the whole creation." This present translation retains the genitive form because it is the basis of Hut's theology of creatures.—Ed.]

24* Note.

25* First.

26* Note.

Paul gives witness to this when he says, "I restore what is lacking of Christ's suffering on my own body for his body" [Col 1 (24)]. Therefore soon—it is about to happen—these wise men will become as fools. For it pleases God "to save those who believe through the foolishness of preaching."[27] To preach the gospel of all creatures should not be understood as preaching to dogs, cats, cows, and calves, or leaves and grass, but rather, as Paul said, "the gospel that is preached to you is in all creatures."[28] He shows this again by saying that the eternal power of God will be seen when it is recognized that it has been present in God's works (or creatures) since the creation of the world [Rom 1 (20)].

So I say (in the Lord)[29] and confess that the gospel according to the commandment of Christ (as Christ and his apostles preached it) is not preached in our time.[30*] All the preachers and civil servants don't know what a gospel of all creatures is! It is hidden and concealed from them, because they do not seek the pure and clear honour of God. Rather, they look after their own honour and their own bellies [Rom 16 (18); Phil 3 (19)]. If you tell them that, they only laugh at it and say we are crafty-headed fanatics. Therefore, my most dearly beloved brothers and sisters in the Lord, mark well what is meant by the gospel of all creatures [Mk 16 (15)], as Paul called it when he said "the gospel which is preached to you in all creatures" [Col 1 (23)].

The gospel of all creatures, as Paul exposits it, is nothing other than the power of God to save all those who believe in it (not only about it).[31] If someone wants to comprehend and confess God's power and divinity, God's invisible essence, through the works (or creatures) of all creation since the beginning of the world,[32] then he must note and consider that Christ always communicated the kingdom of heaven and the power of God to the common man through the use of parables, pointing to a creature or to different handicrafts or different human occupations. He never sent the poor and simple to books (as our scholars

---

27 1 Cor 1:21.

28 Col 1:23.

29 [When Paul spoke with divine authority, he said he spoke "in the Lord."—Ed.]

30* Note.

31 Rom 1:16.

32 Rom 1:20.

do now). Rather, he taught and witnessed the gospel to them through their work[33*]—to peasants by their fields, seeds, thistles, thorns, and rocks (Mt 13 [3–8]; Mk 4 [26–34]; Lk 8 [5–8]; Jn 12 [24]). In Jeremiah 4 [3], he says that seeds should not be sown among thorns. Rather, clear them out first, then hoe them; after that, plow and then plant [Jer 1 (10)]. The power of God that is shown in this is the work of God toward us. The power of God works in us as the farmer works his field. Paul said, "You are God's field" [1 Cor 3 (9)]. God is like the farmer working the field before he sows the seed, preparing us for his Word, so that it might grow and bear fruit.

Jesus taught the gospel to the gardener by using the trees (Mt 7 [16–20]; 12 [33]); to the fisherman by using the catch of fish (Mt 4 [19]; Jer 16 [16]); to the carpenter by using the house (1 Pt 2 [5]; 2 Cor 5 [1]; Mt 7 [24–27]; Heb 3 [3–6]); to the goldsmith by using the smelting of gold (1 Pt 1 [18]; Jb 23 [10]; Ws 3 [6]; Mal 3 [2f.]; Prv 17 [3]; Sir 28 [29]). He taught the gospel to the housewife by using dough (Mt 13 [33]; Lk 12 [1]; 1 Cor 5 [6–8]; Gal 5 [9]). He taught the gospel to the vine keeper by using the vineyards, vines, and branches (Mt 21 [33–41]; Lk 12 [13:6–9]; Jn 15 [1ff.]; Is 5 [1ff.]; Jer 2 [21]); to the tailor by using the patch on old cloth (Mt 9 [16]; Mk 2 [21]). He taught the gospel to the cooper by using old wine casks or skins (Mt 9 [17]; Mk 2 [22]); to the merchant by using pearls (Mt 13 [45f.]). He taught the gospel to the reaper by using the harvest (Mt 9 [37f.], Mk 4 [26–29]; Lk 10 [2]; Jn 4 [35–38]; Rv 14 [15f.]; Jl 3 [13]); to the woodcutter by using the axe and tree (Is 10 [15]; Jer 46 [22]; Mt 3 [10]); to the shepherd by using the sheep (Ez 34 [2ff.]; 37 [24]; Zec 11 [4ff.]; Jn 10 [1ff.]; Heb 13 [20]). He taught the gospel to the potter by using clay (Is 30 [14]; Jer 18 [2ff.]; Sir 27 [6]; 33 [13]; 38 [32–34]; Ps 2 [9]; Rom 9 [21–23]; Rv 2 [27]); to the steward and overseer by using their accounts (Lk 16 [1–13]); to the pregnant woman by using the act of birth (Mt 4[34]; Jn 16 [21]; Rv 12 [2ff.]; Is 26 [17]); [1 Thes 5 (3)]; to the thresher by using the winnowing fan (Is 41 [15f.]; Jer 27;[35] 51 [2];

[33*] Note.

[34] Mt 24:8?

[35] Jer 4:11?; 15:7?

Ez 5 [2, 10, 12]; 22;[36] 29;[37] Ps 43;[38] Mt 3 [12]; Lk 3 [17]); to the butcher by using the slaughter (Is 53 [7]; Ps 43 [44:11]; Rom 8 [36]).[39]

Paul illustrated the body of Christ (that is, the congregation of Christ) by using the human body (1 Cor 12 [12ff.]; Eph 4 [1ff.]; 5 [30–32]; Col 1 [24]). Christ always preached the gospel of the kingdom of God by using the creatures and parables. In fact, he never preached without the use of parables and examples (Mk 4 [34]). David also said, "I will open my mouth and speak in parables."[40]

Noteworthy in all these parables is that the creatures are made to suffer the effects of human activity. It is through this pain that they reach their goal, that is, what they were created for. In the same way, no human being comes to salvation except through the suffering and tribulation [Acts 14 (22); 2 Tm 3 (12); Jdt 8 (20–22)] that is the work of God in him. How this happens through the futility of creaturely life is described throughout scripture.[41]

That is why God gave the children of Israel understanding of his will by use of the creatures and rituals, and announced, preached, and described it through Moses.[42*] God commanded that offerings be made to him of sheep, goats, rams, and bulls.

But Isaiah will not have it! In chapter one,[43] he says, "The sacrifice of bulls, the blood of sheep, calves, and rams, I never wanted." In Psalm 50 [9], he writes, "I do not want the bulls of your house or the rams of your stables."

---

36 Ez 12:14?

37 [Original obscure. Ez 5 ends at v. 17.—Ed.]

38 Ps 1:4?; 35:5?

39 [This list of Bible citations is almost totally different from the one in GOT, 17.—Ed.]

40 Ps 78:2.

41 [Contemporary readers, as much as current ones, found it hard to understand the dense language of this text. In one of the other versions (GOT, 17) this line was altered and translated as follows: "So the whole of scripture and all the creatures illustrate the suffering of Christ in all his members. Therefore the scripture is figured simply in the creatures."—Ed.]

42* Note.

43 Is 1:11.

Therefore the precept of God is not in the commandment of sacrifice; it is in the power of the Spirit [1 Cor 2 (4f.)].[44] The power of this commandment for human beings is that the human stands in relation to God as what is sacrificed stands in relation to humans. It is for that reason that David offered burnt offerings to God, such as rams, oxen, and goats [Ps 65 (66:15)]; in Psalm 51 [16–19], he sacrifices himself instead of a calf. Such ritual sacrifices are signs and witnesses that humans should offer themselves as living sacrifices [Rom 12 (1)]. That is why God commanded (Lv 11 [31–34]; Dt 14 [4–9]) that clean animals should be eaten. The power behind this is that humans are to yield themselves to God to suffer according to God's will, just as animals suffer according to our will. So when God forbids the eating of unclean animals, the power[45] behind this is that one should not have dealings with people who are compared to unclean animals because of their sins [1 Cor 5 (9–11)]. According to Acts 10 [12, 15] there is then nothing unclean, but all things are good.[46]

These rituals demonstrate clearly what the will of God is; they are meant for us as much as for the children of Israel. That is why Christ constantly spoke in parables. The importance is not in what is spoken but in its power and meaning.[47] All animals are subject to humans [Gn 1 (28); Ps 8 (6–8)]. If one wants to use an animal, it must first be dealt with according to human will; it must be prepared, cooked, and roasted. That is, the animal must suffer.

God does the same thing with human beings![48*] If God is to have use of us or enjoyment of us, we must first be justified and made pure by him [2 Tm 2 (21)], both inwardly and outwardly—inwardly from greed and lust, outwardly from injustice in our way of living and our misuse of the creatures.

---

44 1 Cor 4:20.

45 1 Cor 4:20.

46 [A step is missing in the author's argument. His original interest is the comparison between unclean animals and unclean people. In the next sentence his point is that no creature is unclean.—Ed.]

47 1 Cor 4:20.

48* Note.

The farmer does not sow corn among thistles, thorns, branches, and stones. Rather, he clears them out and then does the sowing. In the same way, understand that God does not sow his Word in someone who is full of thistles and thorns, who desires only the creaturely. Worry about physical prosperity, which God forbids [Mt 6 (25–34); Lk 12 (22–31)], must first be rooted out (Jer 31 [18–22]). The carpenter does not build a house out of uncut trees. First he cuts them down and shapes them according to his will. Only then does he build a house out of them. This is how we are to learn God's work and will in relation to us. It's like the steps people go through in getting a house ready before they move into it. We are that house, says Paul [Heb 3 (4)].

People are often called trees in the scriptures. If one is to become a house, one must be cut off from the desires of the world [Gal 5 (24)]. With a tree, one knot points this way and another that way. That is how it is with human desires.[49*] One points toward property, another to wife and child, a third toward wealth, and a fourth toward fields or meadows. A fifth branch points to temporal pomp, arrogance, voluptuousness, and honour.

Therefore we should especially note and diligently ponder our actions in relation to the creatures, for what we do to them is scripture to us. The whole world, with all its creatures, is a book; in it we read our actions, just as we read a written book. From the beginning of the world until Moses, the elect studied[50*] this book of all creatures[51*]—with its descriptions that were inscribed in the nature of things [Rom 2 (14–16)]—and gained understanding from it.[52] Meanwhile, the whole law with its ceremonial works was described, and people behaved toward creatures as the law laid it out.

Even the heathen, who do not have the written law, behave just as people do who have the written law. The scriptural law shows how an animal should be slaughtered before it is offered to God. Only after

---

49* Note.

50* The will of God.

51* Eusibi. lib 7. [Eusebius, Hist. eccl. I, 4.]

52 [The GOT recension (p. 17) adds "Through the Spirit of God" and "This understanding of nature was written on their hearts," as a theological gloss at this point. For this editor, Romans 1 is the interpretive key.—Ed.]

that is it to be eaten. The heathen do that also, because they have the law of nature and do not eat living animals. Likewise, we must die to the world[53*] in order to live in God. In the law, lamps have a snuffer for the light.[54] The heathen also have these for their lights,[55*] as well as almost the same rituals and commandments. That is why Moses describes these rituals with creatures: to remind and admonish people that in these things they may search out and learn the will of God.

Therefore, since the law is inscribed in and demonstrated by all creatures, we may read it daily in our work. It is a book that concerns us daily. The whole world is full of descriptions of the will of God; our own hearts give us witness of this. When we avoid the coarseness of worldly lusts, we may perceive through the work of the creatures God's invisible essence and eternal power [Rom 1 (20)]. One may there recognize how God works with people and prepares them for perfection. This can happen only by way of the cross of suffering according to his will.

That is why all creatures are subject to humans, and humans rule over them.[56] For just as the whole Bible is written in terms of the creatures, so also Christ preached and demonstrated the gospel of all creatures through parables [Mk 4]. This he did himself when he preached to the common man. He did not send them to chapters in books, like our scholars do.[57*] For all that can be shown in the scriptures is already shown in the creatures.[58] Christ had no need of scripture unless he wanted to prove something from it to the soft scholars.

When, according to the Lord's command, the gospel of all creatures is preached, a person is then brought to understanding in a reasonable and natural way.[59*] He sees it in his own work, what he does in relation

---

53* Die to the world.

54 Ex 25:38; 37:23.

55* Note.

56 Gn 1:28.

57* Gloss: This doesn't mean that anyone is deterred from reading Holy Scripture or searching in it. Jn 5:39.

58 [Hut's argument parallels that of medieval Christians who argued that architecture and art were for illiterate people a way to the revelation we find in the Bible.—Ed.]

59* Note.

to the creatures. He can then recognize God's will toward him and may give himself exuberantly in obedience to Christ [2 Cor 10 (5)]. For then he will realize that no one may come to salvation except by suffering the will of God through thick and thin,[60] as is pleasing to God. He says that's how it has to be with me and with all people who want to be saved.[61]

"Faith comes from what is heard" [Rom 10 (17);[62*] Mk 16 (15f.)]. This is the second part of the divine order, that part Christ meant when he said, "Whoever believes." If the person understands the gospel in all creatures,[63] hears and believes it in a way that shows, even that is not enough. For that is something any person may witness and prove. The third part of the divine order[64*] must follow. For as Christ said, "Whoever is baptized will be saved."

Baptism must follow after the other two parts. It comes when the person is ready to accept and suffer all that the Father through Christ has in store for him. He must set his heart to remain in the Lord and forsake the world. He accepts baptism as a covenant of acceptance [1 Pt 3 (21)] before a Christian congregation, who have received the covenant from God. Moreover, they have the authority in the name of God to administer it only to those who long for it with all their heart.

The Lord says (Mt 18 [18]; Lk 17 [3f.]; Jn 20 [23]), "What you bind and loose on earth shall also be bound and loosed in heaven." But no one can be taken into such a community unless he first has heard and learned the gospel, and believes and agrees with what he has heard. For this covenant is an agreement, a demonstration of divine love in relation to all brothers and sisters, in obedience to Christ with love, life, goods, and honour, regardless of what evil the world says about him for it.

And where are such Christians? O God, their number is small [Lk 12 (32)]! Even if no more than two or three were gathered, it doesn't matter, because Christ is there as witness among them [Mt 18 (16)]. The mouths of even two or three are a genuine witness to the truth [2 Cor 13

---

60 [Original: *inn lieb und laid.*—Trans.]

61 2 Tm 3:12.

62* The other part of faith.

63 [Original: *in allen creaturen.*—Trans.]

64* The third part is baptism.

(1)]. Such a person is assured and certain that in baptism, accompanied by a good conscience [1 Pt 3 (21)], he is accepted as a child of God,[65] a brother or sister of Christ, a member of the Christian congregation and the body of Christ, because he has pledged himself to such unity with integrity, according to the will of God. For God commands his saints to gather together, those who hold the covenant more dear than sacrifice [Ps 49 (50:5)]. God does not desire the sacrifice of oxen or rams[66] but rather offerings of thanks and praise. He desires that each person offer his body for justification [Rom 12 (1)], as Paul said, and believe that God will not forsake him in times of need, but will rescue him from all need if he is led into tribulation. Such a faith, although it is not yet perfected, not yet proved, will be counted to him as justification[67] until he is justified and tried, as gold is in fire (Ws 3 [6]).[68]

Baptism, which is preceded by preaching and believing, is not the true essence that makes a person godly. True baptism is a work of faith and a pledge by the person to remind himself of baptism every day. Of it, Christ says that a person is justified of all carnal lusts, as well as impure works and behaviour, if he recognizes that no creature can justify itself and come to its intended being without the person to whom it is subject [Mt 20 (22f.); Lk 15 (50)[69]]. No one can justify himself to his intended end, that is, salvation. This can happen only through God's work in the baptism of all affliction [1 Jn 5 (6–8)], which God proves and gives only to those who submit to justification. Because of that, he will be justified. If a person is to be justified by God, he must be still before the Lord his God and allow God to work in him as God wills. Then God will do all things well, as David said: "Commit your way to the Lord and hope in him, for he does all things well" [Ps 37 (5)].

---

65 Rom 8:16.

66 Ps 40:6; 51:16; Jer 6:20; Hos 6:6; Mt 9:13; Heb 10:5, 8.

67 Gn 15:6; Rom 4:5, 9.

68 [Hut reserves the term *justification* for holiness that God works in us through suffering. He distinguishes it from salvation, in which we come to the faith that we are accepted as children of God and members of Christ's body, whom God would never forsake.—Ed.]

69 [Lk 15 does not have 50 verses. There is no parallel to Mt 20:22 in Luke. Lk 15:20 is related to Hut's topic in this paragraph.—Ed.]

Therefore the water of all tribulation[70] is the real essence and power of baptism, by which the person is submerged in the death of Christ [Rom 6 (4)].[71] Christ accepted this covenant of God in the Jordan [Mt 3 (13–17)]; with it he attested to his obedience to fulfil unto death the Father's love to all people, and became an example for us of one on whom the baptism of all tribulation was richly poured out by the Father [Lk 12 (50); Is 53].

That is why the outer and inner work and essence of baptism must be clearly distinguished from each other. (1) The congregation administers the covenant of baptism through one of her true servants, just as Christ received it from John [Mt 3 (13–17); Mk 1 (9–11)]. (2) The other baptism that is still lacking, let the reader understand, God gives through affliction in the Holy Spirit. Scripture says, he "leads into hell and out again"; he "kills and then brings to life again" [1 Kgs 2 (1 Sm 2:6)]. This is the baptism with which the Lord was yet to baptize (Lk 12 [49–53]). Whoever would be a disciple of the Lord must be baptized (Rom 6 [3–11]; Jn 3 [5f.]; Mt 20 [22f.]) and made pure in the Spirit through the bond of peace into one body [Eph 4 (3f.); 5 (26f.)].

Therefore God saves his own and makes them worthy only through the covenant of the new birth and renewal of the Holy Spirit in faith. God works according to his great compassion, and it is only through this same grace that we are justified and made heirs (Rom 8 [17]) through hope (Ti 3 [5–7]). In this way one is washed, healed, cleansed, and reborn (Jn 3 [3–8]); [1 Cor 6 (11)] into an irreproachable congregation before God (Eph 5 [27]). This is not like the contemporary confederates of the anti-Christ, formed by the usurious and greedy scholars. Just as the people are, so is the priest, as is written in the prophets.[72]

---

70 1 Kgs 22:27; 2 Chr 18:26.

71 [Of the many differences among the versions of Hut's text, the following is significant as a precise theological contrast between GOT (p. 29) and the KB. "This baptism was not first instituted in the time of Christ. It has been from the beginning and is a baptism with which all friends of God, from Adam to the present, are baptized, as Paul said." In the view of the Marpeck Circle, baptism is a mark that distinguishes the new covenant from the old, not a practice common to both.—Ed.]

72 Is 24:2.

That is why beloved David prayed to God to wash him and cleanse him of sin [Ps 51 (2)]. And God graciously heard him, as we read in Ps 68.[73] He was stuck in the water of all affliction and cried to the Lord for help. And from the slime and deep abyss he was rescued.[74] Paul admonishes the brothers in Ephesus to suffer, just as they had seen him suffer.[75] For the kingdom of God consists not in what is spoken, or other external things, but rather in the power of God (1 Thes 1 [5]); [1 Cor 4 (20)], which God alone will give: he makes a person wholly new in speech, senses, and heart—in all actions and conduct. Therefore it is a false gospel the world and its preachers are spreading around:[76*] it doesn't make people better, only worse.

I place this before all Christian brothers to judge [Lk 11 (28)]. But blessed are those who hear the Word and heed it. For a true lamb of Christ hears the voice of the Lord and follows it [Jn 10 (27)]. But whoever hears it and does nothing is a fool (Mt 7 [26]; Lk 6 [49]) and will never be righteous. Whoever wants to come to God without the justification that counts before God throws away the means,[77] that is, the suffering and cross of Christ; indeed, Christ the crucified himself. This is what the whole world is doing now. It will not escape suffering, for no one comes to the Father without the Son [Jn 6 (65)].[78]

Whoever would rule with God[79] must be ruled by God. Whoever would do the will of God must give up his own will.[80*] Whoever would find something in God must lose much in him as well. The whole world talks[81*] about spiritual freedom yet remains in slavery to the world and the flesh. It will not give anything up but constantly wants more. Oh, how subtly and masterfully the world can fool itself!

---

73 Ps 69.

74 [GOT: "The sin was slain and he was made alive again in Christ."—Ed.]

75 Eph 3:13.

76* Note.

77 Rom 1:17; 3:21, 25; 10:3; 2 Cor 5:21.

78 [Justification for Hut is entirely a gift of God received by faith. But faith is surrender to Christ, which involves sharing in his suffering (see Phil 3:8–13).—Ed.]

79 2 Tm 2:12.

80* Note.

81* The world says.

So now everyone is saying that each should remain in his occupation.[82] If that is so, why did not Peter remain a fisherman or Matthew a tax collector [Mk 10 (28); Mt 9 (9)]? Why did Christ tell the rich young ruler to sell all he had and give to the poor [Mt 19 (21)]? If it is right that our preachers want to have so much wealth, then the rich young ruler was right to keep his possessions! O Zacchaeus! Why did you so casually give away your wealth [Lk 19 (8)]? According to the rule of our preachers, you could have kept it all and still been a good Christian! My dear companions, how easy it is to see who the scoundrels are! But this one thing is true: there is a Lord who will judge you.

The heart of a true and faithful friend of God, who waits upon the Lord daily and confidently hopes in him, will be strengthened, so that under the cross he will be able to carry out the will of the Lord [Gal 6 (14)]. All that such a person suffers is Christ's suffering and not our own. For with Christ we are one body and many members, bound together by the bond of love [Eph 4 (4); Rom 12 (4); 1 Cor 10 (17); 12 (13)]. Christ accepts such a person as part of his own body. The prophet says, "Whoever touches you touches the apple of my eye" [Zec 2 (8)]. And elsewhere, "Whatever you do to the least of these my own, you do to me" [Mt 25 (40)]. Christ said to Paul, "Why do you persecute me?" [Acts 9 (4)]. Thus the affliction of Christ must be fulfilled in everyone, until the suffering Christ is brought to completion [Col 1 (24)]. Just as Christ is the lamb who was slain from the beginning of the world,[83] so he will continue to be crucified until the end of the world, until the body of Jesus is perfected (Eph 4 [16]) according to the length, width, depth, and height in the fullness of God [Eph 3 (18f.)].[84]

Under such suffering and such a cross of righteous baptism, a person becomes aware of his faith, is justified and tried as gold in fire [Ws 3 (6); Sir 2 (5)]. Through it, true faith, which consists in goodness and compassion, is revealed. If, after all suffering and affliction, someone is comforted afresh in the Holy Spirit, he is then ready for the Lord and

---

82 1 Cor 7:20, 24.

83 Rv 13:8.

84 [In GOT, 22, the text reads, "*nach der leng, braite, tiefe und höche in der liebe Christi*" ("according to the length, width, depth, and height in the love of Christ").—Ed.]

for doing good works. There cannot be any other way for the truth to be revealed without deception.

The faith that comes by hearing [Rom 10 (17)] will be credited to the person as justification until the time comes when that person is justified and purified under the cross.[85*] Then the person's faith will be conformed to the faith of God[86] and united with Christ. The righteous live out of such faith.[87] Therefore a great distinction must be made between divine faith and human faith at their inception. God's own faith is absolutely true, righteous, and enduring, just in every word, as he promised. In the beginning, our faith is like silver that is still embedded in the ore, full of spots and impurities. But still it is counted as genuine silver until the smelting, in which all impurities are taken out.

That is why the apostles said, "We believe; help our unbelief!" [Lk 17 (5); Mk 9 (24)]. At first, our faith may be compared to unbelief. As someone finds himself in the trial of justification, often neither trust nor faith may be found in him. Locked in unbelief [Rom 11 (32)], he thinks that he has been cast out from before the eyes of the Lord. Nothing can comfort him, no creature at all. It is as David says: "My soul will not be comforted" [Ps 76 (77:2)]. And elsewhere also he says, "I am cast out from before your face, from before your eyes" [Ps 30 (31:22)]. A person is locked in the abyss of hell. Christ calls this the sign of Jonah [Mt 12 (39)]. Nothing can bring him joy, other than the one who has led him into the abyss. He must simply wait until God comes to him with his comfort in the Holy Spirit. Then he will be so joyful that he forgets all the world's desire, joy, and honour, and counts them all as dung [Phil 3 (8)]. Then the person returns from the pit of hell and gains peace in the Holy Spirit.

This is the justification that counts before God; it does not come from an untried faith. An untried faith stretches only as far as justification, where it must be made ready. Of course the whole world fears this justification like the devil, and would rather pay with an artificial faith—and indeed not go on to justification [Jas 2 (14ff.)]. Such right-

---

85* Faith.

86 [The phrase "the faith of God" recurs in this section. Its sense is "faith from God."—Trans.]

87 Hb 2:4; Rom 1:17; Gal 3:11; Heb 10:38.

eousness is not taught or preached by their preachers, for they themselves are enemies of the cross of Christ and of righteousness [Phil 3 (18); Gal 6 (12); Rom 16 (18)]. They seek only what serves their bellies, having only the appearance of a spirituality the likes of which they have never seen! [Col 2 (18)].

If God works his righteousness in us through the suffering of the holy cross, which is laid on each Christian,[88] this reveals God's faith to our faith, according to his promise, so that we are able to believe that God is sure and his faith is demonstrated to our faith. Then all creaturely desires, which we have usurped from the creatures, are rooted out and smashed.[89*, 90] The yoke of the world's sinners will be cast aside,[91] so that it is no longer the world but Christ who rules in us [Gal 2 (19f.)]. Then the law of the Father will be accomplished in us through Christ embodied in his members. Then there is the desire and love (without any hindrance from the creatures) to consummate the will of God in true obedience.

To someone like that, his burden is light, his yoke sweet and inclined to us [Mt 11 (29f.)], so that we might carry out everything, making possible what was impossible. Then someone may truly say, "Christ has commuted my sin and taken it away!" [Rom 8 (2); Col 2 (13)]. But whoever does not submit himself to this discipline and order of the Lord, but rather remains attached to worldly desires [1 Jn 2 (16f.)], will suffer a much greater harm and be overcome. Indeed, he will perish and suffer eternal ruin. Even if they cry out to God in the midst of such suffering, God will not hear them [Prv 1 (28); Ws 6 (6); Dt 32 (20ff.)].[92] By contrast, all who fear God and are surrendered to the truth, who seek comfort in the Lord alone, he will redeem from all affliction here

---

88 Mt 10:38; 16:24; Mk 8:34; 10:21; Lk 9:23; 23:26.

89* Note.

90 Gal 5:24.

91 Gal 5:1.

92 Hos 8:2.

and in eternity [Ws 3 (5f.); 4 (2) Esd 16 (74); Sir 2 (5)].[93] May God help us through Jesus Christ. Amen.[94]

Hans Hut, a comrade
in the affliction[95] that is in Christ,
and servant of all who love and seek God.
His life ended in Augsburg in prison
in the year 1528.[96]

---

93 Ps 37:38–40.

94 [GOT, 24: "but God will scorn him in the same measure as he scorned. Therefore all who fear God should seek their comfort in the Lord, and he will rescue them from all tribulation, so help us God, through the bath of the new birth."—Ed.]

95 Rv 1:9.

96 This date conflicts with contemporary and current sources, which agree that Hut died on December 6, 1527.

7

Concerning hasty judgments and verdicts

To the Swiss Brethren

Pilgram Marpeck

[1542–43]

"Concerning Hasty Judgments and Verdicts" is the first—and longest—of four letters Marpeck wrote to the Swiss Brethren, particularly the most rigorous among them, the Anabaptists in Appenzell.[1] "Even though this letter is not addressed to a specific recipient, the content makes its destination clear."[2] In addition, the next letter in the collection (no. 8), "The Cause of the Conflict," concerns itself with similar matters and addresses itself directly to Appenzellers. Its date is 1543. We know from other sources that in the last years of his residence in that area, Marpeck sought to overcome differences between his circle and the Swiss.[3] Thus, even though the letter is dated 1531, scholars agree that it represents the circumstances of 1542–43.[4]

This text represents Marpeck at his most profound. A mind that is captive to the love of Christ is at work here. Inspired by this love, the

---

Pilgram Marpeck an die Schweitzer Brüder: Von jähen Gerichten und Urteilen; [Ca. 1542/43]. Translation by Walter Klaassen. Previously published as "Judgment and Decision" in WPM, 309–61. Reprinted, with editorial changes, by permission of the publisher.

1 Appenzell is due east of Zurich near Switzerland's border with Austria.

2 WPM, 309.

3 Walter Klaassen and William Klassen describe the setting (MLDC, 185–93).

4 CC, 53–54.

author approaches the baffling problem of persistent sin among people who claim they are living a life of discipleship. Marpeck argues that the most essential trait of love is patience. He makes his point by means of the image of a tree: first there are blossoms, then there are leaves, and finally there is fruit. Blossoms and leaves do not show what the actual fruit will be like. So it is with the Christian's walk. Our motives are mixed; in fact, God can draw them into a higher purpose. For that reason, we cannot pass judgment on fellow believers before the fruit of their life—a consistent pattern of behaviour—appears. We can advise and even warn, but if we come to a premature verdict, we are meddling in the hidden counsel of God.

Marpeck's case is greatly strengthened by his humility and self-criticism. He confesses that every fault he sees in the Appenzellers is also found in him!

At the same time, this text represents Marpeck at his most tedious. His passion to warn against the disastrous outcome of hasty judgments turns obsessive. He can't keep from repeating his argument again and again.

Marpeck's pastoral theology stands on two pillars. First is his view of the church: the body of Christ thrives only in its interdependence. In other words, members owe it to one another to give and receive counsel; they mutually discern the Holy Spirit's work. The goal of this interdependence is the unity of the church, in each congregation but also among all of like faith. As he writes, we see the author grappling with a divided judgment about the Appenzellers: are they or are they not of like faith? The very length of the epistle provides an answer. If they were not ultimately kindred spirits, why would Marpeck beseech them endlessly with entreaties?

The second pillar is his view of life in Christ. Christ's love is the end of the law. The cornerstone of Marpeck's thought is freedom, the liberty in which Christ acted and in which we can act. The mark of the free person is the desire to please God; the prayer of the free person is "Your kingdom come to us." The only command freedom gives is the command to love nonresistantly.

These traits distinguish spiritual from carnal freedom. Premature judging is an act of carnal freedom. Through the presence of the Spirit in our discernment of scripture, the church judges and disciplines members when the fruit of their evil behaviour persists. In our arrogance we conclude that we can fulfil the law without God's love. On the cross Christ defeated this arrogance and freed us from it.

In the middle of the letter the author speaks in an especially confessional tone. He identifies what it means to be part of the kingdom, with a clarity that helps the reader grasp his more complex and rambling arguments. Life in the kingdom is marked by love instead of law, submission to the Spirit rather than commandments, patience instead of violence, the true divinity and true humanity of Christ instead of one or the other, and baptism into the community of the Holy Spirit.

Several distinct themes emerge as the argument develops: the nature of freedom, true and false ways of judging, the place of the Ten Commandments in the age of the Spirit, examples of good and bad fruit, the gospel of all creatures. His treatments of some themes are more or less self-contained trains of thought, prompting the speculation that the author was revising previously written pieces to make a whole out of them.

A comment on the marginal glosses by Jörg Maler toward the end of the text:[5] the passion evident in the glosses suggests that the original dispute was still alive more than fifteen years later, when Maler was compiling the Kunstbuch. He sides with his mentor in his criticism of the Swiss. As a longstanding leader among the Swiss Brethren, Maler had seen at first hand what Marpeck criticizes. Yet in his marginal comments Maler is as critical of Marpeck as he is of the Swiss. He objects to Marpeck's spirit and manner of approach to the Swiss. He regards Marpeck's protestations of humility and weakness as less than genuine. In any event, Maler copied the letters and gave them to posterity, an action indicating that he had not disowned Marpeck. Yet he held to his opinions as strongly as Marpeck held to his, but without breaking fellowship.

---

5 Heinold Fast commented on them in "Pilgram Marpeck und das oberdeutsche Täufertum," ARG 47 (1956): 241; as did William Klassen in "Rothenfelder, Jörg Propst," ME 4:365–67. Both articles establish firmly the fact that Maler sided with Marpeck in the controversy with the Swiss.

This is a copy of an epistle written to those called the Swiss Brethren, and it concerns hasty judgments and verdicts in which some may not concur. 1531.

Grace and peace from God our Father, through Jesus Christ our Lord, be with all who fervently love and seek Christ. Amen.

My dear ones, constrained by the love we have in Jesus Christ, I write this letter because of the schism which until now has existed between us, because we have never recognized in our hearts and consciences the acknowledgement and understanding of Christ Jesus in each other, nor have we ever been able to reach agreement. Nevertheless, in my heart I have always considered—and even now consider—you to be zealous lovers of God and his Christ, although you lack knowledge and understanding of Christ. Every hour and every moment, I am also concerned about this lack in myself, and I have to be, for eternal life depends on such knowledge.

As Christ the Lord said [Jn 17 (3)]: "Father, this is eternal life, that they may know you, the true God, and Jesus Christ whom you have sent." However, contrary to Christ's words Paul says [Rom 12]: "Whoever thinks he knows does not yet know what he ought to know." He says further [(1 Cor 8:2); 1 Cor 8 (1)]: "Knowledge puffs up, but love improves." For this reason, although he had received his teaching from no mortal (Gal 2 [1:12]), but from the Lord himself, Paul was still afraid of and concerned about mixing his own understanding with revealed teaching. For this reason he traveled to Jerusalem at the behest of a revelation, in order to confer with the first apostles, that he might not run in vain.[6]

It happens easily that we depend more on our own knowledge and understanding than on love, which should be preeminent in all things. All knowledge of God subsists[7] in this love of God and the neighbour. Even the law and all the prophets had this understanding of the love of God,[8] which judges and urges all things for the sake of improvement.[9] It is my fervent request to you, for the sake of Christ, that you judge and make decisions concerning my writings according to the true manner of love, which judges only for improvement,[10] and covers many sins.[11] Love has no part in or fellowship with sin,[12] but is always merciful to the heart that mourns over its sin. According to that measure, I desire to have this epistle of mine judged. "Do not condemn, that you may not be condemned!"[13] "Do not judge, that you may not be judged!" [Mt 7 (1)]. That is the commandment and Word of Christ our healer to his disciples. Because of your hasty judgments, which are contrary to the words of Christ the Lord, our master, I find the way of Christ to be missing and lacking among you.

The Lord says [Jn 8 (31f.)]: "If you remain in my words, you will be my true disciples and you will know the truth, and the truth will make you free." As a simple soul, I sincerely desire to discuss this freedom with the mature in Christ. I gladly submit my mind to a clear and more lucid understanding, which is given by the Holy Spirit. I gladly submit to the least among Christ's own,[14] and thank my Lord Jesus Christ if I find the Spirit's witness in my conscience.[15] In this freedom of Christ Jesus the

---

6 Gal 2:2.

7 1 Cor 13:2; Eph 3:19; Phil 1:9.

8 Mt 7:12; 22:37–40; Rom 13:8, 10; Gal 5:14.

9 Eph 4:16. [Comments such as this provide a counterpoint to Marpeck's concern elsewhere for the clear distinction between the old and new covenants.—Ed.]

10 Rom 8:28.

11 1 Pt 4:8.

12 2 Jn 11; Rv 18:4.

13 Lk 6:37.

14 Mt 25:40.

15 Rom 9:1; 8:15.

Lord, and nowhere else, do I find comfort, joy, and peace in the Holy Spirit. Everything that commands, forbids, institutes, orders, drives, or produces anything against this freedom brings quarrelling, wrong understandings, zeal, strife, and unrest in heart and conscience.[16*] Such strife only produces restless, seared, uncertain consciences[17] without the true peace of God. Today one thing is forbidden; tomorrow it is something else. Those who make such impositions do not know what they impose [1 Tm 1 (7)]. Yet, as Paul says, they want to be masters of scripture. More about this matter later.

What follows is a clear witness and account of my conscience and heart concerning the glorious freedom of Christ and his own. If I am in error, I desire to be taught by God, through his Holy Spirit and the scriptures. If by grace I testify to the truth, I desire confirmation of it from those who truly believe. May God the Father give grace through Christ. Amen.

Conceived by the Holy Spirit in Mary,[18] Christ Jesus is the Son as God according to Spirit, Word, and power.[19*] He witnessed to God the Father in Christ through the might of his divine essence, with all powers, works, and miracles. He has also shown and certified his true humanity. As the Lord says in John 14 [10]: "Philip, do you not believe that I am in the Father and the Father is in me? If not, believe for the sake of the works that I do." Thus the Father is certified in the Son as true God and the Son in the Father, one God, manner, nature, and divine essence, all in the Son of Man.

Brought forth from the seed and line of David,[20] he was shown to be, in his weakness, a natural, earthly, true human being. He was born of the human race, but without the seed of man or sin. He was born of Mary, the spotless virgin in flesh and blood, in the manner of the human race; he grew and was brought up by earthly creatures as a truly

---

16* Note.

17 1 Tm 4:2.

18 Mt 1:18; Lk 1:35.

19* Difference between the true divinity and humanity of Christ.

20 Rom 1:3.

earthly man. His physical life was sustained by eating and drinking, and he died a natural death. Like those who also died a natural death, or who will yet die, he rose again from among the dead. By nature he is spirit and Word [Jn 11 (25)], the resurrection and the life (as he said to Martha). He rose again and was taken up into heaven and seated himself at the right hand of his heavenly Father [Heb 12 (2)]. From there we wait for his return and for our resurrection from the dead, according to the flesh [Col 3 (1)] to be received through him. Forgiveness and remission of sins come only through the Lord Jesus Christ.

That, briefly, is the testimony concerning the true divinity and true humanity of Christ. The divinity is testified to and known through power, and the humanity through weakness in death, for death does not come from heaven. I write on this matter because many Antichrists have now appeared who deny both the divinity and the humanity of Christ.[21]

This Jesus Christ is the free Son, of God and Man, and he is without commandment or prohibition against his own, the faithful. For the rebels and transgressors of the commandments, however, the commandments of God are only human commandments, and the whole law only the law for damnation.[22*] For where there is no sin or wickedness, no command or prohibition is needed; there is freedom from all law.[23] Where commandment or prohibition rule conscience, heart, and even God's law, one is not free but in bondage to sin and wickedness.[24] There no free grace, peace, or joy in the Holy Spirit[25] but rather the threat[26] of punishment, fear, sorrowing, and anxiety about the vengeance on sin through the coming wrath of God.

Because of this fear [Prv 9 (10)], external works and fruits of sin are at times abstained from. Such fear of God is the beginning of true repentance, the hope to become free of the law of sin and to become free, through faith in Jesus Christ, in the word of grace. This fear is the

---

21 2 Jn 7.

22* Note.

23 1 Tm 1:9; Rom 8:2.

24 Rom 7:23.

25 Rom 14:17.

26 [Original: *trounuß* = *dräunis* ("threat").—Trans.]

beginning of wisdom [Sir 1 [16)] and the knowledge of God in his Son, who is the wisdom of his Father.[27] In this manner, Jesus Christ, the Son of God, sets one free. He alone, through his Holy Spirit, makes the heart and the entire human disposition godly. He erases the handwriting of the devil, so that it is no longer the law that reigns, but grace and freedom in Jesus Christ [Ps 110 (111:10)], according to the nature of the true love of God and neighbour.

This love in God is the real freedom. Without any coercion, this love truly fulfils all commands and prohibitions[28] that perfectly please God. That is true freedom in Christ Jesus! Whomever he sets free is truly free, for whoever remains in his words is his true disciple [Jn 8 (36)]; he will also know the truth that is Christ Jesus, yes, the Word, the truth, and the life.[29] This truth liberates[30] from all law, command, and prohibition; it rules in the Holy Spirit and fulfils the whole pleasure[31] of God with delight, for it is Christ Jesus himself who is in the hearts of such liberated people.

Does a father command or forbid the son who knows and does[32] the will of the father to have complete pleasure in his own?[33*] For everyone who believes in him, Christ is always the end of the law [Rom 10 (4)]. If we are to please God in Christ, therefore, laws may not rule in the kingdom of Christ. The law and the commandments of God will stand eternally[34] as a means of distinguishing good and evil, and in this knowledge of good and evil[35] is the root and beginning of sin. From it the law emerged,[36] along with sin, and was to be a verdict and condemnation of the knowledge and understanding of our devastated reason, which is the head of the serpent.[37*]

---

27 1 Cor 1:24.

28 Rom 13:10; Gal 5:14.

29 Jn 1:1; 14:6.

30 Jn 8:31f.

31 2 Thes 1:11.

32 Jn 4:34; 6:30, 38.

33* Question.

34 Mt 5:18; Lk 16:17.

35 Gn 2:9, 17.

36 Rom 5:20.

37* Head of the serpent.

The judgment of Christ acts as the stern righteousness of God, for he has given all judgment to the Son [Jn 5 (22)]. The head of the serpent—that is, our reason—must be crushed,[38] either through faith in grace or through the law to condemnation. For the righteousness of God, which is always good and just, judges through grace in faith or through punishment and vengeance in unbelief. The law is spiritual, but we are carnal.[39] To be spiritually minded is life; to be carnally minded is death [Rom 8(6)].

Similarly, the serpent head of our reason must and will be crushed either by the preaching of faith, which takes all reason captive [2 Cor 10 (5)], or by the law in unbelief, which results in eternal destruction. This serpent head must submit to the feet of the woman's seed, to the natural, earthly, human feet of Christ, who is the seed without human origin and without sin. The seed, whom the serpent deceived, crushes its head. How painful it is for pride to have to submit to and be humbled by an earthly creature! But to this our reason, which constantly opposes the good and incites mischief in our mortal life, must submit in grace or perish.[40*] It is certain that the law and the commandments cannot make anyone godly,[41] but only grace through Jesus Christ. The law and commandments of God judge and decide for condemnation, separating the good to the good and the evil to the evil. In our hearts they create nothing but tribulation and sorrowing, since no one living outside Jesus Christ can be justified before God.

The Epistle to the Romans testifies to this fact everywhere, namely, that the law and the commandments only work death in us,[42] which otherwise is life in Christ Jesus. As soon as our devastated reason hears the proclamation of the law and the good commandments of God, she finds herself condemned under it, and would gladly keep the law in order to be saved, of which, however, our own fallen reason is not capable.[43] Because reason herself presumed to be a god and lord, and to

---

38 Gn 3:15.

39 Rom 7:14.

40* Note.

41 Gal 3:11.

42 Rom 7:10.

43 Rom 7:15–25.

have the power that belongs to God alone, the ability to keep the law has been taken away [Gn 3 (5)]. She imagines that she can be saved or condemned by her own power, and not by God's, who alone has all power. That is why God has likened our reason to the head of the serpent. This old serpent constantly resists God and now presumes to be saved through its own ability. Oh, how the poison of the serpent works its destruction in all humanity through presumptuousness![44]

For this reason God the Father has established that his Son should crush this arrogance, this serpent's head. He accomplished this through the weakness, sickness, and infirmity of the nature given to him by the seed of the woman, being born of the seed of David by nature and by human generation, but without sin or human seed. God the Father bruised him[45] and delivered him to death, the wages of sin, for our iniquities [Is 53 (4)].[46] Indeed, all ability, power, glory, grace, strength, wisdom, understanding, faith, love, hope, yes, all service to the glory of God, all blessedness, virtue, and grace can be taken and received only because of this same weakness, this deep suffering of the Lord Jesus Christ, the Son of Man, who was seen by God to be stricken and afflicted, who also cried, "My God, my God, why have you forsaken me?" [Mt 27 (46); Ps 22 (1)]. He is the one to whom all authority is given in heaven and on earth [Mt 28 (18)].

That is the crushing and eternal destruction of the arrogant serpent, which is our own reason, our presumption and attempt to do everything by our own wisdom, law, commandment and prohibition, love and pleasure, in short, all arrogance, doctrine, skill, and understanding that proceeds from our own choice.[47]

Christ's victory over all arrogance, spirit and flesh, is to condemn it eternally. How painful for the arrogant serpent before he is condemned with all his heads, his self-will and arrogance! How he snaps about at the heels of Christ and his own! How he pours out his venom, in many ways, in order to destroy the woman and her seed [Rv 12 (17)] before

---

44 [Original: *O, wie reisst sich der schlanngenn gyft vast in allen menschen durch eigens annemen.*—Trans.]

45 Is 53:5.

46 Rom 6:23.

47 Col 2:18.

he is condemned to be a footstool[48] at the feet of Christ, the human feet that were given into death for the sake of our sin! A mortal, fleshly (but now immortal) creature must rule and judge the immortal, indestructible spirit.[49*] Jesus was delivered to death for our sins and, by this same weakness and sickness, robbed sin, hell, devil, and death of their power.[50*, 51]

Both today and in eternity, the meekness, humility, and patience of the Lord Jesus Christ has the power to prevail in those who belong to him. All that is external, such as baptism, forgiveness of sins, teaching, the Lord's Supper, the laying on of hands,[52] foot washing, and all the external witnesses of faith in Jesus Christ,[53*] we receive from Christ. And, according to the inner teaching of the Holy Spirit, we receive these external things through those who truly believe they are his own and through the love of Christ. How painful for our reason and arrogance! And whoever is still ·a prisoner to what possesses him[54]—as indeed the whole world is—that person is not free in Christ Jesus.[55] For whomever the Son sets free is truly free;[56] he is released from what possesses him, from sin, death, and hell, which possess everyone outside Christ.

In his own body, the Lord Jesus Christ led this captivity captive [Eph 4 (8)], because of his obedience unto death.[57] With no guilt of his own, he has nailed to the cross[58] our guilt and what possesses us, in order that he himself might liberate us from our captivity (2 Cor 5 [19–21]) and take it to himself [Col 1 (13); 2 (15)].

There is therefore now no condemnation for those who are in Christ Jesus [Rom 8 (1)], for Christ is the end of all commandment and

---

48 Ps 110:1; Heb 1:13; 10:13.

49* Note.

50* Weakness of Christ.

51 2 Tm 1:10.

52 Heb 6:2.

53* Note.

54 [Original: *inn seinem eigenthum gfanngen ist.* What Marpeck appears to mean here is the natural state or condition of humanity after the fall.—Trans.]

55 Rom 8:2; Gal 2:4.

56 Jn 8:36.

57 Phil 2:8.

58 Col 2:14.

prohibition—yes, of the whole law—for everyone who believes in him [Rom 10 (4)]. Here there is no longer any servitude but only liberation in God. I am not talking here about the impertinent, self-styled freedoms of the flesh,[59*, 60] which are used as a cloak for wickedness [1 Pt 2 (16)], and of which the whole world is full. Such freedom is the most dire slavery before God and leads to destruction.[61*, 62] The proper, true liberty is in the Son of God and his own,[63] who are made lords of all law, commandment, and prohibition.[64]

They are prisoners to no one, nor debtors to anyone, except to the love that is in God and in them.[65*, 66] They are and remain prisoners and subjects and debtors of love, for the true love of God can never be repaid;[67] it always remains a debtor. Indeed, together with grace, mercy, and goodness, it holds God captive and continually makes him our debtor. And even as love is a debtor to us, so God the eternal Father, Maker of heaven and earth, neither could nor would pay us in cheaper coins[68] than the most costly, deepest, and highest love that he had. We have been paid.

The most high Father, God, and Lord showed himself to be gracious to us in the Son, the Lord Jesus Christ.[69] By himself, in his Son, he paid for our transgression and guilt [2 Cor 5 (18)]. For our sake he suspended his commandment, law, and prohibition, and transferred it from the first man Adam to his Son Jesus Christ; he has established that the love which is Christ should alone be the fulfiller and voluntary keeper of all commandments in Christ and his own. When the Lord

---

59* Libertines.

60 Gal 5:13.

61* Note.

62 2 Pt 2:19.

63 [Original: *Die recht, ware freyheit im sun Gotes und den seinigen ist, unnd send zů Herren gesetzt alles gsatz, gebot und verboth.*—Trans.]

64 Mt 12:8; Mk 2:28; Lk 6:5.

65* Christians are captive to no one, nor do they owe anyone anything but love.

66 Rom 13:8.

67 1 Cor 6:20; 7:23.

68 [Original: *leuchtern werd=leichteren wert.*—Trans.]

69 1 Pt 1:18f.

drops and cancels out[70] the punishment of and vengeance on sin and the transgression of the commandments, the law and the commandments also fall.[71*] They should be fulfilled through the grace that God gives, but he has himself for our sake become the fulfilment of his commandments in his Son and in those who belong to Christ. As Christ the Lord says: "Without me you can do nothing" [Jn 15 (5)]. And Paul likewise: "Whoever boasts, let him boast of the Lord" (1 Cor 1 [31]; Jer 9 [23]); 2 Cor 11 [10, 17]).

Thus the true love of the Father, Christ Jesus, the Son of God, is Lord of all commandments and prohibitions. Even today he fulfils love in his own through the Holy Spirit. All who have died to the law of sin (Col 3 [3]), and have been buried with Christ in baptism (Rom 6 [4]), no longer live. Rather, Christ lives in them, through the law of grace and his free-flowing Spirit [Gal 2 (20)].

But it is not the kind of grace the children of the world hope to receive, which allows them to remain in the lasciviousness of flesh and sin. That can never be called grace![72] Rather, it is the wrath, displeasure, vengeance, and punishment of God [Rom 2 (5)], as it was when David prayed for vengeance on his enemies in Psalm 68,[73] and as (Rom 11 [9f.]) it indeed happens to the whole world.[74*] God allows one transgression after another to come over the children of wickedness,[75] so that wrath and displeasure increase more and more. That is the testimony of God's wrath and not of his grace.[76*]

For such children of wickedness no commandment or law is suspended, yes, not even human law, not to speak of God's commandments and laws, of which they[77] are unworthy, like the heathen. For the

---

70 [Original: *nachlast.*—Trans.]

71* Note.

72 Rom 6:15.

73 Ps 69:22–28.

74* Vengeance.

75 Mt 13:38; Eph 2:3.

76* Note.

77 [Marpeck is referring here to the baptized masses in the Protestant and Catholic churches.—Trans.]

world does not even keep its own laws, although it is a law to itself and thereby condemns itself [Rom 2 (1, 14)].

But the grace from God that we encounter is a complete rebirth from flesh, sin, death, and hell, to peace, joy, and comfort of the Holy Spirit.[78] As the Lord Jesus Christ said to Nicodemus: "Unless someone is born in another way—that is, through water and Spirit—he cannot come into the kingdom of God [Jn 3 (5f.)]. For what is born of the flesh is flesh, and what is born of the Spirit is spirit."

Under the curse the birth of the flesh is a birth into servitude,[79] to the service of the law of sin,[80] under which we are sold and obligated to the life of sin.[81] Thus Paul says: "With my flesh I serve the law of sin, and with my spirit, the Lord Jesus Christ [Rom 7 (25)]." Flesh and blood, in which no good thing dwells,[82] has to be forcibly protected and preserved from sin under the free rule of the Spirit of God. Paul speaks of the desire of the spirit and the action of the flesh, when he says: "I do what I do not want, and what I wish to do, I do not do."[83] For flesh and blood always fight against the law of grace,[84] and so they must serve the law of sin, that is, fear of the wrath and the future punishment of God. Thus Paul does not attribute such a compulsion to the free Spirit of Christ but rather to disobedient flesh and blood. During this time the yoke will not be removed from its neck.

The prayer "Your kingdom come to us!" [Lk 11 (2)] represents the free rule of the Spirit. For whoever submits to the rule of the free Holy Spirit of the Lord Jesus Christ keeps his flesh and blood in obedience, and keeps it so against the will of flesh and blood until death. Indeed, Christ Jesus the Lord himself, although his flesh was weak and his spirit willing, prayed the Father to take the cup from him [Mt 26 (39–41)].

---

78 Rom 14:17.

79 Gal 4:24.

80 Rom 7:23.

81 Rom 14. [Original: *pflichtig zů sein dem gantzen lebenn der sundt zů der maledeyung.*—Trans.]

82 Jn 6:63.

83 Rom 7:15, 19f.

84 Rom 7:23.

But his spirit was willing and ready. He obediently subjected the flesh to death,[85] and said to the Father: "Not my will, but yours be done."

Thus, when we are baptized we are born of his Holy Spirit, who assures us and gladdens our spirit. Together with our flesh and blood, and all its lusts and appetites, we have been buried in the death of Christ [Rom 6 (4)]. As Paul says: If we have died with Christ [Col 3 (3)], and the lust and will of the flesh is dead, then it is not flesh and blood that lives in us, but Jesus Christ! [Gal 2 (20); 5 (1, 13)]. This is the life of freedom, found through grace in those who are free, whom the Son liberates from death to life[86] in free obedience [Jn 8 (36)]. For to be carnally minded is death, and to be spiritually minded is life (Rom 8 [6]). Thus no one is free according to the flesh; rather, he is obligated to obey the Holy Spirit of the Lord Jesus Christ throughout all of life.

Wherever flesh and blood is free to rule, the inner being[87] is neither free nor safe but is made a servant of sin [Jn 8 (34)], and he who otherwise is the image of God is held prisoner for everlasting destruction [2 Pt 2 (9)]. Such are the slaves of sin; they are not free, for they deny him who can set them free. Although it was given to us through grace in Christ in order that we might live,[88] the good, spiritual law of God[89] becomes for them the cause of everlasting death and condemnation. Thus I distinguish between the freedom of the Spirit in Christ, which is life, and the freedom of the flesh, with its will and desire for death. I do not, as I have been accused, stretch the freedom of Christ too far.

The difference is between the liberty of the Lord Jesus Christ and the self-made carnal freedom, which constantly adorns itself with the dead letter[90] as a cover for wickedness.[91]

First of all, every individual must possess true and diligent discernment in conscience and heart, if he is to have a true and certain judgment and

85 Phil 2:8.

86 Jn 5:24.

87 Rom 7:22; Eph 3:16.

88 Rom 7:10.

89 Rom 7:12; 14:1; 1 Tm 1:8.

90 Rom 7:6; 2 Cor 3:6.

91 1 Pt 2:16.

if the self-made freedom of the flesh is not to be taken for the liberty of Jesus Christ.[92*] This self-made freedom is and shall always remain the most profound slavery, from which release is never possible. To act in accordance with this self-made freedom is to sin [Jn 8 (34)], to be led into wickedness and the hardest slavery of sin, for whoever commits sin is the slave of sin. It makes no difference that this self-made carnal freedom always adorns itself with the dead letter [2 Cor 11 (14)] and, posing as the true liberty of Christ Jesus the Lord, covers itself with a false, lying appearance [2 Pt 2; (2 Pt 2:16)]. It finally brings forth no fruit but open depravities, sin, and shame. Such is the case with the hypocrites who, because of their choice to live according to human law and its coercion [Col 2 (22f.)], strut about and, without knowing anything about it, assume the appearance of the Spirit.[93]

Now the true believers are forbidden to condemn all these people before the right time (1 Cor 4[5]), that is, until their fruit, which is open vice, appears. Christ says: "By their fruits (he does not say: by the blossoms[94] or the foliage) you shall know them" [Mt 7 (16)].[95*] For the day of the Lord will reveal everything.[96] But some vices are revealed before that time [1 Tm 5 (24)], for everyone expresses what is within the treasure of his heart [Mt 12 (35)]. Whether it be before or at the time of the last day, to cover or reveal sin is in God's hands [Ps 32 (1)].

For no one may judge the heart until the fruit appears or until the outpouring of the treasure of the heart occurs. Only God, through the Holy Spirit, may judge. He is the true chastiser and judge of the heart. He will punish the world, first, for its sin, for they have not believed, and he will judge them because the prince of this world, who has lost his authority,[97*] is judged. Finally, he will punish the world because of his own righteousness, for he, the Lord, goes to the Father. People grant the prince of this world the authority that is against the authority and judgment of Christ [Jn 16 (8–11)].

92* Freedom.

93 Col 2:18

94 [Original: *pluee = pluet = Blüten.*—Trans.]

95* Fruits.

96 1 Cor 3:13.

97* Note.

Thus, by their own permission, the devil carries out his work and exercises his authority in the children of wickedness. Thus they also deny the righteousness of Christ in themselves, their words, and their works. But Christ, who alone is acceptable to God, is the righteousness of the children of truth before the Father [1 Cor 1 (30)]. This same righteousness does its works in them,[98] and the Holy Spirit [1 Cor 2 (4f.)] witnesses in them through works, power, and deeds.[99]

For nothing is valid before God except Christ; what remains—that is, Christ's work in his own before the Father—is only a testimony of righteousness. That is why he speaks of righteousness, "for I go to the Father."[100]

Whoever therefore establishes, commands, prohibits, coerces, punishes, or judges before the time the good or evil fruit is revealed, lays claim to the authority, power, and office of the Holy Spirit of the Lord Jesus Christ[101*] and, contrary to love, goodness, and grace, runs ahead of Christ Jesus [Jn 10 (8)]. For the Son of God himself has committed this office and work to the Holy Spirit of God, and the office is to be carried out after his earthly,[102] human life has ended. With reference to this work he says: "The Holy Spirit will come and judge because of sin, judgment, and righteousness," judging and searching hearts, for the Holy Spirit works good fruits in the children of light[103] to reveal them before all. Similarly, the spirit of wickedness, who often and in many ways disguises himself as a spirit of light [2 Cor 11 (14)], has his work in the children of darkness. These too are driven by the Holy Spirit to do their own deeds in order that by the power and finger of God they may be known and revealed by their fruits.

---

98 2 Cor 5:21.

99 [These two sentences are an accurate summary of a rather grammatically confused and repetitive passage.—Trans.]

100 Jn 16:16.

101* Note.

102 [Literally, "external"—Trans.]

103 Eph 5:9.

Therefore, even if one is concerned about a lapse[104] or burdened with worry and sees the leaves and blossoms of evil appearance,[105] one ought only to warn and admonish, but not judge, before the time of the fruit [1 Cor 4 (5)].

The Lord does not say, "By their blossoms or leaves," but rather, "By their fruits you shall know them" [Mt 7 (16, 20)]. For love also covers a multitude of sins (1 Pt 4 [8]) and judges all things in the best light.[106] Even though it is concerned about evil appearance and evil fruit, it nevertheless always hopes for the best [1 Cor 13 (7)].

In the same way Christ covers our sin and shame in the love and grace which leads to improvement. Whoever presumes to decide and judge, before the revealing of guilt, is a thief and a murderer (Jn 10 [8]). He runs ahead of Jesus Christ,[107*] who alone is the revealer of good and evil in the heart.

On the other hand, if the sin and wickedness evident from the revealed fruit is revealed through wrath in the righteousness of Christ, one must be ready to judge and decide with Christ, the true judge; otherwise, he too is a thief and murderer. He runs behind Jesus Christ and not with Christ.[108*] All the elect of God with Christ judge in this time with the sword of the Spirit through the Word, and not as the world does, with the carnal sword [Eph 6 (17)]. They too will decide at the last judgment [Lk 22 (30)].

But everywhere the devil selectively[109] uses his weapons against us through the dead letter. Some do not want to judge at all, and take refuge behind Mt 7 [1]: "Judge not, that you be not judged. Do not condemn, so that you will not be condemned."[110] They do not see the contrary statement, Mt 18 [15]: "If your brother sins, discipline him" [Lk 17 (3)]. As long as there are witnesses and they do not listen even to the church, they should be regarded as heathen. Again [Jesus says]: "If

---

104 [Original: *fals*—Trans.]

105 1 Thes 5:22.

106 Rom 8:28.

107* Before Christ's coming.

108* After Christ.

109 [Original: *inn theil und stuckhweis.*—Trans.]

110 Lk 6:37.

your eye, hand, foot offends you, tear it out and cut it off" [Mt 6 (5:29)]. Paul says: "You judge those who are inside"[111] (1 Cor 5 [12f.]); God will judge those outside; [Paul then asks:] "Do you not know that we are to judge angels? [1 Cor 6 (3)]. Now put out what is evil."[112] Many similar scripture passages enjoin the saints to render judgment.

No one may judge except one who has first judged and sentenced his own life through the grace and mercy of God, and pulled the beam[113*] out of his eye [Mt 7 (3–5); Lk 6 (41f.)]. Then, very properly,[114] in patience, humility, meekness, and love,[115*] he may with the greatest care pull the sliver[116] out of his brother's eye without hurting or irritating the eye. That is after all how he has been treated by God. And whoever brings someone to Christ in a different way for judgment, as the Jews brought the adulteress before Christ in the temple [Jn 8 (3–11)], will find himself, together with the hypocritical Jews, running from Christ [Mt 21 (31)] and the adulteress in the temple.[117] Open sinners will enter the kingdom of God before these do. Christ tolerated them less than the adulteress. All transgression is adultery before God, to whom we are betrothed.

Second, the enemy of truth has another trick, worse than the one referred to above. It is to lead people astray with hasty and uncertain judgments.[118*] By doing so they are judging and condemning themselves, making sin where there is no sin, setting up laws, commandments, and prohibitions against the authority and sovereignty of the Spirit of the Lord Jesus Christ, who gave his own no law except the law of love (as stated above).[119] They seek to establish laws and would become the masters of scripture, but they do not know what they are setting up [1 Tm 1 (7)]. Because of this ignorance, the enemy takes hearts

---

111 Original: *was hynnen ist.*—Trans.]

112 1 Cor 5:13.

113* Beam.

114 [Original: *sitlich.*—Trans.]

115* Note.

116 [Original: *spreissen.*—Trans.]

117 Jn 8:59.

118* Concerning hasty and uncertain judgments.

119 Jn 13:34; 15:12; 1 Jn 3:23; 4:21; 2 Jn 5f.

and consciences captive. But to those who are in Jesus Christ and who are justified through Christ, no law is given. For to the righteous, says Paul, no law is given, neither commandment nor prohibition; they are given only to the unrighteous.[120]

However, wherever one establishes, commands, or prohibits, the grace of the Holy Spirit does not reign. Rather, the anxiety and fear of unrighteousness reign. For true love in Christ—indeed, the Spirit and God himself—is a free and willing fulfilment of all that is good [1 Cor 10 (33); 13 (5)].[121] Love denies herself and does not seek her own. She pays all debt (Rom 13 [8]), and can never be paid. She remains a debtor to no one, since she is the payment of all guilt.[122*] Therefore in Christ love is free of all law, commandment, and prohibition. Those who have been captured and bound in true bondage of love in God can never be bound with any other bondage in conscience, heart, disposition, or mind. They are free in all things and owe no one anything but love [1 Cor 13 (1–3)]. Where there is no love, everything is in vain.

Who, then, will accuse God's chosen ones? [Rom 8 (33)]. "For love is stronger than death" (Sg 8 [6]). Love cannot be overcome, and no price can be paid for her in all eternity. Love is the inner anointing of the heart [1 Jn 2 (20)]. Although it is very hot,[123] she feeds among the roses until the cool evening comes,[124] because of her patience of heart, mind, disposition, and all the powers [of the believer]. Love teaches everything, since love herself is the teaching.[125*]

John speaks about this teaching when he says that the inner anointing will teach us many things. Love is a disciple and truly obedient pupil of the Holy Spirit. At the same time, she is the ruler of heaven and earth. In his Son, God the Father has subjected himself to her, for she is in everything God himself.[126] The glorious liberty of Christ dwells

---

120 1 Tm 1:9.

121 Phlm 1:14.

122* Note.

123 Meaning persecution (1 Pt 4:12).

124 Sg 4:5f.

125* Anointing.

126 1 Jn 4:8, 16.

there,[127*, 128] given to no one except to true love in Christ Jesus. Again, the truly free are given no other commandment except to love. This is the bond[129] with which the liberty of Christ is bound, although, as Paul says, to this liberty of Christ all things are lawful [1 Cor 10 (23)]. Nor did he want to subject his liberty to anyone's judgment or decision (1 Cor 6 [10:29]), for the believers judge everything but are themselves judged by no one (1 Cor 2 [15]). But wherever something does not serve or promote improvement,[130] love in Christ acts[131] with all her authority, privileges, and freedom, and never acts against her own nature [1 Cor 8 (9–13)].[132] Nor does true love suspend liberty; rather, she makes us truly free in all things.

That, briefly, is the true liberty in Christ Jesus which all law, Sabbath [Mt 12 (1–8)], commandments, and prohibitions must serve. For they were given for our sake and not we for theirs,[133] and they were given for the sake of God, who alone is to be worshiped and served in Christ. That is why true believers are lords of all with Christ. It is not that they serve the letter of the law[134*] and the Sabbath, but rather that the whole law and commandment of God is servant of the true liberty in Christ.

But the whole law still rules over those who are under condemnation. For cursed is everyone who does not observe all that is written in the book of the law [Dt 25 (27:26); Gal 3 (10)]. These are apart from Christ, guilty in all of life, under the rule of the law, and condemned according to the strict justice of God. They are always in fear and anxiety of torment.[135*] Thus they seek to do the will of God, but since the law rules over them, in truth they can never accomplish it. They are not free from the law by virtue of the grace that God gives [Gal 5 (1)].

127* Freedom of true love.

128 Rom 8:21.

129 Col 3:14.

130 Rom 14:19; 15:2; 1 Cor 14:26; etc.

131 [Original: *begibt.* In the above, Marpeck is one-sided: the point of the passages he cites is that Paul's freedom is subjected to the "other" for whom Christ died.—Trans.]

132 Rom 14:15; Gal 5:13.

133 Mk 2:27.

134* Note.

135* Note.

Rather, they are sold into the slavery of sin[136] to serve the law of sin.[137] They are continually thrown into the fear of damnation without any comfort of conscience.

But the full love of God and the comfort of the Holy Spirit drives out this fear [1 Jn 4 (18)] and releases the imprisoned conscience into the truth and freedom, peace and joy of the Holy Spirit.[138] John is not speaking in this passage about the fear of the flesh. Otherwise it would have to follow that even Christ, who is the fullness of the Father's love, did not possess this full love; when he speaks of the baptism with which he has to be baptized, he says: "How fearful I am until it is done" [Lk 12 (50)]. He also prayed the Father that if it were possible, the cup might be taken from him [Mt 26 (42)]. He did so because of the fear of the agony of the flesh before him. The fullness of God's love receives and retains the victory over this bodily fear, but only in death, when physical life ends. The Lord indeed cried out: "My God, you have forsaken me!" [Ps 22 (1)]. But then, as he gave up his spirit, he said: "It is finished!" [Mt 27 (46)].[139]

Love gets the victory[140] over fear of the body, yet this fear is not driven out before death; otherwise, tribulation would not lead to cross bearing. But the fullness of love erases and drives out the fear of sin and punishment by the law to everlasting damnation, like the devil's bill of charges, about which Paul writes in Colossians 2 [14]. Paul also says: "We have not received a spirit in which we should again be afraid" [Rom 8 (15); 2 Tm 1 (7)].

I discern three varieties of fear. There is also a fourth kind which is without hope, for Judas[141] also had fear.[142*]

Fear of the flesh and fear of sin, as mentioned above—these two are profitable for salvation. The third is the pure fear of God, that one does the right thing according to love; in this fear one regards oneself as an

---

136 Rom 7:14.

137 Rom 8:2.

138 Rom 14:17.

139 Jn 19:30.

140 Rom 8:37.

141 Mt 27:3–5.

142* Fourfold fear.

unprofitable servant [Lk 17 (10)]. This pure fear of God, which endures to eternal life, can never yield to or be driven out by love. The true way of love fears that, in doing all righteousness,[143*] she always does too little or too much, but that it is nevertheless pleasing to God.[144] For creatures must tremble before their Creator, however good they may be. Therefore true fear must be carefully distinguished, in order that one not fall into presumption, tempt God in carnal joy and strength, forgetting the Lord Jesus Christ, without whom the flesh is weak and the spirit willing [Mt 26 (41)]. In him, the disciple is not above his master, or the servant above his lord (Jn 15 [20]); [Jer 9 (23)].

Wherever one presumes to have this love of God to drive out the bodily fear of the Lord before bodily death, a fall and denial will soon set in, as it did with Peter, who wanted to die with the Lord. For in our weakness, of which we ought to boast, as Paul did, God's power and strength is seen [2 Cor 12 (19); 1 Cor 1 (27)], in that the love of God has the victory into eternal life. In this victory all things are clean to the clean and unclean to the unclean [Ti 1 (15)].

Moreover, whoever boasts that he is free and yet commits sin is a liar. He is not free but is a servant of sin; he has been sold under sin[145] because of the law into eternal death [2 Pt 2 (19); Jn 8 (34)].

Again, whoever presumes to preserve, rule, and lead the kingdom of Christ through law, commandment, and prohibition, yes, through the law of God,[146*] thrusts the free-flowing[147] Spirit of the Lord Jesus Christ, the proper ruler of hearts, out of his place and puts himself in the place where he ought not to be. Let us refrain from any mention of human inventions, no matter how pious they appear. This is the greatest abomination against Christ [Dn 9 (27); Mt 24 (15)]. Nothing but sects and popery can come from it, as Christ the Lord and Daniel say.

143* Note.

144 [Original: *dann die recht art der lieb furcht sich inn aller grechtigkheit sy thuee im zevil oderr zů wenig, und ist doch des wolgfallen Gotes.*—Trans.]

145 Rom 7:14.

146* Note.

147 [*Freywillig* means "voluntary," but the sense of the text is the literal meaning "free-willed," perhaps even "free-flowing" or "autonomous."—Ed.]

Whoever has the law is God of the law.[148] If one sins against it, one sins against him who established and commanded it.[149*] Insofar as mortals order and forbid in the kingdom of Christ and those who belong to him, they thrust the Lord out and make sin where there is no sin.

All such are soul-murderers and robbers! [Jn 10 (1, 8)]. They take womanish hearts and weak, seared consciences[150] captive because of commandment*s* and prohibition*s* against them [2 Tm 3 (6)]. They point to and seek an alien salvation, outside Jesus Christ. Like the whole world, they defend everything with the name of Christ; it is all nothing but deceit and lies against the free-willed Spirit of Christ. Even though they point to Christ here or there [Mk 13 (21)], Christ has forbidden us to believe them or to go out to them.[151] The true saints of God and children of Christ are those whose ruler is the Holy Spirit in the word of truth. Where two or three are gathered in his name, he is among them [Mt 18 (20)]. He alone rules in faith through patience and love in his own. I pray God my heavenly Father that he might not allow me to be separated from such a gathering and fellowship of the Holy Spirit; it makes no difference who they are or where they gather in the whole world.[152*] I hope to be in their fellowship and to submit myself to the rule of the Holy Spirit of Christ in the obedience of faith.

But I will have nothing to do with any other sect, faction, or gathering, no matter what they are called in the whole world.[153*] I will especially avoid those who use the bodily sword,[154*] contrary to the patience of Christ. He did not resist any evil [Mt 5 (39); Lk 6 (27–29)] and still commands his own not to resist tribulation or evil, in order to rule in the kingdom of Christ. I avoid those who institute, command, and forbid, therewith to lead and rule the kingdom of Christ.[155*]

---

148 [The German text reads, *Dann wes des gsatz ist, der ist nit ein got des gsatz,* but *nit* ("no") is crossed out.—Trans.]

149* Note.

150 1 Tm 4:2.

151 Mt 24:26.

152* Note.

153* Separation.

154* 1.

155* 2.

I also avoid those who deny the true divinity, Spirit, Word, and power in Jesus Christ.[156*] I further avoid those who destroy and deny his natural earthly humanity,[157*] which was received from the human race and the seed of David, born of Mary the pure virgin without semen or sin. He was crucified and died a natural earthly death, from which he arose and has seated himself at the right hand [Heb 12 (2); Col 3 (1)] of God. I also avoid those who, living in open sin and gross evil, want to have fellowship in the kingdom of Christ but without true repentance,[158*] and I avoid all those who tolerate such a thing.[159*] I avoid all who oppose and fight against the words and the truth of Christ.[160*] Regardless of what they are called in the world, I will have no part or fellowship with them in the kingdom of Christ unless they repent.

My salvation depends alone on Christ the Lord's dying and the shedding of his blood. In him alone have I received the remission and forgiveness of sins from the Holy Spirit in the community of his saints. Into this community I have also been baptized,[161] according to the witness and truth of my heart in the Holy Spirit, on my own testimony and confession of the truth.

I also reject all ignorant baptism which happens without true, revealed, personal faith, whether in children or adults.[162*] For this reason I also was baptized with external water and the external word, on confession of my faith. I was gladly baptized into this community of the Holy Spirit, visibly gathered, for the remission and forgiveness of sins. In it I sincerely desire to remain until my end. Amen to all who desire this with me. That is briefly the testimony of my heart in Christ Jesus.

156* 3.

157* 4.

158* 5.

159* 6.

160* 7.

161 [This is the third reference Marpeck makes to his own baptism.—Ed.]

162* 8. Ignorant baptism.

The difference between true and false judgment, and what the divine biblical scriptures command us to judge and decide according to the example of the Lord Jesus Christ and apostolic teaching.

People today decide and judge for many reasons. First,[163*] it is done out of love for the Word and for improvement. This is the true and proper decision, and the judgment of the saints made in patience. As said earlier, no other patience[164] has any place in the congregation of Christ.

Second,[165*] people judge out of a concern for evil, and they expect to anticipate evil in that way.

Third,[166*] some judge in envy and hatred[167*] because others do not immediately agree with them. They claim that others resist the truth, when in fact these others are resisting their own ignorance. These last two kinds of judgment are false and mendacious and only create schism and sects.

Fourth,[168*] there are a few who do not want to decide or make judgments at all, for fear that they would condemn themselves.[169] They have not judged themselves, nor have they submitted to the Word in the obedience of faith.

The saints of God have been charged by the Lord to exercise judgment through the Holy Spirit. He says: "Receive the Holy Spirit! If you retain sins, they are retained; if you forgive, they are forgiven" (Jn 20 [22f.]). For the Holy Spirit of God is the key of heaven,[170] through which sin is retained or forgiven in the communion of saints![171*] For this reason the apostles wrote to the churches (Acts 15 [28]) and spoke

---

163* 1.

164 [For example, patience with deliberate and open sin.—Ed.]

165* 2. Swiss sect.

166* 3. Note.

167* Pilgramite sect.

168* 4.

169 Rom 2:1.

170 Mt 16:9.

171* Every congregation wants to have and wield this power. They boast of the keys, that they are of the Holy Spirit. The foremost ones are the Hutterites, the Swiss, the Pilgramites. None of them has peace with any other one in God. Each one

against those who were again introducing the law: "It seemed good to the Holy Spirit and to us." No one is commanded to judge without the Holy Spirit, without whom no certain judgment is possible. That is why the Lord Jesus Christ first gave the Holy Spirit to those whom he empowered to judge, so that they should certainly and truly judge and decide according to the word of grace and truth, in order that the witness and fruit, good or evil, may precede and be known in the deed.

This is the only way to bind and loose[172] with certainty and, in the external judgment, to judge according to the testimony of the external fruit, and not of the foliage or blossoms that precede the fruit. As mentioned earlier, Christ says: "You shall know them by their fruits" [Mt 7 (16, 20); 12 (21:43)]. Those who judge in truth may therefore not judge before the time [1 Cor 4 (5)], but must wait for the fruit. Otherwise one meddles with the prerogatives of God's secret and hidden judgment and decision; one judges and punishes before God punishes, as Judas did with Magdalene[173] and as the Jews did with Christ. Christ's saying fits here: "Do not judge, that you may not be judged; do not condemn, that you may not be condemned."[174] In making judgment, one must always distinguish foliage and blossoms from the fruit.

The fruits of wickedness, already judged, from which separation is to be made according to the Old and New Testaments, in order to judge with certain judgment.

First, "unbelief" after hearing teaching proclaimed is the greatest sin, that is, not believing the testimony of the gospel.[175*] That is the sin against the Holy Spirit,[176] for whoever does not believe is already judged and condemned[177*] (Jn 3 [18]; Mk 16 [16]).

---

judges the other, yet all of them fall under judgment. [This gloss, like the previous two, appears to be by the copyist, Maler.—Ed.]

172 [Original: *einzenemen und auszeschliessen.*—Trans.]

173 Jn 12:4–8.

174 Lk 6:37.

175* 1. Distinction between sins as follows.

176 Mt 12:31.

177* Note.

Second, whoever falls away from the sweet gift of God [Heb 6 (4–6)] and the community of Christ, not because of fear, care, and anxiety for his bodily life,[178] but with evident malice [1 Tm 5 (24)], has already gone into condemnation and has sinned against the Holy Spirit.[179*]

Third, there are those who contradict the truth with evil intent, delay it with wickedness and error, and sin against the Holy Spirit stubbornly and with malice[180*] [Heb 10 (26f.); Rom 1 (18)]. Such have already been delivered to the devil in body and soul.[181]

Fourth, there are those who deny the truth because they fear the flesh, as did Peter [Mt 26 (69–75)] and others like him; in them the spark of grace[182] remains in the heart, which leads them fervently to desire and seek repentance[183*] [Gal 6 (1)]. It is the same as for all sin and error that so easily overtakes us. But where the spark of grace remains and the hope in Christ persists, they lead to hearty repentance, the desire to return to Christ and the desire for the improvement of life. People like that sin only against the Son.[184*] They will be forgiven.[185] Although they may be judged by Christ and his congregation, they are nevertheless not condemned with this world.

It is therefore dangerous[186] to fall into the stern judgment of God. For when he sins, no one is assured whether or not through grace he will be given a repentant heart, in order that he may truly repent and be rid of sin. For true repentance is not to sin at all. This repentance is a gracious gift of God and a certain witness of God in the heart for the forgiveness of sins. No one is able to stand by himself or to become

---

178 [Falling away because of worry about the family and physical death was a common experience among persecuted Anabaptists. His concern is not this weakness but malice.—Ed.]

179* 2.

180* 3.

181 1 Cor 5:5.

182 [This is sometimes called "prevenient grace," at work drawing us to God, enabling our repentance.—Ed.]

183* 4.

184* Sinning against the Son.

185 Mt 12:32; Lk 12:10.

186 [Original: *sorgklich.*—Trans.]

good[187*] without the mighty help of God, who alone makes the heart good and who is goodness himself. No one is good but God alone [Mt 19 (17)]. We fall and sin of ourselves, but we do not become good of ourselves.

Therefore whoever sins wantonly tempts God and deliberately falls into his stern judgment [Heb 10 (26)]. For him condemnation is certain, and the grace and mercy of God uncertain. However, in saying this I do not exclude anyone from the gracious hand of God. Although mercy triumphs over judgment, it does not do so over all people and sins [Jas 2 (13)]. Let each one carefully see to it that he does not tempt God.[188] Dear brothers, it is dangerous to fall into the hands of mortals, but it is much more dangerous to fall into the hands of God [2 Kgs 24 (14); Sir 2 (22); Sus 1 (23)].

A parable:[189*] on pain of hanging, the world forbids stealing, and other wickedness and transgressions on pain of death. If someone transgresses, death is nearer than life to him, even though the world occasionally grants life to someone who has deserved death. These, however, are exceptions, and it is the same with God and sin. It is not that God is not gracious and is not merciful to the sinner. It is, however, far more certain and safe not to sin; then one does not need to be concerned about God's wrath,[190] for God is and remains all grace and goodness.[191]

I write about sin because I have been accused by many of using the freedom of Christ as a cloak for wickedness [1 Pt 2 (16)].

Now the root, ground, and beginning of sin[192*] originated with our first parents, Adam and Eve, namely, the knowledge of good and evil. It is the abandonment of the good, according to our nature and birth (what is born of flesh is flesh),[193] and doing evil as soon as recognition and knowledge begin, according to the flesh. All true simplicity

---

187* The world's maxim.

188 Dt 6:12.

189* Parable.

190 [Original: *ungnad.*—Trans.]

191 [Original: *sonnder es ist und pleibt lauter gnad und guet vor Got.*—Trans.]

192* Root of sin.

193 Jn 3:6.

[of infants] is bought with the blood of Christ, but without any law, external teaching, faith, baptism, Lord's Supper, and all other Christian ceremonies [Ez 38],[194] for theirs is the kingdom of heaven without any proviso to change [Mt 19 (14); Lk 18 (16); Mk 10 (14)].[195] But to those who claim to know good and evil, in whom knowledge is the root and basis of all sin, which God refers to as the head of the serpent and enmity against God,[196] the Lord says: "You must become as children." He is condemned who is not born again through faith and baptism [Jn 3 (5)] for the forgiveness of sins, and who is not born again into the obedience of faith, the simplicity and innocence of the child. Before it submits to the simplicity of faith in Christ, reason is the head of the serpent,[197*] which is crushed by faith in Christ.[198] That is the end of all carnal wisdom.

For this reason the adversary, the prince of pride, has invented the baptism of innocents. When the proud head of the serpent, which is reason, receives his strength, he refuses to submit to the baptism of faith, that is, to the crushing of his head by the feet of Christ. That is why the enemy has his way in the absence of reason.[199] He makes the excuse that he is already baptized, claiming innocence in order to usurp the place of the baptism of faith. For it is commanded to preach baptism and faith unto the knowledge of good and evil,[200*] which is mere carnal reason, and to take it captive, so that it may be crushed by the feet of Christ. Faith leads to salvation; unfaith leads to damnation.

---

194 Ez 18?

195 [The way God's grace reaches infants is an anomaly within Marpeck's thought. Elsewhere God's way of reaching humanity is by the union of inner and outer. In "Pilgram Marpeck's Confession of 1532" (WPM, 147–52) and "The Admonition of 1542" (WPM, 242, 257), he lays the groundwork for this claim. In the case of infants, they lack the capacity for faith. And faith is the medium through which an outward act is taken by the Spirit and united with its inward reality. In the absence of faith, the normal medium of grace, God works in an unmediated way.—Ed.]

196 Gn 3:15.

197* Reason, the serpent's head.

198 Gn 3:15.

199 [This sentence does not seem to follow from his argument.—Ed.]

200* Baptism and faith in knowledge.

Reason demands to know, not to believe. Wherever we believe, reason is taken captive under the obedience of Christ!

Thus sin happens where there is unbelief.[201] When one has come to the knowledge of good and evil, disobedience to that knowledge is evil fruit. Similarly, all good fruit comes from obedience through faith in Christ.

Discussion of the Ten Commandments

All false teaching, superstition, idolatry, and self-love are the fruits of sinning against the commandment to believe in one God[202*] [Ex 20 (3); Dt 5 (7)]. Fearing, honouring, and loving anything above or besides God is idolatry; God alone is to be feared, honoured, and loved,[203] in, above, and before all things. Worshiping and serving him alone is, briefly, the first and foremost commandment. And to love one's neighbour as oneself is equal to it [Mt 7 (12); 19 (19)]. According to the words of the Lord, these two commandments comprise all that the law and the prophets preach. One may not honour, love, and fear anything besides God. Whenever one acts against the commandment of love, all other fruits that were the reason for establishing the law of the curse emerge. But the Son of God has become our redemption, granting us the freedom of the Spirit, so that we willingly do what pleases God.

The second commandment: "You shall not use the name of God in vain."[204*, 205] No one who transgresses this commandment will be held guiltless. This guilt includes all the blasphemy of self-made, false worship of God,[206] and all ignorant singing and praying done with the mouth but not the heart.[207] The world is full of this.

The third:[208*] You shall keep the Sabbath holy, that is, the seventh day.[209] This is a ceremonial law, in force until the human coming of

---

201 Sin lies in unbelief.

202* First.

203 Dt 6:4.

204* 2.

205 Ex 20:7; Dt 5:11.

206 Col 2:23.

207 Eph 5:19.

208* 3.

209 Ex 20:8; Dt 5:12.

Jesus Christ, the Son of God, into the world. He is the Lord of the Sabbath of God, his heavenly Father, and he completely fulfils it. If, during an entire lifetime, even unto death, someone is self-seeking in all things, and finds himself only in his work, he breaks the Sabbath of Jesus Christ, the Son of God. To keep the Sabbath is to be unburdened and free of all toil. The Son of God has established for all flesh and blood the rest that comes from obedience to death, yes, the death on the cross.[210] Whoever seeks to save himself will find death, and whoever loses his life finds life [Mt 16 (25)].

That is the Sabbath[211*] which the children of God observe, and of which they are lords with Christ.[212] For their flesh and blood, with all its lusts and with all its sinful works, must rest in Christ, even unto death [Rom 6 (6, 12)]. This is not a reference to the physical work necessary for life; otherwise, we could not eat or drink, nor could we clothe ourselves. Whoever breaks this Sabbath is destroyed from among the people.[213]

However, the literal celebration of the Sabbath is good,[214*] provided it is done in freedom of the Spirit and is not bound by a law to time, state, and person. Otherwise it is not a rest done out of love for God and the neighbour, which is the true rest.

Instead of that, we accept the tyranny of time. But Jesus Christ has already fulfilled time, and thus we now should rule outside time.[215*] If we bind the Sabbath to a place, we cause the kingdom of earth to rule over humanity, when in fact with Christ in patience[216] humanity is lord of the whole earth. If we bind it to a person—for example, to the deceased saints because of their deeds of merit—we bind life to death,

---

210 Phil 2:8.
211* Note.
212 Mt 12:8.
213 Ex 31:14.
214* Celebration of Christians.
215* Note.
216 [This point could be a reference to legal provisions for Sabbath observance, as was the case, for example, in Zurich in 1541.—Trans.]

for I cannot be saved by the works of someone else.[217] Only Christ, the Son of God and Son of Man, is the time, place, and person of the true rest of the Sabbath for God and for the neighbour, in the gloriously free love of God the Father for his own.[218]

That, briefly, is the argument against those who again want to introduce the literal Sabbath.[219*, 220] Jesus Christ is Lord of all ceremonial commandments of both the Old and New Testaments that refer to our material life [Mt 12 (8)].[221]

The new ceremonies of Christ (teaching, baptism, the Lord's Supper, foot washing, laying on of hands) are commanded by Christ the Lord[222*] to be a testimony and a revealing of every heart toward the neighbour; these new ceremonies are to be a witness of true love in order that we all may partake of the same grace, peace, and love.

God knows our hearts.[223] As for us, we are obligated to receive and accept one another on the basis of the Christian testimonies in the love that always believes and hopes the best.[224] And if someone deceives, he has deceived only himself[225] and not those who received him truthfully in love.[226] Thus far, briefly, concerning all ceremonial laws.

---

217 [This is a reference to saints' days, of which there were a great many. In Cologne in the latter Middle Ages, approximately one hundred saints' days a year were observed.—Trans.]

218 [Cf. Roland H. Bainton, *Erasmus of Christendom* (New York: Scribner, 1969), 204.—Trans.]

219* Sect of Sabbatarians.

220 [Other Anabaptists emerging out of the same ferment as the Pilgramites in Moravia included those under the leadership of Oswald Glait. They observed the Sabbath on Saturday because they believed that the Ten Commandments continued in force. This group existed at Jamnitz, Moravia (now Jemnice in the Czech Republic), which was Glait's hometown. See "Sabbatarian Anabaptists," ME 4:396; and Daniel Liechty, *Andreas Fischer and the Sabbatarian Anabaptists* (Scottdale, PA: Herald Press, 1988).—Trans.]

221 [Original: *sovil man brauchen mag usserhalben des menschen hertzen.*—Trans.]

222* What is commanded to Christians.

223 Rom 8:27; Rv 2:23.

224 1 Cor 13:7.

225 1 Cor 3:18; Gal 6:3.

226 2 Thes 1:10.

The fourth:[227*] You shall honour father and mother, so that you may live long and prosper on earth [Tb 4 (3); Sir 3 (3–11); 7 (29f.); Eph 6 (1–3)].[228*, 229] Whoever transgresses this commandment sins not only against God but also against nature. Therefore it has a promise beyond the other commandments, in the nature of a long life. In dumb animals and creatures, nature witnesses to the will and desire of God that every creature loves what gave it birth. For this reason God laid a heavy penalty, vengeance and condemnation, on such transgressors. Whoever strikes, speaks evil of, or curses father and mother shall die and be destroyed from among the people [Ex 21 (17)]. He is called cursed, for to curse or to scold means to maledict or speak evil of; to speak well of means to give benediction or to bless.[230]

The fifth:[231*] You shall not kill. The sixth:[232*] You shall not commit adultery. The seventh:[233*] You shall not steal. The eighth:[234*] You shall not give false witness against your neighbour. The ninth and tenth:[235*] You shall in no way desire or covet the property or wife of your neighbour.[236]

Further, whoever has intercourse with an animal is to be burned and destroyed from among the people [Ex 21; 22; 23].[237]

Following these commandments in Exodus are the rights and the judgments of the natural[238] statutes, which are also the commandment and prohibition of God. Through them, humanity's fallen state is preserved even today, be they Gentile or Jewish laws of nature. This

---

227* 4.

228* Hutterian sect.

229 Ex 20:12; Dt 5:16.

230 Ex 21:17.

231* 5.

232* 6.

233* 7.

234* 8.

235* 9. 10.

236 Ex 20:13–17; Dt 5:17–21.

237 Ex 22:18; Lv 18:23.

238 [Original: *sitlichen,* meaning those laws that apply to all people, and which give order to human life apart from Christ.—Trans.]

cultural statute, even though it is fallen and evil,[239] nevertheless demands order. In it God's character is expressed in human nature, but only for our need, not for God's honour. God is a God of order and not of disorder,[240] and he has firmly united his own omnipotence to his will and order. It is not as the predestinarians[241*, 242] and others say, without any discrimination: that God has the absolute right[243] to save and damn. He has, certainly, but not outside his order and will, to which his power is subordinated. Otherwise one may claim his divine power for every purpose,[244] as indeed Satan and his prophets are doing.[245] Wherever the omnipotence and might of God serves their purposes, they imperiously and indiscriminately use it, without the will of his[246] Father, as Luther does[247*] with the sacrament, child baptism, child faith, and such like.[248] Whenever they find themselves at their wit's end, they save their theology by appealing to the omnipotence of God. There is no more cunning and deceitful article of false teaching than to use and preach the power and omnipotence of God outside the order of God's Word.[249] Further, it is the greatest blasphemy against God and the word of his truth, by which he has ordered all things in heaven and on earth, in which order they shall remain in eternity.

---

239 [That is, belonging to the natural order apart from Christ.—Trans.]

240 1 Cor 14:33.

241* Predestinarianist.

242 [Original: *walbrediger*, that is, those who preach about God's election.—Trans.]

243 [Original: *got vermöges.*—Trans.]

244 [Original: *uff alle weg ziechen.*—Trans.]

245 [Luther and Calvin were the towering Reformation figures who preached predestination.—Ed.]

246 [Although there is no antecedent, the reference is presumably to Jesus.—Trans.]

247* As Luther does.

248 [Here the reference to Luther but not to Calvin or Bucer may be an argument for an early dating of this letter.—Trans.]

249 [Marpeck clearly means God's revealed Word, that Word about which we know. To go beyond that is to deal with things we know nothing about. To do so is presumption and rebellion, for it implies that we are not satisfied with what God has revealed.—Trans.]

For God himself is the wisest order in and through his Word, that is, Jesus Christ, his only begotten from eternity.[250*] Whoever manipulates the omnipotence of God outside this order is a deceiver and seducer. Again, whoever establishes, commands, or prohibits any order outside the divine order and omnipotence denies God's power and glory.[251*] The heathen have done this and by their own violence have become their own law and order [Rom (14–16)]. Thereby they also condemn themselves, according to divine decision, without law, for they are a law unto themselves in imitation of God.[252] This imitation, as their poets say, they have stolen from God. As Paul says, "We are God's offspring"[253] [Acts 17 (28)].

All this—such condemnation and imitation—comes from their own order and law, which is outside God's order and law.[254*] The consequence is that God's wisdom and order are made into foolishness and is despised. He who establishes, commands, or prohibits what has not been established, commanded, or prohibited by the Word of God makes God and his Word into foolishness, as though he did not know or understand God, and thus he makes himself into God. Whoever acts against any statute sins against the Lord of that statute. That is to say, God's honour is stolen, for he alone is sinned against and his place usurped. The whole papacy acts in this fashion.[255*]

May God save and protect those in our time who have been set apart from human statutes,[256*] through the grace of Christ, that they may not be robbed of their new life (Col 2 [20–23]). The serpent is no less cunning now than he was at the beginning. Indeed, according to the words of Christ: "The latter evil is worse than the former" [Mt 12

250* Note.

251* Deny God's power.

252 [Original: *aus der arth gotes.*—Trans.]

253 [Original: *die menschen sein götlicher art.* The translation here is somewhat unusual, but it conveys Marpeck's idea better than a more literal rendering.—Trans.]

254* Note.

255* Papacy.

256* Newly named evangelicals and Anabaptists.

(45)].[257] As Paul also says: "Since we have died with Christ to all worldly statutes, why should we again allow ourselves to be caught and bound by them, as though we still lived in the worldly manner of those who say: 'Do not touch this, do not taste that, do not handle the other!'[258*] All these things only contribute to our harm through misuse; the misuse comes only from human commandments and teaching. Such things have the visage[259] and appearance of wisdom because they do not spare the body. But they are rooted in a self-chosen spirituality and humility, and one should pay no attention to them, since it is clear that to do so is to fulfil the appetite of the flesh" [Col 2 (20–23)].[260]

Again, we are to strive for what is above and not for what is on earth, for we have died, and our life is hidden with Christ in God [Col 3 (1–3)]. Here Paul includes all ethical and human statutes; all of God's external statutes, commandments, and prohibitions have ceased[261*] and, as Christ says, are being fulfilled and carried out in Christ and in those who belong to Christ. Throughout the whole of his teaching, there is a joyful witness to and fulfilment of the power of the Spirit in the heart that freely gives love in Christ; we behave toward others in love and patience[262] and are ready to surrender our own rights in favour of the neighbour and to suffer injustice [Mt 6 (12, 14f.); 7 (1f.); 1 Cor 6 (7)].[263] If anyone wants to sue us for our cloak, we are to give him the coat as well [Mt 5 (38–42)].

All sin is done outside the love of God and the neighbour. Love is the New Testament command of Christ.[264] All law, in both the Old and New Testaments, consists in love from a pure heart [1 Tm 1 (5)]. For all the vices about which the prophets, Moses, Christ, and the apostles

---

257 Mt 27:64; 2 Pt 2:20.

258* Falsely Anabaptist.

259 [Original: *gsait = gesicht.*—Trans.]

260 [Original: *so man ansicht des leibs ersetigung.*—Trans.]

261* Note.

262 1 Thes 3:12; 5:14f.; 2 Tm 2:24.

263 [The original here is confused: *ouch unsers rechtens uerzeihen gegen dem nechsten zu ersushen lossen and uil lieber onrecht than.* This last phrase should surely read *lieber onrecht leiden.*—Trans.]

264 Jn 13:34.

speak are offences against the command to love. There is only one sin from which all the fruit of wickedness begins, namely, disobedience to God's Word.[265*, 266] The works of wickedness are only the fruit and revealing of sin. And the fruits of sin that grow on the evil tree are those to which the prophets, Moses, Christ the Lord, and the apostles in the Old and New Testaments witness and testify. Christ commands us to judge by the fruit [Mt 7 (16, 20)] and not by the blossoms or the leaves that precede the fruit, for blossom and leaf may become good or evil. Evil fruit, when it appears, can never become good. Then the faithful are obligated to exercise judgment.

The beginning of the disobedience to God's Word consists in arrogance, presumption, pride, self-importance, boasting, and stubbornness about one's own self-will and vainglory.[267*] From these follow murderers, those who shed the blood of the innocent, mockers, blasphemers, persecutors of the truth, those who disobey parents, murderers of father and mother, liars, deceivers, and seducers; those who are envious, hateful, and hold grudges; and those who always resist the good, who tend to all wickedness, the blasphemers; those who because of their malice are deniers of the truth, gambling, eating, drinking, whoring, backbiting, slandering the neighbour, denying the truth; idolaters, servants of idols, magicians, and venerators of images.

All these are delivered over to a perverted mind. They change the way of nature and against nature enflame themselves and others with passion, man for man, woman for woman [Rom 1 (24–28)], and for dumb animals; they are seducers of children, brawlers, quarrellers, falsely zealous rioters, rebels, creators of false sects, on whom the sudden judgment of God will fall before long.[268*, 269] Usury, avarice, which is the root of all idolatry,[270] wrath, bad temper, villainy, slanderous talk, disgraceful[271] words, swearers of oaths and perjurers, all these are the

---

[265*] Note.

[266] 1 Jn 3:4.

[267*] Fruit of sin upon which judgment belongs.

[268*] Note.

[269] 2 Pt 2:1–3.

[270] Col 3:5; 1 Tm 6:10.

[271] [Original: *schampere* = perhaps *schandbare.*—Trans.]

fruit of wickedness, and there can never be any hope that such fruit could become good.[272] These all are separated from the body of Jesus Christ; so too are they separated from his holy external congregation, by means of which such fruits are revealed. Whoever has the fellowship of Christ with such a person becomes a partaker in another's sin [1 Tm 5 (22)],[273] shares in his evil works, and crucifies the Son of God afresh in himself [Heb 6 (6)]!

Such fruits of wickedness, which come out of the heart and not from good ground [Mt 15 (18f.)], are subject to the judgment and decision of the children of God whenever they appear in those who call themselves brothers.[274] The believers judge everything and are themselves judged by no one [1 Cor 2 (15)]. Therefore whatever is evil must be excluded (1 Cor 5 [13]) from the community of Christ, but not what might become evil.

Those, briefly, are the wicked actions that Moses also curses [Dt 27 (15–26)]. Therefore our own wickedness should not make the sin larger than it already is; the law of the curse reveals and preaches to us in our conscience.[275]

It follows that many evil blossoms may still turn out good or evil[276*] but do not have fruit by which one could make a judgment.[277*] Similarly, there are many—all liars, dissemblers, and hypocrites—who pretend to desire to bring forth good fruit but who never can bring forth good fruit.

Yet we are forbidden to judge all such individuals before the time of the fruit. We are faithfully warned not to judge prematurely what is hidden but to commit it to the Lord [1 Cor 4 (5)]. This is especially the case with those who appeal to the Lord regarding their evil appearance.[278] Paul commands us to avoid such people [2 Thes 3 (6)] but

---

272 Mk 7:21–23.

273 2 Jn 10; Rv 18:4.

274 1 Cor 5:11.

275 Rom 2:15.

276* False blossoms.

277* Note.

278 1 Thes 5:22.

not to ban them [Ti 2 (3, 10)].[279] These are to be left to the Lord until the revealing of the fruit and are not to be separated from the congregation.[280*] However, good fruit will rarely be found in anyone who remains arrogant and puffed up in spite of brotherly admonition and warning, following an evil appearance or blossom [1 Thes 5 (22)]. Pride should be dealt with by discipline and repentance; otherwise, we must wait for the time of the fruit, which will certainly come and not delay.

Thus one is sure in one's judgment. Certainly, the true shepherds will not drive a patient, humble, meek, and loving heart any further than the chief shepherd, Christ, has driven and bound it,[281] but will let it go out and in, find full and sufficient pasture, and remain victorious over all temptation in Christ Jesus [Jn 10 (11)].

All who act differently are false shepherds, liars, and hirelings, to whom the sheep do not belong.[282*, 283] If one does not immediately agree with their understanding and concur in their judgment, they do not spare the sheep but rather strike and subject them to a false ban, as the pope does.[284] Now when Paul commands that one avoid any brother who walks in a disorderly fashion [2 Thes 3 (6)], he does so because of the chaos of the vices mentioned above [Eph 5 (3–7)]. Furthermore, when Paul says, "Whoever does not follow the sound teaching,"[285] he is not speaking of a salvation that can be achieved by the life or deed of one single work.[286] Not that faith remains without fruit. The fruit, however, is not what saves. Rather, it is the saving teaching that Jesus Christ died and rose again for our sins. He sits at the right hand of God

---

279 [In some Anabaptist circles avoidance was equated with banning; Marpeck separates them and is reluctant to make a final judgment.—Trans.]

280* Note.

281 1 Pt 5:2.

282* That for which one reproved others one now does oneself.

283 Jn 10:12.

284 [The gloss suggests that one of the compilers of the letters, perhaps Maler himself, noticed the very behaviour in Marpeck that he had opposed. It is difficult to locate this accusation in Marpeck's ministry as there is no extant evidence for such a shift.—Trans.]

285 1 Tm 6:3.

286 [Perhaps a reference to Luther's insistence that faith is the one and only "work" required for salvation.—Trans.]

[Heb 12 (2)]; from there we wait for him[287] to judge the living and the dead.[288]

In all this we are to seek what is above, not what is on earth [Col 3 (1f.)]. All the rest is merely the fruit of this teaching of salvation, for which we must wait until the end. Then, as already indicated, the judgment will be certain and just. All creatures without exception were created for good [1 Tm 4 (4)]; they become evil for human beings only[289] because of abuse, which comes from our own rules. Therefore Paul says such things only to warn but not to ban and condemn [Col 2 (16–23)]. Paul commands that our abuse be discontinued, but he does not condemn the creatures that were created for the praise of God and our benefit and not for our hurt, be they food, drink, clothing, including silver, gold, silk, or velvet.[290]

Therefore Paul says he will not allow anyone to judge his liberty, and that all things are lawful for him [1 Cor 6 (12); 10 (23)]. But love is always concerned with improvement [Rom 14 (1); 1 Cor 8 (1, 9)]. Even though all things are lawful, not all things are helpful. Thus true love uses its liberty for improvement (1 Cor 9 [19]). Nor does true love annul liberty. Again, as Paul says, the liberty of love does not justify the rule of ignorance,[291] to order or forbid, to judge[292] or decide [Gal 2 (4f.); 5 (1)]. Everything that is still neither good nor evil, and that may,[293] as already said, become either good or evil, and that occurs frequently, we should not judge or condemn before its time [1 Cor 4 (5)].

Nor are we to exclude, or spew out before their time, the lukewarm and the lame. Rather, the Spirit of God must spew and cast them out [Rv 3 (16)] through the revealing of the fruit they finally produce [1 Cor

---

287 Phil 3:20.

288 2 Tm 4:1; 1 Pt 4:5.

289 1 Cor 7:31.

290 [Evidently there was also criticism of the clothes and house furnishings of some people. Here Marpeck departs from his usual principle of the unity of inward and outward because he sees a danger in passing final judgment on someone's inner life from the appearance of the outer life.—Trans.]

291 Rom 10:2.

292 1 Cor 10:29.

293 [The negative is omitted.—Trans.]

11 (19)]. He does not say that we should cast or spew them out;[294*] he does say that he begins to cast them out and spew them out of his mouth,[295] that is, from his kingdom and the word of his grace, that they may be known by their fruits. Thus one is more certain in one's judgment of them. Otherwise one usurps the office of the Holy Spirit and condemns oneself. Nothing that is external to our heart either benefits or harms us. Only what is in the heart and comes out benefits or harms us [Mk 7 (18–23)], and whatever is external to his heart is the blossom and leaf. They may become good or evil; evil fruit in the wicked, and good fruit in the good.

We have examples[296*] of those who seem to have had evil leaves or blossoms, and in whom all the good was hidden in the secret counsel of God, whose hand even today is not so shortened that it cannot help.[297] Therefore, as we have often said, Christ has commanded us to know them by their fruits [Mt 7 (16–20)], not by the leaves or blossoms that precede the fruit. Those who judge by leaves or blossoms, that is, by the appearance of evil (1 Thes 5 [14]), presume to know God's hidden judgment. This was just as the Jews did with respect to Christ[298*] when he ate with sinners,[299] did not observe food laws,[300] healed the sick on the Sabbath,[301] and much more. From these acts they judged him to be a Gentile and demon possessed.[302]

Then there was Judas with Magdalene.[303*] When she poured the costly ointment of pure nard on Christ, Judas called it folly and pointless waste, as though it were overweening arrogance;[304] indeed, with the world it is pomp and arrogance. Since, however, Magdalene did it

---

294* Note.
295 Rv 3:16.
296* There follows an example of bad appearance.
297 Acts 4:28.
298* The Jews were annoyed at Christ.
299 Mt 9:11.
300 Mk 7:2.
301 Mt 12:10.
302 Mt 12:24.
303* Judas with Magdalene.
304 Jn 12:4f.

out of love for the Lord, the Lord, as the only knower of hearts,[305] said that she had done a good work [Mt 26 (8f.); Mk 14 (4f.); Lk 7 (39)]. For love in the power of God can do everything.[306] Where there is no love, everything is lost and in vain.[307] Had Magdalene done it in arrogance, it would have been a vice before God, even if she had done it to Christ a thousand times.

There was also Judith[308*, 309] of the city of Bethulia, which was besieged by Holofernes. She was motivated by love of the people and God. She made herself up sumptuously, which could have been interpreted as arrogance before the emergence of the fruit. Nevertheless, she did everything for love of the people and with a humble heart, although the appearance or the blossoms indicated arrogance. It was from a humble heart that, using her beauty and affection, she inflamed the heart of Holofernes, came to him, ate with him,[310] and talked to him in words of betrayal, as though she wanted to betray and surrender the city to him. From all this external show an uncertain heart would have judged, before the time of the fruit, that she was a betrayer and a conceited whore.

Moreover, there was Abraham who, because of the divine command and mystery, was prepared to offer up his son [Gn 22 (1–19)],[311*] which was a thing hidden from the understanding of all creatures, even of Abraham himself. If a materialistic, carnal person had seen Abraham before the action was carried out, when he with outstretched arm raised the knife above his son Isaac, he would have judged Abraham to be a murderer of children, of his own flesh and blood, since it would have been indicated in the appearance or in the blossom. But Abraham did not carry it out, preserved as he was by the hand of God. The one who judged would be shown to have been a liar, usurping God's secret judgment and decision. This is what always happens when one does

---

305 1 Kgs 8:39; 2 Chr 6:30; Lk 16:15.

306 1 Cor 6:12; 10:23; Phil 4:13.

307 1 Cor 13:1.

308* Judith.

309 Jdt 10:3f.

310 Jdt 12:17–21.

311* Abraham with Isaac.

not wait for the fruit but judges and decides before the time [1 Cor 4 (5)].

This is what happened to Saul's daughter Michal[312*] when the ark of God was brought into Jerusalem. David was deeply joyful for this in the love of God. Completely forgetting himself, and behaving in a manner unseemly for a king, his love and joy compelled him to dance before the ark of God [2 Kgs 6 (2 Sm 6:14–16)]. Love is stronger than wine[313] and makes one more joyful; love is a strong drink and makes one joyful even in death, for love is stronger than death [Sg 8 (6)]. All this joy constrained and drove David. But Michal was ashamed of it and said in her heart, "The king has become a vulgar fellow."[314] She slammed the window shut and hid her face from him because of shame. Although the blossom of the king's behaviour was that of a dissolute drunk, and had the semblance of loutish immorality, rather than the moral behaviour of a king, God punished her for this false judgment of her heart. She conceived no fruit from David.

In the same way, the Jews judged the apostles to be full of cider or wine, when in fact they were full of the Holy Spirit![315*] If the Jews had waited for the fruit of Christ and the apostles, instead of being offended by the semblance and the blossoms, they would not have sinned against the Holy Spirit. Before the coming of the fruit, they judged Christ and the apostles[316*] to be destroyers of God's commandment, ordinance, and statute, a judgment that was partly justified by the semblance of the literal law (Acts 9 [1f.]; 22 [3–5]; 26 [9–12]); [1 Tm 1 (13)]. Because of the same semblance, Paul, a man zealous for the divine law, persecuted the congregations of Christ. Because of his untimely judgment, Paul refers to himself as an untimely birth [1 Cor 15 (8)]. His judgment was made on the basis of semblance, leaves, and blossoms. Persecution, both spiritual and physical, still happens today because judgment is made on the basis of appearances and not by the fruit.

312* Saul's daughter Michal.

313 Sg 1:2, 4; 4:10.

314 2 Sm 6:20.

315* The Jews judged the apostles.

316* Note.

Similarly, almost throughout the whole New Testament, the learned Jews acted with hasty judgment against Christ and his own before the appearing of evil fruit.[317*] This hastiness hardened their hearts to their own destruction. All this is for each one of you to think about carefully.

Even though they had not seen the fruit of wickedness in any work of his, the friends of Job too judged Job to be an evildoer.[318*] They presumed to meddle with the secret counsels of God. They did so on the basis of Job's own words: he believed God to be so unfailingly just that God would not inflict harm on anyone unless he had first become guilty. Such was their basis of judgment, without the certainty of fruit. In so doing, they acted wrongly against God and Job. Therefore the wrath of God burned against Job's friends, not because of what they said, for they spoke the truth with Job, according to the witness of Holy Scripture, but only because they meddled in the secret counsel of God without certainty about the guilt of Job. Only because of the apparent punishment of God did they take him for an evildoer; when Job was not aware of any wicked deed, they tried to persuade him to confess his wickedness to God. Thus God's wrath will happen to all who pursue and burden consciences and hearts without a sure judgment from God and the fruit of wickedness. What is written is written for our instruction [Rom 15 (4)]. From these evil appearances and blossoms have come good, just, and noble fruits. Therefore one may not judge prematurely, but one must let God be the judge until the time of the fruit [1 Cor 4 (5)].

Another instance will suffice. Jeremiah, the prophet of God, was condemned by the people as a traitor, but he prophesied to Jerusalem only what God had commanded him [Jer 37–39].

Now follows a discussion of good appearance and evil fruit

There are many blossoms and appearances of good that conceal the most gruesome reality, as is true with all hypocrites and liars. By this means, the enemy of truth robs us of the sanctuary; in fact, they have robbed and stolen almost everything. Indeed, the lying dissemblers

---

317* The Jewish scribes laid violent hands on Christ.

318* The vexation of Job's friend.

nowadays[319*] do everything so much like the true children of God that true and pious hearts, even if they have all the evidence of good fruit, can only with great difficulty be clearly recognized. Thus, by false appearances the enemy does his work in his own. He suffers the cross, talks about Christ and his kingdom with a concealed mixture of lies, and endures much according to the external semblance.[320*] Inside, however, his heart is full of envy, anger, and hate. He also does great deeds of love but with a dissembling heart and a disguised disposition, just as Judas did when he kissed Christ.[321*, 322]

Thus every sacred thing is surrendered to the enemy. So too did it happen in the time of Antiochus[323] and Nebuchadnezzar,[324] who robbed the vessels of the temple, stole them for their idols, and used them in all ways as the people of God did.[325*] So too it happens now in the revealing of the kingdom of Antichrist, which is the fulfilment of the kingdom of Babylon and Antichrist.[326*] With all the lying power of wickedness, they portray the sanctuary of truthful hearts, which is the true temple of God, but the appearance of the Son of God, who will reveal everything that is hidden,[327] whether good or evil, will reveal this to be a semblance of truth [2 Thes 2 (3–10); 1 Cor 3 (17); 2 Cor 6 (16)].

Until that time, the life of the truthful is hidden among the hypocrites with Christ in God.[328] They are hidden, not because the fruit of light in the truthful cannot show itself on account of the darkness of the dissembling hearts, but because we have no sure knowledge of who are the righteous, whose light shines warmly because of the light of

---

319* Papist, Lutheran, Zwinglian, and falsely Anabaptist.

320* Note.

321* Kiss of Judas.

322 Lk 22:48. [The Anabaptists were charged with being wolves in sheeps' clothing; this paragraph turns that charge against their critics.—Ed.]

323 Antiochus IV Epiphanes, king of Syria (175–164 BCE). 1 Mc 1:23f.

324 Nebuchadnezzar II, king of Babylon (605–562 BCE). 2 Kgs 25:14f.; 2 Chr 36:18; Jer 52:18f.; Dn 5:2–4.

325* Antiochus.

326* Kingdom of the Antichrist.

327 Mt 10:26; Mk 4:22; Lk 8:17; 12:2; 1 Cor 4:5.

328 Col 3:3.

faith [Mt 5 (16)]; the lying dissembler acts in the same way until God takes away the power of the enemy.[329] Since now the enemy still has the power to put on a show of good fruit, which is the basis of judgment, the elect can only examine and accept wherever the good appears and no evil fruit appears, and leave the choice of election to God, who alone knows the heart.[330]

Gospel of the creatures[331]

What is the gospel of the creatures [Col 1 (23)]? It is preaching the gospel by discerning the nature of God's work in creation.[332] Carnal reason, however, has no right to use the witness of the creatures to the gospel; reason errs in its use, an error that has beset all the philosophers in this world.[333*] Paul warns us (Col 2 [8]) [Col 2 (8)] not to become their prey. But carnal people, who as yet have no understanding of God's law, must first by means of the creatures be led into a knowledge of God. Christ the Lord talked to the people about God's kingdom by means of many parables of nature [Mt 13]. Paul also had to use nature to introduce the Gentiles to the gospel, for the natural, carnal mortal knows nothing of God [1 Cor 2 (14)]. For him the creature of God is a true gospel only until such time as he knows God the Father in the Son, the Lord Jesus Christ, and the Son in the Father [Jn 14 (7, 9)]. According to the flesh, the Son is a creature of all creatures,[334] since all things exist for him.[335] All these things will be fully known beyond this time [1 Cor 13 (9f., 12)].

---

329 [Marpeck warns against claiming to know what is in someone's heart. In Anabaptism great weight was placed on a believer's confession of Christ in baptism and the pledge to follow his way. Christians can be expected to act according to the confession they have made, but that is a different matter from claiming, in an ultimate way, to know what is in someone's heart.—Ed.]

330 1 Kgs 8:39; 2 Chr 6:30; Lk 16:15.

331 [This concept is one of the few in Anabaptist literature that deals with the interdependence of human beings with the rest of creation.—Ed.]

332 Rom 1:19.

333* Philosophical.

334 Col 1:15. [Possibly "firstborn of all creatures."—Ed.]

335 Jn 1:3; Rom 11:36; Col 1:16.

For this reason we all have to remain and work in pieces and fragments until what is whole comes, since, as Paul says, all our knowledge is only fragmentary [1 Cor 8 (2)]. Paul further says, "If anyone thinks he knows, he does not yet know what he ought to know" [Rom 12 (17)]. It is not that something is lacking in the Spirit. Our fragmentation has sprung only out of the weakness and ignorance of our consciences and understanding. If by acknowledging ignorance on my part I could liberate your understanding, I would gladly do so.[336*] According to the measure of God's grace, for your sake and mine, an exposition of the gospel of the creatures might bring us to agreement, to a shared encounter of the heart with God in Christ Jesus our Lord. It is my earnest plea to you that you might patiently read and consider with care the following parables in Christ. I may be more concerned about you than you are about me.

Christ Jesus the Lord, our Saviour, shows nature to be a true physician of body and soul, because he supernaturally healed natural human beings.[337*] Since he has helped natural beings, nature also shows that he was able to help them when they were sick. For he who is well, says the Lord, needs no physician [Mt 9 (12)]. Thus I will present Christ Jesus, my healer.

Does not a physician who undertakes to heal someone command those who care for him to have patience with his illness?[338*] He does not, however, command them to become ill as well; otherwise one ill person would poorly serve the other. Thus it is always the strong one who is the servant of the sick one, in order that his illness may be cured and his weakness become strong while there is breath left in him.

No one buries someone who is still alive, nor does he expel someone in the last stage of illness from the house.[339*] Rather, one waits with patience and endurance for him to get better. Nor does one give him strong food which would only make him become weaker. For this reason Paul commands that caregivers[340] or bishops be chosen who

---

336* Note.

337* Parable of the physician.

338* 1. Parable.

339* 2. Parable.

340 [*Pfleger* is also a synonym for deacon.—Ed.]

will uphold the weak and bear with the wicked. Therefore I desire to be patient with all who are bought[341] with the costly pearl,[342*, 343] the death and shed blood of the Lord Jesus Christ, since God requires patience and long-suffering from us through Christ [2 Tm 2 (24)].

I am not speaking here of those who have died a living death, who have separated themselves from Christ, as shown earlier, because of open wickedness, and who have died before death.[344] In such as these, one cannot hope for life, for they have died twice [Jude (12)]. As both Peter and Paul say, the witness of life in God is to confess Christ in the truth, and to mourn and sorrow for sin [2 Pt 2 (20–22); 2 Tm 3 (1–9)].

Wherever this breath of life is found and whenever it is approached with the word of truth, one is to wait either for death or for recovery of life.[345*] But one is not to thrust others out of the house of God too quickly, to bury them alive and foreshorten life! The true servants of God do not do this. Yet people do exactly this when they begin to beat their fellow servants [Mt 24 (49)], bite one another, and thereby consume one another.[346*] Those who deny the kingdom of God in every little matter regard the precious blood of the Lord Jesus Christ as though it were for sale on the market; they are like those who blaspheme the Son of God, and because of their coarse wickedness, crucify him again in themselves [Ps 50 (49:7f.)].[347] One is the same as the other. It is no small matter to burden someone else's conscience and heart. No creature in heaven or on earth can comfort such a one except the Son of God. It costs too much, says David, to redeem one's brother. In all eternity, one cannot accomplish it.

I testify before my God, through the Lord Jesus Christ, that whoever charges someone with sin and burdens the conscience where there is no sin, accuses the innocent blood of the Lord Jesus Christ, through which all of us are bought and released from all sin. He makes sin where there

---

341 1 Cor 6:20; 7:23; Rv 5:9.

342* Gloss: It has not turned out that way, although it is true and ought to be thus.

343 [Maler evidently regarded Marpeck's behaviour as impatience.—Trans.]

344 Original: *wölchen der tod zům tod vorgeet.*—Trans.]

345* Gloss: Paul says: "You teach others but not yourself." Rom 2 [21–23].

346* Note.

347 Heb 6:6.

is none, which is equivalent to charging someone with murder when in fact he is innocent.[348*] And if he thus accused another, he would be guilty of that other's life and innocent death.[349*] Much more grave is the murder of conscience and soul, both of which belong to God alone. Whoever murders, wounds, and burdens an innocent conscience with his own commands and prohibitions, apart from God's commandment and prohibition, robs God of his honour, murders souls, and tramples the Son of God under foot. He derides and makes a mockery of the sacrifice of Jesus Christ, with which he is bought [Heb 10 (29)].

May God preserve me and every pious heart from participating in a judgment whereby, on the basis of one's own commandment, one accuses an innocent conscience of sin where there is no sin![350*] I know and believe about all of you that you would not take the whole world as payment for sitting in judgment on a known murderer, who in any case deserved death; God willing, I would never do so either. But it is far greater and more terrible to judge those things relating to eternal life,[351*] for life and death, eternal salvation and damnation, are at stake. Whoever regards this matter as trivial and simple has no authority, nor does he know what the judgment of the saints is.[352] Such a one sits in judgment to his own condemnation.[353] Even the world does not judge anyone on the basis of hearsay, suspicion, or appearance, but only on the words of the accused and of reliable witnesses.[354*]

Christ also commands his own that all testimony must be substantiated by two or three witnesses [Mt 18 (16); 2 Cor 13 (1)]. Only when evidence has been presented before the congregation, and he will not hear, does the judgment begin with tribulation, anxiety, sorrow. The other members of the body of Christ experience great pain and suffer-

348* Parable.

349* Note.

350* Parable.

351* Note.

352 Dn 7:22; 1 Cor 6:2.

353 Ti 3:11.

354* Not judged based on rumour.

ing, for a member of the body of Christ the Lord is at stake.[355*] They[356*] must lose a member in order that the other members are not hurt and the whole body destroyed,[357] be it eye, foot, or hand. It should be pulled out or cut off according to the commandment of Christ, our head: "If your eye offends you, or your hand, or foot . . ." [Mt 5 (29)].

The other members of the body of Christ will not be able to do this without great pain and tribulation. If the member is honourable and useful to the body, the tribulation is so much greater. It cannot possibly happen easily or simply. The natural body cannot lose a member without pain.[358*] Nor does it immediately cut it off, even if it is failing and weak; rather, it uses all kinds of medicines. As long as it is not dead and is only painful, the body bears it with patience and long-suffering, and delays the penalty to allow for improvement. If, however, it allows the body no rest, and doesn't improve by means of medicine from the Lord Jesus Christ, through suffering and pain, it must be cut off in order that the other members of the body of Christ remain healthy in the fear and love of God and the neighbour, to whom alone the judgment to retain and to forgive sin has been committed[359*] (Mt 16 [19]; 18 [15–19]; Jn 20 [23]).

My fervent prayer to God is that no truthful heart might be excluded from the true members of Christ.[360*] This is my ardent hope. My conscience also bears me witness that I am grafted into the body of Christ. Even though I am weak, I hope that God's power and strength might be revealed in my weakness. For I can boast of nothing but my

---

355* Gloss: It should be! But where?

356* Healthy members.

357 [The original, which is not clear, reads as follows: *"darnach erst, so vor der gmein bezeugt ist, wo er ouch die nit hören will, so geet erst das urtl mit truebsal, angst und trauren und mit grossem schmertzen und laid, dann es gilt ein glid am leib Christi des Herren. Send die andern glider am leib Christi, so sy ein glid verlieren muessen, uff das dei andern glider nit schadhaft werden und der ganntz leib verdärb . . ."*—Trans.]

358* Parable.

359* Gloss: Every church boasts about this authority.

360* Gloss: Neither the Hutterites, Swiss, nor others believe this.

weakness [1 Cor 12 (5, 9)].[361*] God must have mercy on our destitution and poverty. By virtue of this poverty, God's glory and riches are revealed in us through Christ Jesus. So too is it revealed in our folly, for through him we become wise. Amen.

Oh, my dear brothers, if our hearts and consciences could only meet on the above-mentioned matter! This is my grievance against you. I hope that through the grace of God we might soon be united on the other matters. I am concerned only for you; as I said earlier, I am more concerned about you than you are about me. God knows my heart, and he will judge it. I pray God to give you and me hearts open to one another, so that in Christ Jesus, true Son of God and Man and in whom all knowledge consists,[362] we will know each other[363] and be known by Jesus Christ. For this is eternal life, that they know you, Father, the true God, and Jesus Christ whom you have sent [Jn 17 (3)]. May God the Father grant this knowledge to all who desire it through his Jesus Christ. Amen.

Finally, in conclusion, I find that Christ, Moses, the prophets, and the apostles used divine and biblical scriptures in three ways.[364*]

First, for teaching.[365*] When someone knows nothing of the witness of God and his Word or what is needed to understand it, he claims that everyone already knows it. The letter to the Hebrews mentions not repeating again those matters belonging to the beginnings of Christian life [Heb 6 (1)]. If one is ignorant of something, the scripture serves as guide and teacher.

Second, scripture is used for admonition and warning to him who is already taught.[366*] This is the second function of scripture, and it is especially important where an evil appearance—the leaves or blossoms which precede the fruit—leads to care or fear that there may not in time be good fruit. But from that no certain judgment of good or evil

---

361* Especially if one acts with such impatience, roughness, angry spirit, and hurry. Nor is it the true weakness.

362 Col 2:3.

363 Eph 4:13.

364* Scripture in three ways.

365* 1.

366* 2.

is possible. That function of scripture, which is warning and admonition, belongs here. The book of Deuteronomy is almost all of this kind. That is why it is called the book of repetition, or in Latin *Deuteronomium*.[367*, 368] The same is true of the admonition and warning of the apostles to the congregations throughout the New Testament.

Third, there are commandments and prohibitions. All the writings that announce punishment, the wrath of God, and eternal damnation are directed at the transgression of commandments and prohibitions. Such punitive writings are at times used in the hope of repentance. In such punishment, comfort is also offered, in order that one not sink into too much sorrow [2 Cor 2 (7)]. But in case of apostasy and denial, they even deliver the sinner to the devil, denying him eternal life, as Paul did when he delivered several to the devil in body and soul [1 Tm 1 (20); 1 Cor 5 (3–5)].

Whoever does not use Holy Scripture with these three differences in mind cannot with any certainty handle Holy Scripture. Especially where the Holy Spirit, the true teacher, does not precede in all knowledge of Christ, everything will be misused and wrong when one tries to admonish where one has not yet learned, or to punish where there is no certainty of sin, or to make sin where there is no commandment.[369*] All such approaches lead to error. Some admonition, advice, and order are certainly used to further godliness and the improvement of the body of Christ. And even if one sins against the body, certainly one does not punish by banning, but one is patient again and again in hope of improvement.

Testimony of my understanding of divine scripture

The Lord Jesus Christ says: "Whoever does not deny everything he has is not worthy of me" [Lk 14 (33)]. Paul also says that no one should seek his own but only what is good for others [1 Cor 10 (24)]. The command of Christ and the apostles, that the true spirit of love never seeks its own but always what is of service and of use to others, is a pointed one [1 Cor 13 (5)]. Nevertheless, Paul, Christ, and the apostles exercised

---

367* Dt.

368 [Literally, "second law."—Trans.]

369* Note.

much patience as they did so. Here are examples: when the mother of the two sons of Zebedee asked that one son sit to the left and the other to the right in the kingdom of Christ [Mt 20 (20)], or when Peter asked the Lord what he would get for leaving all for his sake [Lk 18 (28)], or when Christ was asked who would be greatest after his departure. There are many similar examples during the time of Christ and the apostles [Mt 20 (26f.)]. Paul also wrote to the Philippians, and said that he hoped to send Timothy to them soon [Phil 2 (19f.)], since he had no one who was so much of the same mind as Timothy; the others were all self-seekers.

But nowhere do we find that Christ or Paul banned or excluded the others from the fellowship of Christ on that account, even though the true and perfect spirit of the love of God utterly condemns all self-seeking.[370*] Nevertheless, Christ and the apostles waited with patience and longsuffering for improvement, and did not judge before the time of the fruit [1 Cor 4 (5)], which takes the form of the open vices already mentioned. Thus, in the case of Christ and Judas [Mt 26 (23f.)], and Paul and the fornicator and others [1 Cor 5 (1–5)], they were delivered to the devil only after the bearing of the fruit (1 Tm 1 [20]). They were not excluded and banned for minor reasons, even though they were not living in perfect love, as were John with Christ and Timothy with Paul.[371*]

The others were borne in patience, because of the gifts given to them by the Holy Spirit. The foot is not as honourable a member as the eye; it becomes much dirtier in the mud than the eye, but the eye watches the foot, and the foot bears the eye [Rom 12 (4)]. Therefore one does not say to the other: "You are not a member of the body" [1 Cor 12 (14–21)].

It is my fervent prayer that, for the sake of Christ, you get your judgments from Christ and learn longsuffering, forbearance, and meekness from him.[372*, 373] May the merciful Father forgive me my failures and

370* This Pilgram now judges as usury and miserliness.

371* Note.

372* Note.

373 Mt 11:29.

shortcomings, which I find in myself every day. I also pray for all others who, like me, desire forgiveness in and through Christ.

My greatest contention with you in my conscience is that nowhere do I find such precipitate, superficial judgments and verdicts on every little matter in Christ and his apostolic church as I find with you.[374*] Even if one has thoughtlessly offended God the Father, the highest good, the costly treasure of the death and shed blood is nevertheless a reconciliation and an action of the Father's mercy. Mercy triumphs over justice [Jas 2 (13)]. All your precipitate actions make me feel somewhat distant from you;[375*] in my conscience I am not sure that I should have any part or fellowship in such hasty judgments and verdicts.

There are also very few overseers among you.[376*] They have been excluded from you and your gatherings at least once, if not twice. Since God does not repent of his gifts, I do not find in the church of Christ that anyone, having once received the Holy Spirit for the service of the apostolate or the episcopate, has ever been excluded from the fellowship of Christ.[377*] Therefore something must be wrong either with your fellowship or with your overseers; it is something that a weak heart like mine, and like those with me, cannot simply ignore, the moreso since you are yourselves uncertain about your overseers.[378] You seem to say that although these overseers need the discipline and restraint of young children, they should be elders in the maturity of Christ, that is, in the understanding of Christ,[379] and feed the flock of God [1 Pt 5 (2)]. It is a question of maturity with Christ not according to years but according to understanding. That the flock should punish the shepherd is always against the manner of Christ. The shepherd is to feed the flock. Thus the younger do not gather treasure for the old but the old for the young [2 Cor 12 (14)].

I have written to you in the hope that God, through his child Jesus Christ, might grant us the ability to acknowledge one another in Christ

---

374* Contention.

375* Gloss: The same is true in reverse.

376* Note overseers.

377* Gloss: The same is true in reverse and with disorder.

378 [Original: *nit wol lassen mögen.*—Trans.]

379 Eph 4:13.

Jesus with a clean conscience. For all schism, discord, and uncertain consciences come in part from one's own understanding, flesh, and blood, which mixes itself into the knowledge of God. Every moment, I am conscious of this in myself, for division does not come from the Spirit of Christ. May the Lord Jesus Christ redeem us from all evil. Amen. It is my desire that the grace of our Lord Jesus Christ be given to all who long for it. Amen.

Pilgram Marpeck,
God be gracious to him

8

The cause of the conflict

To the Swiss Brethren in Appenzell, especially to Ulrich Scherer and Jörg Maler [Pilgram Marpeck] 1543

"The Cause of the Conflict" is a sequel to "Concerning Hasty Judgments and Verdicts" (no. 7). This letter "deals more bluntly with the issue of schism."[1] "The Cause of the Conflict" shows Pilgram Marpeck at his most self-righteous. For instance, he acknowledges that the Swiss have understood him correctly: he does not regard them as a true church of God! There are two related reasons for the harsh tone. The particular reason is that Marpeck is replying to a letter from the Swiss protesting the accusations contained in "Concerning Hasty Judgments and Verdicts." The more general reason is that this conflict is a fight among friends. Marpeck had been given hospitality and called on by the Ap-

[Pilgram Marpeck] an die Schweitzer Brüder in Appenzell, besonders an Ulrich Scherer und Jörg Maler: Ursache des Zwiespalts; 1543. Translation by Walter Klaassen. Previously published as "Another Letter to the Swiss Brethren (1543)" in WPM, 362–68. Reprinted, with editorial changes, by permission of the publisher.

1 WPM, 362. This bone of contention within two similar streams of Anabaptism recurs in Cornelius Veh's "To the Whole Brotherhood" (KB, no. 24) and Marpeck's "A Warning against the Hidden Fire of the Enemy in Our Hearts" (KB, no. 34).

penzell Anabaptists while he was living among them for twelve years (1532–44).[2]

Marpeck's larger goal was to establish Communion fellowship with the Appenzellers. This matter is addressed in Cornelius Veh's letter (no. 24, "To the Whole Brotherhood") and in Marpeck's letter of 1551 (no. 34, "A Warning against the Hidden Fire of the Enemy in Our Hearts").

"The Cause of the Conflict" is addressed to Ulrich Scherer and Jörg Maler. The latter is the editor of the Kunstbuch, who had also taken refuge among the Appenzellers and was made an elder despite his criticism of some of their practices. Sometime after the letter had been written, Maler or the person from whom he inherited the text apparently attached the title of the epistle as it stands in the Kunstbuch. The original title, "Another Letter Sent to Those Called the Swiss Brethren," stands at the head of the text. The placement of Maler's name together with the Appenzellers' implies that he stands with them over against Marpeck. The glosses on the text that are critical of Marpeck underscore this interpretation.

The other addressee, Ulrich Scherer (so-called for his occupation as a shearer), is also known by the surname Yler. A Strasbourg Anabaptist, he was deported and imprisoned several times before and during his residency in Appenzell.

Marpeck enumerates three causes of schism: false prophets, lack of understanding, and carelessness in faith. He writes that the last of the three afflicts the Swiss, who once believed but "have fallen asleep and grown so careless that the enemy has come in and caused confusion.[3] [Marpeck] insists that they have given him no just reason for not considering his group a true church. For his part, he refuses to regard them as a true church; he has clearly told them that he does not so regard them, because of their 'unjustified censoriousness and use of the ban.'"[4] The intimacy of the conflict is evident in the fact that in the same breath Marpeck accuses the Swiss of zeal and of carelessness.

---

2 Heinold Fast, ed., *Quellen zur Geschichte der Täufer in der Schweiz 2: Ostschweiz* (Zurich: Theologischer Verlag Zürich, 1973), 177–250, 567.

3 WPM, 362.

4 WPM, 362.

The ultimate mark of the estrangement between the two communities is that the Pilgramite congregations "are unable to participate with you in the fellowship of the body and blood of Christ."[5] In the Lord's Supper the unity of the church is enacted. That union with Christ and one another is broken, according to Marpeck, where there is impure fear, ignorant zeal, or a seared conscience. Although his words sound harsh to the modern ear, his argument is consistent: the church is inseparably an inner and outer reality. Believers must be at one in their practice; beyond concrete relationships, there is no "spiritual" unity to which one can appeal.

In his description of judgment, Marpeck makes a rare and revealing aside about government. It contains the germ of a theology of creation. Although earthly government is led by unbelievers, Christians pray for their rulers because God is able to give even them "the spirit of true understanding to judge justly." The implication here is that the Spirit is able to reveal the will of God beyond the church.

This letter is incomplete. Marpeck begins an appendix on the disputed question of the oath, but it and his signature have been removed from the letter. Scholars suggest two possible explanations. Both are based on the claim that Marpeck increasingly disagreed with the rejection of all oaths. He is on record as a critic of the Swiss and of Maler himself on this matter. One explanation is that as editor, Maler wanted to spare the Swiss additional injury by removing an attack on their conviction against all swearing of oaths. The other possible explanation is that he did not want to include in a volume he was publishing a critique of a position he no longer held; we know that Maler moved from the Swiss to the Marpeckian position on the matter.[6]

In this letter, the glosses by Maler are as critical as those in the previous letter. Unless some new sources are uncovered, the confusion and uncertainty surrounding these glosses will persist. Perhaps Maler had come to have sentiments not unlike those found in the last statement of Hans Denck, which reflects a disillusionment with the con-

---

5 1 Cor 10:17.

6 Interlude 4, "Why He Changed His Position on the Oath." See also MLDC, 266–70.

troversy and disagreements of the Reformation era. Or perhaps Maler wished to offer, on behalf of the Swiss Brethren, a response to some of Marpeck's more severe censures.

Another letter sent to those called the Swiss Brethren in 1543.

To the beloved in Appenzell, by virtue of their zeal[7] for God in Appenzell, and wherever they gather, and especially in reply to Uli Scherer[8] and Jörg Maler.

Our fervent desire and prayer for you, and all of us, is the pure and true knowledge of Christ. Amen.

Beloved, we write to you again because of the zeal you have for God and because of the good we hope for in you, which we expect you also hope for in us, to see whether the mercy of God is sufficient for a true unification and fellowship in Christ. May God the Father give and grant us this through his Jesus Christ. Amen.

We have heard from you that you have a serious grievance against us, and you consider it unjust that even now we do not regard or acknowledge you as a congregation of God in Christ,[9] correctly under-

---

7 2 Cor 8:16; 11:2; Gal 4:18; Rom 10:2.

8 [According to Heinold Fast, "Pilgram Marpeck und das oberdeutsche Täufertum," ARG, 47 (1956): 228, n. 66, this man is identical with Ulrich Yler of Strasbourg who was expelled from Basel in 1530. See Manfred Kreps and Hans Rott, eds., *Quellen zur Geschichte der Täufer 7, Elsaß 1* [Gütersloh: Gerd Mohn, 1959] no. 218.—Trans.]

9 [In most of the correspondence in the Kunstbuch, a clear distinction is made between *Gemein* ("congregation"), *Kirch* ("church"), and *Gemeinschaft* ("Communion" or "community"). At the same time—as here—"congregation" sometimes seems to mean more than the people who covenant to meet at one spe-

stood. It is our hope that if you will carefully consider these reasons, you will not bear us ill will but rather praise and thank God for the revelation of his understanding, since eternal life consists alone in the knowledge of God the Father and his Christ [Jn 17 (3)]. Therefore, beloved, accept these reasons diligently and honestly, with humility of heart, and do not slanderously despise them, which only leads to your own bitterness. Remember what injury the enemy may inflict on you and us. No small loss has come to you[10] because through slandering us you have become embittered and resentful. Thereby the enemy of truth has prevented you from believing and from being concerned about this, so that you are now close to destruction.[11] May God preserve you from this. Amen.

All schisms have three causes.[12*] The first is the dissembling and hypocrisy of the lying false prophets who desire that the church and truth of Christ never have unity and fellowship. In them there is no hope of unity, nor will the congregations of Christ ever desire to unite with such false prophets and congregations. Work expended on them is in vain and to no avail.

The second reason[13*] for splits is lack of understanding; ignorance; anger; hasty zeal for old customs, blood relatives, fellowship based on natural love;[14] for one's own teaching, knowledge, and understanding, which loves to puff itself up[15] and which causes communal strife before it has come to self-knowledge. Nearly everyone is burdened with such characteristics of the flesh. Still the law and fear of God is by nature written on their unclean hearts. Because of this, but still not washed

---

cific location. Perhaps this was the case because these pilgrim congregations had no meetinghouse in which to gather.—Ed.]

10 Col 2:8.

11 [Original: *und zů besorgen, noch beschechen möcht gar zům verderben.*—Trans.]

12* All schism from three causes.

13* 2.

14 [The Appenzellers—not surpisingly, considering that they are recent converts to Anabaptism—seem to be torn between loyalty to family and locality on the one hand, and church on the other hand.—Ed.]

15 1 Cor 8:1.

from sin, they accept faith in Christ in baptism, discipline,[16] and the supper, without the accompanying work of the Holy Spirit, presuming in ignorant zeal[17] to be teachers before they have become students of Christ. Such persons bring schism into the congregations of Christ.[18*] Nor may they be called a congregation of God in Christ. But one may be zealous and work for them with hope until they are brought to true understanding. That, briefly, is the second reason for all schism.

The third reason[19*] is that people go to sleep in the faith and become careless, even though through baptism they have been washed from sin through the blood of Christ in the Holy Spirit. Since our enemy never sleeps, so that he might devastate us, they soon fall from the bulwark of faith and true knowledge when they are tempted. If the true believers, especially the watchmen of the people who should give guidance, do not fully wake up, they misdirect the people as well as themselves. The neglect happens through ignorance, which God brings on us because of our carelessness. Thus schism follows, in order that the godly and faithful ones may be revealed. They are the ones who have remained alert through admonition, who arouse those who sleep, who direct the sick to Christ the physician and portray him to them, in order that they may come to true knowledge.

Those who are so neglectful—or to whom God does not graciously send someone, so that they are not admonished—therefore remain in the error of ignorance. For ignorance is not innocent before God. Where there is no one whom God alone gives and sends with the truth to warn, admonish, teach, and preach, there is no grace, and the wrath of God remains on these, as well as on those who do not believe the truth. We write this in order that you might clearly perceive it and open your hearts to God, which we will also properly do with you. Otherwise there is nothing, but if deception and hypocrisy are absent, God will give us his grace for true union. Amen.

For such zeal without knowledge robs and limits the benefits of fellowship. Even if people were to regard such zealots as a congregation,

---

16 [Original: *pann.*—Trans.]

17 Rom 10:2.

18* Gloss: Thus those in Asia and Corinth also were not churches in Christ.

19* 3.

God would not so regard them. For we are unable to participate with you in the fellowship of the body and blood of Christ (which all true Christians have eternally in faith and love) when it is done in impure fear and ignorant zeal[20]—as indeed you have never participated with us,[21*] and still may not do so, because of a seared conscience.[22] False, unjust judgments and verdicts follow from such impure fear, and Christ the Lord denies to his own the rights to these judgments and verdicts. He warns them not to judge and condemn, in order that they be not judged and condemned [Mt 7 (1f.)].

The Lord does not forbid just judgments in this present life, and these the true believers are commanded to make in the Holy Spirit, since the spiritual person judges all things and is himself judged by no one. But the Lord prohibits judgments made falsely and in ignorance, for thereby one judges and condemns oneself. For wherein one judges another and thereby himself becomes guilty, he judges and condemns himself.

Therefore, dear friends, we must properly wake up and exercise the judgments and ways of God, with trembling and fear in just and true knowledge. "Judge with right judgment," says the Lord [Jn 7 (24)]. For where judgment is perverted, all God's action, bodily and spiritually, is suspended.[23*] Wherever the spirit of justice and truth does not rule in earthly[24] unbelievers (that is, where earthly government is concerned), there earthly judgments on a just basis are not possible. This is why

---

20 Rom 10:2.

21* Note.

22 1 Tm 4:2.

23* Gloss: It follows that it was suspended for the Romans, too. But Paul does not do that (Rom 14 [3f., 10, 13]).

24 [Original: *leiplich,* referring to the human state outside of Christ. When Marpeck speaks of the unity of *leiplich* and *geistlich* (on the archtype of the incarnation), the term has no negative connotations and is simply translated as "bodily" or "physical." When body is separated from spirit, as is the case with government, it could be argued that *leiplich* should be translated as "carnal." But in the next sentence, the author states that God gives government a true spirit of understanding. Therefore we have translated those uses of *leiplich* with the more positive "earthly."—Trans.]

true believers pray for human government, that God may give it the spirit of true understanding to judge justly.

How much less is this the case in spiritual judgments, which human reason can never reach without the Holy Spirit of Christ, who forgives and retains sin, and which are concerned with the eternal and not with the temporal realm. For, says Paul, whoever does not have this Holy Spirit of Christ according to the measure of faith does not belong to Christ [Rom 8 (9)]. And John says: "Whoever does not abide in the teaching of Christ has no God" [2 Jn 1 (9)]. For this reason we could not and cannot regard you as a congregation of Christ, for you have no just accusation against us. To this your own conscience will testify. Paul also regarded the Galatians thus (until, with great anxiety, he had given birth to them a second time in the image of Christ) [Gal 4 (19)]. Foolishly and without justification you also have continued to regard us as not being a congregation of Christ. Thus neither of us regards the other as a congregation of Christ!

We are much more justified in making this accusation of you than you of us, since you have no justification for not regarding us as a congregation of Christ.[25*] Rather, you should look to yourselves, since you have not yet shown us a fault that our conscience confirms. Nevertheless, we do not thereby regard ourselves as justified before God, but only through his grace. But because of your unjustified censoriousness and use of the ban, we have until the present justifiably denied you fellowship with us in Christ.

This, then, is your case against us, the reason why you do not consider us a congregation of Christ:[26*] because we exercise the freedom, which we have in Christ, too much, contrary to his Word. If you would prove this to us with a concrete case, so that our consciences could be certain, we would gladly accept your not recognizing us as a Christian congregation. For it is certainly true that the proper and true fellowship of the body and blood of Christ is unity, and unity in the Holy Spirit is true fellowship. For there can be no rift in the body of Christ, since there is only one faith, one Lord, one Spirit, one God and Father of us

---

25* Gloss: God knows who is innocent.

26* Not consider a church of Christ.

all [Eph 4 (5–6)]. And this fellowship is without exception baptized with one Spirit, with water, into one unsundered, undivided body with united members.

Therefore once more our admonition goes to you who are guilty. (We recognize here that all innocent consciences are excepted, and we hold them blameless, as always.) Since you are guilty, bear the charge of this article in the patience of Christ, namely, that we did not and do not consider you a congregation of Christ. Do not let your hearts complain against us any longer, when you correctly recognize the causes. Cast away your own honour, which cannot stand before God, and tread it into the mud! We continue to hope that you will no longer bear us ill will, but that you will rather praise and thank God with us for his grace and revelation. May you pray that knowledge of him may be revealed, to his honour and praise, and pray also for our need of salvation. May he give us, together with you, the teaching of his Holy Spirit for true knowledge of him, in which knowledge alone eternal life consists.[27] May we achieve this through God alone. Amen.

Concerning your understanding of the oath,[28*] on which we have sufficient clarity from you, we cannot bind anyone's conscience or put a rope around anyone's neck, nor are we able to submit our consciences to your understanding.[29]

---

27 Jn 17:3.

28* Oath.

29 [The rest of the letter was cut out of the original codex and is therefore lost. Or did Maler use it in his discussion of the oath in Interlude 4 in the Kunstbuch? It is also possible that he rejected Marpeck's position and did not wish to present both positions in the Kunstbuch. On the oath, see "Oath" in ME 4:2–8.—Ed.]

Rattenberg, Tyrol, on the Inn River. Marpeck's hometown, site of Leonhard Schiemer's martyrdom.

9

Concerning the grace of God
Concerning the little bottle

To the congregation in Rattenberg on the Inn River

Leonhard Schiemer

Rattenberg, 5 December 1527

Leonhard Schiemer (d. 1528) was born in Vöcklabruck, Austria, and brought up in Vienna by devout Catholic parents. He entered the Barefoot Friars, an order of Franciscan monks. Six years later, the disunity in the order prompted him to leave and embark on a spiritual quest. He learned the trade of a tailor and in early 1527 traveled to Nikolsburg, Moravia (now Mikulov in the Czech Republic), where Balthasar Hubmaier and Hans Hut were taking the Anabaptist vision in divergent directions. He heard them in a public debate. Hut was declared the loser and banished from Nikolsburg, but Schiemer was nevertheless attracted to Hut's mystical approach. Schiemer was baptized by Oswald Glait, formerly a Lutheran pastor in Nikolsburg who sided with Hut against Hubmaier, and commissioned as a missionary. In his brief charismatic ministry, Schiemer visited twenty-eight cities, baptized more than 200 people, and wrote profusely. Eight of his essays and several hymns survive in the Hutterite Chronicle and hymnal. One of them, "We plead with you, Eternal God," enjoys pride of place with the compositions of other beloved early martyrs.[1]

Leonhard Schiemer an die Gemeinde in Rattenberg am Inn: Von der Gnade Gottes. Vom Fläschlein; Rattenberg, 5. Dezember 1527. Translation by Walter Klaassen.

His final journey was to Rattenberg, Pilgram Marpeck's hometown. There his zeal led to the immediate formation of a radical congregation. He was soon imprisoned, but the judge, Bartholomeus Angst, was lenient, allowing Schiemer's fellow believers easy access to the prisoner and permitting him enough ink and paper to compose most of his literary output.[2] On 12 January 1528, he was condemned to death by sword and fire. His story is recorded in the Martyrs' Mirror, the most comprehensive and widely used volume recording martyr deaths throughout church history. It was first published in 1660. His death must have made a deep impression on Marpeck, who immediately resigned his office as magistrate. The fact that three of Schiemer's major writings are featured in the Kunstbuch suggests that he had an enduring influence on Marpeck and his circle.

Schiemer's thinking was shaped by late medieval mysticism of the cross, as mediated to him by Hut, among others.[3] Its passion was for Christian conformity to the cross of Christ. This orientation has a spiritualistic bent, in which the inner reality transcends the outer. This is evident, for example, in the section of this essay with the gloss "Law is the first grace; Christ is the second."[4] Schiemer offers a biting parody of the Lord's Prayer for those who mock and blaspheme the cross. The final section of Schiemer's treatise is a heartrending lament worthy of Job or Jeremiah, whose words he borrows. It is one of the few accounts in early Anabaptism of the emotions that can come with the terrifying realization that one has been sentenced to death.

The comments about grace and the little bottle are preserved as separate writings in state archives and Hutterite manuscripts.[5] Maler may well have combined them for the Kunstbuch. Because many of the

---

1 In the Ausbund, "Wir bitten dich, ewiger Gott" (no. 31). There the author is identified as "Leonhard Schöner," but it is generally agreed on the basis of the Ausbund's description of him that the author is Leonhard Schiemer.

2 ME 4:452.

3 MESG, 106–13.

4 Marpeck corrects the theology he inherits, with its emphasis on Christ as the internalizer, with the teaching of the incarnation, in which Christ is the externalizer.

5 For example, see GOT, 43–79.

Bible references in the Maler edition are different from those in other editions, Maler probably supplied the ones in this text. Schiemer's preaching was wildly popular, as was his writing. Despite publication bans and the risks associated with being found with incendiary texts on one's person, his works saw many printings, beginning in 1531, as well as handwritten copies from as late as 1618.[6] Schiemer's other Kunstbuch pieces "The Twelve Articles of the Christian Faith" (no. 10) and "A True, Short Gospel to Be Preached Today to the World" (no. 11) deal with the Apostles' Creed and the content of the gospel. Taken together, the three pieces constitute a rudimentary catechism.

The different versions of the treatise "Concerning the Grace of God" have been shaped by copyists. It might simply be the case that, as was common, the text was read in a service or Bible study and written down to the best of a hearer's ability. But the fact that strikingly different biblical references are used to clinch a point suggests the versions were annotated according to the beliefs and needs of subsequent users. The marginal comments by the editor are emphatically positive, in contrast with other documents where the comments take issue with the text.

6 BSOT, 243–44.

A preamble that covers what God's grace is

The whole world is chattering about and mouthing back and forth the little word *grace,* especially our scripture experts. They notice that there is something in scripture called grace. Since, however, they do not possess it inwardly, they cannot say anything about it, except to regard the word grace as the scholastics do, when they take from Aristotle the word *chimera* or *ens cognitum,*[7] which means that it exists only in the mind, or whenever one thinks or speaks about it. But when thought and words are completed, the essence of a thing is also gone. They call it *en[cia secundum intencionem]* [existing second in the intentions] or *ens non re[a]le* [existing not in reality]. They use terms such as *genus* [type], *species* [species], *d[ifferencia]* [differences], *[proposicio]* [propositions], *kath[egoria]* [categories]. Then they say it can't be translated into German, because the German language is too vulgar! When one thinks about it, one can see that they are so rarified that they can never be *re[a]lia* [reality], for *res* [matter, thing] or *realia* [reality] indicates "some reality" or "thing." But this is no thing or anything and lasts only as long as one thinks about it. Thus, in the end we are left with nothing, and those who can chatter most about this "nothing" are called masters and doctors!

This is precisely the case with our scripture experts. They do not have their skill from God, nor are they taught by God. They have all their knowledge from other Christians and have stolen it out of their books. About them Jeremiah says: "I am against the prophets who each steal my word from one another" [Jer 23 (30)]. They have not been sent by the God of heaven [Jn 3 (34); Rom 10 (15)] but by the god of their belly (Rom 16 [18]), and that is why they cannot preach fruitfully. Christ has not chosen them from the world; therefore they do not witness faithfully regarding the world. For their works are evil [Jn

---

7 [These terms derive from Thomistic thought. The usual phrase for something that exists only in the mind is *ens rationis,* not *ens cognitum,* but they mean the same thing. On Aristotle's and Aquinas's discussion of *genus, species, proprium, differentia, accidens,* see Aristotle, Topics, I.5 102a 18–30; and Thomas Aquinas, Summa Contra Gentiles, I.32.—Ed.]

7 (7)]. The world lets them be and does not hate them [1 Jn 4 (5)]. They are from the world, and the world loves them (Jn 15 [19]) and listens to them. They are just like a person making his living with chopping wood. They do their preaching like any worker who earns his living by his skill [2 Cor 2 (17)]. The results prove it. That is why the Lord says, "A good tree will not bear bad fruit" [Mt 7 (18)]. Further: "As the rain and snow water the earth and make it fruitful, so shall my word be that goes out from my mouth. Wherever I send it, it shall not return empty, but accomplish that for which I sent it, and what pleases me" [Heb 6 (7); Is 55 (10–11)]. But they (the belly preachers!) cannot point to anyone who has been improved by their preaching. The Lord says: "The good shepherd knows his sheep and calls them by name" [Jn 10 (3)].

And these are called masters and some of them doctors of Holy Scripture! But why? They are so called because they have found a word that scripture often mentions, namely, faith. Another is love, and yet another, communion of saints, and others, such as cancelling of sin, brothers, neighbour, Holy Spirit,[8*] God's grace, righteousness, law, Christ, spiritual, preaching, baptizing, the Supper of Christ, hope, remorse, penitence, rising from sin, falling into sin, prayer, justified, Word of God.

They have stolen such words from scripture. If one asks them about the gist of the matter, they say one must simply believe. If one asks, "What is faith?"—since not everyone has faith [2 Thes 3 (2)]—they say nothing, but are after all obligated to give account (1 Pt 3 [15]). They speak about love and faith, but if they are asked how these are to be had, they don't know. If you ask them whether they know Christ, you learn that they know him only after the flesh [Jn 6 (36, 41f.); 18 (20f.); 2 Cor 5 (16)]. The Lord himself condemned this when he said their ignorance has no limit.[9*]

No matter what one asks them, they have words for it. They cannot distinguish the inner Word from the outer. One has to push them to admit that a Christian must be taught by God. However, when they are asked, "Where does God conduct his school and what is the very

---

8* Note.

9* Note.

first lesson?" they have no answer, and then one can see their deceitfulness.

They do the same thing with the little word *grace,* about which I now write. My brothers and sisters, sealed in the Lord [Rv 7 (3–8); 9 (4)], each one of you must share the gift you have received from God and hold it in common for everyone's improvement. It is written, "They held all things in common" [Acts 4 (32)]. If a brother or sister is pleased [with what I write], it shall not be used privately but copied and shared with those who are favourably disposed toward it [1 Cor 12].

The threefold grace, as it is called, is found in the scriptures of the Old and New Testaments.

The first thing to note is that one must carefully distinguish one grace from another. [John says:] "We have received grace upon grace" [Jn 1 (16)], and further [Christ says]: "To those who have, more will be given, and they will have abundance. But from those who have nothing, even what they have will be taken away. And the worthless slave will be thrown into outer darkness" [(Mt 13 (12); 25 (29f.); Lk 8 (18); Mk 4 (25)].

These three graces must remain unconfused, so that one is not mistaken for the other. If scripture speaks about the first, and it is imprudently taken for the second, or the second for the third, the reader is finished and lost in scripture. I will not force the scripture open for the godless with this booklet; indeed, I can't, for it is sealed with seven seals, and no one can open it, except the slaughtered lamb (Rv 13 [8]); [Rv 5 (5); Is 29 (11)]. It is eternally locked to those who do not have the key of David,[10] which is the cross of Christ (Mt 25 [10]; Jn 6 [44, 65]).

If I am to qualify for God's house and love God, I must become the enemy of the lusts of creatures and the world, and turn to the Creator. I can't love two lords (Lk 16 [13]). God wants my whole heart [Prv 23 (26)]. All scriptures that speak of denial, giving things up, and renunciation of what is temporal and worldly are part of this theme. Our love for God grows when we do these things, but so do affliction, persecution, and the cross brought on by the world. In addition, there is inner

---

[10] Is 22:22; Rv 3:7.

and outer affliction: inwardly, the struggle of the flesh; outwardly, the renunciation and deprivation of the body.

Concerning the first grace: the law

In his first chapter (1–5, 7), John writes, "In the beginning was the Word, and the Word was with God. All things were made by it, and without it nothing was made that was made [Col 1 (15–17)]. In him was life, and that life was the light of mortals. The light shines in the darkness." John "bore witness to this light so that they all believed in it," not through John the Baptist, as Luther translated it into German,[11*, 12] but through the light. "It was the true light that gives light to all who come into the world." Here too Luther has got it wrong when he translates, "through his coming into the world." Check all the Latin and Hebrew Bibles!

The reason for the errors is that Luther comes to Christ, to God, to faith, to the light. He will not have any of them *in* Christ but only beside him, under him, near him, as we will soon find in this chapter. [There he translates:] "The Word became flesh and lived among us."[13] But all the scholars know [that it should read:] "The Word became flesh and dwelled in us." That means that he will dwell in us. Further, M. Luther claims that "the gospel among all creatures" is "in a creature" [Col 1 (23)]. But that is Luther's approach through and through. "He hopes for God" and "believes on Christ." I'll let that one go! But we believe not on but in Christ; we hope in Christ. We have the Word in us, not among us.

The text continues with the light of grace. "It was in the world, and the world was made through it, and the world did not know it [Jn 1 (10–12, 16f.)]. He came to his own home, and his own did not receive him. But to those who did receive him he gave power to become the children of God. [It continues:] "From his fullness we have received grace upon grace. For the law was given through Moses; grace and

11* Luther.

12 [See BSOT, 250, n. 2, for the text of the 1522 Luther Bible. Schiemer seems to know that the Greek prepositions in question can be translated with more than one German (or English) preposition. Given Schiemer's mystical orientation, he insists on "in."—Ed.

13 Jn 1:14.

truth through Christ." Here he identifies the law as the first grace and Christ as the second.[14*] When he says that the law was given through Moses externally, having said earlier that the light or Word lives in us internally, he means that the external is always a witness to the internal. Moses is an external witness of the first inner grace, and Christ the witness to the second internal grace. For he says: "John was not the light but witnessed to the light."[15] In order for us to understand this better, take the verse "The eye is the light of the body. If your eye is whole, your whole body will be full of light, but if your eye is a rogue, your whole body will be dark. If the light that is in you is darkness, how great will that darkness be" [Mt 6 (22f.)]. Further, "If your whole body is light, with no darkness in it at all, it will be total light and will illuminate you as brilliant lightning does" [Lk 11 (36)].

From all of this I conclude that God enlightens every person that comes into the world.[16] Those who will not receive this light but extinguish it cannot charge God for their condemnation. It is a Lutheran habit[17*] to blaspheme and revile God, when they say: "I do not have the grace. I would gladly do what is right, but God is to blame, because he withdraws his grace and then condemns me afterward." Thus they make the whole scripture into a liar, as though God is a respecter of persons, more concerned about the one than with the other, giving one grace out of special goodwill but not to another. That is contrary to all scripture. Peter says: "I truly understand that God shows no partiality, but in every nation anyone who fears him and does what is right is acceptable to him" [Acts 10 (34f.)]. It is also written: "God is not far from each one of us, for in him we live and move and have our being" [Acts 17 (27f.)].

"God's grace, his invisible nature—that is, his eternal power and divine nature—have been understood and seen through the things he has made, ever since the creation of the world. So they are without excuse, for though they knew that God is, they did not praise him as God or give him thanks, but they became futile in their thinking and their ig-

---

[14*] Law is the first grace; Christ is the second.

[15] Jn 1:8.

[16] Jn 1:9.

[17*] Lutheran habit.

norant hearts were darkened; although they claimed to be wise, they've been made into fools" [Rom 1 (20–22)].

Paul says further: "God shows no partiality. All who have sinned apart from the law will perish apart from the law. When the Gentiles, who do not possess the law, do by nature what the law demands, these, though not having the law, are a law to themselves. By this they show that the law is written on their hearts, their consciences also bearing them witness. Their thoughts also, which accuse or excuse them on the day when God will judge the secrets of all through Jesus Christ, according to my gospel" [Rom 2 (11f., 14–16)].

In the Gospel, Christ says: "The whole law and the prophets and all the rest are summed up in these two commandments: 'You shall love the Lord your God with your whole heart, with your whole soul, with your whole mind, and with all your strength, and your neighbour as yourself'" [Mk 12 (29–31)]. These two greatest commandments are also written in Deuteronomy [30 (11–14)], when the Lord says: "The commandments which I give you today are not too hard for you, or too far away. They are not above you in heaven, that you should say, 'Who will ascend into heaven and bring them down?' Nor are they beyond the sea, that you should say, 'Who will cross the sea and bring them to us?' No, the Word is in your mouth and in your heart, for you to do it" [Rom 10 (6–8)].

Further, God says through Moses, "I call heaven and earth to witness that I have put before you death and life, good and evil, that you may choose either death and evil, or life and the good, so that you may live and come into the land that God has promised you" [Dt 30 (19f.); 11 (26–28); Sir 15 (17)]. Loving God and the neighbour is the true kingdom of God. John says: "God is love, and whoever remains in love remains in God, and God in him" [1 Jn 4 (16)]. That is why the Lord says: "The kingdom of God is in you" [Lk 17 (21)].

All this makes it certain that there is a light in all people that shows them what is good and evil. Small children,[18*] even before the light shines in them, before they know good and evil, are innocent and will come into the promised land (Dt 1 [21]). That land is not the earthly

---

[18*] Young children are innocent.

land of Canaan but the heavenly Jerusalem. David and Samuel have not yet received this promise, although they knew they were in the land of Canaan. There is more about this in Ezekiel [28 (15f.)]: "You were perfect from the day of your creation until iniquity was found in you. In the abundance of your trade, you were filled with violence, and you sinned." Further [Christ says]: "Let the children come to me, for theirs is the kingdom of heaven" [Mt 19 (14)].

This divine light[19*] reveals in each person what is sin and what is not. God in his eternal goodness, which no one can foreshorten, has not allowed the godless Pharisees to conceal it. They have had to speak the truth, like Balaam's ass [Nm 22 (28–30); 2 Pt 2 (15)], and acknowledge that whoever observes and keeps the Ten Commandments, the Apostles' Creed, the Lord's Prayer, and the Two Commandments to love God and the neighbour, will be saved.[20*, 21] They said the text of the Gospel standing up and heard the lies sitting down,[22] that whoever would be faithful in a few things, to him great things would also be entrusted [Lk 16 (10)]. God will not allow the Lutheran and Zwinglian scripture experts[23*] to conceal God's commandments. I have no direct knowledge of what happens among the Turks and the heathen in all the other countries. Nevertheless, my heart assures me that God is not a respecter of persons [Acts 10 (34f.)], but that he receives everyone and leaves no one out [Heb 13 (5)]. However, no one who has not received it from God himself will believe either me or Paul.

Although the light is equally there in all persons, people's response to the light varies.[24*] It happens in three clearly distinguished ways. The first are those who, when the light shines into their darkness[25] (which is

---

19* Light.

20* Note.

21 [Whereas elsewhere in this text Schiemer is harshly critical of Catholicism and Luther, this summary of the way to salvation is identical to what appears in Catholic and Protestant catechesis.—Ed.]

22 [This line is enigmatic. It could imply that worshipers in Zwinglian and Lutheran churches hear the truth of the Gospel when it is read, but the preaching that follows is false.—Ed.]

23* Lutheran, Zwinglian.

24* Three kinds of people.

25 Jn 1:5.

their flesh), try to extinguish the light in whatever way they can.[26*] This light is not the sun in the firmament of heaven but the eternal living Word [Jn 1 (4)]. The darkness is our flesh and blood. The light draws us on to all that is good; the flesh, to all that is evil. The soul is between the two. Since all of us except Christ have turned with our souls to the flesh, Christ is the physician[27*] who brings us all to life through his Word. Thus we have the will through the power of his Word, but not the performance [Lk 5 (31)].[28]

These first[29] people resist the light of their conscience so vehemently[30*] that they mask it and ceaselessly resist the Holy Spirit (Acts 7 [51]). God withdraws his strength and hardens the hearts of those who wantonly strive against the Holy Spirit, and takes their light from them.[31*] Because they have not admitted that they have knowledge of God, Paul says (Rom 1 [24–32]) God has given them over to a perverted mind, to do what is stupid, full of injustice, fornication, deceit, avarice, malice, overcome by hate, murder, feuding, trickery, poisonous gossip, slander, wickedness, pride, arrogance, swindlers, disobeying parents, enemies of God, ignorant, faithless, unfriendly, stubborn, merciless. These are they who know about God's righteousness; they know that those who commit the above sins are worthy of death. They not only do so themselves but take pleasure in others who do it.[32*] Some people call this light[33] St. Peter's rooster. The rooster crowed as soon as Peter denied Christ [Mt 26 (74)]. The crowing reminded Peter that he had sinned; then he went out and wept bitterly.

26* The first ones.

27* Judah, the son of Jacob, announces the same [Testament of Judah 20].

28 [The editor of this version uses a different biblical scheme to ground Schiemer's arguments. Here, for example, he cites Lk 5 [31], whereas the version in GOT cites Rom 7 [18].—Ed.]

29 [GOT, 71, uses "carnal" here.—Ed.]

30* Note.

31* The reason for the hardening by God and the withdrawal of his light.

32* Note.

33 [Even in the midst of their self-deception, people who do evil cannot say that they have not received the light of Christ. The evidence that they have light is that when they are confronted by their sin, they realize what they have done.—Ed.]

These first people bind up the beak of the cock when he crows in their hearts and suffocate his cry. They are frustrated by his crowing and regard him as their enemy. They continue on this course until they no longer hear him crow, and they no longer fear to sin. They plunge ahead blindly, and no one can get through with a warning about the sin.[34*] These people make the best, most enthusiastic mercenary soldiers, who are unconcerned about danger and who murder, kill, and plunder whatever they can. They are eager to be first over the wall and are effective fighters. They are jolly dancers, leapers, singers, good at cards, good hangmen, accomplished philanderers, suffragan bishops, archbishops, abbots, betrayers, false witnesses! The hearts of these the Lord will harden [Rom 9 (18)]. Concerning this, the Lord says: "If the light that is in you is darkness, how great will the darkness itself be" [Mt 6 (23)]. It is forbidden us to speak the Word of God to these hardened people, wherever we detect them. They are dogs and swine, of whom the Lord says: Do not give what is holy to the dogs, and don't throw your pearls to the pigs, for they will trample them with their feet [Mt 7 (6)] and dismember those who teach them, and they will kill whoever attempts earnestly to teach them.[35*] He will die like a criminal, because he wastefully pours perfectly good malmsey wine into the dirt.

People of the second sort are indolent toward the light.[36*] They do not exactly bind up the beak of St. Peter's rooster, but also don't really like to leave it free. But when their conscience judges them for sin, they are alarmed and fix a hood over the cock's head, which means that they generously allow it to crow but pay no attention to it. The scripture says people like that are overcome by a drowsy spirit [Is 29 (10)]. Elsewhere they are called lukewarm (Rv 3 [15]): "If only you were cold or hot, but now that you are lukewarm, I will expel you from my mouth." These are the five virgins [Mt 25 (1–13)], who indeed are very decent, like most Christians. All they lack is oil, that is, the Holy Spirit. They go their way, halfheartedly fearing God; they are very self-confident but fear the opinion of others. Human knowledge, understanding, good advice,

---

34* Note.

35* Note.

36* The other people.

strength, and skill are highly prized by them. They are very inquisitive, ask many questions, and want to experience everything. These people are very beguiling, for they often appear as angels of light [2 Cor 11 (14)].

Indeed, they are fine Christians, until the cross arrives [Mt 13 (3–8)].[37*] Then they are shown to be servants who are faithful only when the weather is good; when it's bad, they retreat (Is 5 [2]). They care nothing about the grapes. Their biggest problem is that they are prepared too late. They walk too slowly and find the door closed (Lk 13 [25]). They do not pray fervently. In a time of tribulation, they fall away, for they do not truly comprehend their wretchedness [Zec 13]. We cannot deny them a place in our congregation, because they come with calculating words that they should be allowed to grow until the harvest. However, none of them is steadfast. About them the Lord says: "The servant who knows his lord's will, and does not do it, will suffer a severe beating, which will be his reward" [Lk 12 (47)]. That is why a true leader in our congregation must learn to properly discern the spirits,[38] for if he accepts a person who seeks human advice and wants time to consider; the leader will have to let the member take his time. As long as he postpones a decision, he suffers no pain, but he will be like an extinguished ember.

The third group of people are inwardly shocked at the Word of God (Is 66 [2]), as soon as they become aware of the light.[39*] They work unsparingly to resist sin; they pray, often listen to sermons, read a lot, and ask many questions with an honest heart. Although they are sin's enemy, they are not able to resist it in their own strength and are often overwhelmed and taken advantage of by the enemy. But they repent immediately, are sorry for it, and submit themselves humbly. To these God gives grace and more grace [Jn 1 (16)]. He desires to be gracious and merciful to them (Rom 9 [15]). Through the prophet Isaiah, he says: "But this is the one to whom I shall look, he who is humble, and who trembles at my word" [Is 61 (1); 57 (15); 66 (2); Ps 34 (19)]. Like-

37* Seed on rocky ground.

38 1 Cor 12:10.

39* The third people.

wise, David says: "A broken and contrite heart, O God, you will not despise" (Ps 51 [17]).

Christ calls, "Come to me, all you that are weary and are carrying heavy burdens, and I will give you rest" [Mt 11 (28)]. He also says, "The Spirit of the Lord is upon me, because the Lord has anointed me; he has sent me to bring good news to the poor, to bind up the broken-hearted, to proclaim liberty to the captives, release to the prisoners, that I may proclaim the year of the Lord's favour and the day of God's vengeance, that I may comfort all who mourn" [Is 61 (1f.); Lk 4 (18f.); 2 Cor 6 (2)].

Surely these people mourn; they have restless and aching hearts. No scripture or doctrine can comfort them, except God's Word. This fire scorches them and gives them no rest until God gives them light. By this way and means they flee from sin. These know what it means to be in hell.[40*] Their inner sorrow creates such remorse that their outer appearance, in their deportment and speech, does not express much happiness. Since they do not reject this first grace, through which they are made aware of their sin, and use it rightly, they alone are promised the second grace, to which we now turn.[41*]

It is written in Matthew 5 [6:4], "Blessed are those who hunger and thirst after justice, for they shall be satisfied!" That is how they are justified from their sins. "Blessed are those who weep and lament, for they shall be comforted!" This second grace is called justice. To create a person from nothing is a great work of God; it is an equally great work to justify a sinner. This can never happen apart from Christ [1 Cor 1 (30); 6 (14)], who is our righteousness, that is, when his conception, birth, death, and resurrection occur in us. Likewise [Christ says]: "Whoever wants to be my disciple must follow me" [Lk 14 (27)], and again, "Without me you can do nothing" [Jn 15 (5)]. Peter says (1 Pt 4 [1]): "Whoever has suffered in the flesh has finished with sin."

The first light was our taskmaster [Gal 3 (24)][42*] (*idem lex*)[43] in preparation for the second light, which is Christ, the light of the world (Jn 12 [46]). When his Spirit enters me, I am no longer under the task-

---

40* Note.

41* The second grace.

42* The light of our first disciplinarian points to the other light, Christ.

43 [The meaning of this Latin phrase is unclear.—Ed.]

master but under grace. It is the end of the law of works, belonging to sin and death,[44] and the beginning of the law of the Spirit, faith, life, and desire [Prv 1 (23)]. But this Spirit is given only to those who have first surrendered to the cross and discipline of the Lord [Heb 12 (11)]. One has to trim a particular branch off a tree before another can be grafted in [Lk 14 (27)].[45*] Even God in his omnipotence cannot save me without the cross [Mt 16 (24f.); Ps 50 (51:17)]. To have salvation—indeed, to have God himself—is to love nothing except God alone. It is to seek joy and comfort, security and life in the one God alone, and to seek none of these in mere creatures.[46*] If God should let me find comfort, pleasure, joy, and love in him, and then I would enjoy the love, comfort, pleasure, and delight of creatures,[47*] he would charge me with adultery because I loved something besides him.[48*]

God doesn't do that! But he would not be good (perish the thought!) if he allowed it. It is not possible for him to be God and at the same time despise himself. In fact, he is a jealous God, who does not give his glory to another [Is 42 (8)]. In the same way, the more a husband loves his wife,[49*] the less he forces her into unfaithfulness, and she certainly does not desire it from him. If we used to love the creatures and are now to love them no longer, God has no alternative but to trim off the branches, that is to say, to deprive us of the creatures, transfer us naked and exposed into the second birth,[50*] give us his Spirit, and teach us to know and love him.[51*] This cannot take place without pain, suffering, and fear.

It is not that such suffering pleases him, but he tolerates and puts up with it (1 Pt 3 [14ff.]), as a physician puts up with the stench of a sick person when he treats him.[52*] Such troubles and cares have their source

---

44 Rom 7:5, 23.

45* Parable.

46* Surrender.

47* Note.

48* Spiritual adultery.

49* Parable.

50* Poverty of spirit.

51* Note.

52* Parable.

in our unbelief alone. Our unbelief tortures us before it departs. It is like a man who clings to an adulteress.[53*] She abandons him, and he experiences pain. However, no one is torturing him except the unchaste, illegitimate love he has for her.[54*] When therefore God sends us the loss of wife, children, father, mother, brothers, sisters, property, money, or health in life and limb, what alone tortures us is our refusal to believe firmly that it is for our good and that something better is awaiting us in the future [Rom 8 (28)].

An even greater form of unbelief that tortures us is the godless thoughts that invade us,[55*] such as "Yes, but God will forget me. He will not keep his true faithfulness toward me. He is a respecter of persons and won't help me as he helps others." Could there be a greater form of unbelief![56*] Take note of how it thinks, "If I commit myself to God, I will never be secure. I will perish! If I depend on the world, I am safer and won't perish so miserably."[57*] In the same vein, I think, "If I become or remain a Christian, maybe God won't sustain me. However, if I become a heathen, I can easily sustain myself. Or, if I become a Christian, my children will die of hunger, but if I don't, they will survive."

In that case, of course, you are not yet a Christian but a bad heathen, and you will suffer pain until unbelief is separated from faith.[58*] What you need is a good smelting-house, a strong ordeal, some sharp nitric acid, for an uncrucified Christian is like untested ore or like a house whose boards are still uncut trees.[59*] Nothing keeps us from the love of God, except that we do not know him.[60*] For since he is the greatest good, it would be impossible not to love God alone and above all things, if only one knew him [Jn 17 (3)]. Indeed, whoever truly knows God begins so to love him that from now on it is no longer possible to love anything else besides, even if ordered to do so by threat of eternal

---

53* Parable.

54* Note.

55* Godless thought.

56* Unbelief.

57* Mistrust.

58* Unbelief [separated] from faith.

59* Parable.

60* Note.

damnation.[61*] Yes, and if I knew God truly, my spirit and soul would be so jubilant that the inward joy would surge into my body, so that even my body would be completely insensible [1 Cor 13 (3)], impassable, immortal, and glorified.

When someone has been purified from love of all creatures, and of life itself, God will bring about this change by means of sleep. For the saints all sleep until the resurrection of the dead [1 Pt 1 (4f.); Heb 11 (35, 40)]. But we cannot know God unless the cover or net, which is the creature, and which hides the divine light in us, be first removed [2 Cor 3 (13); 4 (3f.)]. The more the creature is withdrawn from us for Christ's sake, the more the light and Word of God shines forth. Whoever surrenders to God under the cross is a child of God [2 Cor 1 (4–7)].

Yet even that is not enough: he must separate himself from all who will not surrender to Christ because of sin[62*] (2 Cor 6 [14–17]) and keep love and communion with all who have surrendered themselves to God.[63*] These are the neighbours (Gal 6 [2]) with whom all the gifts of God must be held in common, whether it be teaching, skill, goods, money [Acts 2 (44f.); 14 (?); 15 (?); 16 (?); Rom 12; 1 Cor 12 (7); 16 (1–3)]. Whatever God has entrusted must be invested for the common good, as we have received it in the articles of our faith.[64]

Third, he needs to be even more committed to brotherly discipline according to the article of faith that speaks of the "forgiveness of sins"[65*] [Mt 18 (18); Lk 17 (3f.); 1 Cor 5]. Whoever has not been loosed by a Christian congregation and accepted by it, that one is also not admitted in heaven. [John says:] "Whoever does not love the brother whom he has seen, how can he love God whom he has not seen?" [1 Jn 4 (20)]. Christ says: "By this everyone will know that you are my disciples, if you have love for one another" [Jn 8 (31); 13 (35)].

61* Whoever knows God and gains love forgets about himself.

62* 1. Separate from evil.

63* 2. Hold everything in common.

64 [That is, the Apostles' Creed. The whole argument that follows assumes that the creed is the faithful summary of scripture.—Ed.]

65* 3.

The second grace is the cross.[66*] Whoever prays for this grace prays for the cross. Those who pray this prayer pray it in the name of Christ sincerely. However, the heathen[67] write the name Christ on a slip of paper and use it to pray with. They have never yet come into Christ.[68*] Christians truthfully say, "I believe in Jesus Christ, our Lord." The heathen have another lord. For whenever one speaks to them of the truth, they reply, "Their lords have forbidden it." Asked who their lords are, they say, "The one from Austria or Bavaria." My response to that is: "Why then do you lie to God, when you say, 'I believe in Jesus Christ our Lord?'"

Paul rightly says: "No one can submit himself to Christ as Lord except through the Holy Spirit" [1 Cor 12 (3)]. "Whoever does not have the Spirit of Christ does not belong to him" [Rom 8 (9)]. Such are the true worshipers [Jn 4 (23)]. Therefore all those who have not yet surrendered life and all that is theirs to the cross of Christ and the communion of the saints, and who have not been loosed from their sins by a Christian congregation, are from the devil [Jn 1 (?); 8 (44)] and the Antichrist. They do not know what they worship[69*] (Jn 4 [22]). They blaspheme, reproach, curse, and mock God our Creator as often as they open their mouth and imagine that they are praying. For God, since he is a Spirit, wants only worshipers in spirit and truth [Jn 4 (24)]. All others pray without the Spirit and in untruth or the lie. For their father, the devil, is a liar from the beginning and does not stand in the truth [Jn 8 (44)].[70*]

A brief discussion of their blaspheming prayer will help you understand better what I mean. It is also a warning to beware of them, so that you don't forget yourselves and ask them, "Say one for me!" For they are unable to pray, except in the Spirit. They would blaspheme and mock God for you, and you would become guilty of their wickedness. So take care.

66* The other grace is the cross.

67 [The text as it appears in GOT, 68, adds, "*Aber die heiden, das ist die namchristen*" ("that is, the nominal Christians").—Ed.]

68* Note.

69* Note.

70* Note.

Now a supposedly Christian or pagan prayer will follow

They say "Our Father"[71] in mocking fashion, for they have not even begun to be his children. They do not want to be his children, and have never obeyed him. Like the Jews they place a crown on Christ's head, put a sceptre in his hand, clothe him in a purple gown, and say: "Hail, king of the Jews!" [Mt 27 (29)]. But they certainly do not want him to be king, saying, "We have no king [but Caesar]" [Jn 19 (15)].

Then they say: "You who are in heaven,"[72] but they are glad to leave heaven to God as long as he allows them their earthly pleasures. They say: "Hallowed be your name"[73] but spit in his eyes and slap his face,[74] for they are the first to blaspheme his name. It is true; if their prayer were not a mockery when they say, "O Father, may your name be hallowed above everything," they would step out and become angry when they heard God's name being blasphemed and spoken against. Sad to say, no devil's or human's name is reviled like the most highly revered name of God.[75*] No teaching of monks, priests, nuns, and other knaves after their death has been so denounced, dominated, and forbidden as today the teaching of Christ is forbidden.

Christ's teaching is called heresy, seduction, and rebellion, so that edicts and mandates against it are sent out from the emperor into every nook and cranny. Here the letter carriers come running; there go the hangmen;[76*] the judge and the civil servant arrive; next comes the prosecutor; and finally a company of cavalry! Not only that: a betrayer is in every house![77*] And even those who don't want to betray anyone talk about it so openly that the brothers of Christ are scattered and killed. Those who don't want to malign them nevertheless say nothing good and excuse themselves:[78*] "I don't do it gladly, but I need to make sure

---

71 Mt 6:9.

72 Mt 6:9.

73 Mt 6:9.

74 Mt 26:67; Mk 14:65.

75* Note.

76* O poor Christians.

77* Note.

78* Excuses.

that I don't earn the displeasure of the prince, for I am innocent." Yes, just like Pilate!

No one steps up and says: "Certainly, God's Word (and name) should not be blasphemed or forbidden, for one must obey God rather than mortals" [Acts 4 (19); 5 (29)]. But they are afraid they will be denounced with Christ.[79*] Thus, when they are called to hallow his name, they run and hide, so that no one will hear it. To this the Lord says: "Whoever denies me before others, or is ashamed of me, him I will deny and be ashamed of before my Father" [Mt 10 (33); Mk 8 (38)]. Paul says that one must confess with the mouth and so be saved [Rom 10 (10)]. But the true children of God when they pray step out with act and word to God's glory, and witness with their blood that one should obey God more than mortals.

When they pray: "Your kingdom come,"[80] Christ answers them: "My kingdom is not from this world" [Jn 18 (36)]. But they want both kingdoms (Mt 11 [8])! They cajole God, like an adulteress who wheedles her husband to lie on her left side and allow her lover to lie on the right in the same bed. Likewise, they pray with their mouth: "Your will be done on earth as in heaven."[81] Yet they don't do the will of God! Rather, they act according to the desires of their flesh and blood, their evil heart, their godless neighbours.

They also say: "Give us today our daily bread."[82] But as soon as God gives it to them, it is no longer "ours" but "mine." And "today" is not enough: they worry about the next day, against God's commandment not to be concerned about the next day [Mt 6 (25)].[83*] They, however, are worried not only about the next day but about the whole year, and not only about one year but about ten, twenty, or thirty years! They are anxious not only for themselves but for their children, not only as youth but as adults, including how to make a profitable marriage. And when they pray that they may have the bread of the soul, the Word of God, today, and God then gives it to them, it comes too early for them;

79* Note.

80 Mt 6:10; Lk 11:2.

81 Mt 6:10; Lk 11:2.

82 Mt 6:11; Lk 11:3.

83* Worries.

they will get it at their convenience, and in any case, it is always a new teaching.

Even as they pray with their mouth: "Forgive us, as we forgive our debtors,"[84] they nurture vengeance in their hearts against those who have offended them, although the Lord said: "Forgive and you will be forgiven." And, "If someone strikes you on one cheek, offer him the other as well, and if someone quarrels with you about your coat, give him your cloak as well. And if someone compels you to go one mile with him, go with him two" [Mt 5 (39–41); Lk 6 (37)]. Paul says: "Do not complain before the judges, but suffer injury patiently" [1 Cor 6 (7)]. They will have none of it! They're praying vengeance upon themselves. It's almost as if they said, "Father, I have a debtor whom I don't want to forgive; therefore don't forgive me either" [Mt 6 (15); Mk 11 (26)].

"Lead us not into temptation."[85] They see that the whole world draws them away from God and tempts them. Nevertheless, they greedily run after the world, never have enough, run ever deeper into sin, and then pray that God will deliver them.

"But deliver us from evil."[86] Whatever keeps us from God is evil, but they desire everything that is against God. Then they say Amen.[87] With this word they confirm their lies and blasphemy. If perchance they had not sufficiently despised God, they complete their deeds with an Amen. Therefore we learn clearly that no Christian should ask a heathen: "Pray to God for me."

A fine preamble, before the third grace begins

In Christ Jesus, God has appeared in his most foolish and contemptible form; at the same time Christ Jesus was himself the fullness of wisdom,[88] because he despoiled the wisdom of the wise [1 Cor 1 (19); Is 29 (14), 33 (6?)]. Similarly, he appeared and entered into the greatest profundity of weakness (Phil 2 [7f.]) [Is 53 (3)], but was at the same

84 Mt 6:12; Lk 11:4.
85 Mt 6:12; Lk 11:4.
86 Mt 6:13; Lk 11:4.
87 Mt 6:13.
88 1 Cor 1:24, 30.

time the most exalted power and might, because he overthrew the so-called might of those called powerful. That was the armed-to-the-teeth strong man, Satan [Mt 12 (29)], and his members. He overcame and bound him and distributed his spoil. David and Paul both say: "He ascended into the height and led captivity captive and gave gifts to people" [Ps 67 (68:18); Eph 3 (4:8)], which means his members, I believe. This is clearly stated by Paul and Christ. First, Paul says: "Since the world in her wisdom did not know God, it pleased God to give salvation through the folly of preaching, but only to those who believe it" [1 Cor 1 (21)]. This is the simple teaching of the gospel, given through the apparently foolish fishermen, the apostles, and even today through working people. This is what Christ meant (Mt 11 [25–27]),[89*] when he thanked the Father, saying: "I praise you, Father and Lord of heaven and earth, that you have hidden this from the wise and intelligent—I mean the wisdom and intelligence of the world—and revealed it to the simple. Yes, Father, because it thus pleased you. All things have been given to me by my Father, and no one knows the Son but the Father only, and no one knows the Father but the Son and those to whom the Son will reveal him" [Mt 11 (25-27)].

The third grace

Now I will tell you about the third grace, which no one may receive unless the first and second grace have already been received. Many people go astray by starting with the last grace without the first two. The Lord speaks plainly in the parable of the man who went down to Jericho and fell among murderers who left him half dead [Lk 10 (30–34)].[90*] A priest came along, who had no mercy on the sick man, and likewise an evangelical. But a simple Samaritan came to his aid and poured oil and wine into his wounds.

To this point I have spoken about the wine. Now I will speak about the oil of joy [Ps 45 (7); Heb 10 (1:9)]. Concerning this oil John says: "You have the anointing from him who is holy, and you know all things. I did not write you as though you did not know the truth. You know it, and you also know that no lie comes from the truth." And, "The anoint-

---

89* 2.

90* Parable.

ing which you have received from God remains with you, and you have no need for someone to teach you. What the anointing teaches you is the truth and no lie. Remain in what the anointing has taught you" [1 Jn 2 (20f., 27)]. About this oil (Jn 14 [26]),[91*] the Lord says: "The comforter, the Holy Spirit, whom my Father will send you in my name, the same will teach you all things and remind you of everything I have said to you." This oil is the Holy Spirit. He cannot teach anyone who has not first despaired of all things human and has raised the heart to God alone. He comforts and strengthens no one who has not first been terrified [over the soul's condition] and alienated from all human comfort and strength. That is why the Lord says, "You have no master on earth. One is your master in heaven, Christ" [Mt 23 (10)].

But Christ receives no one as a learner or disciple [Lk 9 (23); 14 (33)] who does not reject and hate all that he has and follow him and daily bear his cross. One must hope for the comfort of the Lord and sit still [Is 26 (8f.); 30 (15); Dn 12 (12f.); Lk 22 (28); Heb 10 (36)]. The scriptures tell us in many places, especially in the Psalms, the Prophets, in Isaiah, and the Lamentations of Jeremiah (3 [24–26]), that the whole strength of Christians consists in being still. Take note from the Lord's words: it is in not giving up in discouragement but in being patient that we await the comfort of the Holy Spirit, even amid the greatest desolation and misery. This is the true infirmity, about which scripture and especially Paul write: "When I am infirm, then I am strong" [2 Cor 12 (10); 1 Cor 4 (9–13)]. He also says, "Even as the suffering of Christ flows over us, so does the comfort of Christ" [2 Cor 1 (5)]. This is the meaning of Christ's words: "A little while and you will see me, and again a little while, and you will not see me" [Jn 16 (16, 20, 2, 21f.)].

When the apostles asked him what he meant, he answered them: "Very truly, I tell you, you will weep and mourn, but the world will rejoice." "Those who kill you will think that by doing so they are serving God."[92*] "When a woman is in labour, she has pain. So you have pain now, but I will see you again, and your hearts will rejoice, and no one

---

91* Oil of grace.

92* Parable.

will take your joy from you." "I will not leave you orphaned; I am coming to you."[93]

The life of the world has a happy beginning and an eternal mournful end.[94*] Our life has a mournful beginning, but soon the Holy Spirit comes and anoints us with the oil of joy unspeakable [1 Cor 2 (9)]. All eyes shall see him, whom they have pierced [Rv 1 (7); Jn 19 (37); Zec 12 (10)], and he shall wipe the tears from their eyes (Rv 7 [17]; 21 [4]; Is 25 [8]).

It is not a matter of solitary waiting for the comfort of God, but one Christian may encourage another, as is written [Is 40 (1f.)]: "Comfort, comfort my people, says your God. Speak tenderly to Jerusalem and cry to her." James also speaks about this oil: "Any who are sick should call for the elders of the church and have them pray over them, anointing them with oil in the name of the Lord. The prayer of faith will help the sick, and the Lord will raise them up; and anyone who has committed sins will be forgiven" [Jas 5 (14f.)]. James is not referring to olive oil here. The elect saints, who in these days at Salzburg praised God with their holy martyrdom,[95*, 96] could have bathed in bathtubs full of olive oil and would still not necessarily have remained constant in their faith. But the comfort of the Holy Spirit made their torment bearable. This is the oil with which the apostles anointed and with which we still anoint today.[97]

---

93 Jn 14:18.

94* Note.

95* Note.

96 [In November of 1527, less than a month before Schiemer wrote, several Anabaptists were executed in Salzburg. See ME 4:409–11.—Ed.]

97 [In some versions of this treatise, this section that follows is a separate text.—Ed.]

The godless[98] say we drink something from a small bottle, and even the devil does not know what's in it![99*] Those who drink from it are no longer happy and no longer behave as they used to. They put no value on property, money, or life among other people. Now, we are told, they must do what we tell them.

Very well, you godless rabble, let me speak to you! I admit what you say; let it be called a little bottle. And, as you say, the devil doesn't know what's in it. You are that very devil who does not know what's in it! If you want to know, I'll tell you. You prophesy like Caiaphas [Jn 11 (49–51)]. It's true that whoever drinks from it becomes a different person. The drink in this bottle is a beat-up, pulverised, ground up, and sorrowful heart, ground in the mortar of the cross.

The grapes in God's garden all have to be stomped and pressed [Is 5 (1–7)], or there won't be any wine. The book of Canticles speaks about it: "My beloved is for me a packet of myrrh which lies between my breasts in my heart"[100*] [Sg 1 (13)]. Our brother and friend Christ drank from this herbal drink on the cross. He drank it from this bottle, and the drink was mixed with vinegar and gall.[101] He offered the drink from this bottle to the mother of the two sons of Zebedee and said: "Are you able to drink the cup that I will drink?" [Mt 20 (22)]. When this bottle was given to him in full measure on the Mount of Olives, he trembled before it, sweated blood [Lk 22 (42–44)], and collapsed in a faint, until an angel came from heaven and strengthened him. For it is so strong a drink that one becomes such a different person that the neighbours notice it.[102*]

---

98 [The "godless" referred to here were the persecutors of the Anabaptists—in this case the Catholic clergy and governments. The suggestion that the Anabaptists drank something from a small bottle was evidently an official attempt to explain how Catholic believers could suddenly join a non-church sect. Into the nineteenth century, Roman Catholic apologists in Tyrol attempted to account for this phenomenon as a kind of mental illness. See Walter Klaassen, *Michael Gaismair: Revolutionary and Reformer* (Leiden: Brill, 1978), 141.—Ed.]

99* The godless say we drink something out of a little bottle.

100* Note.

101 Mt 27:34.

102* Note.

"Christ suffered in the flesh," wrote Peter; "therefore arm yourselves with the same mind, for whoever suffers in the flesh has ceased from sin" [1 Pt 4 (1, 4)]. "They are surprised when you no longer run with the crowd in a disorderly life, so they blaspheme you" [Ws 2]. The book of Wisdom writes about the bottle: "Eat and drink, beloved friends, and become drunk."[103] "Be drunk, but not with wine."[104] In the psalm, David says, "Oh, how purified is the cup that makes me drunk!"[105] It makes no difference whether it is called a cup or a bottle. The bottle is very narrow at the top, as also is the way to salvation [Mt 7 (14)]. The path is small and narrow, full of anxiety and tribulation [4 (2) Esd 7 (3–5)]. But once tribulation is overcome, the bottle widens toward the bottom. This means that God gives great comfort: "At the time of discipline it is not pleasant but sorrowful. But once over, it gives birth to the peaceable fruit of righteousness for those who have been trained by it" [Heb 12 (11)]. The Lord leaves no one an orphan [Jn 14 (18)], but gives comfort in great distress. This comfort is nothing other than a wonderful foretaste of eternal life. If one searches for it, "he leaves everything he has and buys that acre" [Mt 13 (44)]. There the Spirit of Christ teaches and reveals what can never be expressed by any human tongue [2 Cor 3 (5f.)]. Only they who receive it know it. Neither I nor anyone else can persuade anyone of the truth of such verses, without the Holy Spirit.

Whoever presumes to know shoulders aside Christ, the only master. I, however, and those with me bear witness and direct others into the school in which we were taught, so that they too will take up the cross and enter the brotherly community.

The reason why the godless rage so over baptism, the sacrament,[106] communion of the saints, and indulgences is not that these are so incomprehensible or hard to understand.[107*] For the simplest articles can be understood. Yet they pry into them. And if the articles of faith were harder to understand, no amount of prying would open them. Indeed, if they persecuted pious believers because of our faith with equal zeal,

---

103 Sg 5:1.
104 Is 29:9.
105 Ps 23:5, Vulg.
106 [The Lord's Supper.—Ed.]
107* Ceremonies.

the articles[108] would be even harder to understand. If you do not understand earthly things, how will you understand what is heavenly? [Jn 3 (12); 4 (2) Esd 4 (8–11); 7 (19)]. There are three witnesses on earth, the Spirit, the water, and the blood (1 Jn 5 [7]). The reason why such articles are not pursued so hard is that they are not really taken seriously.[109*] Who would die for the article about the resurrection of the dead, if they could not believe that God would stand by them? And who would die for the article "I believe in the life everlasting," which they have never seen, when they cannot believe in the fullness of temporal life, which they see every day? In like manner I would discuss all the articles.

Simply put, a faith that is learned not from God but only from humans lasts only until it is persecuted [Mt 13 (21)]. After that, faith vanishes as though it had never been. Were I to teach or dispute with someone who had not first surrendered to Christ, as is written, I would be running ahead of Christ;[110] I would be a thief and a murderer [Jn 10 (8)]. For such are darkened in their understanding and alienated from the life that comes from God [Rom 1 (21); Eph 4 (18)]. Such learning would be like providing many lights for a blind person who can never see them.[111*] But whoever has the light, eye, and vision of the Holy Spirit internally, and hears the Word of God externally, is easily taught. External learning and arguing will accomplish only as much as has been revealed in the heart internally. Otherwise Christ and the apostles and Stephen would have converted with their teaching all who externally heard them.[112*] Christ converted only 120 [Acts 1 (15)]. Whoever hears and learns it from my Father comes to me [Jn 6 (37)].

Similarly, no one can know or "become aware that this teaching is from God" except by the Holy Spirit. "Whoever does the will of him who sent me will know whether this teaching is from God" [Jn 7 (17)]. Further: "If you remain in my word or teaching, you will know the truth and be truly my disciples" [Jn 8 (31f.)]. But our teachers begin at the

---

108 [The Apostles' Creed.—Ed.]

109* Note.

110 [This unusual phrase is found in Marpeck's early writings.—Ed.]

111* Parable.

112* Note.

end, put the cart before the horse, and expect to discover and learn the truth in words at the universities. It is as though I hired myself to a goldsmith and expected that he would teach me the craft with words and lectures, but would not go into his workplace.[113*] Or if someone wanted to become a shoemaker and demanded that all the words the master said be written in a book, but would not work with his hands.

That is the way it is with our alleged Christians. If one wishes to know who the good Christians are, one asks whether they have written much about it, or can say much about it, or even make a song about it.[114] John had good reason for saying in Revelation, "The book is written inside and out," but "no one in heaven or on earth or under the earth is worthy to open the book, look into it, and read it" [Rv 5 (1, 3f.); Dn 12 (9)]. But the Lamb that appeared to have been slain opened it. That is why the Lord says, "No one knows the Father, but only the Son and anyone to whom the Son will reveal him" [Mt 11 (27)]. Also: "Whoever loves me will be loved by my Father, and I will love him" [Jn 14 (21)].

Oh, my dear brothers and sisters in the Lord,[115*] I desire to serve you longer in my life, if the Lord should allow it.[116] But if not, I hope and trust that God will give me strength and not forsake me, so that I can serve you with my death. "I won't have much to say to you from now on, for the ruler of this world is coming. He has no power over me. But that the world may see that I love the Father and that I do what the Father commanded" [Jn 14 (30f.)], I am offering myself up. "O Father, save me from this hour! But I have come into this hour." "If it is possible, take this cup from me. But, my Father, not as I will but as you will" [Mt 26 (39)]. "All things are possible for you."[117] O loving Father, you know that I did not begin this in my own power but trusting in your faithful promise. On it I depended. You know and understand what

---

113* Parable.

114 [Perhaps an allusion to the hymns Martin Luther wrote, beginning in 1524.—Ed.]

115* Farewell.

116 [Schiemer was only twenty-seven years old.—Ed.]

117 Mk 14:36.

kind of creature I am: dust,[118] which blows away and does not return,[119] lowly before God, a poor worm[120]—not a person;[121*] yet I am someone born of an ailing woman and surrounded by much trouble. What is my strength? It is all dried up as a potsherd.[122] What good to me is all worldly happiness through which I sinned greatly against my God? "They are like a ship that sails on the sea and leaves no path behind it, or like a swift bird that flies through the air; when the bird has passed, its path cannot be found" [Ws 5 (10f.)].[123*]

Oh, what good is it to me now, that I took such pleasure in the world?[124*] My life is cut off like the cloth from the loom.[125] How pointlessly I ruined my years in my youth. O God, how can I endure before you to give an account of my lost days? [Ps 143 (2); Jb 4 (17f.); 15 (14f.)]. Oh, why did my mother give birth to me on earth so that I learned frivolity and evil intentions from my youth onward! [Jer 20 (14–18); Jb 3 (3, 10–12)]. Oh, where are all those who taught and enticed me to evil? Why did not the earth swallow you before my eyes? You might have alarmed me and driven me to God. Indeed, why did not I myself turn my hands and heart to God?[126*] The Lord has taken note of my last day and has set an end to my life which I cannot avoid [Ps 39 (5); 89 (48)]. What use to me is my blood? The Lord has not given me one extra day to live. If I have used my life badly, who will return it to me? The lion is in his lair[127] waiting for me; the Lord has delivered me to his jaws. The beast with the seven heads has me in his claws and is gnashing his teeth for me [Rv 13 (1)]. I expect him every hour to tear me apart. My food has turned to gall and my drink to myrrh [Ps 68 (69:21); Jn 19 (29)].

---

118 Jb 30:19; Ps 103:14.

119 Ps 78:39.

120 Jb 25:6; Ps 22:7.

121* Humbling oneself before God.

122 Ps 22:16.

123* Confession.

124* Note.

125 Is 38:12.

126* Note.

127 Ps 10:9; 17:12.

O beloved brothers, I had hoped to write some more to you, but when I heard the approach of the leopard, my flesh failed me. I wanted to write more about the teaching, but my heart compels me to write about the grief and terror of my heart. O dear brothers in the Lord, beware of foolish and pointless behaviour; use your time well [Eph 4 (1); 5 (16)]. The days are near. Prepare for the hour of tribulation while there is still peace. I tell you in all truth: unless you turn to God alone, imploring with prayer, mixing your bread with tears,[128] you will not be able to stand in the time of tribulation which will come upon you as a thief in the night [1 Thes 5 (2); Rv 3 (3)], at an hour when you don't expect it. Make sure the Lord finds you awake [Mt 24 (42, 44)], or you will die eternally.

I went in and out easily by night and was well disguised.[129*] I was prepared to escape. But the Lord came and put my wisdom to shame and stopped me. To him be praise, honour, and thanksgiving that he has preserved me and my imprisoned brothers in his Spirit until now. You, dear brothers, remember us in your prayers without ceasing. Imagine you are with us in prison [Heb 13 (3)]; it will help you pray. And I, unworthy as I am, remember your tribulation without ceasing and pray that God might keep you. In terms of my flesh, I am not sure whether I would rather be chased around in the world or be killed soon. It's all the same to me. I have not yet struggled to the point of shedding blood [Heb 12 (4)]; what has happened is only the preliminary terror.[130*] What will it be like when the real battle begins? If I don't fully trust in the Lord, I will fall [Sir 2 (11f.)]. But the Lord is my comfort and confidence. He forsakes no one who trusts in him, as long as we don't break faith with him.

Be strong in the Lord! "Lift up your eyes, for your salvation draws near" [Lk 21 (28)]. Do not neglect brotherly love as long as you have brothers and sisters with you [Heb 13 (1)]. Oh, how you will long for them, how gladly you would carry them with your hands, how gladly you would wash their feet,[131] if they were still with you! Don't quar-

---

128 Ps 42:4; 80:6.

129* Note.

130* Note.

131 Jn 13:3–15.

rel with one another, or you will drive out the Spirit. Bear one another's burdens [Gal 6 (2)]. Let the strong bear with the weak.[132] No one who despises the weak is strong.[133*, 134] While you can, do not neglect Christ's solemn command to wash each other's feet [Jn 13 (14f.)], if you want to be part of Christ.

Dear brothers and sisters, if I have unjustly offended, saddened, or angered anyone, forgive me for God's sake.[135*] I would have had a lot to say to you, but the Day of the Lord has overtaken me, as it will overtake each one of you.

Pray to God for our brother Tischler and his wife, our sister, from Brixlegg, who is imprisoned in Laives,[136] and also for the others, wherever the Lord determined their imprisonment or death. Whoever dies in the Lord receives the better part.

If Jörg Zaunring[137] comes to you, I desire that he should follow my example and marry in the Lord.[138*] I'm saying this deliberately. Whoever takes offence, so be it; such a one is evil to begin with.[139] I commit my Barbara to you, so that she may live honourably. If the Lord summons me from this valley of sorrow, let her marry, if she desires[140*] [1 Tm 4 (1–3)]. Don't imitate the wrathfulness of fools. Whatever is good, do not call evil.[141] Whoever believes marriage to be sin is an anti-Christian teacher and should be banned.

---

132 Rom 15:1.

133* Note.

134 Mt 18:10.

135* Fraternal forgiveness.

136 Benedict Tischler and his wife were executed in 1528 in Brixlegg (in the Inn Valley near Rattenberg, Austria) (see Grete Mecenseffy, ed., *Quellen zur Geschichte der Täufer 13, Österreich 2* [Gütersloh: Gütersloher Verlagshaus, 1972], 257; no. 367). [Laives is a village near Bolzano, in the South Tyrol, now in Italy.—Ed.]

137 Zaunring was from Rattenberg [Marpeck's hometown]; see ME 4:1018–19.

138* Note.

139 Rv 22:11.

140* Note.

141 Is 5:20. [Schiemer is giving expression here to the Anabaptist—and Protestant—view of marriage. He had been a monk whose marriage was forbidden

My brothers and sisters, my heart is the seal of this letter. The Lord has given me retirement from any further learning. I wish to confirm myself now with grace in my heart.[142] Nevertheless, I pray God that he might send diligent workers into his vineyard and harvest.[143] I don't know that I've done anything worse among you than that I was thoughtless, and that I did not take the time as seriously as I ought to have.[144] May God be gracious to me! I commit my spirit and yours with our brother Christ into the hands of the everlasting Father. Amen.

Dated at Rattenberg on the Inn [River], in my chains, on Thursday after St. Andrew's Day in the year 1527.[145]

Your inadequate servant
and unworthy bishop, chosen by God
and his congregation, brother Leonhard Schiemer
from Vöcklabruck, after the flesh,
written with my hand.

On the next Monday after St. Erhard's Day[146] in the year 1528, he was executed by fire. God be praised for his steadfastness. Amen.

---

by the Catholic Church. The forbidding of marriage by the old church was regarded as a sign of the end-time (1 Tm 4:1–3).—Ed.]

142 [An allusion to Heb 13:9, in German.—Ed.]

143 Mt 9:38; Lk 10:2.

144 [Original: *Dann ich weiß mich inn nichte sträfflicher, dann das ich leichtfertig wandlet under euch, das ichs nit so ernstlich anzeiget, als es sein solt.*—Trans.]

145 Thursday, 5 December 1527.

146 13 January 1528.

10

The twelve articles of the Christian faith Concerning the true baptism of Christ

To the congregation in Rattenberg on the Inn River [after 5 December 1527, before 13/14 January 1528]

Leonhard Schiemer

Leonhard Schiemer wrote his commentary on the Apostles' Creed soon after he wrote "Concerning the Grace of God." In the "little bottle" section of the treatise on grace, he mentions his intention to write an exposition of the twelve articles of the creed similar to his treatment of the elements of the Lord's Prayer. In addition to the Kunstbuch version of "The Twelve Articles of the Christian Faith," nine other recensions date from 1566 to 1618. They were mostly copied in Hutterite communities and are preserved in eastern European libraries and a Canadian Hutterite colony.[1] In all of them the text on the creed and that on baptism are separate treatises. The Kunstbuch text has the most comments and explanations, with only minor changes in the text. We see in the author's introduction that he asked for his treatise to be copied.

The preface is vintage Schiemer. It consists in his double affirmation of God's universal goodness in creation and of human responsibility before God. God has revealed the truth to everyone. Even in the most

---

Leonhard Schiemer an die Gemeinde in Rattenberg am Inn: Die zwölf Artikel des christlichen Glaubens. Von der wahren Taufe Christi; Rattenberg, [nach 5. Dezember 1527, vor 13./14. Januar 1528]. Translation by C. J. Dyck, Gerhard Reimer, and John D. Rempel.

1 BSOT, 298–99.

difficult circumstances, God has given us enough light to make moral choices. Citing Old Testament texts that the predestinarians use to argue against free will, Schiemer makes the opposite case. At the same time Schiemer is emphatic that faith and obedience are not our own doing but the work of the Spirit.

In this exposition Schiemer has divided the twelve articles into nineteen. He uses strong, vigorous language. The living Word, Christ, takes precedence over the dead letter of the written Word. This characterization reflects Spiritualist and perhaps medieval mystical influence, but Schiemer is thoroughly committed to the scriptures and the Apostles' Creed. His intention is to add elaborations where he considers them necessary. Thus he makes separate statements on the various parts of the second article, on Jesus Christ. For instance, in article 5, "Born of the Virgin Mary," he avoids any discussion of Mary. His treatment of article 13 includes an extended interpretation of the apocalyptic events of the end-time. It echoes Hans Hut's eschatology, in which the cross and suffering are central themes, as well as Hut's chronology of the end-time. In article 2 he refers to the gospel of all creatures, which he must have learned from Hut (Rom 8:18–23). Like most Europeans in the early 1500s, Catholic and Protestant, he believed that he was living in the last days.

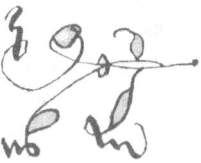

Following is an epistle written to the Christian community in Rattenberg. It contains a nice explanation of the twelve articles of the Christian faith. In the conclusion is a brief basis for the true Christian baptism.

To the elect saints who are of the same faith as we, and who have been scattered hither and yon for the sake of the testimony of Christ, which they bear.

Grace and peace from God the Father and our Lord Jesus Christ be with you all. Amen.

My dearest members of Christ, be mindful of the fact that Paul, our brother in the Lord, tells us that the gifts of the Spirit are diverse [Rom 12 (6); 1 Cor 12 (4); Eph 4 (7)]. If one person has received more gifts from God than another, the one with fewer gifts should not avoid the one with more gifts, nor should the one with more gifts despise the one with fewer gifts. This is what I am writing to you about. I also ask that you would impart this message with diligence here and elsewhere, and to do so by copying this epistle, if necessary, for the promotion of brotherly love.

Dear brothers and sisters in the Lord! Be mindful of me in your prayers. For my flesh is weak and my soul is sad unto death.[2] Pray to God that he might keep me and protect me with his Spirit, that I would not desecrate, dishonour, or deny his holy name, and that he would generate sufficient grace within me that I would not sin against brotherly love [1 Jn 3 (10ff.)], even under pain and torture. For it is a great strain on me that if my God does not stand by me, I will go down.[3]

Dear brothers, do not be so childish that you believe what just anyone says about those who are in jail. For if someone has been put in jail, people can say about them whatever they please. But if you hear something orally from one of us, that is very different. "Hold fast to brotherly love" [Heb 13 (1)]; remember to pray; pay attention to the time,[4] so that you will not let an hour go by uselessly; get together frequently. If you cannot all meet at the same time, let half or a quarter of you meet.

---

2 Mt 26:38; Mk 14:34; Jn 12:27.

3 Ps 69:3, 15.

4 Eph 5:16.

When you read, read mainly from the New Testament and the Psalms. You should know that God spoke to the Jews in a hidden way through Moses and the Prophets. But when Christ himself came (born in due time), then he and his apostles presented everything in a refined manner and with clear understanding.[5] Christ says freely that all of the law and the prophets depend on these two commandments: "Love God with all your heart" and "your neighbour as yourself" [Mt 6 (?); 7 (12)].[6]

Whoever submits himself wholly to God with body and life, whoever trusts him completely, calls on him in whatever tribulation, is patient in suffering, and maintains brotherly love, such a person has no need to go to a school of higher learning. He will find it in his heart and in the testimony of Holy Scripture [Rom 10 (8); Lk 17 (21)]. The Old and the New Testament testify to this, even though it would be good to read the Prophets and the books of Kings and Moses. It is, however, hardly necessary; you can find everything in the New Testament.[7] Everything that has been foretold in the Old Testament is brought to the light of day in the new, and the Psalms contain the excerpt of all the Prophets. Paul says: *"Nos crucem gloriare oportet"*;[8] translated, that means: "We must glory only in the cross of our Lord Jesus Christ" [Gal 6 (14)]. For alone in him is our life and our understanding,[9] through which we become blest and saved.[10]

Dear brothers, don't let anyone know that I have just written to you, but pretend that you've had it a long time already; for if they would find it out, I would not be permitted to write anymore. I know of some

---

5 Heb 1:1f.

6 Dt 6:5: Lv 19:18; Mt 22:38f.; Mk 12:30f.; Rom 13:9; Gal 5:14; Jas 2:8.

7 [This is an untypically strong bias in favour of focusing faith on the New Testament.—Ed.]

8 Gal 6:14; 2 Cor 11:30; 12:1. The Latin wording in the Vulgate is out of order. Presumably Schiemer himself quoted the Bible passage incorrectly from memory. He seems to have connected Gal 6:14 (*mihi autem absit gloriari nisi in cruce*) with 2 Cor 11:30; 12:1 (*gloriari oportet*).

9 Jn 11:25.

10 Rom 5:10.

brethren who have requested this letter of me. So please pass it on from one to the other.

Preface to the twelve articles of the Christian faith

It is a sure indication that one is a child of the devil if one sings the father's song,[11*] which is actually the song of Satan and of all the condemned. They are so haughty that they do not feel guilty for their sins before God; yes, they seem to blame everything on God. He is the one to blame for their sins; they might want to do right, but God hardens them [Rom 9 (14–23)]. He denies them all grace and condemns them accordingly. They are comparable to Pharaoh [Ex 3 (19)] saying that God hardened his heart, but they do not read in the book of Exodus that Pharaoh hardened his own heart. The text continues: "I want to harden Pharaoh's heart," for I knew "that he did not" want to "let my people go" [Ex 4 (21)]. In the same way he hates Esau [Gn 25 (19–34); Mal 1 (3)],[12] knowing about his wickedness in advance, just as in the case of Pharaoh.

God hates sin but not his creature. For it is written: "You have not hated anything that you have created" [Sir].[13] Paul also says: "God does not regret what he has given" [Rom 11 (29)]. Christ says (Mt 23 [37]): "Jerusalem, Jerusalem, how often have I wanted to gather you like a hen gathers her chickens, but you were not willing" [4 (2) Esd 1 (30)]. Likewise, when the king invited the multitude for supper and they did not want to come, they all, one after the other, had an excuse. Then the host became angry and said: "Truly, I tell you, not one of these men that are invited will taste my supper" [Mt 22 (8); Lk 14 (24)]. Thus God hardens them when he invites them and they do not want to come [Lk 9 (5)].

If they got underway, wanted to come [Mt 8 (19–21); Lk 9 (59–62)], and got sick on the way (Is 59; 66 [2]; Ps 44; 51 [19]), if they fell on the ground frequently and tried their best to get up again, he takes pity on the them and looks after them, for they pay attention to his Word.[14*] Christ says: "Come to me, all who are heavily laden; I want to give you

---

[11*] Note.

[12] Rom 9:13.

[13] Ws 11:25.

[14*] Note.

rest" [Mt 11 (28)]. Furthermore, he says: "Whoever comes to me I will not exclude" [Jn 6 (37)], but whomever the Father does not draw through his invitation and call does not come to Christ.[15] Yet he calls all of them. The light shines in the darkness [Jn 1 (5)] for everyone who comes into the world, but he will harden those who do not want to live righteously[16*] (accordingly to the law of Christ) (Heb 3 [13, 15]; 4 [7]; 6 [4–6]; 10 [26]), for they sin against the Holy Spirit[17] [Mk 16 (16)]. And in the Epistle of 1 John 5 [16], it says: "There is a sin that leads to death and a sin that does not lead to death."

God, the heavenly Father, gave a promise to Adam after his fall in paradise.[18*] Christ was to be born of the seed of a woman, and the head of the snake was to be crushed.[19] But Cain, who was born later, did not accept this; he did not want to cast himself on Christ but hated his brother Abel.[20] Then God said to him: "Your desires are under your control, and you must rule over them."[21] Cain did not pay attention to this, and he went ahead and killed his brother Abel.

Furthermore, by the power of God Moses performed great miracles in the land of Egypt and in the Red Sea, and received God's law on Mount Sinai.[22*] Finally, among six times a hundred thousand[23] men, there was no one anymore who remained constant in the faith, but Moses, Caleb, and Joshua.[24] The others did not want to trust God.

Likewise, at the time of Noah, there was nobody in the whole world who wanted to turn to repentance, even though Noah had preached to them for all of a hundred years![25*, 26] This was not God's fault; it was

---

15 Jn 6:44.
16* Unbelief.
17 Mt 12:31.
18* Adam.
19 Gn 3:15.
20 Gn 4:5–8.
21 Gn 4:7.
22* Moses.
23 Ex 12:37; Nm 2:32; 11:21.
24 Nm 14:6, 30, 38; 32:12.
25* Noah.
26 2 Pt 2:5.

their own. Christ says: "As it happened in the days of Noah, so it will happen to the Son of Man" [Mt 24 (37); Lk 17 (26)].

And again, at the time of Lot, there were only four believers in five empires.[27*] Lot invited his sons-in-law to flee with him. God was going to destroy the cities, because the sins of the people were exceedingly great. They did not want to believe him and laughed at him.[28] And Lot's wife did not want to believe either, so she looked back to see if what God had said would really happen to the cities. Then she turned into a pillar of salt.[29] These people had no reason to blame God, for they had the law of God written in their hearts. However, they did not want to pay any attention to God. Therefore God abandoned them to false understanding (Rom 2 [15, 28]).

They also killed all the prophets, because they proclaimed Christ.[30*] They did not want to listen to them (Acts 7 [52]).

Christ himself, when he came into his own, his own received him not[31*] (Jn 1 [11]).

Concerning the apostles of Christ, all of them perished for the sake of the Word.[32*] Their clear cry went forth into all the world (Rom 10 [18]).

Now, in our times, the people excuse themselves, saying they didn't know [Ws 2]; it is God's fault. Yet God in his goodness did not keep the truth from us, as if the truth could be hidden. Had we been faithful in small things [Lk 16 (10)], he would obviously have revealed great things to us too. Indeed, had it been a letter of purchase, a letter of betrothal or of financial interest, people would surely have paid attention. But there was no interest in faith.[33*] They would have had to tell us the truth, even if unwittingly, the same as the donkey of the prophet Balaam [Nm 22

27* Lot.

28 Gn 19:14ff.; Lk 17:29; 2 Pt 2:7.

29 Gn 19:26; Lk 17:32.

30* Prophets.

31* Christ.

32* Apostles.

33* Note.

(28–30)], which heard the text of the Gospel while standing up and the lies of the sermon sitting down.[34]

We have all heard the articles of the Christian faith but have been troubled in understanding them.[35*] In the Lord's Prayer we have learned that we should pray to God for true understanding. In his eternal goodness he would (even to this day) not leave us without understanding. He would have heard us (according to his promises), if we had not prayed so sleepily. These articles are an excerpt of the entire scriptures of our faith; it is no different from what is contained in these articles. Therefore I will (by grace) give a little help, after which those who wish can search the scriptures further. These articles are not to be prayed but to be believed.

I believe in God the Father Almighty

Let everyone notice here that no one can believe for another. Paul says: "The just shall live by faith. But if he were to withdraw" and put another in his place, "it would not please my soul" [Heb 10 (38)]. The prophet Habakkuk likewise said: "The just shall live by faith" [Hb 2 (4)].[36] But the scribes say that when they brought the paralytic to the Lord, "he saw their faith and said to the paralytic," they should really open their ears![37*] The Lord did not heal him immediately but first said to him, "Son, I have seen your trust or faith. Your sins are forgiven you" [Mt 9 (2)].

This is the reason for the foolish error: if we ask whether one may believe for another, we do not know what faith is. Paul says: "Faith is not everyone's thing" [2 Thes 3 (2)]. If they knew what faith is, no one could demand a kingdom in exchange for believing on their behalf, even if God demanded it at the cost of eternal damnation.[38*] They mean that faith is merely something that has already happened, apart from them,

---

34 By "the lies of the sermon sitting down" is understood the sermon, which follows the reading of the Gospel, heard while standing.

35* Note.

36 Rom 1:17. [These repetitive yet disjointed comments are likely due to a copying error.—Ed.]

37* Note.

38* Note.

in Bethlehem, Nazareth, Jerusalem. Or they say that it happened before they were born or will happen after their death. Some of them will admit that faith happens today, but not in them; maybe it happens in other people around them. They cannot account for when or how to believe or even what we mean when we say "faith."[39*]

Faith has never happened to them, so they can give as much account of it as an oak walking stick! They found it outside them but not inside them, perhaps in a dead letter, or a song about it, or someone speaking about it in outward sounds. They think that faith comes simply from external hearing [Rom 10 (17)]. They do not note that the Lord says: "He who hears and learns from the Father comes to me" [Jn 6 (45)]. Yes, they do not know when the Father has spoken to them. It's something that has never happened to them. So I ask someone whom he believes in.[40*] He has a quick retort: "Should I not believe in God the Almighty, even though a Jew or Turk believes that?" Answer: "Yes, you should believe."[41*] It's not a matter of having to believe but simply of saying, "Yes, I believe." Truly, among a thousand people, I cannot find one who believes in the true God, for faith means "an assured expectation of things one doesn't see" [Heb 11 (1)]. But no one wants to trust God unless he sees.

That is their first answer, if you ask them about the Christian life:[42*] "I would no longer be able to feed myself or my children. In the godless life, we are fed well. I would die of hunger if I became a Christian; but if I remain a heathen, I am secure. I would gladly trust, if someone could show me where I might find food and other necessities!" People of that sort are like someone who is extremely hungry and thirsty.[43*] He comes on someone who is well fed and lets himself be persuaded that he has already eaten. Nevertheless, his stomach growls with hunger pangs.

People of that sort do not trust God for tomorrow, even if they've consumed everything they own and are penniless, with no one to help them. You could read them Matthew 6 [19–21, 24–34] six hundred

39* Note.

40* Question.

41* Answer.

42* Unbelief.

43* Parable.

times and they would still worry all night![44*] Indeed, they hear it told in the Gospel how you should trust God and how all the saints have trusted God [Lk 12 (11); Mt 6 (25)]. If they hear it often enough, they let themselves be persuaded that they too trust in God,[45*] all the while feeling the pangs of unbelief in their stomach. They can't claim to be Christians out of fear.[46*] In addition they call God Father but do not know when or how one becomes his child, and they have never obeyed him. They call God almighty but trust the emperor much more. But a Christian surrenders to God [Ps 37 (5, 7, 34)] with all that he has—body, life, honour, and goods; he lets God do with him as he pleases, without murmuring at how God does things.

Maker of heaven and earth

In the wonderful creation of heaven and the earth and other creatures, one may recognize God. Paul says: "God's invisible being, his eternal power and deity, we see clearly in the creation he has made from the beginning of the world" [Rom 1 (20)]. He also says: "God created visible things, that we might recognize invisible things through them" [Heb 11 (3)].[47] Further, he says: "The gospel that I have preached to you is in all creatures" [Col 1 (23)].

God created all creatures in five days [Gn 1], not that the creation should remain in those five days, but that it should come into the sixth day for the benefit of human beings, who were created on the sixth day[48*] [Rom 8 (19–22)]. Then creation was at rest. Yet humanity was not created to remain in the sixth day as humans, but that it might enter into the seventh day to become godly or divinized[49] and come to God [Heb 3 (11, 18); 4 (1–10)]. That is true human rest, a true holiday. Read of it in Paul. This becomes the means through which all creatures benefit humanity, that is, through suffering, in which humans kill, cut up, and prepare them—and the creatures submit to it all, for they can-

---

44* Carefulness.

45* Note.

46* Note.

47 Ws 13:1; Rom 1:20.

48* Note.

49 [Original: *vergotet.*—Trans.]

not prepare themselves.[50*] In the same way, humans come to God, submitting to him and suffering for the sake of the faith. And even as an animal does not benefit humans if it dies of disease,[51*] so also no one is blessed who does not die for Christ's sake (Mt 10 [39]; Lk 14 [26f.]; 1 Pt 4 [1, 13–16]; Acts 14 [22]; Jn 16 [2]). Further, where scripture points to God as mighty, this is its witness, to point to the creation that God has made.

Now in the book of Revelation, the Antichrist's number is six hundred and sixty-six [Rv 13 (18)].[52*] Here read three times six. Our Antichrist, with all his followers, Pharisees and scribes, wants to force us to remain in the six days in which everything was created, and forbids us the seventh day, insisting that we not obey God, thus putting himself in God's place[53*] (Mt 24 [15]; Dn 2 [40]; 7 [25]; 11 [31]; 12 [11]; Is 14; Rv 5; 11; 12; 13 [18]; 17); [2 Thes 2 (4)].

And in Jesus Christ his only Son, our Lord

If someone tells a heathen how a Christian is to live, his first excuse is, "Our lords have forbidden it." But when I ask, "Who are your lords, who have ordered you to believe?" they answer, "This or that prince." Christians obey the rulers of this world with their body and their goods, according to the scriptures [Rom 13 (5–7); 1 Pt 2 (17); Ti 2 (3:1)]. But they obey the prince of heaven, our Lord Jesus Christ alone, with soul and body in all matters of faith. The fullness of God dwells in him bodily [Col 1 (19)]. Also, all power is given him in heaven and on earth [Mt 28 (18)].

Who was conceived by the Holy Spirit

Paul says: "No one can call Jesus Lord, except by the Holy Spirit" [1 Cor 12 (3)]. Since the ruler of this world rages and threatens in such an unchristian manner, no one may boast that they confess Jesus as Lord unless they have first received the power of the Spirit of Christ. Paul says, "Whoever does not have the Spirit of Christ does not belong to him"

50* Mystery.

51* Parable.

52* The Antichrist's number.

53* Note.

[Rom 8 (9)]. We are not the ones who confess Christ; it is the Spirit of our Father speaking through us (Mt 10 [20]).

Born of the Virgin Mary

Christ says: "Unless one is born again of water and the Holy Spirit" (Jn 3 [5]), "he cannot be saved." Peter says (2 [1f.]): "Put off all malice and deceit and be eager to receive the pure spiritual milk as newborn children, in order that you may grow to maturity." The Lord says, "A tree is known by its fruit, whether it is good or bad" [Mt 7 (16); 12 (33)]. Whoever does not lead a new life in Christ and is not one in words, thoughts, and deeds—yes, in all longing and singleness of heart—had better not lie before others that he has been born again,[54*] for he still has only the first flesh and blood of the first Adam.[55]

Suffered under Pontius Pilate, crucified, died

It is surely true (whoever does not want to believe it, let them try!), that as soon as you want to begin living as a Christian, everything that befell Christ will befall you.[56*] For as soon as Christ was born, Herod came and had all the little boys under two years of age in Bethlehem and surroundings killed [Mt 2 (16)]. No one was guilty of these murders but Christ alone, for had he not been born, the children would not have been killed.

The Lord says: "I have not come to bring peace, but a sword. I have come to bring division among people, to turn the son against his father, two against three and three against two, and the enemies will be members of one's own household" [Mt 10 (34f.); Lk 12 (51f.); Mi 7 (6)]. Thus the Jews were right when they said that he was creating unrest from Galilee to Jerusalem. They said: "If we allow him to continue, everyone will believe in him; the Romans will come and take our land and people" [Jn 11 (46–48)]. When they thereupon did kill Christ, the Romans came anyway, not in the same year but 92 years later.

54* Note.

55 [The point here is not a historical one about Mary but a spiritual one about Jesus' birth in each believer.—Ed.]

56* Note.

This same argument was used against Paul when the Jews said: "We have found this man a pestilent fellow, an agitator among all the Jews throughout the whole world, and a leader among the sect of the Nazarenes" [Acts 24 (5)]. That's what happens to all Christians! "The disciple is not greater than the master."[57] "This is grace," says Peter, "to bear sorrow and suffering to God for conscience' sake. What credit is it to you if you suffer because of your own misdeeds? But if you suffer patiently for what is right, that is divine grace. It is to this that you are called, for Christ also suffered and left us an example, to follow in his footsteps, who did not sin, nor was evil found in his mouth" [1 Pt 2 (19–22)].

Further, "Christ suffered in the flesh. Arm yourself with the same thought, or mind. For whoever suffers in the flesh ceases from sin."[58] "Whoever does not hate father, mother, wife, child, brother, sister, and loses their life for my sake" [Lk 14 (26)], and does not carry his cross and follow me,[59] cannot be a Christian. Likewise, "It is given you not only to believe in Christ but to suffer for him and endure the struggle as he did" [Phil 1 (29)]. Note this: "You are heirs of God and co-heirs with Christ when you suffer with him and are lifted up to glory" [Rom 8 (17, 29)]. We must "be conformed to the likeness of the Son." He also says: "If you are without discipline (in which all the saints participate), then you are bastards and not children." "For where is a son whom the father does not discipline?" [Heb 12 (8, 7)].

It is surely true that Christ's suffering destroys sin, even as he suffers in me. As water quenches my thirst only if I drink it, and bread does not still my hunger unless I eat it,[60*] even so Christ does not keep me from sin unless he suffers in me. But if I suffer as an evildoer and not because of his Word, it will not make me pious and righteous [1 Pt 4 (15)]. Therefore the Lord says: "Without me you can do nothing" [Jn 15 (5)].

---

57 Mt 10:24; Lk 6:40.

58 1 Pt 4:1.

59 Mt 16:24; Mk 8:34; Lk 9:23.

60* Parable.

And buried

Paul says: "All of us who are baptized in Jesus Christ are baptized into his death. Thus we are buried with him" [Rom 6 (3f.)]. This is the reason for baptism, namely, a willingness to die with Christ. It is he who comes with water and blood, not water alone. Note this: "There are three witnesses on earth, the Spirit, water, and blood, and these three are one" [1 Jn 4 (?); 5 (6–8)]. Whoever separates these has broken them, like links of a chain.

He descended into hell

You will find this reference to hell in Ephesians and the Epistles of Peter [Eph 4 (9); 1 Pt 3 (19)]. Hell is intimated in the sign of Jonah. Christ told the Jews that he would give them no other sign [Mt 12 (39)]. Yet only Christians can speak of this, when in their martyrdom they sing with Christ: "Eli, Eli, lema sabachthani"; "My God, my God, why have you forsaken me?" [Mt 27 (46); Ps 22 (1)].

In the book of Job it is written: "God will deliver us in six troubles but leave us for a short time in the seventh" [Jb 5 (19)].[61] Further: "I will purify them like silver, which is tried seven times" [Ws 3 (6); Sir 2 (5); Ps 12 (6); Prv 17 (3); 1 Pt 1 (6f.)]. The six trials affect flesh and blood, but in the seventh—martyrdom—one fears that even God will forsake one. Paul also speaks of this, "God has imprisoned everything in unbelief, in order that he might have mercy on all" (Rom 11 [32]).

People in this seventh testing think God does not wish them to be saved.[62*] Let them not leave him, but wait patiently, for his goodness' sake. It is here that one first begins to love God for his own sake, not for selfish ends. This is the highest and last step or degree of a godly Christian life. Victory is at hand! But when the rabid scribes read of it, they speak much of the love of God but know of no way to attain it.

The third day he arose again from the dead

Paul says: "Even as Christ arose from the dead, through the glory of the Father, so we too shall walk in newness of life. If we have been implanted in the same death as he, we shall also be resurrected as he was,

---

61 Is 54:7.

62* Text of Christians.

for we know that our old being has been crucified with him. Then the sinful body shall rejoice that it will not serve sin anymore from here on" [Rom 6 (4–6)].

He ascended into heaven

Christ says: "No one ascends to heaven but the Son of Man alone, who also descended, and is in heaven" [Jn 3 (13); 20 (17)]. Here begins the first article of the Lutheran faith.[63*] They can interpret this verse well, because it is the truth.[64*] Christ spoke it to Nicodemus. He did not mean himself alone, but all those members who partake of his Spirit. For Christ, as head of the church [1 Cor 12 (28); Rom 12 (4f.); Col 1 (18); Eph 3 (5); 4 (11); 5 (23); 2 (20)], sends apostles, prophets, teachers, helpers, rulers, and aspirants forth with his verse, "For where I am, there will my servant be also" (Jn 12 [26]).[65]

They interpret this to mean heaven. But when Christ sweats blood on the Mount of Olives [Lk 22 (44)]; stands before Caiaphas, Pilate, and Herod; or hangs on the cross, they do not want to be his servants, or stand with him, or suffer with him.[66*] They say *he* suffered for *them*. That is true, but note for whom Christ died: if you do not die in him, Christ did not go to heaven for you, and you will also not go to heaven with him. Paul says it another way: "Since you have been resurrected with Christ, seek what is above, where Christ is, sitting at the right hand of God. Be concerned for what is above, not for what is on earth, for you have died, and your life is hidden with Christ in God" [Col 3 (1–3); Heb 12 (2)], and as follows.

Sits at the right hand of God the Father Almighty

Thus says the Lord: "Even as lightning arises in the east and shines to its descent in the west, so shall be the future of the Son of Man" [Mt 24 (27)]. Since I did not see him come, I will let no one persuade me that he has come. We have it in writing: "This Jesus will come in the same way as you saw him go to heaven" [Acts 1 (11)]. Further: "He will

---

63* Lutheran faith.

64* Note.

65 Jn 3:13; 20:17.

66* Note.

occupy heaven until that time when he will restore all the things God spoke through the mouths of his holy prophets from the beginning of the world" [Acts 3 (21); Dn 2; 7; 9; 11; 12].

The things of which the prophets spoke have not all been fulfilled, for they also said that because of their faith a great tribulation and persecution of the children of God would come first. But Christ also prophesied and warned, saying: "If anyone says, 'Look, Christ is here, or there,' you shall not believe them, though they prove it with signs and wonders" [Mt 24 (23f.); Lk 17 (21)]. In addition, Daniel said: "He shall honour the pseudo-god of the powerful, and the god who was unknown to his fathers he shall honour with gold and silver, precious gems and beautiful jewels. He shall honour the fortresses of the mighty—along with the foreign god, whom he recognizes—make them powerful over many things, and lease them the land for a pittance of interest" [Dn 11 (38f.)].

Paul speaks of eating the bread and drinking the cup, which we should do in remembrance of Christ's death until he comes [1 Cor 11 (25f.)]. Thus we note that if he is to come, he has not yet come, and we have the practice of remembering his death; as he died for us, so should we. Therefore Christ said: "This is my body, which will be broken for you" [Mt 26 (26)][67] or crucified. That was the body which sat at table, for the Jews did not crucify the bread. The same is true of the cup. They all drank of it, and yet he said, "This is my blood." Our idolatrous priests switch the order: "That is my body, my blood; eat and drink of it afterward."[68]

From where he will come to judge

The Lord said: "You who have left everything and followed me will judge the twelve tribes of Israel" [Mt 19 (28)]. Paul also says: "The saints shall rule the world and what is above it" [1 Cor 6 (2)].

---

67 1 Cor 11:24.

68 [BSOT, 321, suggests that the implication is: "after the words of institution have been spoken." Schiemer seems to be arguing that Jesus calls the bread his body already before the words of institution have been spoken. Therefore the meaning of the ritual cannot be that the institutional narrative effects a change in the elements *ex opere operato.*—Ed.]

The living and the dead

The Lord said: "The sun and moon will be darkened," "followed by the crying and lamenting of all people on earth," "and they shall see the Son of Man come on the clouds of heaven" [Mt 24 (29f.); Rv 6 (12); 9 (5, 10)]. The crying of the godless will last five months.[69*] Before all this they will lay their hands on us. These days of greatest tribulation have been shortened[70] [Ws 9 (?); Lk 21 (12)], as Daniel 9 [24–27]; 12 [6f.] says; let the reader take note. Further, he says: "When the daily sacrifice," meaning the killing of Christians, "has been established and they sit in the holy place of God, 1,290 days shall pass"[71] (Is 14 [1–20]); [2 Thes 2 (4)].

Note that the man clothed in linen baptizes [Ez 9 (2–4, 11)].[72]

Note the reference to 1 time, 2 times, and a ½ a time (time is a year) (Rv 12 [14]; 2 Cor 11).

Further, the holy place, the Christian people, will be trampled and tempted for forty-two months.[73]

The woman, which is the Christian church, clothed in the sunlight of Christ, shall flee before the dragon for 1,260 days [Rv 12 (1–6)].

A place will be prepared for her in the desert for three and a half years;[74*] that is, God will miraculously feed her for forty-two months. Judgment begins at the house of God [1 Pt 4 (17)]. Understand that this means of the people of God.

Thus the shortening of the days of our great tribulation has been described: time, years, months, and days, in many places of scripture, as just mentioned. If there is someone who would take a year as a day,

---

69* Note.

70 Mt 24:22; Mk 13:20.

71 Dn 12:11.

72 In Hut's stream of Anabaptism, baptism was practised with reference to Hos 9:2–4; Dn 12:6f.; Rv 7:3ff. The sign of the cross was made with water on the forehead (Gottfried Seebaß, "Das Zeichen der Erwählten. Zum Verständnis der Taufe bei Hans Hut," in *Umstrittenes Täufertum 1525–1975*, edited by Hans-Jürgen Goertz [Gottingen: Neue Forschungen, 1975]; MEWLT, 424–37). As a disciple of Hut, Schiemer seems to have baptized this way. Perhaps "the man clothed in linen" is a direct reference to Hut (MESG, 110–11).

73 Rv 11:2; 13:5.

74* Note.

as with the seventy weeks of Daniel,[75] I answer no, for the scripture declares "the day shortened" [Mt 24 (22); Lk 21 (8)]; that is, "a short time will remain."[76] If someone would take a "day" for a "year" the persecution would not be shortened but be the longest of all, namely 1,290 years. No persecution has ever lasted that long, noting that days have been described as years in 4 (2) Esdras [7:43] and Daniel 9 [27]. The plundering of Jerusalem will remain until the struggle reaches its end. "He will make a strong covenant with many, a week long, and when it is half over, he will stop the slaughter and the grain offerings.[77*] A time has been determined, which will come over the abomination of desolation until it is done." He explains: "Right in the middle of the week." A week has seven days and is seven years, and in the middle of the week—that is, three years before the end—the daily sacrifice will be abolished, that is the Christians [Rom 12 (1)].

The Lord says of the grain sacrifice:[78] "I have food to eat, of which you do not know; that is, to do the will of my heavenly Father" [Jn 4 (32); 6 (27)]. Further, it is: "Work for food that does not spoil." Thus the faithful are the sacrificial meal,[79] for the Lord says with loud words: "Whoever would follow me must deny themselves and take up their cross daily—note: daily—and follow me" [Lk 9 (23); 14 (27); Jn 12 (26); Mt 16 (24)]. God has offered us his covenant for the first three and a half of Daniel's years, but scripture says no one will accept it. Listen to the eleventh chapter of Revelation: "It will not rain in the days of their prophecy, and immediately when the 1,200 and sixty days have passed,[80*] "their prophecy will end; the dragon will arise from the abyss to do battle with them; it will overcome them and kill them" [Rv 11 (6–11)]. They will lie unburied for three and a half days—that is, three and a half years—after which the dead shall join those asleep in the Lord.

---

75 Dn 9:24.

76 Rv 17:10.

77* Note.

78 The daily offering (see Lv 6:13; Nm 4:16; 28:31; 29:11; Neh 10:33) is not a grain offering but a burnt offering. But "grain offering" fits better with Schiemer's line of argument.

79 Lv 6:13; Nm 4:16; 28:31; 29:11ff.; Neh 10:33.

80* Note.

Note that at the same time they began to kill brothers from the congregation in Solothurn, Switzerland.[81*] So six days of the week are gone, and one is left (Rv 5). But Esdras says: "My Son Christ will be killed after seven days" [4 (2) Esd 7 (29f.)] This means that one must not separate Christ from his members, but as is written: "The Lamb which has been strangled from the beginning of the world" [Rv 13 (8); Mt 23 (35)]. Christ, as the head of his members, has been strangled only once, and shall never again die. But the slaughter of his members began with Abel [Gn 4 (8)] and will continue to the last half week. Thus has been fulfilled the number of comrades and brothers who must be killed [Rv 6 (11)]. Therefore the Lord said (Mt 24 [21]): "A tribulation will come, of which there has been no equal, or will be," and it is the last one. After this comes the resurrection of the dead (Jn 5 [28f.]) [Dn 12 (1)].

I believe in the Holy Spirit

There are those who feel they do not have the strength to declare that they will achieve something they could not have achieved before their encounter with God. They have not yet been born again of water and the Holy Spirit [Jn 3 (5); Lk 4 (1ff.)]. Likewise, those who do not sense a wisdom [Prv 1 (7f.); Heb 12 (5f.)] that makes them so certain in their faith that no one can disturb them,[82] do not have the Holy Spirit (1 Jn 4 [6]; Jn 13 [17]). But this is given to no one who does not first submit to the cross and brotherly love (and obedience in the truth).

Whoever does not have the Spirit of Christ cannot believe him but believes only externally and will never come to eternal life [Rom 8 (9)]. Many names are given in scripture: as word, light, grace, wind (Jn 1 [1, 4, 16]; 3 [8]); water (Jn 4 [14]; 7 [38]); bread, flesh and blood[83*] (Jn 6 [48, 51, 54]); a door (Jn 10 [1]); a way, a comforter (Jn 14 [6, 16]); a vine (Jn 15 [1]); oil (Jas 5 [14]); anointing (1 Jn 2 [20, 27]); a master (Mt 23 [8, 10]; Jn 4 [31]; 8 [4]; 14 [16f.]; 15 [26]). Whoever does not learn from this master in brotherly life under the cross, to that one the scriptures

81* Solothurn in Switzerland.

82 1 Jn 2:27.

83* Note.

are closed with seven seals (Rv 5 [1ff.]; Is 29 [11]; Mt 23 [13]; Jn 6 [63]; 14 [16f.]).

The holy Christian church

Church or ekklesia is a body of people built on Christ, not on the pope, Luther, or the emperor. Paul says: "You are no longer guests and strangers but fellow citizens and members of the household, built on the foundation of the apostles and prophets" [Eph 2 (19f.); 1 Pt 1 (1)]. For the prophets all had the Spirit of Christ in them. This Christ is the cornerstone [Is 8 (14); 18 (28:16); Ps 8:11 (118:22); Mt 2 (?); 21 (42); 1 Pt 2 (6f.)] rejected by the builders (all preachers). This sign (Christ) will also be contradicted (Lk 2 [34]).

The communion of saints

Paul says: "Whoever declares another gospel" than that of the apostles "is damned and cursed" [Gal 1 (8)]. Thus one does not find the kind of life lived in apostolic times today, but if one finds it it, is called a new sect[84*] and they are killed, as was done to all the apostles. Yes, many lies are invented against them [Mt 5 (11)]. This is a witness to their salvation. Without it they would not be Christians.[85*] This community is found clearly in Acts 2 [42]; 4 [32]; 5 [1–10]; and in 1 Cor 6 [1–8]. They had all things in common; these are the closest brothers and sisters in Christ (Mt 10 [42]; 12 [49]; 25 [40]).

The forgiveness of sins

The Lord says: "If your brother sins against you, go and work it out between you and him alone"; "if he does not hear you, take two others along"; "after that, tell it to the church"—that is, the congregation.[86*] "If he will not listen to the congregation, consider him a heathen. For truly I say to you that what you bind on earth is bound in heaven" [Mt 18 (15–17); Lk 17 (3)]. Similar words are found in John. You see there that the Lord says, "You, you" [Jn 20 (23)]. He requires you first to be a Christian. Take a look, first of all, to whom the letter has been sent.

84* Note.

85* Surrender.

86* The order of Christ.

Make sure the letter is addressed to you, and then you will understand absolution. Note that what is loosed on earth is also loosed before God and before all the saints, here and there.[87*, 88] What is bound on earth is bound before God and before all the saints, here and there. Moreover, no Christian may socialize or have fellowship with them—in matters concerning faith—until they return from sin to God [2 Thes 3 (6); 1 Cor 5 (11f.); 2 Cor 6 (14–18)].

The resurrection of the body

This article speaks of the first resurrection as mentioned, and is taken from the article, "On the third day, he rose again from the dead." There are two resurrections: the first is the new birth in Christ [Jn 3 (3)], a resurrection from sin. Of it we hear: "Blessed are they who are found in the first resurrection" [Rv 20 (6)]. These, if they remain steadfast, will not be lost but have eternal life.[89*] The Lord also says: "Truly, truly I say to you, the hour is coming, and is now here, where the dead will hear the voice of the Son of God" [Jn 5 (25)], as is written in this chapter. The other resurrection is when all who have lived on earth "must appear before the judgment seat of Christ" [2 Cor 5 (10); Rom 14 (10); Mt 25 (31–34)], in which not all shall be saved. Further, the Lord says: "Do not be surprised, for the hour is coming when all who are in their graves will hear his voice and will arise, those who have done good, to life everlasting" [Jn 5 (28f.)]. All flesh will live.

And the life everlasting

No one may firmly believe in eternal life, and no one die for it, unless they have first tasted it. Christ calls this foretaste the comfort of the Holy Spirit [Jn 14 (16, 26); 13 (?); Rv 3 (20)]. For those who truly receive his communion and taste it, for them is it no longer possible to taste worldly joy; rather, they despise the world with its lust, love, riches,

---

87* Note.

88 [In time and eternity.—Ed.]

89* Jn 3:15.

life, and honour.[90*] That is the little bottle of which people speak.[91*, 92] If you are sincere, you will know it. Whoever drinks from this little bottle or cup of the Lord [Mt 26 (27) and 13 (44); Lk 12 (33f.); Prv 2 (4)] sells what he has and seeks this treasure.

This comfort cannot be given to anyone unless he is first placed in utter comfortlessness, robbed of all comfort in creation, even as light cannot enter us until darkness disappears.[93*, 94] To take comfort in a creature is marital infidelity and darkness.[95*] Take note: if one comes to this discomfort and sorrow, one has not learned of Christ and his Spirit; in that case, Christ will not accept them as a pupil or disciple [Acts 9 (16); 14 (22); Mt 5 (10–12); 10 (17–20)]. But the scribes are doctors and masters of scripture, not disciples or pupils of Christ. They have not learned of God;[96] their learning is scribal and pharisaic—exactly what the Lord warns us about. They come along with this verse: "I am sending you scribes!" [Mt 24 (5, 11, 24); 23 (34)]. Notice that if they had been sent by God, their word would bear fruit.[97] A good shepherd knows his sheep and calls them by name[98] [Jn 6 (8:42); Is 25 (Jer 25:4)]. But whoever would know what kind of shepherds they are should read Jeremiah 9 [1–9]; 23 [9ff.]; Ezekiel 34 [1–10]; Hosea 4 [4–9]; Isaiah 1 [23].

Whoever is willing and begins to live as described here, confirms it with the little word: Amen.[99*] But whoever says amen and does not live this life lies to himself and God.[100*]

90* Note.

91* Little bottle.

92 [See "Concerning the Grace of God. Concerning the Little Bottle," Schiemer's previous letter to the congregation in Rattenberg (KB, no. 9).—Ed.]

93* Parable.

94 Jn 8:12.

95* Note.

96 Jn 6:45; 1 Thes 4:9.

97 Mt 13:22; Mk 4:19; Lk 8:14.

98 Jn 10:3.

99* Amen.

100* Note.

Hereafter, as a conclusion, there will be mention of the true baptism of Christ

In the entire scripture of the New Testament, I find no other seal of faith than baptism.[101*] But when one speaks of baptism, it is understood to mean water alone because it's a bargain, even though John says there are three that bear witness—the Spirit, water, and blood—and these three are a unity [1 Jn 5 (7f.)]. One should not be confused with the others, and there is a particular order for them, just as God has created order in all things, according to their measure, number, and weight [Ws 11 (21)]. Paul says, "Let all things happen in an orderly way" (1 Cor 14 [10]; Col 2 [5]).

The first baptism is a baptism of the Spirit, to which we surrender in obedience, just as Christ was obedient to the Father even unto death on the cross[102*] [Phil 1 (2:8); Prv 1 (7); Heb 12 (6–11)]. For as John said (Mt 3 [11]), "He will baptize you with the Holy Spirit." Christ had this baptism, for John saw the Holy Spirit come upon him like a dove. With baptism one surrenders oneself to God with life and body [Lk 14 (26f.)]. Flesh and blood is not capable of such surrender without the Holy Spirit.[103] Therefore it is a sure witness that someone who yields himself to God has the Holy Spirit.

The second baptism is a baptism of water.[104*] We know that, because the eunuch said to Philip, "Look, there is water" [Acts 8 (36)]. Further, Peter says, "Can anyone object that these now be baptized?" [Acts 10 (47)]. Read further yourself. Note that Christ was baptized in the Jordan with water [Mt 3 (13ff.)]—unless you claim that there was no water in the Jordan.[105] But our scripture experts (and other falsely famous people) want to have nothing external. The reason is that they clearly see how we are burned, killed, drowned, and beheaded. In their

---

101* Baptism.

102* First baptism.

103 Mt 16:17; 1 Cor 12:3; 15:50.

104* 2nd baptism.

105 [It seems that part of Schiemer's argument is against people who put no stock in outward signs. He assumes that his readers will accept the plain words of scripture, that Jesus entered the Jordan. The only logical alternative to the conclusion that he was baptized in water is that there was no water.—Ed.]

hearts they support us, but with their mouths they deny us.[106] But the Lord said, "Whoever denies me before others, I will also deny before my Father" [Mt 10 (33)]. Paul says, "One confesses with the mouth and so is saved" [Rom 10 (10)]. The Lord also says (Lk 16 [10]), "Whoever is unfaithful in very little is unfaithful also in much."

Now, gentlemen, dear doctors—whoever you may be! You who care nothing for external things, how will you feed the hungry and give drink to the thirsty, clothe the naked, shelter the needy, comfort the sick and imprisoned [Mt 25 (35-39)], and wash each other's feet?[107] This baptism must not be offered by a faithful Jew or heathen but by those for whom God commanded it, true Christians.

The third baptism is a baptism of blood.[108*] Of this baptism the Lord says (Mt 20 [22]), "Are you able to be baptized with the baptism with which I am baptized?" And again, "I have a baptism with which to be baptized. How afraid I am until it is fulfilled!" [Lk 12 (50)]. Such a baptism is a test for Christians. An untested Christian is like an unrefined metal.[109] If there were only someone who could spare me this baptism, he would be my boon companion! Indeed, if the cross of Christ were not inside the church door, the Lutherans would put no more importance on baptism than on eating meat.[110*] Christ received this baptism from Judas, Pilate, Caiaphus, the Pharisees, scribes, and high priests.[111*] Still today there are children of Judas and Pilate, and those in league with the Pharisees to pour this water of baptism.

To sum up, the water of baptism is a confirmation of the inward covenant with God [1 Pt 3 (21)]. It is like writing a letter and preparing it to be sent.[112] Then you want to have it sealed. But no one will give a seal to a letter without knowing what is in it. When you baptize a child,

---

106 Rom 10:10.

107 Jn 13:14.

108* Third baptism.

109 Prv 17:3; Jer 6:27; 9:6; Zec 13:9; Mal 3:3.

110* Lutheran.

111* Note.

112 [As is often the case, different recensions of the text develop the argument differently. They add to as well as take from the text. See, for example, GOT, 79, as translated in EAS, 96.—Ed.]

you are sealing an empty letter.[113*] Christ sends his disciples, first to teach, second to bring to faith, and third—thereafter—to baptize [Mt 28 (19)]. Likewise, no one waits for a drink unless he knows what is being served.[114*] Whoever is willing to teach children may baptize them, to the extent that they accept the teaching.

For that reason the Lord says (Mk 16 [16]), "Whoever believes"—mark what follows—"and is baptized will be saved. Whoever does not believe will be damned" and needs no baptismal water to get into hell. For God did not permit Lazarus to give the rich man water on his fingertip to cool his tongue [Lk 16 (24)]. Whoever baptizes first and teaches afterward, shoots first and later asks the whereabouts of the target he was aiming for. Whoever lifts a child out of the baptismal font is like someone who shoots while someone else goes in search of the target.[115*]

To sum up, infant baptism has no basis in Holy Scripture. For Christ let no one be baptized who had not accepted the teaching of the gospel—not even the apostles. Thus the Lord said, "Every plant that is not planted by the heavenly Father will be pulled out" [Mt 15 (13)]. Since God did not plant infant baptism, there can't be much of a dispute. It must be uprooted by Christians. Let no one whom we baptize say that he has been baptized twice, because with words like that he is confessing that the old (and new[116]) papal infant bath is also a baptism. We won't admit that!

There are two baptisms, that of John and that of Christ.[117*] John's baptism is past; Christ's baptism is present. We know neither the old nor the new pope! Only those who have already become Christians can offer the baptism of Christ.[118] To make a comparison, no one who

---

113* Infant baptism.

114* Parable.

115* Two parables.

116 Probably a reference to Lutheran practice, since that is Schiemer's main target.

117* The baptism of John and that of Christ.

118 [This sounds like an argument against the traditional Catholic notion that the power of the sacrament is independent of the character and faith of the

is not himself a goldsmith can teach me the craft of goldsmithing.[119*] Similarly, no one can receive me into the Christian life who himself is not a Christian. This matter can be solved without many words or conflicts. Your heart will make it clear to you, if you are good hearted and fair minded. You can't give someone assurance by disputing; it is attained from Christ and his Spirit only through earnest prayer.[120*] The Father sends the Spirit in Christ's name to everyone who asks for it in truth. "For everyone who asks receives. Everyone who searches finds. For everyone who knocks the door will be opened" [Lk 11 (10)].

We have no master on earth; only Christ in heaven is our master [Mt 23 (8, 10)]. We must turn to him with humble hearts, with sighing prayer, with childlike trust [Is 47 (57:15) and 66 (2); Ps 51 (17)]. That's how you experience the foundation of all truth. Without that, nothing can help you, even if you search through the pages of every book there is. You are like a sow in a sugar beet field or a man who goes down one alley after another looking for an argument. Whoever tries the way of Christ and knows it from experience can truly testify of it.

I, brother Leonhard, give a true testimony of what I have certainly experienced. God is no respecter of persons [Acts 10 (34); Sir 35 (16)].[121] He gives everyone who turns to him grace, favour, and comfort. Concerning baptism, there is much more to read: Acts 2 [38, 41]; 8 [12f., 36–39]; 16 [33]; 19 [1–7]; Rom 6 [3ff.]; 1 Cor 12 [13].

To summarize it all, anyone looking for excuses to get around baptism with water would never take upon himself baptism with blood. Never debate with people like that. They'll turn to anything to find an excuse.[122*] But a willing servant does not ask or complain much. But if you encounter a servant who is a scoundrel, he will take issue with something until he can't go any further.[123*] In the end, like a cat he covers the mess he has made, blames God, and declares, "I'd like to do the

---

one who administers it. Schiemer counters that faith is the condition (not the cause) not only of the one receiving but also of the one giving baptism.—Ed.]

119* Parable.

120* Note.

121 Eph 6:9.

122* Excuse.

123* Note.

right thing but I don't have the grace to do it. Nobody is to blame for this but God. He doesn't want to give me his grace."

I write this to you out of love, my God-fearing, faithful hearts, my brothers and sisters in the Lord, so that you take note of the fact that I do not forget you, including in my prayer. I do this to move you not to forget me in your prayer. Be strong,[124] and God be with us all. Amen.

Your servant in the Lord Jesus Christ,
and comrade in the tribulation[125]
which is in Christ,
Leonhard Schiemer

[124] Eph 6:10.
[125] Rv 1:9.

11

A true, short gospel to be preached today to the world

Leonhard Schiemer
Rattenberg, after 25 November 1527

"A True, Short Gospel to Be Preached Today to the World" is the third and final of Leonhard Schiemer's writings preserved in the Kunstbuch. There are no other extant copies or versions. The author's concern in this tract is to identify and warn his fellow believers against false teachers and rulers. For him, the false teachers are Lutheran ministers[1] and the false rulers are the Austrian officials. His hard-hitting diatribe makes use of Isaiah's judgment of his people's leaders.

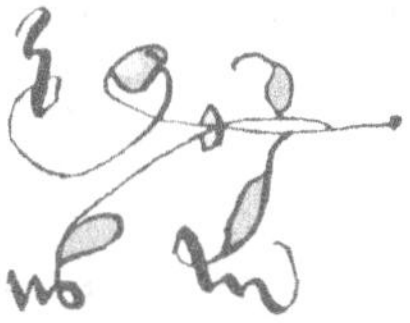

Leonard Schiemer, Ein wahrhaftig, kurz Evangelium, heut der Welt zu predigen; [Rattenberg, nach 25. November] 1527. Translation by John D. Roth.

1 PMLST, 34.

A true, short gospel to be preached today to the world

"Call confidently, spare no one, and do not hold back! Instead, raise your voice like a trumpet and announce to my people their sin and transgression. For daily they seek me; they wish to approach me and demand their rights as a nation that has always done what is right and has never transgressed the judgments and the law of their Lord and God" [Is 58 (1f.)].[2*]

These first ones, regardless of whether they read, understand and know it, have given themselves over to their bellies[3*] [Rom 16 (18)]. Because of this, they risk nothing, but instead fear and protect their own skin. For their own sake they conform to all worldly things, turning their coats to the wind and acting the way people like to hear, see, and have things. In addition, they teach and live whatever pleases them, in order to escape the cross of Christ [Gal 6 (12)]. They do this cunningly, thinking up excuses quickly, and properly under the appearance of godly words and service to God.[4] It's as if one would put a two-pointed jester's cap on a monkey, so that from a distance it appears that it is a reasonable, honourable animal, when it is really only a senseless monkey—one sees this correctly and thoroughly only in the light.[5*] Thus the simpleminded person thinks that what is going on is only holiness, gospel, grace, and bliss, when it is really the devil's specter. They are no longer embarrassed by such lies; rather, for them doing the right thing and or confessing their errors is a terrible abomination.[6*]

2* Gloss: This has been fulfilled today and is still being fulfilled daily among all humanity, including among many who have deceived themselves into thinking that they are also children of God. No one wants to be responsible for his sake. No one wants to have failed. What they lack, however, is problematic. First of all, there are two parties, as teachers and rulers.

3* To the teachers.

4 Col 2:18, 23; 2 Tm 3:5.

5* Parable.

6* Gloss: "Whoever wishes to be my disciple," says Christ "must deny himself and take his cross upon himself and follow me" Mt 16 [24]; Lk 9 [23]. "Truly, truly I say to you, I am the door of the sheep. All those who come before me were thieves and murderers." "So whoever passes in through me shall be saved" Jn 10

They are the other group; they cannot tolerate a judgment any more bitter or sharp.[7*] A new life would be too difficult for them. Frequently they borrow from their old pattern and reap where they have not planted or sown.[8] Soon they demand trust and faith from others, while they, however, do the opposite: killing, strangling, ruining, overeating, tippling, whoring, blaspheming, and living violently in a vain pursuit of pleasure, without mercy to the poor and without any fear of the Lord.[9*]

This is what the worldly government of this age is like; indeed, this is what its nobility and the armoury of its knights amounts to. Therefore the rulers do not believe that God will or can afflict or punish them for this, but merely force their way in with violence,[10] as if God must tolerate their defiance here and there and look on it in silence. For their own sake they gladly retain their false prophets, hypocrites, and liars. They readily scratch where it itches (according to Paul's words) [2 Tm 4 (3)]—yes, namely, the forgiveness of sins without true repentance; grace and peace without true conversion; redemption and eternal life without their life being renewed by God. The false prophets make promises to their rulers and comfort them deceitfully.

As it says in the prophet Isaiah, the sum of both parts—the teacher and the ruler, the deceiver and deceived: these two are the head and tail [Is 9 (14–15)].[11*, 12] They present themselves as fat, rich, full of themselves, and hissing. The Lord Christ also says, it is easier for a camel to go through the eye of a needle than for such a selfish rich person to enter into the heavenly kingdom. The apostle Paul speaks in the same

---

[7–9]. "Watch out for false prophets, who come to you in sheep's clothing but who are inwardly devouring wolves. By their fruit you shall know them" Mt 7 [15f.].

7* The rulers.

8 Mt 25:24.

9* Note.

10 Lk 16:16.

11* The sum of both parts.

12 [The allusions here are cryptic. Isaiah fills out the image: the people of Israel are like a body, or perhaps a beast, whose head and tail and all symbols of its legitimacy are cut off. The "elders and dignitaries are the head, and prophets who teach lies are the tail" (Is 9:15)—Ed.]

way, "Not many wise ones, not many powerful, not many who are noble according to the flesh or the standards of this world; rather, God has chosen what is foolish and weak according to the world."

Where the common masses recognize such things with carnal reason[13] and perceive with the eyes of the body, they see that the head (as the ruler) and the head's eyes (namely, the teacher) wander astray in error;[14*] they are led all the more into all sorts of troubles. For them, swearing and praying, lying and truth telling, buying and robbing—indeed, good and evil alike—are all the same.[15*] They think that just because the abbot throws the dice, the convent brothers[16] are allowed to gamble. But unfortunately, when such games increase so detestably throughout the world, faith is completely extinguished from the earth and love has grown cold in all hearts—Christ has spoken about this [Mt 24 (12); Lk 18 (8)].

Therefore it is right that we should pray daily from our hearts [2 Cor 1 (11)], just as dear Paul did for the Ephesians, that the God of our Lord Jesus Christ, the father of majesty, would give us the spirit of wisdom and revelation to understand him, and enlighten the eyes of our minds [Eph 1 (17f.)]. He prayed that we might recognize the hope of our calling and the richness of the glorious inheritance of his saints, so that we would learn to see and recognize the coarse depravities of this world. Not only that, we are to get them out of our lives and not allow ourselves to be diverted by others from the good or to go astray. We are to recognize and defend ourselves against the devil's cunning; today he is practising it within all groups through great, vexatious divisions and confusions.

Christ has faithfully warned us that we should not allow ourselves to be led astray by their speech. First they say, "Look here"; then "Look there!" [Mt 7 (15–20); 24 (23f.)]; much more, we are to orient ourselves in unity with God through Jesus Christ our only mediator.[17] Ours it is to

---

13 Eph 2:3.

14* Conclusion concerning this word and preaching the gospel today.

15* Note.

16 In German this is a play on words among *Konventbrüder* ("monks"), *Kofent* (a type of beer), and *Kofentjunker* (a handsome youth).

17 1 Tm 2:5.

yield and to commend ourselves to him, to call and plead to him alone, for he wants to teach and lead us, protect and preserve us, through his true Spirit. Aside from this, Paul taught us to be well protected through spiritual judgment, and not to frivolously despise anyone [1 Cor 2 (13–15); 10 (23ff.); 14 (1ff.); 1 Thes 5 (19–21)], and also, that neither angel, human, devil, heaven, earth, nor the elements, nor a single creature can divert us from such faith, hope, and love,[18] which are there in Christ Jesus our Lord [Rom 8 (38f.)]. Amen.

"The curse be upon me, my son, if I deceive you; only obey my voice" [Gn 27 (13)] and do as I say.

Leonhard Schiemer, in his prison in the year 1527

[18] 1 Cor 13:13.

Nikolsburg (Mikulov), Moravia. Anabaptist crossroads.

12

A simple prayer Confession of sin and open confession of faith

Schwaz, 3 February 1527
Hans Schlaffer and Leonhard Frick

Hans Schlaffer was a Catholic priest whose ministry in Austria began in 1511. We do not know when he joined the movement for radical reform. In May of 1527, he and Leonhard Schiemer witnessed the theological confrontation between Balthasar Hubmaier and Hans Hut in Nikolsburg (now Mikulov, in the Czech Republic). Schlaffer, like Schiemer, declared his allegiance to Hut and his message. Since Hut's message shaped Hutterite origins, it is not surprising that the Hutterites included Schlaffer and Schiemer in their canonical writings. In the summer of that year Schlaffer visited Anabaptists in Augsburg, Nuremberg, and Regensburg in southeast Germany. That autumn he traveled to Anabaptist communities in Tyrol. After he left a church gathering in the town of Schwaz (120 kilometres south of Augsburg, near Marpeck's home in Austria) on December 6, he was arrested and imprisoned in the Freundsberg Castle. On 4 February 1528, he and other Anabaptists were executed.

While he was in prison, he wrote several pieces that have been preserved in Hutterite manuscripts copied between 1566 and 1618.

Hans Schlaffer und Leonhard Frick, Ein einfältiges Gebet. Beichte und offenes Bekenntnis; Schwaz, 3. Februar 1527. Translation by C. J. Dyck, John D. Rempel, Gerhard Reimer, and Jonathan Seiling.

Leonhard Frick's name stands with that of Schlaffer in all contemporary copies of this text, but nothing is known about him except two references near the end of the prayer. The autobiographical elements of the piece all refer to Schlaffer. Two of his hymns circulated among Anabaptists after his death. One of them, "I seek not your displeasure,"[1] includes Schlaffer's composition in the same opening section as those of other martyrs of the stature of Manz and Sattler. The other hymn by Schlaffer, "Lord God, my eternal Father" is not extant.

The circumstances under which this extended meditation was composed could hardly be more dramatic: the author was awaiting execution the next day. The reader is let into the soul of a profoundly devout man as he examines his life in the light of eternity. The self-accusations are many, but so are the moments in which Schlaffer gratefully casts himself on the mercy of God. He prays not only for himself but for all who bear the name Christian, for fellow sufferers, and even for the government that persecutes them. Then comes a more stylized (and perhaps exaggerated) section on his decadent life as a Carthusian monk. The story continues with Schlaffer's conversion and desire to follow Christ in his suffering. From here there is an almost imperceptible movement to a meditation on the Lord's Supper; in it we participate sacramentally and ethically in Christ's suffering for us.

In order to make the dense text more accessible and in order to reflect its poetic character, we have rendered it in verse form.

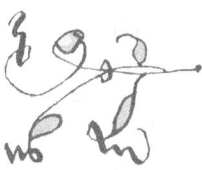

---

1 "Ungnad begehn ich nicht von dir," Ausbund, no. 32.

A simple prayer, prayed by an imprisoned and poor brother in the Lord in Schwaz, troubled unto death.

O Lord, great and terrible God,
you extend your covenant and mercy
to those who love you and keep your commandments.
We have sinned, we have acted wrongly. [Dn 9 (4f.)]
We have been godless and fallen away.
We have abandoned all your commandments and judgments.
We have often sinned against you, you who in times past
have spoken to our fathers through our prophets
and finally through your Son,
whom you made the heir of all things,
him through whom you created the world.[2] [Jn 1 (3)]
You have given him all power in heaven and on earth. [Mt 28 (18)]
Through your goodness in him you have shown us
the way, the truth, and the life. [Jn 14 (6)]

There is no God but you;
you alone are God and none other.[3]
Apart from your Son Christ
there is no way, no truth, no life—
only vain error, lying, and death.
We have refused to heed him or recognize him,
even though true piety and righteousness are in him.

O Lord, all truth and righteousness belong to you alone.[4]
Nothing belongs to us
but untruth, unrighteousness, and public shame.
All around earth's circle
people shout and complain about one another
and their conscience bears witness to their deeds.[5]
To be sure, O Lord,

---

2 Heb 1:1f.
3 Mk 12:32; Jn 17:3.
4 Rom 3:26.
5 Rom 2:15.

our kings and princes, our fathers, priests, and prophets
must all confess to our public shame and disgrace,
that we have all sinned against you.[6]

But to you, Lord our God,
belong compassion and forgiveness of sins.[7]
We have all fallen away from you,
have not followed your voice
nor walked in the commandments which you laid before us
through your servants the prophets[8]
and finally through your Christ,[9] not only in words but in power.[10]
Whoever trusts in him and believes that Christ does not condemn
will be saved:
 that is the reason you sent him into the world.[11] [Jn 3 (16f.)]
But, dear Father,
for so long we neither knew nor understood
how to believe in your Word, in Christ.
In your goodness the content of scripture
has again been revealed to us.
Yet many err and the word of "faith in Christ"
has become a great offence to them.
Those who know how to talk about it as the scriptures show
think that all has been accomplished.
But we, O Lord, enlightened through your goodness,
understand the word of faith also in deed.
Those who have the same faith as Christ,[12] your beloved Son,
whose origin is not human but comes from your work in him,[13]
have surrendered to you, to your will

---

6 Dn 9:8.
7 Dn 9:9.
8 Dn 9:10.
9 Heb 1:2.
10 1 Cor 4:20.
11 1 Jn 4:9.
12 [*Den selben glouben Christi* could also be translated "the same faith of Christ."—Trans.]
13 Jn 6:29.

and to your fatherly discipline.[14]
They have humbled themselves under your mighty hand,[15]
denied themselves, forsaken the world and its lust. (Gal 5:24) [Lk 9 (23)]
They have taken up their own cross
and followed Christ, their master and Lord, even unto death—
he the head, they members of his body.[16]
Therefore every Christian must say with Paul,
"I live, yet not I, but Christ lives in me." [Gal 2 (20)]
"Whoever does not have the Spirit of Christ
does not belong to him." [Rom 8 (23)]

O heavenly Father, whoever is in Christ, your Son,
and in whom Christ lives, suffers, and dies,
will also arise with him in the glory of his resurrection
and enter his eternal kingdom.[17]
That is how we have grasped the holy gospel,
that is how we understand Christ and his teaching;
that is how we understand the word "faith in Christ,"
in such a measure as we have never understood it before.
Now those who believe this and accept Christ accordingly
will be baptized by Christ in the Spirit[18*, 19]
and have the power to become children of God. [Jn 1 (12)]
As an external witness before us brothers and sisters,
as well as the world, they accept water baptism.[20*]
This is the biggest reason why so-called Christians—
members of our own household—
persecute true Christians, disciples of Christ,
and bring them to the holy cross.

---

14 Heb 12:7–9.
15 1 Pt 5:6.
16 Eph 5:23; Col 1:18; 2:19.
17 Col 3:4.
18* Baptism of the Spirit.
19 Mt 3:11; Lk 3:16.
20* Baptism of water.

Therefore, almighty Father,
together we bring you praise and thanks,
that you have so graciously called us
and separated us from this evil world,[21]
this murderous and adulterous generation,
and drawn us into your marvellous light,
Jesus Christ. [Phil 2 (15); 1 Pt 2 (9)]
He lightens our dark hearts;[22]
he seals and marks us with the Holy Spirit;[23]
through him we know you as our true God and Father.[24]
Through him you have made a new covenant with us. [Heb 8 (8–13)]
We left and did not keep the old one,
for no one can keep it without faith in Christ.
This covenant is your law written in our hearts,
where you no longer remember our sins.
Henceforth we are and remain your children forever.

Therefore we pray, dear Father,
that you would uphold us
in all difficulty, offence, fear, and anxiety.
Help us hold still when you discipline us
and do your work in us.
Help us remain steadfast to a blessed end
and joyful departure from this world
in your grace and compassion,
with knowledge and faith in Jesus Christ,
with all patience.

O compassionate God,
we pray to you for all our brothers and sisters
wherever they might be around the world—
persecuted, hunted, scattered, imprisoned, and killed daily.[25]

---

21 Gal 1:4.
22 2 Cor 4:6.
23 2 Cor 1:22; Eph 1:13; 4:30.
24 Jn 17:3.
25 Rom 8:36.

Look down on them and us from your holy place,
your heavenly dwelling![26]
Look down with the eyes
of your fatherly compassion and goodness!
Do not let us be swallowed and destroyed, body and soul,
by lions, wolves, and a seven-headed dragon
with its huge, gaping jaws. [Rv 12 (13ff.); 13 (1ff.)]

Likewise, Father, we pray to you for all true-hearted people,
who grasp the truth through your knock on their heart's door[27]
but are so weak and fearful before tyrants
that they cannot confess it openly with signs and words.[28]
Strengthen them, dear Lord,
and draw them close to your holy congregation,
your poor remnant,
that they may become members of the body of Christ with us.

Once more, O most gracious Father,
we pray for all governments and rulers of this world
to whom you have given and lent authority from above. [Rom 13 (1)]
Grant them, dear Lord, that they may use their power
according to your will, not theirs,
to protect and care for the poor, the pious, the righteous,
to punish evil and evildoers,[29*]
that they may not wash their hands
in the blood of the faithful and innocent,
that an orderly and quiet life may exist among us
in all blessedness and integrity.
For this is pleasing to you, God our Saviour,
You want all people to recover or be saved
and come to the knowledge of the truth. [1 Tm 2 (2–4)]

---

26 Dt 26:15.

27 Rv 3:20.

28 Rom 10:9.

29* Note.

O heavenly Father, we appeal to you
most diligently, most reverently
concerning the hour you alone know,[30]
when you will fully justify us, each of us.
"For your sake we are killed every day
and considered as sheep for the slaughter"— [Rom 8 (36)]
daily they take us to the butcher.
When the tyrants, your servants,[31]
come to interrogate, torture, and kill us,
let us not be so terrified that we fall into dismay
but wait patiently with a willing and joyful spirit
and so overcome the weakness of the flesh.[32]

It is not your will or the intention of
your fatherly goodness and faithfulness
to destroy us, your children,
but to discipline and improve us
as is done with evil and undisciplined children.
[Heb 12 (5–11); Prv 3 (11f.)]

This is to your laud, honour, and praise,
and the glory of our dear Lord, your Son Jesus Christ,
who commanded us to pray without ceasing[33]
and taught us to pray, "Our Father, who art in heaven . . ." [Lk 11 (2)]

O Father, without doubt
this is your most acceptable and pleasing prayer,
if it is prayed in spirit and in truth, for you are a spirit. [Jn 4 (23)]
Give us then your Holy Spirit,
that we might always pray such a prayer in truth,
not as the poor, blind world blabbers it
with many words but without understanding.[34]

---

30 Mt 24:36; Mk 13:32.

31 [The bewildered irony evident in this juxtaposition cannot be lost on the reader.—Ed.]

32 Mt 24:41.

33 1 Thes 5:17.

34 Mt 6:7.

Then you will hear us and grant us our petition. [1 Jn 5 (14)]
O Father, in the end it will be well with us
when we are with you and your Son Christ, our Saviour,
in your kingdom, under your rule,
in your unspeakable glory, always and eternally. Amen. [1 Cor 2 (9)]

Not us, O Lord, not us, but your name be glorified (Ps 115 [1]).

Dear brothers and sisters,
do not let a prescribed prayer influence you to
the extent that the letter becomes your god,
as the Lord's Prayer and other excerpts
from the living Word of God is to the godless
but test everything with your spirit and the scriptures.[35*]
Beware! Satan is more cunning now than before, more desperate.
The fire of which Christ speaks is ready to prevail. [Lk 12 (49)]
Praise God!

Confession and open acknowledgement of my sins to the Lord

Almighty, compassionate, powerful God, heavenly Father,
hear my prayer; let my cry come unto you![36]
The sighs of my heart have made me utterly powerless.
Do not turn your face from me, poor that I am.
Incline your ear[37] to my plaintive voice!
For I have resolved[38] and said to myself
that I want to confess my unrighteousness to you, my God. [Ps 32 (5)]
You alone know our sins,
you alone search our hearts and spirits
for the source of sin. [Jer 11 (20); 17 (10); Rv 2 (23f.)]
You alone can forgive sins, as you yourself say,

35* Note.

36 Ps 17:1; 31:1; 61:1; 102:2; etc.

37 Ps 17:6; 31:2; 71:2; etc.

38 Ps 39:1.

"I am God; I take away your sin for my own sake; [2 Cor 5 (21)]
if you have done wrong, say it; do not hide it.
Then we will judge it between us."[39]
My God, I confess that I have sinned against you alone
and done evil before you.
I have sinned beyond counting,
more than the grains of sand in the sea. [Ps 51 (6)]
The size and weight of my sins has no measure.
If you had not revealed your great compassion to me
and the magnitude of your mercy, I would have to despair.
Nothing could help me:
I would drown in my sins as in a bottomless sea.

But you, Lord, uphold me with your right hand
and will not let me sink.
I begin by remembering the days of my youth
in which you, O faithful God, enlightened me in your goodness
and let me recognize your will in time.
I knew you have no pleasure in sin;
you utterly forbid it.
That very sin which my conscience held against me
through the light of your grace
was the one to which I was most inclined and did not resist.
I didn't even ask you for grace.[40*]
I indulged myself more and more; year after year,
my sin and all its burdens prevailed.

But you, Lord, admonished me in many ways
by your good Spirit, who would not let my conscience rest.
In my wantonness I drove it away.
O my God, what shall I say to this?
My heart is almost breaking.
If I had a thousand mouths
they would not be enough to speak of all my misdeeds.

---

[39] Is 43:25f.

[40*] Note.

Therefore I lay everything before you,
mouth and heart, my whole wasted vessel,
which you created good in the beginning. [Gn 1 (31)]
You loved it; you didn't hate it.[41]
But I have broken and spoiled it and cannot mend it even a little.
But you can and want to do it.
In me there is only corruption
but in you there is help and healing,
Eternal God, even for the most devastated.

I often undertook to help myself out of sin
through confession and the sacrament,
according to the customary annual regulation.[42*, 43]
Yet I kept falling deeper than ever.[44*]
As I grew older I became so conceited that I even dared
to teach and discipline others
while I myself was ignorant and disobedient. [Rom 2 (21)]
O Lord, I sinned grievously
in failing the tender youths who had been entrusted to me,
giving them a bad example and a scandal
in words and deeds, in rage, surly, and inappropriate discipline.[45]

Beyond this, although I was quite inept and lazy
in my supervisory office,
I dared, like Satan, to attempt greater things.
I foolishly took upon myself the vow of the priestly office.[46*]
You know, O Lord, in what frame of mind I did this; I don't.[47*]

---

41 Ws 1:14; 11:24; 1 Tm 4:4.

42* Note.

43 In 1215 the Fourth Lateran Council decreed that every Christian had to take Communion at least once a year at Easter.

44* Schoolmaster.

45 [This suggests that Schlaffer might have been a novice master for his community, guiding novices through the stages that lead to their monastic or priestly vows.—Ed.]

46* Mass priest. [A derogatory term suggesting a cleric who does nothing but say masses because each one of them is paid for.—Ed.]

47* Note.

What shall I say, was it out of arrogance, or on impulse,
or desiring to secure a good life? Or something else?
Outwardly it was—as it appeared—a carnal act.[48]
I administered the office according to custom for a while.
Gradually I became aware of the meaning of the vow[49*]
I had given before the bishop with fingers laid in a book
—poverty, obedience, chastity,[50*]
together with all the other good virtues,
such as moderation, patience, humility.
That you couldn't harmonize such an office and position
with the faith I had, even little children,
let alone adults, would know.
It's an amazing thing!

Take the matter of poverty.[51*]
In all my physical and temporal needs
I had enough, even abundance.
Even in the second lowest status of the order
I had forty to fifty gulden plus food and drink
as my annual income.
But it wasn't enough for me; I wanted more.

Take the matter of obedience.[52*]
I had many privileges, freedom from taxation,
guard and statutory duties, tolls, interest, and service
and other duties performed by the common people
for the authorities or for the common good.

Take the matter of chastity.[53*]
I lived in abundance, eating and drinking, always the best,
lounging around, doing no work.
It was like putting straw on a fire and then forbidding it to burn!

---

[48] Col 2:23.
[49*] Vow.
[50*] Note.
[51*] 1.
[52*] 2.
[53*] 3.

O my God, what I say and confess concerns me alone.
But there is more!
I wanted to earn my salvation with my so-called good works,
like celebrating Mass and praying
(I didn't fast so I wouldn't hurt myself)[54*]
and helping others as a pastor.

How and what was I teaching and preaching?
O Lord, I confess that for several years
I read not a page from the Old or New Testament
in the prescribed order.
I didn't even know what "testament" meant.[55]

Nor could I distinguish the witness of your Word
from that of human words.
I'll let every believer and every scribe in the kingdom[56]
imagine what I must have preached!
Yet, my heavenly Father, even in this old life
your good Spirit would not let me rest.
I was often in fear and without peace—
the work of my conscience—
because of my sinful, damnable, carnal,
and utterly animalistic life, as is written in the psalm. [Ps 49 (13)]

What more shall I say and bemoan
about my disordered and evil life?[57*]
Several times I resolved to become a Carthusian monk.[58]
I ran here and there within the Roman system of grace:
I would go to confession and do—I know not what.
Yet in all of this my conscience could not find peace before you,
my Eternal God.

[54*] Note.

[55] [It is hard to resist the thought that the author is exaggerating his sins and the practices of the church for effect.—Ed.]

[56] Mt 13:52.

[57*] To become a Carthusian.

[58] [The Carthusians were an austere reforming order begun in France in the eleventh century.—Ed.]

At last, in this dangerous and terrible time
you have opened your eternal Word
through the witness of Holy Scripture.
Through the writing and preaching of Martin Luther and others[59*]
I was moved to read the Bible,
the Gospels and Epistles of the apostles.
There I found that no works can justify or save,
O Lord, even works of the law,
which you gave us through Moses—
let alone works invented by humans—
but only faith in Jesus Christ, your only Son, alone,
O heavenly Father.

I realized that your priests, commissioned apostles,
and servants of Christ as proclaimers of your divine mystery
cannot be chosen by people, whoever they may be.
Rather, they are elect, called, instituted,
and sent by you through Christ.
For this office they must surely have the Spirit of God,
without whom their teaching and preaching
cannot have an effect.

I became aware that the Mass, which is celebrated daily,
is not a sacrifice, and that Christ did not institute it[60*] [Rom 12 (1)]
to feed the belly or to be offered for the dead—
that's not its foundation.
A true servant is to proclaim the gospel publicly,
to live modestly, supported by a believing congregation,
and do other possible work (1 Tm 5 [17], 1 Cor 9 [7–11]),
to serve the Lord's Supper,
which is called a Mass, sacrament, or living sacrifice
without scriptural warrant;
it is nothing else than a remembrance of the covenant
of the New Testament, which you with your believers

[59*] Martin Luther.
[60*] Offering.

have instituted through the proclamation of the gospel
of your Son Jesus Christ and through baptism.[61*] [Heb 8 (8–12)]
Through it they are to remember and renew
and proclaim the suffering and death of the Lord,[62]
and what is acquired and bestowed on us, among themselves.[63]
It is that we must help our neighbour and brother as we are able
with possessions and goods, body and life
in Christian fraternal love.

With the witness of scripture I was able by your grace
to assess and understand.
I gave it more credence than councils, popes,
and the long traditions and customs of the fathers.
I turned away from all this, including celebrating Mass,
keeping the prayer hours.
I turned to reading the Bible
and many other writings which had appeared.

Alas, dear Lord, I did not experience much improvement
in myself through this.[64*]
I was no less inclined to carnal, evil lusts
and all other bad deeds.
Alas, my heavenly Father,
how often I had a heavy, lamentable, terrible fall.
My old Adam was so poisoned that he concealed
his malice under your Holy Word and Christ's gospel.
It became offensive to me that I achieved
more fleshly than spiritual freedom.[65*]
Exalted God! Faithful God! What more shall I say?
All the days of my life and being

61* Baptism, breaking of bread.

62 1 Cor 11:26.

63 In this sentence there is a combination of the active and passive voice. At the Lord's Table, believers are to remember; they are also to act out what has been bestowed on them. The church acts out what it has received.

64* Lutheran.

65* Note.

I have grievously sinned against you.
According to your divine justice,
the earth should have opened up often
and swallowed me into the abyss of hell,
like Dathan and Abiram, [Nm 16 (30–34)]
who sinned much less than I—even after I knew the gospel.

The reason for this is that I had knowledge of the gospel
only according to the letter and not in the Spirit[66] and truth.
My heavenly Father, at the very end you did not look upon
my damnable, evil, and sinful life,
and in your pure grace and compassion
drew me to your Son, Christ the crucified.[67]
You revealed it to me—yes, I heard it and learned it from you—
that I have come to him, which is none other
than renouncing the prideful, self-seeking, arrogant world,[68*]
being released from all creatures, [1 Cor 7 (29–31); 4 (2) Esd 16 (42–45)]
denying myself[69] to take up my cross and follow Christ
(Lk 9 [23]; Mt 10 [38]).
That is what faith in Christ means. Through it,
not through works of the law,[70] as Peter says,
the hearts of believers are purified.[71]

Ah! Dear Lord, that is a heavy,
unbearable burden for the old Adam.
To the world it is a foolish and silly
teaching and sermon. [1 Cor 1 (23–25)].
To our Jews, that is, those who confess
you, your Word, and your gospel with their mouth,
it is an irritation, but to us believers
it is divine power and wisdom. [Mt 11 (25f.)]

---

66 Rom 7:6; 2 Cor 3:6f.
67 Jn 6:44.
68* Surrender.
69 Mt 16:24; Mk 8:34; Lk 9:23.
70 Gal 2:16.
71 Acts 15:9.

Beside that, I made many cries and pleas to you with these words,
"Teach me to do your will, for you are my God." [Ps 143 (10)]
I received water baptism as a witness,
according to the command and institution of Christ (Mt 28 [19]),[72*]
in the name of the Father, the Son, and the Holy Spirit,
expressed in these words,
"I believe that Jesus Christ is a Son of the living God," [Acts 8 (37)]
even as you, my God, know every heart. [Jer 17 (10); Rv 2 (23)]

Then arose what was to happen (Mt 4 [1–11]).
You left me in the nest for nine weeks
(and I was imprisoned for the same length of time)
and took care of me in discipline. [Heb 12 (6–11)]
I fled persecution starting on the day of Peter and Paul.[73] [Jn 15 (20)]
Like a lost sheep in the desert of this terrible world[74*]
I wandered here and there as a lost lamb [Heb 11 (38)]
until Nicholas Day[75]
when I was captured here in Schwaz[76*]
that I might turn my poor soul to the faithful shepherd.[77]
I found him! I heard his voice
and in his strength I followed it. [Jn 10 (3–5, 12f.); 4 (2) Esd 2 (34)]
It is your divine power and not mine.
I never want to hear a stranger's voice again.
O Lord, the hireling and day labourer
do not own the sheep; they do not seek what is Christ's
but what is theirs.
They are enemies of the cross of Christ.
Their belly is their god and their end is perdition! [Phil 3 (18f.)]
They come along with many smooth words.[78*]
Outwardly they appear well mannered,

[72*] Christian baptism.
[73] 29 June 1527.
[74*] Note.
[75] 6 December 1527.
[76*] Captured.
[77] 1 Pt 2:25.
[78*] Note.

saying I am right in everything except outward water baptism.
Dear God, I fear that if I deny you
in small matters and become faithless,
I will deny you in large matters. [Lk 16 (10)]
I did not consent to them.
I have been sustained in the comfort and sure promise
that no lamb you have given Christ
can be torn from his hands. [Jn 17 (12)]
He calls all who are heavy laden to come to him;
he will sustain and help them,
for his burden is light and his yoke is sweet. [Mt 11 (28f.)]

He is the life, light, way, truth,
righteousness, and holiness.[79] [Jn 12 (46); 14 (6)]
He is the shepherd,[80] the door to the sheep barn.[81]
He is the reconciler[82] and mediator[83] between you and us,
the spiritual guide and pastor,[84]
food for eternal life.[85]
Whatever we need we must ask and receive
through him and in his name. [Jn 16 (23)]

Through him we have become your children,
beloved, accepted, still becoming.
If we believe in him, you will withhold nothing from us
that would serve your glory and Christ's glory.

This is the goodness, the paternal faithfulness,
that you have shown me, poor soul that I am, in grace.
This I believe;
therefore I have declared it! [Ps 116 (10, 12–14); 2 Cor 4 (13)]
I had been degraded and humiliated.

---

79 1 Cor 1:30.
80 Jn 10:12.
81 Jn 10:7, 9.
82 Eph 2:16; 1 Jn 2:2; 4:10.
83 1 Tm 2:5.
84 1 Pt 2:25.
85 Jn 6:27.

What must I repay you, Lord, for all you have done for me?
I will take up the cup of salvation and call on your name;[86*]
I will give you an offering freely and confess your name. [Ps 56 (54:6)]
I will pay my vow in the presence of all your people.
Those who fear you will see that I hoped in your Word
and will rejoice.[87]

Therefore, Almighty God, manifest your power and benevolence
in my weak, earthly vessel, in which you have hidden
the precious treasure[88] which you showed me—and which I found!
Let it cost what it will— [Mt 13 (44)]
even my weak body
and my miserable life—for I have nothing else.

O my God, what needs and blows I suffer here.[89*]
It is only now that I recognize the immense damage
Adam's fall worked in me. [Gal 5 (16f.)]
The great struggle between flesh and spirit arises,
which none can imagine unless they've experienced it.
O my God, what will happen to me in my hour of greatest need?
So, Lord, I lay all my worry, fear, and need upon you.
Thus far I have mightily known your help.
I hope you will not take it from me in the end
but in my greatest need and weakness
show me your help and strength.
In my dismay and shame show me praise and glory;[90*]
in my time of death reveal eternal life to me.
Accomplish this in all who yield themselves
to you in the faith of Christ,
in those who persist in your will and work to the end
and thus are saved.

86* Note.

87 Ps 119:74.

88 2 Cor 4:7.

89* Note.

90* Note.

It has been determined in your divine counsel from eternity
and verified by scripture, that the whole Christ,
both head and members, must suffer.
For the Lamb has suffered and been killed
from the beginning of the world [Rv 13 (8)].
Christ remains with us—I do not speak physically here—
to the end of the world [Mt 28 (20)].
"For we are members of his body, of his flesh and of his bone.
And the two shall become one flesh.
That is a great mystery in Christ and his congregation." [Eph 5 (29–32)]
When Christ the head lived in a mortal body, but without sin,
he suffered and was killed. [1 Pt 2 (21f.) and 4 (1)]

If we are now his members and with him a whole body,
then the members must follow the head everywhere.
Whoever does not follow is not a member of the body. [Mt 10 (38)]
But most of the suffering of the whole body
happens to the head.[91*] [Jn 15 (20)]
That is why Christ sweated blood in his prayer to the Father
on the Mount of Olives. [Lk 22 (44)]
O my God,
who has ever read, seen, or heard
of a suffering, martyred, dying person
who sweated blood that flowed from him down to the ground,
save Christ alone?

O Lord, strengthen my faith! [Lk 17 (5)]
As a result I firmly believe that when Christ was sweating blood,
he physically felt
the torment, martyrdom, and execution of all his members
and those who believed in him
from the beginning to the end of the world.[92] [Gn 4 (8ff.); Mt 23 (35)]
That was utter anguish for him.

91* Note.

92 [In his torment, Christ took the torment of all his followers on himself. Part of his anguish was that he was conscious of all these torments borne in his name.—Ed.]

For that reason it is that much more bearable and tolerable
for a true Christian to suffer and die
as one of the members of his whole body.[93*]

For just as no Christian lives to himself,
none suffers and dies to himself
but only to the Lord;
whether he is alive or dead it is to the Lord. [Rom 14 (7f.)]
O heavenly Father, that is my present consolation.
In this, Christ will strengthen and preserve me
with the power and force you gave him.
Gracious God, let me never doubt this,
for he is the rock and foundation[94]
on which my spiritual brother and fellow prisoner Leonhard
and I joyfully place our hope.
This is what those who are wise and taught by God also do,[95]
who know that such a building
must be able to withstand a great force
and exceedingly turbulent weather[96]
such as lightning, hail, torrential rains
with all the force of hell.[97]

But by the grace of God they
will not be able to overpower us,
in the same way that next Monday[98] in Rattenberg[99*]
our dear brother Leonhard Schiemer
will demonstrate in a powerful way,
along with many others throughout this godless and blind world,
what still happens in our time. [Rv 6 (11)]
For no one can hinder and oppress

93* Note.

94 Ps 18:2; 31:3f.

95 1 Thes 4:9.

96 Mt 7:24f.; Lk 6:48.

97 Mt 16:18.

98 [Literally, "the Monday after Erhardi"; that is, 13 January 1528—Ed.]

99* Took place in the year 1528.

your Word and your work, O Mighty God.[100*]
Those who are highly regarded by the world
want to demolish and utterly destroy your Word,
but what they do ends up promoting and directing it.
You are wonderful, O my God, in your saints![101]

Therefore it will not come about with sleeping, living comfortably,
or going about idly, laughing madly,
singing, blathering on, ringing bells, burning candles.[102*]
If one wants to be a Christian,
it means risking one's body and life.

Yes, to eat the flesh of Christ and drink his blood
is a tough meal.
Therefore it is also a tough saying for them,
just as it was for his disciples when he said,
"Unless you eat my flesh and drink my blood,
you will have no life in you." [Jn 6 (53)]
Therefore many were troubled, deceived themselves,
and no longer went about with him.[103*] [Jn 6 (66)]

This is what the entire so-called Christendom,
along with their scribes and Pharisees do to this very day.[104*]
They write copious commentaries
on the words of our Lord in John,
and they desire to receive the body of Christ
or his flesh in bread and his blood in a cup.[105*]
It's not tough to eat and drink daily,
in principle it's a good thing to do;
it makes for a good, peaceful day and life

100* Note.
101 Ps 68:35, Vulg.
102* Note.
103* Papist, Lutheran.
104* Note.
105* Lutheran.

to eat plenty and to drink in complete ecstasy—
that's the pinnacle of worthiness.[106*]

But those who only enjoy it once a year
and in one kind,[107] as they call it,
remain in their fleshly lives from year to year,
worldly minded until they reach the end,
even though Christ said:
"Whoever eats my flesh and drinks my blood
will remain in me and I in him,
and as my Father sent me to live
and I live by the will of my Father,
whoever eats my flesh will live according to my will." [Jn 6 (56f.)]

Here one plainly sees that eating and drinking is another,
new life, different from the way the world lives.
That is, one ought to live in suffering, persecution, and death
for the sake of the Lord,[108*]
as it is shown throughout all the blessed scripture.
For everyone who wants to live a life of blessedness
must suffer persecution (2 Tm 3 [12]; Acts 14 [22]).

Our scribes ascribe this passage
to the bread and wine of the Lord's Supper. [Jn 6]
And there are even several of them
who say that it should not at all be understood
as eating and drinking at supper[109*]
but only spiritually, as Luther suggests in his New Testament.[110*, 111]

[106*] Papist.

[107] ["Kind" is the term used to describe the elements. By the twelfth century, lay people were allowed to receive only the bread in Communion. It was feared that if they received the cup, they might spill it, and that would profane the blood of Christ.—Ed.

[108*] Note.

[109*] Note.

[110*] In a gloss by Luther.

[111] [Here the author summarizes the profound debate that took place concerning the Lord's Supper between Catholics and Protestants, and increasingly among

And in this particular matter he is not in agreement with others.
Each faction that presumes to be the Christian church
wants to persuade us to believe them.[112*]
They are never in fuller agreement
than over spilling the blood of Christians.
Some of them wash their hands,
just like Pilate. [Mt 26 (27:24)]

Some of them do not want to go into the pretorium
to avoid becoming contaminated,
leaving it up to Pilate to reply;
they wash their hands and want
the emperor to apportion the blame.

He issued a mandate
that no one should be called a king of the Jews.[113*]
Pilate and Herod became united as one
and in this way became friends, [Lk 23 (12)]
even as they remained each other's enemies in their hearts[114]
and daily held fast to their grudge against each other.
Enough said; these words are superfluous.
May God enlighten them.
We ask this sincerely. Amen.

Let's hear what the Lord explains and says in John 6:
"Anyone who comes to me will not hunger,
and whoever believes in me will not thirst." [Jn 6 (35)]
"Blessed are those who hunger and thirst for righteousness,

---

the various Reformation movements. The early Luther, for example, in "The Babylonian Captivity of the Church," emphasized the spiritual presence; by the mid-1520s he began balancing this emphasis with a sacramental one.—Ed.] Luther's comment next to Jn 6:52–58 in his 1522 translation of the New Testament (called the September Testament) reads: "This chapter does not speak about the sacrament of the bread and wine but about spiritual eating, that is, the belief that Christ as God and man poured out his blood for us."

112* Note.

113* Note.

114 Lk 23:1–11.

as they are worthy of God." [Mt 5 (6)]
For coming relieves hunger, and faith quenches thirst
as one hears from the Lord.[115*]

But in the following it is shown how one comes to Christ
and believes in Christ.
He says furthermore, "If anyone would come to me,
let him deny himself, take up his cross daily, and follow me.
For anyone who gives up his life for my sake
and the sake of the gospel will keep it,"
for and in eternal life.[116*] [Lk 9 (23); 14 (26f.); Mt 10 (38); Jn 12 (25)]

Thus, if we eat the flesh of Christ and drink his blood,
then in death we offer our body—that is, the flesh—
and shed our blood
for the sake of his name, word, and command
(in the small matters as well as in the big ones).

For once again it is no longer our flesh or body,
nor is it our blood, but Christ's.
For that reason he said to Paul (Acts 9 [4]):
"Saul, Saul, why do you persecute me?"[117*]
It is as though he said,
"Why do you kill my flesh
and why do you shed my blood?"
For to put it simply, eating the flesh of Christ
and drinking his blood
happens through no other means than faith,
which is an act and gift from God, that is in us. [Eph 2 (8)]
We want in every sense to become embodied,
participating, conforming—one entity
with Christ in his life,
suffering and death according to the flesh—

115* Note.

116* Gloss: The world wants to have and confess Christ only in the form of a gift but denies him in the form of suffering.

117* Note.

becoming members and heirs of the resurrection
and glory of his kingdom. [Rom 8 (17)]
I can understand it in no other manner
without making all of scripture false,
which is not allowable.[118*]

With Christ we would like to lie in Mary's lap
and receive the offering from the wise men, [Mt 2 (11); Lk 2 (7)]
eat with the tax collectors of this world , [Lk 5 (29)]
with the rulers and princes,
and attend the wedding. [Jn 2 (2)]

But to flee to Egypt and leave everything behind, [Mt 2 (13f.)]
to go to the Mount of Olives,
to sweat in anguish (Lk 22 [39–46]),
suffer imprisonment, mockery, and be killed—
not everyone is up to it.

We would gladly have Communion with him,
and Easter, and foot washing. [Jn 13 (4f.)]
But far be it from us to follow his example
and love one another unto death, as Christ did for us!

However, O merciful Father,
by your grace we have observed the Lord's Supper
with our brothers and sisters to such an extent,
that we became one bread and one body, though we are many.
After that we are all one bread and one body,
if we eat of one bread
and drink from one drinking vessel or cup.
[1 Cor 10 (16–22); 11 (20–34); and 12 (12–31)]

We have accepted the Lord's word about his supper,
where it says,
"In the night when Jesus was betrayed, he took the bread,
gave thanks, broke it apart, and divided it,
giving it to his disciples, saying, 'Eat!'"

[118*] Note.

And they ate the bread. [Mt 26 (26–28); Lk 22(19f.)]
Afterward he said,
"That is my body, [Mk 14 (22–24)]
which will be offered for you;
do this in remembrance of me."

That is, consider that you have the duty to do this
if necessity demands it
for the sake of my name, word, and command,
then also you yourselves
will offer your bodies for another
out of brotherly love even unto death, [1 Jn 3 (16)]
as you have demonstrated among yourselves,
and to which you have consented.
And never forget that!

For that reason he said:
"Do this in remembrance of me, as often as you do this"
and make of this a reminder
during the time that you are weak in faith,
love and understanding
and you will be strengthened.

"Likewise with the cup" (or the drinking vessel),
"he took it, blessed it" (or gave thanks)
"and said: 'Take it and all of you it.'"
And they all drank it.[119]
After that he said:
"That is the cup of the new testament in my blood,
that will be poured out for you."
"Do that as often as you drink," (as Paul said),
"in remembrance of me.
For as often as you eat from this bread and drink from this cup,
you proclaim the Lord's death until he comes." [1 Cor 11 (26)]

[119] Mk 14:23.

That is, just as Christ poured himself out
for you in his death and blood,
he obtained remission of your sins
and reconciled you with the Father,
whose enemy you were,
washing and purifying your evil conscience. [Heb 10 (22)]

Thus you should always be willing and ready
to pour out your blood
as a fortification and strengthening of your beliefs
and to demonstrate untainted brotherly love.
That is a hard trial.

Concerning it Paul says
that everyone should examine himself beforehand, [1 Cor 11 (28)]
and that whenever one eats of this bread and drinks of this cup,
in that way one will not be guilty of the body and blood of Christ,
that is, that the body of Christ will not be offered to no purpose
and his blood will not be offered and poured out in vain,
as it was for Judas.

For if people do not test themselves to such an extent
and discern the mind of Christ in themselves [Phil 2 (5)]
and do not perceive or find such a faith and love in themselves
—or even desire to have faith and love in their hearts—
they eat judgment upon themselves by doing that,
since they do not distinguish the body of the Lord.

That is, they eat the bread just like other bread
and drink the wine just like a normal beverage,
having no respect for the body of the Lord,
that is, for the whole congregation.[120*]
Also in this way, through his suffering
and through pouring out his blood,
we should assist others in ways that are needed,
and in case someone is lacking something,

[120*] Where there are only two or three, there is the body and congregation (Mt 18 [20]).

accordingly that person should be restored,[121*]
as Paul says (Col 1 [24]).

Now Judas ate and drank
of the Lord's Supper with the other apostles.
He barely took his brothers or Christ to heart,
having such love that he sold Christ
for thirty pieces of silver (Mt 26:15).
His thoughts did not lie with Christ or his brothers.
Therefore the devil entered his heart, [Jn 13 (27)]
betrayed him,
told him about the body of the Lord.
And then he grew desperate.
He confessed to having shed innocent blood.
He hanged himself
and burst open in the middle. [Mt 27 (3–10); Acts 1 (18)]
It must still be this way.
Whoever has ears to hear, let them hear.[122]

Now consider the problem the papists and the Lutherans have!
The papists want to make themselves
pure and right with confession, prayers, penitence, repetitions.[123*]
But the others [Lutherans] want to strengthen their faith
and repeat the benefits of the body and blood of Christ,
which they claim to have in the bread and cup,
forever pounding the phrase "believe, believe."[124*]

But what sort of love and other fruit accompany their faith
(otherwise it is not faith)[125]
I will not go into, because I don't want to judge anyone.
You, my Lord and God,

121* Until in the end he himself will distinguish and gather all things together (Mt 25 [31ff.]).

122 Mt 11:15; etc.

123* Papists.

124* Lutherans.

125 Jas 2:18–20.

you are a righteous judge, [Sir 35 (15)]
now and in the age to come over all.

That is how we understand the Lord's Supper
in the simplest way.
We have observed it therefore in this way
and understood it with respect to the departure
and death of the Lord.

That is the table, which you, Lord,
have prepared for us in the presence
of all those who do us harm.
O Lord, you have anointed our heads with oil
and our cup,
which provides us with drink,
is overflowing.[126]

That is the little bottle
of which our dear brother Leonard Schiemer wrote.[127*, 128]
Even the apostles needed to be full of wine (Acts 2 [13]),
as they were speaking
with many languages through the Holy Spirit.
For they also would have drunk
from this cup, this little bottle.[129]
Therefore they also rejoiced,
having suffered disgrace and also death
for the sake of Jesus' name (Acts 5 [41]).

---

126 Ps 23:5.

127* Gloss: This is written up in the epistle concerning the three graces, written from prison after St. Andrew's Day in 1527 in Rattenberg on the Inn River.

128 [The little bottle refers to Leonhard Schiemer's "Concerning the Grace of God; Concerning the Little Bottle," no. 9 in this collection. This line provides evidence that these writings were circulating immediately after they were written and that the radicals were reading one another's writings.—Ed.]

129 [Schiemer speaks in similar ways about the double meaning of the cup. It is the little bottle from which we receive the Spirit's power (See KB, no. 9: Leonhard Schiemer, "Concerning the Grace of God. Concerning the Little Bottle")—Ed.]

Although our enemies say, to some extent at least,
that they are not persecuting and killing us
for the sake of Jesus' name, but for the sake of baptism,
since we regard as null and void
any baptism that does not involve faith in Jesus Christ.[130*]

Therefore in their view
they are killing us for no purpose and in vain.
Merciful Father, let them recognize that. Amen!

Finally and in closing,
Almighty God,
as those who are poor, wretched, destitute,
and mocked in front of the whole world,[131*] [1 Cor 4 (9–13)]
we admonish you
to keep all the agreements
and promises you have made
to your elect and faithful;

that you are a helper of the poor and a comforter to the afflicted,
a strength and power to the weak,
a hope for the despairing,
a refuge, protection and shield[132*]
to the persecuted, destitute, and dying,
for the sake of your name and Word.
In time and eternity
you will keep watch over them in all their ways,
wherever they wander,
and you will send
your holy angels to protect them. [Ps 91 (11)]

In six tribulations you will stand by them
and in the seventh,
that is, in the last one,
you will not leave them. [Jb 5 (19)]

[130*] Note.

[131*] Note.

[132*] O poor Christians!

With such promises you have richly protected us
by your grace
as a sign of your ever-abiding Word,
and covered us like a cloud.
"For your mercy is steadfast upon us,
and your truth remains forever."[133] [Is 40 (8)]

You are a faithful God in all your words
and holy in all your works.[134] [1 Pt 2 (24f.)]
And there is no lack or fault in you.
But in us there is nothing
but hesitation, doubt, fear, anxiety, distress,
and unspeakable lament.

We are surrounded by strife, quarrels, conflict, violence, tyranny,
sword, fire, water, judges, constables, and hangmen.[135*]

Therefore come, dear Father, come!
Great and pressing need is at hand.
The opportune time is surely here.
Keep your pledge! Safeguard your truth abundantly!
Let us have no doubt about it.
Stretch out your hand upon us from above;
release us from fire, sword, and water
and from the hand of alien and evil children,
whose mouths have spoken idle things and lies about us.
Injustice is a force of evil,[136]
but in the midst of the worst afflictions[137] you will save us,
acquit us, and bring us back to life.
We count on that by your grace.

---

133 Ps 117:2.
134 Ps 145:17.
135* Note.
136 Ps 144:7f.
137 Ps 138:7.

Our soul is grieved unto death.*[138] *O Father, help us out of this hour.*[139] *Amen.

This is how the third witness on earth, which is blood,
testifies about us (1 Jn 5 [6f.]).
We will be baptized in it
with the sons of Zebedee, [Mt 20 (22f.); Lk 12 (50)]
in the name of the Father and the Son and the Holy Spirit. Amen.[140]

Father, into your hands we commit our spirits (with Christ) [Lk 23 (46)]. Amen.

We go up to the Mount of Olives to pray with the Lord:
"O Father, not ours, but your will be done" (Mt 26 [39]). [Lk 22 (42)]
Help us through this night of torment
to your holy, eternal Sabbath. Amen.

Given on the Monday after Candlemas
during this dangerous year of 1528.[141]

Tomorrow your fellow brothers in the Lord
(poor and imprisoned in Schwaz)
Hans Schlaffer and Leonhard Frick will be released.

Glory to God alone!

---

[138] Mt 26:38; Mk 14:34.

[139] Jn 12:27.

[140] [This is the formula for baptism with water.—Ed.]

[141] [Candlemas is the popular name for the Presentation of the Lord, the feast on February 2 commemorating the presentation of Jesus in the temple (Lk 2:22–38). Candlemas refers to the custom of an elaborate procession with many candles in the service for that day.—Ed.]

Interlude 1

Petition through the profundity of Christ

Petitioning through Christ must happen through the profundity[1] of Christ, exhorting the Father about what he has done on our account, and about that, what he presently is or was, as he was and is from eternity. For in this regard, the Son like the Father, and the Father like the Son, is to be prayed to in spirit and truth.[2] The profundity of Christ is our salvation, the victory of Christ is our comfort, and the majesty of Christ is our joy. This is also the throne of grace where Christ is sitting in majesty. A throne from which there is no longer movement is no longer effective. We in Christ are better off than Adam was before the fall, since everything that Adam should have become has taken place for us through Christ.

Zwischenstück 1: Bitten durch die Tiefe Christi. Translation by Leonard Gross.

1 [Elsewhere in this collection, *Tiefe* is translated "lowliness" (see, for example, "Concerning the Lowliness of Christ," no. 35). Both translations are theologically and literarily plausible.—Ed.]

2 Jn 4:24.

Fuggerei. The world's oldest social housing project still in use, founded in 1516 and sponsored by the Fuggers, Augsburg's wealthiest family.

13

Concerning the love of God and the cross of Christ

Pilgram Marpeck
Augsburg, 1546/47

"Concerning the Love of God and the Cross of Christ" is undated and unaddressed, but the letter contains a clue to its date and place of writing. Near the end is a strong outcry against the Roman Catholic Church in its reliance on the emperor to defend its interests. Later the letter makes the same accusation against the magisterial churches. The likely reference is to the Schmalkaldian War of 1546, in which Protestants and Catholics were allied militarily. If this date is correct, Pilgram Marpeck would have written the letter during his stay in Augsburg.[1]

This treatise dares to speak about the impenetrable mysteries of life: the love of God, time and eternity, the bliss of the saved and the horror of the damned in eternity, as well as the suffering of the righteous in time. Its language rises to the occasion in the poetic reach of its most inspired portions and in the structure of its contrasting concepts.

Marpeck begins with thoughts about the eternity of God and therefore the eternity of love. Love is known by means of God's Trinitarian

---

Pilgram Marpeck, Von der Liebe Gottes und vom Kreuz Christi; [Augsburg, 1546/47]. Translation by Walter Klaassen. Previously published as "Concerning the Love of God in Christ" in WPM, 528–48. Reprinted, with editorial changes, by permission of the publisher.

1 BSOT, 372.

nature. Reinforcing the conjecture of 1546 as the date of composition is the similarity between this succinct statement about the taking of the incarnate Word into the Trinity, and the much longer treatment of this audacious theme in his most densely theological tome, his reply to Caspar Schwenckfeld's *Judicium,* written about the same time.[2] His proposal is that the taking up of the humanity of Christ into the life of the Trinity shows that it has become essential to Christ's—and God's—identity. The consequence of this claim is that humanity itself belongs to eternity because of the incarnation and ascension. The other creatures do not share this status.

"Christ in his humanity is complete love since he sought and accepted no benefit for himself which could have caused or initiated love. We in our humanity are weak, and therefore love is patient,"[3] ready to wait and suffer, not coercing but drawing us to itself. Here again we see that for Marpeck nonviolence emerges from the very nature of love. "The psychological insight, reflected in this and similar passages, into the nature and ways of love is further evidence that the writing comes from his later years."[4]

Following his musings about love, his meditation on time and eternity describes "the difference between eternal bliss and eternal damnation," a central theme of art, literature, and preaching in his day. It is not God—whose patience is unending—but our persistence in evil that condemns us. This arrogance leads to the delusion that human might can save. Thus the resort to violence is not simply a question of ethics but the pursuit of a "deceptive consolation," a false salvation. "The author is especially critical of those who claim to believe in God but who believe that they will be saved by violence and coercion. He mentions especially Jews, Catholics, Protestants, and certain sects. Such so-called salvation is temporal and does not last, since it has no relation to love, which is rooted through Christ in the eternal God and which works in time through patience. The whole letter is as powerful

2 LWPM, 114–19.

3 WPM, 528.

4 Ibid.

a statement on the power of love and nonviolence as one can find in Anabaptist literature."[5]

The concluding section of the letter presents a final contrast, between the innocent cross of Christ, the guilty cross of believers, and the damnable cross of the condemned. The detail that characterizes the argument suggests that this theme was highly disputed. Believers can bear two different crosses. They share in the cross of Christ's innocence when they obey him; they share in the world's cross of guilt when they continue to sin after coming to faith. The tragedy, beginning with Adam, is that people sorrow over the suffering they must endure but not over the sin that is its cause. Marpeck presents Joseph and Job as people who suffered not because they sinned but because injustice was done to them. Through "gentle patience" and "passionate intercession" they overcame evil with good. They are part of the narrative of nonresistance Marpeck sees in the Old Testament.

This treatise includes more glosses than most of the other pieces in this collection. They offer further definition to some of the concepts Marpeck introduces. Their likely source is Jörg Maler.

5 Ibid.

What follows concerns the love of God in Christ,[6] and the love that has been poured out by God upon humanity and the creatures,[7] together with other clarifications. Then there is a conclusion concerning the sacred cross of Christ and the guilty cross of the believers, as well as the condemning cross of the condemned.

Grace and peace from God our heavenly Father through and from the Lord Jesus Christ abide with us eternally.[8] Amen.

My dear ones, loved in and by Jesus Christ our healer, Lord, and God, with an eternal love which is God himself eternally through and in everything that is called divine love and which is loved by God in Christ.[9*]

For whoever abides in love abides in God, and God in him.[10] He is and remains eternally with God. For God himself is the eternal in him, about him, and with him. God cannot pass away or diminish; he cannot come to an end or be changed, for he is self-subsistent forever.[11*, 12]

Love is all power, authority, strength, might, wisdom, reason, skill, understanding, truth, righteousness, mercy, forbearance, patience, meekness, in all humility and lowliness. She is fully God in all, in, with, and through her summation [who is] Jesus Christ our healer. He is the complete, whole, eternally coming true love of the Father, and the Father himself is the true love of the Son, one Spirit, God, and Lord forever, not mixed but one from eternity to eternity, not separated into two or three but three in one eternally. Only what God himself is from

---

6 [On the upper margin: "There is some solid stuff in this epistle. Read it with understanding." By a later hand identified as Jacob.—Trans.]

7 Rom 5:5.

8 Rom 1:7; etc.

9* Gloss: The difference between what is from eternity and in eternity. They are separated by the time in between which has a beginning and an end.

10 1 Jn 4:16.

11* Gloss: By the power of the love which is God, and is in those who according to the measure of faith by faith enter into God and God into them.

12 Rom 12:3.

eternity in and of himself is everlasting (understand: not "in" but "from" eternity), and nothing can be added to him.

For the eternal is one from eternity and remains eternally, God the Word and Spirit. Only the incarnate Word is taken into the unity, and according to the measure of time, one in and with God. He is two natures, one person, two natures, one God, divine and human in one. But whatever is taken in has a beginning, a middle, and also eternity to eternity (understand: "in" eternity not "from" eternity). Those are the creatures that have eternal existence with God, in God, and from God. They are, for example, the angelic creatures as well as human spirits and souls. These, even though they did not desire it, must be and exist and remain in eternity.

The charm of the creaturely species and characteristics that must exist and remain eternally is still not the blessed, blissful, and joyful eternity. Rather, such blissful eternity occurs when what is creaturely exists in the creaturely love in which she was created in dependence on the Creator and is taken unperverted into God, Word and Spirit, who is blissful and everlasting love. For this love, for the sake of Christ, humanity was created. That is, grace and more grace,[13] love and more love, faithfulness and more faithfulness, truth and more truth, the unity of God and the creature in love eternal.

But those who fall away from this first creaturely love, be they angelic or human, will exist and remain in eternity against their will. As a recompense for the works they have committed against the creaturely ways and the nature in which they were created in love and for love, it may thus be revealed to them by the stern righteousness [of God] that they have wantonly forsaken the proper way of their Creator and embraced wickedness. This stands firm and must stand firm eternally: they must endure an agonized eternity.

When time ends (after which the amnesty of Christ's grace and the time of repentance ends and eternity begins) they can never again become good, for agony and sin must remain eternally evil, eternally surrounded by death, pain, and hell. Thus the creatures are taken into and come into everlastingness according to the divine nature. Understand

---

13 Jn 1:16.

that "taken into" means being given grace and more grace, and "coming into" means guilt and more guilt, evil and more evil, agony for sin, into which they come through their fault eternally. Those who are taken in, however, through grace and more grace, in love and more love, remain in everlasting love and glory with Christ Jesus. For his sake all things are, for through him and to him and in him are all things, and everything exists in him.[14] It is not that they are absorbed in God or will no longer be what they were before the creation, as some erring spirits desire, and that God should remain alone and everything be absorbed in him. Such error be far from us![15]

Thus the pardoned and the elect, who have been justified and who live in love in God and God in them, enter into the one eternal essential love, which remains eternally and is God himself.[16] But it is impossible to have or come by the power of love, which God has and himself is eternally (as stated earlier), wholly in this time of grace. It is available only up to the measure of the power people are given and receive, and not in their own powers.[17*] I speak here about that complete power that is in its fullness and without measure only in Christ, and not about the measure of love that is poured out into mortals. For in Christ the fullness of Godhead dwells bodily;[18] in us, in this time,[19] it is only in part.[20] Love is our teacher through the Holy Spirit: especially in this time we should be led and directed by her, and learn of her. We remain seated at the feet of Christ[21] with Magdalene,[22] who loved much and therefore received much forgiveness and remission according to the

---

14 Col 1:16f.

15 [This is a reference to the mystic Spiritualists such as Johannes Bünderlin and Caspar Schwenckfeld, who in the Neo-Platonic manner held to the idea of absorption in the divine. See MESG, 155–75.—Trans.]

16 1 Jn 1:16.

17* Gloss: The difference between the love that is the very being of God and Christ himself, and the love that is poured out by God upon humanity and the creatures and which works in and reigns over that which is incomplete.

18 Col 2:9.

19 [*In dieserr zeit* ("in this time") connotes both the urgent and the earthly.—Ed.]

20 1 Cor 13:9f.

21 Lk 10:39.

22 Lk 8:2; Lk 7:36ff.; Jn 11:2; Lk 10:38–42.

Word of the Lord [Lk 7 (36ff.)].[23] That love is intended for our benefit and salvation.

But in Christ love is complete, since he sought and accepted no benefit for himself that could have caused or initiated love. He is the fullness of everything eternally. In the creatures love is awakened and given for their benefit to the praise of God. For complete love has no defect. But mortals, in whom she already dwells, are full of weakness; therefore love is full of patience [1 Cor 13 (4–7)]. They know that they fail constantly under love's rule, but love replaces all failure and shortcoming. They are often unwilling, but love is willing.[24*] They are idle, but love acts. They are unfriendly, but love is friendly. They are arrogant, but love is humble. They are quarrelsome, but love is conciliatory. Love suffers all things, endures all things, and bears all things. Even today, true love often dwells in a believing soul and spirit, in order that she alone may assert her sovereignty against the ill-mannered, contrary flesh. Such evil obstructionism was not found in the humanity of Christ, for he is the fullness of love, and God himself. This obstructionism should not lead us to make excuses but should awaken fear and shame.

For in this time we cannot lay claim to the fullness of love with its power to convince. But we can follow her path with sincere desire, and mark her footprints and tracks with earnestness, as love pleads with and speaks to love in the Canticle: "Draw me after you and let us make haste."[25] May we never lose sight of her until we completely possess her in that day with Christ. For he who possesses her to the fullest degree possible in this time is merely given greater desire for her, but can never see her form clearly or embrace her as she has embraced him.[26] She is like a stag or deer that, when it sees someone, dashes out of sight.

Yet she is swift to let herself be seen and to grant us our desire to see her form and to prove with power why she is called love.[27*] She is not to be bought. She cannot be coerced, driven, or urged. Even if one gave

---

23 Lk 7:47.

24* Note.

25 Sg 1:4.

26 Phil 3:12.

27* Note.

his wealth for her, he would not gain her,[28] for she is priceless and unconquerable. With her beauty and ornament she is beyond price, and her praise is unspeakable. Even the Holy Spirit himself has not found a perfect expression for love in all the creatures to show or reveal her transfiguration[29] of all virtue, beauty, ornament, or form. He seeks to show her form and to bear witness to it, to demonstrate with sufficient power and deeds, to search out and seek to fathom the depth of her patience, to show her sympathy, the means and abundance of her friendliness, the expression of the loveliness with which she is adorned, and to make visible her form. Her mildness no one can tell, nor can anyone fully receive what she bestows, distributes, and gives in abundance. For the overflowing of her mildness is fullness and sufficiency[30]—indeed, the fulfilling of all hope. Whatever and however much there is to be hoped for blushes in shame in the presence of her mildness and generosity, for in her all hope and faith must come to an end and vanish.

Only love, who is most beloved, remains eternally independent. This self-subsistence and immovability[31] of love no one can achieve or comprehend. For this reason she is compared to a rock, a wall, and a strong tower, on which creatures and people (who have been set ablaze by her flames and heat) build silver bastions that will survive the terror of the night because of her dependability and strength. Those are the temptations by which people are afflicted until her brightness, light, and dawn fully break forth, and her morning star rises,[32] taking away the darkness of the night, and all darkness passes away by her perpetual light, as it must.

Love is patient in time; who can recount her patience[33] or declare her end or her measure? In her patience and forbearance[34] lies human blessedness. The delay of love is in its time the highest reward of wait-

---

28 Sg 8:7.
29 [Original: *verclärung.*—Trans.]
30 Jn 10:10; 2 Cor 9:8.
31 Heb 11:1, Vulg.
32 2 Pt 1:19.
33 1 Cor 13:4.
34 Patience. 1 Cor 13:7.

ing. For even the angels wait with longing to see[35] what fulfilment her patience will accomplish. For in the patience of love's delay lies human blessedness.[36*] No creature has been found to express, teach, and witness with power what love is, along with its virtues and powers, except the man Jesus, Jesus Christ, the Son of God. None but he was brought forth, glorified, and revealed by the Father with that glory which he, as the incarnate Word, had in the presence of the Father from eternity.[37] With love he declares himself to be the true Son of God, commissioned even to the condemnation of death, and has achieved the fullest, greatest, and most exalted love in that he gives his life for his friends. For no one has greater love than he who gives his life for his friends [Jn 14; 15 (13)].

To this, Christ has witnessed and in love declared himself, with the incarnate Word, deed, and power. This is the Lamb that was found worthy to open the sealed and closed book [Rv 5 (5, 12)], that is the hiddenness of all virtue, power, and effulgence of love, and himself to reveal before the Father the glory of love in himself, according to his holy humanity. This Lamb declares that the Father himself has glorified him with that glory which he had with the Father before the foundation of the world was laid.[38] And as he was glorified in love in and before the Father when the world had not yet begun, so he also glorified himself before people and angels, and so the Father will glorify him again. In him fullness of virtue, such as the power of love, is completed and revealed before time, in the time of his flesh, as well as after this time to eternity.

As this power of love is declared and witnessed to in that manner before the Father, so the Father will fully glorify the Son in the fulfilment of time in all Christ's elect,[39] and they will be as he is, and he will be as those who belong to him in God and God in them eternally.[40*] It

---

35 1 Pt 1:12.

36* Gloss: The difference between the transfiguration of the Word from eternity and the transfiguration of the incarnate Word to eternity.

37 Jn 17:5.

38 Jn 17:5.

39 Jn 17:10.

40* Note.

is not as though he had just become love, but this shows that he exists from eternity. Thus the incarnate Word is God and man, man and God, two natures, one God, and also two natures, one man, the beginning of time, the centre and end of all things, the A and the 0[41] [Rv 1 (8)]. For his sake all things exist.[42] He is the breaking in of time out of eternity and into eternity.

For the sake of love the Lamb of God, which has taken away the sin of the world [Jn 1 (29)], was slain in love from the foundation of the world (Rv 13 [8]). He, without guilt and sin, was sacrificed in history for human guilt and sin, in order to restore the fall of humanity from their original love of creation and raise them up into blissful, joyful, eternally enduring love—taken into Christ out of grace and in grace, accounted worthy, to the glory, praise, and honour of God as an eternal thanksgiving.[43*, 44]

All this has been written so that one may be able to distinguish what is from eternity (for example, three in one) from what will yet be and remain in eternity. We are to perceive inbreaking time. It is not what is from eternity but what came to be and will remain into eternity. In this inbreaking time, the Word became incarnate as the beginning, centre, and end, for[45] the sake of all creatures.[46*]

---

41 [The alpha and the omega, the first and last letters of the Greek alphabet.—Ed.]

42 Jn 1:3.

43* Gloss: Paul says that all creatures exist for our sake; we exist for Christ's sake; and Christ exists for God's sake.

44 1 Cor 3:22f.

45 [Original: *das die umb des vermenschten worts als umb anfanng, mitl und endt allerr creaturen willen sey.*—Trans. This is the first of several uses in this text of the term *vermenschtes wort* (humanized word). The reference is clearly to the incarnation and has been so translated. But the usual German for "became incarnate," as in the Nicene Creed, is *leibhaft geworden.* It seems that either Marpeck or a source on which he depends is trying to make the notion of God's humanity in Christ more vivid. This fits with the use of *menschheit Christi* (humanity of Christ) as his description of the incarnate Word, the church.—Ed.]

46* Gloss: The difference between the creatures that pass away and end with time, and the creatures that are and remain eternally.

Time will cease to be.[47] Sun, moon,[48] stars,[49] and everything that exists in time and for the sake of humanity (not created to remain eternally) must cease to be for the sake of what is and must remain eternally [Rv 22 (5)], such as people and angels who are taken up into God and God into them. For there will no longer be any need for time or the creatures of time, such as animals, birds, fish, light, or day. For in eternity time ceases, and God himself is day and light. Darkness and night will depart from the light, that is, from the incarnate Word and Spirit, and go to their eternal place, where no grace or creaturely light will ever again be seen. Only the hellish and eternally deadly fire is the revelation and illumination of everlasting torment.[50] They will suffer eternally,[51] be and remain eternally in the darkness[52] of God's wrath, yea, in eternal envy, hate, anger, murder, and in agonized crying because of the fire which will never depart from them.[53*]

For all their sin and guilt, along with their wickedness, remains eternally in them and with them. For salvation and mediation are no longer available, so that they do not have even the smallest particle of comfort.[54*]

The fallen angels and people are delivered over to each other as the greatest enemies with never-ending enmity, envy, and hate, in order to completely fulfil in each other their hellishly incorporated wantonness and their envious, hateful, and wrathful manner without the means of any adjudication, judgment, or restraint. Whatever in their greed and lustful wrath they invent and scheme to torment, insult, and hurt each

---

47 Rv 10:6.

48 Rv 21:23.

49 Mt 24:29.

50 [A marginal gloss from another hand reads: *Hie vacht er an sagen von bin [pein] der verdampter in der hellen.* (Here he begins to speak about the torment of the damned in hell.)—Trans.]

51 Mt 3:12; 25:41; Mk 9:43, 45; Lk 3:17; Jude 7.

52 2 Pt 2:17; Jude 6, 13.

53* Gloss: The difference between eternal bliss and eternal damnation.

54* Gloss: God has ordained the governing power for this time and for the sake of the godly; as a protection, arbiter, and punishment; and as intermediate gods between the evil and the good. (Ex 21:6; 22:8f.; 1 Cor 8:5.) [It is to be noted that Luther also referred to the princes as gods on the basis of Psalm 82.—Trans.]

other, they completely carry out. Beyond that, all the evil they do to each other will be most bitterly salted with fire when the torment and great pain of eternal fire will be their arbiter. Thus the great pain of eternal fire together with everlasting despair will by far exceed their own torment, and all this in immortality. It would be as though a mortal being had many deadly pains in his body, each pain far exceeding the other, with no surcease.[55*] Thus the lesser pains would be a small relief compared to the greater torment, but added to the greatest torment, be even unto death. Thus not a single remedy will be available for all those condemned, each according to their deserts. For in this time all authorities are gods and mediators between goodness and evil, between the just and the unjust, established to provide physical rest and peace and to restrain evil and protect the good.[56*] For evil and good now exist together in this physical life undifferentiated and unseparated[57] until the day when judgment takes place and good and evil are separated. This will take place when the last person to be saved is brought in.[58] Then all worldly authority will be dissolved, one house will fall upon the other, there will be war and the cry of war without any means of peace or rescue, and all piety, faithfulness, love, truth, faith, and confidence will cease.

For the pious and the godly, for whose sake the world with its wickedness is spared, will be saved. They will be separated from all wickedness and gain rest and eternal joy as Christ said: "When you hear war and the cry of war, lift your heads, for your salvation approaches" [Mt 24 (6); Lk 21 (28)]. Only then will goodness and wickedness be separated one from the other,[59*] love and truth from envy, hate, and lying, hope from despair, belief from unbelief, peace from strife, patience from vengeance, joy and comfort from mourning and despair, mild-

---

55* Parable

56* Gloss: The reason for governmental authority in this time.

57 [The negative prefix does not appear in the original, but the context demands it.—Trans.]

58 [Marginal comment: *Merckh* ("Take note")—in the hand of a later owner (Jacob)—next to a pointing finger.—Trans.]

59* Note.

ness from greed, mercy from mercilessness, humility from arrogance, meekness from pride and haughtiness, and truth from lying.

That will be the salvation and final decision for all the godly, who in themselves and among the wicked are now attacked, prone to fall, and imprisoned, afflicted, sorrowful, anxious, tormented, and molested daily against their will by evil, abominable behaviour. Thus they will be redeemed and led out of all temptation. Because the kingdom of Christ is not of this world,[60] and because the kingdoms of the world and the kingdom of Christ are the complete opposite of each other, Christ says: "In the world you are afraid, but in me you have peace. Be glad, for I have overcome the world" [Jn 16 (33)], that is, in patience, hope, and faith. You will be in need of patience (that is, patience in time of evil tribulation).[61] And do not resist evil with evil, but overcome evil with good [1 Pt 3 (9); Rom 12 (17, 21)]. Thus and in no other way has Christ overcome the world, so that we may be joyful in hope and also overcome, awaiting our Saviour, according to his promise. He will be our victory and our overcoming![62][63*]

Far be it from us that we should seek to be redeemed like the Jews and these present alleged Christians. They comfort themselves and hope to be redeemed by human power and the arm of mortals. The Jews, contrary to Christ and his own, claim to expect a Messiah or Christ who will redeem them from all power of the Gentiles by means of the human arm and carnal weapons, and lead them into the promised land. The alleged Christians are now blinded by this Jewish error (contrary to the bright light and word which they claim to have and of which they boast).[64*] They assume that with carnal sword and the human arm, Christ will release and redeem them from those who justifiably coerce and frighten them through the appearance of his coming. The old Latin Roman Church, which is ruled by imperial power, also hopes the emperor will achieve victory in the semblance and name of

---

60 Jn 18:36.

61 Heb 10:36.

62 1 Jn 5:4f.

63* Gloss: The distinction between the redemption of Christ and the redemption of humanity.

64* Note.

Christ against all those who resist her, and rigidly insists that this will happen. It will happen in order that all those will be punished who, in the semblance of Christ, suppose that they will decide with the carnal sword[65*, 66] and themselves become coercers of faith, and persecute with the carnal sword those who do not agree with them, and insist on maintaining violence against violence with the carnal sword in the semblance of Christ.[67*]

Christ himself, in his holy humanity submitted to every authority in patience, who himself had and has all authority in heaven and on earth.[68] For whoever takes the sword to protect Christ and himself in the semblance of the Word, takes and uses it like Peter, who cut off Malchus's ear, which Christ put back on and healed [Mt 26 (51f.); Jn 18 (10f.)]. If someone today takes and uses the sword thus and fights for Christ, the same person must and will, according to the words of the Lord, perish by the sword. The guilt rests on their heads as long as they boast of Christ and do not believe his words. The Jews boasted that they were children of God and Abraham[69] and did not believe the words of his Christ but crucified him under the authority of Caesar. They set themselves against the imperial authority deliberately and with a perverted mind. Into this perverted state God delivered them and has to this day abandoned them. Because of this they were coerced by the authority of Caesar with great persecution, devastation and destruction.[70*]

Everyone is confident in a false hope and illusion concerning his healer and Saviour.[71*] The Jews console themselves with the Turk [that he will help them] against the emperor and all sects of the Christian

---

65* The Lord says the Holy Spirit would come and judge the world for sin. But now human authority presumes to do what belongs to the Holy Spirit alone and to punish unbelief.

66 Jn 16:8.

67* The difference between physical (bodily) authority and the authority of Christ.

68 Mt 28:18.

69 Mt 3:9; Lk 3:8; Jn 8:39.

70* Gloss: The distinction between the consolation of redemption by Christ and the deceptive consolation of redemption by human beings.

71* 1.

name.[72] The Roman Latin Church with its old language,[73] its seeming churchliness, the renown of its age and traditions under all the Roman emperors,[74*] is confident in the emperor as its protector and saviour from all the opposing sects of Christian name and also from the power of the Turk.[75*] In the same way, the self-styled evangelicals are confident about all those who set themselves against the Roman authority and church, as though they were all means of their own salvation from the Roman authority and church.[76*] Wherever an insurrection against the emperor as the Roman authority occurs, be it the Turk, the French, the city states,[77] or other rulers, lords, and people, they regard it joyfully as a hope of their own salvation.

There are also alleged sects and Christians rejoicing in the false hope and consolation of salvation not by the human arm or authority but by miracles.[78*] They believe that God will exercise vengeance on all who oppose them, and wait for newly sent prophets and miracles with vengeance in their hearts.[79*, 80] They are enemies of their enemies (and not friends and benefactors, according to the teaching of Christ), and think that because of their supposed sanctity they should be saved from bodily tribulation and the cross of Christ. They hope to achieve a human and bodily rest within history, which might well happen.[81]

---

72 [The Turks at this time treated the Jews with much more favour and respect than did the Christians. Jews held high and influential political, social, and economic positions in the Ottoman Empire.—Trans.]

73 2 Tm 3:5.

74* Note.

75* 2.

76* 3.

77 [The free cities of the empire, which in many ways were a law unto themselves.—Trans.]

78* 4.

79* Note.

80 [This is quite possibly a reference to the Münsterites or some remnants of Müntzer followers. The latter especially continued for a long time in sections of Thuringia.—Trans.]

81 [This last clause is a sarcastic reflection on the fact that they will die and thus achieve the rest of the body.—Trans.]

That joy, however, is not for Christians, but rather the sorrow of human corruption. It is proper for the believer, however, to rejoice in the righteous judgments of God, to which is added the sorrow over human corruption. Abraham interceded for Sodom because he was sorry for the destruction of those souls [Gn 18 (22-32)], but he nevertheless rejoiced in the righteousness of God and the salvation of the godly. Thus we are to rejoice, that is clear.

But all those described above know Christ (like the Jews) only according to the flesh and not in spirit and in truth. They seek rest, peace, and joy where none can ever be found in eternity.[82*] For this is the rest and redemption of Christ, that we are redeemed from sin to renounce wickedness (never to fulfil it), henceforth to live for Christ. That is peace, joy, and comfort in the Holy Spirit[83] and our true redemption. I know of no other salvation in Christ within history. Whoever hopes in any other salvation is truly imprisoned in his own vengeance, builds on the sand of this passing life,[84] and is in the company of all the false hopes described above, having to do with war and the cry of war, utterly imprisoned by their own vengeance.[85, 86*]

All these can never rejoice at the approach of salvation, for it brings forth only fear, misery, and distress, and never accomplishes redemption. For temporal and eternal death takes everything into bondage again. Whoever imputes such a redemption to Christ, imputes all bondage to him and makes of him a servant who traps and ensnares in behalf of death. In its bonds humanity is kept against its will. From this imprisonment Christ alone is the Redeemer. For such temporal consolation and hope can never be called the consolation or hope of Christ.

82* 5.

83 Rom 14:17.

84 Mt 7:26.

85 Rom 12:9.

86* Gloss: Whatever waits for temporal salvation and is already temporally saved will pass away again and come to an end because of the nature of time. For death takes everything again into its bondage. Such a salvation cannot be imputed to Christ, for he is an eternal Redeemer [Heb 9:12].

Those who trust in it suffer not for the sacred, innocent cross of Christ, but for the cross of their own guilt.[87*]

For there is a great difference between the light burden and the sweet yoke of Christ,[88] which is the sin-forgiving cross of Christ washed, cleansed, and hallowed in the innocent blood of Christ, and the cross of guilt. For the cross of guilt can never be called the sacred cross of Christ. Not that I am including those cleansed from sin that is done in unbelief, in contrast with those who were born again through faith in Christ, in the original guilt. Never! But those who sin again after faith in Christ bear the cross of guilt, even though they gain forgiveness through grace under chastisement and punishment.[89] Yet it is a cross of guilt because, according to the words of Christ, no evil goes unpunished and no good unrewarded.[90]

Saint Paul writes to the Corinthians, charging them with disorderly living: "For this reason many of you are weak and ill, and a number have fallen asleep" [1 Cor 11 (30)]. Certainly, he means the sickness and sleep of the spirit in unbelief, in which one becomes ill and even sleeps the sleep of death. But he definitely also means the believers whose guilt and sin has been forgiven under chastisement and punishment, but who are often caught in the plagues and vengeance of the world such as pestilence, hunger, war, and destruction, which are the greatest plagues and penalties of vengeance in this mortal time.[91*] The psalmist witnesses to the same thing—one should read it!—saying that God does not allow faith to fail but punishes transgression with a rod [Ps 107 (10–18)]. Thus believers retain the sin they commit in the cross of guilt. That cannot be the hallowed cross of Christ, but may be called the cross of guilt that brings the pardon of Christ in the form

---

87* Gloss: The distinction between the holy, innocent cross of Christ, the guilty cross of believers, and the damnable cross of the condemned.

88 Mt 11:30.

89 [The concern about post-conversion sin, first raised in Heb 4–6, esp. 6:4–6, became a preoccupation of the early patristic period and of parts of Anabaptism. It was a greater concern among the Dutch and Swiss than among the Marpeck Circle.—Ed.]

90 Mt 10:42.

91* Note.

of a rod of discipline, a humble submission to the folly in which they have transgressed. Stupidity and folly must be humbled in us because of our transgression. Whoever is thus humbled will be made great in Christ. However, we may never say of anyone that he bears the cross of guilt; it is known only as everyone finds it himself in his own conscience before God. If someone has a clear conscience, he may endure torment, revenge, punishment, or sickness in faith, but such torments, no matter how great they are, will not make him guilty any more than Job was. For all mortals must suffer physical death no matter what form it takes.

The world's cross of guilt is greatly to be distinguished from the believers' cross of guilt.[92*] For this we have a plain, clear history and figure in the two thieves who were crucified with Christ, one to the right and one to the left [Lk 23 (33)]. The one on the right confessed his sin and guilt to the innocence of Christ, who in innocence was crucified and tortured beside him on the most hallowed and purest cross in torment and suffering. The thief did not desire to be rescued from the cross of guilt but only that he might receive grace. That's why he begged the Lord to remember him when he should come into his kingdom [Lk 23 (40-43)]. Moreover, he chastised the other thief for blaspheming God and not fearing him when he said: "If you are the Son of God, help us and yourself down from the cross."[93]

This is what the world does with its cross of guilt; it desires constantly to be released from it. And yet, because of its guilt it must hang and remain on the eternal cross of guilt, namely, its own condemnation, without pardon, in everlasting torment. For the world and its children, like the thief on the left, are sorry only for the suffering and not at all for the sin. Thus those who have received pardon have sorrow under the weight of their cross of guilt only for their sin and not at all for the suffering. Although it terrifies them, with a fear that they might be condemned after death, they confess that death and all suffering is the result of sin. Therefore they desire to be released from sin—which is the actual root of all suffering. You can see how great the difference

---

92* Cross of guilt.

93 Lk 23:39.

is between the believers' cross of guilt and that of the world. Although in this life they are punished with similar torments, the manners and ways of those who have been pardoned are far removed from those of the damned.[94*]

The sacred, easy, light, sweet, and innocent cross of Christ is as greatly to be distinguished from the believers' cross of guilt, not to speak of the world's, as heaven and earth are to be distinguished. The innocent cross of Christ can never be taken up and carried in this age by any believer. For it has its source and beginning in the word of promise to restore the fall of Adam. This is the source of the hatred and enmity of the serpent against humanity.[95] For the sake of the seed of the incarnate Word,[96] it was given the promise of restoration. For the serpent there was no restoration, but the crushing of his head through the seed of the woman, that is, the incarnate Word. The head of the serpent must be understood to mean that all his intention, cunning, and plotting against the incarnate Word will be destroyed and crushed with the feet of Christ, and together with his seed made an open shame.

Nevertheless, the serpent will bite the heel of the incarnate Word and the seed of the woman, which is born through the generation of the Word (that is, of the mother, the church), and who still walk in the flesh as members of the body of Christ. This biting of the heel is the affliction of flesh and blood with much cross, tribulation, and torment. On this point one should read Psalm 56 (6f.): "They band themselves together, they lurk and watch my heel, how they may seize my soul. Deliver him because of wickedness." This means the seed of the serpent. Flesh and blood, led in obedience to the Spirit in the word of truth, is the very heel and lowest part of the inner being who is fashioned after God.[97*]

The Holy Spirit walks and makes his footprints on such a person against all the plots of the serpent and the gates of hell.[98] Whatever pain and torment the serpent (as the source of all agony) inflicts on the

---

94* Gloss: The believer's cross of guilt does not have the fullness of patience of the sacred, innocent cross of Christ. The cross of guilt is bitter.

95 Gn 3:15.

96 Jn 1:14.

97* Note.

98 Mt 16:18.

flesh and blood of believers, and thus bites the heel of Christ, his head is nevertheless crushed, overcome, and executed by the heel. The heel is all the weakness of the flesh and blood of Christ in all patience in his saints. This holy cross of Christ is the occasion of the enmity between the seed of the serpent and the seed of the woman, so that no peace or harmony can ever be between these two.

The serpent, together with his seed and children of his innate wickedness, envy, and hatred, desires to destroy the seed of the woman through every cunning, lie, and the deceit of sin, death, suffering, and martyrdom. That is the enmity between the seed of the woman and the serpent and his seed. The former hates and opposes the wickedness, deviousness, deceit, and cunning of the serpent and his seed, and resists it with all power by the word of truth. The seed of the woman carries out the strife and battle against all pain, death, sin, and hell, of which the serpent is the ruler and head, with true and proper patience, and thus will overcome eternally with Christ (the Lamb of patience) and achieve the victory.

Thus Abel's lamb was killed by Cain according to the flesh (meaning not the physical killing but because of patience),[99] but it was victorious in the Spirit according to creaturely love and faithfulness through patience which he showed to his brother. The same was true of the seed of the woman, Sarah's son Isaac, against Ishmael. Rebecca bore Isaac two antagonistic sons, Esau and Jacob, who began their hatred, cross, and struggle in the womb. That the children were contrary to each other through the enmity of the[100] seed of the serpent and the woman by nature and from the time of conception and birth, shows that the wicked one hated the godly one and that the godly one overcame the wicked one with patience.[101] Jacob was the father of Joseph, who also through patience overcame the brothers who hated him (repaying them good for evil), and although he was innocent, they sold him into Egypt.[102]

Thus many of the ancients (Job and others) overcame evil by means of good deeds through patience in tribulation. Afterward they over-

---

99 Gn 4:8; Mt 23:35; Rv 13:8.

100 [Marginal comment: *feintschaft der* ("enmity of"—Trans.]

101 Gn 25:29–34.

102 Gn 42.

came everything in and through[103] patience and waited for the redemption of Christ. With gentle patience, love, and truth he overcame evil with all goodness, love, faithfulness, truth, and mercy. When evil was done against him, he returned passionate intercession for his enemies and surrendered his human life and eternal bliss on the cross in unbroken patience, a submissive and silent Lamb of sacrifice for the sins of humanity and its salvation. This is the universally hallowed cross of Christ—and no cross of guilt. By it, in the innocence of Christ, all the followers of Christ overcome; through the cross they have free access in and to God,[104] provided their hearts do not accuse them in guilt.[105] For they are washed from their sins[106] through the innocence of Christ to be a pure and sanctified co-sacrifice pleasing and acceptable to God, as Paul says, which is our reasonable service to God [Rom 12 (1)].

In it the highest joy can be expected and had, namely, that one does not have to suffer as a debtor or an evildoer but may praise God in the matter according to the words of Peter: "Let no one among you suffer as a murderer, thief, evildoer, or a covetous one. If someone suffers as a Christian, however, he should not be ashamed; let him praise God in the matter. For it is time that judgment begins in the house of God." Furthermore, "those who suffer commit their souls to the faithful Creator with good works" [1 Pt 4 (15–17, 19)]. Thus the cross of Christ is a holy, innocent cross, if one suffers innocently as a witness of God in the truth and for the truth, to the praise of God.

To this holy cross of Christ, our highest shelter and shield, we have surrendered with holy patience (not obliged or forced patience) to overcome all our enemies in the victory of Christ. May the heavenly Father and the Lord Jesus Christ establish, strengthen, and keep us in this patience to his praise and our salvation until life's end. Amen. All the chosen of God greet you by name in the peace and grace of Christ.

Pray to God for us with all your heart and for all of the concerns of the union and fellowship of the saints in Christ. We desire to do the

---

[103] [Marginal comment: und *durch* ("and through")—Trans.]

[104] Rom 5:2; Eph 2:18; 3:12.

[105] 1 Jn 3:20.

[106] Rv 1:5; 7:14.

same for you as your debtors. The grace of our Lord Jesus Christ be and remain with us eternally. Amen.

In the Lord Jesus Christ,
servant to you and all true believers,
and comrade in the tribulation of Christ,[107]
Pilgram Marpeck

[107] Rv 1:9.

Interlude 2

"Whoever is not useful"

Children who still are nursing at their mother's breast do not know what good or evil is. Nor can they differentiate between the two. Thus a fool is not helpful in anything that needs to be enacted rationally. Therefore both are appropriately in no covenant. For Paul says: "When I was a child, I acted like a child and reasoned like a child" (Dt 1 [39], 1 Cor 11 [27]; 13 [11]; Ws 12 [24f.]). Between a person who has been baptized in Christ yet does not hold to the commandments of God, and an unbeliever or heathen, there is no difference. They both will suffer blows according to their measure, and such persons are in the ban (Jas 1 [23f.]; Mk 16 [16]; Lk 12 [47]).

Zwischenstück 2: "Wer nicht zu gebrauchen ist." Translation by Leonard Gross.

14

An attempt to win him for Christendom

To Ulrich Ageman in Constance

Jörg Maler

St. Gall, 15 October 1552

Of the five writings by Jörg Maler in the collection, "An Attempt to Win Him for Christendom" is the only letter. It was written after his two-year imprisonment and subsequent expulsion from Augsburg. Maler returned to the Appenzell congregation in St. Gall, where he had served as a reader from 1541 to 1547. This was the congregation Pilgram Marpeck accused most sharply of legalism.

From Sigmund Bosch's letter (no. 26, "Concerning the Office of Peace") we learn that Maler's plan was to itinerate through the Swiss and Marpeckite congregations, beginning with St. Gall. The fact that Maler's wife remained in Augsburg suggests that it was his intention to return there as soon as it was safe to do so. We know that he did so, because in late 1552 or early 1553 Maler delivered a letter (no. 16, "Concerning the Service and Servants of the Church") for Marpeck from Augsburg to Moravia.

The epistle is addressed to Ulrich Ageman, director of the poor house run by the city of Constance, on the Swiss-German border near St. Gall. For years Ageman had been in friendly contact with Anabaptists and

---

Jörg Maler an Ulrich Ageman in Konstanz: Versuch, ihn fürs Christentum zu gewinnen; St. Gallen, 15. Oktober 1552. Translation by Victor Thiessen and John D. Rempel.

offered them refuge. The fact that he lived outside the city wall allowed for less scrutinized encounters. This letter sounds like the continuation of a conversation already in progress. One senses that Maler wrote to Ageman[1] out of an inner prompting to urge him to make an unequivocal commitment to Christ and the Anabaptist church. The tone is set by opening words from Paul, "I am not ashamed of the gospel . . ." (Rom 1:16). This was an especially tall order after the Schmalkaldian War. Part of its outcome was the stern return of Constance to Catholicism, to the point of obliterating all manifestations of Protestantism.[2] Maler is asking a longstanding friend of Anabaptists to risk his life! Although Maler's appeal is audacious, the fact that he wrote it immediately after his own jail term for matters of conscience gives it integrity.

Maler's letter is cast into two distinct parts. The first and longer one makes an appeal for a confession of faith that is visibly sealed in baptism. The second part, the declaration, lays out the life of discipleship and an urgent appeal for decision. Written out of deep conviction, this letter by the editor of the Kunstbuch is, ironically, the least edited piece in the collection! Topics change quickly—almost arbitrarily. It gives the sense, with its piling up of biblical references, of having been worked on right up to the time Maler set off for Zurich to have the collection bound. Out of his work as its translator, Victor Thiessen has concluded that this is most obviously the case for the last section. By placing this letter in the Kunstbuch, Maler was offering a highly personal appeal for commitment as a model for evangelistic ministry in the church at large.

Were Maler's theology and piety representative of Anabaptism as he knew it? Asking this question (and studying the Kunstbuch itself) reminds us how fluid and diverse the movement remained well into its second generation. The first part of the letter exhibits traits we know from other writings of the Swiss Brethren and the Marpeck Circle. The accumulation of quotations from both testaments and the Apocrypha

---

1 Maler addresses him with the polite form of you, *euch*. But in the concluding section of his epistle, the declaration, he uses *euch* in the plural, suggesting that he is addressing not only Ageman but also a likeminded circle of people around him.

2 BSOT, 389.

on a given theme as a form of apologetics has precedents among the Swiss.[3] The emphasis on an uncoerced but urgent forsaking of old loyalties for Christ and his reign, acted out in believer's baptism, typifies both communities.

The word *order* (*Ordnung*), as most Anabaptists used it, refers to the visible forms the life of discipleship takes. Its first use comes at the very beginning of the letter, when the author writes about Christ's resurrection bringing "an enduring existence . . . in the order of his Holy Spirit." At the end of the first section, Maler says that "outside the order of the Holy Spirit and Christ there is no grace." At the start of the second section the term is "order of the Lord Jesus Christ and the custom of the apostles." The rest of the title ("on which those who believe differently stand and live together") as well as the immediately following paragraphs make clear what is meant by this term: being a Christian happens through incorporation into the community in water baptism, is worked out in discipline, and is renewed in the Lord's Supper. Maler has no doubt about Ageman's sincerity but insists that being a disciple involves more than an inward disposition. Maler's passionate concern is to make clear that the life of Jesus in believers, the freedom and the suffering it brings, can happen only within the Spirit's ordering of community.

3 BCSB.

This following epistle was written to Ulrich Ageman in Constance, caretaker of the poor people.

Like Paul, "I am not ashamed of the gospel of Jesus Christ, because it is a power from God to all who believe on it" (Rom 1 [16]).

Dear Ulrich, with my whole heart I wish you the true knowledge of God and his beloved son Jesus Christ (in whom alone rests eternal life) [Jn 17 (3)], who has robbed death of its power, and has brought to light[4] an enduring existence through himself, in the order of his Holy Spirit. May we follow him in true submission and loss of ourselves, through true humility, in humbleness of heart. This is what I wish you with all my heart, together with all those truly eager souls, desiring spiritual and pure milk [1 Pt 2(2)]—indeed, also those hungering and thirsting after justice. God will certainly satisfy them according to his promise and assurance [Mt 5 (6)], though we might wish it in other ways. For the kingdom of Christ is not a forced or imposed kingdom, as the Holy Scripture has shown in many places; that is, "God has given his people the power to take their own counsel. If you desire this, then obey his commands, and go forth faithfully in his favour. He has laid before humanity fire and water, death and life," darkness and light, etc. "Stretch your hand to that which you desire; that which pleases a person will be given to him" [Sir 15 (14–17); Dt 11 (26)].[5] Furthermore: "Come and buy wisdom without money. Bow and incline your neck under his yoke" (as Christ has also said), "and your soul will receive wisdom; it is near, and lets itself be found" [Sir 51 (25f.); Mt 11 (2f.)]. This is true for those who incline toward it with desire and love. "For God's wisdom does not come to an evilly inclined attitude, and finds no dwelling in those who are subject to sin." He, "the Holy Spirit," has indeed a disregard and an abhorrence for those who play at discipline and wisdom; "he also withdraws himself from those thoughts that are without understanding, and he avoids those places where sin gains the

---

4 2 Tm 1:10.

5* Gloss: The tree of good and evil stands yet before us, just as before Adam and Eve.

advantage." Rather, "he lets himself be found by those who do not test him, and reveals himself to those who trust him," who "search for him in the simplicity of their hearts." But "perverted thoughts depart from God" [Ws 1 (4, 5, 2, 1, 3)].Furthermore, God calls through the prophet Isaiah: "O all you who thirst, come to the water. And you who have no money, come and buy so that you have food to eat, wine and milk beyond money and price. Why do you give your money out to that which does not nourish, and your work for that which does not satisfy?[6*] Choose me instead; then you will eat of the best, and your souls will enjoy their finest desires" [Is 55 (1f.); Jn 7 (37)]. So speaks Judah, a son of Jacob's, to his children: "My children, realize that two spirits join themselves to people, the spirit of truth, and the spirit of error. And the Spirit mediates an understanding of the sense of things; the one who has it is free to go where he will."[7*, 8] "Thus the sinner should forsake his way and the unjust his attack and turn to the Lord; God will then have mercy on him, for he is inclined to forgive."[9]

Furthermore, "Behold, the hand of the Lord is not too short, that it cannot help, and his ear not so plugged that he will not or might not hear you; but your misdeeds have hidden his face, so that he cannot hear you" [Is 59 (1f.)]. And the Son himself also calls and says: "Come here to me, all you who are weary and heavy laden; I will strengthen you. Take up my yoke, and learn from me, for I am gentle and by nature humble; thus you will find rest for your souls. For my yoke is easy and my burden is light" [Mt 11 (28–30)]. "Whoever has ears to hear, let him hear."[10] Moreover, "Everything that my father gives to me comes to me, and whoever comes to me I will not cast out" [Jn 6 (37)]. Further, "He has come to proclaim the gospel to the poor," (to call them to repentance), "to heal the crushed and sick, to preach pardon to the captives" (of conscience), "the release and sight to the blind, freedom to the shattered through their release, to preach the acceptable year of the Lord" [Is 61 (1f.); Lk 4 (18f.); 2 Cor 6 (2)], that is, to those who are rueful and

---

6* Note.

7* The most ancient father of Judah.

8 Testament of Judah 20.

9 Is 55:7.

10 Mt 10:15; etc.

repentant, who with Magdalene sit at the feet of Christ [Lk 7 (37ff.) and 10 (39)].

For God hears (or pardons) no sinner (that is, those who continue and remain in sin), except those who fear God and do his will [Jn 9 (31)]. Thus speaks the prophet, in the person of the Lord: "Even as you stretch out your hands, I turn my eyes from you, and even as you multiply your prayers, I will simply not hear them. For your hands are full of injustice. Wash yourselves, become pure, put away that evil from my sight, desist from doing evil, learn to deal justly, be diligent in simplicity." "If we do this, our sins (though they be red as scarlet) will be whiter than snow" [Is 1 (15–18)]. That is, one receives grace upon grace [Jn 1 (16)], if one desists (Rom 6 [12ff.]), quits doing so, as Christ speaks to the thirty-eight-year-old as he made him well, saying, "Sin no more, that nothing more horrible may befall you" [Jn 5 (14)].

Briefly, whoever wishes to become a Christian cannot serve two masters [Mt 6 (24)];[11*] (that is), we cannot hang onto things for the sake of the world and its creatures (so that we will not be persecuted by it). We cannot leave aside God's business and order and act according to our own discretion and better judgment. If we do so, we fool ourselves by our natural pious appearance, in order that we can maintain our friendship with the world. James says this is enmity with God [Jas 4 (4)]. Sirach also said: "Woe to the sinner who walks along two streets" [Sir 2 (14)]. For Christ said, "All the plants that my heavenly Father did not plant" (that is, did not order or command) "will be uprooted"[12*] [Mt 15 (13)], also of those among his own, inasmuch as they reveal by their fruit [Gal 5 (19)] (not their leaves or their blossoms)[13] (Mt 13 [28–30]) in the communion of saints. For as Paul says, those outside our community are not our concern (1 Cor 5 [12]); God will judge them and punish them and give to each according to his works and how each one had acted, be it good or bad, as will be discussed below. Further, Paul also says in Gal 1 [8], "If we or an angel from heaven should preach

---

11* Gloss: Christ does not speak of physical service.

12* Gloss: [He] speaks here of drawing not the physical sword but the sword of truth, which is the ban of the love of Christ.

13 [This is Pilgram Marpeck's favourite image of the stages of discipleship; see especially no. 7, "Concerning Hasty Judgments and Verdicts."—Ed.]

something else than what I have preached, may he be damned" [Rom 2 (6); 2 Cor 5 (10); Rv 2 (2)].

We must not begin constructing this building in the middle or from the top (or overrunning the costs), but start at the beginning, and at the bottom [1 Cor 3 (9ff.); Lk 14 (28–30)]; these were the orders Christ had given before he ascended to all those who wish to follow him in truth [Mt 28 (19f.); Mk 16 (15f.)]. In the stories of the messengers,[14] and the letters of Paul, Peter, and John also it is shown from time to time (Acts 2 [41]; 8 [36–38]; 9 [19]; 16 [33]; 19 [4f.]; Gal 3 [27]; 1 Cor 12 [13]; Eph 4 [5]), as you well know. Christ blesses all those who also do likewise (Mt 7 [21–27]; Lk 6 [47–49]; 11 [28]). For it is dangerous outside the house. If we wish to learn from Christ, we must enter into his school, that is, into his fellowship that he has won through his death and the blood he shed, that he continues to gather today through his Holy Spirit in and through the preaching of the gospel. One must have faith in it with remorse, suffering, sorrow, and repentance of sins, after which the believer should submit to baptism in the name of Jesus Christ for the forgiveness of sins[15*] [Mk 16 (15f.); 1 Pt 3 (21); Rom 6 (3f.); 1 Jn 5 (6–8); Col 3 (2:12f.; 3:1)].[16*] Whoever boasts of faith without true baptism deceives himself [Jas 2 (14)]. Even if he should do all the external works of love, it would not be of any use unto salvation (so it will be told and shown to him from the Holy Scriptures); unless (as stated) he takes the side of Christ according to his ordinance through rebirth [Jn 3 (5)], through the revelation of his church and spouse, as he imposed and commanded it, at the end as it was at the beginning [Mt 28 (19); Mk 16 (15f.)].[17*, 18]

---

14 Acts of the Apostles.

15* This gathering does not consist of many people; rather, where there are two or three, Christ is in their midst.

16* The baptism of Christ is not for the ignorant (like among the anti-Christians), but [is] the covenant or announcement of a good conscience with God.

17 Gloss: Three give witness in heaven, the Father, the Word, and the Holy Spirit. And three witnesses on earth, the Spirit, water, and blood. These three serve as one.

18 Jn 5:7f.

Taking Christ's side happens not only inwardly (as some confused spirits claim) but also outwardly, not only as the world does with its ignorant, invented pedobaptism. But whoever rejects and flees it (of which he is not worthy) for the sake of fear, the favour of the world (that he does not upset it), or temporal glory, wealth, loss of goods and persecution (as the world rages against it and angrily sets itself against the teachings that they have placed upon him, according to the teaching of Paul): he must be baptized by fire [2 Tm 3 (4f.)]. "I speak the truth of Christ and do not lie, as my conscience is witness through the Holy Spirit."[19*, 20] St. Peter offers true counsel and says, "Save yourselves from the uncircumcised and perverted generation" [Acts 2 (40)]. Likewise, "Those who happily accepted his word were baptized," namely, by faith (as faith follows from preaching) [Rom 10 (17)] and the confession of their sins with regret and sorrow for the forgiveness of Christ, as Holy Scripture surely assures us [Is 53 (5)].[21*]

It amazes me, beloved Ulrich, that you heard the truth from the brothers so many years ago and offered them hospitality. You showed and proved your love and faithfulness to them. Still today you have a humble spirit and accept as right the actions and ordinances of Christ. Nevertheless, you hold yourself back, or allow the world together with Satan to hold you back (for he is the hinderer of all good). However, as the Holy Spirit bears witness and says, "Whoever hears my voice today, do not harden your hearts" [Heb 3 (7f.)]. "Truly God does not have any joy in the sinner's death, but rather that he repent and live" [Ez 18 (23); 33 (11)]. Further: "God desires that every one be saved and come to the knowledge of the truth" [1 Tm 2 (4)].

As Peter says of God, "Forgive and be patient with people, that no one is lost but rather that everyone repent" [2 Pt 3 (9)]. "For this reason the healing grace of God has appeared among us," says Paul "that ad-

---

19* Gloss: At the age of thirty, Christ let himself be baptized, to be an example; because he was complete in all righteousness, he did not need it.

20 Rom 9:1; Lk 3:23; Mt 3:15.

21* Where one did not first believe, there it cannot be (Acts 8 [37]). On the other hand, where true faith exists, one should not omit baptism (and all that Christ has commanded), for just as faith without works is dead, that is true of the opposite (Jas 2 [17]).

vises us to forsake our ungodly existence and worldly desires and from now on live virtuously, justly, and godly in the world" [Ti 3 (2:11f.)].[22*] For the God of love has never hindered his command and Word. Indeed, in all that he has commanded, or has prescribed or promised any single creature (that has reason), there is nothing that says it is not possible for us to do what is commanded and persevere through him. Woe, woe to all those who hinder or prevent any single creature from following his command and Word or offering obedience, as Moses had said, also as Peter bore witness in Acts: "God will awaken a prophet from among your brothers; him you should listen to him as you would me, in all he says to you; and it will come to pass that whichever soul does not listen to him shall be destroyed" [Dt 18 (18f.); Acts 3 (22)].

As the true prophet Jesus Christ says, whoever loves his father, mother, wife, child, brother, sister, lands, carpets, goods, honour—in sum, all things that can be named, yes, even his own life—above him is not worthy of him [Mt 10 (37)]. And whoever will not leave all this in his name cannot be his disciple [Lk 14 (26)]. Stated briefly, he wants our heart alone. Solomon writes that God suffers no god besides him.[23] "Where your treasure is, there your heart is also" [Lk 12 (34)].[24*]

As he (the Lord) answered and said to the young man (who had held all the commands of God from his youth onward), "'You lack one thing, sell what you have, give it to the poor, and follow after me.' But he departed from him with sadness, for he had many goods" [Mt 19 (21f.); Lk 18 (22f.); Mk 10 (22f.)]. That meant: his heart was set on them, as it is recorded in the text. Thus everyone should look at what he depends on, that he will not stand exposed on his day (understand, the day of the Lord). Blessed, blessed are all those who deny themselves, and daily, in patience, take upon themselves the cross [Lk 9 (23)], and submit to following him now and in the future—that is, to accept the covenant of Christ together with a good conscience with God, according to his command and word [1 Pt 3 (21)]. "For God has overlooked the times of

---

22* If one is incorporated into the communion of saints (Rom 8).

23 1 Kgs 8:23.

24* Gloss: It is natural that a lord of the house would not like it if his spouse yearned for another. How many thousand times more true of God. We should keep this in mind, for God will not be trifled with (Gal. 6 [7]).

ignorance. Now, however, he bids all people at all times to do penance, for he has set a day in which he will judge the entire earth with justice through one man (who is Christ), in that he has decided and held out faith to everyone after he raised him up from the dead" [Acts 17 (30f.)]. As Peter also said to the Jews, "Beloved brothers, I know well that you and your leaders have done it (to Christ) without knowing what you did. But [God] had previously proclaimed through the mouth of all his prophets that his Christ should suffer, and has fulfilled it. So repent and turn around, that your sins may be wiped away" [Acts 3 (17–19); 1 Cor 2 (8)].[25*]

"You ask just as some of them did as they had heard the preaching of the apostles and had their hearts pierced, saying, 'Beloved men, what should we do?' Peter said to them, 'Repent and let yourselves be baptized in the name of Jesus Christ for the forgiveness of sins'" [Acts 2 (37f.)]. From this text we can clearly understand that when we do not do this, or do not wish to, then none of our sins are forgiven. In summary, it cannot be otherwise; the so-called Christians can say what they wish. For this command will neither rot nor die until the Lord Jesus Christ comes again, in the end as in the beginning (which the Lord knows). And cursed is the one who acts according to those words that state: "Do not add anything to his words, lest he punish you and you be exposed as a liar" [Dt 4 (2); 12 (13:1); Prv 30 (6)]. For no liar will have any part in or communion with Christ (Ps 5 [6]; 101 [7]; Sir 7 [13f.]; 20 [26]; 25 [4]; 26 [6]; Eph 4 [25]; Rv 22 [15]). But selfish reason and intentions will be ever present and will invent something for their own benefit with the illusion of truth and false interpretation, so that they will not be persecuted with the cross of Christ, maintain the favour of the world, and be left in peace [Gal 6 (12)].[26*]

[25*] Gloss: True repentance, which is according to God, the death of humans unto obedience—it drives away the darkness and illumines the eyes and gives knowledge to the soul and shows the way to blessedness; indeed, what one cannot learn of people, that one knows through ready repentance. Gad, a son of Jacob.

[26*] Gloss: I speak of such partiality that allows one to ignore God and his holy Word, twist it, and nonetheless claim to be saved.

Oh no, it must be one or the other, day or night, light or darkness, Christ or Belial, temple of God or of idols.[27] The one cannot have any part or common ground with the other. Thus Paul says of this issue: "Separate yourselves and go out from their midst; do not touch any unclean thing. Then I will be your God, and you will become my sons and daughters" (Jer 51 [6]; Ps 24 [3f.]; 26 [4f.]; 101 [6f.]; Sir 12 [3–6]); [2 Cor 6 (17f.)]. Furthermore, "Do I preach to please either God or people? For if I wish to please people, I will be no servant of Christ" [Gal 1 (10); 1 Thes 2 (4); Lk 6 (26)]. May the Lord Jesus Christ grant you to reflect on these things seriously and in the fear of God [Sir 12 and 18]. Do not preserve anything from one day to the next, for we are not certain what tomorrow will be like. May it not happen to you as it did to the foolish virgins, who wished to buy oil only after the door had been locked shut [Mt 25 (9f.)]. They were left standing outside, saying: "We ate and drank with you; you taught us in the streets. Have we not prophesied in your name? Have we not driven out devils in your name? Have we not done many great deeds in your name?" (Mt 7 [22]). The Lord will answer them (as they knock and say: "Lord, open up."):[28] "'I do not know who you are; depart from me, you evildoers!' Then there will be wailing and gnashing of teeth" [Lk 13 (26–28)].

Beloved Ulrich, plead earnestly with God that he might direct your heart and spirit to take a happy step into Christendom (that is, the communion of his saints) as Christ has commanded and indicated to this end, that you might come to a good mediator (who is Christ) and end up in the Holy Spirit. May you be found to be a true warrior and knight of Christ, together with all those who have given themselves through grace with all their heart to that end [2 Tm 2 (3); 4 (7); 1 Cor 9 (24f.)]. What I am wishing for you I wish for my own soul. Amen.

Dear Ulrich, let us fear much more him who has power to throw body and soul into hell, not him who has no more power over the body after he kills it [Lk 12 (5)].[29] Christ also, the physician of the soul (Lk 5 [31]), says, "What does it profit someone if he should gain the whole

---

27 2 Cor 6:14–17.

28 Mt 25:12.

29 Mt 10:28.

world and yet suffers harm to his soul? Or what can a person give that will rescue his soul again?" "For whoever will cling to his life here will lose it" [Mt 16 (26, 25)]. "There is no lasting city here, but one should search for the future one" [Heb 13 (14)]. One should set his mind on and search for what is above and not what is of the earth [Col 3 (1f.)]. The whole world follows a way of life that says we will be here forever—with their invented worship and deceitful infant baptism and their ways of buying off heaven[30] and taking it by force [Mt 11 (12)]. (They blindfold the people and sneak around them to mislead them and leave them unjustified.[31] Through their deceitful works[32] they offer the appearance of truth against the truth and remain enemies of the cross of Christ [Eph 4 (14); 1 Cor 16; Rom 1; Phil 3 (18)].) It is as plain as day that neither God nor the Holy Spirit had called for or commanded them. And the priest is like the people, as the prophet has stated,[33] needing to twist everything, speaking of peace where none exists[34]—but rather destruction.[35*]

They all claim they want to enter, but do not want to enter through the right door. Those who want to go in, they will not let inside. Thus they are also thieves and murderers and remain so according to Christ's Word [Jn 10 (1); Mt 23 (13)].[36*]

In summary, outside of the order of the Holy Spirit and Christ there is no grace, favour, or forgiveness of sins, and where one is not born anew (that is, with a changed life), one cannot be saved and enter into the kingdom of God [Jn 3 (5); Rom 6 (4)]. Everyone should know how to orient himself according to this, if he wishes to enjoy eternity with

---

30 [This is probably a reference to purchasing indulgences that are supposed to shorten a believer's time in purgatory.—Ed.]

31 Gal 5:7.

32 2 Cor 11:13.

33 Is 24:2.

34 Jer 6:14; Hos 13:10, 16.

35* Gloss: Christ broke bread with his companions and commanded and taught them also to pray not as the world understands it (which it only appears to understand) and is thus a judgment of their very being.

36* Just as Christ is Christ before one believes it, so also teaching is correct teaching before one is baptized. And do not baptize before one is taught and believes the teaching; otherwise it is a betrayal.

Christ. And thus we advise people, because God is to be feared [2 Cor 5 (11)]. Those who are driven by the Spirit of God are the children of God [Rom 8 (14)], and in them is nothing damnable, as long as they are (incorporated) in Christ (namely, through the externally acknowledged, personally desired baptism with water) and no longer walk according to the flesh but according to the Spirit.[37] "This certain foundation of God persists and has this seal: God knows his own. Let those depart from injustice who call upon the name of Christ" [2 Tm 2 (19)]. For through the fear of God one avoids evil, does right, follows the just path, repents from his heart, neither doubts nor opposes God's Word, prepares his heart, and humbles himself before God [Prv 14 (2) and 16 (6); Sir 2 (17)].

Declaration of the order of the Lord Jesus Christ and his apostles in brief, how one obeyed it and still should (the foundation on which those who believe differently stand and live together),[38] as far as I can grasp, through the Lord's grace.

What follows is the order of the Lord Jesus Christ and the custom of the apostles (as an example to us). Above all it consists in the teaching and preaching of the gospel [Mt 28 (19f.); Mk 16 (15f.)], through which one comes to the knowledge of God and Christ and also oneself, and comes to faith (in which alone eternal life consists) [Jn 17 (3)]. It includes sorrow and ready repentance regarding sin, through faith in the forgiveness of sin in and through Christ.

Thereafter follows, first of all, baptism, through which one is incorporated into the church of Christ, that is, into the community of saints [Rom 6 (3)]. Brotherly love and friendship hold this community together as members of one body [Rom 12 (4); 1 Cor 12 (13)], as do brotherly punishment, discipline, warning, admonition, and the Christian ban, if one sins and acts blasphemously and in a troubling manner

---

37 Rom 8:1.

38 [This line is a gloss. The translation is suggested by the author's intention to stay with the basics of faith.—Trans.]

against God's Word and love [Mt 18 (15–18); Lk 17 (3f.); 1 Cor 5 (1ff.); 6 (1ff.); Gal 5 (19ff.); Eph 2 (3–5); Rom 1 (26ff.)].

Next there is the breaking of bread to the memory of the broken body and shed blood of Christ offered on the cross, with which his death is to be proclaimed until he returns, and to give thanks for all good deeds (1 Cor 11 [23–26]).

Likewise, we should continue in prayer (Col 4 [2]) for all the concerns of the brotherhood we have in the world, and for the authorities and all people, according to Paul's teaching and words (1 Tm 2 [1f.]).

We also pray for the community [Rom 12 (13); 2 Pt 1 (2); Heb 13 (1–3); 1 Cor 16 (1f.); 6; 2 Cor 8 (1ff.)], that is, aid for its needs according to the Word of God (Mt 26 [11]): "You will always have the poor but not me forever" (understand: his presence as a human being). And "whenever you wish, you can do good to them" (Mk 14 [7]). For what you do to the least of my brothers, you have done to me;[39] it will not go unrewarded.[40][41*]

This should all be done without human compulsion, command, or sanction [2 Cor 8 (8)], but rather according to the nature of love and the motivation of the Holy Spirit, to maintain the body of Christ, of which body he is the only head [Eph 4 (15f.); 5 (23)], as it is also stated in Acts: "They remained faithful to the apostles' teaching and in the community, and in the breaking of bread and in prayer" [Acts 2 (42)]. Whoever does not wish to enter in or considers it unnecessary and does not wish to believe in Christ, he will also be ruined and damned in his unbelief [Mk 16 (16)]. Such a one runs around outside the house. He must look out for himself, that he not be devoured by the dogs and wild animals outside [Phil 3 (2); Rv 22 (15)].[42*] O God, grant grace and true hunger of the soul, also knowledge, and open the eyes of understanding [Eph

---

39 Mt 25:40.

40 Mt 10:42.

41* Gloss: Christ does not speak here of the poor, beggars, or needy of this world but of those poor who believe in him, as Jas 2 [5] says, "who are rich in faith." For whoever does not have the Spirit of Christ is not his (Rom 8 [9]).

42* Gloss: Thus just as Pharaoh and his army was drowned in the sea, reason fears that it will also drown in baptism and die, as it must be according to the scriptures.

1 (18)], that we might sufficiently recognize our poverty and blindness, so that we might become rich and receive sight through you. For surely the existence of this world shall pass away,[43] but whoever does your will shall remain in eternity [1 Jn 2 (17)]. O God our Father, allow us, the needy, to sit with Mary Magdalene in stillness and diligent attention [Is 30 (15)] at the feet of your Christ (so that we might be helped) [Lk 7 (37ff.); 10 (39)], and from him alone learn how to be obedient, as he, in his true humanity, was obedient to you until his physical death [Phil 2 (8)].[44*]

Protect us, Lord, from our own desires and babbling knowledge according to our own reason. Let us gladly come into the light and remain constant in the Christian life, order, and being, as it has been the case for you, Ulrich, to this point. Whatever the reason may be, God and you know best. Ask God to free you, through his grace and mercy, of all things that prevent you from beginning the Christian life, so that you may freely sacrifice yourself for the Lord Jesus Christ [Rom 12 (1)]. May God send you, together with us, an orderly being and life that is Christian, as is often reported, so that your behaviour will not be a witness against you on the last day. I esteem, as you will probably recall, the last time I was with you and spoke with you. You said you wanted to reflect on Christ—and asked if I would be at your service when I should next come into your territory. I was not inclined to miss out on that visit. But dear Hans Gutenson told me you had decided to go to Schaffhausen. I let it stand at that; otherwise I would not have continued on my way, together with my fellow travellers, not because we wanted anything from you, but because we wanted to search for you, since we sensed your desire and sympathetic attitude toward all of us. For we are debtors according to love to everyone, especially those who hunger and desire God's Word and truth, as much as has been imparted to us through grace [1 Pt 2 (3:15)]. We are to seek the salvation of others, to their improvement and admonition (as one expects of us).

---

43 1 Cor 7:31.

44* Gloss: One's own reason does not wish to be taught, but it wishes only to teach through its own knowledge and pleasure; thus it must remain a fool (before God).

After all, we leave the work, the honour, and the glory to God the Lord, so that it might be fruitful. This is what I wish for you and your wives from the bottom of my heart, according to God's will.[45] You almost certainly have need of it, though you probably claim that life is not so bad, that I should desire this for you. But it is far, far from the mark. Natural piety is not enough for the kingdom of God. (When a scribe asked what the foremost command of God was, Christ gave him a wise answer, saying that he was not far from the kingdom of God [Mk 12 (34)].) We must cross over to the supernatural life and existence (through the new birth, throwing off the old person with all his works, putting on the new person, who is "created by God, in upright righteousness and holiness" [Jn 3 (5); Col 3 (9f.); Eph 4 (22–24)]). Otherwise it is in vain.

For scripture will not orient itself according to us: we must orient and measure ourselves in all our ways and life according to scripture, because it is a measuring stick for both the wise and foolish. As Christ himself says: "Search the scripture, for you claim life in it, and it is that which bears witness of me. Yet you do not wish to come to me, that you might have life" [Jn 5 (39)]. Paul says: "Everything that is commanded of us has been written to instruct us" [Rom 15 (4)]. He also writes to Timothy—because he had known Holy Scripture from his youth—that it might make him wise in the same fashion, to salvation through faith in Christ Jesus. "For all scripture given by God is useful to us for teaching, punishment, improvement, discipline in righteousness, that the godly person may be moved without compulsion to all good works" [2 Tm 3 (15–17)]. Christ also said: "'Whoever believes in me as the scripture says, from his body will flow rivers of living water.' This he said, however, of the Spirit, whom those who believed in him would receive" [Jn 7 (38f.)]. In the same way St. Paul says: "The letter kills (namely, for those who do not follow the intention of the letter of the law), but the Spirit gives life (that is, for those who follow obediently and carry it out" [2 Cor 3 (6)]. As Christ says: "Whoever despises me

---

45 [For the most part, in this letter the formal second-person pronoun *euch* ("you") is singular, addressed to Ageman as an individual. In these paragraphs the reference seems to be to a group of people; hence Maler's well wishes to *eurer hausfrouen* (the wives—plural—of these men).—Ed.]

and does not take up my words, he has his judge already—namely, the Word which I have spoken; it will judge people at the last day" [Jn 12 (48)]. "Each will be given according to his works," that is, "according to that which he did, be it good or evil" [Rom 2 (6–10); Eccl 12 (14); 2 Cor 5 (10)]. "Praise and honour, even eternal life, will be given to those who sought imperishable existence with patient and good works" (that is, those works that flow from true faith) [1 Pt 1 (4)]. "Strive for eternal life. Eternal disfavour, revenge, punishment, sorrow, and fear will fall on those who are disputatious and disobey the truth" (that is, his commands) and "obey what is unjust. They will fall upon all mortal souls who do evil, be they Jew, heathen," Turk, or supposedly Christian [Rv 2 (23); 22 (12)]. For "just as his mercy is immense, so also his punishment is great: each will be judged according to his works"; "and each will be found out according to his actions" [Sir 16 (12, 14)].

The prophet Jeremiah said that of all living things the human heart is the most deceitful. "Who then can know it? I, the Lord, guardian of the heart, I protect the kidneys and repay each one according to his ways and according to the fruit of his counsel" [Jer 17 (9f.)]. Thus, dear mortal, "experience," examine, and discipline "yourself before this judgment comes; then you will find grace for yourself in the time of punishment." Before you become sick, seek healing and humble yourself with Christ, and give yourself to his healing teaching. Let nothing hinder you from that, but instead show yourself ready in good time by stepping back from your own intentions [Sir 18 (21f.)]. Do not act as one who wishes to tempt God,[46] but rather ponder the severe wrath that will come at the end, and the hour of vengeance when God will turn away his face [Sir 35 (22–24)].

For God is pleased when we depart from sin and foolishness, when we pull back from unrighteousness [Sir 12 (6)]. This reconciles us with him. No one should be ashamed to confess his errors and sin; no one should try to force his way against the current of the river. Do not bind two sins together, for this will not help you avoid punishment for the first one [Sir 4 (31); 7 (8)]. Furthermore: "those who received their rewards here in this life and did not acknowledge me have suffered dis-

---

46 Dt 6:16.

tress because of my commands and words—for they wanted rather to have freedom instead of my healing and my return; and they did not understand or desire it but rather despised it" (they left it untouched) [4 (2) Esd 9 (10–12); Lk 16 (25)]. "They must acknowledge it after death in suffering" [Ws 5 (3ff.)]. "But praise and honour, also peace," says Paul, "to all who do the good and are obedient" (according to the order of his word), "be they Jew or heathen," woman or man [Rom 2 (10f.); Gal 3 (28); Col 3 (11)]. As Peter spoke in the house of Cornelius: "Now I experience in truth that God does not respect the person, but among all peoples whoever fears him and does right is acceptable to him" [Acts 10 (34f.)].

O God and Lord, give whatever, however, and to whomever as you wish! God does this to those who believe and truly trust in him. I do not speak here of the supposed faith that comes from speech without putting one's heart into it. This is how the world together with Satan believes—that there is one God; indeed, they also confess that Christ is the Son of God [Jas 2 (19); Mt 8 (31); Mk 1 (24)]. But this does not help them to salvation. And why? Because they do not wish to humble themselves before Christ, in his humanity. They are too proud, too uncommitted, these supposed Christians with their invented faith. I speak of a faith that is active through the love of God, empowered by the Holy Spirit [Gal 5 (6)]. As Paul himself says, whoever believes from his heart will become holy, and whoever confesses him with his mouth will be saved [Rom 10 (10)]. Such a person, whose heart the preaching of the gospel (that is, the joyful, grace-filled message) penetrates with regret and suffering, will also ask (as mentioned above): "Dear men, what shall we do?" [Acts 2 (37)].

The Holy Spirit answers someone with such a humble, shattered spirit and broken heart (who puts his ego aside and obeys the Word of God) [Is 57 (15); 66 (2); Ps 34 (18); 51 (17); Lk 1 (52)], and says even today, "Repent and let each of you be baptized in the name of Jesus Christ as a promise and for the forgiveness of sin. Then you will receive the gifts of the Holy Spirit, which are promised to you and your children, and to those who are far away."[47] As Christ said: "I have other sheep;

---

[47] Acts 2:38f.

they are not from this fold" (that is, from this people), "and these also I must bring here to me" (indeed, those who willingly let themselves be led), "and they will hear my voice" (that is, they will accept it). "There will be one herd and one shepherd" [Jn 10 (16)], that is, Jews and heathens or so-called Christians who come to the faith and will enter in and remain within according to this rule of Christ [2 Tm 4 (17); Rom 15 (8–12); Acts 13 (48); Ps 49 (1); Gal 6 (16)].[48*] Paul draws upon the witness of the prophet Isaiah: "I have been found by those who did not seek me, and appeared to those who did not ask after me" [Is 56 (65:1); Rom 10 (20)]. As Esdras also said against the Jews, under the influence of God: "Judah, since you have not wished to be obedient, I will offer myself to another people. I will give my name to them, for they will do and hold true to my words. Those who have never heard me will believe on me, and those to whom I never gave a sign will do what I call them to do. They have never seen any prophets and will nonetheless search out and confess their sins. Although they have never seen me with their physical eyes, they will nonetheless believe in what I say through the Spirit" [4 (2) Esd 1 (24, 35–37)].

In the same way also, the man who was uncircumcised asked Philip (as he preached to him of Christ and explained and helped him understand the scriptures): "There is water; what hinders me from letting myself be baptized? Philip answered, 'If you believe with your whole heart, then it may certainly be'" [Acts 8 (36–39)]. (If one has not believed beforehand, baptism cannot be performed, and is false [Acts 19 (1–6)].) The man who was uncircumcised answered him; "I believe that Christ is the Son of God." Thus he was incorporated and taken into the community of saints (wherein alone is the forgiveness of sins) and drove along the road rejoicing.[49*] I do not speak here about baptizing

---

[48*] Gloss: The goats also have a stable together with their princes, whom they serve and follow. These are all the unbelievers of whom Paul spoke: "Behold, those who despise and wonder at you and destroy you. Then I shall do a work in your times that you would not believe if someone had told you" (Hb 1 [5]; Acts 13 [41]).

[49*] Gloss: Just as a flowing spring cannot hide the fact that it springs forth, thus also a just, true believer desires baptism without any qualifications, and pursues everything that Christ has commanded.

those who are ignorant, as Peter and Paul point out. "Do you not know," he says, "that all whom we have baptized are baptized into his death," which means nothing other than the death of the previous way of life [1 Pt 3 (21); Rom 6 (3)] and a drowning of our own reason, a washing and removal of our sins (from inside out) through the blood of Christ. Likewise, those who were baptized in the house of Stephen had committed themselves to the service of the saints [1 Cor 16 (15)]. What then is left of the ignorant pedobaptism of the old and new popes? It is excluded before God and Christ and also in the community of saints as the most outrageous atrocity. It is not necessary to present more evidence of this. "Whoever has ears to hear, let him hear," and "whoever can understand it, let him understand it" (for it is the truth) [Mt 13 (9, 43) and 19 (12)]. But "faith is not everyone's thing," says Paul [2 Thes 3 (2)]. The people will find God's Word and teachings too hard (for it does have a conclusion and an end). For he says: "Whoever follows (or serves) me, let him deny himself and take up the cross every day and follow me" [Lk 9 (23); Mt 16 (24); Jn 12 (26)]. (But people do only one thing—they follow the world and its false teachers and go along with the rich young man away from Christ [Mt 19 (22)].)

One does not consider, however, how difficult the word will be: "Depart from me, you accursed, into the eternal fire"—that is, all those who disobey his commands and words [Mt 25 (41)—"that has been prepared for the devil and his angels, where the worm does not die and the fire is not quenched" [Mk 9 (44)]. But it burns us (creates unbelief) even now just as a quenched coal, and they maintain that it is not so bad, it holds no danger, until destruction suddenly befalls us like the labour pains of a pregnant women [1 Thes 5 (3)]. People will cry out "to the cliffs and mountains, 'Fall upon us, and hide us from the anger of the Lamb. For the great day of his anger has come; who can withstand it?'" [Rv 6 (16f.)]. "At the same time," says Christ, "the people will quake and shake with fear, for they will not know how to escape. They will lick their lips in fear and expectation of things that shall come to pass around the whole earth, which the powers of the heavens will bring about. And at this time they will see the Son of Man coming in the clouds with great power and glory" to sit in judgment [Lk 21 (25–27)]. Then a terrible fright will fall upon them [Ws 5 (2ff.)], all those who despised the patience and longsuffering of God and Christ, and did not improve themselves, since their own hiding places will no longer cover them [1 Pt 3 (9); Lk 13 (3)].

In summary, no excuse will help them, as the Lord spoke in a parable of the guests invited to the wedding, who tried to make excuses to get out of it [Mt 22 (2–14); Lk 14 (16–24)]; and this continues to today from those who wish to avoid God's wisdom—it can be heard constantly in the streets. It cries out, still in the time of grace, through its servants and workers, in the doors and gates and among the people [Prv 1 (20–33)]. "They speak their words in the city and say: 'How long do you people want to remain foolish, you mockers enjoy your mockery, and you fools hate my knowledge? Turn to my discipline; then I will pour out my Spirit to you and proclaim my words to you.'"[50*] "I continue to call, however, and you turn away; I stretch out my hand, and no one takes heed of it; my advice is allowed to go unnoticed! No one wants my discipline and admonition! Thus I will laugh at your destruction and mock you when your fear arises! When, however, fear comes upon you like a storm, and your destruction like a thunderstorm [Rv 6 (13f.); Lk 21 (26)], when fear and need come upon you, then you will call to me, but I will not answer you. You will wish to search for me early in the morning and not find me.

Since you hated my knowledge and did not choose to fear me, since you did not want my advice and hated all my discipline, you shall therefore eat the fruit of your ways and will be satisfied by your own advice, for what the ignorant desire kills them, and the happiness of fools brings them death." (As stated in the book of Wisdom, that is the way of the world. Whoever relies on it finds nothing more than a fool's paradise, like a wind that passes and is gone.) "But whoever chooses me" (relies on godly wisdom), "he will remain secure" (from all that mentioned above) "and have enough without fear of evil" [Ws 5 (14)].[51*] Thus St.

50* Gloss: "How often have I wished to gather you under my wings," says Christ, "like a hen her chicks, and you did not want this" (Mt 23 [37]).

51* Gloss: Wherever someone does not let go of all visible things (with Christ) (1 Cor 7 [22]), he will always be hindered. One is compelled first to bury one's father or to wish his family goodbye, and it is a burden and sorrow (Lk 9 [59–61]).

Paul said, whatever someone sows, that he will reap. Whoever sows according to the flesh will reap destruction according to the flesh [Gal 6 (8)]. Christ says this: If one wishes to save his live, he will lose it (Mt 16 [25]). However, he who sows according to the Spirit will reap eternal life from the Spirit. This refers to those who lose their lives for Christ's sake. They will retain it in eternity. Further: "Whoever sows injustice (that is different from what was just announced) will reap trouble and will come to his senses through the rod of plagues" [Prv 22 (8)].

For now I will end with this, beloved Ulrich. Accept this writing and admonition of mine for your salvation, with best wishes from me, a poor man (in truth!). Out of love I did not wish to leave it unsaid, especially since at this time I was not able to come to you in person. I pray to God, that if it be his will, I might come here again and find you surrendered to his holy truth. That would be to God's praise, to your usefulness, and to his people's comfort. May God the Father grant this in grace and mercy through Jesus Christ our only mediator and Saviour. Amen.

Greetings from Hans Gutenson and Hans Falck and their wives. I also greet you with the friendship of the Lord Jesus Christ, including your wives, daughters, and those dear to you.

Dated at St. Gall, 15 October in the year 1552.

In the Lord Jesus Christ,
servant in truth to you and to all who are eager for God,
a comrade in grace through the tribulation of Christ,[52]
Jörg Probst Rothenfelder, whom they call Maler

[52] Rv 1:9.

Interlude 3

It has been proclaimed to you, O mortal

"It has been proclaimed and made known to you, O mortal, what is good, and what God the Lord requires of you, namely, to do justice; to love him and your neighbour, kindness, good deeds; and to walk humbly with your God, so that you might be called a city of the Lord, and justice might be your name" (Mi 6 [8f.]; Dt 3 [10:12]); [1 Cor 15 (1); Acts 20 (20)].

For nothing common or unclean will go into this city [Rv 21 (27) and 22 (15)], but rather, as the prophet Isaiah says: "Those who are diligent in loyalty and truth" [Is 26 (2)].

My God and Lord, grant grace through your Jesus Christ, that we might gain it. To you be every honour and glory, in the Holy Spirit, in eternity. Amen.

Zwischenstück 3: Es ist dir, o Mensch, verkündigt. Translation by Leonard Gross.

Interlude 4

Why he changed his position on the oath

Jörg Maler

Most Anabaptists of the first generation, including the Swiss Brethren in St. Gall and Appenzell—to whom Jörg Maler had belonged between 1535 and 1548, flatly rejected taking oaths, on the basis of Matthew 5:34.[1] Marpeck, on the other hand, apparently held that taking oaths in legal civil transactions was legitimate within certain limits. Maler must have changed his position on the oath in connection with his alignment with the Marpeck Circle, with which he stayed in epistolary contact after 1543 at the latest, and with which he associated more closely after his return to Augsburg in 1548.[2]

Zwischenstück 4: Jörg Maler, Warum er seine Stellung zum Eid geändert hat. Translation by Leonard Gross.

1 This commentary is a translation of the introduction by Martin Rothkegel to *Zwischenstück* 4 (BSOT, 407).

2 Edmund Pries, "Anabaptist Oath Refusal: Basel, Bern, and Strasbourg 1525–1538" (PhD diss., University of Waterloo, 1995); MLDC, 227–30.

I have been questioned about the oath, how I stand in relation to it, since some hold to it, while some do not, on account of the words of Christ (Mt 5 [33–37]).

The answer I gave is that my position was not to take the oath, as described above. But that is no longer the case. My reason is also based on Christ's words (Mt 23 [16–22]; 5[33–37]). They lied and claimed that if they swore only by something creaturely, the law could not kill them and they could still magnify God. But the commandment was that anyone who did not keep what he had sworn by should be stoned, if whatever he had said was not simply Yes, yes. According to James, Christ does not pick up on this and say that the Christian has no law, commandment, or prohibition concerning the honour of God and the love of the neighbour. For love must soften all laws, commandments, and prohibitions. Some people thought that Paul had gone too far in calling on God as a witness to his soul when he criticized believers.[3] They would have believed him simply on the basis of his Yes. Paul also writes to the Hebrews that people swear by someone greater than themselves, and an oath puts an end to all dispute.[4] The Hebrew believers were of the same mind. This is not abolished in cases where it applies. The exception is a false oath, one that stands against the honour of God and the love of neighbour. No Christian is allowed such an oath; it is sin.

---

3 2 Cor 1:23.

4 Heb 6:16.

15

Concerning the humanity of Christ Concerning the Son of Man

To the believers in Ulm and in the Leber Valley

Pilgram Marpeck

Augsburg, 22 January 1555

"Concerning the Humanity of Christ" is the last known letter from Marpeck's hand and the final one to be included in the Kunstbuch. He died in 1556 in Augsburg. It is only in the conclusion of the text that we see that it was addressed to two congregations, one of them in Ulm (75 kilometres due west of Augsburg), led by Abraham Schneider, and the other one near it, in Langenau. It was also sent to believers in the Alsatian Leber Valley.

In this epistle the veil that covers the Augsburg Anabaptist congregation from 1528 to 1561 is lifted a little. We have no more than fragments of information about its inner life and its relation to the city and its policies.[1] In Pilgram Marpeck's advice to the beleaguered community in Langenau we hear words of caution about provoking the authorities and encouragement to remain quiet. Martin Rothkegel describes

---

Pilgram Marpeck an die Gläubigen in Ulm und im Lebertal: Von der Menschheit Christi. Vom Menschenshon; Augsburg, 22. Januar 1555. Translation by William Klassen, based on a transcription by Torsten Bergsten. Previously published in "Two Letters by Pilgram Marpeck," MQR 32 (1958): 196–200; and "Concerning the Humanity of Christ" in WPM, 507–15. Reprinted, after revision by William Klassen and John D. Rempel, by permission of the publishers.

1 Hans Guderian, *Die Täufer in Augsburg* (Pfaffenhofen, Germany: W. Ludwig, 1984), 101–6; MLDC, 231–44, 287–98.

the Augsburg congregation as "moderate to the point of compromise but remarkably realistic."[2] Heinold Fast makes a similar assessment: "In 1528 Marpeck joined the Anabaptist movement under the influence of the messenger Hans Hut, whose expectation of the end of the world put the established order of things into question. By the end of his life Marpeck has become a representative of the 'quiet in the land.' Contrary to his own expectations, he survived the tumult with which the movement began. Now he knows that survival is possible with moderation and modesty."[3]

Fast and Rothkegel seem to be damning Marpeck with faint praise. It is hard for an early twenty-first-century reader to respond to Marpeck's choice with integrity. In counselling the beleaguered believers in Langenau, Marpeck has two pieces of advice. First, do not confuse the voice of the Spirit with your own. Second, do not give the authorities occasion to persecute you. On the one hand, his recommended approach (which he practised in Augsburg) looks remarkably like the course mainstream Mennonites (and other Christians) in North America have chosen. On the other hand, Marpeck's piece of worldly wisdom seems to fall far short of his own vision of the resurrection of Christ and the reign of God, in which in fact the established order of things is put into question. The patient, passionate minister and self-taught theologian has stepped down from his pedestal, and we do not know what to do with him.

The two distinct themes of the letter are made clear in its opening lines: Christology and the nature of the spiritual life. "Although Marpeck never developed a comprehensive theological system, it is generally agreed that Christology formed the center of his concern. In respect to his doctrine of Christ he laid emphasis on the humanity of Christ and its implications for church order. For him Christ was truly divine and truly human: the implications of the latter for the Christian life and for the corporate body of Christ attracted him like a magnetic field."[4]

---

2 BSOT, 408.

3 Bern MS, no. 15, 1–2.

4 WPM, 507.

The author's thinking initially developed in response to the celestial flesh Christology of Caspar Schwenckfeld, which was quickly taken up in Dutch Anabaptism. What we have here is a digest of Marpeck's convictions set forth to make it clear that he and the movement around him opposed the Christology of Melchior Hoffman, which had taken root in most of the Dutch Anabaptist communities, including the most orthodox, led by Menno Simons. Marpeck reiterates his most controversial conviction: the flesh is of the creaturely nature that is taken up into and entered into the Godhead, and the Godhead is united and one essence in the flesh.

Having made the necessary point, the author goes on to describe the living presence of Christ in the believer and the revelatory role of the Holy Spirit in making Christ present. He deals with the "difference between servile and filial obedience and gives some indications about how to discern whether we are being led by the Spirit."[5] He cautions against zeal, a concern reflected in his later comments about the relationship between church and state. It is possible that Marpeck's "four reasons for having assurance" are oblique words of counsel to the persecuted people in Langenau, especially that no one should open a door God has not opened.

5 Ibid.

This epistle deals with the humanity of Christ and the Son of Man, also with the Christian life and calling, as well as the difference between servants and children[6]

Grace and peace from God, our heavenly Father, and from the Lord Jesus Christ,[7] his beloved Son, abide with us and all who love and seek Christ with a pure heart. Amen.

Dearly beloved, loved in God the Father and in Christ: First, we thank God for the bestowal of all his graces, which he accomplishes in us through Jesus Christ, and for his sake. Indeed, the Lord Jesus Christ himself works in us, ruling, directing, and leading us through his Holy Spirit in all truth of his divine will and good pleasure. He does this in all who love and seek Christ Jesus with a pure heart. In them he accomplishes the good pleasure of our heavenly Father.[8] Therefore no one (indeed, no creature in heaven or on earth) is accounted as anything before the Father, but alone the Son of Man.[9] The Son was born of the Father from the virgin of the tribe of Judah, and of the seed of David.[10]

This Son of Man (I say "Son of Man") is appointed a lord and ruler of all things; yes, indeed, humanity is taken up into God the Father and God the Father into the Son, who from eternity has been one essence, Spirit, and God.[11] Indeed, he has been the right way, the truth, and the life[12] in true humanity by nature and kind, born of the generation of mortals in and of Mary, the pure virgin, a true, pure, immutable human being. In him alone the fullness of the Godhead dwells bodily.[13] From the fullness of the Son of God[14] all true believers are filled with the Holy Spirit, so that they may not speak anything unless Christ (the

---

6 Jn 15:15; Rom 8:15; Gal 4:7; etc.
7 Rom 1:7; etc.
8 Phil 2:13.
9 Mt 3:17; 12:18; 17:5; Mk 1:11; Lk 3:22; Col 1:19.
10 Mt 1:1, 18ff.; Lk 2:4ff.; Rom 1:3; Rv 5:5; 22:16.
11 Jn 1:1–4.
12 Jn 14:6.
13 Col 1:19; 2:9.
14 Eph 1:23.

Son of God and of Man) works, completes, acts, and rules in them himself.[15] This is written so that all human actions—however lofty they may seem, however often the Lord is called a lord by people, indeed, even recognized as the Son of God—may truly confess Christ. Even the devil confesses and acknowledges him![16]

This does not please the Father unless the Lord confesses himself through his Holy Spirit in faith, by means of the physical voice of the believing person.[17] Likewise, no one can call the Son of Man "Lord" without the Holy Spirit.[18] Even the unclean spirits can call him a Son of God—indeed, even a Lord. However, to ascribe honour to the Son of Man as a true man of the human race and to confess him as their Lord and God—this no unclean spirit can do.[19*, 20] Either they consider him (the Lord) as purely human, to whom they do not want to ascribe the honour that he is also Lord and God, or else they confess him as purely the Son of God also according to the flesh, thereby failing to ascribe to him the honour of being a Son of Man, of the human race, flesh, blood, and human.

The flesh that is taken up into and entered into the Godhead is of a creaturely nature. And the Godhead is united and of one essence in the flesh as the true Word that became flesh;[21] it is truth and life itself.[22] To the flesh, body, and blood I ascribe all the honours the Father has ascribed to the Son. My reasonable service is to honour him as much as the Father. Yes, I also grant him all judgment that was committed to him by the Father.[23] Because he is the Son of Man, he will be a judge—and not because he is also the Son of God, one essence with the Father.[24] The Spirit of the Father and the Son judges apart from and

---

15 Mt 10:20; Mk 13:11.

16 Mt 4:3, 6; etc.

17 Rom 10:9f. [This is a play on this verse, underscoring the role of the body in confessing Christ in its emphasis on the physical voice.—Ed.]

18 1 Cor 12:3.

19* Note.

20 Mt 8:29; Mk 3:11; 5:7; etc.

21 Jn 1:14.

22 Jn 14:6.

23 Jn 5:22f.

24 It is in his humanity that Christ is God's agent on earth.

prior to that. The transfer of power that took place, took place for the sake of the humanity of Christ, that it might be honoured like the Father as essentially true Son of God and Man. He, the man Jesus Christ alone, accomplishes in the believers the good pleasure of the Father. He, the Lord, a true Son of Man, is Lord, ruler, leader, and director of his saints.

Through the Holy Spirit they know that all their actions are governed and led in and through Christ, so that they do not live (understand: unto the good pleasure of the Father) but Christ lives in them[25] and does and accomplishes the good pleasure of the Father. Thus St. Paul says that he dares to speak nothing but what Christ works in him [Rom 15 (18)]. Further, "Those whom the Spirit of God moves are children of God" [Rom 8 (14)]. Elsewhere he says, "Test whether Christ is in you; if not, you are cast aside!" [2 Cor 13 (5)]. That witness is given in order that we may be reminded and know what our committing and omitting is made up of. I mean this of believers, in matters of faith, namely, that in Christ nothing else shall move, lead, and guide believers than Christ, the word of truth.[26] It is not we on our own who speak, read, write, run, gather, or assemble. It is the Lord himself who brings it about. Without that, truly all is in vain and not pleasing to God the Father, whatever may be its appearance.

Therefore it does not depend on our willing or running but rather on the mercy of God[27] and on his grace in and with Christ. The one who gives the willpower can also accomplish it in those who belong to him.[28] In all our actions we must simply stand idle, as if we had died to ourselves, if Christ is to live in us. It is only Christ's life and walk that are pleasing to the Father. For human wisdom, especially the human wisdom of the scribal kind, can disguise itself as an angel of light.[29] Indeed, it is often coarse, carnal simplicity that deems its simplicity

---

25 Gal 2:20.

26 2 Cor 6:7; Eph 1:13; Col 1:5; 2 Tm 2:15; Jas 1:18.

27 Rom 9:16.

28 Phil 2:13.

29 2 Cor 11:14.

to be a self-chosen spirituality.[30*, 31] On its own it runs, impels itself, and erects sensual sects, that is, ones that have no spirit. Indeed, these have neither natural nor divine understanding. These the apostle calls "clouds without water" (understand the water of the graces of Christ, his Holy Spirit) "driven about by a whirlwind."[32] Ah, my brothers, how diligently and carefully we have to take heed that we do not consider our own movement the movement of the Holy Spirit, our own course the course and walk of Christ.[33*]

I must differentiate it a little and show how it can be tested and recognized, first of all in me, after that also in others, whether our actions are moved by the Holy Spirit or flow from a carnal mind. In the first place, it often happens—I've experienced it in myself as well as through many biblical narratives—that natural piety hates what is evil and is zealous about what is good. It does so even according to the divine manner, which people have in them by nature. They eagerly further the good and hinder the evil as they are able; in fact, they are overwhelmed with zeal, driven by it, totally exerting themselves.

Yet this is not the compulsion of the Holy Spirit of Christ, nor do they become children through it; it is only a servile compulsion and not a fatherly one—without the gains that are possible for children of God. This happened to Paul, who persecuted the church of God out of the compulsion of his zeal [Acts 9 (1ff.)]. Likewise, Peter was driven to cut off Malchus's ear.[34] Even today this happens through zeal for the sake of Christ, for the sake of good against evil. False apostles in the semblance of Christ were driven out of zeal for themselves. Some—who thought one ought to keep the Sabbath, refrain from foods, be circumcised—were even driven by true faithfulness. They were driven by many things.[35] Similarly, even today and to the end of the world, many people, who do not know or suppose otherwise than that they are

---

30* Note.

31 Col 2:23.

32 2 Pt 2:17; Jude 12.

33* Note.

34 Jn 18:10.

35 Gal 4:10; Col 2:16; etc.

driven by the Holy Spirit, act because of zeal concerning the good.[36*] [37] In part it is probably true that this zeal is often of God, though not under the office of the true Holy Spirit of Christ, but driven to serve in a slavish way. God uses such servants now, often in provisional ways, as forerunners and preparers of the way for those who are rightly driven by the Holy Spirit of Christ. They may make the path and the road, clear it, and weed it.[38] They are, however, only servants and not friends or children; they do not know what their master is doing or what he has in mind.[39] Such a servile compulsion has frequently taken place in our time for quite a while now and contributed to all divisions and sects, in order that the righteous who are moved by the Holy Spirit of Christ may become manifest.[40*, 41]

I write all this in order that each one may well perceive for himself what moves him, from what source it flows, and what the reason behind it is. This the servants do not know. However, the friends and children know what their Lord does and why the compulsion of the Holy Spirit is in them. Paul knew that he must be led to Rome to preach the gospel to the Gentiles.[42*, 43] Peter was moved by revelation to speak the gospel to the centurion Cornelius.[44] Philip also was moved to encounter the eunuch in the carriage.[45] Paul had no peace until he came again to Jerusalem to converse again with the leading apostles.[46] Peter was moved to arise and preach to all the nations.[47] Thus the apostles and their followers were each moved according to the measure of their

---

36* Gloss: Paul says: you have not received a servile spirit but one that is childlike.

37 Gal 5:1.

38 Mt 3:3; Mk 1:2f.; Lk 3:4f.; Jn 1:23.

39 [Marpeck develops these themes in relation to the creation and the fall in "The Admonition of 1542" (WPM, 232–27).—Trans.]

40* Gloss: Luther, Zwingli, M. Hoffman, C. Schwenckfeld, S. Franck, and others have been only servants who did not know what their Lord would do.

41 Gal 3:23; Jn 15:15.

42* Note.

43 Acts 19:21; 23:11; Rom 1:13–15.

44 Acts 10:9ff.

45 Acts 8:29.

46 Acts 2:14.

47 Acts 2:14–36.

faith.[48] So also they are moved even today through the Holy Spirit as children and not as servants, who with good and true knowledge know what their Father and Lord has in mind, namely, in such a way that they always know and are assured[49] of the basic reason why they are moved by the Holy Spirit. This assurance and certainty consists principally in four things, or reasons.

Four reasons for having assurance

First is love for God and granting my neighbour what God has granted and given to me, for his praise and the salvation of my soul.[50*] Second is to count it as loss and to give up life to the point of death, to suffer for the sake of Christ and the gospel in all patience. Third, to realize when God unlocks or opens a door,[51] that one enter the same with the teaching of the gospel. No one shall open a door that God has not opened, in order that the office of the Holy Spirit remain his own and free. For it is he who opens, and no one closes; it is who he closes, and no one opens,[52] in order that the pearls be not cast before swine or the holy things before the dogs, lest they turn about and mangle them.[53] Fourth, that one be free and sound in teaching and judgments and in truth, in order that none speak unless Christ works through his Holy Spirit.[54*, 55] By this one can recognize if the listeners are eager, thirsty, and hungry, weak, sick, tired, and fatigued; to them belongs the nourishment, the bread and the drink of the physician, and the salve. For the healthy and the despisers need no physician,[56] or salve, which salve is the word of truth that serves for the health of the nations.[57]

These four parts are the true proof that the movement is of the Holy Spirit; also that it brings forth fruit at each season. Where Christ does

---

48 Rom 12:3.

49 [Original: *gewiß*.—Trans.]

50* 1.

51 Acts 14:27; 1 Cor 16:19; 2 Cor 2:12; Col 4:3.

52 Rv 3:7.

53 Mt 7:6.

54* Gloss: The spiritual person judges all things and is judged by no one.

55 1 Cor 2:15.

56 Mt 9:12; Mk 2:17; Lk 5:31.

57 Rv 22:2.

not find this fruit through the Word that is proclaimed, a curse and barrenness soon befall them, as they befell the fig tree [Mt 21 (19); Lk 13 (6–9)]. All trees are to have fruit, wherever and whenever Christ arrives, be it in season or out of season. Therefore it behooves us to give diligent heed that we distinguish our own movements sharply and diligently from the movement of the Holy Spirit. I do not write this to weaken, detain, or set aside anyone's progress or compulsion, but only that it may be well and truly discerned, through the pure fear of God, which fear is the beginning, root, and ground of all wisdom, understanding, and knowledge of God.[58] May the Lord grant us this to his praise and our salvation in eternity. Amen.

Concerning the brothers from Langenau, we thank God, who always bears with our weakness and gives us a way of escape in all temptations. Nevertheless, it seems to us, as I also said to them here, that they should try to return there. Perhaps God would grant them a sojourn there for a while, especially the old brother and the very old sister. We do not think that their councillors' command would be so strict that they would be expelled from the territory. A threat often occurs in order to get people to keep quiet and not give the authorities occasion to persecute, in case people gather together unnecessarily. Exercise moderation and discretion in such a case. Governments often stand in fear of their own punishments; as a consequence they do not like to persecute us. Hence it behooves us to spare the government any occasion to act, in order that it may not wrongly seize believers. I write this especially to you, beloved brother Abraham.[59] For your sake and the sake of other brothers and sisters, use discretion and moderation, in order that we do not lose through lack of moderation the place which God has granted us. If the old sister does not want to remain, try to have her cared for by one of her friends, so that she can leave you. It would bring a special persecution upon you and her. Hence one should proceed with moderation and wisdom. However, if God's honour and truth are at stake, then we are obligated to hold to everything we own

---

58 Ps 111:10; Prv 1:7; 9:10.

59 Abraham Brendlin Schneider, a gardener in Ulm, in southern Germany.

lightly and to endure all persecution unto death. So much concerning the brothers in Langenau.

For the sake of the wife of Lawrence in the Leber Valley, it is my advice, dearly beloved brother Lawrence, that you let her continually drink of the valerian herb. Don't mix in any other liquid so that the strength of the herb is not diluted. Do not boil it, but only place one, three, or four herbs in one batch and then let it stand three or four days, continuing to add more. At the same time, a dry healing salve can be used for the injury. The quiet brother Lienhart Schuhmacher used it; he had serious wounds but was healed. She should have no cabbage,[60] pork, and no liquid food and drink like strong wine. Bathing is harmful unless the trouble is not in the head. All this, as said, only draws the rheumatism into the head. Food that does not smell will be good for her. At the moment I have no further advice.[61] May the Lord grant us that we bear all things with patience, since, as pertains to the flesh, we are subject to all infirmities and weaknesses.

Concerning Bartle, he will report to you how graciously we dealt with him. According to what you write, he has given us every other report.

We thank God for all grace. May the Lord grant us all to persist to the end.[62] Amen. The grace of our Lord Jesus be with you[63] and us all, who desire it with a pure heart. Amen. We greet all of you, each one of you especially by name, with peace and love in Jesus Christ. Pray to God earnestly for us. By grace we desire to do the same for you. When

---

60 [Original: *kabaskraut.*—Trans.]

61 [A similar prescription clearly attributed to Pilgram Marpeck found its way into a medical codex (no. 11, 182) in the Vienna Royal Library. Entry no. 36 discusses how to make blackthorn juice to cure syncoma. It is dated 1555. See Johann Loserth, *"Zwei biographische Skizzen aus der Zeit der Wiedertäufer in Tirol, "* in *Zeitschrift des Ferdinandeums für Tirol und Voralberg* 11 (1895), 288–90. Did Marpeck derive his interest in medicine from Otto Brunfels in Strasbourg? For Brunfels's interest in gynecology and his publications in the area of medicine and botany, see F. W. E. Roth, "Die Schriften des Otto Brunfels 1519–1536," *Jahrbuch für Geschichte, Sprache und Literatur Elsasslothringens* 16 (1900): 257–88.—Ed.]

62 Mt 10:22; 24:13; Mk 13:13.

63 Rom 16:20; Phil 4:23; 2 Thes 3:18; etc.

you have read the letter, (if it pleases you in the Holy Spirit) pass it on to the Leber Valley and other places.

Dated at Augsburg on the twenty-second day of January, 1555.

In the Lord Jesus Christ,
your servant and comrade
in the tribulation[64] which is in Christ,
Pilgram Marpeck

64 Rv 1:9.

Interlude 5

Jörg Maler's interrogation by three evangelical preachers and one Dominican

[Augsburg, before 26 August 1551]

Jörg Maler depicts his interview with three evangelical preachers and one Catholic ecclesiastic in the Augsburg prison.[1] It must have taken place after Maler's imprisonment in April 1550 and before the expulsion of evangelical preachers from Augsburg on 26 August 1551.[2] As for the three specifically named evangelical preachers, they were Johann Held, pastor at St. Anne; Johann Flinner, pastor at Holy Cross; and Johann Meckart, pastor at St. George. The Dominican is presumably to be identified as the cathedral preacher Johann Fabri (also spelled Faber), OP, from Heilbronn, who by 1550 had come out against the Anabaptists through his published writings.

Despite his at least partial recantation in 1533, this time Maler does not equivocate. His interrogators responded by jailing him for two years. (See the commentary on no. 40: "Confession of Faith according to Holy Scripture.")

Zwischenstück 5: Jörg Malers Verhör durch drei evangelische Prediger und einen Dominikaner; [Augsburg, vor dem 26. August 1551]. Translation by Leonard Gross.

1 The first part of this commentary is a translation of the introduction by Martin Rothkegel to *Zwischenstück* 5 (BSOT, 416). Translation by Leonard Gross.

2 [As part of the conditions the emperor imposed on the Schmalkaldic League, all Protestant ministers were forced out of Augsburg for part of 1551.—Ed.].

Take note, reader, of several summarized conversations of my response, as requested in prison from three preachers and one preacher-monk, concerning baptism.

The first one maintained that if the father in the family is a believer, he may also have his household baptized.[3*, 4] His point was that there must have been children included. I answered that Paul said the house of Stephen had organized itself in the Lord's service. He did not want to admit this, until I made mention of 1 Cor 16 (15).

Further, I asked two questions, wondering whether Christians persecuted others, or allowed themselves to be persecuted. He said the disobedient and stubborn need to be persecuted.[5] I said he should substantiate to me on the basis of Holy Scripture where I had been stubbornly and disobediently against truth. But [they said] I did not understand.

Second, on the one hand, they say the world keeps getting better, because it has become Christendom[6] through infant baptism. On the other hand, they preach that the longer they live, the more wicked and evil the devil's work in the world becomes. When I said that, my interrogator went away from me.

The other person said that since Paul reports that the adults passed through the sea,[7*] and that they were baptized with the sea and clouds [1 Cor 10 (1f.)], along with their children whom they had taken along

---

3* Here.

4 1 Cor 1:16 [16:15—Ed.].

5 1 Sm 15:23.

6 [That is, Christianized.—Ed.].

7* Flinner [one of the interrogators—Ed.]

and did not leave behind, the children thus experienced the same. Why would that not be the same at the present time? I said little by way of a response but remained with the words of Christ and the apostles (Mk 16 [15f.]; Acts 2 [38, 41]; 8 [37]).

The third person thought that since Paul called children holy and clean, one ought also to baptize them, incorporating them into God's congregation.[8*] I said that according to my understanding, Paul had not thought about baptism in this place but about marriage, as the text reads (1 Cor 7 [14]). And so it remained.

After all this a monk came to me, asking me that I should tell him whether it is not true that one person may believe for another, and that Holy Scripture says that. I said he was a scribe; he should show it to me and I would listen. He pointed to Mt 9 (2), that they had believed for the paralyzed man,[9*] for the Lord said: "He saw their faith." I said: no one may believe for another concerning eternal life. But in terms of the body, they may well have believed that he might make him well, for they had seen that the Lord healed all sorts of sickness.

He continued: the child was conceived and born into sin (Ps 51 [5]). I said: in the sin of the father and mother. For it stands written: "You were pure from the time of your creation, until misdeeds were found in you" [Ez 28 (15)].

Further, he stated that the child had original sin, which needed to be taken away from it through baptism. I said Christ took it away. He did not want to believe this. I said: why then did Christ come? Otherwise he would have become human to no avail. But he did not accept this answer. I did not want to believe him. There the interrogation came to an end. I remained imprisoned; he went away from me.

8* Meckart [another one of the interrogators], God be gracious to you.

9* Gloss: What he meant is that the godfather and godmother can believe for the child.

Moravian village.

Austerlitz (Slavkov), Moravia. Oldest Hutterite community, center of radical activity.

16

Concerning the service and servants of the church

To the congregations in Moravia
Pilgram Marpeck
Augsburg, 1552–53

The Marpeck Circle was widely dispersed geographically.[1] The people to whom this letter was addressed lived in Moravia, which is in the southeast of the present-day Czech Republic, due north of Vienna. The saints in Moravia were not Hutterites but seven congregations located at Austerlitz (now Slavkov u Brna in the Czech Republic), Poppitz (Popice), Eibenschütz (Ivančice), Jamnitz (Jemnice), Znaim (Znojmo), Vienna, and one referred to as "am Wald." They were brought into being through the work and inspiration of Pilgram Marpeck himself. This letter was carried to Moravia by Jörg Maler and shoemaker (Schuhmacher) Jacob Schultz, both members of the Augsburg fellowship.

The letter is a pastoral admonition on the nature of Christian service. Jesus as the Son of Man is the model. He served humanity even to the loss of his soul, an unusual turn of phrase that is part of Marpeck's frequent reference to the letter to the Hebrews. All creatures are simi-

---

Pilgram Marpeck an die Gemeinden in Mähren: Vom Dienst und von den Dienern der Kirche; [Augsburg, 1552/1553]. Translation by William Klassen. Previously published as "The Servants and Service of the Church" in WPM, 549–54. Reprinted, with editorial changes, by permission of the publisher.

1 This commentary is taken (with minimal adaptation) from the introduction to "The Servants and Service of the Church," no. 19 in WPM, 549.

larly now expected to serve; this includes angels as well as humans. Christians know that they could never pay the debt they owe to the love of Christ, so they serve in a "freely self-giving spirit," in the inspiration of the Holy Spirit. Thus they do not fall into pride and destruction like the fallen angels, who wanted to serve in pride and power.

There is specific reference at the conclusion to twenty copies of "The Admonition of 1542,"[2] Marpeck's most widely read book, and to two other letters by him which have not survived, so far as we know. They deal with surrender (*Gelassenheit*) and the Lord's Supper. Both were carried to Moravia by Maler and Schultz. They were second copies; they had been sent earlier by another carrier. There was some doubt about whether the letters had arrived the first time. The answer to this letter is no. 17 in the Kunstbuch (to Pilgram Marpeck and the congregation in Augsburg); it expresses "Gratitude for the Letter We Received," which testifies to the fraternal love among the congregations in Augsburg and Moravia. The date of no. 16 is deduced from that of no. 17. This is the only instance in the Kunstbuch where both sides of a correspondence have been preserved.

2 WPM, 152–302.

This epistle concerns the service and servants of the church.

To God's elect, the holy ones, our beloved in Christ in the margravate[3] of Moravia, gathered at Austerlitz, Eibenschütz,[4] and in other places.

Grace and peace from God our heavenly Father and from the Lord Jesus Christ[5] be and remain with us and you and all who love and seek Christ with a pure heart through voluntary patience under the acquittal of Christ. Amen.

Dearly beloved in Jesus Christ, beloved as a witness to the truth! Our dear brothers Jörg Maler and Jacob Schultz Schuhmacher[6] have decided voluntarily to journey to you in order to become acquainted with your way of living and the knowledge of God our Father and of his Christ (in whom is our salvation) among you. They come that you may receive from them both a spoken and a written testimony to the truth of the state of our life. They do this in order that all of us may have received the same comfort, peace, and joy and bear the same compassion in the tribulation of Christ[7] in the fellowship of his body.

In this body the gifts of the Holy Spirit are manifest in each member according to the measure of faith[8] in Jesus Christ for service in the growth of the body of Christ.[9] By this service the weakest, least, and smallest members are strengthened, comforted, led, guided, and pastured by the strong, leading, and most able members. Thus they are trained, preserved, increased, and nourished until they reach the full maturity of Christ. For whoever would be the greatest must be the

---

3 [Margravates were originally frontier German provinces of the Holy Roman Empire. Margraves were the noblemen who governed them; by the twelfth century they had all become princes in their own right.—Ed.]

4 [The lords of Eibenschütz granted religious freedom to all. In addition to a Hutterite gathering, there was also a circle of Marpeck followers.—Trans.]

5 2 Thes 1:2; etc.

6 [A shoemaker, about whom nothing is otherwise known.—Trans.]

7 Col 1:24.

8 Rom 12:3; Eph 4:7.

9 Eph 4:16, 19.

vassal and servant and not the ruler of all the others, says the Lord [Mt 20 (26f.); Lk 22 (26); Mk 10 (43f.)]. Their service is not compelled or forced or for the sake of shameful gain; rather, it flows voluntarily from an affectionate disposition. They do not rule over the heritage of God but become an example to the flock, says Peter [1 Pt 5 (2f.)]. For it is certain that the highest good treasure, which is the Son of the Father, was not (in this time) sent to rule in order that he should be served, but rather that he voluntarily presented himself to us all to serve our salvation, and never desired that he should be served. In the Lord is a true example for all who are his disciples and servants.[10]

Thus the eternal Father subjected the angels, as the highest of the creatures, to the Son for Christ's sake[11] because he served humanity as the least of the creatures (although he is the image and likeness of God).[12] This was so that they (the angels) should properly and voluntarily serve (as the Son of the Father), without compulsion or urging. Those angels who did not present themselves to the Son voluntarily in all humility and lowliness, for service with him on behalf of mortals, were thrown into the abyss and eternally rejected.[13] This is the just judgment of God, since they had received knowledge of it from the Son (in the divine intention that it was to happen) through the preaching of the everlasting gospel [Rv 14 (6)].[14]

This intention of God was proclaimed in the midst of heaven by an angel and will be proclaimed eternally, that all creatures of God should, like the Son of the Father, submit freely and without compulsion to such service and lowliness. Any creature that has not thus voluntar-

---

10 Jn 13:12ff.

11 Heb 1:4–14.

12 Heb 1:3; 2 Cor 4:4.

13 2 Pt 2:4.

14 [This phrase was given new significance by writings attributed to Joachim of Fiore, who in a mystic experience had a vision of the "everlasting gospel." This was identified with the true gospel, in contrast to the watered-down gospel of the church's teaching; it was not tied to the earthly institutions of church and empire which were temporal in nature. In this sense the idea was picked up by the Spiritual Franciscans and came to have currency in mystic circles and so ultimately found its way into Anabaptist writings. The Pietists of the seventeenth century were also fond of it.—Trans.]

ily served humanity with and in Christ, prior to the revelation of the mighty glory of the Son, is cursed and eternally damned. The fall of the angels on account of humanity took place in immediate response to the intention of God in the eternal gospel, preached from eternity to eternity, through which the envy and hate of the serpent, the fallen angel, has come upon mortals.[15*, 16] In this same envy and hatred he also turned humans away from service together with the Son, from the law and from obedience of God. Even today he continues to turn people away from believing the eternal gospel and giving free obedience and fellow-service in and to all, with and in Christ. For this reason humanity too comes under condemnation, together with the enemy of all truth and obedience.

The true servanthood of the Son, even to the loss of his soul, which he has shown us voluntarily, has become our salvation through faith in him. Thus we again serve humanity, together with all the holy angels of God, until the glorious appearance of the Son of God from heaven, together with his holy angels and mortals.[17] The Son himself did not come into this time of his servanthood that he should desire or allow himself to be served, or to enjoy even the smallest honour or benefit from any creature [Mt 20 (25–28)]. Instead he regarded as nothing all the service he rendered to the honour of God and to our salvation, even to the loss of his soul. It was as though he had done or deserved nothing, when in fact he earned, achieved, won, and conquered all alone, without any assistance or collaboration from angels or mortals or any creature. The presumed contribution of all other creatures is only the hopeless, unpayable debt of unworthy servants who cannot earn anything [Lk 17 (10)]. Whatever is given to them is given from pure, unsullied goodness, faithfulness, grace, and mercy, alone through the merit of Christ. Whoever does not serve in the freely self-giving Spirit of Christ, even to the loss of his soul, or serves from fear and threat of condemnation, the same seeks his own satisfaction and the shameful

15* Note the fall of the angels.

16 Gn 3:25.

17 Heb 12:22.

benefit of a vain, proud, purloined reward and honour. His reward is destruction.

Some people neglect to serve humans in and through Christ with the gift God has given them,[18] because of scorn, fear, idleness, laziness, carelessness, or any other cause. Let them take heed that they not receive the same judgment along with the angels, whom God did not spare even though they were the highest and most honoured creatures [2 Pt 2 (4)].

To all his true servants God promises a sharing with Christ in the reward and heritage. The true childlike servants do not look to the reward, as though they could earn it with their service;[19*] they look alone to the rewarder and the giver and not to the gift or the reward. Nor do they measure their services according to the size of the reward. God does not measure or weigh the reward or gift, but he constantly gives freely an overflowing measure of his kindness and goodness. Similarly, all our conduct will be judged regardless of how good it may be. (In any event, it has all been given to us by God in the first place.)

Therefore everything has been given to us for service, in order that we should not wantonly waste it, as though it belonged to us, and regard it as of no account, in opposition to the inexpressible goodness and grace of God.[20] In truth, it does not flow from our ability and conduct [2 Cor 3 (5f.)]. It is only that God in his love takes pleasure in us, his children, and we receive everything from the Father in Christ. It is this love alone that motivates us to perform the services of Christ to one another by grace. Thus the angels too, who were created holy and pure, rejoice to serve humans (those who are justified in Christ and washed and cleansed from their sins). Since even the Lord himself desired and rejoiced to serve mortals for their salvation, although he was Lord and master [Jn 13 (13f.)], how many hundred thousand times more should we perform our service to one another eagerly, joyfully,

---

18 1 Pt 4:10.

19* Note.

20 [Original obscure: *Darum ist es unns alles geben, damit zů dienen, das wir wider gegen der unaussprechliche guet und begnadung Gotes, on einig alefanntz, roub, name, alles wieder verschätzt und bey uns nicht geacht werden soll . . .*—Trans.]

and freely? We do not serve ourselves but rather serve to the praise of God and our own salvation, because the Lord himself has served us. The angels also continue to serve us to this day,[21] without any pleasure of their own.

O dearest friends of God, if we really reflect on it let us not become lazy, dull, or careless. It will cheer up our hearts, regardless of all the offence, frustration, and affliction of the enemy and our own flesh and blood and what we must endure and suffer because of it. None of this compares with the inexpressible glory we have through the knowledge of Christ. What therefore should prevent, vex, and hinder us in our godly life, conduct, and service in the love which is in Christ? [Rom 8 (18, 26, 35, 39)]. May the Lord Jesus Christ give us the gifts and aid of his Holy Spirit.[22] Indeed, may the Holy Spirit himself, as the mind, will, and pleasure of the Father and the Son, be in us the giver and doer, ruler and accomplisher, teacher[23] and leader,[24] reminder[25] and urger,[26] that we may be found to be free servants of one another in Christ until our end. Amen. May the heavenly Father grant this to you and all of us who desire it from a pure heart. Amen.

Further, we send you twenty testimonies of the covenant[27] and two epistles. The one about true surrender and poverty of spirit we had already sent earlier by an older brother from Silesia by the name of Thomas.[28] Can it be that you have not received it? The other deals with our latest thinking on the Lord's Supper. We hope you will receive everything as servants without merit[29] to the comfort of our salvation in

---

21 Ps 91:11f.

22 Phil 1:19.

23 Jn 14:26.

24 Jn 16:13.

25 Jn 14:26.

26 Rom 8:14.

27 [Original: *Bundtzeugknussen.* This is likely a reference to copies of "The Admonition of 1542," which was also called "The Testimony of the Covenant" (*das buch der bundesbezeugung*).—Trans.]

28 [An otherwise unknown Anabaptist from Silesia, which in the 1520s and 1530s had many Anabaptist congregations.—Trans.]

29 [Original: *inn der schuldigen dienstbarkheit.*—Trans.]

Christ. The Lord Jesus Christ make it fruitful[30] to grow[31] and increase[32] in all things. Amen.

The grace of our Lord Jesus Christ be and remain with us in eternity. Amen.

In the Lord Jesus Christ,
your servant of all the faithful
and comrade in the tribulation[33] which is in Christ,
Pilgram Marpeck

---

30 1 Cor 3:6.
31 Eph 4:15f.
32 1 Cor 15:58.
33 Rv 1:9.

17

Gratitude for the letter we received

To Pilgram Marpeck and to the congregation in Augsburg
The elders and congregations in Moravia[1]
Eibenschütz,[2] 19 March 1553

This epistle was written by the leaders of the Marpeck Circle in Moravia in gratitude for Pilgram Marpeck's writing to them "Concerning the Service and Servants in the Church," no. 16 in this collection. Jörg Maler and Jacob Schultz Schuhmacher were couriers of the Marpeck letter. This letter had been carried to Augsburg by Maler and Valentin Schneider. The list of signatories provides us with rare information about leaders in Moravian and Austrian congregations of whom we have little other information. For example, there is no other record of an Anabaptist congregation in Vienna in the 1550s. This letter is moving evidence that in the instability and insecurity of the times, these congregations treasured every opportunity for contact.

Älteste und Gemeinden in Mähren an Pilgram Marpeck und an die Gemeinde in Augsburg: Dank für den empfangenen Brief; Eibenschitz, 19. März 1553. Translation by Leonard Gross.

1 Moravia is the southeastern region of the Czech Republic near its border with Slovakia and Austria. It has a long history of religious radicalism going back to Jan Hus (1372–1415) and the Unity of the Brethren.

2 Currently Ivančice, in the Czech Republic.

There follows a reply to the above-mentioned letter, written in Moravia

To our dear brother Pilgram Marpeck, dwelling in Augsburg, including the congregation itself, wherever it gathers in the name of the Lord, and to our dear brothers in the Lord at hand.

May grace and peace from God the Father and from the Lord Jesus Christ[1] be and remain with you and us, including all the saints of God. Amen.

Dearly beloved in the Lord, in and through Jesus Christ our cherished Saviour, in particular to you, much loved and faithful brother and servant Pilgram, including your congregation in Christ, namely, at Augsburg, or wherever it is gathered in the name of the Lord.

The dear brothers Jörg Maler and Jacob Schultz Schuhmacher have come to us, your and our dear brothers in the Lord. They have disclosed the love in the Spirit which you have and show us through word of mouth and written communication. We listened to the epistles being read, the one on the Lord's Supper, the commemoration of our Lord and Saviour Jesus Christ, and another regarding ministers and the ministry of the churches. They were then read in all congregations that stand with us in the same faith in Christ in the land of Moravia. They filled us all with heartfelt joy, for which reason we thank God our heavenly Father through Christ for such love and support, which the Lord Jesus Christ allows to descend upon us through you, our esteemed ones in the Lord.

---

1 Rom 1:7; etc.

Indeed, we cannot thank our God enough for his unspeakable goodness, grace, faithfulness, and mercy, which the true God and heavenly Father bestows on us, which the Lord Jesus Christ supplies to us poor and needy ones with his riches and treasures—unworthy though we are—for our spiritual prosperity. Yes, we experience and see the Lord richly and abundantly in all his works and gifts of grace in these most dangerous last days. The Lord admonishes and cautions us not to become languid or negligent in our undertakings[2] and walk, and this all the more—much more!—since the time of our redemption is drawing near.[3] Oh, you beloved in the Lord Christ, we are too simple, too lowly, and too immature to thank our God the Father for such faithfulness and blessing. May the Lord graciously foster, speak, and write within us his praise, honour, glory, and blessing, unto the hallowing of his majestic name—indeed, that what we do may be pleasing before God the Father, so that the God and Father of our Lord Jesus Christ may work and carry out such in us and all believers[4] through Christ our Lord and Saviour, to his eternal praise. Amen.

Dear brothers, we covet always the truth and all that is good, as much as this has been and will be revealed to us, including keeping up with you vigorously, through the help of the Lord and the helping hand of his Holy Spirit.[5] We also sense and see richly the Lord's help and undergirding, as he is revealing from day to day the fragrance and taste of his mystery[6]—the longer, the more completely—on account of our adversity, that we straightaway need to marvel that the Lord supplies us so faithfully with all sorts of provisions. Indeed, exactly this is being handed over and delivered to us from you, through the helping hand of the Holy Spirit. We are to—and want to—confess, to the honour of our God the Father and Lord Jesus Christ, all that the daily needs among us require. In this, we sense the overwhelming love and goodness of our

---

2 Eph 3:13; Heb 6:12; 12:3.

3 Lk 21:28.

4 Eph 3:20.

5 Phil 1:19.

6 2 Cor 2:14–16; Phil 4:18.

Lord and Saviour Jesus Christ (which he extends to us as his saints), that he does not want to leave us orphaned.[7]

May the Lord grant that we surrender ourselves in these and other areas. Through faithful service and labour we plow them and then attain fruitful results—not forgetting him. God adorns and bestows honour and teaching on his church, his bride, so that in Christ it will be carried home to the heavenly Father, and we as his pupils and disciples may grow, going from one divine blessing and virtue to another.[8]

We also thank God our Father for all of you, that you have not become tired and languid toward us in things that bear on our salvation, improvement, edification—indeed, advancement of our most holy faith in Christ.[9] May the Lord reward you for your efforts and labours (which you have exerted to our benefit for a long time) and hold you in great vigour and strength, including steadfastness—something we also want for ourselves. We wish this for you with all our heart, to all and to each individually, according to the way of love through Christ, our Redeemer and Saviour. Amen.

Our and your beloved in the Lord, Jörg Maler and Valentin Schneider, will be able to report to you how things stand with us in Moravia. They departed from us in the peace and love of Christ—for now they are no longer here! Hearty and genuine greetings come to you from all of us and from each individually, in the peace of the Lord Jesus Christ—especially to you, much-beloved brother Pilgram, along with all of the saints with you. It is also our deepest heartfelt wish and desire for you, beloved brother Pilgram, and for all the brothers and sisters in the Lord, for you or someone else to contact the beloved brother Leupold Scharnschlager, and also the old and beloved brother and father Sigmund Bosch. Greet them from all of us, orally or by letter, for their faithfulness in the peace and love of Christ.[10] For we have received much that is good through their gifts (from God) and the helping hand of the Holy Spirit. May the Lord reward them for all this, now and on that day, along with all the faithful in Christ. Amen.

---

7 Jn 14:18.

8 Ps 84:7.

9 Jude 20.

10 Eph 6:23.

May the Lord grant us to remain wakeful in all spheres of life, that we not be outmanoeuvred, overcome, and exposed to shame by them. This is especially the case given the thorny temptations and deceptions that have happened and continue to happen under the name of Christ.[11] May no one seize our crown[12] through the thousandfold trickery of the enemy, but under all sorts of tribulations may we patiently persevere in the truth (as revealed to us) with all the saints of God (known to the Lord), even to the end.[13] Amen, amen.

All the Christian congregations in Moravia greet you as well, including their ministers and elders, namely: at Austerlitz,[14] Poppitz[15] and Um den Stein, Eibenschütz, also at Jemnitz[16] and at Wald, also at Znaim[17] and Vienna. It is also the entreaty and admonition in the Lord of all of them to you, desiring that you pray for them to the Lord earnestly and heartily. This, as debtors of love, they also desire faithfully to do for you. Amen.

Dated at Eibenschütz, the Fifth Sunday of Lent, 1553.[18]

From us ministers: Andre Schuster at Austerlitz;
Peter Fruewirt at Um den Stein and Poppitz;
Balthasar Grasbanntner, Tischler at Eibenschütz;
Rup Dachensteiner, Pfannenschmidt at Wald and Jemnitz;[19]
and Bastel Schlosser at Vienna—and from the elders
and congregations in the land of Moravia,
your brothers in the Lord Christ

11 Rv 3:17; 16:15.
12 Rv 3:11.
13 Mt 24:11; 1 Cor 1:8; 2 Cor 1:13; Heb 3:6; Rv 2:26; etc.
14 Now Slavkov u Brna in the Czech Republic.
15 Popice.
16 Jemnice.
17 Znojmo.
18 Judika, which was on March 19 in 1553.
19 [These towns were within a 50 kilometre radius of the city of Brünn (now Brno, in the Czech Republic), near the centre of Moravia.—Ed.]

Interlude 6

Concerning true patience

This piece sounds like an excerpt from a longer writing. Its themes are typical of the South German mystical piety evident in many Kunstbuch texts. Its extolling of patience echoes Marpeck's thinking. The theme of the innocence of Christ comes up late in no. 13, "Concerning the Love of God and the Cross of Christ."

Zwischenstück 6: Von der wahren Geduld. Translation by Leonard Gross.

Take note of true patience

Nature brought nothing with itself into the world but destructibility and fragility. To be sure, the natural human being is subject to suffering of necessity, as long as he carries around the natural body on earth, until he again turns into the earth from which he came.[1] And as soon as this same suffering comes, piercing and perforating the natural person, the only response befitting humanity is impatience. For all people flee suffering, not desiring to be subject to it or needing to experience it.

There is no true patience within humanity but only self-will, which makes itself known, not desiring anything else than that no suffering be present where it touches on a person's existence. This is not yet true patience but rather impatience, as noted above. From where, then, comes true patience, or upon which basis does it flow our way? It comes to us when we are mindful with all our heart of our entry into the world, which brings with it all sorts of suffering and fragility.[2*] It has its beginning in each young infant as soon as it leaves its mother's body, evidenced in the fact that it cries for the first time.

The second basis of true patience is that every injustice and sin people have committed must be punished with the severe justice of God.[3*] The third basis is that a person must completely offer up his own will and surrender himself into the will of God.[4*] Fourth, if someone arrives at this point and has achieved all this, then the innocence of Christ becomes his innocence, and he suffers as one who is innocent.[5*] This is so because with his innocence Christ redeemed and justified us with his blood from all guilt and injustice. Genuine, true patience flows from this basis. It is the greatest wisdom on earth when someone accepts all things on the basis of truth, testing them on it.

---

1 Gn 3:19.
2* 1.
3* 2.
4* 3.
5* 4.

18

Concerning five fruits of true repentance

Pilgram Marpeck
Augsburg, 24 August 1550

The introductory comment provided by the original editor describes this writing as "a thorough report." This pastoral epistle seems to have been written as a general teaching for all Marpeck Circle congregations rather than for a particular one. Pilgram Marpeck's basic train of thought makes clear his debt to Martin Luther and to the mystical piety mediated by Luther.[1] At the same time, the Anabaptists claimed that the fruit of these insights was not evident in the daily life of members of Catholic and magisterial Protestant congregations. Their clergy "claim the name of Christ, talk much of repentance, confession of sin, and even the ban."[2] But where is the evidence of existential faith, the practice of repentance, and transformed lives flowing from it? "For Anabaptists the nature of repentance was of the greatest importance—

Pilgram Marpeck, Von fünferlei Früchten wahrer Buße; Augsburg, 24. August 1550. Translation by William Klassen. Previously published as "Five Fruits of Repentance," in WPM, 484–97. Reprinted, with editorial changes, by permission of the publisher.

1 Luther acknowledges his great debt to the *Theologia Deutsch* or *Theologia Germanica* (modern translation by Bengt Hoffman, *The "Theologia Germanica" of Martin Luther* [New York: Paulist Press, 1980]). Marpeck quotes the *Theologia Germanica* at length in PMA, 212–16. See PMLST, 25–30.

2 WPM, 484.

it had to do with the integrity and the visibility of the church."[3] The author warns his fellow church members not to be found among this "generation of vipers."

To show the distinctiveness of Marpeck's understanding of repentance it is helpful to compare it with the streams of Anabaptist spiritual life closest to him, at least geographically. The most systematic presentation of the subject among the Swiss Brethren is found in Balthasar Hubmaier's writings.[4] He rejoices in Christ's work of salvation accomplished for us, apart from us. Hans Hut, who embodies early South German mystical Anabaptism, talks about "a baptism of affliction" in which our inward suffering is essential to salvation.[5] In Hut's view our suffering is an ascetic means of purgation, an understanding typical of late medieval mysticism. Marpeck incorporates elements of both views. Most simply, he sees suffering as the just punishment for our sin: acceptance of this punishment is an essential step toward true repentance.

To give a frame of reference for the experience of forgiveness Marpeck reminds his readers of the meaning of the Lord's Supper. In it they experience the communion of the body and blood of Christ. We know from his other writings that for Marpeck the Christian knows Christ only within his body, understood both eucharistically and ecclesiologically. Thus "there is no forgiveness of sin apart from the fellowship of Christ." His identification of the Spirit with the communion of saints reinforces this conviction. Even though the experience of repentance is inescapably existential, it does not happen privately, in an independent relationship of the believer with Christ.

The first fruit of repentance is the confession of guilt. Sinners tremble before the face of God, forsaken by all creatures. This is "the solitary experience of the descent into hell,"[6] which Christ made in our behalf and which we now make in his behalf. Only in this depth does one find Christ. Here we encounter a central element in Marpeck's piety. There is another aspect to the descent into hell: Christ offers himself not only

---

3 Ibid.

4 BH, "Summa of the Entire Christian Life," 81–89.

5 See Hut's "A Beginning of a True Christian Life," no. 6.

6 WPM, 484.

to unbelievers from all past generations but also to sinners of every succeeding generation, who can count on meeting Christ at the deepest point of their sin and lostness. It is this encounter that is acted out in believers baptism.

"The second fruit is the recognition that one must wait for God's grace and cannot seize it with superficial words about repentance. The third fruit is that sinners are in sorrow for their sins and not for the consequences they must suffer. All they want is to be remembered by God.

"The fourth fruit is the determination no longer to commit sin. Without this everything is in vain and a sham.

"The fifth fruit is the full acceptance of responsibility for one's own sin and the refusal to blame anyone or anything else. To do this is ultimately to blame God."[7] Here the author makes a significant theological claim: "Wickedness has its source only in itself." The positive side of the fifth fruit is that the sinner affirms God, together with his creatures, as true and good. To lessen one's culpability by revealing someone else's transgression is judged severely; to do so is to intrude into the mystery of God. Such strong language might have been occasioned by the temptation Marpeck's communities faced when they aspired to perfect holiness and didn't know what to do when they fell short.

"This letter is the most unified and concise statement of a subject in Marpeck's correspondence."[8]

7 Ibid.

8 Ibid.

Here follows an epistle presenting a thorough report of five fruits of true repentance

The grace of our Lord Jesus Christ and his compassion be with you and all who are poor in spirit.[9] Amen.

We have reason to thank God our heavenly Father when someone grieves because of his sins, when there are those who come to true repentance through grace, and appear before Christ, the throne of grace,[10] with remorse and regret, confess their sins to him, recognizing them, through the law of grace, by which they receive "grace upon grace."[11] "For the law" of vengeance "was given through Moses. Grace and truth have become ours through Christ."[12]

This grace and truth in turn lead on into true comfort, peace, and joy of the Holy Spirit.[13] In this Holy Spirit alone there is forgiveness of sin through the sacrifice of death on the cross and the shedding of the blood of Christ. Such forgiveness, however, takes place only in the fellowship of saints, in which alone such power is received from Christ.

Therefore Paul says: "The bread which we bless" (which means: to speak well of, to praise and thank our God), "is the communion of the body of Christ, and the cup with which we give thanks" (which means: to thank our God for the forgiveness of sin), "is the communion of the blood of Christ" [1 Cor 10 (16)]. For this reason there is no forgiveness of sin apart from the fellowship of Christ, however much the whole world may claim for itself grace and forgiveness of sin with false boasting. I write you this so that you may be in possession of genuine and true evidence of your hope for pardon and the forgiveness of sins, and produce the honest fruit of repentance in order to escape the coming wrath of God, and that we may not be found among the generation of vipers.[14]

---

9 Mt 5:3.

10 Rom 3:25; Heb 4:16.

11 Jn 1:16.

12 Jn 1:17.

13 Rom 14:17.

14 Gn 3:15; Lk 3:7f. [Mt 3:7; 12:34; 23:33.—Trans.]

This generation and kind belongs under the law of the curse[15] and is eternally condemned and exiled. Even if this generation feigns repentance a thousand times, with its confession of sin and acceptance of the ban of Christ, the poison of vipers still remains in it, in order to poison others as well as itself with the future wickedness and to become an offence. In spite of it they fall from one sin into another. However much warning, scolding, reproof, and admonition is attempted, it does no good, for their whole performance has the one aim of leading astray and deceiving themselves and others.

Concerning this generation John, the baptizer to repentance, spoke gravely and terribly, saying: "You generation of vipers, who told you to flee from the coming wrath of God? Do not say: 'We are Abraham's children,' for God can make children for Abraham out of these stones!" [Mt 3 (7, 9)]. That means: "Do not boast that you are the generation of Christ (of the seed of the Word).[16] For even today the axe is laid to the root of such barren, unfruitful, and twice-dead trees[17] (yet when the Word shines upon them they become green), to cut them down,[18] especially when no work, digging, or cultivation will any longer benefit them."[19] Christ may come to them whenever he pleases; he will find only his name, that is to say, only green leaves. Although they correspond to the name of Christ, they certainly do not serve for the healing of the nations, and bear no fruit [Rv 22 (2)].

The curse of Christ applies to them just as it does to the fig tree. For when Christ arrives hungry, desiring and seeking fruit, but finds no fruit, nothing can follow but the curse, as with the fig tree, so that it dries up and—as those who do not bear fruit are cut off the vine which is Christ[20]—is prepared for the fire [Mt 21 (18f.)].

I write this in order that we may take careful note of the witness within our hearts,[21] so that when we sin we may perform and complete

---

15 Gal 3:10, 13.

16 1 Pt 1:23.

17 Jude 12.

18 Lk 3:9.

19 Lk 13:8.

20 Jn 15:6.

21 Rom 2:15.

the true fruit of repentance, in order that the wrath of God and the curse of Christ may not come over us to our destruction, as they will certainly come upon all the enemies of God so that the last evil is worse than the first [Lk 11 (26)].

The psalmist David pleads for vengeance on people like that when he says: "Lord, let one evil after another come upon them; turn their table into a trap" [Ps 68 (69:27, 22)]. For no greater punishment or vengeance can be found than to fall from one transgression and sin into another[22] and still assume that one participates in the table fellowship of Christ.[23] In truth they are and remain only at their own table, which has become a trap for them and from which they eat judgment to themselves,[24] and not from the Lord's table. Although they have been invited or else appear at the wedding banquet with soiled garments, they will nevertheless not taste the Lord's Supper eternally, but rather eat their own meal from their own table perverted into a trap. They will be judged so that they will depart exiled and condemned. For they cannot stand in the judgment, as the psalmist says and prays: "Let them be condemned when they are judged."[25] The Lord commands such dishonest people to be bound hands and feet and to be thrown into outer darkness [Mt 22 (11–13); Lk 14 (24)].

Those are all terrible and hard sayings, which cause consternation and fright when one seriously considers them. Happy are those who allow themselves to be alarmed by the Word of God and who are earnestly shocked because of it.[26] Salvation draws near to them! For they are prepared for and led to the Lord Christ through the genuine fruits of repentance so that he bestows his grace upon them. This fruit of repentance proves itself true in suffering, sorrowing, fear, and pain of conscience, in deep affliction and in true fruits of repentance.

---

22 Jb 34:37.

23 1 Cor 10:21.

24 1 Cor 11:29.

25 Ps 109:7.

26 Is 66:2.

The first fruit of true repentance

This is the first fruit: the sinner confesses himself guilty of eternal death under the stern, serious righteousness and wrathful vengeance of God. He becomes ashamed and completely battered and broken in his own eyes, and with fear and trembling appears before the face of God[27] helpless, comfortless, and completely forsaken by all creatures in heaven and on earth. The sinner knows, seeks, and recognizes no help in himself or in anything else. He recognizes only his sin and guilt, which condemn him with the devil and his following to hell.

That is the first and most bitter fruit of true repentance. Prior to all other fruit, we test and experience what kind of fruit the sin that we have committed produces—and that we taste and eat this fruit. Yes, prior to all other fruit, a true penitent must taste what he himself (through the deceit of sin) has done and sown.[28][29*]

For what each of us sows, he will and must reap or harvest [Gal 6 (7)]. For all pain, anxiety, distress, and suffering, together with eternal death, are the true fruit and reward—yes, the true wages—of sin.[30] These wages are given to all sinners who have not received grace; by them they are condemned to eternal destruction. Whoever does not find Christ in this depth (that is, in this true baptism for the remission of sin) will not find him in the height in joy and glory eternally. For he who descended is the one who has ascended.[31] Whoever desires to eat this Paschal Lamb must eat bitter herbs with it [Ex 12 (8)]. Nevertheless, it still depends on God's free grace. When someone has an experience of sin that is to blame for his woes, or even if it is innocent bitterness, we don't know whether or not he will grant the sinner to partake of the Lamb of God who takes away the sin of the world.[32] Even if we

---

27 Ps 34:18; Ps 51:17; Ps 109:22.

28 Prv 22:8.

29* Gloss: It is not enough that one merely say: "I would gladly repent and confess my sins." A part of it is to recognize what kind of fruit sin brings.

30 Rom 6:23.

31 Eph 4:10.

32 Jn 1:29.

drink the cup of the suffering of guilt, we are not for that reason given the kingdom of God.[33*]

Cain, Esau, Saul, Judas, and all other sinners felt that bitterness, but partaking in the Lamb was eternally denied them [Heb 12 (16f.)]. Whoever therefore would contemplate God's goodness must first contemplate God's severity [Rom 11 (22)]. Thus far briefly concerning the first fruit of repentance.

The second fruit of repentance

The second fruit is that God allows a glimmer of the hope of his grace to shine along with his condemnation, in order that the sinner may anticipate that grace with patience and become aware that he cannot rob God of his grace or seize it. In the meantime he regards as his blessedness the divine hesitation and withholding of grace, comfort, and peace in the Holy Spirit. Then the light—the day of grace at the pool of the water of grace—appears in brightness, and the water is stirred in hope of recovery; in other words, until Christ finds him in such hope and patience, in the Portico of Solomon[34] after thirty-eight years of illness, in order to take pity on him [Jn 5 (2–5)]. Then he bids him rise, takes away the agony of sin, the anxiety and distress of conscience, as well as sin itself, and freely gives him comfort, peace, and joy in the Holy Spirit.[35]

Oh, God, how utterly impatient we are to await your comfort! We like to assume that you would prostrate yourself at our feet with your comfort and mercy; all we need to do in order to be received into the fellowship of Christ is confess our sin and devise sorrow and fictitious remorse, and then the whole matter is made right. Whoever thinks thus will go far off the mark and be a victim of self-deceit.

The third fruit of true repentance

The third fruit of repentance is that the sinner sorrows more about what he has done against God than about what he must suffer in con-

---

33* Gloss: We are not to boast of suffering but of grace, since all suffering proceeds from sin and guilt. [This scribal insertion tilts the argument toward the Swiss and away from the mystical South German position, as mentioned in the commentary.—Ed.]

34 Jn 10:23.

35 Rom 14:17.

sequence. Thus he desires from God (in the hope of his grace) that he not be delivered from cross and suffering until God's will has been satisfied in him and until (like the evildoer on the cross to the right of Jesus) he desires to be remembered by God.[36] For the thief on the cross had no thought of being delivered from his cross of death. He committed his own guilt to the care of the innocence of Christ.[37] Rather, it was the unrepentant evildoer on the left, whom the other admonished for not fearing God, who said: "If you are the Son of God, deliver us and yourself from the cross."[38]

That is what viperish penitents still do today: they are sorry only that they must suffer because of sin but have no sorrow for the sin itself, which is the cause of their suffering. True penitents, however, desire to be rid not of their deserved suffering but of their sin. They commit their guilt to Christ's innocent intercession. They confess that they suffer justifiably by their own guilt, and that the Lord Jesus Christ suffered innocently for our sins. They wait patiently for release from their suffering, through him who has delivered them from their sins, never again to carry out sin,[39] in order that henceforth they may live completely to please their God.[40] Thus far concerning the third fruit of repentance.

The fourth fruit of repentance

Although sin is lodged within us (according to the first Adamic birth of the flesh), a true penitent does not allow it to rule[41]—because of the sin he is still suffering on the cross with the innocence of Christ. For what evildoer still desires or does the evil deed when he is imprisoned and suffers tortures because of his evil deed, unless indeed he is in blasphe-

---

36 Lk 23:42.

37 ["The innocence of Christ" is a favourite concept of Marpeck. See especially no. 13, "Concerning the Love of God and the Cross of Christ." It is a parallel notion to the "sinlessness of Christ" but has an additional connotation. Elsewhere Marpeck talks about the innocence of children when they are born. The sense of the present usage is that Christ never lost his innocence.—Ed.]

38 Mt 27:40; Lk 23:39.

39 Jn 5:14.

40 2 Cor 5:15; 1 Pt 4:2.

41 Gn 4:7.

mous despair?[42*] Even less do these sinners allow sin to rule because they are true prisoners of God and suffer agony of conscience because of sin and still have no certain comfort. All they can hope for is to be rid of sin.

It would indeed be a monstrous wickedness and impertinence against God to commit sin while one repents, is captive in conscience, and has hope for deliverance! For this reason a true penitent does not allow sin to rule, but along with his repentance, insofar as it is true persevering repentance, accepts the command of Christ, that he should no longer commit sin, lest the latter evil be worse than the first [Lk 11 (26)].[43] For that is the highest, greatest, and most beneficial repentance: henceforth to live in the will of God and not in wickedness. Without this, all repentance is in vain and the Son of God is crucified and trodden underfoot [Heb 6 (8); 10 (29)].

The fifth fruit of repentance

The fifth fruit is that I do not blame any creature in heaven or on earth for my sin or point to it as the cause of my sin, as follows: "If this or that had not been so, I would have been pious enough not to have done it." For original wickedness has its source only in itself.[44] It takes its beginning in and through itself, as though it were eternal, as a lying false god who of himself creates an eternity out of identical, true divine honours.[45*] It is a thief and a murderer[46] who robs the true God of all honour and murders those who yield all honour to the true God.[47]

Thus he is the beginning of wickedness, a father of murderers, of lies,[48] and of all malice and wickedness, a hater of all good and lover of all evil. Consequently he is lord, god, and potentate of all the pain that because of the guilt of wickedness he bears in himself. Sin, death, and

---

42* Parable.

43 Jn 5:14.

44 Jn 8:44.

45* Note.

46 Jn 10:1.

47 [Evil is not created by God; it is an imposter of good, claiming to be like God.—Ed.]

48 Jn 8:44.

hell follow their god. For deception and all wickedness is, as was already mentioned, a veritable god, uncreated, who (like the eternal and true God) created himself out of nothing, as though wickedness (along with its god) were from all eternity.

Thus this god (as prince of the world)[49] remains eternally in his own domain. Hell, death, and sin, with all their agony, follow him as their god. Whoever therefore points to any creature in heaven and on earth as the cause of his sin, deceptiveness, and wickedness, in order to excuse himself, accuses his own God, Creator, and Maker of all creatures, even though these creatures have been created for all goodness.[50]

To make excuses amounts to blaspheming God, as though I had said: "If it were not for God, I would not have sinned." The opposite is true: if it were not for the wicked "god" (his and all my own wickedness), no sin would occur. However, anyone who attempts to excuse himself with some other cause of sin really wishes that instead the true God, with his creatures, were the liar and doer of wickedness.

This, however, is a fruit of true repentance: that God together with his creatures is regarded as true and good, as indeed he is true and good. Indeed, it is better that all mortals be liars and that God be true, as Paul says. But it is the way of a viper and its poison to be full of pretense in order to conceal itself and plunge others into guilt [Ps 115 (116:11); Rom 3 (4)].

Wherever there is such hidden poison, no genuine fruit of repentance can ever follow. Rather, one is compelled to confess with David and say: "Lord, I, I, I myself am the transgressor. Therefore, my God, do not accuse or punish any other work of your hands because of my sins [2 Kgs 12 (15)]. All the guilt with its torment and penalty comes justly upon me, me, me. For I have constantly followed that prince, namely, the god of all wickedness, and given consent to him by my own impertinence. For you are always my God, Lord, and deliverer. You have reconquered the power and capability to withstand all wickedness for me and all humanity, and freely bestowed and given it to us.

---

49 Jn 12:31; 14:30; 16:11.

50 Gn 1:21; 1 Tm 4:4.

"But I have again wantonly surrendered the power you conquered, the judgment and righteousness you achieved and with which you have judged, bound, and overcome the rulers of this world.[51] Of my own free will I returned it to the enemy of my salvation, and have permitted him to rule over me with his wickedness and perversity. He has again taken me prisoner and taken the power from me!

"Thus I have again lost your might, your judgment, your truth, and your righteousness. With them you conquered, and surrendered it to him whom you have bound with your power, and from whom you had wrested all his weapons, his power, and also all the riches he had stolen from the human race [Mt 12 (29)]. You have given them to us again as spoils, distributing his plunder, and giving back to us the might, power, and strength.[52] I should have held on to them and should have watched better over the welfare of my soul! Carelessly I slept until the enemy, thief, and murderer undermined my house [Mt 24 (43)]. Through the deceit of sin he sowed weeds in my heart,[53] so that the fall of my house was very great.[54] Nor will it be built up again, and my heart and my soul will not recover. But then, Lord Jesus Christ, you stand surety for the fall and the breach.[55] This I hope for from your mercy and grace, that you will again save and deliver me from the hand of my enemy, rebuild my house, root out once again the weeds of sin, have compassion on my distress and great poverty, and be merciful to me a poor sinner."

Moreover, I desired that God should cover my sin and not hold me accountable for the greatness of my guilt but forgive my transgression. Only thus are we prepared to do the same in true repentance to all creatures, and not to reveal or to receive confession of the sin of any other person if God has not first uncovered, witnessed, brought forth, and revealed it to them by a public deed.[56] The person who confesses and reveals his sin to others only after they have disclosed or revealed it to him acts as the whole world acts and says: "At any rate, I am not the

---

51 Jn 12:31; 16:11.

52 Ps 68:18; Eph 4:8.

53 Mt 13:25.

54 Mt 7:27.

55 Ps 106:23.

56 1 Tm 5:24.

only one or the first one; another has also done this and that, one thing and another, or still does it."[57*] According to the command of Christ he could have confessed his sin first, but did not submit to this discipline.

He uncovers his sins and brings them out against the whole order of God, since according to God's command he could have done it first, prior to the revealing of his sin and shame. But he does it only after God has brought out and revealed his sin and shamed him. But it is the way of the viper to intrude itself into the mystery of God and the Holy Spirit and reveals its shame and sin in order to appear in a better light.

Much more could be discerned concerning true and false repentance for our instruction and the cleansing of our conscience. May God our heavenly Father and the Lord Jesus Christ grant us grace to be truly humble before the great majesty and goodness of our Father, and that we might present and reveal ourselves and confess honestly and truly without any falseness of spirit. We can never humble ourselves sufficiently before our God, against whom we have sinned. Wherever such remorse, which is true sorrow and suffering, is found in sinners, it produces a "repentance that no one will regret" [2 Cor 7 (10)]. Wherever sin abounds in sorrow (not in the works of wickedness), there grace also abounds![58] Without this eternal regret, pain and agony of conscience remain, along with eternal torment. This is the case wherever we forsake the right and the good and again return to lies, sin, wickedness, together with all unrighteousness.

Let us receive this admonition and reminder along with other parts of Holy Scripture. They do not direct us against the discipline and obedience of the word of truth[59] but lead us into it and show us what serves the praise of God and the salvation of our souls. And even if it makes for remorse, suffering, and sorrowing, no one sustains any harm, except those who deliberately persist in stubbornness and despair and who begrudge God his glory. For all discipline, penalty, threatening of conscience, as well as all suffering in spirit, soul, and body—in short, everything that contributes to cleansing and sanctification—is regard-

---

57* Note.

58 Rom 5:20.

59 2 Cor 6:7; Eph 1:13; Col 1:5; 2 Tm 2:15; 3:16; Jas 1:18.

ed as a melancholy thing, and if one is stuck in it, as a heavy anxiety. Afterward, however, says St. Paul, it yields the peaceable fruit of eternal blessedness.[60]

Please accept this writing for the sake of your and our improvement and in all things look forward to the comfort and strength of peace, grace, and love in true hope and patience. For this I pray to God our heavenly Father and the Lord Jesus Christ: that he would grant you and us the working and moving of his Holy Spirit, to expect such things from him. Amen, amen, amen.

The grace of our Lord Jesus Christ be your comfort and ours. In him we can rejoice in the truth with you, and be given comfort and joy in our sorrows.[61] Amen.

Dated at Augsburg, 24 August
in the year of our Lord 1550.

In the Lord Jesus Christ,
servant to you and all true believers,
and comrade in the tribulation which is in Christ,
Pilgram Marpeck

60 Heb 12:11.

61 Mt 5:4.

Interlude 7

The time is near

“The Lord knows his own,” writes Paul (2 Tm 2 [19]). “When the Son of Man comes in his glory, and all the holy angels with him, all the nations will be gathered before him. And he”—note “he”[1]—“will separate them from one another as a shepherd separates the sheep from the goats, the sheep as his right hand, the goats at his left” [Mt 25 (31f.); (Mk) 13 (26f.)].

Then the prophecy of Daniel will be revealed. Many shall be running back and forth [Dn 12 (4)], holding various views, concerning what time has come upon us. Many congregations want to be congregations of Christ. They boast of their power to include and to exclude and compete with one another in the extreme.[2*] May God look on this with grace. The time is near. Amen.

I hope that our redemption is finally near,[3] according to the words of the Lord. The blossoming of summer makes certain the coming glo-

---

Zwischenstück 7: Die Zeit ist nah. Translation by John D. Rempel.

1 [The author is emphasizing that it is Christ rather than any human authority who will act as judge.—Ed.]

2* Note.

3 Lk 21:28.

ry of Christ and the revelation of his kingdom. Together with the ten sleepy virgins,[4] we know that it is at hand.[5] Christ wants to encourage them, that they already have the armour of light and the witness of faith in Christ.

No one will be able to ask someone else to share this oil with her. Everyone has to acquire it on her own, so that she has enough for herself. We have reason enough not to look to other people or congregations; all of them are stumbling in the face of judgment and no one trusts her sister on the basis of prophetic speech.[6] Everyone pleads with God for a vigourous heart and a bright light, so that she might not stumble in this dark time and extinguish the inner light unto everlasting blindness and darkness,[7] where no one will ever be able to see light. Each of us is commanded to walk while it is still day. For the night comes, when no one is able to walk.[8] To all appearances, the Lord wants to close the door. Whoever delays during the time of grace[9] will be left standing outside forever. May the Lord uphold each person in his grace; he alone knows who and where they are.

---

4 Mt 25:1–12.

5 Lk 21:29f.

6 [This pessimism about finding revelation in the visible church is a trademark of Spiritualism.—Ed.]

7 Mt 6:22f.

8 Jn 9:4.

9 2 Cor 6:2.

19

Congregational order for Christ's members in seven articles

Leupold Scharnschlager

"Congregational Order for Christ's Members in Seven Articles" is the first writing by Leupold Scharnschlager to appear in the Kunstbuch.[1] He was Pilgram Marpeck's most intimate partner in ministry and the second most esteemed elder in the Marpeck Circle. Like the Marpecks, Scharnschlager and his wife, Anna Honigler Steger, came from the Tyrol, a region that lies on both sides of the current border between Austria and Italy. It was an area where a variety of religious radicalism was in the air.[2] The most significant Anabaptist leaders were Leonhard Schiemer and Hans Schlaffer, whose writings are included in this collection. Nothing precise is known of our author's early formation in Anabaptism until 1530 when Leupold, Anna, and their daughter Ursula fled the Tyrol for Strasbourg. There he quickly took on a leadership role among moderate Anabaptists, where Marpeck was already active.

In 1534 the Scharnschlagers were exiled from Strasbourg because of their convictions. Martin Rothkegel says, without elaboration, that they lived for a time in Augsburg. About 1544 they took up residence

---

Leupold Scharnschlager, Gemeinde Ordnung der Glieder Christi in sieben Artikeln. Translation by William Klassen.

1 See "Scharnschlager, Leupold," in ME 4:443–46; MLDC, 193–200.

2 PMLST, 12–24.

in Ilanz in the Grisons (Graubünden), a canton in eastern Switzerland. There he became a schoolteacher and for the rest of his life led the Anabaptist congregation, forced to live high in the mountains, in its precarious existence. Both Scharnschlagers died in 1563. Leupold remained a close collaborator and fellow author of Marpeck throughout the years of leadership they shared.

Recent research by Werner Packull has demonstrated that Scharnschlager's congregational order is an adaptation of a 1527 order devised by the Swiss Brethren. Packull has also shown that another order, later taken up by the Hutterites, is based on the Swiss original.[3] Community of goods is held to in the Swiss and Hutterian versions but rejected in Scharnschlager's.[4] In addition, his patient approach to discipline and his emphasis on a notion of the priesthood of all believers grounded in 1 Corinthians 14 distinguish Scharnschlager's work from that of the Hutterites and associate it with Marpeck's views. Heinold Fast notes that the practices spelled out in our document give the sense of emerging from years of pastoral experience as well as from disputes with the Hutterites. Therefore he dates it at about 1540.[5]

Scharnschlager's congregational order significantly enlarges its instructions on how to order worship, discipline, and mutual aid. The expansion on eschatology is noteworthy. The anticipation of the return of Christ was intended to inspire believers to continue to be faithful in the ordinary tasks of discipleship, not to interrupt those tasks with an interim ethic. In preparation for the Day of the Lord, believers should "follow the order through which we exist in love" with wisdom and quiet demeanour.[6] Gatherings for worship are always to include intercessions not only for members but for all people. Those outside the Anabaptist church are not condemned—surely a temptation for people under persecution—but prayed for. Discipline and stewardship are to be without coercion; the poor are to be helped in an organized way:

---

3 HB, 33–53. The text of the three orders is found on HB, 303–15.

4 HB, 308–9.

5 BSOT, 440–41. This dating fits with arguments against compulsory communalism similar to Scharnschlager's in Marpeck's "The Admonition of 1542," WPM, 278–81.

6 This is in the spirit of 1 Pt 4:7–10.

this is what the church is to be about as it prepares for the Day of Judgment.

The congregational order notes an urgent need under the harsh conditions of persecution for "workers"—that is, ministers—who are to be respected and prayed for. The implication is that this is not happening. Where people are overtaken by sin, there shall be modest and sincere admonition by leaders who act in trembling and the fear of God. No quarter is given to leaders who claim special revelations that put them above the requirements of discipleship. The ordinances of the church and the witness of each member are to be guided solely by "the commission and practice of the Lord and his apostles."

Congregational order for Christ's members set forth in seven articles

"Children, let all your works be done in order with good intent in the fear of God, and do nothing disorderly in scorn or out of its due season"[7*] (TNaph).[8]

Paul says (1 Cor 14 [40]): "Let all things be done decently and in order." Likewise (Col 2 [5]): "I rejoice when I see your order and the steadfastness of your faith in Christ."[9*]

Preface

Our heavenly Father, to whom be eternal praise, honour, and thanksgiving, has in these last days called us out of the anti-Christian kingdom and delivered us from the darkness of the world into his

7* Yesterday.

8 Testament of Naphtali 2 [9—Trans.].

9* Today.

marvellous light[10] through knowledge of his holy truth. We are all baptized and have decided to become one body in Jesus Christ, regardless of where we may be located in the world. Therefore, if we are to achieve our calling not only in words but also in deed and in truth,[11] it is necessary that we follow the order through which we exist in love and can be exhorted and corrected, since indeed all things exist through order. In the words that follow such an order is written down in articles. Nevertheless, we allow for daily changes for improvement, according to the nature and opportunities of the times.[12]

The first article

First: because manifold deceptions are everywhere making inroads, it is necessary that the called, committed, and obligated members of Christ's body, wherever they may be in the world or in distress, insofar as it is possible, should not neglect the assembly[13] [Heb 10 (25)]. Wherever and however they may, according to the place and the persecutions, they should gather together for the sake of their love for Christ, be their number small or great, 2, 3, 4, 6, 10, 15, 20, more or less. Such meetings should take place with wisdom, modesty, reason, discipline, friendliness, and quiet demeanour, especially since we see the Day of the Lord drawing near. The Lord says: "Where two or three are gathered together in my name, there I am in the midst of them" [Mt 18 (20)].

The second article

Second: when they come together, they shall, where there is no special leader,[14] select someone competent from among them and admonish him in a friendly and loving manner to read or speak to them according to the gift he has received from God. Someone may also volunteer to serve out of love. One may follow another in speaking according to

---

10 1 Pt 2:9.

11 1 Jn 3:18.

12 [Original: *doch uff tegliche verennderung nach gstalt und glegennheit der zeit und alweg eins pessern unferzigenn.*—Trans.]

13 [Original: *versamlung*, a common term for the gathering of the congregation.—Trans.]

14 [Original: *vorsteer*—Trans.]

the way they receive something, as Paul teaches, and thus exercise his gifts for the improvement of the members [1 Cor 14 (26f.)], so that our fellowship may not be the same as that of the falsely renowned,[15] where only one and no one else can speak.

However, before they begin to speak, let them fall on their knees and faithfully call upon God [1 Tm 2 (8)], that he may add fruit to their speaking. After the talk, diligently admonish one another to walk according to the will of the Lord, to remain constantly in him, to watch faithfully and to wait for the Lord until he comes [Mt 24 (42); 26 (41)]. This is so that we may be found without blemish before him (Phil 2 [15]), and that not only here but much more in the next world we may together be with the Lord [1 Thes 4 (17)] and may also rejoice eternally. Furthermore, before dispersing, call upon the Lord and intercede for all members, also for cases of special need, and for all people according to the directive of our beloved brother Paul (1 Tm 2 [1f.]). Offer thanksgiving for all God's gifts and good deeds [1 Thes 5 (17f.)]. On occasion and according to opportunity, before dispersing break bread among yourselves in memory of the death of the Lord (1 Cor 11 [23-26]).

The third article

Third: when you are assembled in this manner, a leader if present (if not, any other elderly brother) shall remember the poor members for the sake of the Lord with words that are wise, sincere, gentle, transparent, uncoercive—and yet earnest, emphatic words. Thereby hearts may be moved to a voluntary expression of compassion and grow into the nature and power of love that is genuine and pleasing in the sight of God. Above all, a brother known to all the members of the church should always be present with a purse of money. Then each member may know where to place a freewill offering and his gift of blessing, either in the meeting or after, when the Lord admonishes him to, so that at all times when the need arises the poor may be assisted according to the amount available at the time. Then the brother who cares for the fund shall distribute it with a good conscience and in the fear of God, paying diligent heed, whether they are needy or not, whether greedy or

15 [*Valschberuemten* seems to refer to the one-pastor system of the state church.—Trans.]

not, not as the world deals with the poor, without testing and inquiring about their manner of life and walk. For this is a holy commission (Acts 6 [1–7]).

The fourth article

Fourth: there is a shortage of faithful workers who correctly, wisely, and in good conscience faithfully seek for the lost and labour for the Lord in his vineyard.[16] Every day this shortage causes much confusion, error and offence. Thus, when such a faithful worker is found and discovered, there is an urgent need that he be given due respect and obeyed [1 Thes 5 (12f.)], for he is worthy of a double honour, according to the words of Paul [1 Tm 5 (17)]. Share every good thing and all the support possible with him [Heb 13 (7)], as he may need in addition to work he is able to do on the side. Our concern is that we not depreciate the messengers and workers of the Lord for whom we pray daily [Lk 10 (2)], lest the Lord allow us to be scattered abroad without shepherds.[17] This applies not only for the sake of the ones who have seen the truth but also for the sake of the weak, milk-drinking[18] vegetarians[19] and for the sake of those who will be gathered to the Lord in the future.[20]

The fifth article

Fifth: The example of the primitive church in Jerusalem is misunderstood by some, giving rise to error and contempt. Special sects and the like arise; some of them have made of this example a law, a requirement, a fetter, even almost a carnal righteousness, demand, and the like. Therefore let us recognize that in the early church at Jerusalem the sharing of goods was a voluntary matter, and further observe what took place after the dispersion of the church from there [Acts 4 (34f.); 5 (1–13)]. Even Paul wrote about sharing material possessions and community of goods [Rom 15 (26f.); 1 Cor 16 (1f.); 2 Cor 9 (1f.)], and we likewise in true apostolic character are to pay heed that the bride and flock of Christ be not forced but led and fed voluntarily [1 Pt 5 (2)].

---

16 Mt 9:38; 20:1–16.

17 Nm 27:17; Is 13:14; 1 Kgs 22:17; Ez 34:5; Mt 9:36; Mk 6:34.

18 1 Cor 3:2.

19 Rom 14:2.

20 Jn 17:20.

Therefore the one who gathers funds[21] is to pay heed, to accept the smallest gift without despising it, just as he does the greatest (Lk 21 [1–4]) from both the rich and the poor, and to faithfully thank both God and the giver. After that, leave it to the Lord.[22*] For even though someone says, with worldly wisdom, "Ah, after all everyone has agreed to this and committed himself to it, why not diligently demand whatever is necessary?" We answer: the order of the Holy Spirit will not permit it. This is not a human work, just as it was not the flesh that initially agreed. Therefore it must be sought not in the fleshly nature but in the spiritual. Otherwise we disrupt the voluntary nature of God's relation to his people.

The sixth article

Sixth: when a brother or sister is overtaken by vices of the flesh, false teaching, licentious living and being, or other such transgressions in word or deed, there shall always be disciplined, modest, sincere admonition and correction from the leaders, elders, and fellow members[23] in trembling and fear of God, in love. Diligent attention is to be paid in each case of transgression, be it secret or open, large or small, one warning or more, how the person is dealt with according to gentleness and sharpness, patience and impatience [Gal 6 (1); Mt 18 (15–18)]. For correction and excommunication must be distinguished according to the actual circumstances and according to the witness of the scriptures, so that everything take place according to the spirit of love and not according to the nature of the flesh [Ti 3 (10); 1 Cor 5 (11); Rom 2 (1); Eph 5 (2–13); 1 Cor 6 (1–8)]. The power of Christ is not a power to destroy or to exercise tyranny, but to improve.[24*] We do this so that the bride of Jesus Christ may be kept pure,[25] everywhere, both for those within as well as for those outside the church, so that an honourable, inoffensive walk may result and no one block or make difficult the way and road to Christ and his kingdom.

---

21 [Original: *steursamlerr*—Trans.]

22* Note.

23 [Original: *gschwisterten.*—Trans.]

24* Note.

25 Eph 5:26f.

The seventh article

Seventh: concerning teaching, baptizing, and the Lord's Supper, these are to be observed according to the content of the commission and practice of the Lord and his apostles. They are not to be changed or perverted, nor is anything to be added to or taken from them,[26] as it happens among the Antichrists and the falsely renowned [Dt 4 (2); 12 (13:1); Prv 30 (6)]. At all times each brother and sister is to be guided by the secrets of the essential Christian faith in what they do and what they let go of, and whatever the Lord has entrusted to him to bear before the world with a clear conscience,[27] to prevent the blasphemy of Christ's name,[28] Word and honour.[29*] Whatever other matters and errors arise in daily life, they are to perceive them and act with godly fear according to the gospel of Christ, corresponding to the faith[30] and serving for the improvement and edification of everyone [Phil 1 (10)]. We are to follow him faithfully and renounce all unrighteousness of words, works, and manner of life; flee from it, abstain, and separate ourselves from it [2 Cor 6 (17)]. We do this to the honour of God and of our bridegroom Jesus Christ [Mt 24 (25:1–12)], in order that when he comes we may joyfully appear before him in holy adornment arrayed in the Holy Spirit so that we may fully possess what he acquired for us and prepared through his precious blood [Jn 14 (3)]. Therefore we pray to our heavenly Father that he may help us accomplish this and achieve it through Jesus Christ, his beloved Son, our Lord, to whom be praise and honour and laud in the Holy Spirit from eternity to eternity. Amen.

In the Lord Christ,
a brother by grace and a servant of the truth,
as well as a comrade in the tribulation[31]
which is in Christ,
Leupold Scharnschlager

---

26 Rv 22:19.
27 1 Tm 3:9.
28 1 Pt 4:14.
29* Note.
30 Rom 12:6.
31 Rv 1:9.

20

General admonition and reminder for reformation

Leupold Scharnschlager

This treatise continues the concern of the previous one (no. 19, "Congregational Order for Christ's Members in Seven Articles") for a kind of order in the congregation that is receptive to the initiative of the Spirit. It is not focused on the institutional structure of church life but on the form discipleship must take if believers are to be faithful to the promises made in baptism. The author laments that Anabaptist Christians have lost their first love. The attitudes and practices he describes suggest what sociologists of religion describe as the "second generation" phenomenon, when the radicality of first-generation conviction is not replicated in the next generation.

The content of Leupold Scharnschlager's lament may indicate that it was written after 1544, when he became a leader of the Pilgramite congregation in Ilanz (in the Grisons, a canton in eastern Switzerland), which was dispersed around the mountainside. If this dating is accurate, we have at work two puzzling phenomena, not usually found together. First, Scharnschlager's description of laxity suggests a community integrated into its surroundings. Second, the dispersal of the congregation in Ilanz suggests the opposite, a setting of separation and

---

Leupold Scharnschlager, Gemeine Vermahnung und Erinnerung. Translation by Victor Thiessen.

nonconformity. Heinold Fast conjectures that the problem of marrying outside the congregation was a result of the isolation of believers: they were so widely dispersed that normal communal life, including functions such as seeking a mate, was not possible.[1]

The author uses strong language to give voice to his lament. He draws on John's description in the book of Revelation of the unfaithful congregations in Asia Minor: they are lukewarm. Later he describes these Christians as foolish virgins, and finally as the people in Jesus' parable who kept making excuses for not heeding the king's invitation. The gist of the matter, according to Scharnschlager, is that "they once again acquire a love for the world . . . —a love from which they had once departed." That love expresses itself, the author claims, in the following: they don't meet with the congregation; they are preoccupied with getting rich; they cynically deflect the giving and receiving of counsel.[2] Marital life is plagued with disputes over material comforts.

Is the letter writer speaking in hyperbole to arouse his hearers from their sleep? The specificity of the charges he levels suggests that he is describing the situation literally, as he sees it. If that is so, what explains the profound erosion of conviction from one generation to the next?

Martin Rothkegel suggests that the Marpeckian model of personal freedom, patience, and the reluctance to turn to rules for conduct resulted in individualism and minimalism in the second generation.[3]

This pastoral letter invites the reader to look into the mirror that it holds up.

---

1 In 1567 Hutterites wrote a blistering critique of the life of Swiss Brethren congregations in Moravia and Switzerland; it echoes this self-criticism (see "Reply Given by the Brethren," Elisabeth Bender, trans., Brünn Codex, 1567; typescript in Associated Mennonite Biblical Seminary library, Elkhart, Indiana). This was not an impartial account. But if there is truth in it, it raises a similar problem. The Swiss were a persecuted and nonconformed minority. Did the relentless strain of living under such conditions erode their discipleship?

2 The image of foot washing is evoked twice to describe the offer and the refusal of counsel.

3 BSOT, 446.

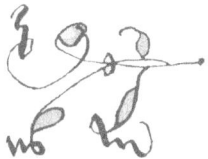

General admonition and reminder for the reformation of the body of the Lord Jesus Christ, and as a warning to all those spiritually asleep and careless in the Lord in these last times, in all four corners of the earth.[4]

First, it is the will of God, to whom we have all committed ourselves in obedience, to live solely for him.[5] Therefore we do not forsake the assembly, the discipline, the admonition, and all things that are appropriate to a congregation, members of Christ, and belonging to his and his apostles' teachings in love [Heb 10 (25); 2 Pt 1 and 2 (20–22)]. Nonetheless, many of these things regarding the will of God and Jesus Christ have been completely and utterly forgotten in these times [1 Tm 4 (1)]. Some members have even fallen away completely (2 Thes 2 [3]), and others have become weary in the walk and the struggle of faith [Heb 12 (1); 2 Cor 4 (1, 16)]. Yet others, who should have been teachers in these last days (Heb 5 [12]), require that once again they be given milk to drink. Through the power of God's love, those who still try to persevere in God's grace are encouraged by a general call to arms concerning what must be done, as follows, so that they examine themselves, whether and to what degree they belong to the day or the night [2 Cor 13 (5)].

There are, first of all, some members, men and women, who have been baptized with water, of whom people in the congregation say that they are baptized and members,[6*] but they care little, if at all, for the

---

4 Is 11:12; Ez 7:2.

5 1 Pt 4:2.

6* 1.

members of Christ, and concern themselves with the assembly little or not at all.[7] These are those of whom the Holy Spirit bears witness that they have left their first love and faith (if they ever believed) and will receive their judgment [Rv 2 (4)].[8] There are also those who are neither cold nor hot, also those who live in name only (that is, they are members of Christ and have been baptized with the Holy Spirit) and yet are dead. Of these Christ says that because they are lukewarm and neither cold nor hot, they give him a bad taste and he will spit them out of his mouth. They say they are rich and have become rich and need nothing yet do not know that they are miserable and pitifully poor, blind and naked [Rv 3 (15, 1, 16f.); 1 Cor 11 (30);[9*] 1 Cor 10 (5)[10*]]. Christ admonishes them regarding their beginning and says: "Consider what you have received and heard. Hold fast to it and be converted! If you do not awake, I will come upon you like a thief, when you do not know the hour" [1 Thes 5 (2); Rv 3 (3)].

Some of these people have engaged too readily in the affairs and trade of this world;[11*] they concern themselves with getting rich, with acquiring things for their children and taking care of them [1 Tm 6 (9); 2 Tm 2 (4)]. They once again acquire a love for the world and the things of the world—a love from which they had once departed [1 Jn 2 (15); 2 Tm 4 (4)]. They pursue the very foolishness they had once spat out [2 Pt 2 (22); Prv 26 (11)], devoting themselves to the temptations, the snares, the harmful and foolish lusts of greed (Sir 13 [2ff.]; 31 [5]; Ps 42 [43:1]; Prv 17 [1]; Eccl 4 [6]); [1 Tm 6 (4)]. Through this folly their hearts have become obstructed and held back from the Lord, his Word and will. They do not want to increase in the knowledge of the truth, or grow in spiritual judgment and heavenly gifts and goods.[12] Rather, they have become sleepy, awkward, and totally listless in the faith and all good works, and will miss out through this sleep, like the five foolish virgins [Mt 25 (5)]. This is always the case with such sleepyheads, from

---

7 Heb 10:25.

8 1 Tm 5:12.

9* Sleep.

10* Has no pleasure in most of them.

11* 2.

12 Heb 6:4.

the first to the last, as it has obviously happened to many in these latter days. I cry out in lament before God!

When you tell this to a Christian assembly, they block it out, making excuses such as: "This very night—as well as today or tomorrow, I have this or that to do." It's like the excuses people whom the Lord had invited made: one had bought a house; another had taken a wife; and so on, as the text indicates [Mt 22 (3–5); Lk 14 (18–20)]. Once again they have become so blind that they would rather attain temporal goods and live their own lives instead of following the Lord and gaining their soul's salvation. Indeed, they walk in their own paths rather than the Lord Christ's. These words of Christ, "Whoever wishes to be my disciple must deny himself, take up his cross daily, and follow me" [Lk 9 (23); 14 (27); Mt 10 (38); 16 (24); Jn 12 (25)] apply much less than do the words that foretell: "Go hence, you damned, to the eternal fire" [Mt 25 (41); 10 (39)]. Such people do not take to heart the words of Christ: "Whoever prefers his own life to me is not worthy of me." Indeed, they are not worthy of him, nor will they taste his supper according to the Word of Christ (Mt 22 [8]).

With respect to fraternal correction,[13] it is lacking among the brothers and sisters.[14*] When one speaks to them in the Lord regarding an issue, or admonishes them in a brotherly way, in order to purify them through Christ by spiritually washing their feet[15] or the rest of their lives[16] or doings in this world, they then say in a lighthearted way, "My friend, who do you think you are? Don't you also do this or that?"[17*] And in this manner they silence such supposed failings and counter-accusations, until one punishes or admonishes them for this failing. They know full well that the one who has admonished them also stands under such obedience to brotherly correction. He does not use their own arguments and rationalizations against them, and they have no witness that he acted disobediently in meting it out. Concerning these, a passage of scripture applies. It speaks of people who are enemies of

13 Lk 14:24.

14* 3.

15 Jn 13:14.

16 1 Pt 4:2.

17* Note.

those who admonish before the gate. On top of that, these people are disobedient to their parents [Am 5 (10); 2 Tm 3 (2)]. That is the Word of Christ against Peter: "If I have not washed you, you have no part of me" (Jn 13[8]).

Ignorance has arisen regarding marriage, for some sisters marry and desire to be married so that they might be better nourished, because they might not be able to feed themselves on their own.[18*] They forget the teaching of Paul to marry solely to protect against fornication [1 Cor 7 (2)]. For this reason some brothers and sisters marry outsiders,[19] with the result that many have fallen. Some say they want to marry so that they have someone who can teach and guide them in the ways of God, whom they may trust, and so on. But what trust do they then have in their fellow members in Christ, or for what reason do they mistrust them in such matters?

Moreover, there is also this weakness among some of the brothers and sisters in their marriage.[20*] One spouse is satisfied with the relationship they have, with the mate the Lord has wisely given them, and abides happily by this even in times of dearth, hunger, thirst, frost, and cold [Heb 13 (5); 1 Tm 6 (6)]. With Paul and all faithful servants and followers of Christ they carry the sufferings of his cross, according to Christ's and Paul's call [2 Cor 11 (23–27)]. They prefer to discipline their appetites for the sake of the things of the Lord and his truth and do not neglect their souls' salvation and nurture. They are satisfied with little, but the other partner is there and will simply not suffer along or do without. Regardless of what one spouse admonishes regarding the suffering and cross of Christ, the other one shamelessly dares to say: "Suffering, schmuffering—just make sure that we have enough to eat and drink in the kitchen and cellar at home." One day there is too little lard, another day too little meat, cheese, wine, bread, eggs, and on it goes. There is no end to the murmuring, as the children of Israel did when God tested them in the wilderness, where God sent them scarcity [Nm 11 (4); 14 (12); 1 Cor 10 (10)]. This proves that they love their

---

18* 4.

19 2 Cor 6:14.

20* 5.

stomachs more than God's honour,[21] will, and command, and that they are only members of Christ when they have no lack of food. As soon as there is a shortage, their faith and Christianity comes to an end.

Where then is the cross and patience of Christ? Concerning them, the Word says, "Whoever does not share in suffering and endurance will also not have a share in ruling" [Sir 2 (5); 2 Tm 2 (12)]. They lack heavenly and spiritual riches, gifts, and knowledge, peace and joy in the Holy Spirit.[22] Otherwise they would dispose themselves differently, and they would not find sharing in another's suffering to be so difficult. Nor do they seek food for the soul, which lasts forever [Jn 6 (27); Mt 4 (4)]. They are sleepy (Is 29 [10]; Rom 12 [11, 8])—too lazy to read, ask, and listen! They are satiated, without hunger, claiming they know everything and have everything [Rv 3 (17)]. If one wishes to speak with them of spiritual things and the gifts of discernment, through which we are to grow in the kingdom of God and receive the power that lies in spiritual joy, their only concern is the disgrace of poverty, nakedness, and blindness in their midst. Little fruit of the Spirit for the common good can come from such trees.[23]

In conclusion, let everyone be warned (Ez 3 [18f.]); whatever a person sows, that he shall reap (Gal 6 [7]). "Whoever does not sow properly will reap trouble, and through the winnowing of torments he will be exposed" (Prv 22 [8]). "Whoever loves danger will die from it" (Sir 3 [26]). O God, protect us from evil,[24] through the intercession of your son Jesus Christ. Amen.

L. Scharnschlager

---

21 Phil 3:19.

22 Rom 14:17.

23 Mt 3:10; 7:17–19; etc.; Gal 5:22.

24 Mt 6:13; Lk 11:4.

21

War ordinance of the heavenly emperor for his captains

[Hartmut von Cronberg][1]

Circa 1522

It is the range of texts as much as their content that makes the Kunstbuch noteworthy today as an aid in understanding the Marpeck Circle. This collection helps answer the kind of question that leads us closer to the soul of the movement. To what did people turn in order to confirm their most dearly held convictions? Where did they look, largely on the basis of religious instinct, for sources of wisdom and inspiration that complemented what their own tradition could offer?

In that regard the most striking selection in Jörg Maler's manuscript is the "War Ordinance of the Heavenly Emperor for His Captains."[1] For a largely pacifist movement, as Anabaptism was, military images require subtle interpretation; such interpretation occasionally used the model of Ephesians 6.[2] What made this allegorical writing appealing

---

Kriegsordnung des himmlischen Kaisers für seine Hauptleute. Translation by Victor Thiessen.

1 See my argument below for my contention that Hartmut von Cronberg is the author.

2 See Thomas R. Yoder Neufeld, *Ephesians,* Believers Church Bible Commentary (Waterloo, ON, and Scottdale, PA: Herald Press, 2002), for an insightful and nuanced presentation of the use of military language in the early church and today. Note also Leupold Scharnschlager's "general call to arms" in the previous letter (no. 20), "General Admonition and Reminder for Reformation."

to Maler and his fellow believers? Was it the language itself, with its urgency and the importance of unquestioning obedience? Was it the eloquence and intensity with which this text articulates a grand vision of God's cosmic purposes and expresses the aspiration for costly discipleship? Was it the description of the life-and-death struggle Christians face, with cosmic as well as human enemies, that rang true to the Anabaptist experience of persecution?

The language of spiritual warfare is at home in the Marpeck Circle. Most strikingly Marpeck and Scharnschlager use it in their introduction to "The Admonition of 1542." Jesus is called the church's general. At the same time, the authors are unequivocal that the general's kingdom is not of this world and cannot be found with a sword.[3]

Newer textual criticism reveals the process by which the Marpeck Circle appropriated a document from outside its universe. Until very recently scholars assumed that Maler borrowed an existing anonymous text. Victor Thiessen has made the convincing case that the "War Ordinance" of the Kunstbuch is based on the soldier's manual of the imperial knight Hartmut XII von Cronberg (1488–1549).[4] Cronberg had taken a stand for Martin Luther's cause already early in the movement, most likely under the influence of his fellow nobles Franz von Sickingen and Ulrich von Hutten. The enthusiastic Lutheran entered into imperial service as a soldier and returned in 1541 to his castle. In the years 1521–23 he composed numerous pamphlets, including this one.[5] He apparently had no ties to Anabaptist movements.

Thiessen has shown that Cronberg's pamphlet has been seriously altered and expanded by another hand, probably Maler's. This edited version consists of an introduction, a paraphrase of Cronberg, a discussion of Christian armour, and a call to watchfulness.[6] Thiessen mentions three possible explanations for the differences between the

---

3 WPM, 164–65.

4 Victor Thiessen, "Flugschriften eines Ritters im Kunstbuch des Marpeck-Kreises," MGB 60 (2003): 65–79.

5 Together with a letter from Luther and Cronberg's answer to Luther, the "War Ordinance" was published in pamphlet form by Wolfgang Köpfel in Strasbourg in 1522.

6 Thiessen, "Flugschriften," 65–79.

versions: deliberate editing, working from an inaccurate copy, and working from memory.[7] The probability that Maler knew Cronberg to be a Lutheran and a warrior suggests an openness on his part—and perhaps on the part of the community in whose behalf he worked—to receive truth from other sources. The "War Ordinance" appears in several editions of Luther's collected works.

Jesus is the narrator of the editor's new opening section of the treatise. Inclusiveness figures prominently: under the theme of payment for service, no difference is to be made on the basis of health, age, or wealth. The captain accepts all volunteers—Turks, heretics, schismatic Christians, whores, and so on. By the same token, all who reject the "service of the Almighty," whether emperor or pauper, will reap his anger. The editor adds two short paragraphs on the equipment listed in Ephesians 6, warning against "the armour of human teaching," and later returns to discuss the subject at length. Might this phrase refer to fighting according to human power and calculation? Allowing for the fluidity of allegorical language, it can be said that for peaceful Anabaptists the emphasis of the following sections on renouncing human attachments and powers implied nonviolence. The point throughout this text is that the battle facing the Christian is a spiritual one.

7 Ibid., 67.

The all-powerful and invincible emperor admonishes his avowed and sworn captains that they be armed and ready immediately without delay.

Call to arms of the most powerful and invincible emperor of all, to his avowed and sworn captains that they be ready and prepared in all regards without any delay (4 [2] Esd 16 [41]).[8]

Dear captains, a great tumult comes up to us from the abyss below, for the first murderer, liar, and perverter of the human race has arisen against us with all his might. For the battle that he lost to our servant Gabriel[9] (when he wished to be established as our equal), which caused him to be dethroned and robbed of all his glory and cast into the abyss of hell, still burns within him [Rv 12 (7–9) and 20 (1, 3); Jb 4 (11); 2 Pt 2 (4)]. Although his power is nothing compared to ours, and he may achieve nothing, nonetheless one must not scoff at any enemy, however small he is.[10*] For I have in my household no worm so small that it does not curl up when one steps on its tail.[11] Although he cannot win anything from us, he will nevertheless attempt to do whatever he can to harm us, for this was his habit from the time he was first cast out. With this he is satisfied, for he knows well that whatever happens to any of mine happens also to me.[12]

He uses his armour in various ways, for he is the master of a thousand deceits; here with force, there with offerings and gifts, third with all sorts of physical pleasures, with which all his commanders have been enslaved. Therefore it is necessary to equip ourselves with all power

---

8 [The Apocryphal book of 2 Esdras is conventionally subdivided into three parts. 4 Esdras includes chapters 3–14. The intended reference, 16:41, "Let the one who sells be like the one who flees; let the one who buys be like the one who loses," however, comes from 5 Esdras.—Ed.]

9 Jude 9.

10* Note.

11 Mt 10:29.

12 Mt 25:40.

and be prepared to campaign in the whole world, to rescue those who belong to us from the fierce lion that continuously prowl*s* around to find something to mangle and devour [1 Pt 5 (8)].

Therefore be reminded and warned in light of this letter. Rouse yourselves, so that I lose none of those who are mine; tell everyone to be armed and ready! For the foe is already prepared to attack us without any warning. Our imperial majesty asks, desires, and commands these things of each of you as our chosen friends, who alone know what is our pleasure.[13] But where anyone among you becomes careless, and one of our citizens is killed as a result, our imperial majesty will demand that citizen's blood from your hands and throw you into the abyss [Ez 3 (18)].

Thus we desire that you not take money secretly from any other lord but be satisfied with our payment alone. No one may serve two lords [Mt 7 (6:24); Lk 16 (13)], but everyone should promote our command alone, that they[14] might pursue these alone, and be on guard against my future burning anger, for the end is truly at hand, and this will be the last admonition [Ps 2 (5)].

Thereafter all things will be renewed, a new heaven and earth will be created through fire [Is 65 (17); 2 Pt 3 (12)], and this new creation will be given to all those who faithfully fulfilled our commands, who fought[15] and died nobly on earth for our sake, just as Jesus Christ had led the way for you, my beloved Son and also your Lord and Saviour, whom you should imitate to be a pleasant scent to me[16] and salvation to you [Lk 9 (23); Jn 12 (3); 1 Pt 2 (5)]. To this end I will help you with my grace. Take comfort that I will provide for you.

---

13 Jn 15:15.

14 [There is frequent movement between the third-person singular and plural pronouns.—Ed.]

15 2 Tm 4:7.

16 2 Cor 2:15f.

Kunstbuch text

Now follows a selection of some chief articles of the almighty field general's troop installation to all estates of the entire world, and to all cavalry men and infantry, comforting and acceptable, but terrifying to all enemies of the general.

First, the great and all-powerful emperor, our true heavenly general, promises to his soldiers service not for a month or a year but freely forever without termination.[18*]

The payment is eternal life, and each one who has taken up service with him shall be accepted as a son and heir of eternal life.[19*] He has permission to make use of all treasures for himself.

The soldiers' wives and children and all those attached to them shall all receive full payment, that is, everyone, young or old, healthy

Kück text[17]

A compendium of some chief articles drawn from the contract of the almighty king, comforting and acceptable to all emperors, kings, princes, and lords of the whole world, and to all cavalrymen and infantry, mounted and on foot, and terrifying to all enemies of God's Word.

First of all, our heavenly king promises service to his soldiers not for a period of one month or year but freely for eternity.

The payment of the heavenly king is eternal life, and that each one who commits himself to God's service shall be accepted as a son in the heavenly eternal kingdom, that he may make free use of the heavenly treasure as his own inheritance, which shall never run out.

The soldiers' wives and children shall all receive full payment, that is, each one, young or old, healthy or sick, rich or poor, whoever sub-

---

17 [Eduard Kück, ed., *Die Schriften Hartmuts von Cronberg,* Flugschriften aus der Reformationszeit, no. 14 (Halle a.S.: Max Niemeyer, 1899).—Ed.]

18* 1.

19* 2

or sick, rich or poor.[20*] Whoever enters his service shall receive payment from that hour onward and be paid in accordance with each person's degree of faith and trust in God.

mits to the Lord's service; his payment shall be as large and certain as the measure of faith and trust that each one has to the Lord and his faithful, certain promises.

No difference shall be made regarding payment among the various soldiers, whether they be mounted or foot soldiers; emperor, king, prince, or lord; or even the most despised.[21*] Only those who do not have living faith will have no eternal reward (Mt 25 [34]).

No difference shall be made regarding payment among the various soldiers, whether they be mounted or foot soldiers; emperors, kings, princes, or lords; or even among the most despised of the poor. For whichever person believes and trusts, he shall receive, and whoever does not believe will receive nothing of the heavenly payment, be he lord or servant.

When the trumpets of the Word of God sound the battle cry, whoever makes himself available with steadfast faith to the general, enlists and lets himself be incorporated, binding himself to the captain, and accepts and carries the sign of the corps as his insignia, he shall receive his wage from that time onward, and he will be assured of present and eternal advantage [Mk 16 (16); 1 Pt 3 (21); 1 Jn 5 (6–8)].[22*]

Each one who enters the Lord's service with steadfast faith and trust will receive his payment from that time onward, and he shall be assured of eternal riches, now and forever.

The general will also make good any damages to each soldier, and

The heavenly captain will also make good any damages, temporal

[20*] 3.
[21*] 4.
[22*] 5.

all that is owed him shall be made good, be it physical or spiritual damage.[23*] For he [the general] has committed himself to each one who is bound to him, so that whatever damage, lack, theft of goods that they may suffer will be restored one hundredfold, and a future of eternal life; this he has promised (Mk 10 [30]); [Heb 10 (34)].

or eternal, of all those who believe and trust in him. To those who lack faith and trust he may request this of God diligently and seriously; faith and trust will be given to him as much as he needs.

By means of his boundless power, the heavenly king will restore a hundredfold all things that one loses in his cause to those who believe and trust and remain true in faith.

The general will accept everyone who comes to him, Turks, heathens, heretics, schismatic Christians, whores, and knaves and all sinners.[24*] Whoever served the hated king beforehand should come, for the promised payment is certain (and paid for), and the general is faithful, true, and constant (Jn 2 [12:25]; Mt 16 [25]).

All Turks, heathens, Jews, heretics, and schismatic Christians are called upon to join the service of this Lord. Whoever believes and trusts this almighty, true Lord through the grace of God, may enter into the service of this Lord and be assured of the eternal kingdom. Whoever does this will not rue it. For all the power and riches of the Turkish emperor, even if he brings the entire world under his power and obedience—may God prevent this according to his will—it means little or nothing to him; it is to be reckoned as a shadow compared to the lowest pay of the poorest soldier who believes and trusts in God.

[23*] 6.
[24*] 7.

Furthermore, the general promises to all his allies great grace, and help and strength against all their foes.[25*] He will also give them power and strength and victory, to triumph through true patience. For he is all-powerful; without him no one can overcome sin, death, and hell (Jn 15 [5]); [Jn 16 (33); Ps 40 (41:3); Heb 2 (9f.)]. He wants to be their helper, protector, and refuge, to save them in all distress and protect them from all evil.

Almighty God promises each and every one his faithful grace and strength against all foes. They will triumph and be victorious against the world, the devil, and gruesome death, through the power of God, without any cares.

All those, be they of whatever estate and honours—emperors, kings, princes, or lords, rich or poor; all those who reject the calling and service of the Almighty, despise his Word, truth, and command—should know that the Almighty Lord and general will let his terrible anger and naked sword sweep over them. He will destroy, crush, and overthrow them with his weapons [Ps 7 (6)].[26*] As he says himself (Ps 2 [9]; Prv 1 [26f.]), all the human power in the entire world will not be able to protect them (Lk 19 [43f.]; Is 10 [3]).

All people, be they emperors, kings, princes, or lords, poor or rich; all those who despise and spurn this most high, almighty Lord and his Word and truth and grace, that he alone once and for all freely offered us out of his obvious leniency and mercy, and who stubbornly remain out of their own arrogance in their endeavour; they should know that the almighty Lord will let loose his gruesome anger and justice upon their temporal bodies and goods and condemn and damn their souls with eternal hellish punishment. Against this no human power or riches in the entire world can protect them.

25* 8.

26* 9.

Here follows an outline of the letter of articles.

All common and Christian soldiers shall know that if anyone does not hold the above-mentioned articles, he may be assured that he will be relieved of service by the chief of staff (Mt 25 [41]).[27*]

Outline of the letter of articles, which must be diligently obeyed by the common Christian army. And whoever does not obey this letter of articles, he may be assured that he will be relieved of his commission by the supreme heavenly Lord and general.

Take note: whoever has taken up service and allowed himself to be enlisted on the list, regardless of rank, he shall forgive and excuse all his brothers in arms, as then the Lord's Prayer requires [Mt 6 (12)], and from then on conduct himself in friendly demeanour through words, deeds, and gestures toward all his brothers-in-arms [Eph 4 (2)], so that we may more easily conquer all God's enemies as Christ has conquered and triumphed (Jn 16 [33]); [Rom 12 (21); 1 Pt 3 (9)].[28*]

Whoever enters into the service of the heavenly almighty Lord, be he emperor, king, prince, lord, or servant, he shall forgive all his brothers and comrades in arms, as we ask in the Lord's Prayer, through which we may withstand more successfully the enemies of God, with united spirits and hearts.

From now on, each and every one shall conduct his words and deeds out of love for the general and his neighbour.[29*] For love is the fulfilment of the law[30] (1 Tm 1 [5]).

Each and every one shall conduct his works out of love of God and neighbour, so that these same works all arise from the same attitude, thereby to be of help and assistance to one's neighbour; for through the love of one's neighbour all God's laws will be fulfilled, as St. Paul teaches.

27* 1.

28* 2.

29* 3.

30 Rom 13:10.

Each one who has enlisted should also be equipped with a good weapon and armour, developed by Paul in his armour chamber (Eph 6 [11–17]).[31*] He should be warned of strange clothing and the armour of human teaching that does not resist the smoke (much less the shot) of battle. He should be warned of the displeasure of the general and fulfil strictly his earnest commands (Mt 7, 13).

Each one shall listen to the commands of God, which are grounded in the two next articles, and shall preserve himself against all mutiny that might be preached against the aforementioned two articles. For namely, wolves disguised in sheep's clothing will approach us, as Christ himself has portrayed for us. They do not come through the door but like thieves and murderers climb into the sheep stall, solely to slaughter and destroy the sheep. To which end these thievish wolves pronounce and preach to us human laws and empty announcements instead of the Word of God. These same have taken from us our daily bread, God's Word, the heavenly food, and other things that might make them money, concerning which we have no commands or

31* 4.

promises from God, but because of which many thousands of souls are miserably murdered.

These are the devilish fruits by which we may recognize them.

St. Paul has told us of these same seducers in their special clothing and their own sects, and has illustrated them for us. These same groups teach us to differentiate between foods and days, and take for themselves a false chastity and many other similar things against God's command and against love of one's neighbour. Thus one should guard oneself against these hypocritical seducers as much as against the most serious enemy of Christ and his entire Christian people, so that he will not be discharged from the heavenly troop by the highest general.

Take note: you should know (at the expense of your soul, body, honour, and goods) that no one wishes to pay homage to the enemies of the general either publicly or secretly, or enter into any contracts with them at the risk of losing honour and favour, and of the above-mentioned penalty.[32*] This is shown in more detail in the large letter of

Conclusion of this contract.

So that each one is entirely certain and assured of all things that are contained in these articles above, each one should know that these things are confirmed in the Word of God and the death of Christ, sealed with his blood. Heaven and earth will pass away, but the Word of the Lord must

32* 5.

articles,[33] as 2 Cor 6 [14–17]; Mt 25; Jas 4 [4]; Rv 18 [4]. Let no one shrink from reading the complete letter of articles frequently, for the entire contract is reported in it, as well as the entire equipment. In the New Testament, namely, we see how one should behave in all articl*es* and actions against all his foes, to conquer them and protect the victory forever [Mt 5; Lk 6 (20ff.); Rom 12]. All this comes with the help of the high commander, who has offered and written to us that he will give assistance to every single serviceman in all actions and needs. Everyone can rely on it, refreshed and confident.

Everyone may be completely certain and secure, because the commander-in-chief, called Jesus Christ, has promised it. You should know that all this has been confirmed and reinforced through God's Word, and printed and sealed with the blood and death of Christ. You are to hold to all the contents of this letter irrevocably, though heaven and earth them-

remain eternally. Let everyone be admonished not to shrink from reading or hearing repeatedly the entire contract of Christ the Lord, that is, the holy gospel. In this text each one can receive much more completely a clear understanding of these above-mentioned excerpted articles, and grasp the grace of God more fully. Let everyone learn how to behave in all circumstances toward friends and enemies, find actual reports and truly achieve eternal victory thereby, all this through the assistance of the highest heavenly general, upon whom every serviceman may call in all actions and distress, who will forcefully help and conquer all enemies. No one need ever doubt this!

33 [Original: *grossen articklbrief.* The term artikel commonly refers to a list of doctrinal or ethical points. Here the sweep of the text in both columns suggests that the letter of articles in question is the New Testament itself.—Ed.]

selves are destroyed.[34] Thus the commander-in-chief who is called faithful, true, steadfast, and eternal truth binds himself to his own (Mt 24 [35]; Jn 14 [6]).

Printed in Steinburg for the furtherance of the holy Word of God and to the shame of all enemies of the cross of Christ. In the year 1522.

Weapons of the Christians, so that every soldier knows what he should put on and take off in the battle.

The above was clearly intended to refer to weapons, but it was not expressly stated just how and what they are. Thus it is necessary to write out the meaning of these weapons for the good of simple people, so that they might not improperly arm themselves and mistakenly hurt themselves, to their own destruction. The soldier who is fearful and fainthearted should not take to the field with the captain, but must return home, so that he will not make his brother despondent along with himself. Steadfast faith and confidence must be brought to the captain for him to defend and protect the soldier (and the whole bright army) against all the forces of the enemy. He says in Deuteronomy 20, "When you march to war against your enemy, and if you see that his elite troop and wagons are greater and more powerful than those you have on your side, do not fear [Lk 12 (4)], for I, the Lord your God who led you out of Egypt, am with you."

Nowadays the enemies of the captain are not temporal; they do not make war against contemporary kingdoms. Therefore other means and other weapons must be used to destroy the enemy [Heb 8; 2 Cor 10 (4)]. The captain will not allow a man to put on woman's clothing, or a woman man's clothing.[35] The soldier's words should not be "half-

---

34 Mk 13:31; Lk 21:33.

35 Dt 22:5.

linen or half-wool"[36] but should confess plainly and simply by words and deeds[37] without hypocrisy. He will reject all other clothes that are not simple and of one colour. For strange people wear strange clothing. Thus his soldiers must be lightly and simply clothed.

But the consequences are clear: they must first of all renounce all their own righteousness and good works[38*] (which are in truth nothing other than dirty linen)[39] and allow him to work all things through grace as it pleases him, whether or not he takes it up. For this is why Christ came into the world and let himself be baptized as a sinner—though he committed no sin (1 Pt 2 [22])—but was God's righteousness, his true light and life[40] [Mt 3 (15)]. Thus he says in Luke, "Though you do all these things, you are still useless knaves" (Lk 17 [10]).

Second, they must reject all temporal creatures and goods.[41*] Thus Christ says, "Whoever does not forsake house, farm, field, pasture, father, mother, wife, child, and follow me, he is not worthy of me."[42] But one should not throw away what God has provided for him, and give to others so that he suffers want. In this case love knows how to act. But whatever the commander demands, he should be willing to carry out.

Third, he must renounce himself and his own life,[43*] and for the sake of the commander leap into battle as Christ also offered and gave his life for his own, to be an example for his own to follow him.[44] Now it is obvious that those who do not have true faith in Christ do not follow him in any matter. Even though some follow him for a time, they do not persevere to the end.[45] It is not enough to renounce good works for Christ's sake. For when they are commanded by him to renounce

36 Lv 19:19.
37 Dt 22:5.
38* Note.
39 Rv 3:4.
40 Jn 1:4.
41* 2.
42 Mt 10:37; Lk 14:26.
43* 3.
44 1 Pt 2:21.
45 Mt 10:22; 24:13; Mk 13:13.

creaturely things and themselves, they fall away from the commander and curse him. Indeed, they commit perjury.

Thus it is necessary in this confusion that each one throw off all that may hinder him[46] from joining the elite troop, unencumbered, prepared, and without surplus baggage. Temporal, dedicated foot soldiers do so, taking along only what is necessary for warfare, in which one has very few easy days until the war comes to an end. This the soldiers can do with the following weaponry.

Paul writes to the Ephesians (6 [10–13]): "My brothers, be strong in the Lord, and in the power of his might. Put on the armour of God that you can withstand the evil attacks of the devil, for we do not battle with flesh and blood" (alone), "but with princes and powers, with the regents of darkness in this world, with the spirits of evil under heaven. Therefore take hold of the armour of God, with which you can resist on that evil day and be armed with all things."

Paul explains from the start how God will strengthen us in the battle, so that we might not quickly despair, or rely on our own strength, for this serves more to our loss than to our victory. To which the prophet says, "Cursed be the one who places hope and trust in mortals" (Jer 17 [5–7]), who trusts in "and takes his arm for flesh, and whose heart turns from the Lord" (in battle). "That kind of person will never see the future treasure." "But blessed is the one who trusts in the Lord" (in battle), "and whose hope is in the Lord." Also, cursed is the strong one who hopes in his strength. For all human help is like a reed which will break apart and stab you in the hand if you try to lean on it.[47]

Further, "the wise one should not depend on his wisdom, or the strong one on his strength, or the empire on its imperial treasury, but that he knows and acknowledges me. For I am the Lord, who carries out mercy, justice, and righteousness on the earth. Thus I take great pleasure in such things" (in my soldiers), "says the Lord" [Jer 9 (23f.)]. Thus we should put on the armour of God (as mentioned above). It can withstand all arrows of our enemies, which are the devil with his cohort and the forces of darkness, and if we turn to these, we are al-

46 Lk 9:62; Phil 3:13.

47 2 Kgs 18:19–21; Is 36:4–6.

ready equipped for battle and may withstand all the evil times—understand—through love and patience.

There is more to do! "Let your loins be girded with the truth, and be covered with the breastplate of righteousness, your feet shod with the armour of the gospel of peace. In all things, however, hold fast to the shield of faith, with which you can extinguish all fiery darts of the evil one, and put on the helmet of salvation, and the sword of the Spirit, which is the Word of God."[48][49*]

Now, however, after one has put on the armour of God, one should persevere within it.[50*] For it is not enough that a soldier swear and enlist in service to his captain, or that he also receive payment for it.[51*] He must also persevere and stand fast against the enemy, not lag behind, so that he will not be exposed as a perjurer. Clearly one must persevere in this war until death. Through this the captain senses the faith of his people.

But so that they may persevere fresher and stronger, they should gird their loins with truth. For the enemy (of this people) fights only with superficial glory, vengefulness, fleshly zeal and lies,[52*] for their commander the devil is the father of lies from the beginning [Jn 8 (44)]. In contrast, therefore, true soldiers must be girded about their loins (where one attacks first of all in wrestling to throw a man down) with the truth, and decked out with the breastplate of righteousness.

Here Paul offers true soldiers only the breastplate, so that they protect the chest, as a sign that whoever marches to war should persevere and attack the foe from the front and not run away, thereby showing them the back where they are exposed [1 Cor 9 (25); 2 Tm 4 (7)]. For the enemy might soon hit the weak spot and gain the victory. Thus they should put on the breastplate of righteousness, give their due to God and their neighbours, and owe no one anything other than love, according to the teaching of Christ and Paul [Rom 13 (8)].[53*]

---

48 Eph 6:14–17.

49* 1.

50* 2.

51* Parable.

52* Note.

53* 3.

The enemies are unable to do anything against this, even though they steal from God and his troops, robbing and murdering against God, honour, and justice. Nonetheless, the true soldiery should be satisfied with their pay and the commitment of the captain, always pressing forward (not turning aside in pursuit of booty) to proclaim the commands of the emperor to everyone. For this reason they should always be shod, to proclaim the gospel of peace, which—thanks be to God—has been gaining ground for a long time (by the blood of Christ's witnesses and warriors) and still undaunted by the frenzy, raging, and counterattacks of the enemies (let it be understood, the world with its Goliath) [1 Sm 17 (4ff.)].

Thus let everyone increase his efforts to accept and do (the job) with thanksgiving, as befits a true warrior and knight of Christ. Thus one also should wield the shield of faith against the devilish enemy (the two animals [Rv 13 (1ff., 11ff.)]). He thereby does in the archenemy of the human race[54] through patience. For with it one puts out all his fiery darts. If one believes in Christ, living water will flow from his faithful body,[55] which douses all Satan's wily military challenges, temptations, and fires.

One must also protect one's head in this battle, just as one has facial protection in all storms and strife. That should be the helmet of salvation.[56] Following that, one should take a double-edged sword in hand (and set to with manly courage). That is the Word of God.[57] This is what our commander Christ did in the wilderness (Mt 4 [4, 7, 10]).

What you have here is a just Christian soldier, decked out from top to bottom not with fleshly weapons but with spiritual ones. Paul proclaimed this in 2 Cor 10 [4ff.]: Dear brothers, we walk not according to the flesh, nor do we fight in this way. "Though we are still of the flesh, we do not battle according to the ways of the flesh. For the weapons of our knighthood are not fleshly but powerful before God, to disrupt the battlements and thereby disrupt the attacks" (of the enemy) "and all the high and mighty who rise up against the knowledge of God." Nothing

---

54 Acts 13:10.

55 Jn 7:38.

56 Eph 6:17.

57 Heb 4:12.

is said here of worldly authority, for it has its special service and office from God concerning the evils in the world, from which they protect the pious [Rom 13 (1–7); 1 Tm 2 (2)].

All of this is not yet enough. One thing has to be added in conclusion. It concerns quarrels and conflicts and is common among soldiers on the march. That is, the guard or watch. You may be as well armed as possible, but nothing can substitute for being prepared to the hilt, so that the enemy does not attack the camp at night and strangle everyone. Thus Christ says, "Watch!" [Mt 24 (42)]. *A*nd Peter adds: Dear brothers, "be sober and watch, for the grim lion, the devil" (the old snake) "continuously prowls around and searches whether he might nab something" (through lies and false teaching) [1 Pt 5 (8)]. Such guarding and watching is brought to our attention constantly in scripture; thus it is not necessary to explain further. It is also common in worldly dealings and battles that everyone seeks to do his utmost when he notices that the enemy is present.

Now whoever perseveres patiently in this battle, so that the emperor, along with Christ, the captain, finds him watchful—he will triumph over all the world (through faith in Him), and will give him an imperishable crown as he always promised [4 (2) Esd 2 (43–46); Rv 7 (9–17)]. May the Almighty God and our Lord Jesus Christ, together with his Holy Spirit, help us all to fight our way through this roiling and raging ocean [2 Tm 4 (7f.)].[58] Amen.

---

[58] Is 17:2f.

23

Concerning the comfort of Christians under persecution

To his followers in Windischgraz[1]

Hans Has von Hallstatt

Graz, before 2 December 1527

Hans Has von Hallstatt was a Catholic priest in southern Austria. In 1525 he began to preach an evangelical message. With opposition from the parish priest but with the support of the town council, Hallstatt promoted reform along the lines of radical early Zwinglianism. Among other things, he married; he simplified the sacraments, celebrating Communion around tables and baptism without the old rituals; and he allowed laymen and women to preach. He was imprisoned sometime after Pentecost in 1527 and hanged on December 2 of that year.[2] Hallstatt was not an Anabaptist, but—as his inclusion in the Kunstbuch testifies—he shared a commitment to radical reform and radical disci-

---

Hans Has von Hallstatt, *An seine Anhänger in Windischgraz: Vom Trost der Christen in der Verfolgung; [Graz, vor dem 2. Dezember 1527].* Translation by Victor Thiessen.

1 Or Windischgrätz; now Slovenj Gradec in northern Slovenia.

2 For biographical studies, see Karl Amon, "Der Windischgrazer Prediger Hans Has von Hallstatt und die 'Neue Synagoge' von 1527," *Jahrbuch der Gesellschaft für die Geschichte des Protestantismus in Österreich* 78–79 (1963): 3–15; Michaela Kronthaler, "Die Epistel des frühreformatorischen Predigers Hans Has von Halstatt," *Zeitschrift des historischen Vereins für Steiermark* 89–90 (1998–99): 57–84.

pleship. Some of his followers fled, but one, Kasper Maler from Graz, was baptized as an Anabaptist in 1528.[3]

This pamphlet is a riveting and extravagant sample of persecution literature. It is Hallstatt's last will and testament, written from a prison cell. The ominousness of the political situation for dissenters is suggested by the fact that a papal visitation and inquisition came to this region in 1528.[4] The intensity of the writing suggests that Hallstat was struggling to make sense of his fate—to himself as much as to fellow believers. The outcome of his struggle was a trembling but inspired confidence in the unshakably gracious purpose of God for all who love God. Two factors suggest that Hallstatt's story, preserved only in the Kunstbuch, was part of the Marpeck Circle collection from early on. The first is the closeness of Hallstatt's convictions and location to those of the Marpeckites. The second factor is the fact that his testimony does not appear in any other record. The fact that the Swiss and the Marpeckites continued to experience waves of persecution gave Hallstatt's testimony immediate relevance.

When we remember that the author had joined the cause of evangelical reform only in 1525, we are amazed that only two years later his thought was steeped in biblical language and images. Yet their selection and interpretation is different from that of most Anabaptists. Two matters stand out. One is Hallstatt's emphasis on the absolute sovereignty of God in the lives of individuals and nations. This accent suggests Augustinian influence: confidence in the providence of God, belief in God's preservation of the elect and rejection of the damned, and conviction that even in their perversity the damned carry out the divine purpose. The other difference is that Halstatt's presentation of the cross of suffering makes almost no reference to Jesus' own cross bearing or his teaching about the cross.

The key to the riddle of innocent suffering in this letter is God's absolute sovereignty and the security of the elect in their ultimate salvation.

---

3 BSOT, 464.

4 Johann Loserth, "Zu den Anfängen der Reformation in Steiermark: Die Visitation und Inquisition von 1528 und ihre Ergebnisse," in *Quellen zur Geschichte der Täufer 11, Österreich 1,* ed. Grete Mecenseffy (Gütersloh: Gerd Mohn, 1964), 149–60.

At one point a gloss qualifies this security: "as long as it did not arise from our guilt," a typical Anabaptist concern. Suffering Christians take heart from the fact that the tyrants who persecute them do so not out of their own intention but solely out of God's. Thus believers need not fear, because their enemies are already damned and ultimately powerless. This is the thrust of the many Old and New Testament references. Hallstatt concludes from his claims about God's power that Christians should not oppose oppressive rulers with violence, wish them evil, or curse them.

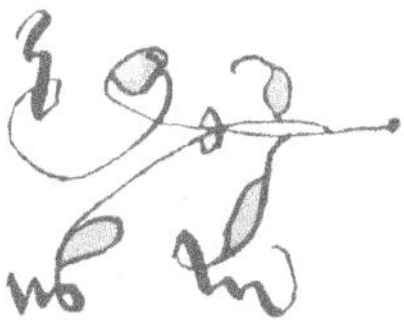

The grace and strength of Christ be with you in your tribulations.[5] May he give you a spirit of hope to fight boldly against all persecution and oppression of the anti-Christian powers. Hans Has of Halstatt (now a prisoner for the sake of the Word) wishes these things for all the elect and good-hearted in Windischgraz and all others scattered here and there in misery. Amen.

Now I acknowledge first and foremost, dear brothers, that either you, together with those who are now imprisoned and hunted, are true Christians, or that the overwhelming riches of fatherly mercy[6] see fit to make you true Christians through his most beloved Son Christ, our Redeemer. For persecution and oppression make genuine Christians and strengthen them,[7] so that they become truly experienced and well practised in true faith and strong reliance on God. Indeed, they become truly educated and experienced, more bold and unwavering, since one learns and studies more of the

5 This epistle gives an account concerning the comfort of the faithful under persecution and all attacks of the devil and sin.

6 Eph 2:7.

7 2 Tm 3:12.

gospel through a little tribulation than in any other way in one's entire life. Thus the elect must undergo all misfortunes as best they can. For no persecution or tribulation will come upon them that is not entirely profitable for their salvation [Rom 8 (28)]. They will become even stronger and more fruitful in their faith in God, and boldly trust him. For one sees, notices, and acknowledges how all of this together rests solely on God's power, might, and strength. Indeed, not a hair will fall from the heads of the truly faithful against his will[8] (according to the words of Christ) [Mt 10 (30); Lk 21 (18)].

In addition, the persecutors of the gospel are solely servants and slaves of our Lord (as was Pharaoh against the children of Israel [Ex 14 (4)]). Indeed, they are instruments through which God, the Almighty, the most gracious Father, tests, provokes, and drives his elect, so that they may be recognized as true Christians, for they remain steadfast (in the truth). For as gold in fire, they are proved worthy through tribulation, suffering, and fear, and thus they learn in such need to flee to God, to truly call upon him from their whole heart and set all their comfort and hope on him [Ws 3 (6); Sir 2 (5)].

In summary, in all troublesome situations they enjoy the taste of the gospel. They love Holy Writ above all gold and silver.[9] For they discover how all things happen only through God, of God, and in God, as it has always happened with God's elect [Jn 5 (39)]. And the more God has loved saints, the more he sent them tribulation and persecution [Jb 5 (17); Mt 10 (21f.); Lk 12 (4)].[10] This is evident with the holy David, who was persecuted not only by Saul but also by his own son Absalom [2 Sm 17]. Thus those whom God loves he allows to suffer here all the more [Heb 12 (6)].

When they have sunk deep down, God often lets them swim a long time, until they are about to go under and drown in their suffering. Then he comes to them at the last minute and helps, showing himself

---

8 Acts 27:34.

9 Prv 8:10; 16:16.

10 [Here and elsewhere the text switches from the third-person plural to the singular. In order to distinguish pronouns with human referents from those with divine referents, I have generally used the third-person plural for pronouns with human referents.—Trans.]

to be God and a gracious, loving Father. For he helps most when no other help can be found, when all comfort and hope of the creaturely is completely gone.[11*] When the proper time comes for help, then he comes forth. For he is called "a help in times of trouble"[12] [Ps 9 (9)], that is, a helper at an opportune, convenient, and appropriate moment. When no other comfort and help are available, he shows himself to be a strong, mighty, and powerful God, who is the Lord of heaven and earth, and that all creatures[13] are in his hand [Mt 11 (27)]. Through such help God pours out his grace into the chosen, so that they might increase and dwell all the more in the truth, and trust completely in God, so that God may do with them whatever his will deems proper. Thus they set their whole hope on him.

For that reason he sets up mighty and powerful people before us, who have formidable reputations of strength in the eyes of the world, and not simple, lesser, weak people of no value.[14*] Why this? So that he can demonstrate his might and strength through the least of creatures against the great and mighty. The least overcome the mighty with their patience, so that it becomes known that God is even more mighty and powerful than all powers on this earth. This is how he dealt with the mighty king Pharaoh, demonstrating his power over him, and thus showed his chosen people with deeds that he alone was the God and Lord of Israel [Ex 14 (4)] and no one could harm them against his will, however mighty, powerful and strong they might be.

Take note: when we experience and recognize in our misery the fact that our Lord is the one God of heaven and earth, and no one may harm us without his fatherly will, then we believe for the first time in our hearts that he is God and all-powerful, mighty Lord of all things [Rom 8 (28)]. Now if the power and might of the children of Anakim[15] had not been revealed, God's greater power and glory also would not have been revealed to us [Nm 13 (22ff.); 14]. Then we would not have

---

11* Note.

12 [Original: *auxiliator inn oportunitatibus inn tribulatione.*—Trans.]

13 [There is solidarity between humans and the animal kingdom; salvation is not only for humanity separate from the other parts of God's creation.—Ed.]

14* Note.

15 Dt 1:28; etc.

recognized that he is our mighty, strong God, who could stand by us in all our needs.[16*] We would not see of what great help his provision is, and never, ever experience in this life that he alone is a mighty Lord, who holds all things together in his power. Therefore, if something should arise against us, we should believe fervently that it comes from God. He does it himself; he brings it to pass to test our faith in Christ. This must serve to his praise, power, and glory, and to our salvation.

Behold, the great tyrants must therefore serve us and be beneficial for our salvation without any regard for their own wills and thoughts, even if they condemn us and give us over to the devil. May they be despised (I mean this not according to the flesh) for thinking that they could do differently from what God plans for them! [Is 41 (10–14)]. When a true Christian becomes aware of and recognizes the great power which God demonstrates to the godless, he will become completely bold and take heart. For he will realize that such raging and tyrannizing does not come simply from mortals, or their own power, but that God pushes them and blinds them to it (because of their own guilt). God has them, as he has us, in his power. He moves their hearts wherever he wishes [Prv 21 (1)]. As Solomon says, they persecute his elect regardless of their own thoughts, so that through our weakness God reveals his power over them to all the world. Soon it will be shown mightily and powerfully (believe this steadfastly!) that he is our God and Father, as much as he ever did for the people of Israel when he rescued them from the bloody hand of Pharaoh and humiliated their enemies before all the world. Only flee to him boldly (he will not leave us as orphans) and sincerely ask him for grace! [Jb 14 (18); Heb 13 (5f.); Ps 119 (8) and 56 (5)]. We may thereby see that he is the Lord of all things [Eph 1 (21f.)], and that all things work in all ways according to his pleasure.

Second, though they have nothing good in them, he works in the same way through the damned to his honour and glory [Ps 18 (46f.)]. For they have been ordained to demonstrate God's justice upon themselves, just as we have been ordained to demonstrate his fatherly mercy upon us [Rom 9 (15)]. For he is God, who must be acknowledged as

---

[16*] Gloss: As long as it did not arise from our guilt, that is, not from evil deeds.

mighty and powerful. Since these things must be revealed, it is necessary that something must be available to demonstrate them. Thus the great powers and strengths of this world exist, against which God's might and omnipotence should be shown. God brings forth his vessels of wrath, which he ordained as a means to exercise his justice upon them: thereby God proves his omnipotent justice upon them [Rom 9 (22)]. When he chooses to reveal this, he has a servant, Satan, whom he uses through his omnipotence in order to awaken such things in the damned, which then erupt from within them [Ws 2 (25)].

It becomes clear to all what kind of vessels they are, what evil roots are buried in their hearts.[17] For God looks more on the heart than on works.[18*] Thus, if the heart is evil and damned before God, he lets such impurities break forth from their hearts and manifest themselves in such deeds,[19] so that it will become public that these vessels are vessels of wrath.[20] Thus the damned show their faithlessness with their works: just as the Amorites had not yet carried out their misdeeds [Gn 15 (16); Dt 20 (17)] because God did not wish to drive them out of the land or kill them. For as Moses said, their misdeeds had not yet come to fruition. First of all they had to show convincingly through their works that they were vessels of wrath and then be tossed into eternal damnation by God's justice.

He does likewise with the vessels of his mercy, that he according to his foresight had already ordained for salvation in order to demonstrate the riches of his mercy on them.[21] In order to reveal what kind of spirits they were, he aroused the mercy he had placed in them through the Holy Spirit. He moved them so that the fruit of their roots had to come forth.[22] Athough God already foresaw and acknowledged that the roots before him were just and good, these fruits had to emerge nevertheless, so that it would be publicly revealed that these were vessels of

---

17 1 Mc 1:11; Heb 12:15.

18* Note.

19 Mt 12:34f.; 15:19; Mk 7:21; Lk 6:45; 1 Tm 5:24.

20 Rom 9:22.

21 Rom 9:23.

22 Mt 7:16.

his mercy, which he had prepared beforehand out of pure grace, before any good work had come from them.

Thus he demonstrated both his mercy and his justice through his divine omnipotence, that he is an almighty Lord, who with his power creates and carries out in all creatures all things, except for sin [Eph 1 (11)]. Powerful and almighty, he rules, has power, and dispenses his wealth over all things; regardless of the number of lands, peoples, and powerful lords to rule over them, none is God's equal. Indeed, like a strong captain and mighty king we have triumphed! He, the very same, goes before us in all strife; he intervenes and battles for us.[23] This is Christ our Redeemer, who has such power given to him by the Father, to be Lord in heaven and earth [Mt 28 (18)]. He is also the one who speaks heartily and comfortingly to us, for he says, "Rejoice, for I have conquered the world" [Jn 16 (33)]. So we shall rejoice, for the joy is certainly ours. It is ours, for he has gained the victory for us.[24*] Since the victory is also ours, thus we are lords together with him above all creatures.

Since we are lords, who can harm us? The entire world with all its allies can do nothing to us [Rom 8 (28–34)]. "For there is one in us who is greater than he who is in the world" [1 Jn 4 (4)]. Since this one now lives within us [2 Cor 13 (5)], we have far less reason to fear. For "since God is with us, who may be against us?"[25] If death, hell, and the devil—even the entire world—now confront us, we have one who steps forward for us, takes us under his wing,[26] and keeps careful watch over us [1 Jn 2 (1)]. "Who will then raise charges against God's elect?" [Rom 8 (33)]. Indeed, even though sins should fall upon us in droves, nonetheless Christ is here; he defends and justifies us before the Father (Heb 5 [9]; 1 Jn 2 [1]). Who can then harm, kill, and damn us?[27*] Christ is the one who will give life; he is the one who rose from the dead, sits now at the right hand of his father [Heb 12 (2); Mk 16 (19)],

---

23 Ps 24:8.

24* Note.

25 Rom 8:31.

26 Ru 2:12; Ps 17:8; 36:7; 57:1; 63:7; 91:4.

27* Gloss: past or adhering [The original—*vergangen oder anklebisch*—is hard to interpret.—Trans.]

and intercedes mightily. Therefore we are certain that neither sword nor persecution, neither death nor hell, neither martyrdom nor terror can turn us away from the love of God which dwells in Christ our Lord [Rom 8 (34–39)].

For this reason, dear brothers, I rejoice with all my heart over the trials and persecutions that have arisen among you and yours. God, the Father of all holiness (may he be blessed for ever and eternally), has seen fit through Christ to send to you a small tribulation. For it is a great, noteworthy proof that he has sent Christ our Saviour together with his blessed Word to announce that he also accepts you as true, proper Christians. For where Christians are found, the cross must also be found. And where there is no cross, there is no true Christian.

Therefore call undaunted to God in faith, that you may become worthy to suffer such insult and shame for the sake of the Word of God. For it is a special gift of God, as Paul says, to suffer for the Word of God [Phil 1 (29)]. O God, we are not worthy of this suffering, not worthy to bear the precious cross [Heb 11 (26)]. For Christ has made it precious and blessed it with his suffering and dying. There are very few among you on earth who are worthy of it.[28] He gives such worthy suffering only to those who are specially blessed and chosen for that. He himself especially chooses true Christians, and lays this cross upon them, so they might learn to recognize him as the one to whom they should flee when it comes to the decisive battle.

Such persecution is nothing more than a skirmish in which we learn to fight and to find refuge in Christ.[29*] Therefore, when we at last come before God's stern judgment in great fear and distress, we will know from previous experience what will comfort us and where we will find refuge. Thus we may be bolder when the last battle begins (when flesh and spirit shall part), when human wrath turns on us with such brutality [Ps 124 (2)]. Therefore do not fear their threats, arrogance, and violence, but look alone upon Christ and desire him alone in your tribulation and persecution, "as the deer longs for cool springs when he is hunted" [Ps 42 (1)]. Then you will quench your thirst and be powerfully

---

28 Heb 11:38.

29* Note.

strengthened against all your foes and persecutors, and speak boldly with your whole heart: "The Lord is with me; I shall not fear what anyone will do to me" [Ps 118 (6)]. And though they bring a mighty army against me, nevertheless my heart shall not fear. Though a battle arise before me, I will rely on this promise.

Why is this so? Because "the Lord is my light and my salvation, whom shall I fear? The Lord is the strength of my life; who shall terrify me?" [Ps 27 (1)]. Indeed, "though I were in the midst of death, I would fear no evil, for you, Lord, are with me."[30] "For I would leap over the walls" with my Lord [Ps 18 (29)]. And though my God should slay me, even so I would hope in him.[31] Yes, even if I see nothing else before me but vain terror and sorrow, even the horrible wrath of God himself, even then I would believe "in hope where there is no hope" [Rom 4 (18)]. It must certainly come to pass that we of the faithful will be tested hardest, to the utmost degree. At this point Satan will show us God's most terrible wrath, that he might make us despair and rebel. Satan is the master of a thousand arts, utterly cunning and subtle. An ancient warrior, he has done this for thousands of years, cutting down many a proud hero.[32*] Precisely for this reason we must equip ourselves with the sword of the Spirit, that is, with the Word of God, with which we may extinguish Satan's fiery darts [Eph 6 (16f.)].

But in order that we may become more adept at such a battle, we must first learn in this life, as I said above, that when it comes time to fight, we will be ready at arms. Thus our gracious God and Lord, out of his grace, for our good and piety, raises up those who take us for the greatest fools on earth. Then God the Almighty awakens someone in order to persecute us relentlessly.[33*] It is irrelevant to God who it is. He would as soon take for this purpose a great lord, a powerful prince, as a simple man; indeed, he'd prefer a big shot like Pharaoh! He had to persecute God's people, even if he had not wanted to do so. Similarly, he raised up Saul and Shimei against pious David, so that they afflicted him with much trouble. Even so, David did not want to seek

---

30 Ps 23:4.

31 Jb 13:15.

32* Note.

33* Note.

revenge against anyone—indeed, to the extent that he commanded his own servants not to lay a hand on them [2 Sm 16 (5ff.)].[34*] For he knew the reason for these things; he certainly observed that the Lord had arranged and commanded this, as he also confessed when he obstructed his servants so that they did nothing to Shimei. For he said, "The Lord has commanded him to persecute me."[35]

A true Christian becomes aware of this fact and recognizes that these things come from God, serving his good and God's praise. The godless do not know this but assume it is in their power. When he is plagued by tyrants, such a Christian will endure all suffering without despair. He is now certain and believes steadfastly that all misfortune must bring about the best for him. Then he will become joyful and defiant in the Spirit, like a joyful warrior against all trials, strong as a rock.[36*] He considers it an especially great joy and grace whenever a variety of tribulations come to him.

When tribulation and persecution come to an end, when he has experienced and learned from it that God deals wonderfully and kindly with his own, he would not exchange many goods for the misfortunes he suffered and the friendly grace of God he experienced in them [Rom 5 (3–5)]. He becomes intimately aware of how powerful, gracious, and merciful God is, that all things are in his hands, and that our free will can do nothing in such matters. And when tyrants seriously undertake to deal with Christians doing this and that to them, inflicting this and that sort of martyrdom upon them, threatening them hard and fast with the sword and other things [Lk 12 (4f.)], a true Christian knows, however, and is certain that they may not harm a hair on his head, may inflict no harm upon him any more than God will allow [Mt 10 (30)]; Lk 21 (18)]. No matter how they might rage, the look of tyranny in their eyes, we see often enough in the Bible that God's eye is on them and cares for his own.

34* Note.

35 2 Sm 16:10.

36* Parable.

For example, when more than forty of them swore to one another that they would neither eat nor drink until they killed Paul, nonetheless God saved him from their murderous hands [Acts 23 (12f.)].

He freed Peter from the prison and the chains fell from his feet [Acts 12 (7)].

When some men sought Paul's life, God helped him over the wall [2 Cor 11 (33)].

How often God rescued pious David from the hands of bloodthirsty Saul. When he threw his spear at him, even then God protected him. Yes, even as Saul surrounded him for a time on the mountain, which drove even David to despair of any escape, God again rescued him and helped him escape [1 Sm 19 (2); 23 (27f.); 24 (1ff.)].

God also helped the prophet Jeremiah escape [Jer 39 (17f.)].

The prophet Daniel from the middle of the lion's den and Susanna from the rigged court of capital crimes [Dn 6 (22); Sus (45ff.)].

He saved the entire city of Bethulia from the strong and mighty Holofernes through a single woman. How wonderful is God's help, that he would send help in a time of need through a weak woman [Jdt 12; 13].

God also helped the three young men out of the fiery furnace, though they were already in the midst of death [Dn 3 (25f.)].

And there are many other examples that God had shown to his own, as he led the people of Israel through the great deep sea and saved them, though the sea was before them, high mountains on either side of them, so that they could not run away even if they may have wished to. Behind them was the mighty Pharaoh with weapons in hand. Yet again God demonstrated his power and helped them escape, just as all hope and help appeared to vanish with no consolation of escape [Ex 14].

This and many other examples happened so that we could learn to recognize that it rests in God's might and power alone to rescue his own from these things, regardless of how great and how terrible the enemy and the persecution might be. Even today God moves the hearts, courage, and intentions of tyrants to inflict all manner of plagues and misfortunes on his elect, just as he moved the hearts of the

Egyptians.[37] As David says, he transforms the hearts of those who are harmful to his people and act maliciously to his servants.[38*, 39] Of what good is that blind and miserable people on this earth than that they behave as God's rods and instruments to be used on his Christians, as God ordains them to do, and reveal his glory through them, as has been noted above?

Do not be daunted! If God sends suffering to you, he will also send grace and comfort to you [1 Cor 1 (6)].[40*] May you suffer all the adversity with great patience, praying earnestly that his fatherly will might come to pass.[41] He is the father and knows how to deal with his children in a proper manner. There is no emergency as long as this almighty Father is present and keeps a diligent eye upon us. The scriptures cannot show often enough the great love that God has for his faithful. They often demonstrate that he loves us all as a father loves his children, as one spouse loves the other, yet divine love exceeds all earthly love. For the love of a spouse, one leaves father and mother and goes to the one given by God [Gn 2 (24); Mt 19 (5)].[42*] It could well come to pass that this great love may be extinguished and split up and from then on be given to others, which will cause a great, endless division, so that they may never forgive those who were separated and accept them in grace.

How often we have departed from our God, as Jeremiah says, to be a whore with idols of stone and wood, clinging to creatures and replacing God with them,[43] and devoting our comfort and love to them! [Jer 3 (9)]. Nevertheless, our almighty, gracious Father is so kind and loves us so much that he accepts us in his grace at any time, as the father accepted his squandering and disobedient son in honour [Lk 16 (15:20)].

How often God has called us through his prophets to leave off with our evil lives and turn to him, for he wishes to remember our previous

37 Ex 4:21; 7:3; etc.

38* David.

39 Ps 105:25.

40* Gloss: Joseph tells [of] his brothers and children and reports how God saved and preserved him [often] from serious temptation (Gn 39 [7ff.]).

41 Gn 45:5–8.

42* Parable.

43 Rom 1:25.

life no more![44] [Ez 18 (21f.) and 33 (11)]. Why is this? For this reason, that out of great love he won us through Christ his Son; yes, such was his love that he said, "Is it possible that a mother forget her suckling child, that she not have a heartfelt sympathy with him? And though it might even be possible that she could forget her child," says the Lord, "nevertheless I cannot forget you" [Is 49 (15)]. Behold, what joy overflowing with grace there might be to a believing, troubled person, when he notices and acknowledges the paternal mercy the eternal Father has for him.

One takes note of and recognizes this most clearly, however, when one is in fear, need, and tribulation; there he learns best what the eternal providence of God is, what good it is, how comforting it is [Is 26 (16)]. Otherwise one cannot lay hold of and experience it without danger, regardless of how attractively or beautifully one may debate the issue.[45*] All this can obviously be received and acknowledged only through the living Spirit. Here one learns with the heart that all our deeds and salvation arise from no other power than God's might. However much and often one rants against the elect, however much one wishes to push them into hell and afflict them with all plagues, nonetheless they are certain that no one may harm them [Rom 8 (38f.)] and rip them from the hand of God, though all the world were against them—indeed, all the might of the devil [Jn 10 (28); 17 (12); 18 (9)].

Behold, this is why God sends his elect so many trials: so that his fatherly faithfulness might be recognized. For no misfortune comes to God's elect in which they do not experience something wonderful of the depths of God. For in all cases he reveals to them something lovely and wonderful, through which they love him more and become bolder in the face of all misfortune. Thus the great harm with which tyrants afflict us is useful for us, specifically that we become more manly in faith, learning and experiencing that they are utterly miserable, blind, poor people, mere instruments and vessels of God's wrath who cannot do anything of their own accord [Rom 9 (22)]. God uses them for his needs; thus we fear their power as much as if it were a falling leaf from

44 Jer 31:34.

45* Note.

a tree, whereas we otherwise rightly believe from the heart in God our Father.[46*, 47]

Wherever tyrants forbid the Word of God, we will be all the more desirous to hear it, read it, and publicly spread it and preach it with joyful heart. Thus faith grows within us. The Word of God moves, trains, and renews us [Col 3 (10); Eph 4 (23)] so that we become different people, teaching our neighbours also of the great deeds that God reveals to us in his gospel.[48*] With their prohibitions the tyrants create this. The more they prohibit, hinder, and fight against the gospel, the more bravely and joyfully it is proclaimed and revealed. We have such examples in the Acts of the Apostles. When they earnestly threatened the apostles to keep quiet and not speak in the name of Jesus, they really began to speak out, stepped forward in the temple and in their houses, proclaiming the gospel with joyful hearts every day as never before [Acts 5 (28)]. This is what the godless produced with their prohibitions! Thus it turns out that all their tyranny and havoc against us only promote and drive us to study the scripture more diligently and reveal it to others.[49*] Take notice, dear brothers: God is great and merciful, for he is able to turn everything, including their thrashing and havoc, to the best,[50] and even without our will moves us to grasp the Word of God with our hearts and not only externally with our ears.

To conclude: do you, dear Christians, believe that Christ spoke in vain, saying that those will be blessed who suffer persecution for the sake of righteousness—that the kingdom of heaven belongs to them? [Mt 5 (10)]. The eternal truth does not lie: Christ calls us to rejoice and be happy when they persecute and reject us for his sake. Truly, when he tells us to rejoice when we suffer persecution, we should not be sad. Since Christ has said so, we need nothing else. Although they take our goods, our body, our very life from us (more they cannot take [Lk 12 (4)]), nonetheless we have another who can give us far, far more, as he

---

46* Note.

47 [The relationship between the second and third clauses in this sentence is puzzling.—Ed.]

48* Other people.

49* Note.

50 Rom 8:28.

has promised [Mt 19 (29)]. Whoever leaves house, home, goods, honour, wife, and child for his sake, to him he will restore these things a hundredfold and will give him eternal life. Pay attention: he will give us more than they can take from us.[51] They take from us what is temporal, earthly, transitory, but the Lord gives us eternal, heavenly, unending, inexpressible joy and blessedness [1 Cor 2 (9)]. The miserable blind people harm themselves much more than us. They want to take what is temporal from us, and thereby they themselves lose what is eternal.[52*]

Thus one should have a heartfelt pity for them, and pray to God regarding their ignorance, whether he might have a Saul among them whom he would transform into a Paul. For goodness' sake, do not oppose them with your fist, or wish something horrible upon them or curse them. For they will all be richly rewarded by the stern judge who will not suffer any injustice [Lk 23 (34)].

My dear brothers and sisters, have you understood (I hope) how all of this comes together from God alone, be it persecution or any other misfortune? God brings us this out of pure grace and love. All these things assist us greatly to eternal salvation; they provoke and motivate us, that we may learn to recognize God more and more [Jn 17 (3)]—he who is wonderful in our eyes through the deeds he does for his elect. Even the evil that is present in the world has to serve the good of the pious, and the glory and honour of God [Rom 8 (28)]. To us, however, who remain steadfast in the Word of God, it brings eternal life. Amen.

May all of this be a farewell and last word to you, written before my end. May God give grace through his Jesus Christ, that it may be fruitful for many and bring healing to many to God's praise. Amen.

Hans Has of Hallstatt, a sometime preacher
(of the Word of God) at Windischgraz,
was hanged by a rope on 2 December 1527 at Graz
for the sake of the gospel.
He began to preach in the year 1525.
Praise God.[53] Amen.

---

[51] Rom 8:18.

[52*] Note.

[53] [Original: *Laus Deo.*—Trans.]

24

To the whole brotherhood, especially those in Appenzell as well as in and around Zurich

Cornelius Veh
[Austerlitz?] 8 March 1543

"To the Whole Brotherhood" is the only letter in the Kunstbuch from Cornelius Veh, but the collection does include a letter sent from Pilgram Marpeck to Veh: no. 3, "Concerning the Libertarians."

The earliest report we have about Veh appears in a Hutterite account.[1] He is described as a teacher in the congregation in Austerlitz (now Slavkov u Brna in the Czech Republic), which was in regular correspondence with Marpeck. This bond is reinforced by by Veh's use of his mentor's signature phrase, referring to himself in his salutation as a comrade in the tribulation of Christ. According to the report, in 1541 Veh and others came to the nearby colony of Schäkowitz (or Tscheikowitz; now Čejkovice in the Czech Republic) to speak to the assembled congregation about unity. But instead he shamed and mocked them, hoping to weaken the comrades in faith. The report continues with a similar account of a visit by "Bilgram" (Pilgram) soon thereafter. These incidents are typical of the initiative members of the Marpeck Circle took in seeking unity among Anabaptist groups.

Cornelius Veh an die ganze Bruderschaft, besonders die in Appenzell sowie in und um Zürich; [Austerlitz?] 8. März 1543. Translation by Victor Thiessen and John D. Rempel.

1 A. J. F. Zieglschmid, ed., *Die älteste Chronik der Hutterischen Brüder* (Ithaca, NY: The Cayuga Press, 1943), 224.

Veh casts a wide net in his appeal for unity, addressing himself especially to the Swiss congregations in Appenzell and Zurich. Appenzell is significant for both Marpeck and Jörg Maler. The former found it to be the most legalistic of the Swiss congregations, while the latter was attached to it during his years of exile. The two recurring themes are the gifts given to each Christian and the willingness to die for love's sake, in the confidence that one will live again. Alongside these themes is a prickly polemic against "false Christians."

Early in the epistle the author uses a telling phrase: "We, together with all true witnesses of Christ's resurrection, we have received gifts from Christ." It puts into words a common conviction among Anabaptists that they were one with the apostolic church and part of its experience of encountering the risen Lord. Veh links "the old and new law of love" intimately with walking in the resurrection. True Christians persevere in a life of love to the point of death, both spiritually and physically, following the pattern Christ has set.

Continuing from this thought Veh turns to the unusual image of Christ as the "mint-master" and asks if believers, the "coins," are stamped with his likeness. Beware of false stampings, he cautions, those impressed on untreated iron. Treated iron bears the engraving of Christ, the Spirit, and the scriptures. Veh then proceeds with a series of comments that might have raised the ire of his Hutterian hosts. On the one hand he criticizes those who claim they are the only ones engraved by Christ. On the other hand, he decries people "like the Pharisees," who place the emphasis on outward scrupulosity, locating Christ in "temporal goods." His targets are Catholics and Lutherans but also the Swiss (to whom he is writing!) and the Hutterites. Soon thereafter Veh moves from practice to piety, asking his audience to examine themselves to see if Christ lives in their heart. If he does, they are justified by grace through faith. Veh is not consistent in his line of argument. We are left uncertain whether the stamp of Christ is concrete practices of discipleship, orthodox theology, or the experience of justification; he mentions all three. Perhaps he is trying to say they are all of a piece.

From here Veh returns to the notion of gifts and with it gives his treatise a pastoral turn. We depend on the gifts, both spiritual and material, we share with one another. It becomes clear that the "we" now refers to the Swiss and well as the Pilgramites. Together the Pilgramite elders ask the Swiss, whose names are written and known by God, to intercede for them. A candid list of prayer requests follows, in which Veh unashamedly lays out his weakness and need.

This letter preserves an instructive sample of the conflicting convictions, emotions, and personality traits that came into play as different streams of Anabaptist vision both feared and sought unity with one another.

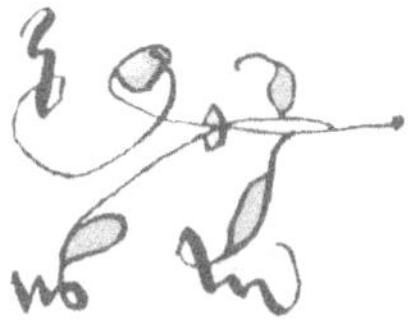

To be read to all our members and comrades[2] (also Christ's), in the kingdom and tribulation of Christ,[3] elders and ministers together with the whole brotherhood, wherever they are scattered, here and there in the flesh, but united in the Spirit, or in the desire to become united.[4]

Grace and peace from God our Father and the Lord Jesus Christ[5] in heaven is with you and us; may it continue to be with all of you and us, and also all those who have trusted and continue to trust in the same knowledge of the Spirit and of faith in our Lord and God in Christ. May they not be put to shame, but rather be preserved in living hope and love, to the honour of our God and to our mutual improvement and comfort, even to eternal blessedness. Amen, amen, amen.

---

2 [The exact translation of the original—*mitglidern und mitgenossen*—is "co-members" and "co-comrades," terms suggesting mutuality and reciprocity.—Trans.]

3 Rv 1:9.

4 1 Thes 5:27.

5 Rom 1:7; etc.

Dearly beloved in and of God, loved by Christ (for the sake of the obedience of faith), certainly it is not impossible that we, together with all true witnesses of Christ's resurrection, have received gifts from Christ on high,[6] and every true believer has received from him a gift as a seal for each faithful heart.[7] Indeed, we also offer our gifts to one another, so that each one may enjoy the other,[8] so that we join hands according to the inner effects and movement of the Spirit and conscience and do not reject or neglect it. Rather, each one should invest such gifts or acquisitions at higher interest [Mt 25 (27)] to the honour of the Lord and for the needs of his children, our members and brothers. Truly, each one should bring what is old and what is new from the treasure of his heart[9] to the exchange table of the Lord, who looks upon the treasure of his children in his kingdom. In his kingdom all children of the kingdom who so diligently work (to gather more riches) will receive more, that they will enjoy its fullness and abundance.[10] For whoever has will be given, but whoever does not have, from him will be taken also what he does have (and yet does not have, for he does not use it or let others use it). It will be taken away and given to the true servant, so that he has even more. However, the lazy one will have nothing and go away without honour.[11]

Dearly beloved sisters and brothers, I write this so that we may be properly grounded to proceed correctly with the treasure of our Lord, who has moved to a foreign, unknown land [Lk 19 (12)]. There the Lord has taken it away from all the old, unreborn[12] people; certainly without this rebirth no one may come to him,[13] much less see or comprehend him. This Lord is now at home with the Father (we, however, are absent because of our bodies [2 Cor 5 (6)]). Christ refreshes the old and

6 Lk 24:49.
7 2 Cor 1:22; Eph 1:13; 4:30.
8 1 Cor 12:7; 1 Pt 4:10.
9 Mt 13:52.
10 Mt 13:12; 25:29.
11 Mt 13:12; 25:29.
12 [Original: *unwidergebornen.*—Trans.]
13 Jn 3:3.

new law of love,[14] which had become as cold as ice[15] and extinguished through the false self-promoting[16] spirits who are like horrible south and north winds[17] which are driven about as a whirlwind[18] on land and sea by the source and father of all error.[19] These are nothing but clouds without water,[20] driven about by false spirits in the form of angels with words and gestures that appear as day and night.[21] But they contain nothing; though they utter threats, they produce neither water nor rain.[22] They promise freedom and peace, but behold there is nothing but coercion, insecurity, and disturbance![23]

For they themselves are not only slaves of perdition but also servants and children of sects and error, as my most recent letter also discusses; all of whom, or at least the largest part, have died twice, are barren and fruitless trees. They have departed from the right way of truth and have now devoted themselves not only to useless babbling but also to shameful, harmful lusts and error,[24] doing things that are unseemly. In his grace, God has protected us from all these things to this point, to his glory and to our salvation. Thus whoever purifies himself from such erring stars,[25] and vessels or spirits of error and dishonour, does well and will be useful and capable of good things for Christ, the Lord of the house.[26]

Dearly beloved in Christ Jesus, the fire of divine love has been partly blown out in us in these sad, hard, and cold times.[27] God has allowed them to come upon us through false, babbling, deceptive spirits, or

---

14 1 Jn 2:7.
15 Mt 24:12.
16 Col 2:23.
17 Eccl 1:6.
18 Eph 4:14.
19 Jn 8:44.
20 Jude 12.
21 2 Cor 11:14.
22 Jude 12.
23 Ez 13:10, 16.
24 Jude 12.
25 Jude 13.
26 Ti 1:16.
27 Mt 24:12.

foggy, illusory clouds. Let us therefore rekindle one another once again through the blessed and temperate wind (the Spirit of Christ), so that the glowing wick is not extinguished,[28][29*] but the first—that is, the original—law of love is renewed and refreshed to become even more fervent in our hearts. May we strive for greater love of Christ Jesus, the honour of God, and the increase of his kingdom; may we strive for the possession of the one law of charity, refreshed and renewed in us. Let it bring us, as his children and members, to victory in love, through faith, in true patience. Through faith and perseverance, in living hope, for the sake of the noblest love, as children and members of love, we are buried in this temporal world of the dead for the sake of love—for the sake of highest love, which is God, Christ, and the Holy Spirit. In the same way, love itself was buried through no guilt of its own but for the sake of our guilt. How could—and should—we otherwise be resurrected from the earth through love and then given honour, if we are found to be without love in these days?

How can someone who does not die in love for the sake of love be awakened through love to honour? It is possible only for someone who does not seek his own to the point of death and the grave but rather suffers shame and dishonour with Christ on the cross and in the grave. Would to God that we might lose ourselves for the sake of love![30] Even if we were ruined and died for the sake of love, we should not worry about how we will rise again. Even if it were possible that love itself could die, as it did once for our sake (so that we could know it), love would also then rise again in its own power, as it has already done of itself. No one who has suffered sorrow and persecution, and continues to suffer it daily even unto death—solely for the sake of love—in true love should worry or doubt! This is the case even though he is already buried (as was love) in the realm of the dead, even though the dead do everything to keep him from spiritual or physical resurrection. He will be raised again through the Lord of death (who died for our sake and became alive again for the Father's sake). He will be resurrected from

---

28 Is 42:3.

29* Note.

30 Lk 17:33.

the realm of the dead and be led into the kingdom of the living through Christ, the true life, to live and rule with him eternally.[31]

What I have just said and what I now say belong together. It is necessary that we take a close look at the treasure or currency of Christ our king, the true director of the currency exchange. We should ponder it often; indeed, we should turn the coin over in our hearts and consciences, and check to see that the proper image or portrait of our Lord and God is embossed there with the right and true seal or stamp, namely, the Holy Spirit, who is the true deposit[32] and seal on this letter written for us, that is, the believing heart.[33*] It bears the stamped impression, that is, the true, proper epigram and portrait of Christ according to the correct form, embossed upon our hearts according to the likeness and witness of the entire Holy Scripture. The Lord himself says, "Whoever believes in me, as the scripture says" [Jn 7 (38)], and [as] Paul adds, "I have not proclaimed or believed anything beyond the law and the prophets" [Acts 26 (22)].

For the scriptures testify of Christ; thus one should examine them,[34] so that we are not fooled by false coins and stamps, believing that God the true mint-master had stamped and embossed them. As soon as one examines the epigram, one can tell if it is of King Christ, and if it bears his portrait and true epigram, namely, "JESUS OF NAZARETH, A KING OF THE JEWS,"[35] that is, the Saviour from Nazareth, king of the Jews. If that is not found, but the opposite, namely, "the God of the earth, a prince of the world,[36] error, and evil," then we would be fooled by the treacherous workers and false mint-masters. How lamentable that many, many of these sorts of coins have been stamped with false shepherds' staffs or false stamps by those who hypocritically uttered and stamped lies upon untreated iron. Immediately it is brought to the test in the heat of the smelter[37] to be melted in truth and community

---

31 Rv 22:5.

32 2 Cor 1:22.

33* Note.

34 Jn 5:39.

35 Jn 19:19.

36 Jn 12:31.

37 Prv 17:3; Ws 3:6.

(meaning in the school of Christ), that is, to be judged according to the witness of the entire holy, indivisible, and indestructible scriptures. As we mentioned above, the Lord says, "Whoever believes in me, according to the scriptures."[38]

Truly, as soon as this happens the impression reveals itself, how many false characters, symbols, and letters were forged into it, that is, in the unplowed and unbelieving heart. It is as if iron has been embossed contrary to the true fashioning and image of Christ—indeed, against Christ and his church, truly against the Holy Spirit itself and against the entire holy and indestructible biblical scriptures. All those who have been thus struck or minted shall receive injustice or error as their reward, as it should be, if they have not otherwise been melted or pressed.

Not all silver or gold can be considered pure unless it has already undergone the work of the goldsmith so that the slag can be removed from it until it is pure.[39*] Not only does it undergo the test on the anvil, as a single strike, which can be deceiving, but it also passes the scrutiny of a master craftsman who is a goldsmith. Only then will—or should—the noble coat of arms or names, together with noble stones, be pressed upon it. No false mint-master or coin can survive, neither there in the judgment of Christ and his saints or here in the congregation of the righteous. Unrepentant sinners cannot stand unless they purify themselves and are purified through the Word (which explains and illuminates all things). Whoever allows himself to be cleansed of his error, sin, or unrighteousness, no harm will befall him from the second death [Rv 20 (6)]. But whoever does not do so will remain subject to death.

Some Christians occasionally carry this confession on their tongues. They insist that they have proclaimed his righteousness, even that they have minted many, many, hearts. They boastfully portray that this is the coinage of Christ, claiming to act in his name and to use the letter of the scripture. This is what Satan, the father of lies and error, employed against Christ while leaving out certain passages or words of scripture

---

38 Jn 7:38.

39* Parable.

[Jn 8 (22); Mt 4 (6)], just as today his members and false apostles forge or water down scripture.

In the same manner, Pilate, ignorant of the Hebrew, with its foreign and unfamiliar letters and script, wrote without God's or Christ's special verbal command, "JESUS OF NAZARETH, KING OF THE JEWS."[40] Yet it was not without the special preordained judgment of God, though without benefit to him, but much more a testimony against him and others. When you test this, however, against the true proof-stone of Jesus Christ, or against his epigram on coins,[41] it will reveal something else. That is, an "X" should refer to Christ, and indicate Jesus who alone was crucified for our sins—he is "struck" onto people's hearts through the true preaching of the gospel of Christ, so they might believe in him. Thus they translate the "X" to refer to Christ in German, but this is a false designation for the cross, in that it makes "Jesus" into the name of a sinful human being, and "Nazareth" into the name of a ruined village or temporary city. And they apply the expression "King of the Jews" to themselves, that they alone have been commissioned, that they alone are children of God.[42] Accordingly, people are either named after this city for its own sake or because they were directed there, or they have called themselves by the same name as those who have sent them there. They have settled them in a foreign place and identified them by their own X and place, yet against Christ and the guidance and order of his Holy Spirit, and against Holy Scripture. This has happened time and time again and will continue to happen until the end.

They have searched for Christ in the wrong place but have not found him. Yet they search daily and still do not find him. Nonetheless they think they are showing him to others, though he was never there and never will be![43] Much less will he be found by them, here or there.[44]

---

40 Jn 19:19.

41 [Original: *numisma epigrama.*—Trans.]

42 [Veh appears to be identifying a group (or groups) that claim only they have been called. The reference is most likely to the Hutterites who were missionizing not only the Moravian population as a whole, but specifically other Anabaptists at the time the author was writing.—Ed.]

43 Mt 24:23.

44 Mt 24:26.

They actually look for Christ in the desert, as though they can do without the normal and natural need for food, drink, clothing— indeed, spirituality—as ordinary people or Christians do. They are among those who have been refuted by the apostles, myself and others.

Their false images and errors have been confirmed according to scripture, as the life of John or his disciples bears witness.[45] Those of little or no faith are uncomprehending disciples. They have in part—like the Pharisees—placed more emphasis on externals like watches, fasting, praying, eating, drinking, washing, almsgiving, working, and similar things that are neither dear to Christ their Lord nor commanded by him. And they did these things for the sake of the powerful sect of the Pharisees, or for the strict, serious, and pious lives dear to John's heart. They would gladly have become like him at the time of Christ, so that no one would be better than they and those like them. Furthermore, Christ spoke and warned us, saying: "If they," the false Christians and false prophets, "will say to you, 'See, he is in the chamber,'"[46] that is, in their own special room, where no one may come to him except those who alone have the key to knowledge. But in the same way that those did not come inside, these and all those who point to Christ in the wrong place will also not come inside, because they not only don't want to come in but they try to prevent others from coming in.[47]

Christ properly warned us against such people. Truly, he speaks not only of the pope and his following, but also of those who point to Christ in the chamber, or in the desert,[48*] or of others who point to him in bread and things like that, such as Luther and his followers.[49*] He warned us against those who point to Christ outside the human heart, regardless of the form it takes. Whatever is the custom of the false Christians, some of whom are called—and wish to be called—brothers, that is, Anabaptists, some of them insist that Christ can be found only here or there. On one occasion they point to him in scripture, on another to lifeless creatures, like handicrafts or other things

---

45 Mt 3:4; Lk 7:33; etc.

46 Mt 24:23.

47 Mt 23:13.

48* Pope.

49* Luther.

we are forbidden to use.[50*] On yet another occasion they locate him in temporal goods and the community of goods.[51*] They claim that those who do not give over or forsake all such things shall not come to Christ, shall not find him, much less be saved, unless they sell it all, that is, give to "the poor children of God" and the like. The two dangerous and destructive sects, called the Swiss and Hutterites, have had their own approach; in the case of the Hutterites it has to do with temporal goods.[52*]

Regarding such things, beloved in the Lord, let us pay attention to the faithful warning of Christ, because he said it so that we would not be misled. But let us take this to heart among ourselves. Let us all examine ourselves, testing whether we are and stand true in faith and whether Christ lives in us, that we recognize him in us and experience him living in our heart through the Holy Spirit [2 Cor 13 (5)]. Where not, he is of no use to us outside our hearts—then we would be as outcasts. For whoever does not have or recognize or experience the Holy Spirit in his heart, and in whom the Spirit does not live in this form, he is no Christian[53] but an outcast. Nor can he in truth call Christ the Lord, since he will not be ruled or led by the same Spirit, who is love [1 Cor 12 (3)].

Thus, beloved in Christ Jesus, lest we in this windy, dark, cold, and dangerous time should forget love and forsake its works [Rv 2 (4)], let us continually remind and challenge one another, truly one to the other [Heb 10 (25)]. Let us offer ourselves to one another with respect and prove our service one to another in the manner of Christ our master (Jn 13 [15]) and true example, and do so with deeds and truth unto death,[54] as is the way of love, that she[55] is not left without love even unto death. And should we have lost the way of love, let us run to the Lord of heaven and buy from him, yes, plead with him, that he give to us what we need, for he is both willing and wealthy enough to do so.

50* 1.

51* 2.

52* Two sects.

53 Rom 8:9.

54 Rv 12:11.

55 [*Liebe*—"love"—is a feminine noun.—Trans.]

If we trust him, he will give gold that is tried by fire [Rv 3 (18)], which is unblemished[56] and active love. And that he does—he gives us grace with no strings attached. Who would not want to run to him and ask, for we have a rich, strong, and great high priest,[57] who lives bodily in heaven and spiritually in us [Heb 5 (1–10)]. He wants to live in us; for that reason he wants to represent us as his children and members. He is our intercessor, our mediator,[58] our throne of grace[59] [1 Jn 2 (1)]. He does that for the sake of our faith in him, so that we might be found in him, that we might give evidence of the righteousness that counts before him through faith,[60] so that all who are justified through faith might boast that they belong to him and live their faith in him [1 Cor 1 (31); Is 53 (11); Jer 9 (23)]. May God the Father give us grace, that we may be found in Christ, to his glory and to our salvation. Amen.

I write this to you so that both you and we might be reminded of our calling, walk, and diligence, that we might have communion with one another, as easily and with the many good gifts as valuable treasures of our Lord and God, Jesus Christ, the original and heavenly giver. Just so, he had communion in and with God the Father and still has it—they have never left each other.[61] Likewise, we faithfully pass on to one another gifts according to the inner working of the Spirit to the betterment and preservation of our conscience and inner being. Wherever we are, we do not abandon true community of both kinds of gifts, including our meeting together [Heb 10 (25)]. And that all the more wherever the times are dangerous, the errors great and frequent (Dn 12 [1]) [Mt 24 (11)]. All of us, especially me, are weak and in need.

Thus it is my heartfelt desire for all true believers and students of the most high and true teacher and doctor, the Holy Spirit, that they share their spiritual gifts with me, needy and poor soul that I am.[62] With these gifts I could thrive and improve, to the honour of Christ the

---

56 2 Cor 6:6.

57 Heb 4:14.

58 1 Tm 2:5; Heb 8:6.

59 Heb 4:16.

60 Rom 1:17; 3:21, 25f.; 10:3; 2 Cor 5:21; [Phil 3:8–9.—Ed.]

61 Jn 10:30; 17:11.

62 Rom 1:11.

heavenly king and to my—and your—salvation and comfort.[63] I want to be victorious in the witness of Christ through faith in true patience. Amen. This is my heart's need and desire.

All this, beloved in the Lord, is my heart's desire and plea. Again and again I admonish you and all the faithful: complete the work in the Lord's vineyard! [Mt 20 (1–16)]. Indeed, we should use the gifts with which the Lord has entrusted us in the time of grace to profit God's kingdom and his honour. Thus we shall meet with approval on the day of Christ's reckoning and repay what he gave us with interest for the increase of his reign and honour. May he give us greater responsibility. For he gives us these things that we might enjoy and use them together to give him honour and thanksgiving. God gives them to his children, that is, our members, for improvement—not to keep them for ourselves, bury them, or live for ourselves. No one should live for himself but live for the Lord[64] and his members, who gave himself to his own. The lazy servant did not do so; in the end he attempted to put the blame on the lord, saying: "Lord, I knew that you were a hard man; you reap what you did not sow; you gather where you did not scatter. So out of fear I buried your money; here, I give it back to you" [Mt 25 (14–30); Lk 19 (12–27)]. It is not necessary to record what the lord gave him as payment and answer. What is written is written for our improvement [Rom 15 (4)].[65] Therefore let us deal faithfully with the Lord's goods, whether they be temporal or spiritual gifts and goods, for he will demand repayment from many with interest or profit.

Let us invest them with interest or give them to the money managers and servants of the Lord Christ in his house and on his table.[66*] And if anyone fears using these because of the hard, stern justice of the Lord Christ, it does not follow that he should also not use them for himself, not to mention others. It follows, however, that he should have borne them for his table companions and asked them what he should do with them so that he could pass the muster.

---

63 Phil 2:1.

64 Rom 14:7.

65 2 Tm 3:16.

66* Unforced submission, without command, without law.

With various admonitions and true warnings they should have advised him, instead of giving back to Christ his pound or pence, to use the gifts he was given for his and others' true physical needs (as love teaches) in good conscience, to live through this time and successfully pass the judgment of Christ's congregation and that of the Lord [Mt 25 (19); Heb 13 (?)].

Those who do not follow this advice, however, will not be helped by an excuse, as is the case with some people who are called believers yet say or think, "Yes, it is true and good that we should learn and also believe, act, and live. I was taught it early on, believed it, and was baptized on it. I committed myself to live by grace and for this reason have received a gift from the Lord. I know very well that I must work for it in his house and vineyard. But I fear that it has turned into a den of iniquity and has been utterly destroyed. I do not know for the life of me with whom I should make common cause or with whom I should share life and be in community!"[67*]

Such people do not believe the messengers, as it were, the "bankers" of Christ, through whom they once came to faith and were baptized in Christ's place. Now, however, they do not want to submit themselves in obedience to the teaching that follows baptism, which they should previously have both learned and obeyed as the basis of truth. And now they leave off doing good. Indeed, they celebrate, sitting around and remaining lukewarm.

We should commend people who think like that to God and leave them alone until the Lord, through his Spirit, punishes them or spits them out, and they are cut out from the vinestock of the vineyard and cast out of the kingdom and body of Christ [Jn 16 (15:6); Rv 3 (16)]. This can and shall surely happen, if not here then hereafter. What, indeed, will happen to someone who resorts to blaming Christ with lies in order to cover his laziness, by saying (as mentioned above), "You reap where you have not sown, and gather where you have not scattered."[68] This is simply not true! For God will demand nothing from anyone to

---

67* Gloss: No wonder there is such fear! They're all stumbling toward judgment, the servants foremost. [*Diener* is a general word for "servant," but it was also a common Anabaptist designation for "minister."—Trans.]

68 Mt 25:24.

whom he gave nothing. At the same time, no one may excuse himself before God, for God has already poured out his Spirit on all flesh [Acts 2 (17)]. Thus the gospel of the kingdom of God is preached to the whole world to be a witness to all [Mt 24 (14)]; Paul also points to the psalmist, who says that the sound has gone out into all lands, and the Word into all the world [Rom 10 (18); Ps 19 (4)].

In such matters, beloved, I did not wish to refrain from admonishing you, along with me, to aspire to spiritual gifts,[69] as also to more understanding of ourselves, of God,[70] and of our Christ.[71] Our goal is that we might increase and grow in every way,[72] as in wisdom and understanding, in perseverance, humility, friendliness, gentleness, love and mercifulness, peace and unity, faith, patience and steadfastness, together with other fruits of the Spirit.[73] We want to grow in the inner being, under the head, Christ.[74] We want to hold to him and thus grow together to great stature according to the blessing of our God and the image of Christ,[75] in which we have an unshakeable joy, in living hope, persevering unto that day,[76] that we may be found faithful.[77]

Not that you—and we—did not already know this beforehand through grace, but that you together were reminded and admonished—indeed, strengthened and comforted— especially through us, poor and small though we be; and likewise we, by you. All of this is for the Lord, through his granting of the Holy Spirit and his gifts. May he uphold you and us in the true unity and community of his Spirit and kingdom unto eternal life, through Jesus Christ our Lord and Saviour. Amen.

In the meantime we stand together with you through grace, in one faith, attitude, and spirit, as we also hope and believe that you stand with us. We yearn and desire, yes, we hope that nothing will happen

---

69 1 Cor 14:12.
70 Col 1:9.
71 Eph 4:13.
72 Eph 4:15.
73 Gal 5:22.
74 Eph 3:16; 4:15.
75 Eph 4:13.
76 1 Jn 2:28; 4:17.
77 1 Cor 4:2.

either against you or the truth.[78] We offer thanksgiving with prayer that we might be held together among, with, and through one another, for the honour of Christ our Lord, and for everyone's healing and steadfastness. Amen. Amen.

May the grace of Christ Jesus be and remain with you and all of us. Amen.[79] In addition, it is my special desire, and that of the elders here and throughout the land, as well as the entire brotherhood, that you all might not forget us in your prayers and pleadings before God the Father and through Christ. By grace, we will do the same.

I, Cornelius would like to greet all of you, and each of you specifically, as many of you whose names are written before God[80] and known by him. I write not only on my behalf but on behalf of the entire brotherhood. It is unnecessary to write all of you, for the time is too short, and I am too poor at writing, as you can see from the beginning of this epistle. Once again, greetings (out of love) to all of you from myself and all of us. We plead continuously, as you have been instructed in all the concerns we have brought to you, that we, together with you, might be upheld to the praise of our Christ. It is our firm intention not to forget you, and we know that is your intention toward us. May God replace and restore whatever pleases him and is useful and necessary to you and us, through the grace of Christ and the power of his Holy Spirit. He is with you and us; may he also be with all of us in all places in all dangers unto the end. Amen.

If anyone of you wants to know more, share your request with this brother, who can send you a report on any subject. Bear with my poverty of spirit and accept what I—and we—are able to describe. Plead with God the Father through Christ, especially for me—weak, timid, and poor as I am, that he might be my strength in all temptation and give me wisdom and understanding to serve his people faithfully, without any self-interest, honour, love, or commendation. May I, together with all true servants, be preserved, to his honour and to the comfort and improvement of his people—indeed, in all things to attend to the body

---

[78] 2 Cor 13:8.

[79] Phil 4:23; 2 Thes 3:18; Rv 22:21.

[80] Lk 10:20; Heb 12:23.

of Christ,[81*] that none are killed and destroyed by birds of prey. Plead also with the Lord for even more true workers, to help me and others in our great need, in the work of the Lord, reaping and harvesting,[82] for they are few who undertake this task without selfish gain, wishing only to serve the Lord's honour and the people's improvement.[83] Many, however, are opponents and false ones who mislead and allow themselves to be misled. May God the Father take pity on his own; may he save and protect them from evil. Amen.[84]

And thus we commend ourselves and all true believers under the blessed and sweet yoke [Mt 11 (30)] to carry the holy cross of our Lord and Saviour Jesus Christ in true patience to the end, so that we together may be comforted under Christ and also may inherit and rule with him[85] eternally. Amen.

In great hurry and pressure, the eighth of March, this year of Christ 1543, abundant with grace.

As you in Appenzell are able, please make certain that this messenger and this letter are shared with our beloved brother and co-worker Mathes Wiser and the entire church of Christ (also in and around Zurich),[86*] and greet him from all of us for the Lord Christ's sake.

In the Lord Jesus Christ,
I am your most insufficient and unworthy servant,
assistant, comrade, and brother
in the kingdom of Christ,[87]
though made worthy by God through Christ
in the cause of truth
against the untruth of the Antichrist,
Cornelius Veh

81* Note.
82 Mt 9:38.
83 Phil 2:21.
84 Mt 6:13.
85 2 Tm 2:12.
86* May they find grace in God.
87 Rv 1:9.

25

An account of faith

Jörg Maler
Appenzell, 1547

"An Account of Faith" is the earliest of Jörg Maler's extant writings, written when he was forty-seven years of age. A decade earlier he had been chosen as the elder of a congregation that met just beyond the city gate of St. Gall, in eastern Switzerland. At the time of writing he was living in nearby Appenzell, making his livelihood as a weaver and serving in the congregation as a reader of and commentator on New Testament passages, because, unlike many, he was literate.[1]

Maler's account of the faith is directed to believers and seekers alike. The first part describes the work of Christ for humanity. The second part is a lyrical retelling of the promises of God to the church. It consists of seamlessly linked scripture passages that set forth the themes of the gospel.[2] The reader senses that Maler writes his convictions in the confidence that his audience in the Swiss as well as South German settings shares them. At the same time, Maler's unmistakable emphasis on grace and justification, as well as his lifting up of Paul, might have

---

Jörg Maler, Rechenschaft des Glaubens; Appenzell, 1547. Translation by Victor Thiessen and John D. Rempel.

1 "Vom Amt des 'Lesers' zum Kompilator des Kunstbuches. Auf den Spuren Jörg Malers," BSOT, 42–70.

2 For a contemporary comparison, see BCSB.

been intended as a corrective to the influence in some strains of Anabaptism on the stages of purgation found in mystical piety or on rules for discipleship.[3]

To the twenty-first-century ear, the author's movement from one thought of Holy Writ to the next without much commentary might lack originality; in the sixteenth century it was welcome evidence of a mind completely shaped by the message of the Bible. Because he was well educated, Maler's treatise would have been a model for faith formation and a digest of the Christian testimony that hearers could memorize.

The flow of thought is straightforward, yet a number of concepts are worth noting. Believers are justified "so that we would become without sin"; "Christ is the example and source of eternal salvation." Suffering looms large, both because we struggle with the flesh and because we follow a master who was persecuted.

Maler's account of faith has the ring of authenticity. What he says emerges out of his own and his hearers' sharing in the tribulations but also the triumph of Christ.

3 Pilgram Marpeck's thought was influenced by the mystical piety of early South German radicalism, but he shared Maler's conviction that the life of discipleship emerges out of the experience of grace. Steven E. Ozment, *Mysticism and Dissent: Religious Ideology and Social Protest in the Sixteenth Century* (New Haven: Yale University Press, 1973); see esp. 14–31, 133–36.

A simple account of faith in Christ, drawn together with other evidence from the Holy Scriptures, Old and New Testaments, to all the faithful for their comfort and steadfastness in the tribulations and dangers of the world; also as a report to those who seek and desire the truth with all their heart.

Our faith and hope in God is a call out of the sin and dead works[4] of darkness,[5] out of the unrighteousness[6] and uncleanness of the world. It is a call to the one, true, living God the Father [Eph 4 (1); 2 Tm 1 (9)] in a penitent life [1 Thes 1 (9)], through the preaching of Christ in the gospel's word of truth to one faith, one baptism [Eph 4 (5)] in the name of the one true Son of God and our Saviour Jesus Christ [Mt 28 (19); Mk 16 (16)] for the forgiveness of sin [Acts 2 (38)]. That is a covenant, a sure announcement of a good conscience before God [1 Pt 3 (21)]. He died for the sake of our sins (Rom 4 [25]) and was raised from the dead for our justification, so that we would be without sin and live according to righteousness[7] through the power and gift of the Holy Spirit from now on [Acts 10 (44f.)].

The Spirit has been promised to all those who have faith in God through him (1 Jn 3[24]) (who raised Christ from the dead) and who cleanse themselves and keep themselves clean of all stain of the flesh and spirit [Mt 5 (8); 2 Cor 7 (1)]. They proceed with the saints in the discipline with which Christ has made us holy and cleansed us in his blood, through the water bath in the Word), so that he might present to himself, now and on that day (Mt 25 [34]), a glorious congregation without spot or wrinkle or any such thing, that it might be holy and unblemished in the fear of God [Eph 5 (26f.)]. It must be dedicated to discipline and brotherly admonition in the communion of saints [Mt 18 (15–19); Lk 17 (3f.)] (where they can be with one another) through

---

4 Heb 6:1.

5 Eph 5:11.

6 2 Pt 2:8.

7 Rom 5:21; 2 Cor 5:15; 1 Pt 4:2.

obedience to the truth in a spirit of unsullied brotherly love.[8] This is what the dedicated children of God recall together when they break bread with one other in memory of the Lord's death [1 Cor 11 (23–29)].

In this act of love Christ is an example and source of our eternal salvation [Heb 5 (9)]. We believe in him with all our heart and together are obedient to him in the Father [Phil 2 (8)]. According to his will we follow in the footsteps [1 Pt 2 (21)] of the one who has gone up to heaven [Acts 1 (11)] and is seated at the right hand of the Father (Mk 16 [19]; Heb 12 [10:12]; Col 3 [1]). He will be there in the future to judge the living and the dead. Those who have done evil will rise again to judgment, but those who have done good, to life [Jn 5 (29)]. Thus all those who have become holy through his grace and truth will be heirs of eternal life,[9] according to the hope that they shall not be put to shame [Rom 5 (5)]. For "this solid foundation of God stands firm and has this seal: God knows his own, and: whoever calls upon the name of the Lord shall turn away from unrighteousness" [2 Tm 2 (19)]. For if one believes in his heart, he will become holy, and if he confesses with his mouth, he will be saved (Rom 10 [10]).

These people are a congregation of the living God, a pillar and foundation of the truth [1 Tm 3 (15)]. There is no contradiction here; Paul says if we understand, according to the institution and ordinance of Christ (to the apostles), that they have been incorporated by baptism according to their faith[10*] [2 Tm 2 (19); Mt 28 (19); Mk 16 (16)] (and with the confession of their mouths[11] of their own desire), which comes through preaching (Rom 10 [17]); [Acts 2 (41); Rom 6 (3f.); 8]. "Great is this blessed secret, which is revealed in the flesh, is made holy in the Spirit, is preached to the heathen, is believed by the world, has appeared before angels, and was taken up into eternity."[12]

All these people who kept the faith [2 Tm 4 (7)] will be with the Lord; they no longer conform to this world [Rom 12 (2)], that is, they

---

8 1 Pt 1:22.

9 Ti 3:7.

10* God knows them.

11 Rom 10:9.

12 1 Tm 3:16.

no longer pull together with the world in the yoke of their sinful, infuriating lives [2 Cor 6 (14)] but allow themselves to be changed through the renewal of their minds in Christ (Jn 3 [5]; Gal 6 [2]); [Eph 4 (23); Col 3 (10)], so that we may prove what the will of God is—what is good, pleasing, and mature,[13] fleeing the passing desires of this world and all that is in it, so that we might take on a godlike nature [2 Pt 1 (4)]. For "if anyone loves the world, the love of the Father is not in him. For everything that is in the world (such as the lust of the flesh, of the eyes, the pride of life), is not of the Father, but of the world. And the world with its lusts will pass away. But whoever does God's will abides in eternity" [1 Jn 2 (15–17); 1 Cor 7 (31); 4 (2) Esd 16 (42–45)]. And those who "hate the stained cloak of their flesh" [Jude 1 (23)]. And in this grace and truth that has come to us through Christ [Jn 1 (17)], all children of our discipline and of God comfort one another in all sorrows, persecution, and hatred of the world (Mt 24 [9]).

It follows that they know they have no continuing city, but through the love of God they seek a future city [Heb 13 (14)]—as Paul announced in a warning to the Colossians [Col 3 (2)].[14] And Christ our Lord and master says, "You are not of the world, but I have chosen you out of the world. If you were of the world, the world would have loved you, but since you are not of the world, the world hates you [Mt 10 (22)]. Remember the words that I have spoken to you. For the servant is not above his lord, or the student above his master.[15] If they persecuted me, they will also persecute you. If they have held to my word, they will also hold to yours" [Jn 15 (19f.)]. "They will do everything to you that they did to me, for they do not know me or my Father" [Jn 16 (3)].

Peter also commented and said, because Christ has suffered in the flesh, so we should arm ourselves with the same mindset [1 Pt 4 (1)]. As it is written in Acts, "We must go through much affliction to arrive at God's kingdom" [Acts 14 (22)]. "All who wish to live blessedly in Christ Jesus," says Paul, "must suffer persecution" [2 Tm 3 (12)].

---

13 Rom 12:2.

14 [The reference is to Heb 11:8–16.—Ed.]

15 Jn 15:20.

"The word of the cross is foolishness to those who are being lost, but to us who are being saved it is a power of God" [1 Cor 1 (18)]. For as we suffer in the flesh, Peter continues, we cease sinning, that for the time that remains in the flesh, we do not live from human desires but according to the will of God [1 Pt 4 (1f.)]. With Paul "we are not ashamed of the gospel of Christ, for it is strength from God that saves everyone who believes in it" [Rom 1 (16); Mk 8 (38)]. Do not be earthly minded but heavenly minded, "where Christ is, sitting at the right hand of God" [Col 3 (1f.)] Because of that, the world does not recognize us and does not recognize him either.[16] It curses us, because "we no longer wish to walk in the excesses of its disordered, sinful being," "for which all must nonetheless give a reckoning to him who is prepared to judge the living and the dead" [1 Pt 4 (4f.)]. He is the avenger (to us is given only true patience in Christ), as it is stated, "Vengeance is mine; I will repay" [Rom 12 (19); Dt 32 (35)]. "Herein lies the patience and faith of the saints" [Rv 13 (10)]. "For patience is a perfect work";[17] it overcomes all enemies of the truth [Jas 5 (7–11)]. For "it is given to us not only to trust in Christ but also to suffer for him" [Phil 1 (29)]. Only those who do so will be his heirs [Rom 8 (17)].

For all who fear the truth "in God will not be unfaithful or opposed to his Word, and those who love him will attend to his ways." We "who fear the Lord will diligently do his pleasure; those who love him will fulfil his law, prepare their hearts, and humble themselves before him." Without this, "it is better if we fall into the hands of God than into human hands" [Sir 2 (18–22)]. Understand: this means that we refuse to accept the mark [of the beast] or to worship its image [Rv 13 (16); 14 (9); 2 Pt 2 (1)].[18]

---

16 1 Jn 3:1.

17 Jas 1:4.

18 [An elaborate but seldom articulated eschatology, based on Ecclesiasticus, Maccabees, and Revelation, underlies the author's thinking. The fact that explicit references are sparing suggests that his audience knew what he was referring to. In different writings, the beast is government or the Roman Catholic or magisterial churches.—Ed.]

"For the souls of the pious are in the hand of God. And no torment" of the other death "may touch them [Rv 20 (6)].[19] In the eyes of the unwise they are despised, as if they were dying; their demise and end, even their ways, are regarded as a disaster. But they are" secure in rest[20] and "peace, and even though they presently suffer pain at the hands of mortals, nonetheless their hope is in indestructible things. In little suffering they are tested; much good will be given back to them [2 Mc 6 (18ff.); 7]. For God tests and purifies them" in their faith "and finds them acceptable. Indeed, as gold is purified in the refiner's fire [Dn 3; Ps 12 (6)], God has tested and refined them [Rom 8 (36)][21] and has accepted them as a burnt offering [Ws 3 (1–7)].[22] At the appropriate time he will look upon them," for the pious will remain steadfast in eternity, and their reward is with the Lord [Rv 6 (11)]—though they search for no reward for their deeds, and their thoughts are with the Most High. "Thus they will receive a glorious kingdom and a beautiful crown from his hand" [4 (2) Esd 2 (45); Rv 7 (13); Ws 5 (6:17–21)].

For we speak as we are able with Paul, "Our citizenship is in heaven" (Phil 3 [20f.]), "from which we expect our Lord and Saviour Jesus Christ" with great desire. "He will remove the body of our humiliation," if we "hold fast to the end to the fame of our hope" [Heb 3 (6)] through faith "and conform our bodies to the body of his transfiguration." In his mortal humanity Christ asked the Father that they (meaning his faithful followers) might see his transfiguration and be where he is [Jn 17 (1, 24)]. But in the present exile they carry "this transfigured treasure in earthen vessels, in which the power is God's and not ours. We are pressured but not cornered; we suffer toil, need, and poverty, but we do not despair; we suffer persecution, but we are not forsaken;[23*] we are struck down but not destroyed, always carrying around the dying of the Lord Jesus upon our bodies, so that the life of the Lord Jesus might be revealed in our body. For we who live will ever be put to death for

---

19 [Ws 3:1—Ed.]

20 Rv 14:13.

21 Sir 2:5.

22 [Ws 3:1–6.—Ed.]

23* O poor Christians.

Jesus' sake, so that the life of Jesus might be revealed upon our mortal flesh" [2 Cor 4 (7–11); 5 (1–8)].

Paul speaks further, "We have died" (meaning to sin) "and our life is hidden with Christ in God. But when Christ, our life, will reveal himself, then we will also be revealed in glory" [Col 3 (3f.)]. "For it is certainly true, and for this we labour and are despised, that we hope in the living God" [1 Tm 4 (9f.)], and for the sake of this hope that we have for the future, we "do not turn our faces away from spite and spit, and we offer our backs to the whips and our cheeks to the punches," "but the Lord God comes to our aid" [Is 50 (6f.)].

"They scold us," says Paul, "and we bless them. They persecute us, and we bear it with patience. They slander us, and we plead earnestly. We are the garbage of the world and have become everyone's junk" [1 Cor 4 (12f.)]. We consider our lives as Paul does, as of little worth, so that we might fulfil our race (our calling) with fullness of joy in Christ [Acts 20 (24)].[24] Through God's grace we will also not let up; "although our outer humanity wastes away, our inner life is renewed from day to day. Our sorrow, which is temporary and light, creates an eternal, weighty, and appropriate glory beyond all measure. We do not look to what is visible but to what is invisible; what is visible is temporal, but what is invisible is eternal" [2 Cor 4 (16–18); 1 Cor 1 (18)].

We expect this through the help of the one whom the Father and Son have given us as a surety [Heb 10 (16)], and say once again with Paul, "Who will separate us from the love of God? Sorrow, fear, persecution, hunger, nakedness, danger, or the sword? As it is written, 'For your sake we are being killed all day long. We are reckoned as sheep for the slaughter'" [Rom 8 (35f.); Ps 43 (44:22)]. To summarize, "whoever turns from evil is fair game for robbers" (Is 3 [14]; 59 [15]); [Heb 10 (34); 4 (2) Esd 16 (47f.)]. "But in everything we are more than conquerors," says Paul, "for the sake of the one who loved us. For we are certain of one thing, that neither death nor life, angels nor principalities, powers, nor things present nor future, height nor depth nor any other creature could separate us from the love of God, which is in Christ Jesus our Lord" [Rom 8 (37–39)].

---

24 2 Tm 4:7.

Thus St. James admonishes us to "count it as pure joy"[25] when we fall "into various temptations" [Jas 1 (2f.); 1 Pt 1 (6)], but not to allow ourselves to be drawn in to act against God. "Know that faith that is tested brings patience." This is St. Paul writing. He continues, "Since we have been made holy and righteous through faith" (for "whoever does not believe is damned" [Mk 16 (16)]), "we have peace with God through Jesus Christ our Lord, through whom we have access to this grace in faith, in which we stand and in which we praise" "the future glory that God shall give. Not only that, but we praise our affliction,[26*] for we know that affliction brings patience, patience brings experience, experience brings hope, and hope is not put to shame." The reason for all this is that "the love of God is poured into our hearts through the Holy Spirit, who is given to us" [Rom 5 (1–5)].

The apostle continues, "There is goodness in weakness." (By this he means not the sort of weakness that the world speaks of in its maxim: sin, and then appeal to God's grace; blame your weakness.) He means "weakness that comes through disgrace, need, persecution, and fear for Christ's sake" [2 Cor 12 (10)].[27*, 28] Furthermore, Paul says (2 Cor 11 [24–28]) he received "thirty-nine lashes five times" from the Jews. He was overworked, overwhelmed in blows, often imprisoned, and frequently close to death. More than that, he was "beaten with rods three times, stoned once, shipwrecked three times, spending day and night in the depth of the sea. He was frequently underway and in danger from water, murderers, among Jews and heathens. He found himself in cities, in deserts, on the sea, and among false brothers, in trouble and toil, waking, hungering, thirsting, fasting, and frostbitten—all this without considering the usual difficulties, that is, daily existence and worry about the congregations."

St. Paul admonishes the Christians "to show themselves to be servants of God" and followers of Christ, "with great patience in tribula-

---

25 The text reads *freund* ("friend"), but the reference is unmistakably to Jas 1:3, to *freud* ("joy").

26* Gloss: Truly, the so-called evangelicals do not ask for this kind of fame.

27* Gloss: All this has been written as an example to us (Rom 15 [4]) for God's glory alone.

28 Prv 18:12.

tion, in need, in fear, in beatings, in prison, in riots, in persecutions, in work, in waking, in fasting, in purity,[29*] in insight, in longsuffering, in friendliness in the Holy Spirit, in untainted love, in the word of truth, in the power of God through the weapons of justice to the right and left, through honour and shame, through evil slander and good praise [Mt 5 (11)], as deceivers yet having integrity, as unknown yet known, as dying and behold we live, as punished but yet not dead, as sorrowful yet at all times joyful, as poor yet making many rich [1 Tm 6 (7)], as those who have nothing and yet have everything" [2 Cor 6 (4–10); 1 Cor 4 (9–13)]; (Lk 9 [58]). All this the world does not wish to have—and is unworthy of [Heb 11 (38)]. They want Christ only for his gifts. Unfortunately, they invent a conclusion by a logic that goes against God's Word, and in this way they preserve their own faith. They resist with their defences in all impatience, which is obviously false, against the patience of Christ and all apostolic teaching, so that their idle honour and fame will become a shame before God and humanity [2 Tm 3 (9)], together with their blind guides,[30] whom they themselves have chosen and established. According to Paul's words, "their ears itch" and "turn from the truth" [2 Tm 4 (3f.)]. What they fear will overcome them.[31] For whoever fears a frost must expect a blizzard. As scripture witnesses, flee, whoever can do so! Flee from yourself, from the world's sin and injustice! [Jer 51 (6); Rv 18 (4)]. So that God's wrath and punishment upon the entire Sodom-like world will not take hold of you for eternal damnation [2 Cor 6 (17)]. O God, help us to realize this!

In closing, I pray to God, my heavenly Father, the Father of our Lord Jesus Christ, that he might uphold all of us under his holy cross (to which we have submitted ourselves in baptism), in all patience (to honour the truth), that our boast, with Paul, might be in the cross of our Lord Jesus Christ, through which he was crucified to the world and the world to him. Upon such people, he says, let there be peace and mercy [Gal 6 (14, 16)]. Amen.

29* Note.

30 Mt 15:14.

31 Jb 3:25.

For all who bear these things in truth (as mentioned above) will also partake of comfort. As the beloved Paul says, "Just as the suffering of Christ comes upon us, much comfort will come upon us through Jesus Christ [2 Cor 1 (5f.)]. Whether we have sorrow or comfort, all these things come upon us for good" [Rom 8 (28)]. This is true to the extent that we do not suffer as doers of evil but as doers of good. As Peter says, "What is praiseworthy about suffering for your misdeeds? But if you suffer and remain patient for your goodness, this is the grace of God" [1 Pt 2 (20)]. Moreover, "let no one among you suffer as a murderer, thief, or evildoer, or one who desires a stranger's goods. But if he suffers as a Christian, he should not be ashamed, but should praise God for this" [1 Pt 4 (15f.)].

To summarize, it cannot be otherwise: in truth, whoever will have God and his Christ as a friend must make the world, with its false Christians, his enemy [Jas 4 (4)]. As Christ himself said, "Truly, truly, I say to you, you will cry and weep; the world will rejoice, but you will be sad" [Jn 16 (20)]. For they will persecute you and kill you and think they are doing God a favour![32] "But I will see you again. Then you will rejoice, and no one will be able to take your joy from you."[33] "In me you have peace, but in the world fear. Take heart, for I have overcome the world."[34]

May Christ also overcome in us, through his Holy Spirit, in these most dangerous times, and "present us blameless before his glorious face with joy," to his praise, honour, and glory in eternity [Jude 1 (24f.)]. Amen.

Dated in Appenzell in the year 1547.

Jörg Probst Rothenfelder,
whom they call "Maler"[35]

Faith is not everyone's thing [2 Thes 3 (2)], but the appearance of faith seems to be everyone's thing. Glory to God alone.[36]

---

32 Jn 16:2.

33 Jn 16:22.

34 Jn 16:33.

35 ["Painter."—Trans.]

36 [Original: *Gloria soli Deo.*—Trans.]

26

Concerning the office of peace

To all holy congregations and children of God

Sigmund Bosch

4 July 1553

The first epistle in the Kunstbuch (no. 1, "Concerning the End-Time") was also written by Sigmund Bosch. Pilgram Marpeck, Leupold Scharnschlager, and Bosch are talked about as the most revered leaders in the Marpeck Circle. Letters no. 16 ("Concerning the Service and Servants of the Church") and no. 17 ("Gratitude for the Letter We Received") document Bosch's place in the movement. The present writing is a round letter to all congregations, dictated to Martin Damm, a tailor[1] and church member, because of Bosch's frailty.[2] For this reason, and because he is eager to get a personal greeting to Jörg Maler, Bosch addresses different audiences in this pamphlet: Maler himself at the beginning, and then all the congregations.[3]

The rule that guides the "office of peace," with which the church has been commissioned, is found in 2 Corinthians 6:3–10. It is to be read to the people "repeatedly, as often as possible." Bosch wanted Paul's words to shape the consciousness of believers. These words deal with nonre-

---

Sigmund Bosch an alle heiligen Gemeinden und Kinder Gottes: Vom Amt des Friedens; 4. Juli 1553. Translation by Victor Thiessen.

1 In German, *Schneider.*

2 No. 17 speaks of "the old and beloved brother."

3 The message to Maler is bracketed by two greetings to the congregations.

sistant peacemaking: enduring affliction and imprisonment with patience and truthfulness, which are the weapons of God. In this seeming defeat God is at work: everyone thinks Jesus' followers are dying—and see, they are alive. For Bosch there seems to be no distance between the charge and the experience of faithful Christians in the first century and the sixteenth. Paul's description of tribulation and of the experience of God's intervention is as true now as it was then.

He concludes by reminding his hearers of the oath they made to fight nobly in the Lord's alliance. They allowed themselves "to be buried through baptism unto death." That was the practice run for what is now before them.

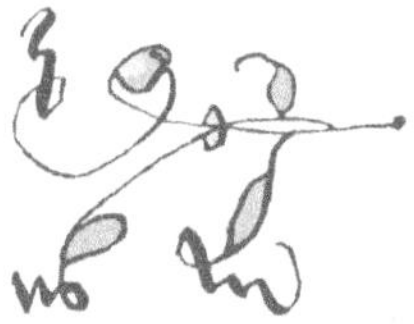

This epistle should be read to the congregations of God repeatedly, as often as possible.

Grace and peace and mercy from God our heavenly Father and the Lord Jesus Christ[4] be with all who love God's justice with all their hearts. Amen.

Beloved brother Jörg Maler, I have accepted your admonition in the Lord with joy, together with the living letter[5]—our dear brother Veitenn Maurer—whom you have sent me. I thank God and you for the eagerness with which you have undertaken to visit the congregations of the children of God. The Lord grant you grace and guide you through his Holy Spirit. Amen.

---

4 Rom 1:7; etc.

5 2 Cor 3:2f. [Maurer is mentioned in Marpeck's letter (no. 38) to Magdalena von Pappenheim, 9 December 1547: "Concerning Three Kinds of People in the Judgment and Kingdom of Christ."—Ed.]

To all holy congregations and children of God who are scattered here and there, yet are one body with us in Christ.

Grace, peace, and mercy from God the Father and the Lord Jesus Christ, along with true love and unity in the Holy Spirit,[6] be with you and with us all. Amen.

All the beloved in the Lord: first I exhort you regarding the unsearchable treasure, which has been proclaimed and granted to you through grace, because you have become part of the common salvation of all the saints. O how great is the office with which you and we have been entrusted! O how difficult it will be to give account of ourselves if it should be defamed through us![7] O how rich and unfathomable is the crown and glory[8] that has been set aside for those who remain true in the battle pertaining to this office to which we are called and which is entrusted to us.[9]

O how blessed are the feet of the messengers who proclaim peace.[10] These are the people and messengers of God who walk uprightly with their whole lives, in the fear of God in truth, justice, gentleness, and heartfelt humility. The Lord has commanded us to learn from him, and has called us to take up his yoke [Mt 11 (29)]. He proclaims peace to us with the same command and says, "My peace I give to you, not as the world gives it" [Jn 14 (27)]. Paul says, "Keep peace with everyone, as much as is possible for you" [Rom 12 (18)]. That is, as much as the world hates and shamefully persecutes you, show them only peace with patience in all tribulation, thereby confessing the truth.

This rule, in 2 Cor 6 [3–10], should be read often and diligently. Those who agree to follow this rule will know that they have the spirit of peace—indeed, the Spirit of Christ. "But whoever does not have this Spirit of Christ does not belong to him." "Those, however, whom the Spirit leads are children of God" [Rom 8 (9, 14)], through Christ and

---

6 Eph 4:3.

7 2 Cor 6:3.

8 [1 Pt 5:4.—Ed.]

9 2 Tm 4:5–8; [2 Cor 5:18.—Ed.]

10 Is 52:7, Rom 10:15.

with Christ. How then shall they not be holy and blessed, for they have been born of the Holy Spirit [Jn 3 (5)]; thus they are of a godly nature (Acts 17 [28]) and manifest a godly nature. For he who is in them "is greater and stronger than he who is in the world." For a single child, even the weakest child of God, conquers the entire world [1 Jn 4 (4)] with only the peace that Christ has left for us and given us.[11] Therefore "blessed are the feet" of such "messengers, who" with a godly nature "preach" and demonstrate "peace" [Is 52 (7); Rom 10 (15)]. This they proclaim and prove, conquering all peacelessness through peace.

For this reason, beloved brothers, examine yourselves, whether the guidance of the Holy Spirit (the sweetness and foretaste of eternal life) is properly realized and established within you. Where some have been careless, the rule of Christ will box their ears, as stated above; it will persist both roughly and tenderly, making them alert and sober [2 Cor 6 (1–10)]. It will lay low all evil lusts[12] and desires of the flesh [Gal 5 (16)], recalling that the time is short,[13] limited, and evil. It awakens those with weak knees and tired hands [Heb 12 (12)]. Let lips that mumble wearily practise giving a thank offering to the Lord—ceaselessly as a tribute. For he is not far; he will not neglect to give to each one according to his deeds [Rom 2 (6); Rv 2 (23)]. His promise is true. The time is here; the day has come and is passing! [Ez 7 (10)].

Consider the serious oath you have sworn to him, according to the announcement of the gospel. Upon your own faith you agreed and promised to fight nobly to the end in his holy alliance; upon this oath you allowed yourself to be buried through baptism unto death[14] [1 Pt 3 (21); Rom 6 (4)]. Keep this fresh in your memory and "rejoice in hope"[15] and know that the Lord is true,[16] that he will never forsake any of his servants in battle. The hairs on their head have been counted [Lk 12

---

11 Jn 14:27.

12 Col 3:8; 1 Pt 2:1, 11; 4:2; Jas 1:21.

13 1 Cor 7:29.

14 [Original—*bis inn den tod*—could also be translated "into" or "until" death.—Trans.]

15 Rom 12:12.

16 Jn 3:33.

(7)]. I have nothing more to add at this time. May the gracious hand of God and his eternal peace be upon you and us all.

Date: written in haste on St. Ulrich's Day, 1553.[17]

Sigmund Bosch, your most unworthy servant
and comrade in the cross and tribulation
of Christ Jesus our Lord[18]

I, Marty Damm Schneider, who have written this letter, wish all true children of God much peace and mercy from God our heavenly Father and from our Lord Jesus Christ. The grace of the Lord be with you and with us all. Amen.

17 July 4.

18 Rv 1:9.

27

Concerning the heritage, service, and menstruation of sin

To Leupold Scharnschlager
Pilgram Marpeck
[Augsburg] 1545

Pilgram Marpeck's letter to Leupold Scharnschlager in Ilanz,[1] where the congregation was dispersed on the mountainsides, "is one of several personal letters in the collection."[2] Aside from bits of domestic news, the tone of the letter is one of theological exposition rather than personal conversation. We do not know whether other private letters Marpeck might have written were more self-disclosing and informal, or whether he was by nature private and reserved.

"This epistle was prompted by one which Marpeck had received from members of his group in Moravia who were concerned or confused about the feuding among Anabaptist groups there."[3] Marpeck's response is in the form of allegories focused on freedom from sin and freedom for suffering. If this principle and the spirit behind it were

---

Pilgram Marpeck an Leupolt Scharnschlager, Von der Erbschaft, dem Dienst und dem Blutfluß der Sünde; [Augsburg,] 1545. Translation by Walter Klaassen. Previously published in WPM, 412–17. Reprinted, with editorial changes, by permission of the publisher.

1 Ilanz is in the Grisons (Graubünden), in eastern Switzerland, where there were several Swiss Brethren congregations.

2 WPM, 412.

3 Ibid.

clear, the argument implies, there would be no reason to feud about other matters.

"Marpeck again casts his reflections in an allegorical or typological interpretation";[4] grasping it depends on a number of fine points. This time his text is Gn 31:34, 35, "the incident of Rachel hiding the family gods under her skirts and getting away with it by feigning menstruation. Marpeck draws an analogy between this incident and the sinful human state."[5] In our embarrassment, he writes, we concealed God and made off with his divinity, so that our sorry humanity would not be exposed. God was lenient and gave us a fuller revelation of himself. Now "we no longer need to deceive others about God"[6] but can "publicly carry" him about without fear.

The author makes the startling claim that "death is no longer death for us" and lays out what he means by it. Those who have struggled through from death to life (in conversion and baptism, as well as in persecution for Christ's sake) know that the love of Christ is as strong as death. The enemies of the gospel cannot take away the Christian's existence, because she already has the gift of eternal life. Out of this experience of the deathlessness of love comes the freedom to spend one's life for it.

Such people no longer seek to govern others but serve them. They do not judge prematurely. When they do serve others, the pattern of redemption (Christ "suffering in all patience") becomes the pattern of discipleship. "This is a favourite theme, elaborated at greater length" in ['Concerning Hasty Judgments and Verdicts' (no. 7) and] 'Concerning the Lowliness of Christ' (no. 35). Christians will certainly rule with Christ, but only after they have gone through the depth of tribulation with him."[7]

The inclusion of the same theme here might suggest that trying to rule others was the source of the feuds in Moravia. But the reference to "temporal and spiritual tyrants" seems to be broader, perhaps referring to the physical coercion imposed on dissident believers by their

---

4 Ibid.

5 Ibid.

6 Ibid.

7 Ibid.

government, trying to force them into unity with the official church. "In any event, [Marpeck] suggests that if Christians serve as Jesus did, there can be no disunity in the church."[8]

An epistle concerning the heritage and service, as well as the blood flow[9] of sin, which was established through Christ, together with other scriptural parables. Finally, also concerning the Christian's service and false messengers.

Grace and peace from God our heavenly Father, through Jesus Christ our Lord,[10] be and remain with us in eternity. Amen.

My dearest brother Leupold![11] Recently, I wrote you and brother Martin[12] a letter which I hope you have received. In it I indicated something about how matters stand with us in the Lord by his grace. We continue to thank God for his great mercy; he has given us the privilege to live in his house of peace[13] (yes, in the house of grace and love), not as slaves, strangers, or hirelings, but as friends, children, brothers, and sisters.[14] Unlike Jacob, we are not like those who work for the inheritance (I mean the inheritance of sin) and for wives. Nor do we serve another seven years for the beautiful Rebekah,[15] that is, the church and bride of Christ. Because of his blood and death

---

8 Ibid.

9 [Original: *plůtfluß* (literally, "menstrual flow").—Trans.]

10 Rom 1:7; etc.

11 [On Leupold Scharnschlager, see ME 4:443–46.—Ed.]

12 [Martin Plaickhner; see ME 1:351; and MLDC, 235, 279, 285.—Ed.]

13 Is 32:18.

14 Jn 15:15; Rom 8:15; Gal 4:7.

15 Gn 29.

on the cross, we are already given[16] and married to him, and are as handmaidens to Rebekah, his bride.

Nor may we ever steal or make off with the God of our father, or cover up and conceal[17] him with female embarrassment.[18] God our Father has revealed himself to us in Christ—yes, Christ himself—as both God and man.[19] From the beginning, God has known of our embarrassment, and yet we have used this embarrassment to deceive. Ashamed of ourselves, we have tried to cover up, hide, and make off with his divinity. He, however, has been lenient with our sin; he did not want to uncover our sickness and female embarrassment.[20] Until the time determined for the revelation, he will bear with it.[21]

Consequently, we now publicly carry about the God and Father of our Lord Jesus Christ, our spouse with the Father, along with all the treasures of Christ,[22] and call him our own.

Everything has been given to us with him.[23] The wearisome female flow of blood,[24] by which we mean sin, has been staunched and cleansed.[25*] Along with our blindness from birth,[26] it has been healed and given sight. Yes, like Lazarus, four days dead and stinking,[27] we have been raised to life. Thus we now participate in the first resurrection,[28] which began with Christ, the firstborn from the dead.[29] The second death no longer has power over us,[30] because of his liberating power,

---

16 [Original: *vertraut.*—Trans.]

17 Gn 31:34f.

18 [Original: *blödigkheit.*—Trans.]

19 Mt 11:27.

20 Gn 31:34.

21 1 Tm 5:24.

22 Eph 1:3.

23 Rom 8:32.

24 Mt 9:20–22; Mk 5:25–34; Lk 8:43–48.

25* Note.

26 Jn 9:1.

27 Jn 11:17ff.

28 Rv 20:5f.

29 1 Cor 15:20; Col 1:18; Rv 1:5.

30 Rv 20:6, 14; 21:8. [In many interpretations of this text the first and second deaths occur at the second coming of Christ. In Marpeck's understanding,

delivered from above.[31] Moreover, we now rule with Christ[32] by virtue of the power and working of his Spirit over sin and death, and the working of his Spirit over the devil and hell, over all their power, gates,[33] bonds, and cords,[34] and even over ourselves and all creatures under heaven.

Death is no longer death for us.[35] Rather, through faith in Christ we have struggled from death to life[36] with love that is as strong as death.[37] Thus neither death nor hell can now overpower us. Previously, we were deceived by self-love and idolatrous love of creatures.[38] We loved in spite of God, and arrayed ourselves, in confusion and disorder, against God and our neighbour. But the love of God has been shed abroad in our hearts,[39] and, for the sake of that love, all else is surrendered to him, for it is regarded as valueless.[40] For the sake of the love of Christ, we have now achieved this freedom, this release from the slavery of sin under which we were all sold.[41]

However, now that we have this liberty, we no longer serve ourselves and the creatures,[42] nor do we serve for the sake of reward. We serve in the freedom of grace. Christ works in us and gives us his aid. He lives in us—not we in ourselves:[43] he is our heritage. No slave himself, the Spirit of the Son, Lord and God is his pledge in us.[44]

Christ's resurrection restores creation from the fall; believers participate in that reality now.—Ed.]

31 Lk 24:49.

32 Rom 5:17; 2 Tm 2:12.

33 Mt 16:18.

34 2 Sm 22:6; Ps 18:5; 2 Tm 2:26.

35 1 Cor 15:55; Heb 2:14.

36 Jn 5:24.

37 Sg 8:6.

38 Rom 1:25.

39 Rom 5:5.

40 Phil 3:8.

41 Rom 7:14.

42 Rom 1:25.

43 Gal 2:20.

44 Eph 1:14.

Whatever we serve in this life, we serve under the sweet yoke of Christ,[45] and whatever we suffer in the flesh, we suffer in Christ's stead.[46] Without reward or pay, Christ has taken our place—his service and suffering have reconciled us to the Father.[47] Until we have entered the kingdom and, through his suffering,[48] have been endowed with power from on high,[49] we too serve. Whatever is still lacking in our members of the suffering Christ[50] we make up in all patience and faith, something that is needful at this time. In no sense do we receive a reward or inheritance for what has already been earned by Christ and given to us. And whatever right we have to govern, rule, overcome, judge, condemn, or acquit, Christ does it all together with the Father;[51] he has all power over heaven and earth[52] until the time of his appearance. Then his glory and brightness shall glorify our bodies,[53] and his splendour shall raise us into splendour with him.[54]

Now Christ did not come to condemn or to destroy the human race.[55] Nor did he come to be served.[56] He came to offer people salvation and, through his suffering in all patience, to save[57] and serve them. Even so we have been appointed by him not to rule over, judge, condemn, destroy, or inflict any suffering or evil on others. We are to serve them, to offer and announce to them his grace and healing, and in his name to proclaim the forgiveness of sin.[58] People may then be converted to their Creator, God, and Lord; repent for the forgiveness of sins; and believe in and trust God and the Lord Jesus Christ. To proclaim the

---

45 Mt 11:30.
46 Col 1:24.
47 Rom 5:10; 1 Jn 4:10; etc.
48 Rom 5:1f.; Eph 2:18; 3:12.
49 Lk 24:49.
50 Col 1:24.
51 Rv 3:21.
52 Mt 28:18.
53 Phil 3:21.
54 Rom 8:17.
55 Lk 9:56.
56 Mt 20:28.
57 Mt 18:11; Lk 19:10; Jn 12:47.
58 Lk 24:47.

virtues and grace of him who called us is our service and appointment at this time.[59] In his name and in his place[60] we now serve in patience and love, as members of his body. We serve under him as our head.[61]

Such servants are in short supply! In his great mercy, may God send many of them. The opposition is powerful in manifold ways and forms. There are many rulers,[62] many temporal and spiritual tyrants who, while appearing to be Christian, violate, judge, and condemn.[63*] They run ahead of Christ and seize his power like thieves and murderers;[64] they rob him of his honour and glory[65] and arrogate it to themselves! They rule before they have known patience, distress, and suffering, even though tribulation has to precede glory. They become powerful before they have humbled themselves;[66] they rule and govern before they serve; they condemn and judge before they have judged themselves. The world is full of those who run before they are called.[67] They are clouds without water, as Peter says, driven by a whirlwind.[68] But perhaps the world does not deserve anything better.[69]

I have written this epistle to you because the brothers in Moravia have written to me, and because it has been reported to me by a brother, Heinrich Schneider,[70] how those who live there are full of schisms and deceit. May the Lord preserve us. Amen.

Also, please note that I, my Andle,[71] and the other sisters and brothers are spiritually and physically well through the grace of Christ. We heartily wish you all the same. Greetings from all of us to you. Pray

---

59 2 Cor 5:18; 2 Tm 1:9; 1 Pt 5:10; 2 Pt 1:3.

60 2 Cor 5:20.

61 Eph 4:15f.

62 Lk 22:25; 1 Pt 5:3.

63* Note.

64 Jn 10:1, 8.

65 Rom 2:22.

66 Prv 18:12.

67 Jer 14:14f.; 23:32; etc.; Rom 10:15.

68 2 Pt 2:17.

69 Heb 11:38.

70 [Apparently an Anabaptist, of whom nothing further is known.—Trans.]

71 [An affectionate form of Anna, the name of Marpeck's wife.—Ed.]

God for our sakes, especially for mine, and we, as debtors to love,[72] will faithfully do the same for you. The grace of our Lord Jesus Christ[73] be and remain with us forever. Amen.

In the year 1545,
your comrade and fellow-contender for the truth
in the tribulation of the Lord Jesus Christ,
Pilgram Marpeck

Andre Nessling sends faithful greetings to you. He is employed as a servant with Fränzli's master.[74*] Amen.

---

72 Rom 13:8.

73 Rom 16:20; etc.

74* May God be gracious to him.

Interlude 8

The Athanasian Creed

Following: Bishop Athanasius's confession of faith

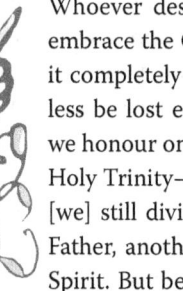

Whoever desires to be protected from all things must embrace the Christian faith. Unless each person holds to it completely in its undestroyed meaning, he will doubtless be lost eternally. But this is the Christian way, that we honour one God in the Trinity: the Three—that is, the Holy Trinity—in-One. [We] still intermingle the persons, [we] still divide the essence, where one person is of the Father, another of the Son, and yet another of the Holy Spirit. But being of the Father and of the Son and of the Holy Spirit composes one Godhead with an identical glory, and a co-eternal majesty or splendour—just as the Father, so also the Son as well as the Holy Spirit: uncreated Father, uncreated Son, and uncreated Holy Spirit; immeasurable Father, immeasurable Son and immeasurable Holy Spirit; eternal Father, eternal Son, eternal Holy Spirit; and yet

---

Zwischenstück 8: Symbolum Quicunque ("Athanasianum"). Translation by Leonard Gross. [The Athanasian Creed, so called in honour of an early champion of orthodoxy, is referred to historically as *Symbolum Quicunque.* It is a "symbol" of the church's path. It was written in about 500 by a follower of the orthodox teaching on the Trinity.—Ed.]

not three eternal but one Eternal—consequently, not three uncreated or three immeasurable but one uncreated, one immeasurable; at the same time, almighty Father, almighty Son, almighty Holy Spirit, and yet not three almighty but one Almighty; thus, God-Father, God-Son, God–Holy Spirit, and yet not three gods, but [there] is one God; therefore, Lord-Father, Lord-Son, Lord–Holy Spirit, and yet not three lords, but [there] is one Lord. Consequently, just as we are forced in Christian truth to confess each different person as God and Lord, so also, however, it is forbidden to us with Christian sacredness to speak of three gods or lords.

The Father was made, created, and given birth by no one. The Son is solely from the Father, not made or created but born. The Holy Spirit is from the Father and Son, not made, created, or born but originating from both. Consequently there is one Father, not three fathers; one Son, not three sons; one Holy Spirit, not three holy spirits; and in this Trinity there is no before or after, no greater or lesser, but the three persons as a totality are in and of themselves eternal and kindred. Thus, as is written above, this is always to be honoured: the Three-in-One and the One-in-Three. Therefore whoever so desires to be protected (and there is no other way), he shall [embrace] the Trinity; but it is also essential for eternal salvation that he truly believe in the incarnation of our Lord Jesus Christ. Therefore the true faith that we believe and confess is that our Lord Jesus Christ is the Son of God—God and man. He is God, out of the substance of the Father, born before the world [was created]; and he is human out of the substance of the mother, born in the world, perfect human, consisting of rational soul and human flesh: equal to the Father according to divinity, lesser than the Father according to humanity. Although he is God and human, there still is—not two but rather—only one Christ, but not the Godhead transformed into flesh, but rather in the adopting of humanity into God.

One, overall: not in the amalgamation of the essence but in the unity of the person.

Just as the rational soul and the flesh is one person, so also God and man is one Christ, who suffered there (and who died a natural death for the sake of our sins), and on behalf of our salvation, descended into hell. He arose from the dead. He ascended into heaven, sits at the right hand of God, the almighty Father, from where he shall someday judge the living and the dead.

Concerning the future, all people will arise bodily and will account for their own works, and those who have lived well will enter eternal life. Those, however, who have lived evilly will enter eternal fire (where their worms do not die and their fire never subsides).

This is the Christian faith that each believes in (holds to and carries out, and also confesses), faithfully and firmly, apart from which (as noted) one cannot be saved or (as regards life) protected.

To God alone be the glory.[1]

1 [Original: *Gloria soli Deo.*—Trans.]

Interlude 9

Prophecy of Albrecht Gleicheisen of Erfurt, to take place in the year 1528

This word of prophesy was preserved in the sixteenth century in at least three publications and a number of handwritten manuscripts. No one has yet discovered an original on which various recensions are based.[1] Theories have been advanced which locate the allusions in the text in Catholic, magisterial, and Radical Reformation events and persons.

Apocalyptic utterances of this sort were commonplace at the time and may be found not only among apocalyptic Anabaptists but also among others. The Marpeck Circle (and the Kunstbuch) typifies the peaceful streams of Anabaptism in its marginal attention to these themes.

Zwischenstück 9: Prophezeiung des Albrecht Gleicheisen von Erfurt auf das Jahr 1528. Translation by Leonard Gross.

1 BSOT, 508–10.

In the year 1372 an old man named Albrecht Gleicheisen of Erfurt uttered a prophecy, speaking the following words:

"If from this time forward one adds 128, and again 28, at that time a great happening will take place in Germany which will have strength and power in and of itself over all things, and will be so powerful that it will permit no power to exist alongside, and it will be a power over all. Let anyone who responds with force against it be cautioned: he must surely suffer! At the same time, a child-emperor will appear with a weak magistracy of clerical and secular leaders, but because of the Romans[2] and clerics, they will oppose the above-mentioned power. But this same power is bold enough to rise and equal the [power of the] child-emperor and his regents throughout the empire, displaying a crown on its shield. Its strength flows from its innermost being; it will find a place under the same lord whose crown is on the shield. Radiating the powerful force from within itself, it will sojourn in the old named free cities, whose residents will suffer unusual affliction on account of this mighty power. But this same constant power will emerge victorious, thanks to the strong power from within itself."

"What they fear I shall allow to come upon them"
(Is 66 [4]).[3]

---

2 [Roman Catholics.—Ed.]

3 [Jb 3:25.—Ed.]

28

Confession of guilt

Helena von Freyberg

Helena von Freyberg was a remarkable person whose story has only recently become known. Her biography and her confession provide rare insight into the mind of an articulate woman and into the understanding and practice of repentance and forgiveness in that era. She was born in about 1491 at Münichau, east of Rattenberg, Pilgram Marpeck's home, in the Tyrol region of Austria. By 1506 she was married to Onophrius, Baron von Freyberg. They had four sons. In 1523 Helena and Onophrius became the owners of the Münichau castle. Under the leadership of a former priest, Paul Rassler, Anabaptist meetings were held in the castle between the fall of 1527 and December 1529. Helena was baptized in 1527 and became a leader in the congregation.[1] It is possible that her acquaintance with Marpeck goes back to this time.

Helena von Freyberg, Schuldbekenntnis. Translation by Linda A. Huebert Hecht. The original handwritten copy of the confession is in the Burgerbibliothek Bern. It was previously published as "Helena of Freiberg, Confession (as follows) on Account of Her Sin" in Linda Huebert Hecht, *Women in Early Austrian Anabaptism, Their Days, Their Stories* (Kitchener, ON: Pandora Press, 2009), 247–52. It is reprinted here, with editorial changes, by permission of the publisher.

1 Grete Mecenseffy, "Anabaptists in Kitzbühel," in MQR 46 (April 1972): 99-112. *Helena von Freyberg, Schuldbekenntnis.*

In January 1530 any immunity Freyberg might have enjoyed as a noblewoman ended. She left Münichau in order to escape the threat of imprisonment by the Catholic authorities, while her Lutheran husband and their sons remained in Bavaria. From then on she lived the life of a fugitive. She moved to Constance, on the German-Swiss border, where she came into contact with Marpeck, and she stayed there until she was banned by Protestant authorities in November 1532. Freyberg was willing to make a private recantation and oath to the civil authorities in order to return to her family. But since she was unwilling to make a public recantation under oath, Freyberg could not return.[2] Maler himself had offered such a recantation, as had other Anabaptists. This shared struggle must have contributed to his inclusion of her confession in the Kunstbuch. With the help of her well-connected husband and sons, she settled in Augsburg. Even there she suffered a short imprisonment in 1535 and then banishment outside the city limits.[3] She lived there until her presumed death in 1545, a member of the small and secret Anabaptist congregation. At the same time she had contact with Caspar Schwenckfeld, who had followers who were relatives of her husband.

This undated confession of guilt was directed to the Augsburg congregation and especially to its leaders, Pilgram Marpeck and Valtin Werner. It gives an intimate snapshot of the practice of communal discipline in the Marpeck Circle. Freyberg, a distinguished woman, probably in her mid-fifties,[4] is brutally honest about herself. Her thoughts are marked by psychological as well as theological depth. Perhaps the recantation she had once made lies behind the remorse she names

---

2 MLDC, 255.

3 Her husband died in 1538. On 3 January 1539 her sons appealed to the Augsburg city council to give her sanctuary. "They remind the Council that all of her life she has been advocating only a better way of life than violence, an alternative to killing people, that she has stood up for the rights of people to have their own faith, but that she has never harmed anything." William Klassen, personal correspondence, 4 September 2006, 3.

4 Merry Wiesner writes that for upper-class women in early modern Italy, the average age of marriage was fifteen (*Women and Gender in Early Modern Europe* [Cambridge: Cambridge University Press, 1993], 57). Helena married in 1506, so her birthdate would have been about 1491.

here.[5] Embarrassment at such a level of self-disclosure is the reason for writing down her sins instead of addressing them to fellow members personally, as was the custom.

Freyberg divided her undated confession into eight parts. According to the first one, she realized that she was doing wrong when none of the gifts of the Spirit were evident in her life. Second, she admits that she had become a cause of stumbling with respect to "the dogs." Scholars have disputed about whether this line refers to extravagance in the keeping of pets; more likely it is a Tyrolean colloquialism for local officials, before whom she gave her recantation. In her fourth admission, Freyberg laments her inward bitterness of heart and her outward glibness. In the eighth part she casts herself on the mercy of God, as did the prodigal son. Before us stands a painfully penitent sinner but also a person with the strength of character to confront herself, acknowledge her guilt, and move on to forgiveness.

Helena Freyberg's confession of her transgression follows

Beloved in God, I ask you through God's will that you hear my accusation of myself, and the recognition of my guilt, in writing, since I truly cannot speak of it with my mouth, without turning red with shame. For flesh and blood have refused to confront it; they have sought escape where possible and remained mute when I have tried for a long time in the past to deal with it. Flesh and blood can no longer avoid being disgraced because of their malice and trickery. The devil has covered me over many times,[6] distorted the light, made me white while I was black, and perverted the

5 PAW, 132; William Klassen, personal correspondence, 6 October 2006.

6 1 Pt 2:16.

Holy Spirit into a spirit of the flesh. This is what the devil does in all spiritual things. He presents himself as if he were white as an angel and very humble.[7] But God my Lord is even stronger and deprives him of his power and might through Jesus Christ, his beloved Son [Mt 12 (29)]. To him be honour and praise. Amen.

First of all: I confess and acknowledge my guilt from the bottom of my heart before God and all his saints in heaven and on earth, how I have transgressed and incurred guilt in the matter that has now been revealed to me by God's grace through the goodness of the Holy Spirit through the mercy and goodness of God my Lord and Father. God does not neglect to discipline his wicked, quarrelsome child;[8] unfortunately, I have rebelled against God and as a result I have lost the grace of the Holy Spirit. The fruit of the Spirit—patience, righteousness, gentleness, humility, kindness, true love, faithfulness, peace, self-discipline [Gal 5 (22)]—can no longer be seen in me, which mocks true faith[9] and the Word of God.

From the bottom of my heart I am guilty of great impatience before godly discipline and punishment, which has resulted in the bitterness of my heart, in many unfruitful, irresponsible words and behaviours, inwardly and outwardly. Also, I confess that I have carelessly sworn by the name of God and in disobedience to the holy gospel, and have not followed its rule, the teachings of Christ my Lord (and Redeemer), where he says, "Learn of me; I am gentle, patient, and humble from the bottom of my heart" [Mt 11 (29)]. He was patient and did not object when injustice was done to him [1 Pt 2 (22)], and yet I do not want to suffer because of my guilt. This is far from the mind of Christ,[10] which a Christian should also have; for children of the heavenly Father should have his nature. Christ teaches us to leave ourselves and the life of self behind, not to seek ourselves, and to follow him faithfully [Lk 9 (23)], in simplicity and uprightness, like a child[11] without falseness or deceit.

---

7 2 Cor 11:14; Col 2:18.

8 Jb 5:17; Prv 3:11; Heb 12:5–8.

9 1 Tm 6:1; Ti 2:5; 2 Pt 2:2.

10 Phil 2:5; 1 Pt 4:1.

11 Mt 18:3.

I also confess that my prayer is not righteous, for I do not gladly allow the Lord's will to happen to me, in that I resist what goes against my will or wants to break it.

I am guilty from the bottom of my heart of not being genuinely god-fearing [Sir 1 (16)], of not having God constantly in my sight.[12] In that I lack the godly wisdom that comes from the fear of God [Ps 110 (111:10); Prv 9 (10)]. I exhibit this in my walk; I barely grow or increase in the body of Christ,[13] as a woman who is mature in the faith should,[14] so that I feel worthless and shameful before God and his own. I am weak, miserable, lukewarm, and tired in my watching and praying [Acts 3 (16)].[15] Wherefore all my trouble has befallen me [Mt 24 (42)]. In this I have only myself to blame and no one else.

I confess myself to be guilty and to have failed completely in loving God first and my brother. I have broken the command of God, wherein the whole law is contained, that is, in forbearance and kindness [Mt 7 (12); Lk 10 (27)]. For love has no evil passion, and is neither contrary nor complaining, neither boastful nor puffed up; it is not undisciplined, bitter, or ever angry [1 Cor 13 (4–7)]. Love endures and forbears all things and trusts that all will go well, has no evil suspicion, does everything for the best according to the prompting of the Holy Spirit, and also does not seek its own advantage [1 Cor 10 (24)]. In all this I have failed and broken faith.

I wanted to teach and discipline my brother, but I was not teachable or amenable to discipline myself. I have sought the twig in him and not seen the beam in my own eye [Mt 7 (3)]. Also, I have been troublesome in the way I have acted toward my brother and foremost in my great impatience, with which I caused anger and great impatience, from which regretfully no good thing followed and happened. Thus the fault is mine alone and falls on me and no one else.

---

12 Ex 20:20; Rom 3:18.

13 Eph 4:16.

14 Eph 4:13.

15 Mt 26:41; Mk 13:33; 14:38; Eph 6:18; etc.

Especially I have transgressed and become guilty concerning the dogs,[16] those in civil authority, about which I was spoken to in the beginning; according to my understanding and intention, it was not sinful according to the evangelical order. I have resisted at this point with impatience and tactlessness in word and deed. I forcefully wanted to retain the freedom I thought I had, not wanting to be restricted or compelled, seeking my own good to the detriment of my neighbour, which caused my brother to stumble, resulting in his vexation. In this I did not take into consideration the love or the good of my brother, and have loved the creature for its own sake. This I confess before God and his own. I have been completely uncooperative and impatient toward those who have resisted me in this. I have often wanted to separate myself from them. In all of this I confess, that I have done wrong, above all with the dogs, those in civil authority (having the improper attitude and excessive conduct). Unfortunately, I have not been able to understand it otherwise until now, but God has revealed it to me, through his holy, charitable Spirit, to whom be praise eternally. Amen.

Thus I am guilty from the bottom of my heart of committing a sin and becoming indebted to God and my brothers and neighbours, both knowingly and in ignorance, as God my Lord knows best for me, inwardly and outwardly. Because of me the name of God has been blasphemed. Consequently, many evil, careless, unfruitful, and blasphemous words[17] have been said before the face of God.

I confess before God that I well deserve every punishment because of my transgression and guilt—yes, probably even more than he has given me—and am worthy only of humiliation, disgrace, and ridicule. Surely it would not have been a wonder, for all that I have deserved

---

16 [This is a Tyrolean colloquial reference to local officials. See Hans Fink, *Tiroler Wortschatz an Eisack, Rienz und Etsch* (Innsbruck: Universitätsverlag Wagner, 1972), 134. Here *hůndt* is defined as *"der Gemeindediener, mancherorts noch heute 'Gemeindehund' genannt."* ("Dog" is defined as the clerk, in many places today still called "dog.") Huebert Hecht's viewpoint has been challenged by, among others, Heinold Fast (Bern MS, no. 28, 1–3). Klaassen and Klassen (MLDC, 256–57) have weighed the evidence and side with Huebert Hecht's interpretation.—Ed.]

17 Mt 12:36.

from God, if he had readily allowed me to perish. But God acts as a faithful father to his angry, quarrelsome child, and punishes me until I become aware of my sin. Because of God's great love through Christ, I have experienced grace and compassion, which will speak for me at the judgment [Jas 2 (13); 5 (20)]; to God be given thanks eternally.

So I am in the same position as the lost son: I have uselessly squandered what my Lord and God the Father in grace has given me—yes, have used it unfruitfully. I say I am no longer worthy to be called his child [Lk 15 (21)], and I say along with public sinners, "God, be gracious and compassionate, and forgive me, needy as I am, my sin and transgression [Lk 18 (13)]. Provide for me—poor soul that I am—a perfect and fitting repentance in all yieldedness, humility, and self-denial, through the holy blood of Jesus Christ."[18] For I am sorry from the bottom of my heart; God knows what I have done. Therefore I also ask his holy congregation, especially here at Augsburg, whom I have offended greatly, in particular Pilgram and Valtin, to forgive and pardon what I have done against you, for which I am sorry from the bottom of my heart, as I have already mentioned and as God knows.

And now, however, the consolation and assurance in the shedding of the holy blood of Jesus Christ my God and Lord promise sanctification and reconciliation. For he says that in the hour in which sinners sigh in their hearts over their sins, they are forgiven. To this I cling in faith, that my sins are forgiven through Jesus Christ. This prepares me for death. This I say in praise, honour, and thanks for God's immense grace and compassion, to whom be laud, praise, and honour from eternity to eternity. Amen.

I ask and plead to God from the depths of my heart through Jesus Christ and through the intercession of the saints[19] and children of God and his holy congregation, whom the Lord knows. I ask them from the bottom of my heart, with desire, that they would pray in my behalf to God for help and strength, that in future I may withstand all that is op-

---

18 Mt 6:10; Lk 11:2.

19 [This plea seems to refer to the saints who are still on earth. Otherwise it would be an unusual assertion in Anabaptism and in the Reformation as a whole. The argument was that since Christ is the all-sufficient mediator, believers do not need to turn elsewhere to come before God.—Ed.]

posed to God and end my life following God's will, to the honour and praise of his holy name. Amen.

Thus I yield myself to the discipline and punishment of God my heavenly Father, his holy congregation and Christian church, as long and however much as is pleasing to the Holy Spirit. May the will of God be done[20] in me according to his grace, along with all those who desire it and who are in need. Amen.

This is my will and final decision at present. May God the Lord require of me whatever he wills. I forgive (forget), and pardon from the bottom of my heart those whom I suppose to have done things against me. I ask God also to forgive and pardon them, yes, that God would give them grace to help them recognize their sin (as has happened to me through grace). Amen.

Praise God![21]

---

20 Mt 6:10; Lk 11:2.

21 [Original: *Laus Deo.*—Trans.]

29

Whether a Christian can hold a government office

L[eupold] S[charnschlager]

The following text continues the instructional mode found in Leupold Scharnschlager's earlier epistles (no. 19, "Congregational Order for Christ's Members"; and no. 20, "General Admonition and Reminder for Reformation"). It reminds us that he was a teacher by profession. No date is given, but the text has affinities with the author's thoughts on government in his "Farewell to the Strasbourg Council."[1] Here he briefly states his position on a central social-ethical question: can a Christian fulfil an office of political authority? This was a query every peaceful Anabaptist had to be ready to answer. The form of the text strongly suggests that Scharnschlager had prepared a handy standard answer for church members who routinely faced this question in court hearings and public disputations, rather than as an apology to the authorities and their interrogators.

L[eupolt] S[charnschlager], Ob ein Christ ein Amt in der Obrigkeit wahrnehmen kann. Translation by Victor Thiessen. *Obrigkeit* is commonly translated "government" or "magistrate." The title speaks of "an office of," suggesting the more generic term.

1 William Klassen, trans., "Scharnschlager's Farewell to the Strasbourg Council," MQR 42 (1968): 211–18.

The answer to this question, the author notes, depends on the answer to another question: what is a Christian? He answers it succinctly and revealingly, paying greatest attention to the love of enemy. If an officeholder binds himself to the Christian way, as described here, he can remain in office. The reference to Michael Sattler's "booklet," the Schleitheim Articles of 1527, is instructive. It is evidence for the claim that these articles by the Swiss Brethren were accepted as authoritative in the wider Anabaptist world. In addition, the full acceptance of the separatist argument suggests that the well-known differences between the Swiss and the Pilgramites, sharply highlighted in some of the correspondence in this volume, had less to do with theological principles than with the spirit in which they were applied. Scharnschlager adopts the earth-heaven dualism of the articles and then adds a contrast of his own, between weapons of the flesh and weapons of the Spirit.

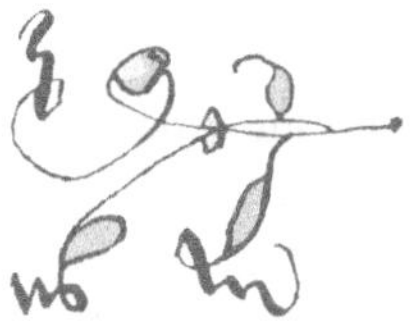

A question: You do not want a Christian to become a magistrate?[2]

Answer: Do you mean those Christians in name only, be they adherents of the papacy, Lutheranism, Zwinglianism? I mean those whose walk is limited to nature and natural love, who live according to the flesh, outside of the love and Spirit of God, and the new birth from God. They live without the discipline of the Holy Spirit; they do not have, observe, or willingly undergo brotherly discipline or other ordering[3] of the Holy Spirit. These people are not our concern. Nor do we deny them anything, or have any grounds to judge or discipline them whether or not they wish to be

2 [Original: *obrer.*—Trans.]

3 [Original: *ordnung.*—Trans.]

rulers of the world. For Paul says, "Of what concern are those of the world to us?" [1 Cor 5 (12)]. This means those who do not do the will of Christ or walk according to the content of the gospel in love, patience, and other forms of obedience. And therefore when you ask us whether a Christian can be a magistrate, it is necessary to discuss and come to understand what is the essence of a true Christian, or how he must live.[4] That is, someone who lives, abides, acts, and forsakes in such a way that he may be saved.

The things he must obey if he wishes to be a Christian—that is, a child of salvation and of God, also a disciple of Christ, and considers God to be his God—are the following. He must do the will of God, that is, obey his commands.[5] Further, he must abide by the sayings and teachings of Christ,[6] for these teachings of Christ are like the law of God: to love God with the whole heart and all strength, and one's neighbour as oneself[7]—indeed, in addition, to love his enemies[8] [Mt 5 (39f., 44)]. He does not resist evil: when someone strikes him on the right cheek, he patiently offers the other one without resisting; also, he does not seek revenge for himself or for others. Moreover, he blesses those who curse him, does good to those who hate him, prays for those who insult and persecute him. Likewise, he shall be saved who walks in the patience of Christ[9] without impatience, and lives without any sin. That is, he has died to the old life, submits to brotherly discipline,[10] does not rule over, pressure, or make demands of anyone in the church of Christ [Rom 6 (10f.); Col 3 (3)],[11] walks in the fruit of the Holy Spirit—that is, love, joy, peace, longsuffering, friendliness, goodness, gentleness, and the like, as the gospel generally points to and commands [Gal 5 (22)].

And when you ask us about these Christians, whether we admit that they may become a secular magistrate, we answer thus. If it is equal-

---

4 [Original: *wie er sein můß.*—Trans.]

5 Mt 19:17; Jn 14:15, 21.

6 Jn 8:31.

7 Dt 6:5; Lv 19:18; Mt 22:37–39; Mk 12:30f., 33; Lk 10:27.

8 Lk 6:27, 35.

9 2 Thes 3:5; Rv 1:9.

10 Mt 18:15–18.

11 Mt 20:25f.; Mk 10:43f.; Lk 22:25f.; 1 Pt 5:3.

ly possible to remain true to these things—observe, obey, and retain them—upon which his salvation rests, namely, those things that have been mentioned above, without which no one can be saved or enter into the kingdom of heaven, or have God as his God, then it is equally possible for him to become a secular ruler and act and continue as one, just as it is also written in Michael Sattler's booklet, in the article about magistrates.[12] He says there that it is not appropriate for a Christian to be a magistrate. The reason is: "The magisterial authority[13] is of the flesh, whereas the Christian authority is of the Spirit. The houses and dwellings of the former are grounded in this world, whereas those of Christians are in heaven. Their citizenship is in this world, whereas the citizenship of Christians is in heaven.[14] Their battles and weapons are fleshly and directed solely against the flesh; the weapons of Christians, however, are spiritual, aimed against the fortress of the devil. The worldly are armed with steel and iron, but the Christians are armed with the armour of God, with truth, justice, peace, faith, well-being, and with the Word of God" [Eph 6 (12ff.); 2 Cor 10 (4)].

"God has ordained magistrates for every people, but Israel is the Lord's portion" [Sir 17 (17)]. Christ the Lord says, "The worldly kings rule, and the mighty are called 'gracious lords'; but it is not so with you" [Mt 20 (25f.)]. This is where the ways part! "But the greatest among you shall be as the youngest, and the most esteemed as a servant" (Lk 22 [25f.]; Mk 10 [42f.]).

Written by him whose name is an L. and an S.

---

12 [The reference is to the Schleitheim Articles of 1527, whose chief author was Michael Sattler. See John H. Yoder, trans. and ed., *The Schleitheim Confession* (Scottdale, PA: Herald Press, 1977).—Ed.]

13 [Original: *regiment.*—Trans.]

14 Phil 3:20; Heb 13:14.

30

Admonition and comfort in all manner of sorrow

To the brothers in the Grisons (Graubünden) and Appenzell

L[eupold] S[charnschlager][1]

[after 24 May 1544]

This letter and the next one (no. 31, "An Epistle of Comfort concerning the Love of God") by Leupold Scharnschlager have to do with the same events. In May of 1544 the government of the Swiss district of Chur responded to pressures from clergy of the state church to take legal action against the local Anabaptists. Martin Plaickhner, Ulrich Hafner, and Anna Schererin were threatened or were actually served with expulsion papers.[2] Plaickhner was able to report to Scharnschlager in the midst of the tumult, and in Scharnschlager's first letter (no. 31), he replies immediately to Plaickhner. Placing the first reply after the second one might simply have been an editorial error, or it might have been a considered decision: first there is an admonition to faithfulness, and second, a call to rejoicing in the midst of persecution.

L[eupolt] S[charnschlager] an die Brüder in Graubünden und Appenzell: Vermahnung und Trost in Allerlei Trübsal; [nach dem 24. Mai 1544]. Translation by Victor Thiessen and John D. Rempel.

1 This use of initials was probably an attempt to veil the author's identity in a setting of political oppression.

2 Heinold Fast, ed., *Quellen zur Geschichte der Täufer in der Schweiz* 2: *Ostschweiz* (Zurich: Theologischer Verlag Zürich, 1973), Letters 630 and 631, by Johannes Comander to Heinrich Bullinger, the head of the state church in the canton of Zurich.

Writing that arises from within the experience of persecution is a type of literature people who have not faced the threat of annihilation cannot fully grasp. For example, the claim by the writer that it might be God's will for the congregation he shepherds to suffer is incomprehensible to people outside that experience. Similar to that is his warning against the temptation to think that compromise on a small point might ease the conflict. That would be a denial of the unblemished community God has brought into being! Later in his epistle Scharnschlager reminds his friends that "we must enter the kingdom of God through much tribulation." Quoting scriptures that one senses the community knew from memory, the author promises that God will not fail them during this supreme testing of their faith.[3] He concludes with a nakedly honest phrase of solidarity: "I will sigh to the Lord on your behalf."

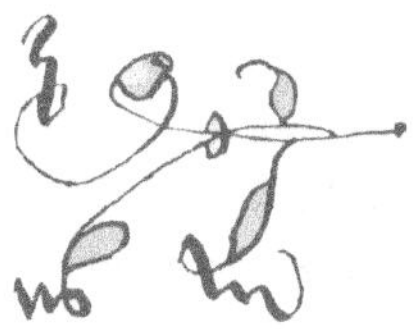

3 It is likely that the BCSB or a similar thematic collection of biblical texts was used in the Pilgramite congregations. Scharnschlager might well be taking scripture citations directly from a section of a concordance whose subject was "comfort under tribulation."

A letter of comfort to all believers, including the simple and weak members in the faith, useful to all for their admonition and comfort in all tribulations.

To my beloved brothers in the Lord scattered here and there, especially those located in the Grisons (Graubünden) and Appenzell.

Grace be with you and peace from our heavenly Father and the Lord Jesus Christ.[4] Amen.

The persecution and tribulation of these days have come upon us, beginning with our beloved brother Ulrich Hafner and brother Michael Maurer. In all probability we also, one after the other, will be next, according to the will of God. All of this, however (God be praised), is only for the sake of the Lord and his holy Christian evangelical truth and holiness, of which we should not be ashamed,[5] and in which we desire to live and remain through his grace and power, and not depart from them either in the least or the greatest part. Out of the duty of love (in which we are debtors to one another in Christ),[6] I have considered it good to encourage and strengthen you through grace, that you all, beloved brothers and sisters, might be comforted thereby, especially wherever and whenever such tribulation or persecution falls upon each and every one of you.

Do not forget to watch and pray according to the Lord's words [Mt 26 (41)], but stand fast in grace, wrapped and girded [Lk 12 (35)]—yes, armed in your disposition, spirit, or heart [Eph 6 (14); 1 Pt 1 (13)]—so that you may not fall into doubts or temptations of the enemy through the weakness of the flesh, to become shaky or depart from the Lord and his truth. Instead, remain in unshakable love[7] and steadfastness in the smallest as well as in the greatest things,[8] and do not become overwhelmed by the so-called Christians or other figures with their caresses or other methods, with all their attractions or even their com-

---

4 Rom 1:7; etc.

5 Rom 1:16.

6 Rom 13:8.

7 Eph 6:24; 1 Pt 3:4.

8 Mt 25:21; Lk 16:10; 19:17.

fortless words, saying: "Where will you go? You will find no place anywhere—give in just a little!" Be alert especially to those who say to us: "Hey, only something minor is at issue, or it depends on such a small point. Neither salvation nor damnation depends on it. Can't you take it or leave it, so that you will not be persecuted and remain on peaceful terms with the world?" [2 Mc 6 and 7]. But it is written: "Whoever will be a friend of the world will be God's enemy" [Jas 4 (4)]. Let us preserve our hearts entirely in love and faithfulness to the Lord, according to the requirements of his command to love him with our whole hearts [Mk 12 (30)].[9]

For if we were unfaithful or unjust in the smallest things, how could the Lord proclaim us to be faithful and true in great matters, according to his words, where he says: "Whoever is faithful in the little things, he will also be faithful in the greatest things, and whoever is unfaithful in the smallest things will also be unfaithful in the greatest matters" [Lk 16 (10)]. Thus we would become punishable or impure before him through the abdication, negligence, or denial of even the littlest thing. This is even though he purified us "through the water bath in the Word, upon which he established for himself a glorious congregation that is without blemish or anything of the sort; rather, it must be holy and beyond accusation" [Eph 5 (26f.)].

And therefore let us be honourable, "honest, and genuine as children of God, beyond accusation in the midst of the crooked and perverted race, that we appear among them as a light in the world" [Phil 2 (15)]. This is so that we remain upright and strong like "a pillar and foundation of truth," bearing witness to the certain path and word of truth and life [1 Tm 3 (15)].[10] From our steadfastness many brothers and those who are kindhearted will receive all the more comfort, courage, and confidence in the Lord and his truth, and we ourselves will not become bereft of comfort at any time, or turn away,[11] or "be shaken by the enemy" or their threats. To them it is a sign of damnation; to us, however, it is a sign of salvation before God [Phil 1 (28); 1 Pt 3 (14)].[12]

---

9 Dt 6:5.

10 Jn 14:6.

11 Gal 1:6.

12 1 Cor 1:18.

Let us be true unto death; then the Lord will give us the crown of life, according to his promise [Rv 2 (10)]. Yes, let us honour and kiss his Word and truth, which is he himself, so that he might not become angry and we might not lose the way (Ps 2 [12]). Carefully observe the great treasure trove; it is the goodness in this tribulation and the promise that comes with it to comfort us. For as the Lord says, "Blessed are those who are persecuted for the sake of righteousness, for theirs is the heavenly kingdom. Blessed are you when everyone reviles and persecutes you and speaks all manner of evil against you, you who remain committed for my sake.[13] Be happy and rejoice; you will be rewarded for this in heaven! For they also persecuted the prophets who came before you" [Mt 5 (10–12)]. Paul says, "I consider therefore that this time of troubles has no value, compared to the glory that shall be revealed to us" [Rom 8 (18)]. And furthermore, "our tribulation, which is temporary and light, creates an eternal glory that is great and beyond all measure for us who do not look to the visible but to the invisible" [2 Cor 4 (17)].

My beloved brothers, let us also measure these tribulations against the much heavier tribulations our fellow believers[14] have suffered. Indeed, they have remained faithful unto physical death. It will be much easier for us, and we will be strengthened and more greatly comforted, that we may battle worthily in patience and receive the crown,[15] indeed achieve glory, because no one will rule with us or become an heir who has not also suffered and persevered [Rom 8 (17); 2 Tm 2 (5)].

Such tribulations must always be with us, as it is written, "We must enter the kingdom of God through much tribulation" [Acts 14 (22)] that will confront us in order to test our faith. It is written, "All those who have ever pleased God have been tested through troubles and found firm in the faith" [Jdt 8 (20)]. And: "You are presently troubled for a short time—as it should be—in various testings, so that the perse-

---

13 [Today it is considered important to make a clear distinction between a quotation and additional commentary. This was not so in the sixteenth century. It was common to expand a quoted thought with one's own words, without separating the two.—Ed.]

14 [Original: *mitbrueder.*—Trans.]

15 Rv 2:10.

verance of your faith might be revealed, much more precious than perishable gold that is tested by fire" [1 Pt 1 (7)]. Thus misery goes before honour [Prv 15 (33); 18 (12)].

Therefore, my beloved sisters and brothers in Christ, though you do not know immediately or soon when or where your persecution will end, nevertheless do not become timid in faith but remain courageous in wakefulness and prayer [Ps 37 (5)].[16] The Lord will take care of us according to his faithfulness [1 Cor 10 (13)]; he will help us and save us at our request and calls [Lam 3], in our fear and time of need, to his praise, according to his words of promise [Mt 7 (7f.); Lk 18 (7)]; (Ps 3 [8]; 4 [3]; 18 [4]; 22 [4f.]; 34 [4]; 50 [15]; 65 [3]; 107 [6]).

For what kind of test, what kind of faith and hope would it be, in which our future comfort, location, or place did not remain hidden, invisible or unknown, but were physically or visibly present? The Lord and Peter only pronounce blessed those who believe yet have not seen [Jn 20 (29); 1 Pt 1 (8)]. And Paul says it is not hope if one sees it (Rom 8 [24]), so that we become like the faithful Abraham who is a father and shaper of the faithful [Rom 4 (11)], who went out "to the place that he should receive as his inheritance, though not knowing where he would end up" [Heb 11 (8)]. Let us rejoice in such testing and tribulations, because they will produce only goodness and patience [Jas 1 (3); Rom 5 (3)]. Consider that they come upon us only for our good; that is why he sends you such tribulations.

Circumcise your heart[17] of everything creaturely and of your very selves, so that nothing obstructs you or hinders you in the work of the Lord. Do not worry or say anything to yourself from lack of faith, as though the Lord does not know of or see our tribulations. For the faithless, who are our opponents, say that God does not know or see any of this [Ps 94 (7); 73 (11)]. For "the Lord looks down from heaven and sees all the children of humanity. From the seat prepared for him, he sees all who live on the earth. He instructs all their hearts. He takes note of all their works," and "his eye looks upon those who fear him, who wait upon his goodness, that he may save their souls from death

---

16 Mt 26:41; Mk 13:33; 14:38; Lk 21:36.

17 Rom 2:29.

and nourish them in the famine" [Ps 33 (13–15, 18f.); and 37 (13)]. Moreover, "the eyes of the Lord look upon the righteous, and his ears hear their cries. But the face of the Lord is turned against those who do evil; he will wipe their memory out of the land" [Ps 34 (15f.); 1 Pt 3 (12)]. Therefore let us remain firm in the faith, love, fear, and will of the Lord, and remain in prayer to him [Ps 13 (5)]. Then the opponents and foes of truth cannot boast that they are more powerful than we are; nor may they rejoice, as though we had fallen and been overthrown, nor that we encourage them in injustice, nor be the source of slander against the truth. Not at all! The opponents and foes who seek to trap our souls and wish us evil shall be put to shame [Ps 35 (4); 40 (14); 70 (2); 71 (13); 83 (17)].

Not long ago I sent out an epistle of comfort; in it I touched upon the love of God.[18] Whoever has that letter should read it together with this one. By the grace of God, I hope that that letter, together with this one, will be a comfort to you.

I will sigh to the Lord on your behalf, just as you do for me, that he might commend us to the defence and protection of his blessed and mighty hand. Amen.

In the Lord Jesus Christ
by grace, your true servant, fellow elder, brother,[19]
and comrade in the tribulation of Christ,
whose name, well known to you, is an L. and an S.

---

[18] Rv 1:9. [See the letter to Plaickhner, which follows as no. 31.—Ed.]

[19] [Original: *mitalter bruder.*—Trans.]

31

An epistle of comfort concerning the love of God

To Martin Plaickhner in Chur
Leupold Scharnschlager
24 May 1544

Martin Plaickhner was an elder in the Marpeck Circle and one of the co-authors of the response (*Verantwortung*) to Caspar Schwenckfeld's judgment (*Judicium*), the circle's most systematic and comprehensive theological treatise.[1] Marpeck's letter no. 26, "Concerning the Heritage, Service, and Menstruation of Sin," is addressed to Plaickhner and Leupold Scharnschlager. The courier of Plaickhner's letter of lament was one N. Goldschmid.[2]

This letter as a whole is addressed to Plaickhner. But in the final paragraph the author asks that it be read to the weak in faith. Like the

---

Leopolt Scharnschlager an Martin Plaickhner in Chur: Trostespistel von der Liebe Gottes; 24. Mai 1544. Translation by Victor Thiessen.

1 MLDC, 235.

2 It is not clear whether the name *Goldschmid* ("Goldsmith") is intended to veil someone's identity or whether it merely reflects the custom of naming people according to their trade. Martin Rothkegel suggests that the goldsmith is Lorenz Rosenboom, a member of the Anabaptist congregation in Schaffhausen. He lived in Augsburg from 1539 to 1546, overlapping with Marpeck's residence in the city by two years. BSOT, 527; see also Heinold Fast, ed., *Quellen zur Geschichte der Täufer in der Schweiz 2: Ostschweiz* (Zurich: Theologischer Verlag Zürich, 1973), 92–105.

previous letter, it is a sample of persecution literature.[3] There the message was an admonition to faithfulness; here Scharnschlager's emphasis is on rejoicing—jumping for joy!—in the spirit of the Beatitudes, in anticipation of a reward in heaven. The writer inhabits the Bible verses he quotes, writing as if the original message had been written for the present hearers. Most moving is the personification of love, Christ as the bridegroom and the church as the bride, using an interpretation of the Song of Solomon that had been traditional in the medieval church.

Here follows the other epistle of comfort concerning the love of God, as mentioned above[4]

This letter has been written to Martin Plaickhner, since he, together with others, was exiled from Chur; it is also intended for the good of every believer who is in danger, need, and persecution.

Grace be with you and the peace from God our Father and the Lord Jesus Christ.[5] Amen.

My beloved brother in the Lord, I have received your letter, sent with Master N. Goldschmid, and have understood from it that you, together with brother Ulrich Hafner and sister Anna Schererin, have received notice from the city official. Praise be to God for your willingness to allow the Lord to lead and preserve you in faith in his sacred power and comfort. For, my brothers, there is

---

3 See the commentary that introduces the previous letter in the collection, no. 30, "Admonition and Comfort in All Manner of Sorrow."

4 [The editor has inserted a reference to the preceding letter, no. 30.—Ed.]

5 Rom 1:7; etc.

nothing else to be done but to have our loins girded at all times [Lk 12 (35–37)], our lights shining and our aprons tied as those who have prepared themselves for wandering [1 Pt 1 (13)]. Indeed, we are as those who wait upon their Lord,[6] already prepared, until he signals to them. In this matter our flesh certainly has no reason to boast, because it is miserable and completely weak;[7*] the Lord alone deserves the honour and praise.

Christ himself bears the burden he has called us to take up and carry after him [Mt 11 (29f.)], through his Holy Spirit and the love of God poured out in our hearts.[8] That is the true power that makes the burden of Christ light. Thus I ask of you that this love shape us, encircle us, and take us captive. May this love give us its strong wine to drink,[9] that we may forget ourselves. Let love inscribe herself in our hearts[10] through her self-revelation and the inflowing confirmation of her faithfulness, friendship, and goodness. Let her ignite our hearts toward her with fiery brilliance and become such a lovely aromatic bag of myrrh[11] that we will never relinquish it in eternity.[12]

O that God might grant this! My beloved, please say with me: Amen, amen, amen. So then love—just as she ignites us—is equally held captive by us and we by her, in an indivisible unity. O Holy Love, great is your power! Through you the tribulations of all the saints become light, even negligible! Let us behold you and your holy eternal visage forever, O sweet and pungent aroma! Let us share delight with you; reach out your hand to us and draw us onto your loving way, that we may go with you and you with us through all waters and streams! We will be like those who drink the sweetest new wine from the noblest vines and are joyful and stouthearted; in the tribulations we have undergone for your sake—that is, the journey of our persecution by the world—it will be just as if we were to go to a wedding of great honour, where one rejoic-

---

6 [Phil 3:20.—Ed.]

7* Note.

8 Rom 5:5.

9 Sg 5:1.

10 Prv 3:3; 7:3; Jer 31:33; 2 Cor 3:2f.; Heb 8:10; 10:16.

11 Sg 1:13.

12 [Mt 11:29.—Ed.]

es, or as when one plays a joyous piece of music with flair and springs up with joy.[13*] Just so, the love we find in Christ speaks and comforts: "Be joyful and rejoice! Your reward will be given to you in heaven" [Mt 5 (12)]. Truly, "Rejoice and leap for joy, for your reward will be great in heaven. The kind of persecution you have endured is what their fathers did to the prophets as well" [Lk 6 (23)].

Certainly, my most beloved, I have no doubt that you have already been comforted through grace and can comfort each other. Do this especially by acknowledging goodness, tribulation, and the cross, for, as has been written repeatedly, they are a proof of our faith and love.[14] O that God might grant that we bear up in this, as Paul says: "Their joy was boundless when they were preserved through much tribulation" [2 Cor 8 (2)]. Hear James's words of comfort: "Consider it a pure joy if you fall into various temptations, and know that your proven faith brings forth patience" [Jas 1 (2f.)]. For your suffering is a grace and gift of the Lord,[15] as he says: "It has been given to you that you not only believe in Christ but also suffer for him" [Phil 1 (29)].

Paul continues: "Our tribulations, which are temporal and light, create for us an eternal and immeasurably weighty and splendid glory, one that cannot be seen in what is visible but only in what is invisible" [2 Cor 4 (17f.)]. For love looks upon the love that cannot be seen.[16]

Judith said, "Let your minds meditate on this admonition, that years ago our fathers were also tempted and embattled, by which they were tested to see whether they had true love for God and honoured him. Keep in mind that they remembered how our father Abraham also was tempted, and through much tribulation was proved to be a lover and friend of God. In the same way, Isaac and Jacob, also Moses—indeed, all those who ever pleased God—are proved through much tribulation and found to be firm in the faith" [Jdt 8 (18–20)].

Thus Paul says that those who live without discipline are bastards; those who accept discipline are children born to a marriage [Heb 12 (8)]. All of this, my dear ones, is a great comfort, though you prob-

---

13* Parable.

14 Jas 1:12; 1 Pt 1:6f.

15 1 Pt 2:19.

16 Rom 8:24.

ably have already been comforted. May you be even more certain and stronger with this comfort. I have wanted to comfort you through grace; I wanted God to grant me that, so I could place you in my debt so that you would comfort me when I am in need of comfort. May God grant this through Jesus Christ, the true comforter. Amen.

Retain this letter for me! I have just written it by hand and have no copy or transcript.

Dated this twenty-fourth of May in the year[17] 1544. May the Lord give each one whatever is helpful and necessary, according to his grace and goodness. Amen.

Dear ones, read this letter to the ignorant and weak in faith, especially the sisters, for their admonition and comfort, so that no inconstancy of heart develop and grow but that all of us might be prepared and armed through grace in their hearts and in truth, however the Lord sees fit. We willingly take this reality into account with thanks. In this manner our hearts are tested before him, for who knows why he moves and decrees all things. He alone knows our hearts and minds[18] (Jer 17 [10]).

In the Lord Jesus Christ,
servant of all of you and comrade
in the tribulation of Christ,[19]
Leupold Scharnschlager

---

17 [Original: *anno.*—Trans.]

18 [Original: *nieren* ("kidneys").—Trans.]

19 Rv 1:9.

32

Concerning true faith and common salvation in Christ

To all true believers, especially in the Alsace

Leupold Scharnschlager

This undated, substantive, and probing theological treatise[1] is the only one of Leupold Scharnschlager's pieces in the Kunstbuch devoted to questions of faith. He writes it upon request. His concern has been church order, and he tells his readers he has relied on Pilgram Marpeck and other ministers to instruct members on the nature of faith. Scharnschlager challenges his hearers to take up the message "worthily and with hunger, not as my word but as the Lord's." Either as an assumption or as a hope, the author asserts that his considered thoughts, arrived at by giving and receiving counsel with others, bear God's authority.

Scharnschlager's concern is the right order of faith and works. Because the heartbeat of Anabaptism was "walking in the resurrection,"[2] it was dissatisfied with the teaching of justification by faith—if it meant

---

Leupolt Scharnschlager an alle Wahrgläubigen, besonders die im Elsaß: Vom wahren Glauben und gemeinen Heil in Christus. Translation by Victor Thiessen and John D. Rempel.

1 Heinold Fast (Bern MS, no. 32, 2) offers no definitive date but suggests that the letter may have been written in 1545. Because of internal evidence, Martin Rothkegel believes it must have been written shortly before Marpeck's death in 1556 (BSOT, 530).

2 John H. Yoder, trans. and ed., *The Schleitheim Confession* (Scottdale, PA: Herald Press, 1977), 10.

that salvation is complete in the act of believing. The good news, according to Anabaptism, was not only that one can be reconciled to God but also that one can become a different person. But Swiss Anabaptism, in both its Swiss Brethren and Hutterian expressions, Scharnschlager argues, placed the weight of the Christian life so strongly on works that works were in danger of displacing faith.

Scharnschlager's soteriology at this point is steeped in Paul's thought. His interpretation of Paul is so close to that of Luther that he uses Luther's concepts word for word: it is "faith alone" that saves. The believer is reconciled with God through the sacrifice of Christ, and made a partaker of Christ. One senses that Scharnschlager is so emphatic because he fears that his hearers do not have clarity on this most important matter. When he is confident that the point has been made, he asserts that works demonstrate that one has faith.

One other statement is noteworthy because it offers a rare insight into what Marpeckite Anabaptists read aside from the Bible—or rather, what they read along with the Bible. On the subject of surrender, a familiar stage in the mystical spirituality abroad in South Germany,[3] Scharnschlager refers his readers to *Theologia Germanica*[4] and "the booklet about discipleship." The former was a popular late medieval spiritual guide that also won many adherents in the Reformation. The latter was most likely Thomas à Kempis's *The Imitation of Christ*. This list of resources for the surrendered life of the justified believer (itself an oxymoron to some polemicists) reminds us that despite the passionate rivalries to which the sixteenth century gave birth, many Christians of various groups considered these teachings and practices authentic expressions of the gospel.[5]

For Scharnschlager, faith and works, experience and ethics, make up a seamless garment. He offers not only the experience of grace but also the continuous indwelling of Christ. And it is the very nature of

---

3 MESG, 17–34.

4 *Theologia Deutsch* or *Theologia Germanica* (modern translation by Bengt Hoffman, *The "Theologia Germanica" of Martin Luther* [New York: Paulist Press, 1980]).

5 This reality did not keep our author from castigating "Papists, Lutherans, Zwinglians, false Anabaptists."

this deep inwardness that it constantly manifests itself in outward acts of surrender and sacrifice. The agent of this seamless spiritual reality is always the Spirit.

Announcement of truth faith and common salvation in Christ

To all true believers in Jesus Christ, first in Alsace, and also other places here and there, scattered physically over the earth but gathered in faith and spirit, my beloved brothers and comrades at hand.

Grace be with you, and the peace from God our heavenly Father and the Lord Jesus Christ.[6] Amen.

My beloved brothers and sisters in Christ, until now I have waited for the Lord our Redeemer to give me an opportune time to write something fruitful and comforting to you, according to the measure of my gifts in the grace of Christ.[7] I say this so that it might be evident to you that you have not been forgotten by me in the Lord. Alas, until now it was not possible to write you, because of time and effort spent elsewhere for good reasons and the Lord's business; it is not the case that this situation has come about because of my inattention.

In addition, I confess my hope and comfort that, my writings notwithstanding, through the grace of God you have been (and will be) visited and cared for in your need through a visit in the flesh by our beloved in the Lord, brother Pilgram, and other ministers of yours. May the Lord be thanked, and may they be thanked in the Lord. But as a result of repeated pleas from your messengers, and out of the press-

6 Rom 1:7; etc.

7 Rom 1:11; Rom 12:3; Eph 4:7.

ing debt of love in Jesus Christ our Lord,[8] I cannot refrain any longer but must write you a little note in short order, and a special summary of our common salvation. I write in the hope that it might be taken up worthily and with hunger, not as my word but as the Lord's. Don't consider it unfruitful or indifferent.[9] Show yourselves worthy to receive similar consolation from the Lord through his own in the future.

My beloved in Jesus Christ, the Lord Christ himself has said that one shall not live by bread alone but from every word that proceeds from the mouth of God [Mt 4 (4)]. In this case it should be understood as two breads: bodily and spiritual, the bodily bread that sustains the natural body, and the spiritual bread that sustains the spiritual life. Just as someone cannot live physically without material bread as food, likewise he cannot live without the Word of God for the soul, or in the spirit. For this reason St. Paul taught that we ought not to forsake coming together as has become the custom for some [Heb 10 (25)].

The Word of God, however, in which we live, is above all the holy gospel preached by Christ and his apostles. Through faith in Jesus Christ, through whose Word or sermon all of us believed by grace, we came to life. For, as the Lord said, "Whoever believes in me has eternal life" [Jn 6 (47)]. Truly, my brothers, we must not become careless by diligently and eagerly embracing this message without ceasing,[10] so that the newly begun life in us is sustained, improved, and strengthened through growth and secured to the end, since we no longer have any reason to live in the world,[11] but more and more concern ourselves with spiritual things.

Since we have been made alive through faith and live solely through faith, as Romans says [Rom 1 (17)], how then could such a life come about through works, as some of the Swiss seek after, as if life, salvation, or the kingdom of God consisted in works?[12] For it consists in faith alone. I say, however, of such faith, that it exists only after Christ's

---

8 Rom 1:14; 13:8.

9 Ti 3:14.

10 Heb 6:1.

11 Col 2:20.

12 Lk 17:20; Gal 4:3; Heb 9:10.

resurrection and ascension to heaven.[13] It did not exist before that. God offered it to everyone after he had raised Christ from the dead [Acts 17 (31)]. Of this faith the gospel says: "But I say that such righteousness before God comes through faith in Jesus Christ to all, and upon all who believe" [Rom 3 (22)]. Further, "They are made holy by his grace without works through the redemption that happened through Christ, which God has made into a throne of grace through faith in his blood."[14]

Moreover: "Since we have been made holy and righteous through faith, we have peace with God through our Lord Jesus Christ" [Rom 5 (1)]. It is clear, then, that we receive eternal life and the essential piety and justification that counts before God[15] solely through faith. Therefore those who push external works—who clean the cup on the outside [Mt 23 (25)], who say, "Do not buy that," "Do not carry that," and so forth [Col 2 (21)]—should remove themselves from all this. They should see that faith is not a human gift but a divine one[16] and be built up and planted in it.[17*]

Such faith consists above all in two things. First, if I believe in the death and blood of Jesus Christ, the Son of God, who suffered and poured himself out for our sins in the fullness of time,[18*] I am reconciled,[19] and the wrath of God[20] is laid aside. Thus I am made righteous and holy before God, as Adam was before the fall. Second, I (who am now reconciled with God by Christ's blood[21]) continue to

---

13 [Like others in the Marpeck Circle, Scharnschlager emphasizes the contrast between the Old Testament and the New Testament. Faith, in the New Testament sense, is possible only in the power and the revelation released through Christ's resurrection and ascension and the descent of the Spirit.—Ed.]

14 Rom 3:24f.

15 Rom 1:17; 3:21; 3:25; 10:3; 2 Cor 5:21.

16 Jn 6:29; Rom 12:3; Eph 2:8.

17* Note.

18* 1.

19 2 Cor 5:19.

20 Jn 3:36; Rom 1:18; etc.

21 Rom 3:25f.

believe in the message of the future kingdom of God with its heavenly being and glory.[22*, 23]

That, my brothers, is the faith, the great treasure that we should never let slip from our attention but rather should look upon without ceasing. No one can enter the kingdom without acknowledging his sins and nothingness, and that all the things we possess are nothing. Only Christ, his suffering, holiness, and righteousness, has been given to us and is ours. Those who rely on works do not recognize this. They know nothing of Christ and of God's love, generosity, and grace; they cannot love both Christ and God in return. Of this aforementioned faith a great deal could be said, but a little bit will be enough for now.

O brother, what great grace we receive through this faith! We are fellow heirs[24]—indeed, a newly married bride, the very spouse of the Lord Jesus Christ.[25] We are partakers of Christ and all his riches:[26] whatever Christ has is ours, and whatever we have is his. To begin with, he made our sins his own; he took them on[27] as though he had committed them himself. He nailed them to the cross,[28] so that the believer might set his hope on the future time, on the proclaimed kingdom of God you heard about above, and the future glory. With outer works and appearances[29] I cannot acquire the tiniest part of these things from God or stand before him just, holy, reconciled, and filled with life.

Faith alone is the centrepiece and source; those who want to be justified before God with external works remain in darkness. Above all, external works can be performed only through faith. Faith must be present beforehand; only thereafter can works of faith follow according to the measure and portion of faith,[30] which God alone gives, and through which alone—not through works—one can be called a believ-

---

22* 2.

23 Rom 5:1f.

24 Rom 8:17; Eph 3:6; 1 Pt 3:7.

25 Sg; Eph 5:23–32; Rv 19:7.

26 Eph 1:3.

27 Is 53:3.

28 Col 2:14; 1 Pt 2:24.

29 Rom 3:20; Gal 2:16; Col 2:23.

30 Rom 12:3.

er in Christ.[31] And any believer who should fall into this blindness and presumptuousness, claiming to become holy or a Christian before God through good works, falls from faith and from all aforementioned gifts that come through faith. But whoever has the faith stated above has a comfort that works can never achieve. Indeed, those in the Old Testament did not achieve it through the external keeping of God's laws and commandments,[32] not to mention other works of human invention. For what can harm, horrify, or damn a believer, as Paul proclaims? [Rom 8 (33–35)]. If sin and death come upon the believer, faith resides in his heart—faith that Christ died for his sins, that Christ has become his, and that his unrighteousness and sins are no longer his but Christ's.

This is what we have to say about faith in Jesus Christ.[33*] No one should claim that faith, which comes from the preaching of God's Word,[34] is merely a historical or dead faith, without effect or fruit. No doubt that is what people held at the time of James [Jas 2 (17)]. According to his Epistle, James replied with a demonstration of faith at work. Even today some understand Christ and Paul as ascribing righteousness and life to faith alone, as if a faith without deeds and fruit is enough for salvation.[35*] For how can it be a barren, that is,. a dead faith, when life—and much more—comes forth from it? That is what we intend to recount here briefly.

First, such faith in Christ reconciles sinner*s* to God.[36*, 37] Through its[38] ways and attributes it brings about the cleansing of the conscience from sin and death against God.[39] With it come repentance and cessation of all sin. We have been reconciled from our sin, in which we had

31 [Original: *christgloubig.*—Trans.]

32 Rom 9:31f.

33* Speaking of faith.

34 Rom 10:17.

35* Note.

36* 1.

37 [Original: *Erstlich versueneth solcher glouben inn Christum die sundt vor Got* ("First, such faith in God reconciles sinners before God."—Trans.]

38 [The nouns to which "his" refers are both masculine, so the pronoun could refer either to "faith" or to "Christ."—Ed.]

39 Heb 9:14; 1 Pt 3:21.

previously lain exposed to God's wrath, so that we might not fall into it again.

Second, this faith expressly offers us a word about the future kingdom and glory through the inner eye, instead of what is earthly, temporal, and visible.[40*] This preaching about the future being and glory releases us and lets us surrender our love of creaturely things.[41] With Paul we can say, "I forsake what is behind me and strain toward what is before me" [Phil 3 (13)].

True, free, unsullied, and unfeigned surrender[42] follows solely from such faith.[43*] This is written about in the *Theologia Germanica* and in the booklet about discipleship. There can be neither true surrender nor discipleship in someone in whom the gist of such faith and foundation is not rooted. There is only a façade: you can read this book or that, but you will not find true rest. For a person purifies himself through such demonstrable faith and hope, just as Christ is pure, as John says in his Epistle [1 Jn 3 (3)].

Thus the person of faith will be inwardly affirmed, comforted, strengthened, purified, and changed through both levels of faith in Christ, and through such faith receive the promised Holy Spirit. Through the Spirit he is assured of being a child of God[44] and moved to all goodness,[45] washed from all impurity and sin [1 Cor 6 (11)]. Through this Holy Spirit he embraces the love of God; for such an attitude is love as God himself in us. This happens in every believer according to the measure of his faith in Christ.

First of all, good works, the fruit of the Spirit, and the love of God all originate from faith. Of these fruits Paul says: "The fruit of the Spirit is love, joy, peace, patience, friendliness, goodness, faith and faithfulness, gentleness, self-control" [Gal 5 (22)]. Likewise, "The fruit of the Spirit is all manner of goodness and righteousness and truth" [Eph 1 (5, 9)].

40* 2.

41 [Original: *macht in gelassen von liebe der creaturen.*—Trans.]

42 *Gelassenheit* appears to refer both to peace and to obedience, with only a weaker implication of submission or yieldedness.

43* 3.

44 Rom 8:16.

45 Rom 8:14.

Likewise, "Love is patient and friendly; love does not burn with jealousy; love is not unruly or difficult, or puffed up, improper or shameful; love is not awkward, does not seek its own good, is not bitter or resentful, does not attempt to aggravate, does not rejoice in misfortune, but rejoices in the truth, bears all, trusts all, hopes all, is patient in all" [1 Cor 13 (4–7)]. All these things come from God.

When someone has received the Holy Spirit[46] of godly birth and adoption[47] through the love of God, this is the true baptism of Christ that comes through the faith we've talked about [Mt 3 (13–17)]. The Holy Spirit, who is life itself [Rom 8 (10)],[48] raises up the person to do the will of God. Then the believer finds an opposing will in his flesh;[49] yet in his inner person, set aflame through God's Spirit and love, he does not want to follow it and reaches for the crucifixion of the flesh. As Paul says: "All who belong to Christ crucify their flesh with its lusts and desires" [Gal 5 (24)]. Thus the believer subdues his body, that is, his flesh, and tames or disciplines it, to make it serviceable for the Spirit. When one no longer goes along with the sinful masses of the world, the external cross or tribulation[50] arises [1 Pt 4 (1f.)].

The believer places himself willingly and patiently under the cross and the ban of Christ and brotherly discipline,[51] as well as admonition for improvement and purification. A believer who has such evident faith in the blood of Christ and the life to come is someone who has planted a good tree according to the command of Christ. Such a good tree brings forth good fruit of its own in its appointed time [Mt 7 (17); 12 (33)], for it has been planted on a water reservoir [Ps 1 (3)], that is, the water of the Holy Spirit and love of God [Jer 17 (8)], which we were promised and given, which we received through the kind of faith

---

46 Jn 3:5; Ti 3:5.

47 Gal 4:5; Eph 1:5.

48 [Marpeck and his companions are fond of equating God and love, as can be seen earlier in this letter. Here the equation is repeated, not of the three persons of the Trinity together, but of the Spirit.—Ed.]

49 Rom 7:23.

50 Rom 5:3.

51 Mt 18:15–18. [He probably refers here to the ban, or the discipline of the Christian community.—Ed.]

we've already talked about. The good tree, like faith (or the faithful person) continues to be fruitful in all good words and works through the Holy Spirit and the love of God. That happens internally with respect to God and self, and externally with respect to other people, working in all ways to obey and please God, according to the demands of the evangelical Word,[52*] be it with baptism, the Lord's Supper, the spiritual walk, love, patience, not repaying evil for evil,[53] and much more in that vein. Living water flows from such things [Jn 7 (38)], and the fruits of such trees or waters are good to eat [Ez 47 (12)]. Hence someone who is learned in the things of faith or spirit can discern how a person may be made a Christian, or be brought to Christianity, that is, to life and to a God-pleasing righteousness through works or through faith, which is not a human gift but a divine one,[54] not earned but given by grace.

And therefore, as is proper, a person is made holy, just, blessed, a child of God who is fully alive by faith alone, a well-planted tree that brings forth good fruit. It is not the fruit that makes him good, for he has already been made good. Similarly, evil works do not make a person evil; rather, someone who is evil does evil. In all senses a person must be good and holy first, then good works proceed from a good, holy person. The fruit does not bear the tree, and the tree does not grow from the fruit, but the fruit grows on the tree. The tree bears the fruit and must come before the fruit.

To summarize, the fruit makes the tree neither good nor evil, but the tree does so for the fruit. Thus the person must first be evil or holy before he does either good or evil works, and his works do not make him either good or evil, but he commits either good or evil works [Mt 12 (33)]. Works do not bring forth faith; they do not make holy. But faith, which makes one holy or good, also produces good works. Thus the person must become and remain alive, holy, and righteous before God. This happens through faith alone and not through works. Whatever good a true believer brings forth, he does not do so to become holy through it, because he has already become holy through faith. No,

---

52* Note.

53 Rom 12:17; etc.

54 Eph 2:8.

he does it as a free act of love and desire for God's praise and his neighbour's good. As Christ says, because of his godly[55] nature and birth he cannot do other: like a good tree standing by good water, he cannot bring forth bad fruit [Mt 7 (17f.)].[56*, 57] Nothing but faith can make a person good, and nothing but unbelief can make him evil before God.

As Paul says, without faith it is impossible to please God [Heb 11 (6)]. He does not say "without works," but "without faith." And furthermore, whatever does not proceed from faith is sin; for without faith in Christ, one is still subject to sin and the wrath of God [Rom 14 (23)].[58] All things will be united or brought to peace with God through faith in Christ,[59] and not through works, as one's own righteousness, which the Jews sought in order to become holy before God. Whoever teaches that one can be holy through works and not through faith is blind and a leader of the blind.[60] He torments himself and others with works that have no juice, power, spirit, or life, and never comes to true holiness. Such people undoubtedly have the appearance of holiness, but its authority is denied in the process [Col 2 (23); 2 Tm 3 (5)]. They continue to learn without the knowledge of true holiness (2 Tm 3 [7]).

This is how to understand good works—how they can be reprehensible and not reprehensible—and to understand the teachings of Christ and the apostles. Through them we learn to do good works: they must proceed from faith in Christ accompanied by the Holy Spirit and the love of God. When that happens, you don't have to evaluate if they are good and righteous, evil or unjust; based on what has been said above, you know they are pernicious. Then they do not proceed from freedom and the right approach. When that happens, faith in grace and in the blood and death of Christ are denied and forgotten.

---

55 [Original: *götlicher* ("godly" or "divine").—Trans.]

56* Parable.

57 Ps 1:3; Jer 17:8.

58 Jn 3:36.

59 Rom 5:1.

60 Mt 15:14; Lk 6:39; Rom 2:19.

Although Christ and the apostles preached the promise of salvation through good works,[61] this occurs only for the sake of faith, from which such works proceed and are good. There is one good work of God, from which flow all works in and through love, power, and the Holy Spirit of God [Jn 6 (29)]. As stated above, all righteousness and holiness that counts for eternal life is manifest through faith in Christ. Likewise, St. Paul says: "Not the righteousness that comes from the law but that which comes through faith in Christ, that is, righteousness that comes from God. By faith I know him and the power of his resurrection and the fellowship of his suffering, that I become conformed to his death, if I wish to encounter the resurrection from the dead" [Phil 3 (9–11)].

For it is in faith, as we have spoken of it, that we recognize God, in his grace and love toward us through Christ, and receive them. We recognize the power of the spiritual resurrection,[62] which faith possesses through the Holy Spirit. Further, we recognize the fellowship of Christ's suffering. We remain in such faith through repentance or turning from sin and works of the flesh,[63] which bring the believer inner and outer suffering, strife, and crucifixion of the flesh. In this faith we stand firm in the fellowship of the suffering of Christ and his own. We become conformed to his sufferings and death, and encounter the future resurrection of the dead both spiritually and physically.[64]

As has been said above, it is fitting to preach Christ's faith and sanctification, together with those things that go along with it, not without including its accompanying treasures, fruit, works, consequences, accompaniments. These flow from the very nature of faith and must not be left behind.[65*] Otherwise it is no faith, at least not a true faith, only a historical faith, without life, spirit, love, fruit, repentance, resurrection, or cross, without God's spiritual gifts. We don't want that; we want what Paul says: "To you is given not only to believe in Christ but also to suffer with him" [Phil 1 (29)]. And, "If one believes with all one's heart,

---

61 Mt 16:27; 25:35ff.; Rom 2:6; 1 Cor 3:13f.; 1 Pt 1:17; Jas 2:24; Rv 2:23; 14:13; 20:12.

62 [Elsewhere the author calls this the "first resurrection," based on Rv 19.—Ed.]

63 Gal 5:19; 1 Pt 4:1f.

64 Rom 6:5.

65* Note.

one will be righteous, and if one confesses with one's mouth, he shall be saved" [Rom 10 (10)]. Likewise, Peter adds, "Show" Christian "virtue in your faith" [2 Pt 1 (5)]. These passages speak of true, proper, living, saving faith in Christ, and bind together faith and the works of faith, for there is no other way for them to exist; one flows from the other, that is, proceeding from faith. Just as faith, the Holy Spirit, and love of God proceed and work together, one proceeds from the other, and yet one cannot be without the other. The conclusion of all this is that one becomes holy, righteous, and saved through faith and the works of faith, or through faith and the Christian life that ensues from it [Rom 10 (17)].

In the sadness of your many tests of tribulation, my dear brothers, this faith shall carry you and help you bear up in your sorrow,[66] so that your faith comes through well practised, enlightened, and evident before the Lord, all angels, devils, and the entire world. That is true faith. According to the Lord's Word, a lighted candle will not be hidden [Mt 5 (14)]. Through its confession of faith, the body or church of Christ must take upon itself the devil, hell, death, and the entire world, Papists, Lutherans, Zwinglians, false Anabaptists, together with all other opposing sects and opinions, according to the prophet Zechariah: "For I will make Jerusalem a stumbling block to all peoples, on which all those who wish to rise against it will be torn, and against which all peoples of the earth will gather" [Zec 12 (3)].

I interpret this simply and solely to mean that because of persecution, this city of God, the true Jerusalem,[67] must withstand being taken by storm, battle, bombardment, and attack. Every race, people, and person attempts to achieve its salvation. In the process the city bears sadness and fear [Is 26 (17); Jn 16 (21)] and lets itself focus on the glory and victory that appears to be on the side of its enemies and persecutors. It is as though they are right, and the church of Christ suffers shame, embarrassment, and injustice, as though God, Christ, scripture, and all angels appear to be against us, just as the Lord Christ himself had to endure as he hung on the cross [Ps 73 (9); Jb 21 (7ff.); Jer

---

66 1 Pt 1:6f.

67 The church.

12 (1); Hb 1 (13)]. His enemies "blasphemed him, shaking their heads at him and saying: 'You who would destroy the temple of God and rebuild it in three days, help yourself! If you are God's Son, climb down from the cross!' Likewise, the high priests ridiculed him, together with the scribes and elders, and said, 'He has helped others and cannot help himself. If he is the king of Israel, let him climb down from the cross; then we will believe him.' He trusted in God; let God save him, if he cares to do so. For he said: 'I am God's Son.' And those who were crucified with him reproached him as well" [Mt 27 (39–44); Mk 15 (29–32)]. "The soldiers also ridiculed him, coming to him and saying: 'If he is the Christ, the chosen, and the Jews' king, let him help himself!'" [Lk 23 (36f.)]. "'Behold the Christ, the king of Israel; let him come down from the cross, that we might see and believe.'" [Ps 22 (8); Is 53 (4)]. "For the disciple is not above the master, or the servant above the lord. It is enough for the disciple to be like his master, and the servant like his lord. If they called Beelzebub their housefather, how much more should they be called his comrades and work with him" [Jn 15 (20); Mt 10 (24)].

Nevertheless, the church of Christ is preserved in God's grace and favour through the great treasure of faith we have mentioned. This grace and favour are the church's constant help. However dark the times may appear, faith persists all the way, with its attendant love and accompanying Holy Spirit as comforter.[68*, 69] The church of Christ remains inseparable from God and his love (Rom 8 [35]); fellow travellers and mercenaries damage only themselves—and the gates of hell will not overcome the rightly built church of Christ.[70] May God help us to that end, through Jesus Christ. Amen.

This, my dear brothers, is the great treasure of the true middle[71] way, the short path to eternal life. This, in brief, is what I wanted to show you for your comfort, so that you could stand all the more steadfast and remain immovable—and therein all the more edified and forti-

---

68* Gloss: The Lord knows his own, says Paul (2 Tm 2 [19]). He will distinguish between them on his day (Mt 25 [32] and 13 [49]).

69 Jn 14:16; etc.

70 Mt 16:18.

71 Turning neither to the left nor to the right.

fied. I wanted you not to be led astray, neither to the left or the right, but simply following this path to the end in patience in Christ [Dt 5 (32); 17 (11, 20); 18 (28:14); Jo 1 (7); 2 Kgs 22 (2); 2 Chr 33 (34:2); Prv 4 (27); Is 30 (21)]. For that reason I ask God to make you and us skilled and worthy, fulfilling this in and through us, through Jesus Christ, so that his name might be praised through us, and we through him, according to his grace. To him be honour and praise and thanks in all eternity. Amen.

Commend me to the Lord in all your prayers.

I admonish you, my dear brothers, keep in mind the words of Paul, who says: "Be obedient to your leaders, and submit yourselves to them, for they watch over your souls as those who have to give account of them, that they can do so with joy and not sighing, for this is not helpful to you" [Heb 13 (17)].

My brothers, see to it that those who work among you and lead you in the Lord do not suffer want in temporal nourishment,[72] that they do not devote to other things time they should be spending in service to you, being forced to do physical labour and hindered from doing the Lord's work, to your improvement and encouragement. I say this for your sake: keep in mind that such words of the Lord bring you nourishment.[73] Therefore be co-workers in the kingdom of God.[74]

In the Lord Jesus Christ,
your servant, fellow elder, and
brother in grace,
Leupold Scharnschlager

[72] 1 Tm 5:17f.

[73] Mt 10:10.

[74] Col 4:11.

33

Concerning the Christian and Hagarite churches

To the believers in Württemberg and elsewhere
Pilgram Marpeck
Chur, 15 August 1544

Two riddles accompany this pamphlet. It was written in August of 1544 in Chur, a town in eastern Switzerland. We know from Leupold Scharnschlager's urgent response (nos. 30 and 31) to communities in that region in May of 1544 that they were being threatened with expulsion. The first riddle concerns the question of why is there no trace of this crisis in "Concerning the Christian and Hagarite Churches." Had Scharnschlager overreacted to the threat? Was Marpeck deliberately silent, so as not to endanger spiritual comrades? Two possibilities suggest themselves. One, the intensity of the imagery used and the way it keeps building throughout the letter suggest that the author was in a deeply meditative and inspired state, removed from everyday affairs. If we remember that Marpeck had already written on this theme (no. 5, "Concerning Unity and the Bride of Christ"), it is conceivable that the substance of the present text had been written at an earlier time and sent when confidence in the visible church of Christ's fellow sufferers

---

Pilgram Marpeck an die Gläubigen in Württemberg und anderswo: Von der christlichen und der Hagarschen Kirche; Chur, 15. August 1544. Translation by Walter Klaassen. Previously published as "The Churches of Christ and of Hagar" in WPM, 390–401. Reprinted, with editorial changes, by permission of the publisher.

was most urgently needed. Two, since the letter is addressed to congregations in Württemberg (the German province immediately to the east of the Alsace), perhaps Marpeck is simply focusing on the pastoral needs in that setting.

The second riddle concerns Marpeck's place of residence. One possibility is that he was still living in Chur at the time of writing, and the turmoil there hastened his departure for Augsburg. This thesis is complicated by the fact that a notation in the municipal records of Augsburg shows that as of February of that year, Marpeck oversaw the wood supply for the city. A similar entry about his work appears in October. These facts suggest that the author was already living in Augsburg but traveled to Chur on a pastoral visit, perhaps because of the dangerous situation.[1]

This epistle is an ode to love and an extended allegory about the church. Marpeck is concerned to show that love is both the essence of God and the essence of the church. Considering the subtlety of his subject, it is not surprising that the train of thought he develops is complicated and difficult to follow. One reason for this is the writer's distinctive attempt, often in the same sentence, to combine flowery poetic allusions and methodical dogmatic claims about the persons of the Trinity. Marpeck's belief that as the Father works inwardly through the Spirit, so the Son works outwardly through the church, is evident here. His point is that all three persons of the Trinity are at work in the church, drawing individuals into it.

The author's goal is to show the blessedness of the true church and to warn against the curse of the false church. Halfway through it, his lovely allegory becomes polemical. To begin with, he takes the imagery of the Song of Solomon and applies it to the church. He unfolds this figurative language to the point where the children of the bride take succour from the bride's breasts. Then he takes a flying leap, by means of the typology Paul develops in Galatians 4:21–5:1, to argue that in addition to the true bride, Sarah, there is also a false bride, Hagar, with

---

1 Walter Klaassen concludes from an assessment of all the fragmentary biographical evidence that Marpeck had been living in Augsburg for two years before he traveled again to Chur (personal correspondence, 15 November 2006).

poisoned breasts. The children of the true bride can be known inwardly by their surrender to God's love and outwardly in their being washed by water in the Word, that is, through baptism upon confession of faith.

Marpeck's emphasis is on the visible church as the mediator of grace. And in the understanding of his age, the Song of Solomon was a treatise about the church. "He begins and ends with the already familiar interpretation of the Canticle, which, he says, is a 'natural parable of love.' By means of this love, 'all faithful hearts are led into the real, supernatural love,' the mark of the true church."[2] The details of the allegory become more and more graphic as the author proceeds!

"He identifies many who claim to be in the covenant as Ishmaelites, that is, children of Hagar. God is their Father, but they are not children of the true mother, the church of Christ. He charges that they are concerned with, and have, only the letter of scripture, and not the Spirit. Their faith, then, is a mere external faith which has not permeated and changed all of life, as it has done for the children of promise. He is clearly thinking here of other Christians, perhaps of the Reformed variety found in Strasbourg."[3] Others claim to have been conceived through the Spirit, though without a mother. They might be the Spiritualists.

2 WPM, 390.

3 Ibid.

An epistle about the churches of Christ and of Hagar

To all the faithful elect in Christ Jesus in the land of Württemberg and scattered elsewhere but gathered in faith and spirit, my dear brothers and comrades.

Grace and peace from God our heavenly Father through Jesus Christ our Lord[4] be and remain with us eternally. Amen.

My deeply beloved, in God the Father through Jesus Christ: This love is the true source from which all love flows.[5*] For this love from the one God flows from the heavenly Father in Christ and from Christ in the Father. In the Holy Spirit this love brings about the unity of all faithful hearts. She is a bond,[6] an inseparable unity, an eternal beginning stretching from the highest height.[7] She takes to herself the influx of whatever is loved and may in truth be loved. In particular, love, which is God in all, is the observer of what she herself has created and formed in the likeness of her image.[8] In God the Father, according to her manner and her nature, love has an eternal likeness. The model and parable of love is humanity.[9] In us, love, as the essence of all reality, has a likeness from eternity, and her form is perfectly seen. When she lives in the new heaven and the new earth as a holy city, the new Jerusalem, her form will be fully seen in him [2 Pt 3 (13)]. Prepared as a bride for her husband,[10] she will come down out of heaven from God,[11] himself the essence of love. A dwelling of God, she will be the most beautiful of all.[12] She shows her-

---

4 Rom 1:7; etc.

5* Love.

6 Col 3:14.

7 Lk 1:78.

8 Gn 1:27.

9 [In these dense sentences the author's focus is on two matters. He describes the vastness of God's love, constituting his very being. At the same time he emphasizes that the church is the perfect likeness and embodiment of that love.—Ed.]

10 Rv 21:2.

11 Rv 21:3.

12 Sg 1:8; 5:9; 6:1.

self to her bridegroom and husband, and she is the banner above all.[13] She is the seal[14] imprinted on the hearts of all the faithful, and she is the pledge[15] for eternal security, victory, and conquest against all hate and enmity.[16] Unmoved, unspotted, and unchanged, she will eternally retain her name against them.

Love's garments, which are the virtues of the Holy Spirit, remain eternally unspotted, untorn, and undamaged. Only love wears the virtues unspotted; for her honour they were prepared and made in eternity. Whoever does not contemplate or know love in her finery and adornment knows neither love nor himself. She is the daughter who has left her father's house and who has been brought to the king in her embroidered dress.[17] Whoever wishes to see her form should behold her in the adornment of her king.[18] Her Christ and king, who is himself thus dressed and adorned, has dressed her. Whoever, even once, truly sees this loveliest of all brides in her adornment and form will praise her in wonderment. He will exalt her honour, praise, and adornment among the nations.[19] Because he has seen her, he is also able to speak the truth about her apparel and crown from foot to head, and because of her beauty and adornment he has great desire to serve at her feet and to entice all who gladly hear it to serve love together with him.

I, along with many others who testify to it through faith, have had only a glimpse of her form. This glimpse has created great longing in our hearts to see her again, fully and as she really is. Perhaps we, with all who desire it, may get another glimpse of her and see her form, so that our hearts may be more eager with desire to seek her and see her form. Then we too may be clothed with her apparel and please her with fervent service.

First, I hope that all who have, by virtue of the Holy Spirit in true faith, had a glimpse of her form will witness with me to her apparel and

---

13 Sg 2:4.

14 Sg 8:6.

15 2 Cor 1:22.

16 Eph 2:14–16.

17 Ps 45:10, 14.

18 Is 33:17.

19 1 Chr 16:24; Ps 96:3.

adornment as the loveliest of all.[20] I hope too that they will witness to her king, who has been clothed and crowned by his mother on the day of his joy.[21] This day is the occasion of eternal wonderment in all the creatures.

First, the Holy Spirit witnesses with all faithful hearts in the Canticle of Praise[22] to her beauty and adornment. Similarly, the prophets, patriarchs,[23] evangelists, apostles, and all who have seen and recognized her form, have acknowledged it and testified to it. What they have said and testified I here set down as a seal of our testimony not only to truth but also to our certain faith. This love testifies to herself from her spirit concerning her friend. In the Canticle, she says: "He kisses me with the kiss of his mouth, for his breasts are sweeter than wine. They smell of the fragrance of your ointment; your name is like ointment poured out. That is why the maidens love you. Draw me after you, and let us make haste. The king brings me into his chamber. We rejoice and are glad because of you; we will remember your breasts more than the wine. All who are upright love you."[24]

Partly drawn, as it is, from nature as a parable, these brief words show the artistry of love. Nearly the whole of the Canticle recalls, presents, and illustrates the real, supernatural love by means of the natural parable of love. By this means, all faithful hearts are led into the real, supernatural love, into God himself; yes, into God himself, and God into them.

First, the Holy Spirit says: "He kisses me with the kiss of his mouth." That is, the eternal Word has gone forth, and continues to go forth,

20 Sg 1:8; 5:9; 6:1.

21 Sg 3:11. [Mary's role in Christ's enthronement is taken over from high and late medieval allegorizing on the Song of Solomon. For the most part Protestant reformers rejected this role for Mary, as well as the teaching of her bodily assumption on which it depends.—Ed.]

22 Sg.

23 [It was commonly believed in the sixteenth century that Christ was known in the events of the Old Testament prior to his incarnation.—Ed.]

24 Sg 1:1–4. [This translation is accurate; it depends upon the version of the Bible Marpeck used. See CC, 146–47.—Ed.]

from the mouth of the Father,[25] from God himself.[26] With this Word, he kisses the hearts of all the faithful. Thus the divine nature of the children of God is conceived and born from the love of the Word, the imperishable seed.[27] This seed is the congregation, bought through the blood of Christ,[28] and the church is his spouse and bride, the loveliest and most beautiful among women.

All who are thus kissed by the mouth of God, and who have conceived a divine nature by the seed of the Word, are brought to this bride and mother, the church, by the Holy Spirit. In her, as the mother, spouse, consort, and church of Christ, are they born. Conceived by the action of the Holy Spirit, she bears the children of the Word in her body. As stated above, that body is the body of Christ, for while Christ is the husband and head,[29] the two are one flesh.[30] Her children are washed by the blood of Christ for the forgiveness of sins, and washed in the water of the Word,[31] they are cleansed of all filthiness of the flesh,[32] that is, sin. To reveal that the mother has conceived this child through the Holy Spirit and the Word from God, this child is then included in the covenant of a good conscience with God[33] in Christ. The covenant reveals that God is the child's Father, that it is not illegitimate but is born out of the marriage with Christ. This child is a true heir of the Father and the eternal kingdom.[34] Their mother, the church, has conceived these legitimate children, and they are from the Father, and they are born again through the washing of the water of the Word.[35] Thus

---

25 Sir 24:4.

26 Jn 1:1.

27 1 Pt 1:23.

28 Rv 5:9.

29 Eph 5:23.

30 Gn 2:24; Eph 5:31.

31 Eph 5:26; Ti 3:5.

32 1 Pt 3:21b.

33 1 Pt 3:21c.

34 1 Cor 15:50; Gal 4:7.

35 [This reference, from Eph 5:26, refers in this writing to baptism. It is noteworthy that it did not require an explanation, making clear that baptism may be received only by faith. That it stands for spiritual birth is brought out in the allegory and was understood by the author and his readers.—Ed.]

they are the legitimate children of the true Abraham, that is, of God the Father, who is the Father of all such children,[36*] and of the true Sarah, who is the mother of all such children.[37*] As Peter says: "You have become her daughter" [1 Pt 3 (6)]. Again, as Paul says: "Sing, you who are not pregnant, and bear children, you who have not been in childbirth. For she who is left alone will have more children" in the eternal kingdom, "than she who has a husband" [Is 54 (1); Gal 4 (27)]. Without this,[38] there is no heir, nor is there any divine birth.

However, practically everyone quarrels and boasts that they are of Abraham's seed, that they are born of God the Father's Spirit.[39*] Nevertheless, their boasts are pretentious and false. They are, and remain, only Ishmaelites;[40] they boast of being born of God, but without a legitimate mother, for their mother is neither promised nor married to God. Their mother is Hagar, the servant woman.[41*] Thus, because they are children born of the flesh, theirs is only the first birth. And although they are of the father Abraham's seed, she and her children serve only in the interests of reward. Their Creator, God, is their Father, but they are not born from Isaac, the child of promise,[42] that is, Jesus Christ through the Holy Spirit. Nor are they conceived or born of Christ's espoused bride.[43*] Therefore they cannot feed at the breasts of the true, espoused bride, the true Sarah, which are filled by the Holy Spirit.[44*] They suck the alien and false milk[45] of the maid, and not of the married one. Hagar's breasts are not filled by the Holy Spirit; her breasts are filled by her own cleverness in the dead letter of scripture.[46]

36* Abraham.

37* Sarah.

38 [The antecedent is not clear. Likely, "it" refers to the washing of the water of the Word.—Ed.]

39* World.

40 Gn 16f.

41* Hagar the slave.

42 Gal 3:29; 4:22–28.

43* Isaac.

44* Sarah.

45 1 Pt 2:2.

46 2 Cor 3:6.

The children of the true Sarah suck the pure milk of her breasts, filled as they are by the Holy Spirit. They are lovelier than wine.[47] Without deceit or wrong, the mother, the true Sarah, bears her children to the Father. The pure milk flows from her body as the bride and spouse of Christ through the fervent love and kiss of the Father. Her breasts are lovely and give sensible and pure milk.[48]

The children of the mother are all eager for her milk and suck from her breasts to their hearts' content. They are raised and nourished, and grow and increase, in the discipline the mother applies to them. Thus they are not destroyed in the filth[49] of their carnal nature by sin through which they are made unclean in ignorance.[50] Rather, when they reach their mature adulthood in Christ[51] their bridegroom, they are taught and instructed in the discipline of the Holy Spirit. Then, possessed with wisdom, understanding, and perception, they are given over to the Father, who receives them as heirs of the eternal inheritance and kingdom with Christ.

Thus such an inheritance, bequeathed to them only by the Holy Spirit, gives comfort to the Father's heirs. In faith, hope, and true love,[52] they are confident that they are conceived by the Father and that they are born of the spouse and consort of Christ, as the married spouse, who is promised and wed to Christ the Son of the Father. She is the true and honourable mother, the married one. Through his blood, she is promised and espoused to Christ, the Son of the Father, and because of the washing of water in the Word [Eph 5 (26)], her children are born again.[53] Therefore, in order that God may be revealed before the world,[54] the mother bears the Father's children, conceived by him

---

47 Sg 1:2.

48 1 Pt 2:2.

49 1 Pt 3:21.

50 Lv 5:2. [Here the story line almost becomes literal. It concerns everyday children: they are not condemned by their ignorance. As they are able, they are instructed in the ways of the triune God, which are laid out in the paragraphs that follow.—Ed.]

51 Eph 4:13.

52 1 Cor 13:13.

53 Ti 3:5.

54 Jn 7:4.

through the Holy Spirit. Christ's blood then ensures the washing and forgiveness of sins. This child of inheritance is of the seed of the Word. Raised, increased, and nourished by the breast of the mother, whose unadulterated milk, the word of truth,[55] comes from the Holy Spirit, this child and Christ are of one flesh, one bone, one blood, the seed of the Word. Thus the sure pledge, the Holy Spirit, instills in this legitimate child confidence in the inheritance.[56] This child is legitimately born of Father and mother, has the divine nature and manner, and has been grown, nourished, and raised honourably. All these children may with unshakable hope, and without worry of shame, look for the inheritance of the eternal kingdom. Apart from this rebirth, no one will inherit the kingdom of Christ.

For the others, all may boast as they please that they are born only of the Holy Spirit, without the legitimate mother, Christ's espoused bride. If they are not conceived by the Father in the legitimate spouse, and if they are not born of her in the washing of water in the Word [Eph 5 (26)], they are bastards; they are not heirs.[57] Again, whoever is conceived and born of the maid, and not the legitimate spouse, is illegitimate, and no heir.

Hagar does not feed her children with the milk of love but with lifeless water,[58] kept in a little barrel. The desert destroys the water, so that in the end neither mother nor child has any nourishment. Then the mother in despair abandons the child in the wilderness to die of hunger and thirst. Hagar's children boast of being a church and the spouse of Christ. In fact, they are only Egyptian maids and mothers who bear only Ishmaelites, reared on the dead letter and skill in scripture, and fed on keg water.[59*] All these Ishmaelites establish a church on the dead letter, and not on the living water of the eternal source,

---

55 2 Tm 2:15.

56 2 Cor 1:22; 5:5.

57 Heb 12:8. [Although the language is fanciful, its intention is clear. In Marpeck's eyes the Spiritualists are "unitarians of the Spirit," those who believe that the Christian life is concerned only with inward realities. They want nothing to do with the Father or the church, the bride of Christ.—Ed.]

58 Jer 2:13.

59* Ishmaelites.

which flows from the Holy Spirit, out of the body of Christ who sits at the right hand of God.[60] This water flows only into the spouse and bride who is one body with Christ: from her body, in turn, flow living waters.[61] However, the Hagarite mothers cannot give such waters, nor can they give drink to their children. The children of such mothers suck from shrivelled[62] breasts, to which there is no flow of grace or aid from the Holy Spirit, and drink lifeless barrel water which has no living source. Nevertheless, they all call themselves mothers and churches of Christ. They claim that they are conceived by Abraham, and that their children are Abraham's seed, God's children.[63*] But when their barrel water and their sack lunch[64] are consumed, when the dead letter and their skill in scripture come to an end, their faith and hope are also finished. And mothers and children despair in the terrible wilderness of this world.[65]

Therefore those mothers and children are not to be believed. These mothers have children without God the Father and the Holy Spirit, without the seed of the living Word. They are mothers who produce children as a result of the dead letter, a technical knowledge of scripture, and their own cleverness. That is the origin and source of all sects. Nor can any child be believed who claims to be a child of God but who is without a legitimate mother. He is a false spirit and a liar who boasts that he lives only as the offspring of the Spirit and Word, that he is

---

60 Mk 16:19; Lk 22:69; Acts 7:55f.; Rom 8:34; Col 3:1; Heb 10:12; 12:2; 1 Pt 3:22.

61 Jn 7:38. [Original: *inn die gsponns und prauth, ja, eegmahl, als zwey ein leib, fleusst, von wölcher leib lebenndige wasserr fliessen.*—Trans.]

62 [Original: *gesignen* = *versiegten* ("dried up," "withered," "shrunken")—Trans.]

63* Note.

64 [Original: *eingfasste speiß.*—Trans.]

65 [This is likely an allusion to Martin Bucer's covenant theology, in which Christians are referred to as children of Abraham because God's covenant with Abraham is an eternal covenant and did not end with Christ. See Marpeck's "Strasbourg Confession of 1532" (WPM, 107–57); Bucer's reply (Manfred Kreps and Hans Rott, eds., *Quellen zur Geschichte der Täufer* 7, *Elsaß 1* [Gütersloh: Gerd Mohn, 1959], 416–528); and Marpeck's response (in the same volume, 529–30). On Bucer, see Martin Greschat, *Martin Bucer: A Reformer and His Times,* trans. Stephen Buckwalter (Louisville: Westminster John Knox Press, 2004).—Ed.]

born only by virtue of the Holy Spirit, that he is nourished, raised, and taught without a mother.

Yet the Holy Spirit has no child without the legitimate spouse of Christ. The spouse of Christ bears, cares for, and trains the children of God, and the heavenly Father in Christ provides, preserves, and feeds the mother and her children. Whoever despises the birthgiving, care, and training of the mother[66] despises the Father along with her and has forfeited the heritage of both father and mother. These are the functions of the paternal and maternal heritage: the father is the eternal promise of that heritage; the mother, because she is his espoused bride, is the mediation of all the grace of the Father, given by the Holy Spirit to the hearts of all the faithful to aid the mother's discipline of her children. All the despised children are disinherited; they are excluded from the heritage, grace, and discipline of the Holy Spirit, and given over to everlasting destruction.

Therefore St. Paul faithfully warns us not to forsake the mother, spouse, and consort of Christ, which is the gathering and unity of the church of Christ. In Paul's day, some did forsake her, and some still do today. Even though the time is 1,500 years closer than in Paul's day, much less should we now forsake her, in order that we may enter into the kingdom of the Father together with our bridegroom Christ, and with all prudent and wise hearts. Unlike the five foolish virgins, against whom the Lord closes the door, nevermore to open it, we will not be without oil. The Lord does not know from where these others come [Mt 25 (1–12); Lk 13 (25)]. They are born, raised, and taught neither by him nor by his spouse. They lack the oil of faith, virtue, and true skill in the knowledge of the Father and of his Christ, wherein is eternal life in the eternal kingdom and heritage. They know neither the Father, nor the Son, nor the Holy Spirit, nor do they know his espoused bride, which is his congregation and church [Jn 17 (3)].[67] Nor are they taught

---

66 Prv 1:8.

67 [For the most part, Marpeck makes a careful distinction between "congregation" (*gemein*) and "church" (*kirch*). Perhaps he means that "the foolish virgins" don't recognize the church in either its local or its universal dimensions.—Ed.]

by her. How, then, can the Father, Christ, and his congregation know them?

So much concerning the birth of the legitimate and true children of God, who are legitimately born, bred, and nourished by the heavenly Father and the spouse and consort of Christ. The breasts of this Father and mother are lovelier than wine. All the patriarchs, prophets, and apostles have prophesied and witnessed to it, and they have affirmed that the name of the bridegroom and the bride is like ointment poured over all peoples for eternal salvation through his Word. That is why the bride's maids love him. He draws the bride with her maidens and children after him, and together they hasten on the upright way to the eternal kingdom. The king leads the bride into his chamber, that is, to his mystery; he shows her all the glory, understanding, and mystery of faith, all of which she, her children, and her maidens will receive from the king and eternally possess. Thus they rejoice in the bridegroom and king, and think of the breasts which they sucked rather than of the wine. That is, they remember his great love, faithfulness, and compassion, shown them in his death, resurrection, and ascension to the right hand of God. His love is the only source of joy and salvation to those born of God, and they rejoice eternally. Therefore the upright of heart love him; the unfit, the faithless, and the false cannot love him.[68]

I write this to you in the hope that we may earnestly contemplate the birth and beginning of our life. Because of faith, we have received this life out of the seed of the Word, implanted by the Holy Spirit in our legitimate mother, who is the spouse and consort of Christ, the giver and Creator of life.[69] As true children of God, we are sanctified and consecrated to the eternal kingdom and heritage, to our heavenly Father and his eternal praise, and to the everlasting royal priesthood.[70] We will reign eternally.[71] Together with all the elect of God, we will eternally sacrifice offerings of thanks in the purity of our hearts.

Such is the goodness, grace, and faithfulness with which he has crowned us and made us worthy for this royal priesthood. As the only

---

68 Sg 1:2–4.

69 Jn 6:63.

70 1 Pt 2:9.

71 Rv 22:5.

high priest[72] and king, he has made us heirs to this royal priesthood, and we are to take this inheritance. To his eternal thanks and praise, magnification, and exaltation, we are to take away from our heads, dispositions, and consciousness the inheritance he has given us. Similarly, the twenty-four elders took from their heads the crowns with which they had just been crowned, and said: "You, O Lord, are worthy to receive praise, honour, and power; you have made all things, and for your sake they exist and were created" [Rv 4 (10f.)]. It behooves all his creatures to give thanks to God, but especially those creatures who have been exalted to his glory. In the purity of their hearts, they should gratefully offer that same glory and honour, with which God has adorned them, to their Creator and bestower. Yes, and that mark of gratitude should be offered with clean, willing hands; it should be offered without any concern for their own honour, even as God, as one who cannot be coerced, has given everything freely to them. Such a heart is the free offering of thanks for everything it has received from its Creator, God, the Lord Jesus Christ, and the Holy Spirit.

Therefore, my loved ones, let us eternally thank God with such hearts. All his gifts are given for the sake of such gratitude; then, all thanksgiving, praise, and honour is and will remain his alone. For to him alone it belongs. It is to him that I, together with all the faithful, gladly and eternally give praise.

Dated at Chur the fifteenth day of August in the year 1544.

In the Lord Jesus Christ,
servant to you all,
Pilgram Marpeck

---

[72] Heb 10:21.

34

A warning against the hidden fire of the enemy in our hearts

To the congregation in St. Gall and Appenzell

Pilgram Marpeck

Pilgram Marpeck's concern for what he considered graceless legalism among the Swiss goes back to the early 1540s (no. 7, "Concerning Hasty Judgments and Verdicts," and no. 8, "The Cause of the Conflict"). In 1551 Marpeck tried once again to reach the Swiss Brethren with his message. This letter is one of a series written at this time by both parties. Marpeck had written at least once and had received a reply but was unsatisfied and mystified by their response. What the "demand" of the Swiss Brethren (to which he refers) is, is not clear, but it may well be that they resented his long admonitory letters—which, like Paul's, were sometimes "hard to understand"—and that they had suggested that if he would only stop, things would right themselves. In any event, he took their attitude to be an attack on him.

He counters with the claim that wisdom can be gained and good can be done only at the urging of the Spirit. Believers flirt with the sin of presumption when they start acting and speaking as if it were within their own power to discern God's will. He warns his listeners that Satan secretly starts fires in our inmost heart, and he immediately proceeds

---

Pilgram Marpeck an die Gemeinde in St. Gallen und Appenzell: Warnung vor dem verborgenen Feuer des Feindes in den Herzen; Augsburg, 9. August 1551. Translation by Walter Klaassen.

to the accusation that this has happened with the Appenzellers: they expose themselves to the wiles of the devil by being censorious and quarrelsome. He laments the divided state of the Anabaptist fellowship and emphasizes that the Holy Spirit reveals itself in many ways and not necessarily according to human rules and regulations. Marpeck's impulse is to see the fault entirely on the side of the Swiss. But then he prays a moving prayer of repentance in which he unmistakably includes himself. The Holy Spirit can do its uniting work only if Christians talk with one another, or in his case, write to one another.

In this letter Marpeck is torn between setting his fellow believers straight and accusing himself. Even though he charges the Swiss with unwillingness to listen to the Spirit, in the end he includes himself in that judgment. It is not hard to see how his letter might further antagonize the Swiss—but it is also not hard to see how Marpeck's vulnerability might convince them of his genuineness in pursuing the unity and peace of Christ's church.

This letter was carried to the churches at St. Gall and in Appenzell by old Thomas Schuhmacher, for reasons you will understand.

Grace and peace from God our heavenly Father, through and from the Lord Jesus Christ,[1] be and remain with us to eternity. Amen.

Dearly beloved, loved in Jesus Christ, our healer.

We, and especially I, Pilgram, have received your letter at the hand of the carrier, your and our dear brother. Even now I am unable to discover or understand from the oral or written account any reason for your demand and desire. How might a movement caused by the grace of God, and not a human or carnal impulse, follow from it?

Recently I wrote you requesting information and anything else that was pertinent, but you did not acknowledge our letter or indicate whether it had reached you and how you thought and felt about it. Similarly, your messenger was unable to report to us. Nor did he know whether our letter had been brought before the congregation.

Because of this we are gravely concerned, especially I, Pilgram. Your whole demand is shrouded in uncertainty.[2] Consequently I also find in me no urging of the Holy Spirit, without whom all striving and intention is in vain.[3] I am ready, however, to take the blame myself rather than to blame you. Perhaps God does not consider me worthy to serve you in the grave concern about which you wrote and complained in your letters, twice before and again now. Nevertheless, I would have to do it even if I would rather not. Even if a whale, that is, any human power, regime, or temporal service[4*]—which would not hinder me if I trust in God—had swallowed me,[5] I would still have to emerge, as frequently occurred, and carry out the bidding for which God sent and urged me. In such matters and situations I would rather have God urge me, drive,

---

1 Rom 1:7; etc.

2 Cor 9:26; Gal 2:2; Phil 2:16.

3 Rom 9:16.

4* Note.

5 Jon 2:1.

press, and even thrust me out by force, than that I should act of my own accord—to say nothing of an unknown cause.[6] Please understand me right when I say that strife, error, disunity, and antipathy flow from fleshly acclaimed wisdom and self-chosen feigned spirituality.[7]

Let me add that I might even be justifiably censured without discernment by spiritual people, if I had a strong urging of the Holy Spirit in me to engage in the strife, error, and attacks referred to above. Then I would slowly and sadly submit and desist. It is not that I desire to resist the prompting of the Holy Spirit! God forbid! Rather, my reason is to test the prompting carefully, not because of the Holy Spirit, but because of my own human inability, weakness, ignorance, lack of understanding, folly, inconstancy, and fickleness.[8, 9*]

The following must be included in testing the urging of the Holy Spirit. Have I been clothed with power from above[10] to cover my weakness, to turn my inability into an ability? Do I sense and recognize the true knowledge, wisdom, and understanding of God over against my ignorance and folly, in order to know wisdom? Have I laid hold of steadfastness based on the firm foundation of truth to counter my fickleness?[11] Only then may I accept the urging of the Holy Spirit with fear, anxiety, and trembling, in order to act with certainty and not uncertainty.[12]

However, no one should hide behind what I have just written with a deceptive appearance or deliberate obstruction, but persevere in good

---

6 [Here the author makes his central point: good can come only from the urging of the Spirit; our own motives and goals, as well as "unknown causes," cannot be our foundation.—Ed.]

7 Col 2:23.

8 [These are densely written thoughts. Marpeck seems to be caught between powerful convictions he wants to put forth and the realization that his motives are mixed and his understanding is partial.—Ed.]

9* Gloss: The Holy Spirit often drives the guilty to their own fall because of their presumptuousness, in order that they acquire self-knowledge. [Inserted here, this gloss leaves the impression that the editor is addressing his judgment against Marpeck rather than (or as well as) his opponents.—Ed.]

10 Lk 24:49.

11 Prv 22:21; 2 Tm 2:19.

12 1 Cor 9:26.

faith in the fear of God. For the enemy of our salvation does not sleep or even take a nap[13] with his cunning and deception, to lead people astray everywhere.[14] He stirs up much discord and fighting in humankind—and they do not know why. He makes a persuasive appearance of godly zeal, although he is concerned only for himself and not for divine honour and truth. Thus he mortally wounds people and brings them to the verge of destruction, from which they are saved, won, and healed again only with great difficulty. Whoever meddles to separate people[15] without a specific urging and command of God sustains great harm, indeed destruction. Examples of this abound.

I am not writing this to show that you are forsaken by God but to admonish you earnestly not to enter into quarrelling and strife with one another. Bear with one another in sincere love[16] and confess your sins to each other[17] in trust, to bring about true repentance. For we are not ignorant of the designs of our enemy,[18] for he is the greatest envier and hater of human salvation.

Therefore it behooves us to watch over our souls,[19] our own and each other's,[20] especially to observe and search out whether the enemy has secretly started a fire in our innermost heart, conscience, and soul, in order to consume soul, conscience, and heart in the wrath of God. There is a hidden fire among you which has an evil, stinking smoke and the taste of fire, which the enemy of truth is seeking to conceal in order that he may ignite, destroy, and burn to ashes many hearts before it is discovered, as the means of the wrath of God which burns brightly everywhere.[21*, 22] He kindles his strife with deceit, lies, cunning, false suspicion, evil faultfinding, mistrust, gossip, blandishment, flattery, greed

---

13 [Original: *entnuckt = einninken* ("To take a nap").—Trans.]

14 1 Pt 5:8.

15 [This seems to be a reference to excommunication.—Ed.]

16 Eph 4:2.

17 Jas 5:16.

18 2 Cor 2:11.

19 Heb 13:17.

20 Heb 10:24.

21* Hidden fire.

22 [Original: *Alsdann, mitl im feur des zorn Gotes, so es zům höchstenn prynnt an allen orten.*—Trans.]

for personal honour, scolding, slandering, anger, envy, hate, antipathy, unfriendliness, stubbornness, boastfulness, and pride. From this it follows that no one will yield to anyone else.

These are the weapons of his knighthood,[23] with which he conducts his campaign to sneak up on and slay people. Now when the fire in the houses (that is, human hearts in which God should dwell) burns most fiercely—so that fire and sword, hunger after the truth[24] and famine,[25] meet—then he looks about for help lest it be too late.[26*, 27]

The time to rescue and defend with haste is before it is all but burned down. First you need to intervene and obstruct the cunning, deadly strokes of the enemy with the sharpness of the word of truth,[28] even if you have already been fatally wounded.[29*]

First, the hungry must be given bread to eat, and the thirsty good wine to drink (that is, the comfort of the Holy Spirit), so that the heart may be made glad,[30] since the enemy has ravaged and consumed it, scattered and slain the builders and workers, and devastated the earth (that is, us mortals). What can one worker do in such a situation? He really ought also to be burned, killed, or die of hunger, since the earth has been cursed, laid waste, and execrated.

I do not write this to point at someone specifically but only for our mutual warning, so that we put out the fire and save one another, and that we apply the greatest earnestness, care, and diligence to get each other out of the fire before we perish. We must learn to fight with the sword of the Word[31] before we are attacked, wounded, and killed by the enemy with the weapons described above. We must not allow our land

---

23 2 Cor 10:4.

24 Am 8:11; Mt 5:6.

25 1 Sm 2:36.

26* Gloss: The fire must be understood to mean the wrath of God, the sword to mean the deceit and cunning of the enemies. On the other hand, there is the sharp sword of God's Word that slays those who resist. Then comes the withdrawal of the word of grace and the faithful builders, workers, and servants.

27 Heb 4:12.

28 2 Tm 2:15.

29* Note.

30 Ps 104:15.

31 Eph 6:17; Heb 4:12.

and soil to be wasted and to bear thorns and thistles;[32] if this happens, the curse is near.[33] We are not to surrender it to the destruction of the enemy, but rather build up our earthly body and root out the weeds which grow from the evil seed of the enemy.[34] This is in order that the blessing of God may follow our labour, so that the fruit may prosper. If there are faithful builders and labourers, they should be loved and respected.[35] If fruit is produced by the blessing of God, it should be supported, cared for, and given diligent attention. Let us not leave the bread lying underfoot or carelessly throw out the wine that gladdens our hearts.[36] Thus, when hunger and thirst come, we can be comforted by them, made glad, satisfied, and guided.

I declare before God that great gifts and the fruits of God's blessing could have come in our time through many faithful workers. If only we had been more careful of the fruit, if we had stored and kept it in the cupboard of our hearts, since it came to our doors so utterly without cost! Had we truly cared for and gathered it and thanked God for it, it would surely not have been possible for us to go to someone else for bread and run around begging. We would have our fill,[37] and enough for all other peoples.

Still, my God, we can only lament about ourselves before you, for the fault is ours and not yours! You have richly given to us, but we have given meagre thanks. Nor have we listened diligently. That is why we are in dire need in all places and in many ways, so that we must now search for what we did not care for and have lost. Now we have to call on you with shame on our faces. And even if you should continually turn us away,[38] refusing to hear or advise us, you would do no wrong. For first you recompense us for our carelessness and idleness, in order to rouse our sleepy spirits and warm our lukewarm hearts with the fire of poverty. Thus, my God, you have ample right to tell us that we ought

32 Is 5:6.
33 Heb 6:8.
34 Mt 13:25.
35 Lk 10:7; 1 Tm 5:18.
36 Ps 104:15.
37 Jn 10:10.
38 [Original: *verweisst* (could also mean "approve").—Trans.]

to be ashamed of our request because we have regarded as trifling your gift and grace.

Nevertheless, we will continue shamelessly and importunately[39] to beg with hope that you will listen to us for the sake of your own peace. And we will not be surprised or deterred from our urgent prayer by your delay, in the hope that you will grant us assistance to fill our needs.

No one who has not felt it knows how hot the fire of God's wrath is. Nor does anyone who has not often gained salvation and victory in battle know the strategy of the enemy and the injuries he can inflict with his poisoned weapons. Likewise, only someone who has been thirsty and hungry knows what true hunger and thirst is. In these experiences God teaches his own to care for,[40] protect, and watch over[41] their souls for his sake, and to pray earnestly not to be led into and be destroyed by temptation,[42] should it come.

Truly, my dear brothers, in a variety of ways the Lord sends a concise, direct word[43] to those people to save their souls. Regardless of the form, whether it be in writing or in speech, it behooves us to accept (as Christ himself) whatever in them is the testimony and the truth. Because of our carnal mind, many things are difficult to understand and incomprehensible; because of guilt and human weakness, we may not immediately be able to understand or grasp something, yet the time does come when we grasp and receive it with thanksgiving.[44] It is when we are in tribulation, under the rod in the school of Christ, that we truly learn to understand and become wise with the wise.

Thus St. Paul says: "Test everything; keep the good, and discard the evil."[45] He has written many things in great wisdom and divine earnestness, some of which are hard to understand. Peter testifies to this when he says: "About which our dear brother Paul writes much (no-

---

39 Lk 11:8.

40 2 Chr 6:27; Ps 25:4, 9; etc.

41 Heb 13:17.

42 Mt 6:13; Lk 11:4.

43 1 Sm 3:1.

44 Am 8:11.

45 1 Thes 5:21.

tice, much!), of which some things are hard to understand, and which the ignorant twist—as also they do other scriptures—to their own destruction."[46]

Thus it behooves us to examine and test all things carefully, and not judge, reject, misinterpret, or falsify what we do not understand, in order that in so doing we do not condemn ourselves and be plunged into error. For the gifts of the Holy Spirit are weighty.[47] He moves as,[48] when, and where he wills, giving them to whomever he desires, through scriptures, speech, discipline, terror, tribulation, and judgment, as he desires and pleases. He gives gifts through profound as well as mediocre understanding, in length as well as breadth, in height as well as depth.[49] Everything is his.[50] He is Lord and sovereign over all, over written and spoken scriptures which people test, learn, experience, witness to, and judge, to the praise of God and their own salvation. With them they judge themselves and others.

Therefore whoever despises and scorns the written and spoken aid of the Holy Spirit[51] accuses him and all that he offers.[52*] Such a person acts as though it would do more harm than good, as if it were better not to write or speak so much. He scorns and mocks what he has never known,[53] the very thing that serves his salvation. He wants to teach the Holy Spirit how to give his gifts, thus putting himself in the place that belongs to God the Holy Spirit alone.[54]

Thus it would be well for everyone to take care what he says against the spoken and written gifts of the Holy Spirit, against whom he complains[55] and speaks, and whether it is human beings or God that he

---

46 2 Pt 3:15f.

47 [This sentence and the following one appear incomplete: *Dann schwär ist, die gaben des h[eilige]n geists, die er geistet, etc.* There is no main verb.—Trans.]

48 Jn 3:8.

49 Eph 3:18.

50 1 Cor 12:6; Eph 1:23; Col 1:17.

51 Phil 1:19; 1 Thes 5:20.

52* Note.

53 Col 2:18; 2 Pt 2:12; Jude 10.

54 Mt 24:15; Mk 13:14.

55 [Original: *wurmle*. Possible copyist's error for *murmle* ("murmur," "complain")—Trans.]

mocks and scorns. Only evil is not of God; all good gifts come from God.[56] Therefore one must hold on to what God loves and let go of evil, which God hates. May God save us from such judgments, despising, scorn, and accusation. For it would be an abominable error to despise the written and spoken gifts of the Holy Spirit. Far be it from us!

I write this because you have never given me a co-witness in the Holy Spirit[57] or gratitude to God for my repeated writing. We owe him this because these are his gifts. Fear and worry have seized me and have caused me to write you in my faithful care for you, to save and shield our souls from the deceit and cunning of the enemy of our salvation.

May our heavenly Father grant this through Jesus Christ our Lord from now on to eternity. Amen.

Fervent greetings in Jesus Christ to each of you by name from me and all of us. Let us pray to God earnestly to save us from this and all our temptations. Amen.

Dated at Augsburg, the ninth day of August in the year[58] 1551.

In the Lord Jesus Christ,
servant to you and all the truly believing servants
and comrades in the tribulation of Christ,[59]
Pilgram Marpeck

---

56 Jas 1:17.

57 [For Marpeck the notion of "co-witness" is integral to the dynamic of God's work. Just as the persons of the Trinity co-witness with one another, so also bread and wine are co-witnesses with faith to the presence of Christ in the Supper. In this instance Marpeck is asking for corroboration that what he had written the believers in St. Gall is true.—Ed.]

58 [Original: *anno*.—Trans.]

59 Rv 1:9.

35

Concerning the lowliness of Christ

To the congregations in the Grisons (Graubünden), Appenzell, St. Gall, and in the Alsace

Pilgram Marpeck

Augsburg, 1 February 1547

"Concerning the Lowliness of Christ" is a pastoral letter of theological substance. Author Pilgram Marpeck's interest is ultimately a pastoral one, but to make his case he turns to the incarnation and the relationships within the Trinity. His description of the role of the Spirit in relation to that of the Son is especially well developed in this epistle. The way to church unity, according to Marpeck, is to follow the pattern of Christ's willing humiliation, most strikingly demonstrated by his descent into hell. This treatise manifests Marpeck's ongoing commitment to achieving unity between the Swiss and Pilgramites. Metaphors and allegories abound in his argument. He begins by offering his hearers a belated New Year's wish. He follows the custom of giving gifts on this occasion by commending Christ as the great treasure. Those who receive the giver and the gifts are his temple and his priests, as well as his earthly vessels.

Marpeck addresses his hearers—among whom are Swiss Brethren congregations—as "elect and saints." This spirit of generosity toward

---

Pilgram Marpeck an die Gemeinden in Graubünden, Appenzell, St. Gallen und im Elsaß: Von der Tiefe Christi; Augsburg, 1. Februar 1547. Translation by Walter Klaassen. Previously published in WPM, 427–63. Reprinted, with editorial changes, by permission of the publisher.

other Anabaptists continues throughout. The date of the letter, "this critical time of great danger," is significant for a second reason. It was written during the Schmalkaldian War of 1546–47, a contest between Catholic and Lutheran forces for the dominance of south German cities. It was financed largely by the Fugger family of Augsburg.[1] Marpeck had worked for the Fuggers as a young mining magistrate, so his critique of the financing of warfare later in this epistle is an informed one.

His theological starting point, as usual, is the Gospel of John. At its heart is the claim that no one knows the Father except the Son and those to whom the Son has made him known (1:18). It is by means of his "physical"— outward—words and actions that the Son makes the Father known: "by means of the earthly and in his earthiness [the human being] may become heavenly through the incarnation of Christ." This single pregnant concept is the starting point for almost everything in Marpeck's theological and pastoral writings.

In his description of the treasures Christ has brought the world, the author turns to the analogy of an ark. "Everything that God had to give humanity was 'locked up' in the human body of Jesus, just as things are 'locked up' in an ark. The cross represents the opening of the ark to all those who believe. That happened, however, because Christ was willing to accept complete and utter humiliation, even to the *descensus ad inferos*, which Marpeck specifically states was not a triumphant descent but the nadir of his humiliation."[2]

"Such a belief provides a direct link to Marpeck's concern for the Swiss Brethren. Christ's saints do not rule or exercise power. They first follow Christ in his humiliation."[3] Indeed, "here, only the deep humility

---

1 See photograph on page 304.

2 WPM, 427. Schwenckfeld misrepresented Marpeck's view of Christ's descent into hell. In a 24 March 1549 letter, written under a pseudonym to two of his followers, Schwenckfeld accuses Marpeck of teaching that Christ had to complete his sufferings not on the cross but with his descent into hell, and that "in Hell the Devil installed him as High Priest." See E. E. Schultz Johnson, ed., *Letters and Treatises of Caspar Schwenckfeld von Ossig 1547–1550*, Corpus Schwenckfeldianorum 11 (Leipzig: Breitkopf & Härtel, 1914).

3 Ibid.

of Christ brings any possibility of salvation." Appeals to his divinity that avoid sharing in the sorrows of his humanity are bad theology.

Marpeck makes the case that every believer has been given gifts but that they have been given to human beings "in earthly vessels which easily break. Therefore they must be handled with care, patience and love. Patience is, in fact, the 'ark' which preserves all that God has to give his own. . . . Indeed, Marpeck insists that there is a close relationship between hasty judgments and actions against fellow saints, and the violence practised by Catholics and Protestants in their religious intolerance. Faith cannot be coerced in any form, and to justify coercion on allegedly Christian grounds does not make it any less the devil's work. He emphasizes that all such violence brings only ruin in its train. In a marginal gloss, editor Jörg Maler provides the examples of Ulrich Zwingli's war with the Catholics, and the Schmalkaldian War between Catholics and Protestants."[4] War, "Marpeck reminds his readers, is what happens when people do not abandon all claims to power and submit to the lowliness of Christ."[5]

"If, then, Christians live in absolute liberty in Christ, how are they guided in their actions?"[6] Marpeck answers that it is both through the "external service" of Christ, such as teaching, baptism, and discipline, and through the inner guidance of the Holy Spirit, to whom the ministries of Jesus in his humanity point. The outward does not automatically embody the inward: the two become one only when the Spirit copies the law of Christ onto the hearts of believers. It is in them, rather than in buildings or "external rites in and of themselves,"[7] that God dwells. "It is an eloquent description of a pilgrim church."[8] Heinold Fast concludes that this dynamic is what distinguishes Pilgram Marpeck's attempt to develop an alternative ecclesiology and ethic from that of Spiritualism and sacramentalism.[9]

---

4 Ibid., 427–28.

5 Ibid., 428.

6 Ibid.

7 Ibid.

8 Ibid.

9 Bern MS, no. 35, 1.

Concerning the lowliness of Christ, together with other fine expositions also concerning the New Year

To all the elect and saints of God in the Grisons (Graubünden), Appenzell, St. Gall, in the Alsace, and wherever they are scattered hither and yon, my dearest ones in Christ.

Grace and peace from God our Father and our Lord Jesus Christ[10] be and remain with us forever. Amen.

My dearly beloved in God the Father and the Lord Jesus Christ. Especially in this critical time of great danger, my fervent prayer and desire now and always is that one of these days,[11] before my end, God might open the way to come to all of you. There together we might rejoice in the way, truth, and life which is Jesus Christ;[12] discuss his will, mind, and Spirit which are given in word, deed, and act; and share our delight in the love and truth of the gospel of Christ.

This is the message that Christ in his grace has given, commanded, and delivered to us. It is the costliest and most esteemed treasure, for it is Christ the Lord himself [Col 2 (3)]. In this treasure are hidden all the treasures of the secret will and pleasure of the Father. No one has seen the Father, much less known him, except the Son who is in the bosom of the Father.[13] Similarly, no one has known the Son except the

---

10 Rom 1:7; etc.

11 1 Sm 3:1.

12 Jn 14:6.

13 Jn 1:18.

Father who sent him.[14] The Son reveals his Father in his holy, physical[15] teaching. And the miracle and power of his works on earth are the Father's physical testimony to the Son's teaching. He to whom the Father has not been revealed cannot, and may not, know the Father of lights.[16] Similarly, no one can know that Jesus Christ is the Son of the living God unless the Father reveals it to him.[17] Thus the Son is glorified through the Father and the Father through the Son[18] in the sight of humankind on earth.

He was born to the Father from the human race for our sake to liberate us from the power of the devil,[19] sin,[20] death,[21] and hell, that is, from the guilt of Adam into which all human beings have come through the guilt of sin, and because of the pains of hell and death which were laid on mortals.[22] In addition, they have been given over to the devil, who has the power of death and torment[23] as well as of sin. And it is sin that causes the wrath of God[24] so that for those among the whole human race who do not possess the salvation given by the Son of God, there can be no cessation of sin.[25] Thus the wrath of God delivers us to sin, death, hell, pain, and the devil. Because of the one sin of disobedience, humankind is no longer ever able to know its God, Father, and Creator.[26] Even today we are utterly under the wrath of God and because of sin[27] we are outside of Christ, the Lord and Saviour. However, because of our sin the Father did not spare the Son.[28] He has given him up for

---

14 Mt 11:27.

15 [Original: *leiplich* (literally, "bodily" or "physical").—Trans.]

16 Jas 1:17.

17 Mt 16:17.

18 Jn 17:1.

19 1 Jn 3:8.

20 1 Tm 1:15.

21 Heb 2:14f.

22 Rom 5:21; 1 Cor 15:21.

23 Heb 2:14.

24 Rom 1:18.

25 Jn 3:36.

26 Jn 16:3; 17:3.

27 Gal 3:22.

28 Rom 8:32.

the sake of many and delivered him into the suffering and pain of death, even to condemnation, as salvation for all people.[29]

Thus Christ's sufferings enable us to regain the original purity and innocence in which we were created pure and good, to be prepared for our God, Father, Creator, and Maker [Ws 1 (14)].[30] The Holy Spirit, who cannot be where sin is, can again find a place and gain a dwelling in people, and then transfer them from the earthly to the heavenly. The human being is created in what is earthly; by means of the earthly and in his earthliness he may become heavenly through the incarnation of Christ.[31]

Had Adam not fallen, there would be no need for suffering. But because of sin, suffering and death came upon Christ.[32] And unlike us, who experience suffering and death because of guilt, Christ is without guilt. Grace, and the justification that leads to true devotion and which proceeds from faith,[33] transfers us from the earthly to the eternal, heavenly state.[34] Therefore all earthly creatures are made subject to us[35] in order that we might be made subject to the Lord Jesus Christ in his heavenly state and glory. Similarly, in true humanity the Son is subject to the Father.

By the will of the Father, he was born of a virgin from the generation of the fathers. He was born the true Son of God, full of grace and truth[36] and according to the Spirit. He is the eternal Word and the only born Son of the Father. He is filled with every counsel and knowledge, wisdom, understanding, and perception of the Father's will. As announced in Is 9 [6]: "For to us a child is born, a son is given, and the kingship shall be upon his shoulder." As Samuel told the people of Israel when

---

29 Mt 20:28.

30 1 Tm 4:4.

31 [The wording for this foundational construct of Marpeck's thought is crucial: *Darum dan der mensch inn das irdisch erschaffen ist, durch das irdisch und im irdischen himlisch zů werden durch die vermenschung Christi.*—Ed.]

32 Rom 5:12; 6:23.

33 Rom 1:17.

34 [Original: *wesen.*—Trans.]

35 Gn 1:26.

36 Jn 1:14.

like the Gentiles they desired a king, the kings of this world rest their kingship as a heavy burden upon the shoulders of the people [1 Sm 2 (8:11–18)]. Such a king had the right to expect that his kingship should rest on the shoulders of the people, that they should bear the burden of the king.

However, this king, I mean the Lord Jesus Christ, has liberated his people from their eternal burden; he has put it on his own shoulders and has fastened it to the cross [1 Pt 2 (24)].[37] Can we conceive of a more glorious kingdom, priesthood, kingship, or king? Isaiah further says that his name is "Wonderful Counsellor, the Mighty God, the Everlasting Father, the Prince of Peace. His kingdom shall have no end, and peace will be multiplied."[38] This child has been given to us by the Father with all his treasures and gifts.

That same Lord, king, and true God has given himself with all his treasures and gifts, and he himself will be the acceptable new year.[39, 40*] These treasures were hidden and locked in the trunk[41] of his body, the ark of the covenant.[42*] This ark he destroyed on the cross, and then he pried it open, which was the finishing of his work.[43] The child fulfilled the Father's promise to us. The suffering and death on the cross completed his work on earth. Then he made the descent into hell and dwelled with the condemned, with those imprisoned in perdition, and with those held by death.[44] As Christ himself said on earth and in the abyss: "My God, why have you forsaken me?"[45]

In the depth of death and in the abyss of hell, the Lord of both life and death proclaimed the gospel to the dead. Here the soul of Christ preached the gospel. On earth, Christ's physical suffering and death proclaimed the Word to those living in the body. Just as it was on earth,

---

37 Col 2:14.

38 Is 9:5f.

39 Lk 4:19.

40* New year.

41 [Original: *der truhen* ("the chest" or "the coffin").—Trans.]

42* Ark of the covenant.

43 Jn 19:30.

44 1 Pt 3:19f.; 4:6.

45 Ps 22:1; Mt 27:46; Mk 15:34.

among the dead in the prison of hell, all faith and hope had disappeared. Because of the guilt of the first Adam, death and hell had seized and held captive the promise of the salvation to come on earth as well as to the prisoners of death and hell in the abyss. Then all faith and hope disappeared from the earth and from the dead in the pit.

The parable and prediction of the prophet Jonah was fulfilled in Christ. Even as Jonah was swallowed by the physical leviathan[46] in the physical depth of the sea [Jon 2 (1)], so too was the Lord, together with the rest of the dead, swallowed and made captive by the spiritual leviathan, the lord of the spiritual sea, of torment and death, who has power eternally. Contrary to the view held by some erring spirits, Christ did not descend in triumph to the dead.[47*] Such a fabrication contradicts the true teaching of Christ. Even as Jonah sang a song of triumph in the whale,[48] Christ triumphed in hell and death. The Lord himself points to it and says: "No sign will be given except the sign of Jonah. Just as Jonah was in the belly of the whale three days and three nights, even so, the Son of Man will be in the middle of the earth three days and three nights" [Mt 12 (39f.)]. Just as Jonah was in the whale only a short while, Christ remained in death and hell until for our sake he had completely paid the guilt of sin.

Thus the Father did not spare the Son but gave him up so that all who believe in him may have eternal life [Rom 8 (32); Jn 3 (16)]. The Father sealed the guilt of sin (the human spirit and soul)[49] in death and in the prison of hell forever. In his human poverty, the payer of the debt, the true warrantor, went into the depths of hell with our sins, and yet without any sin of his own, through his torment on earth in order to make payment with his body. Moreover, he took the power away from death and from him who has the dominion over pain and death [Heb 2 (14)].

The whale could not hold Jonah, nor could the pit hold him there. Life broke through in its power, which the Lord had had in himself

---

46 Jb 3:8; 41:1; Is 27:1.

47* Schwenckfeld, etc.

48 Jon 2:3–9.

49 [This parenthesis is difficult to interpret. Perhaps it means that the guilt of sin is incurred by the spirit and soul.—Ed.]

against all the power of hell. By means of the glory, dominion, and power of life, he took life back again out of the midst of death, together with all who had hoped for the Lord and his salvation![50] Their hope, and also the hope of the apostles on earth,[51] was gone. For their very sakes the joy, splendour, and glory of Christ has ascended to the heights, not only with all the imprisoned, but with the prison itself.[52] Paul's question is appropriate here: "Death, hell, devil, and sin, where is your power and dominion?" [1 Cor 15 (55)].

Thus, for the first time, death has been swallowed up in victory, and Christ has emerged from death to life with all his chosen ones.[53] To do so, he had both to descend and ascend, for his soul did not remain in hell.[54] Death could not possibly keep the life of all life imprisoned [Ps 15 (16:10)], and darkness could not put out or comprehend the light,[55] even though the light had come into the darkness of hell. Since the light himself was imprisoned and held by darkness, there were three hours of darkness over the whole earth[56] not from some natural cause but from the irruption of the pit, which is the source of all darkness. The true light, which had the most right to shine, did not assert his power, and since he himself had commanded all other lights to shine, the natural lights then had to surrender their brilliance.[57]

But the Lord, as the true light,[58] has broken out of the darkness of the devil, death, sin, and hell, through the brilliance of his light and clarity and returned alive from death. In his own power he took life back; he ascended and seated himself to the right of the majesty of God the Father[59] and in the glorification of the Father, with that eternal,

---

50 [That is, all the believers of the Old Testament who were saved by their hope and expectation of God's salvation.—Ed.]

51 [At the death of Christ.—Ed.]

52 Ps 68:19; Eph 4:8.

53 Jn 5:24.

54 Eph 4:8f.

55 Jn 1:5.

56 Mt 27:45; Mk 15:33; Lk 23:44.

57 Gn 1:16–18.

58 Jn 1:9.

59 Mk 16:19; Heb 1:3; 10:12; 12:2; 1 Pt 3:22.

preexistent glory which he had with the Father before the foundation of the world was laid.[60]

The Son conquered the sin of many precisely by this skilful descent into the depths,[61] this greatest humility with which he humbled himself before the Father, and by which the Father afflicted and humbled the Son.[62] All the saints of God must learn the depths of Christ,[63] these same depths of humility and damnation, into which the leaven of our sin brought Christ. They must learn the consequences of sin. Provided the devil completes[64] sin's work in us, sin brings us into death.[65] Here only the deep humility of Christ brings any possibility of salvation. Whoever does not grasp that he must be condemned with and in Christ in the depths can never understand or achieve the height of Christ.[66] Indeed, the whole world does not want to grasp this depth of Christ; it does not want to be condemned, to recognize its lostness, and so be saved [Mt 16 (25)].[67]

However, almost everyone babbles and boasts deceitfully about the height and divinity of Christ, and uses reason and scriptural subtleties[68] to find a false sufficiency of joy in themselves. Yet no one is prepared to go down with Christ through baptism into death and be buried with him [Rom 6 (3f.)]. They reach for the height [of Christ], in order to deceive themselves and others. Thus they must go down to destruction and suffer eternal exclusion from the height of Christ.

Baptism is a secret, severe water which drives all reason down into the depth to die with Christ and be buried in his death.[69*, 70] How else can we rise with Christ and become a partaker of his gifts and the treasures of his kingdom, which he distributes to all his chosen ones

60 Jn 17:5.
61 [Original: *kunst*.—Trans.]
62 Is 53:12.
63 Eph 3:18.
64 [Original: *verbracht*; likely, *vollbracht*.—Trans.]
65 Rom 5:17; Jas 1:15.
66 Eph 3:18.
67 Mk 8:35.
68 Original: *kunst*; the context suggests subtlety in a pejorative sense.
69* Baptism.
70 2 Cor 10:5.

and gives to his own?[71] That is how the Son makes the Father known, and the Father makes known and reveals the Son.[72] The elect are glorified in them, just as the Father and Son are glorified in and with themselves.[73]

But all this has been revealed and learned first through the incarnation of Christ, in the depth and humiliation of Christ through his holy humanity. His power and miracles proved that we could believe what the Lord said, did, and accomplished on earth.[74] He has received it all from the Father. To his honour and glory, he has opened it to us. Thus our lives are renewed in order that we should eternally honour, praise, and thank the heavenly Father through his beloved Son.

To the honour and glory of the Father, he has sealed us with the Holy Spirit.[75] As the true Prince of Peace, he has established eternal, perpetual peace with us in our hearts and consciences.[76]

He never ceases to increase the kingdom of his peace,[77] not in the world's manner,[78] but eternally and without end. He gives not only peace but also joy and comfort. Hence, no disaster may ever come near the dwelling which is God and man eternally, Jesus Christ himself, in whom all believers dwell and he in them.[79, 80*]

After this temple or tabernacle of his body had been broken, he raised it up again on the third day.[81] The hearts of all the faithful were made temples and dwellings of God, in which God, Father, Son, and Holy Spirit live, govern, and reign in righteousness, godliness, faithful-

---

71 Ps 68:18; Eph 4:8f.
72 Mt 11:27; Lk 10:22.
73 Jn 13:31f.; 17:1ff.
74 Jn 17:4.
75 2 Cor 1:22; Eph 1:13; 4:30.
76 Eph 2:14.
77 Is 9:6f.
78 Jn 14:27.
79 Ps 91:10; Jn 14:23.
80* Gloss: The faithful have their dwelling and safety in the temple of Christ's body. Thus the Father and Son, after the manner of deity, have their dwelling in the hearts of all the faithful through the action of the Spirit.
81 Jn 2:19–21.

ness, and truth, from now until eternity.[82*, 83] Thus all the faithful live and dwell in the risen temple of the body of Christ,[84*, 85] which is built, raised, and erected to the right of the majesty of God, the almighty, heavenly Father.[86] The Father himself has prepared and erected this temple for himself, for in it the one God, the Father, Word, and Holy Spirit, dwells eternally. He dwells nowhere else, and God cannot be found or comprehended at any other place or location eternally; nor can he be known, seen, or heard anywhere else.[87]

In this inner chancel,[88] the sublime and holiest place, God allows himself to be apprehended, seen, and heard. As the true mercy seat,[89] the place of worship in the Spirit and in truth is now this sole temple [Jn 4 (23f.)].[90*] Because of the sharp sword of the Word, which proceeds out of the mouth of him who sits on the throne,[91] nothing unclean can approach this holiest place,[92] the transfigured body of Jesus [Heb 5 (4)]. In this temple all the faithful find pardon and rest for their souls,[93] yes, all that is needful for their life, and all the treasures, glory, and pleasure of the temple, in which God himself is the highest adornment, treasure, and glory eternally. For this reason all the faithful, like David, properly demand what they have prayed for: that they may remain in the house of God their whole life and behold the pleasure of his temple.[94] They

---

82* Temples and dwellings.

83 1 Cor 3:16f., 19; 2 Cor 6:16; Eph 3:17; Rv 3:12.

84* Note.

85 Jn 2:21.

86 [It is not just Christ who is seated at the right hand of the Father; his body the church is also seated there.—Ed.]

87 [Marpeck is here directing himself against the Roman teaching, which propounds the presence of God in the Eucharist. Marpeck also directs criticism against the popular assumption that he is to be found in temples "made with human hands," that is, in church buildings.—Ed.]

88 1 Kgs 6:16, 19; etc.

89 Ex 25:17; etc.; Rom 3:25; 4:16.

90* Worship.

91 Heb 4:12; Rv 1:16.

92 Lv 21:21; Ps 24:3f.; etc.

93 Mt 11:29.

94 Ps 27:4.

would rather be doorkeepers than live in the dwellings of the godless.[95] For your soul, and for my own, I fervently wish you all these things, that you might have an acceptable year,[96] which all the faithful ought properly to explore.[97]

I wish to briefly discuss this acceptable year, in which everything, including the treasures given us with Christ, has become new in Christ.[98*] We should see and observe the pleasure of the temple of his body[99] and thus comfort and make glad our souls. Indeed, we should fall into wonderment and thank our God and Father for it. Whoever does not contemplate the gift in order to attend to the giver rather than the gift cannot understand either the gift or the giver. He may neither love either of them properly nor truly thank the giver.

All gifts are given to us by God,[100] and they are given for two reasons. First, in them we can learn to know our Creator, God, and Father, and thus with a pure heart we may glorify, praise, and thank him.[101*] Second, we are to use the gifts to serve one another[102] and not to lord it over one another.[103, 104*] And if we accomplish something to the praise of the Lord and the benefit of the neighbour, we do not rejoice over it. Our highest joy shall be that in heaven our names are written in the book of life (Lk 10 [20]). To show, with unwavering faith and certain hope, love toward our neighbour, and thus prove our love of God,[105] is and shall be our highest joy. Not the work but love itself, to serve and to be a guardian of the salvation of all the elect of God, is heavenly joy.[106]

---

95 Ps 84:10.

96 Is 61:2; Lk 4:19.

97 [Given the time of the letter's writing and the following gloss, this seems to be a New Year's wish.—Ed.]

98* New year, etc.

99 Jn 2:21.

100 Jas 1:17.

101* 1.

102 1 Pt 4:10.

103 1 Pt 5:3.

104* 2.

105 1 Cor 13:13.

106 2 Cor 1:24.

Therefore we are obligated to contemplate and pay attention to the treasures and most precious gems of Christ;[107*] we are obligated to explore, to fathom, and to observe them diligently, and in the shrine of our hearts[108] to protect them carefully from thieves and murderers. Thus one may discover what a wonderful, acceptable new year the heavenly Father has given and committed to us to proclaim through his child Jesus Christ.[109] Isaiah 61 [1-3] speaks about the child and Lord and his kingdom; he also speaks of the Lord's servants, messengers, and ambassadors, and their office, and what they are to accomplish in the power of the Spirit.

Therefore the Lord has given the Holy Spirit to his ambassadors and servants for this office. Isaiah says: "The Spirit of the Lord is upon me, for the Lord has anointed me and sent me to announce good news to the poor, to bind up wounded hearts, to announce deliverance to the captives, and to open the prison-house of those in bondage. I am to announce the year of the Lord's favour and the vengeance of our God, comfort all who mourn and give beauty instead of ashes to those who lament in Zion. I am to give them a happy anointing instead of a stench, a beautiful garment instead of a heavy heart. They will be called gods of righteousness, a planting of the Lord in which he will exult."[110*] This text clearly describes the service of the Lord himself and the office of his ambassadors in this time of our mortal life, which all ambassadors still have. We should take care that we do not speak evil of this precious treasure.[111] Paul says: "That we may comprehend, together with all the saints of God, the depth and the height, the length and the breadth of Christ, yes, the love which surpasses all understanding and knowledge" [Eph 3 (18)]. To this end, all the chosen of God must strive to follow the pattern and example given to us by the Lord himself.[112]

107* Observe treasures.

108 Mt 12:35; Lk 6:45.

109 2 Pt 1:3f.

110* Gloss: Christ's garment of innocence for sin. The prisoners, the sick, and those wounded in spirit.

111 Rom 14:16.

112 1 Pt 2:21.

The servant is not, nor will he ever be, above his Lord,[113] nor will the disciple be above his master, or the apostle above him who sent him.[114] The Lord himself has tested this principle; so too will it also be tested in his servants.

The Lord has opened, given, and revealed his priceless treasure and gift without price. Through his divine skill, he has unlocked and released the scriptures, the most sublime and learned old and new treasure,[115] written for himself by the Holy Spirit. All the patriarchs, law, and prophets point to him. Then, according to the fullness of understanding and knowledge of the Father, the fullness of Godhead appeared bodily in Christ himself [Col 2 (9)]. Indeed, this was said and will be said.

This is the conclusion concerning the old and new treasure. Moses gave the law,[116] and the prophets predicted the future grace, until John,[117] the baptizer unto repentance, prepared the way of the Lord. The old treasure was given because of sin,[118*] and it was to point sinners and to lead them, in faith and hope, to the future grace accomplished by the Spirit of Christ[119] in the law, the prophets, and John, who pointed with his finger to the Lord as the true Lamb of God that takes away the sin of the world.[120] Through the Lamb, the Lord Jesus Christ, grace and truth have appeared.[121] On the cross his death and blood,[122] offered up for the remission and forgiveness of sins, fulfilled grace and truth. There on the cross, the old was completed, and there the new treasure, the grace and truth which Christ brought with him,

---

113 Mt 10:24; Lk 6:40.
114 Jn 13:16.
115 Mt 13:52.
116 Jn 1:17.
117 Mt 11:13.
118* Old treasure.
119 2 Pt 1:21.
120 Jn 1:29.
121 Jn 1:17.
122 Acts 3:18.

was offered.[123*] Thus our greatest scribe and treasurer gave everyone his due in his time.[124]

Similarly, it behooves all the apostles and evangelists, who are the scribes of the Holy Spirit, to give to each in his time his due out of the old and new treasure [Mt 24 (45) and 13 (52)]. The old treasure, the law and the prophets, still minister to the old Adam. They live in his sin and under his sin, for they live only in their first birth according to the flesh. As his first grace, Christ in his fullness gives them the old treasure. God's stern wrath, his penalty and vengeance, are proclaimed against all ungodly creatures.[125] They are shown that they must repent, forsake sin, and show regret and remorse for their sin. A genuine sorrowing is begun in their hearts, by which they are bruised and made captive and ill in their consciences. Thus they are prepared for the Lord, the true physician.[126] The old treasure applies solely to the children of the first Adamic birth, and their repentance from sin rightly comes from the old treasure. Thus, through the Holy Spirit who preceded him, the Lord Jesus Christ worked in John and the prophets.[127]

In the same way, according to the measure of his will,[128] he fills his servants with such skill, wisdom, and understanding, in order that they may administer in the right manner, according to time, measure, and apportionment, his treasures and wealth. The true treasure is Christ himself. He is the fulfilment of all in all,[129] be it skill, wisdom, understanding, or knowledge. His body and true humanity are, moreover, the genuine temple and treasure-house, the true dwelling and abode of God. As the true dwellings, treasure-houses, and temples of God, in which Father and Son themselves, the most sublime treasures, live and remain in the power of the Spirit, the hearts of all the faithful are prepared and built up by him for [the enjoyment of] these treasures.[130]

123* New treasure.
124 Ps 104:27; 145:15.
125 Rom 1:18.
126 Mt 9:12; Mk 2:17; Lk 5:31.
127 2 Pt 1:21.
128 Eph 1:5.
129 Eph 1:23; Col 2:3.
130 1 Cor 3:16f.; 6:19; 2 Cor 6:16.

He adorns and consecrates this temple with all its utensils and glorious gems, the gifts and virtues of the Holy Spirit, and anoints them with the oil of gladness,[131] with which the Lord himself has been anointed by the Father above all his equals. Thus he is the high priest before the Father, and he accomplishes the priestly office in the hearts of the faithful. He establishes his own as fellow priests[132] to rule and reign with him forever.[133]

That is the length and the breadth of Christ,[134] the highest treasure, who is from eternity and who eternally spreads himself out in the hearts of all the faithful. In this new and acceptable year, he has been given to us in our earthen vessels.[135] These vessels are easily broken or damaged if we do not take care of ourselves, or if we speak evil of the treasure.[136] If struck, these earthen vessels will break [2 Cor 4 (7)]. One must also diligently watch that his own earthen vessel, in which the treasure is given, is not exposed to offence;[137] one should not easily become offended by Christ and his own, and thus sustain damage. Moreover, it behooves us not to give offence or scandal to others,[138] or to take it ourselves.[139] Rather, we should cling firmly and immovably to the truth, and preserve from offence the earthen vessel into which the treasure of Christ is laid by God the Father, Son, and Holy Spirit.

Thus we should allow ourselves neither to be offended nor scandalized by anything. Also, we are to watch diligently that our earthen vessel does not cause offence to anyone else. Otherwise our own or our neighbour's vessel might be broken. If we carnally attack one another, or fight one another in the spirit of the flesh, in arrogance and conceit, such breakage will occur. It also happens if we give room and place to

---

131 Ps 45:7; Is 61:3; Heb 1:9.
132 1 Pt 2:5, 9; Rv 1:6; 5:10; 20:6.
133 Rv 22:5.
134 Eph 3:18.
135 2 Cor 4:7.
136 Rom 14:16.
137 1 Thes 4:4.
138 1 Cor 10:32; 2 Cor 6:3.
139 Lk 7:23.

the lust of the flesh. To do so, under the guise of the liberty of Christ,[140] is to assume that one is free to do anything;[141] such an assumption is contrary to the manner of Christ and defiles the treasure of the love[142] that is in Christ. In whatever form offence happens and manifests itself, the earthen vessels and containers are easily shattered and destroyed, and the treasures, along with all the gifts of Christ, are defiled and slandered. Yes, in us Christ himself is shamed, despised, blasphemed, and crucified anew.[143] What is even worse is if someone is injured by deception and cunning, and polluted by abominable vices. Even in the law of Moses, such vices did not remain uncondemned; much less may they have room under the grace of Christ.

Therefore, my beloved ones, let us be aware of the high priest Christ[144] in our hearts, and of his joyful anointing of us, with the oil of gladness, comfort, and peace.[145] This anointing gives us all learning,[146] wisdom, understanding, and comprehension, and then we may understand what is best and most pleasing to the Father of our Lord Jesus Christ [Rom 12 (2)].

We should often take the treasures out in one place and diligently discern what God the heavenly Father has conferred upon and given to each for the service of building up the body of Christ [1 Cor 12 (7); Eph 4 (16)]. The gifts in every single member must be acknowledged, heard, and seen. There can be no unendowed member who has not been given something of the treasures of Christ, such as virtues and the fruits of the Holy Spirit on the body of Christ. Everything has been given to us by the Father of lights with and in Christ [Jas 1 (17)]. Always the gifts of the Father are only good gifts, which he gives to his children who ask him. There are no stones for bread, or scorpions for eggs, or serpents for fish [Lk 11 (11–13)]. Thus the Father does not regret[147] that he gives

---

140 1 Cor 8:9; 9:18; Gal 5:13; 1 Pt 2:16.
141 1 Cor 6:12.
142 Rom 14:15.
143 Heb 6:6.
144 Heb 3:1.
145 Heb 1:9.
146 1 Jn 2:27.
147 Rom 11:29.

the gifts to his children. Nor does he give his gifts and treasures to unclean wild animals, for he never throws the pearls before swine or what is holy to the dogs; the Lord himself forbade his own to do it [Mt 7 (6)]. His holiness is the pearls, treasures, precious stones, and gems with which he has sanctified himself for his own. And these treasures that he gives are given only to those who are sanctified. Thus, with such sacred treasures, yes, with Christ himself, his own may cleanse one another and to the pleasure of their God and Father sanctify one another with all the virtues and gifts, and with the Holy Spirit's adornment and finery [2 Pt 1 (5)].

The Father of our Lord Jesus Christ desires and expects the mother, the bride of Christ and sanctified by Christ, to nourish, raise, and preserve the children for the Father in all sanctification, adornment, and ornament. Isaiah says: "[Such children] will be the Father's boast, his honour, glory, and majesty, and the mother with her children will express and give eternal praise, laud, honour, and thanks to the heavenly Father forever."[148]

Such housekeeping is demanded not only of the mother and the bride of Christ herself but also of her servants, the highest angels of God, who freely serve.[149*] Indeed, the angels desired to see this housekeeping of Christ and his bride.[150] Those angels, because of their willful pride, did not freely surrender themselves to this service to his spouse, bride and children, in the deep humility of Christ. They did not humble themselves with Christ, the Son of God, in the time of his mortal life, and were eternally cast out and bound in hell.[151, 152*] Whoever therefore serves from pride, or because of pride refuses to serve, relates to this housekeeping of Christ and his espoused bride as the whole world does, which wants to rule and not serve, and what it serves, it serves

---

148 Is 54:1.

149* Household.

150 1 Pt 1:12.

151 2 Pt 2:4; Jude 6.

152* Gloss: Jacob was deceived with his first wife, but he served again for the beautiful Rachel [Gn 29:25–30]. These two wives represent the old and new marriage.

from pride. They are all like their ruler, the devil, the angel who was cast out.

Therefore the precious gems, pearls, and sacred things are to be given to all who are washed, cleansed, and redeemed through the blood of the Lamb [Rv 1 (5)].[153] They are children of and fellow-heirs[154] to all the treasures of Christ's grace. To them belong all the gems, pearls, and holy places, and they are to be adorned and beautified with them to the honour of their God and Father and the Lord Jesus Christ. For the others, Christ, his riches[155] and treasures are a mockery and derision.

Therefore, my dear ones, let us be aware of our calling.[156] Let us rightly look to our High priest and forerunner.[157] Let us see the treasure, gems, and ornaments, the fullness of grace and truth[158] with which he himself has adorned the temple of his body.[159] Look and see the glorious, beautiful, and priestly garments, all the virtues and gifts of the Holy Spirit, with which he, as the true God, was clad by his heavenly Father.[160] His faithful ones should learn from his example and be amazed by it. Just as the whole of the true and chosen ones, the royal priestly generation and God's own people, are clad with the virtues and gifts of the Holy Spirit, so should the faithful ones long to be similarly clad [2 Pt 1 (3)]. They are all fellow-priests [1 Pt 2 (9)]. Through Jesus Christ and the Holy Spirit, their God and heavenly Father clothes them with the same gifts and virtues.

Moses prepared the figurative temple and the Aaronic or Levitical priesthood.[161*] God had showed him the design on Mount Sinai.[162] The temple was to be adorned with glorious ornament[163] and lavishly decorated with gold, silver, copper, bronze, and iron, and all kinds of

---

153 1 Pt 1:19; Rv 7:14; 12:11.

154 Rom 8:17.

155 [Original: *reichtungen*; read *Reichtümer*.—Trans.]

156 Heb 3:1.

157 Heb 12:2.

158 Jn 1:17.

159 Jn 2:21.

160 Ex 28:6; Rv 19:16.

161* Yesterday and the figurative temple.

162 Ex 25:9.

163 Ex 25ff.

precious wood and stone. Everything was washed, anointed, sanctified, consecrated, and cleansed. Thus God was worshiped and honoured with great external pomp and splendour. The high priest used no unclean or unconsecrated vessels in his high priestly function.

Much more glorious, however, is the most exalted form; the real manner and way is not according to any model but according to the glory of the true priest, the Son of God himself.[164] More glorious is he himself who came down from the highest mountain, the eternal God and Father in the Son, and proclaimed the will, pleasure, and commandment of the heavenly Father. That commandment was no longer written in stone tablets, that is, in hardened hearts; it was written by the finger of God in broken hearts of flesh [2 Cor 3 (3)]. It is not adorned with earthly gold[165] but with the spiritual gold of divine love; it is fired, purified, and cleansed and made steadfast in all tribulation in the power of faith. This gold is love, that is, God himself, and it does not pass away but endures forever.

Similarly, all the other sacred gems of the temple and of the royal high priest Christ and of his own are not of earthly production, of elemental or creaturely birth. Given to the Son himself, to his fellow-priests and the spiritual temple,[166] the Father bestows these treasures in the power and working of the Spirit. This compactly built temple is not cleansed, nor is it consecrated with the blood of animals. It is consecrated with the precious blood of Christ Jesus.[167] The washing, cleansing, and purifying through baptism are the basis of faith in the forgiveness of sins.[168] They are a co-witness of the Holy Spirit of the Father of truth which is believed.

This temple and its priesthood receive the treasures, gems, and gifts, which are not of silver, gold, or precious stones, or apparel of silk. Rather, such treasures, gems, ornaments, and honour are spiritual gifts, produced and prepared by the Holy Spirit. Of them St. Paul (Gal 5 [22,

---

164 Heb 9:1–14.

165 1 Pt 1:7.

166 1 Pt 2:5.

167 Heb 9:19–25; 1 Pt 1:18f.

168 Rv 1:5.

23]) and John[169] wrote: "The virtues of the Holy Spirit are love, faith, hope,[170] patience, joy, peace, long-suffering, piety, goodness, kindness, gentleness, purity."

Our apparel is justification and chastisement; it is the grace of our heavenly Father, who does not allow his own to appear in the shame of nakedness.[171] Therefore it behooves us to keep our priestly garments unsullied, unspotted, and clean,[172] so that they may not be taken from us, and we be found unclothed in the shame of nakedness.[173*] All this belongs to our priestly office and priesthood, and to our hearts, the temples of God. In them God dwells [2 Cor 6 (16)].[174*] They are the most precious treasures and gems, given to us by our Father God and Lord with Christ. With them we may eternally offer thanksgiving, laud, and sacrifices of praise [Heb 13 (15)].

No high priest serving in the temple and spiritual house of God may ever use an unholy, unclean, or unconsecrated utensil. Every utensil must be sprinkled with the blood and the grace of Jesus Christ in the forgiveness of sins. Whenever so-called Christians do use unclean utensils—and it happens today—God's anger flares. The gifts of the Holy Spirit are withdrawn and the hearts of the faithful destroyed and desecrated. So it happened with the figurative treasures, temple, and priests. The same happens daily before our eyes through deceit. But in the house and temple of God, no vessel is used in dishonour. In and for his wrath, God uses such unclean and unholy vessels outside the house.[175] But in the house and temple of the Father, our high priest uses only pure, holy vessels in all holiness [2 Tm 2 (20)].[176*] He has himself hallowed them in his holiness. In them, and in the hiddenness and pa-

---

169 Rv 3:4, 18; 16:15.

170 1 Cor 13:13.

171 2 Cor 5:3.

172 Rv 3:4; 16:15.

173* Note.

174* Priestly office (2 Cor 3 [16]).

175 Rom 9:22. [This is a reference to the order of society outside of the church, for example, the state.—Ed.]

176* God uses unclean vessels outside the house.

tience of their hearts,[177] he conceals his treasure and gems according to the mystery of his will.[178] Yes, they are hidden from the whole world and all unclean animals.

The ark or coffer of the new covenant or testament is the patience of Christ and the faithful saints,[179] who are prepared for the Father's praise in all patience.[180*] In this coffer, all the household furnishings of God, the treasures, virtues, and gifts of the Holy Spirit, are safely kept and locked away from all enemies of God and his own. Neither the violence, aggression, pride, or pomp of the world, nor anything else that may rise up against it, will be able to open, destroy, or shatter this ark or coffer,[181] which is the patience of Christ itself, bound, mounted, and locked away with the band of his love,[182] humility, and surrender.

Without this ark or coffer, our treasure, the virtues and gifts of the Holy Spirit that are placed in our hearts as temples of God, cannot be locked, protected, or preserved. Therefore, as the Lord says, we must arm and prepare our souls with patience,[183] for we will need patience if we wish to preserve the treasures and the true rod of our high priest Aaron,[184*] which, together with the golden bucket,[185*] blossomed in our souls [Heb 10 (36)].

The true bread from heaven is in the loving hearts of the faithful, which the Father gave us from heaven[186] and which has given us life, kept for a perpetual remembrance.[187] This bread is his broken or creaturely flesh[188] and blood, given up for our life.[189] The pure flesh and

---

177 1 Pt 3:3f.

178 Eph 1:9.

179 2 Thes 3:5; Rv 1:9.

180* The ark of the new covenant is patience.

181 2 Cor 10:5.

182 Col 3:14.

183 Lk 21:19.

184* Rod of Aaron.

185* golden bucket.

186 Jn 6:32f.

187 Heb 9:4.

188 [Original: *geoberuert oder guwurckt fleisch.*—Trans.]

189 [Marpeck is here using as an analogy the contemporary practice of reserving some of the consecrated bread of the Mass for emergencies. It was kept in a

blood of the Virgin Mary prepared this flesh and blood for us, and this heavenly bread, which the Word made flesh, raises us from death to life.[190] It is the true food and drink, given for our life;[191] it nourishes and preserves our souls. The true bread of remembrance belongs in the golden bucket, and this bread is kept locked in the ark of the New Testament.[192*] In all patience, united with his own gentleness, humility and surrender, our high priest has locked the treasures in the ark. Thus the temple of his body is preserved in the ark of the covenant of the New Testament so that we have a perpetual remembrance of him.[193*] Had our high priest himself not so carefully locked his treasure for us, every covenant and witness of the eternal covenant would be pillaged by the enemy, who steals all divine treasure [Heb 5 (10)]. Wherever impatience breaks the ark of the covenant, all the treasures of our temple, that is, of our hearts, are lost, pillaged, and stolen, and the temple of God is destroyed and broken down.[194*]

Therefore, if indeed we wish to preserve the treasures of our temples in this new and acceptable year, in this time of grace,[195] and if we wish to save these gems from the Philistines, we need patience.[196] The ark of the New Testament is not compatible with the Philistines, I mean with the world. The impatience of the Philistines opposes the true patience of Christ. When they gain the victory over the ark and presume to use it, it does the opposite of what they expect. When tribulation comes, which is inevitable if indeed it is the ark of the New Testament called

---

special vessel and locked tightly to protect it from sacrilege. During the feast of Corpus Christi, this special vessel was carried in the procession. By the time of the Reformation, this kind of public manifestation had become a major festival of the church. Most likely, he also had in mind the golden urn containing the manna, or—as Luther renders it—"*der goldene Krug mit dem Himmelsbrot*" which is mentioned in Heb 9:4. Froschauer has "*der guldin eimer, der das himmelbrot hatt.*"—Ed.]

190 Jn 5:24.

191 Jn 6:55.

192* Bread of remembrance.

193* Note.

194* Impatience destroys the ark of the covenant.

195 Is 49:8; Lk 4:19.

196 1 Sm 4–6.

patience,[197] they return it with much impatience by the hands of ignorant and untamed beasts, soldiers with armour, weapons, and guns [1 Sm 6 (12)].[198*] For the tribulation of Christ is for them a plague and a shame in an unsavoury place![199]

Thus, along with an offering, which God despises, they send the ark back to its place.[200] They endure their suffering and death to death in much impatience. If one wishes to, one can see that such is the case these days.[201*] There are those who have adopted the gospel, but they only appear to adopt the patience of Christ. As the Philistines, they now send the ark back home again. Are these not truly the unspiritual Philistines who, together with their Goliath,[202] trust only in human power? Such a trust is contrary to the true manner of the patience of Christ;[203] it contradicts the genuine and true David. Armour and sword do not fit him. He kills all his enemies with their own sword [1 Sm 17 (38f.; 50f.)]. Under the name of David, their own impatience consumes them. As the Lord says: "Whoever fights with the sword will be destroyed by it" [Mt 26 (52)].

Human coercion will destroy all who support a human, forcibly imposed faith and all who claim the word of faith but who trust and depend upon human protection and power; like Peter, they will be driven to a denial. Peter also thought that Christ would be a temporal and earthly redeemer who would save them with carnal weapons.[204*, 205] Thus Peter pledged that he was prepared to give his life for the Lord.[206] However, he received no help from the Lord in his carnal fighting; Jesus

---

197 Rom 5:3; Rv 1:9.

198* Note.

199 [Original: *plag und scham ann geheimem ort.* Marpeck seems to mean that they regard the tribulation of Christ as something disreputable, to be assiduously avoided.—Trans.]

200 1 Sm 5:6.

201* That is the way it was in the Schmalkaldian War and in Switzerland with Zwingli.

202 1 Sm 17:4ff.

203 1 Sm 17:45.

204* Note.

205 Lk 22:49f.

206 Mt 26:35; Jn 13:37.

helped the one whose ear Peter had cut off [Jn 18 (10f.)]. Then Peter denied the Lord three times and swore that he had never known the man.[207*, 208]

This happens to all who know Christ only after the flesh, who know him only in terms of temporal aid and the saving of temporal life and property,[209] and who know nothing of the Holy Spirit's heavenly treasures and gifts, which are given to all faithful believers in Christ. God grant that they fall into no worse denial, or into a betrayal like Judas did, or that they have become thus toward one another.[210] Rather, God grant that they should later confess their sin and repent[211] like Peter, who in his ignorance and fear denied the Lord. Nevertheless, he risked his life and entered the fray with no thought about what might happen to him.[212*] He did not, like Judas, betray the Lord for the price of shame.[213*, 214]

Would to God for their sake that it were not true that today there are worse and even more evil merchants than the Jewish Pharisees, who bought the Lord from Judas out of envy and hate. But today whole lands, populations, and armies (many hundreds of thousands of people, even though they are not good people)[215] are betrayed, sold, and bought by their loans, finance, and usury. It is done out of avarice, envy, and hate, an attempt to preserve their earthly pomp, pride, and vain honour. Moreover, all the actions of those who compel faith, both the old and new,[216] are done in the semblance of Christ and his gospel.[217*] I am concerned that, shortly, the words of James, "Howl and weep, you rich,"[218] will be fulfilled in them.

207* Peter denied.

208 Mt 26:74; Mk 14:72; Lk 22:61; Jn 18:27.

209 2 Cor 5:16.

210 [Original: *undereinander wurden und schon worden send.*—Trans.]

211 Mt 27:3.

212* Note.

213* Judas.

214 Mt 26:14–16; Mk 14:10; Lk 22:3–6.

215 [That is, not good by contrast to the blameless Jesus.—Ed.]

216 [Catholic and Protestant.—Ed.]

217* Those who compel faith.

218 Jas 5:1.

Those who have been violently compelled to hold a faith cannot bring forth better fruit. Whatever is preached from the dead letter of scripture or ancient, idolatrous custom, and whatever is taught under human power, protection, and patronage will also by human coercion and power be destroyed and scattered again in mutual denial and betrayal. Even though all creatures are clean, the riches, treasures, gold and silver, precious stones, pearls, velvet and silk garments of the world can produce no better fruit in the heart than eternal condemnation [1 Tm 4 (4); Ti 1 (15)]. I do not intend to judge or condemn the world: along with its prince, the devil, it has already been judged and condemned before God.[219] Rather, I write this letter as a testimony to Christ that their works are evil. Just as the light is distinguished from darkness, or the riches and treasures of Christ from the treasures of this world, I distinguish them from good works. The children of light[220] always bring forth good from the treasures of their hearts, and the children of evil bring forth evil from the evil treasure of their hearts [Mt 12 (35)]. Where the treasure is, there the heart is also [Lk 12 (34)].

Therefore it behooves us to look again to our calling[221] and to him who called us from the horrible darkness of this world to his marvellous light [Jn 15:16; 1 Pt 2 (9)]. For he called us from the world, not we him. He has revealed to us the will of his heavenly Father. He has taught and instructed us with full understanding. He has also sent us the teacher in the heart, and the comforter to comfort,[222] and to teach us with Jesus' own words and teaching. He equips and empowers us with the heavenly, inner, hidden power from above;[223] he leads, instructs, and guides us, and he anoints us, as the Father of lights[224] anointed the Lord himself, with the oil of gladness.[225]

---

219 Jn 12:31; 16:11.

220 Lk 16:8; Jn 12:36; Eph 5:9; 1 Thes 5:5.

221 Heb 3:1; 2 Pt 1:10.

222 Jn 14:26.

223 Lk 24:49.

224 Jas 1:17.

225 Heb 1:9.

Our life is hidden with Christ in God;[226] it is not we who live, but Christ who lives in us.[227] We are not taught by the human voice, by the literal, external teaching of Christ and the apostolic preaching of the gospel.[228] We are taught not by humans but by God, the Holy Spirit himself.[229] The Spirit takes the treasures and good things of the Father and the Son,[230] and has poured into our hearts the love[231] which is the mind of Christ and the true and only understanding. Only what Christ himself has said and taught,[232] and no other word, does the spirit of wisdom bring to remembrance in his own.

Therefore, no matter how holy they may appear, all those who take away and add to this word and teaching are false spirits. Nor have they been taught by God who only hear the Word from the mouth of Christ, the apostles and other saintly people, nor does he teach those who read their writings only according to the letter, without the reminder of truth and teaching of the Holy Spirit.[233] They are thieves and murderers who run before and lag behind Christ [Jn 10 (8)]. With their own inventions and sophistries[234] in scripture, they either run ahead of the Holy Spirit of Christ, before they have been driven by him, or else they lag behind Christ and presume to teach those from whom God has withdrawn his grace.[235*, 236]

---

226 Col 3:3.

227 Gal 2:20.

228 [In "A Clear and Useful Instruction" (WPM, 77–86), Marpeck emphasizes the "physical" teaching of Christ as the medium of the gospel. There he is arguing against Spiritualists; here he is arguing against reformers who outwardly coerce faith rather than relying on the Spirit.—Ed.]

229 1 Cor 2:13; 1 Thes 4:9.

230 Jn 16:14.

231 Rom 5:5.

232 Jn 14:26.

233 Jn 14:26.

234 [Original: *kunst,* with a negative meaning.—Trans.]

235* Before and behind Christ.

236 [Original: *denen Got sein gnad entzogen hat.* This is an unusual statement for Marpeck. While he proclaims God's judgment, he almost never claims that God has withdrawn his grace.—Trans.]

Thus, without being called, and without any discrimination about who is drawn or sent by the Father,[237] they throw pearls before swine and what is sacred before dogs [Mt 7 (6)]. They pay no regard to the admonition the Lord gave to his own to distinguish between people.[238] Instead these others without discrimination dump their teachers and teaching, like the useless salt, in front of everyone, so that people trample it underfoot[239] and, as one can now see, mock it. Like swine and ravenous dogs, they turn around and rend them.[240] These are clouds without water, driven by the whirlwind [2 Pt 2 (17)]; they are not driven, taught, or recalled by the Holy Spirit, nor are they led by him in the truth [Jn 14 (26)].[241] "Those whom the Spirit of God moves are children of God" [Rom 8 (14)]. All these teachers, self-appointed or reestablished by human violence, who teach for the sake of carnal gain and self-indulgence under human protection [2 Tm 4 (3); 2 Cor 2 (17)], who have not drunk at the streams of living water but have stolen their human sophistry of scripture from stagnant cisterns;[242] all these, as the prophet says, build with crumbling mortar [Ez 13 (10f.)].

Therefore their building immediately collapses, and they perish along with it. They are destroyed by the human violence and protection under which they build their edifice. Through the deceit and error of human teaching, they fall and are overcome by the debris. Whoever has ears should hear;[243] whoever has eyes should see what has happened everywhere to these so-called Christians, who have only the semblance of the gospel. Such righteous judgments by the almighty, righteous God, our heavenly Father of the Lord Jesus Christ, rightly follow. It is the judgment of the Holy Spirit, who now because of sin judges the world together with its prince [Jn 16 (8)].[244] With the justice of Christ,

---

237 Jn 6:44.
238 Mt 10:17.
239 Mt 5:13.
240 Ps 80:13.
241 Jn 16:13.
242 Jer 2:13.
243 Mt 11:15; etc.
244 Jn 12:31.

the potentate of heaven and earth,[245] who now sits at the right hand of the majesty of God,[246] the Holy Spirit judges the sin of the unbelief into which they are rejected and thrown. His is the true righteousness. He went to the Father for the sake of exercising this righteousness and judgment of the Holy Spirit.[247] From above, he now creates and effects the same righteousness, which alone is valid before God,[248] and which exists and remains eternally before the Father in his saints.

Prior to this ascension of Christ and access to the Father, no one was justified in the justification of grace. Before his departure to the Father, even the physical teaching, power, and miracles of Christ could not justify the apostles, or anyone else, to this eternal justification. For this reason, even though the physical teaching of Christ, the Son of Man, was testified to by his miracles and the divine power that the Father had in him and he in the Father, the apostles could not bear,[249] understand, or comprehend[250] the teaching of Christ so that they might have remained steadfast in it. Thus, since only God could do the works he did,[251] the apostles were led to believe and to confess[252] him as the Lord Jesus Christ, the true God, the Son of the Father. This faith, however, was received from the physical teachings and miracles. Without the true teacher and reminder, the Holy Spirit who comforts and leads into the truth, and whom Christ promised to send,[253] such faith was not valid. After his resurrection from the dead, Christ sent the Spirit and made the promise [Acts 2 (33)], which still stands, that he would eternally be[254] with all the faithful believers who have been taught,

---

245 Mt 28:18.
246 Mk 16:19; Lk 22:69; Col 3:1; Heb 10:2.
247 Jn 16:10.
248 Rom 1:17; 3:21, 25; 10:3; 2 Cor 5:21.
249 Jn 6:60.
250 Jn 12:16.
251 Jn 3:2.
252 Jn 5:36; 10:25; Acts 2:22; 14:3.
253 Jn 14:16; etc.
254 Jn 14:16.

reminded,[255] and led into truth by the same Holy Spirit.[256] He comforts us in our repentance and sorrow for sin, and forgives.

Therefore all external service—of Christ and those who belong to him in the time of this mortal life—serves and prepares the way for the Holy Spirit. This external service consists in the external preaching, teaching, miracles, baptism, foot washing, the Lord's Supper, discipline, chastisement, and admonition. Such service also includes the ban of exclusion and separation from the fellowship of the body of Christ. In order to preserve the true communion of all the faithful, we are commanded to keep the ban, together with the Lord's Supper, in remembrance of the true love of Christ and the gracious deed of his death. In the time of his mortal life, Christ did not rule; he served. Thus he sent his own to serve, not to rule [Jn 13 (4–17)]. People are to be served by Christ and his own, and they are to be prepared for the Holy Spirit. Some spirits either regard such preparation as unnecessary, or else they regard it too highly.[257*] But wherever this service of Christ is not carried out in all its provisions, there the Holy Spirit cannot do his work.

To believe, like Peter, that such a Lord should not wash one's feet [Jn 13 (8)], and to refuse to have the act performed on the basis of such carnal reasoning, is to rely on private invention rather than the Holy Spirit.[258*] Even today Christ says to these individuals that they can have no part in his kingdom. For the Holy Spirit may not and cannot function, nor can he find an abiding place without preparatory teaching. Service is commanded by Christ, and it is the means by which, according to the command of Christ, we are prepared. Moreover, the key of David is also a means, for it is the key of understanding with which our earthly mind is opened.[259] Then the Holy Spirit, as true God with Father and Son, can move[260] where he will, namely, in those whom the Father draws to Christ [Jn 6 (44)], even today to the same apostolic church

---

255 Jn 14:26.

256 Jn 16:13.

257* Note.

258* The foot washing of Peter; etc.

259 Is 22:22; Rv 3:7.

260 [Here Marpeck makes "spirit" into a verb: "the Spirit spirits."—Trans.]

and bodily service, preaching and teaching, baptism, foot washing, and the Lord's Supper. We submit to this service in the obedience of faith in Christ and under the discipline of the Spirit. When we mortals are renewed and born again of the Holy Spirit, the Holy Spirit becomes the pledge[261] and the third witness[262] of salvation.

The apostolic service of the church is properly carried out by the servants of the church or the communion of the bride of Christ, in accordance with the commands of Christ, and through their service as helpers of God they prepare, cultivate, fertilize human hearts as a newly broken field [1 Cor 3 (9)],[263] sowed and planted with the word of truth and watered with the water of baptism through the Word,[264] which has to be received in faith [Mk 16 (16)].[265*] But even if all this is done according to the command of Christ, with external service to the external person, the Spirit still moves in glorious liberty wherever he will, and he gives the increase and the growth[266] to whomever he will. Such is the prerogative, in eternity, of the Godhead, which the Spirit shares with the Father and the Son.[267*]

It is sheer fabrication and deception when some insist that the Holy Spirit moves apart from the apostolic service of the church, that such service, commanded by Christ, is unnecessary. What other teaching, word, or work can the Holy Spirit teach, bring to remembrance, and lead into truth, if not the actual spoken words, commands, and laws of Christ, reminded and taught by the Spirit? For the Lord himself promised that the Holy Spirit would remind us of all that Jesus said or commanded [Jn 14 (26)].[268*] Certainly, a spirit who teaches contrary to the

---

261 2 Cor 1:22; Eph 1:13f.

262 1 Jn 5:7.

263 Hos 10:12. ["Breaking" here means the initial plowing of virgin soil.—Ed.]

264 Eph 5:26.

265* Order of Christ.

266 1 Cor 3:7.

267* Gloss: The Antichrist has destroyed the apostolic service, and therefore Christ moves wherever he is prayed for.

268* 1.

Son of Man, who taught human beings with a human voice, is a deceiving spirit.[269*]

On the other hand, they also deceive themselves who think that when they serve, teach, and baptize, simply because the apostolic service is performed, it follows that the Holy Spirit also moves and teaches.[270*] Nor is the church of Christ merely where the external service is properly done. Not so! If the inner, through the Holy Spirit, does not co-witness to the external, through faith,[271] everything is in vain,[272*] for "where the carcass is, the eagles gather" [Mt 24 (28)]. The true communion and gathering of Christ cannot be identified with a place, nor can it be called a human name.[273] Wherever such a gathering is, according to the Word of the Lord, there Christ is with the Father and the eternally abiding Holy Spirit.[274] They love him who keep his Word and commandment. To them he and the Father will come and dwell [Jn 14 (21, 23)].

Therefore whoever says that Christ is anywhere else than living on earth as in heaven, in the power and clarity of the Spirit and in the heart of each faithful believer, he is a deceiver.[275] Whoever does not find Christ dwelling in his own heart, eternally, will not find him elsewhere.

However, where such hearts as temples and dwellings of God, are built into a spiritual dwelling for the Lord, these places are named and identified only so long as the faithful live there.[276] Thus that place is holy for the sake of the saints,[277*] even as God sanctified the figurative

---

269* Deceiving spirit.

270* Note. 2.

271 Rom 8:16.

272* Gathering of the church.

273 1 Cor 1:12; 3:4.

274 Mt 18:20.

275 Mt 24:23f.

276 [In other words, there is a church in Strasbourg only so long as the faithful actually live in Strasbourg. The presence of the cathedral in and of itself does not say anything about the presence of God, nor does the meticulous preaching and the performance of the sacrament.—Ed.]

277* Note.

temple.[278*] When it was destroyed, its place was profaned. The same is true of a place without saints.[279*] Where they do not dwell, it is a curse and malediction; it is desecrated, destroyed, and profaned before God. At this time, we see it clearly in the whole world.

The whole world imagines that it has Christ living here or there, because of the sectarian, external, coerced religion, by which they deceive themselves.[280*] Since the physical and true service of Christ did not come into force in the hearts of the apostles without the moving of the Holy Spirit, how can the forced and coerced faith, or the faith based on old custom, stand before God?[281*] This forced, coerced faith, based as it is on sophistic interpretation of scripture or on ancient custom, is not from God, nor is it taught by the Holy Spirit and his manner, birth, artistry,[282] and wisdom;[283*] it is unrelated to the Spirit's reminding and leading us into truth. Rather, it is from the generation and will of the flesh of man (Jn 1 [13]), who is steeped in his earthly, fallen nature and human reason, sophistry, and wisdom.

Thus one should preach the apostolic service and teach the teaching of Christ in the power of the Holy Spirit before earthly people; it flows out of the inmost being of believers as a fountain[284] flowing into eternal life.[285] Still, there is the second teaching of the Holy Spirit, which alone reminds and leads us into truth, and which teaches the divine artistry of wisdom; the second teaching must always accompany the first. Those who are thus taught are not taught by mortals but by God.

All the others continually learn from and are taught by mortals [2 Tm 3 (7)]. But these others never come to the knowledge of the truth, which is eternal life (Jn 17 [3]). They can never through the inspiration of the Holy Spirit know God the Father as the true God, and Jesus Christ as the one whom the Father has sent. Therefore the Lord

---

278* Yesterday.

279* Today.

280* Christ here and there.

281* 1.

282 [Original: *kunst.*—Trans.]

283* 2.

284 Jer 2:13; 17:13.

285 Jn 4:14.

says, "Not everyone who cries 'Lord, Lord' will enter the kingdom of heaven. Only he will enter who does the will of the heavenly Father" [Mt 7 (21)]. Since no one knows the Father but the Son and him to whom the Son reveals the Father (Mt 11[27]), no one but the Son could do the will and pleasure of the heavenly Father. Thus no one but the Father knows the Son.

Therefore Paul writes that no one can call Christ Lord except by the Holy Spirit (1 Cor 12 [3]). Also, no one can do the will of the Father without the Son. It follows that those who are in Christ do not themselves live, but Christ lives in them (Gal 2 [20]). Moreover, whatever they ask the Father, Christ himself will do and perform in the hearts of all the faithful. Such is the true righteousness, the reason why Christ went to the Father (Jn 14 [13f.]).[286] Thus St. Paul says that everyone should examine himself to see whether Christ dwells in his heart (2 Cor 13 [5]). If he does not, that individual is cast off. Therefore whoever calls Jesus "Lord" and God "Father" without the Holy Spirit does not for that reason enter the kingdom of heaven. To those God says: "You call me Father, but where is my honour? You call me Lord, but where is my fear?" (Mal 1 [6]). Without the artistry and teaching of the Holy Spirit, who pours out love, which is God himself, into the hearts of all the faithful,[287] and which surpasses all reason and understanding, everything is in vain [1 Cor 13 (2)].

The Holy Spirit proceeds from the Father and Son, and witnesses to the Father and Son in the hearts of all the faithful;[288] he copies and repeats the perfect law of the liberty[289] of Christ. The faithful look into this law of liberty, in order that they may fervently do what Christ spoke and commanded. They have a blessing, but not a temporal or temporary one, as Moses did, who engraved the written literal law through twelve witnesses from the twelve tribes of Israel with physical blessings and maledictions.[290*, 291] The Father, as true God, himself witnesses to

---

286 Jn 16:10.

287 Rom 5:5.

288 Jn 15:26.

289 Jas 1:25.

290* Twelve witnesses yesterday.

291 Dt 27:11ff.

the Son and the Son to the Father. Hence, all who believe in the Son have an eternal blessing.[292]

Moreover, twelve witnesses are established from the twelve tribes of Israel; they are the twelve apostles of which the Lord speaks in Acts 1 [8], where he says that they should be his witnesses to the ends of the earth.[293*] They had been with him from the beginning;[294] to empower their witness, he gave them the Holy Spirit, so that they should announce to all nations repentance and forgiveness of sins through his death and blood. Whoever believes and is baptized for the forgiveness of sins shall be saved. Whoever does not believe is condemned [Mk 16 (16)]. The Holy Spirit is the true, complete copier of the law of Christ in the appointed messengers and witnesses of Christ. The Holy Spirit renews and copies Christ's law in the hearts of believers, so that all things are rightly understood, recognized, and known, even as the Lord spoke, taught, and intended what he knew and received from the Father.

Without this copier of the law of Christ, I mean the Holy Spirit, the apostles could neither understand nor bear the teaching of their master [Jn 6 (60)]. He repeated in them again what Christ had said, taught, and commanded.[295] He is the true pledge[296] of our salvation, and the true witness[297] to our faith; he is the true repeater,[298] teacher, and reminder of our perfect law, no longer written on stone tablets, but in the hearts of the faithful [2 Cor 3 (3)]. The Holy Spirit no longer takes from the image[299] or the mediation of angels,[300] nor does he take it through fire, clouds, or darkness, as Moses received it and took it from God.[301] He takes it from the Father and the Son, and gives it to the hearts of all

---

292 Jn 3:16.

293* Twelve witnesses today.

294 Jn 15:27.

295 Jn 12:16.

296 2 Cor 1:22; 5:5; Eph 1:13f.

297 Rom 8:16; 1 Jn 5:6.

298 [Original: *äfrer.*—Trans.]

299 [That is, the plan of the tabernacle and its furnishings which Moses saw on the mountain with God (Ex 25:9).—Trans.]

300 Acts 7:38, 53; Gal 3:19; Heb 2:2.

301 Ex 19:18; Dt 5:22.

the faithful.[302] In them the laws and new commandments of Christ the Lord are written by the finger of God [Heb 8 (10)].[303]

That is the true copybook[304] for all the faithful, written by the three heavenly witnesses and affirmed by the Father, the Word, and the Holy Spirit [1 Jn 5 (6f.)].[305] Physical action, the power displayed with signs and wonders,[306] testifies to it on earth before mortals. The Father performed it in the Son, and the Son in the Father. As the Lord says: "My Father has worked until now, and I do as well" (Jn 5 [17]). The Father, the Spirit, and the Word are the three witnesses who witness in the incomprehensible, invisible, heavenly Being,[307] and these three witnesses have also witnessed before human beings on earth in visible, tangible, and bodily form. The physical miracles of the Son showed the Father.[308*] The Son taught the physical words, which he himself was as the Word of the Father, and revealed the Father.[309*] Thus he was glorified before humanity as true God.[310] The Holy Spirit, in the visible form of a dove, testified to the Son that God, the Creator of heaven and earth, was his Father.[311*, 312] He also appeared as tongues of fire to the apostles [Acts 2 (3)]. Although God is and remains a Spirit in three persons, Father, Word, and Spirit, an eternally invisible heavenly unity, Father, Son, and Holy Spirit nevertheless witnessed before humanity

---

302 Jn 16:14.

303 Lk 11:20.

304 [Original: *äferbůch* (literally, "copybook," which is somewhat obscure). Marpeck seems to have coined this word; it does not appear in the dictionaries of early High German. It is the copybook in which the teacher repeatedly copies the lesson for the student. The noun *äfrer* which appears just above, is followed by the synonyms "teacher," "reminder." It is the Holy Spirit who brings to mind in the believer the new law of Christ written on the heart.—Trans.]

305 [This reading follows earlier translations. More recent translations, based on older manuscripts, have "Spirit, water, and blood."—Ed.]

306 Acts 2:22.

307 1 Jn 5:7.

308* Father 1.

309* Son 2.

310 Jn 17:4.

311* Spirit 3.

312 Mt 3:16f.; Mk 1:10; Lk 3:22; Jn 1:32.

on earth in visible, physical form, as stated above, is one unitary Spirit, God, Father, and Son.

The Holy Spirit witnesses on earth with water and blood to the Lord Jesus Christ as truly human on earth.[313*] But there is blood as well as water, so that all three in one are active from heaven in the one Lord, Jesus Christ, on earth (1 Jn 5 [6]).[314*] If, with integrity of heart and with the co-witness of the three names and persons, God the Father, Son, and Holy Spirit, one is baptized in an exact copy of Christ's command, and if that baptism[315] is witnessed to in heaven as on earth, this witness is the subject of a fine new copybook written in the hearts of all the faithful. This law and copybook cause no curse but only blessing for mortals. It has not only human witnesses on earth but also divine witnesses in heaven, for it is witnessed to by Father, Son, and Holy Spirit, along with the co-witnesses of the apostles and servants of Christ. As the Lord said to the twelve: "You are my witnesses because you have been with me from the beginning" [Jn 15 (27)].

So too have the apostles patiently witnessed to the spiritual law of complete liberty[316] and to the copybook. As the true ark of the covenant of the New Testament, they are preserved in patience together with all the other gems of the temple of Christ's body. Their deaths and their lives preserved it from all enemies. To our heavenly Father's eternal praise, they possessed the power of the love that was poured out so that in this ark of patience we could bring home the treasures and vessels and all the gems of our temple to the heavenly Jerusalem, to the true temple of the body of Christ.

This temple was erected for perpetual worship, and it is [served by] a royal priesthood[317] that is not perishable or destructible but remains forever. Thus the Lord himself, in all gentleness, humility, and patience, determined and has preserved it from all the enemies whom he has overcome through his descent to the depths.[318*] Today, as they travel

---

313* Witnesses on earth (1 Jn 5 [6]).

314* Witnesses on earth.

315 Mt 28:29.

316 Jas 1:25.

317 1 Pt 2:5, 9.

318* Christ has overcome his enemies in the depths.

through the wilderness of this world, it behooves all faithful believers to exercise the greatest care for this ark of the new covenant and ensure that it may not be broken and seized by the enemy, and the treasures of Christ robbed. If indeed we want to be glorified with Christ and share his joy, all the treasures and gifts of Christ are kept in this ark of patience until death, the last enemy, is overcome.

Misery always precedes honour.[319*, 320] In the Lord's case, tribulation, sorrowing, and grief were followed by joy, bliss, and glory.[321] Our treasures will then no longer be mocked, nor will they be seized by any enemy.[322] Indeed, the ark is no longer necessary, for all the treasures and gems, as well as the garments of honour, are in discipline and virtue taken out of the ark of patience to the praise and glory of the heavenly Father, and to the eternal honour and glory of the Lord Jesus Christ. These gifts and virtues of the Holy Spirit are then returned and offered up again. There, before the eternal glory and unique majesty of God, they will be used without any fear or care in eternal worship. Only there, with all the angels, will the hallelujah be truly sung and understood![323]

Finally it will be revealed that the sufferings of this world are not worthy to be compared with the future glory and that all the tribulation and poverty is worthless by comparison with the unsurpassed riches[324] and glories of the treasures of Christ [Rom 8 (18)]. This acceptable new year has been announced, revealed, and proclaimed for all the faithful, in order that we may fervently rejoice over it and in it,[325*] and thank and praise our heavenly Father. We invite all creatures to rejoice with us and to sing praise to our God. Together with David let us heartily sing the song of praises:

"I will extol you, O king,
and praise your name forever and ever.

319* Misery before baptism.

320 Prv 15:33; 18:22.

321 Rv 21:4.

322 Rom 14:16.

323 Rv 19:1, 3f., 6.

324 Eph 2:7.

325* Such a new year; etc.

Every day I will bless you
and praise your name forever and ever.
Great is the Lord and worthy of all praise;
his greatness is unfathomable.

"Children's children will praise your deeds
and speak of your power.
I will speak of the glory of your praise
and of your wonders,
so that others will speak of the power of your deeds
and extol your glory.
They shall tell the story of your great goodness
and praise your justice.

"Gracious and merciful is the Lord,
forbearing and of great goodness.
The Lord is good to all,
and his mercy is over all his works.

"All your works thank you,
and all your saints praise you.
They tell of the glory of your kingdom and of your power,
so that all our children might know your power
and the glorious gifts of your kingdom.
Your kingdom endures for all time,
and to your dominion there is no end.

The Lord preserves all those who fall
and raises up those who have been beaten down.
All eyes are lifted up to you,
and you give them their food when it is time.
You open your hand and fill everything that lives
with what is pleasing.
The Lord is just in all his ways and holy in all his deeds.
The Lord is near to all who call on him.
He does his pleasure to those who fear him;
he hears their cry and helps them.

The Lord protects all who love him
and will exterminate the godless.

My mouth shall announce the praise of the Lord,
and all flesh shall praise his name forever and ever" [Ps 145 (1–21)]. Amen.

That is my heart's desire for all of you, as well as for my own soul. Amen. Pray to the Lord faithfully for me, and all true believers with me. Send everyone the greeting of peace and love in Christ Jesus our Lord from me and all true and faithful believers. Amen.

The grace of our Lord Jesus Christ be and remain with us all forever. Amen. Dated at Augsburg, the first day of February in the year of our Lord[326] 1547.

Servant and comrade to all of you
in the tribulation[327] which is in Christ,
P. Marpeck

---

[326] [Original: *anno domini.*—Trans.]
[327] Rv 1:9.

36

To her improvement

To Sophia von Bubenhofen, born von Pappenheim

Hans Bichel

Waiblingen, 7 January 1555

Hans Bichel was a shoemaker and an Anabaptist leader from the area around Salzburg, near Germany's southeastern border with Austria. He is on the record as a hymn writer, with five hymns included in the expanded Ausbund of 1583.[1] Equally suggestive of his esteem in the community was his participation in two defining disputations (Pfeddersheim, 1557; and Frankenthal, 1571) between the state church and the Swiss Brethren. This letter of comfort is his first extant piece of writing. The fact that he has a personal connection to a well-known member of the Marpeck Circle suggests, as do other letters in this collection, that the Swiss Brethren and Marpeckites overlapped more than Pilgram Marpeck's censorious epistles to the Swiss and much recent scholarship suggest. Bichel's greeting to Sophia from Marpeck and Hans Jacob Schneider indicates that Bichel had recently been with them. Von

Hans Bichel an Sophia von Bubenhofen, geb. von Pappenheim: Zu ihrer Besserung; Waiblingen, 7. Januar 1555. Translation by Arnold Snyder. Previously published as "Letter to Sophia von Bubenhofen, born Marschalkin von Pappenheim," in PAW, 120–21. Reprinted, with editorial changes, by permission of the publisher.

1 No. 9: "Ambrosius klärlich beschrieb"; no. 29: "Als man zählt tausend fünfhundert Jahr"; no. 45: "Es b'gab sich auf ein Zeite"; no. 46: "Ein g'fahre Zeit vor nie erhört"; no. 71: "Herr, starker Gott, ins Himmels Thron."

Bubenhofen was a relative of the Anabaptist von Pappenheim sisters. See letter no. 38, "Concerning Three Kinds of People in the Judgment and Kingdom of Christ," which is a letter from Marpeck to Magdalena von Pappenheim. Sophia had married into a noble family in Swabia (the area around Augsburg in southern Germany) and hosted Anabaptist gatherings on her estate.

It is common in texts in our collection to refer to taking part in "the first resurrection," a term taken from the Revelation of John, as a description of conversion. This reference underscores the Anabaptist emphasis on newness of life, spiritually and ethically, as the defining mark of Christian identity. The corollary term, "the second death," is also from Revelation. It is striking that this language had an immediate, existential meaning in an age so charged with eschatological thinking.

Apparently Sophia von Bubenhofen continued to be burdened by a sin long past. Did Bichel know this because he and von Bubenhofen were friends, as is suggested by the greeting he passes on to her from his wife? Or had Marpeck or Schneider drawn this worry to Bichel's attention? In any case, his declaration of Jesus' pardon was intended to release her from the past. This very personal letter probably merited inclusion in the Kunstbuch because continuing remorse over past sin is a common affliction among scrupulous Christians.

This following writing was done by a brother to Sophia von Bubenhofen, born Marschalkin[2] von Pappenheim, for her improvement.

Dearly beloved sister in hope Sophia. The brothers at Augsburg, above all Pilgram and Hans Jakob, greet you in particular, and also the others who are with you and who live in the faith. Everything is going well, as usual, for the brothers at Augsburg, as far as I know. May the Lord again have mercy on you and also on us, and grant you true love and peace, and also take from you and remove the heavy burden and grave stone with which you have been tortured and weighed down (for a long time now, because of your transgression), even unto death.

But God our Saviour did not leave the distressed woman comfortless, who grieved with tears and cries concerning her son who had died, as one reads (Lk 7 [12–15]). God had mercy on the mother and spoke a command to the child, "Stand up!" and he did. The Lord Jesus gave him to his mother again, free and alive. This also will be the comforting hope (for your sake): God will always grant the requests of the mothers of the church of Christ, and give them back their sons who have died [Lk 15 (24)]. Saved and holy is the person who has taken part in the first resurrection, that is, when one is resurrected through true repentance into a new life (through trust in faith that God forgives and is able to awaken one from death, no matter how great the transgression may be, for nothing is impossible for God), to the praise and honour of God their Creator, who can call into being what is not [Jn 11 (43f.)]. The second death (understand: the eternal death) will have no power over such a one, but this death will follow for all the unbelievers who do not unite with God in the time of grace, while they are still on the way [Rom 1 (18); 6 (23)]. The Almighty God wishes to grant you and us what we require, to our salvation and to his praise, through Jesus Christ our Saviour. Amen.

Receive a true and sincere greeting from me and my wife, which we pass on to all those who are with you, who fear God.

---

2 [A Marschalk was a manorial lord.—Ed.]

Dated at Waiblingen, on Monday following Holy Three Kings' Day in the year[3] 1555.

By me, Hans Bichel,
a comrade in the faith of Christ

3 [Original: anno.—Trans.]

37

On the inner church

To the congregations in Austerlitz and elsewhere

Pilgram Marpeck

Circa 1545

The title of this letter follows the usual pattern of Pilgram Marpeck's letters. It is addressed to a specific group, but what concerns one part of the body of Christ is held to be relevant to other parts as well. This epistle was inspired by the visit of messengers from Austerlitz (now Slavkov u Brna in the Czech Republic); conversation with them confirmed that they and Marpeck were of one mind. A web of connections lies behind this meeting of minds: Marpeck's closest colleagues, Sigmund Bosch and Leupold Scharnschlager had also been in correspondence with the Austerlitzers, particularly with their elder, Cornelius Veh. At the conclusion, "the brothers from Strasbourg" are mentioned as sharing in this consensus. All things considered, the letter probably dates from 1544 or later.[1]

Pilgram Marpeck an die Gemeinden in Austerlitz und anderswo: Von der innerlichen Kirche. Translation by William Klassen and John D. Rempel, based on a transcription by Torsten Bergsten. Previously published in "Two Letters of Pilgram Marpeck," in MQR 32 (1958): 201–5; and "On the Inner Church," in WPM, 418–26.

1 Bern MS, no. 37, 1; Martin Rothkegel allows for 1548 and 1553 as possible but unlikely dates of composition (BSOT, 588).

Marpeck's ecclesiological references are almost always to congregations (*Gemeinden*) because the church exists in concrete form. In this case, he uses *Kirche*, which designates the church collectively. The implication of this usage is that the author is going beyond particular statements about particular congregations to talk about the church in a general and universal sense.

This epistle has a unique place in Marpeck's writings, in that it complements what he normally emphasizes about the nature of the church, namely, its outwardness, its physical character. For reasons similar to Marpeck's, Anabaptism and its descendent movements have made the visible character of the church the cornerstone of their ecclesiology. Marpeck insists that the church is both visible and invisible, because the formative work of the Trinity happens beyond what we can see or track. This emphasis makes clear that the church is God's creation and not ours. Thus the church is more than the sum of its parts, more than the aggregate of human choices to accept Christ. At the same time, it is not less than that.

Two interwoven themes stand out; they carry over from letter no. 35, "Concerning the Lowliness of Christ." One of them is the now familiar Johannine notion of the relationship of Father and Son. This is summarized early in the present epistle in a way that suggests that believers are drawn into the relationship that exists among members of the Trinity. Thus God the Father dwells in Christ, Christ dwells with God the Father in us, and we dwell with Christ in God. The second theme, which describes how this divine-human dynamic expresses itself, is the notion of co-witness. As far as we know, this is an original concept of the author. On the one hand, outward expressions of the body of Christ—believers, scripture, and ceremonies—co-witness with the Spirit to the living presence of Christ. On the other hand, the Spirit also co-witnesses with the church to that presence. God's work in the world is known by the distinct but inseparable activity of outward manifestation and inward origin. As can be seen in no. 34, "A Warning against the Hidden Fire of the Enemy in Our Hearts," the Spirit always has priority in this dynamic.

By means of the notion of co-witness, Marpeck wanted to avoid two errors. First, he had in mind the mass churches, both the Catholic and magisterial Protestant. In his view, they ultimately "reduced the outer to a mechanical performance"[2] because it was not always based on the living presence of Christ. Second, he aimed at the "purely mystical or spiritualistic approach, which stressed only the inner"[3] and thereby abandoned the incarnational nature of God's presence.[4]

"In this letter, Marpeck [re-]affirms the central importance of worship,"[5] using the image of the temple. This temple is, surprisingly, not the church but the heart of the individual believer. It is possible that this individualizing of a corporate reality (the body of Christ) is intended as a criticism of the emphatically communal understanding of this term found among the Hutterites. Only the Holy Spirit can enter the inner sanctuary of the human heart: the church must not enter it and seek to discipline its members until the Holy Spirit has done his work. "At this point the concept of co-witness becomes central"[6] to the argument.

---

2 WPM, 418.

3 Ibid.

4 There are moments when Marpeck speaks with more nuance. At one point he expresses gratitude for his godly parents who remained Roman Catholic. In the midst of his passionate debates with Caspar Schwenckfeld, Marpeck is sometimes able to acknowledge the common conviction Spiritualists and Anabaptists have about the indwelling Christ.

5 WPM, 418.

6 Ibid.

This epistle reports on the inner church. First, it is God's temple, dwelling place, revelation, and inner choir.[7] Second, it has an external work that deals with order, where and how one should worship and confess sin, along with other matters.

To the elect, sanctified by God in Christ Jesus, our beloved in Austerlitz and other places, we offer an answer.

Grace and peace from God, our heavenly Father, through the Lord Jesus Christ, abide with you and all of us,[8] who love Christ from the heart. Amen.

Dearly beloved sisters and brothers in the Lord Jesus Christ. By the grace of God, the messengers you sent us have arrived. Along with your epistle to us, in which we perceived your disposition, mind, and spirit in Christ, we received them and their report with sincere joy in Christ. Through the Lord's grace, we understood everything and accepted it with sincere joy. On your behalf and ours, we also praise our God and Father through Jesus Christ our Lord, and thank him for his mercy and grace, which he has shown to us and all the children of humankind.

It was our heart's desire to know how the faith of Jesus Christ,[9] its knowledge and confession, stands with you, because eternal life consists in the knowledge of the truth of Christ. As the Lord Jesus Christ, the true Son of God and Son of Man, says: "This is life eternal, that they know you, Father, true God, and Jesus Christ whom you have sent" [Jn 17 (3)].

---

7 1 Kgs 6:16. [The inner choir or sanctuary of the temple was furthest into the building, a structure within a structure. It was described as the holy of holies.—Ed.]

8 Rom 1:7; etc.

9 [Original: *imm glouben Jesu Christi.* Marpeck makes much use of this formulation, which has caused recent debate in NT studies. See Richard B. Hays, *The Faith of Jesus Christ: An Investigation of the Narrative Substructure of Galatians 3:1–4:11* (Chico, CA: Scholars Press, 1983); and Mark Husbands and Daniel J. Treier, eds., *Justification: What's at Stake in the Current Debates* (Downers Grove, IL: InterVarsity, 2004).—Ed.]

Human salvation and eternal life consist only in the knowledge of God the Father and his Christ, and it remains so in eternity. To hear that we are of one mind in the truth of Christ and the Father is a joyous thing. And what more joyous thing can we experience than to confess to one another that we know that Christ Jesus is in the Father and God the Father is in Christ[10] and remains so eternally? Indeed, we know, recognize, and also sense that Christ is in us and we in Christ[11] and remain so eternally. Moreover, we know and recognize that the dwelling of God the Father and his Christ is built in our hearts. Now in this time they have made a dwelling and live in us.[12*, 13] Indeed, we also know and recognize the fruit and work of the Son, which the Father works in the Son and the Son in us,[14] whereby we remain in his Word.[15] The fruit is perfect love. In it we recognize that the Father and the Son have made their dwelling in us and live in us.

These are the ones who love the Father and the Son and keep their words in unity.[16] But those who do not love him do not keep his words.[17] Furthermore, we must also recognize that we love one another as he loved us; thus we are perceived as his true disciples.[18] Whoever has this command and keeps it loves him. He too will be loved by the Father. And Christ will also love him and reveal himself to him.[19]

The true revelation of Christ Jesus is to sense and recognize that the will, work, and good pleasure of the Father is performed in us through Christ.[20*] Thus God the Father dwells in Christ; Christ dwells with God the Father in us; and we dwell in Christ with God. This place and dwelling was first prepared for us through Christ [Jn 14 (2)]. Before Christ's

---

10 Jn 14:11.
11 Jn 15:4; Rom 8:10; Gal 2:20.
12* Dwelling of God and Christ in us (Jn 14 [23]).
13 Jn 14:23.
14 Jn 14:10.
15 Jn 15:10; 1 Jn 2:5; 4:12, 17f.; 5:3.
16 Jn 14:23.
17 Jn 14:24.
18 Jn 13:35.
19 Jn 14:21.
20* Revelation of Christ.

ascension, such a place and dwelling was not ready for anyone.[21] But this dwelling means that we have the presence of God the Father and the Son in us; thereby we keep his Word and his commands, which are not heavy but light.[22]

Consequently we also dwell in God, in God the Father and in Christ, in the Jerusalem that is above and not here below upon the earth.[23] The only place of worship is above.[24*] There the true worshipers worship in spirit and in truth and in the fellowship of the saints. Eternal life consists in such true and similar knowledge. To achieve it we must truly learn to know God the Father, and Christ who was sent by God: this is eternal life.[25]

If we received it by grace and prayer, such knowledge in Christ is also life eternal. Hence our joy toward one another is complete in God,[26] and thus we rejoice in you and hope that you are also rejoicing with us in the truth. Because the Jerusalem that is above[27] is only built by Jesus Christ in the Spirit, the heart is the inner and only temple.[28*] This Jerusalem is the place of worship, namely, in spirit and in truth. Human hearts, the hearts of the true believers, are the inner sanctuary,[29] the holy of holies into which no one can enter except our high priest.[30*, 31] To him alone the sanctuary and the holy of holies have been dedicated by God the Father, who is able to search the heart, thoughts, and soul [Jer 17 (10)].

---

21 [Marpeck makes the same claim elsewhere, namely, that prior to Christ's resurrection and the descent of the Spirit, believers in life and in death were not "hidden in Christ" (Col 3:3); at death they entered Hades and awaited the Messiah's coming.—Ed.]

22 1 Jn 5:3.

23 Gal 4:26. [But the author goes on to describe believers on earth as the temple.—Ed.]

24* Place of worship (Jn 4 [23f.]).

25 Jn 17:3.

26 Jn 16:24.

27 Gal 4:26.

28* The heart is a temple.

29 1 Kgs 6:16.

30* The inner sanctuary of the human heart.

31 Heb 9:7.

This sanctuary and holy of holies is known only by the high priest, Christ; in it he prays to the Father for the sins of humanity. Only this high priest Christ Jesus in the Holy Spirit[32] can see how the inner sanctuary and holy of holies are decorated and formed. This church is seen only by the Spirit and only in the Spirit.[33*] In it alone is there forgiveness and remission of sins through the high priest Christ. That is the inner church of Christ, in which eternal life is found.

Eternal life means that everyone shall and must now know for himself whether Christ dwells in him [2 Cor 13 (5)]. At the same time, God alone through Christ knows the condition of the human heart, whether it is right before God.[34] This inner church will be revealed only by the coming of the Lord Jesus Christ, at which time he will transfigure and reveal the hearts that belong to him. However, when Christ our life is revealed in the glory he had before that time, we too will be revealed with him.[35] Before this, his glory is revealed to no creature in heaven or on earth, not even to the angels, because liars and hypocrites can also do the external work Christ already commanded and ordained to his church,[36*] and they can change their external appearance into that of angels of light [2 Cor 11 (14)].

In collaboration[37] with the Holy Spirit, this inner church of the Holy Spirit is also directed to perform outer works, to be a light before the world.[38] It witnesses inwardly between God and humanity, but it is also formed externally and testifies in love shown toward the neigh-

---

32 [Marpeck uses various prepositions (not only "in" but also "through" and "with") to describe the relationship of Father, Son, and Spirit among themselves. His underlying point is their interdependence and mutuality.—Ed.]

33* Inner church.

34 [This statement shows in concrete form how Marpeck holds together the visible and invisible dimensions of the church. Those who are part of the body of Christ know that Christ dwells in them. On the other hand, only God knows what is in each believer's heart.—Ed.]

35 Col 3:4.

36* Note.

37 [Original: *mitwurckhung*. Marpeck's emphasis on the cooperation between the human and divine is expressed here in a novel way. As the paragraph unfolds, it implies a synergy between the two.—Ed.]

38 Mt 5:14.

bour. This love is demonstrated toward all people with baptism and the Lord's Supper, according to the measure of the internal working of the Holy Spirit, to the betterment of the outer person in Christ.[39*] It leads to the outer forgiveness of sin. In this manner, the Spirit, mind, and will of the Father are revealed by the outer person,[40] Jesus Christ;[41*] they are revealed bodily, by word and deed, in the same form as the internal working of God the Father.[42] The point is that no one comes to the Son unless the Father draws him [Jn 6 (44)]. And no one knows the Father except the Son and him to whom the Son reveals him [Mt 11 (27)]. Therefore today, as long as it is "today,"[43] the full knowledge of the Father and of his Christ consists in the inner and the outer workings of the Holy Spirit. St. Paul also says: "In him the fullness of the Godhead dwells bodily. And you share in that fullness" [Col 2 (9f.)]. "There is one faith, one baptism," one teaching, one Lord's Supper, "one God, Father of us all," who rules over the one church, inner and outer, in eternity [Eph 4 (5f.)]. Amen.

What the Father does as Spirit and God, the Son immediately does likewise [Jn 5 (19)], but he does it as an external human being who performs outward works. The Father loves the Son and has given all things into his hand.[44] Those who are born anew in Christ, according to the inner working of the Holy Spirit [Jn 3 (5)], are those who are baptized with fire,[45] who are aglow with love. Moreover, these children, born of the Spirit, see what the Father working through Christ does for the inner being; they too by co-witnessing in the Holy Spirit immediately do likewise for the outer being. Thus the body of Christ is built inwardly through the Holy Spirit and outwardly through the co-witness of human works. This is his church or congregation, his bride,[46] internally in

---

39* Inner is not without the outer.

40 [Original: *mensch*.—Trans.]

41* Note.

42 [Jn 5:19—Ed.]

43 Heb 3:13.

44 Jn 3:35.

45 Jn 3:11.

46 Eph 5:25–27; Rv 21:9; 22:17.

the Spirit and truth,[47] outwardly through the word of teaching to which we owe obedience. When they are brought together, they praise God before the world as a single light.[48] But this church is separated from the world to be a witness to it [2 Cor 6 (17)]. Similarly, the gospel must be preached through word and deed before the coming of the Son of Man.[49]

I do not mean to suggest that the mission to the cities of Israel should be accomplished by anyone other than the commissioned apostles, nor should it be carried out before the Day of the Lord.[50*, 51] I write merely to ensure that those whom God the Father draws and gives to the Son will be fulfilled [Jn 6 (44); 17 (12)] and will have salvation proclaimed to them. These he will keep, and he will lose only the children of perdition. The children who are kept will often suffer great loss, because of the children of perdition. It may even seem that they come to destruction and fall victims to it. Yet not one of them will be cast aside. I refer to those in whom hope remains, for—as God pleases—hope is a spring from which one may again receive grace for the future. Those who do not lack hope, and who do not as a consequence harden their hearts, may all be brought again to Christ while "today" is still a day of grace [Heb 3 (13); 4 (7)]. His body, which at the present moment is still upon the earth, will assist them. It is in the communion of the saints that remission of sins is available through Jesus Christ.

The Holy Spirit rebukes[52] a committed sin before his saints carry out any external rebuke.[53*] He alone rebukes first.[54] If, however, the Holy Spirit reveals this sin, then the church of Christ first rebukes through

---

47 Jn 4:23f.

48 Mt 5:14.

49 Mk 13:10.

50* Note.

51 Mt 10:23. [The abruptness with which Marpeck moves on to his next point suggests that the matter was contested. It sounds as if some fellow believers held that human initiative could hasten the kingdom. Marpeck emphasizes that it is God who calls workers and who calls those in the world whom he has chosen to faith.—Ed.]

52 [Original: *straffen* (may also be translated as "punish")—Trans.]

53* Discerning and punishing sin. Note.

54 Jn 16:8.

the co-witness[55] of the Holy Spirit. That is, it is the Spirit who reveals sin.[56] Thus the saints co-witness[2] that sins may not be tolerated in the body of Christ and separate them from the body of Christ [1 Cor 5 (11) and 11 (29)]. Wherever the Holy Spirit rebukes inwardly in a hidden way—from grace to grace,[57] with the comfort of forgiveness—no creature, either in heaven or on earth, is authorized to inflict punishment, which some do out of a false concern.[58*] They judge the hearts and desire to reveal them before the time [1 Cor 4 (5)].

As the psalmist says: "Blessed is the one whose transgression is forgiven, whose sin is covered, and in whose spirit there is no guile" [Ps 32 (1f.)]. Whoever does not confess his sin before God, who knows and sees all things, him the Holy Spirit punishes by manifesting the sin before others. If he then refuses to recognize or confess it either to God or to a person, if the sin is openly known and seen on him, and if he still refuses in spite of admonition and punishment to confess his transgression, then he belongs to the world, and the Holy Spirit will punish him for the sin of unbelief [1 Cor 5 (5)].

If, however, the Holy Spirit rebukes unto grace, the hope the sinner has received remains as long as remorse for the sin continues. It often takes a long time before this sin is forgiven by the Holy Spirit and the erring one is blessed with inward comfort. Such forgiveness and comfort naturally precede all forgiveness and comfort in the individual.[59*] It is like a spark of grace.[60] Through this divine fire (out of the fullness of Christ to give grace upon grace),[61] the inner may be kindled with the admonition and intercession of the saints.

So until someone confesses his sin before God and the communion of his saints in Christ, and until he confesses against himself and judges himself,[62] he is borne up during that time only by the prayer of

---

55 Original: *mitzeugen,* a term which Marpeck uses frequently, especially in his later writings. See CC, 80, 82; and AB, 121–27, 134, 137, 140.

56 1 Tm 5:25.

57 Jn 1:16.

58* Not to judge the hidden.

59* Note.

60 [Original: *funckhli der gnaden.*—Trans.]

61 Jn 1:16.

62 1 Cor 11:31.

the saints for such sinners.[63] All sin must be atoned for with prayer through the death of Christ.[64*] Only when there is no deceit in confessing sin, and only when the prayer of the saints is pure, does the Holy Spirit put comfort into the heart of the sinner and forgive the sin. Only then may the saints forgive him through Christ and the Holy Spirit. This whole process is a single act of forgiveness. Whoever grieves God has also grieved his saints, and whoever grieves his saints has also grieved God.[65*, 66]

I write this letter to you, my beloved, so that we do not run ahead of the Holy Spirit in anything, either ban or forgiveness of sin, either command or restriction, either order or custom. Indeed, there are many people today who make laws and ban people; they capture the conscience[67] and sear the cheek.[68*, 69] There are also many deceivers who completely despise and seek to discontinue admonition, prayer, ban, punishment, teaching, baptism, the Lord's Supper, and the forgiveness of sins in the communion of saints.[70*] Therefore, my beloved, let us allow nothing to take away from or rob us of the grace given to us. Rather, let us hold on to our unwavering hope[71] in Christ, which I and all the elect of God in Christ desire from the heart and ask on your behalf and ours. Amen.

Since both brother Leupold[72] and the brothers from Strasbourg have written to you and revealed my heart and mind along with theirs, I consider it unnecessary to write more and in greater detail. The brothers will inform you by word of mouth; they will be like living letters from

63 Jas 5:13.
64* Sin atoned by prayer.
65* Note.
66 2 Cor 2:5.
67 2 Tm 3:6.
68* Many lawmakers.
69 1 Tm 4:2. [The author of 1 Timothy writes of those whose consciences are seared.—Ed.]
70* Order suspended.
71 Heb 10:23.
72 [Leupold Scharnschlager, Marpeck's closest co-worker. Apparently, he was with Marpeck in Augsburg at this time.—Ed.]

us to you.[73] I pray God, if it be his pleasure and serve his honour, that he might allow us to read the letters written in our hearts by the finger of God[74] from mouth to mouth. I hope—without any doubt—that this will take place.

Pray to God the Father through Christ that we may all fulfil and complete the suffering of Christ, which remains in his body [Col 1 (24)]. May all of us, as faithful co-witnesses to the tribulation of Christ,[75] do so even unto death, according to the way of love.[76] May we also suffer one for another, as Christ suffered for us[77] until the end. Amen.

Jörg Stadler[78] and his matrimonial sister[79] Anna, both unknown to you in person, send greetings. So do my matrimonial sister Anna, along with me and all those who are personally known to us, and we to them. God knows all of our names. Pray to God for us fervently and earnestly, according to our need. As debtors to love, we will do likewise for you and all who desire it, who are bound to us in the debt of love. The grace of our Lord Jesus Christ abide with us and with all who love and seek Christ from the heart. Amen.

In the Lord Jesus Christ,
your (and all true believers')
servant and comrade in the
tribulation of Christ,[80]
P. M.

---

73 2 Cor 3:3.

74 2 Cor 3:2.

75 Rv 1:9.

76 Rom 14:15.

77 1 Pt 2:21.

78 [Nothing further is known of Stadler.—Ed.]

79 [This unusual reference to a wife as *mein eeliche schw[este]r* would seem to support the idea that for the Anabaptists marriage was seen as a partnership for the purpose of more effective service in the kingdom. Roland Bainton writes: "This third Christian attitude to marriage, which considers companionability as the prime ingredient, came into its own most fully with the more radical varieties of the Reformation such as the Anabaptists, later the Quakers" (*What Christianity Says about Sex, Love and Marriage* [New York: Association Press, 1957], 91.)—Ed.]

80 Rv 1:9.

38

Concerning three kinds of people in the judgment and kingdom of Christ Concerning the peasant nobility

To all the elect, especially Magdalena von Pappenheim Pilgram Marpeck Augsburg, 9 December 1547

"Concerning Three Kinds of People in the Judgment and Kingdom of Christ" is Pilgram Marpeck's second extant letter (see no. 2, "Concerning Those Dead in Sin") to Magdalena von Pappenheim,[1] the Anabaptist noblewoman who became his theological conversation partner. The basic image of the letter is a play on words. It uses von Pappenheim's noble rank as a metaphor for the "nobility" of the true Christian. At the same time, there is no explicit personal reference to von Pappenheim. The title says that the epistle is also addressed to several others. It has the character of a typical Marpeck circular letter.

"The title of the letter is somewhat misleading: Marpeck actually deals with five different types of people in judgment. Evidently, he began writing and found as he proceeded that there were not three but five kinds of people under the judgment of Christ"; only three of those

---

Pilgrim Marpeck an alle Auserwählten, besonders an Magdalena von Pappenheim: Von dreierlei Menschen im Gericht und Reich Christi. Vom bäuerlichen Adel; Augsburg, 9. Dezember 1547. Translation by Walter Klaassen and John D. Rempel. Previously published as "Men in Judgment and the Peasant Aristocracy," in WPM, 464–83. Reprinted, with editorial changes, by permission of the publisher. There were many textual variants between the recension used in the original translation and the one used in BSOT.

1 WPM, 464.

have entered the kingdom. "However, he did not return to revise his introductory sentences. The copyist apparently did not wish to take the liberty and make the revisions himself."[2]

In addition to the problem of form, there is also a problem with his central concept, not only for the modern mind but also for contemporary church members, who came from all classes. Because his metaphor is both literal and figurative—that is, it refers to a member of the nobility as well as to all faithful Christians—it degrades peasants as a class.

Marpeck begins with the same frame of reference that opens letter no. 7 ("Concerning Hasty Judgments and Verdicts"), 8 ("The Cause of the Conflict"), and 37 ("On the Inner Church"): the true knowledge of Christ.[3] A false knowledge of Christ is evident where grace is known but not received. The detail in which he rehearses claims that must already have been well known in the Marpeck Circle makes it clear that his audience is in jeopardy. It is not easy to identify the audience. Is it current members of the circle's congregations? Their lapsed members? Or their critics? Suggestions in the text point to all three possibilities.

Five types of people come under God's judgment, and ultimately under God's grace. The first are repentant sinners whom grace reaches and transforms. The second are those who strive to be naturally devout but finally open themselves to grace. The third are weak and desperate people who can't imagine being able to do the will of God. In the end God raises them up. Then there are hypocrites who claim that in being honest about their sinful ways they are more virtuous than the devout. And finally, there are sectarians, people who run from one assembly to another, looking for the perfect church, not knowing that they must meet God first of all in their own heart.

Marpeck mounts a sharp attack on a crucial aspect of the foundational claim of the Lutheran Reformation, as Anabaptists experienced it in the everyday life of Lutheran congregations. Martin Luther summa-

---

2 Ibid.

3 The German word *Erkenntnis,* generally translated as "knowledge," is knowledge in the sense of recognition. It is not that the believer is in possession of empirical facts that save her but that she recognizes and takes to heart truth that is revealed in Jesus and taught by the Holy Spirit.

rized his profound discovery, gained through his study of Romans and Galatians, with the phrase *simul justus et peccator* ("at the same time justified and a sinner"); that is, even though Christians are declared righteous through Christ's work on the cross, they always remain sinners. Marpeck's observation bristles with resentment. Such "so-called Christians . . . claim that the devil still holds power over those who truly believe in Christ Jesus."

Marpeck's formulation of the issue is as problematic as the alleged Lutheran practice of it.[4] Marpeck is in agreement with Luther (and Paul) that salvation comes by grace through faith. Where they differ is on the question of whether saving grace changes only our status with God or also our nature. While Marpeck "does not adopt perfectionism, he does insist that those who claim Christ as Savior but continue in sin, even if reluctantly, are still under judgment. He does grant them the status of believers: 'they are sinners under Christ, but they are not yet in the kingdom of Christ.' When he says that 'there are no sinners in the kingdom of Christ,' he is not saying that Christians do not sin. Rather, he asserts that they are to be distinguished from those who have not committed themselves to the freedom of Christ. Living in the freedom of Christ is living in liberation from sin; sin no longer rules over them."[5]

What might Luther have said about the practice of Anabaptist congregations? Even if he had admired their striving for holiness of life, in that very striving he might have observed the judgmentalism and self-righteousness toward others that Marpeck himself challenges in the letters preserved in this volume. He might also have observed that as soon as works become the evidence of faith, the danger is that faith itself is seen as a human capacity rather than as a gift.

God appointed Adam to be a noble whose charge "was to rule over creation. But all his dominion was lost when Adam disobeyed God. In consequence, he and his descendants became boorish peasants, doomed to live 'in the great village of this bleak world's wilderness.' But

---

4 Most Marpeck scholars agree on his indebtedness to Luther, particularly in his Christology. See Neal Blough, *Christ in Our Midst* (Kitchener, ON: Pandora Press, 2007), especially 40–46.

5 WPM, 464.

Christ came, and brought with Him the power to once again confer nobility on those who unite themselves with Him.[6] To those who do unite themselves with Him, He gave the virtues and the treasures that go with nobility." At this point "Marpeck's theology echoes the patristic recapitulation theory,"[7] in which the fall is completely undone and creation is restored.

As bold as the image of nobles and peasants, and theologically more provocative, is the rich picture Marpeck paints of God as the Father and the church as the mother of believers. Immediately after that lofty portrayal, and in pointed contrast to it, Marpeck launches into an uncharacteristically detailed rant against every imaginable evil. He lays out five categories of people who spurn the love of Christ and its transformative power and instead follow the path to perdition.

6 Another of Marpeck's pithy epigrams summarizes God's ultimate purpose in redemption: "All creatures exist for our sake, we exist for Christ's sake, and Christ exists for God's sake."

7 WPM, 465.

To all the elect of God, but especially to my beloved in Christ, Magdalena von Pappenheim, and also to all other sisters and brothers and beloved in the Lord who are scattered here and there; to all my deeply beloved ones in Christ.

Grace and peace from God our heavenly Father and the Lord Jesus Christ our Saviour[8] be and remain with us forever. Amen.

This is a treatise concerning three kinds of people who find themselves in judgment; it also concerns itself with the peasant nobility.

Dearly beloved in God the Father, loved in Jesus Christ after the manner of true faith, the true understanding and knowledge of Jesus Christ. According to the words of the Lord, eternal life lies in such knowledge: "Father, this is eternal life: that they know you, the only true God, and Jesus Christ whom you have sent" [Jn 17 (3)].

What is the true understanding and perception of the eternal and blessed life of Christ? God can be perceived only in the teaching and instruction of the Holy Spirit. The Lord himself had chosen and called disciples who had surrendered themselves wholeheartedly to his school and discipline, in order that they might follow him in the new birth of the Word[9] [Mt 4 (19, 21)]. To them he said, "If you remain in my words, you will be my true disciples. You will know the truth, and the truth will set you free" [Jn 8 (31f.)].

Thus only those who remain in the teaching of Christ are the true disciples. The others have no God, says John in his Epistle [(2) Jn 1 (9)]. To have true knowledge of salvation is to recognize the truth in Christ's teaching, which is the right word of truth. For this purpose, Christ, the Son of God, was sent by the Father, that he might give his people knowledge of salvation;[10] bind up hearts that have been wounded

---

8 Rom 1:7.

9 1 Pt 1:23.

10 Mt 18:11; Jn 3:17; 1 Jn 4:14.

by the deceit of sin[11] and by the devil, the enemy of truth;[12] open the prison for the captives and proclaim liberty to them; and "proclaim the acceptable year of the Lord and the day of vengeance of our God" [Is 61 (1f.); Lk 4 (18f.)].

The Spirit of the Father came into the world with the sending of Jesus.[13] He is the spirit of glory himself,[14] the one whom the Lord promised to send to his apostles,[15] and upon whom, as true human being,[16] he rested.[17] The Lord himself is the Spirit of the Father,[18] one God and one essence.[19] He is the true pledge[20] of our salvation. Even today he will rest upon all true disciples of Christ;[21] he will dwell in them,[22] be the legitimate teacher of the true understanding and knowledge of salvation; he will remind and teach them everything that Christ, the true ambassador from the Father, said, taught, and commanded.[23]

He is rightly acknowledged as eternal life, as true God[24] and as a true human being of the generation of humanity.[25] Born of the chaste, virginal, pure Mary[26] and conceived by the Holy Spirit, he is born of

---

11 Heb 3:13.

12 Jn 8:44.

13 [Marpeck often speaks of the incarnation of the Son and the descent of the Spirit on him as tandem events. But the gift of the Spirit to believers does not come about until Pentecost.—Ed.]

14 1 Pt 4:14.

15 Lk 24:49; Jn 14:16; etc.

16 [Original: *mensch* (meaning both "human being" and "person"; it is gender inclusive).—Trans.]

17 Lk 4:18.

18 2 Cor 3:17.

19 [It is a mark of Marpeck's theology that he sets forth the role of each person of the Trinity. Yet at times he is so concerned to preserve the unity of the Trinity that here and elsewhere he conflates the persons of the Son and Spirit.—Ed.]

20 2 Cor 1:22; 5:5; Eph 1:13.

21 1 Pt 4:14.

22 Jn 14:23; Rom 8:9, 11; 1 Cor 3:16; 2 Tm 1:14; Jas 4:5.

23 Jn 4:26.

24 Jn 17:3; 1 Jn 5:20.

25 Phil 2:7.

26 [Even though Protestantism rejected Mary's mediatorial role, Protestant theology continued to honour her unique role in the coming of salvation, as can be

God.[27] He is the eternal Word of the Father. He who is of the nature of God, who is one God with the Father and himself God the Word,[28*] became flesh of and in Mary, and was born a true human being from her faithful pure flesh as of the seed of Abraham.[29] His speech, teaching, and life are the truth and eternal life;[30] the healing of all the wounded; the redemption and liberation of all prisoners;[31] the faithfulness, love, and goodness of all believers, and it is this goodness which leads them out of the wickedness and deceit of sin into all truth, faithfulness, and love. He reminds and teaches them nothing but what he himself is,[32] namely, love, faithfulness, truth, and goodness, all of which come from true faith in Jesus Christ. That is the true knowledge of salvation, and that knowledge is eternal life.[33]

All other knowledge, that is, knowledge that is falsely acclaimed and foreign, is death and not life before God. Such knowledge is condemnation, not salvation; it is lies and sin, not goodness or truth. From this enmity, anger, even hatred against God,[34] one wickedness follows after another in the children of unbelief.[35] Thus they persist in their sins. What Isaiah said about the Israelites, I say about all so-called Christians, whose numbers are like the sand of the sea: that only a few (the remainder of the Gentiles)[36] have remained true to the Lord, and only they will be saved.[37] Like the Jews at the time of Christ, the time of the Gentiles is almost over. The fulfilment of their time is at hand.[38]

Therefore everything that speaks and teaches against the knowledge of the teaching, Word, life, and walk of Christ is falsely acclaimed

---

seen throughout this section.—Ed.]

27 Mt 1:20.

28* Note.

29 Gal 3:16.

30 Jn 6:63; 14:6.

31 Is 61:1; Lk 4:18.

32 Jn 16:13.

33 Jn 17:3.

34 Rom 8:7; Jas 4:4.

35 Eph 5:6; Col 3:6.

36 Zec 14:16.

37 Is 10:22; Rom 9:27.

38 Lk 21:24.

knowledge; it teaches and persists in sin. All true believers have died with Christ, and thus have risen from sin and death.[39] Yet, boasting of a grace and forgiveness that bears only vice, the whole world falsely believes the claim that Christ established before God a grace and mercy which demands no repentance, no forsaking of sin, as though Christ had not delivered his own from sin, death, and hell, and all the powers of the devil. Such deceit assumes that Christ did not redeem his own from sin, death, and hell, and from all the power of the devil.[40]

"Whoever commits sin," the cause of death,[41] "is the slave of sin" [Jn 8 (34)], and he serves the devil and the power of the devil.[42] Whoever truly believes serves Christ in all goodness, love, faithfulness, and truth. Through Christ, we are justified to love, faithfulness, and truth. This comes from faith and not the power of the devil, which is his deceit and our imprisonment in sin; it makes us the imprisoned servants of the devil.[43*] But, through Christ, the devil never will rule over us.[44]

However, these so-called Christians deny and slander the Lord Jesus Christ, as though Christ did not take away the power of the devil. They claim that the devil still holds power over those who truly believe in Christ Jesus, and that he still has his way with the children of faith and light,[45] just as he has with the children of unbelief[46] and wickedness. They slander God and his dwelling in heaven.[47] Darkness and light, goodness and wickedness, Christ and Belial can never be compared, nor can they have fellowship one with the other.[48] Therefore it is a terrible slandering of God and his dwelling, that is, of his saints in whom God dwells, to say that the devil and his power of sin should live along-

---

39 Rom 6:2ff.; Col 2:12.

40 Heb 2:14.

41 Rom 6:23; 7:13; Jas 1:15.

42 Heb 2:14.

43* Gloss: The highest power and might of the devil, which is sin, wherewith he overpowers people and holds them prisoner.

44 Mt 12:29; Mk 3:27; 1 Jn 3:8.

45 Jn 12:36; Eph 5:9; 1 Thes 5:5.

46 Eph 2:2.

47 Rv 13:6.

48 2 Cor 6:15. [This language is also found in the Schleitheim Articles of 1527.—Ed.]

side God, as though Christ had not taken away his power, overcome him, judged him, and cast him out of the true believers. I insist that to speak in this manner is to speak where it is improper[49] and to slander God and his dwelling.

It behooves them[50] therefore to search diligently, investigate, and test themselves, according to the words of Paul, whether Christ dwells in them [2 Cor 13 (5)]. If Christ lives in them with the action of his grace, they are no longer sinners. But if they are still sinners, they are cast off. They have time to repent, forsake sin, and confess their sin to God. If God extends his grace and again liberates them from the bonds, cords, and power of the devil,[51] and if Christ lives in them again through his Holy Spirit, they are justified through Christ and no longer sinners. Their sins and the stain of their wickedness have been washed away and cleansed[52] through the blood of Christ,[53] and God does not hold sin against them (Ps 32 [2]).

The true discernment is that those who are in Christ and in whom Christ dwells are not sinners. If they do sin, however, they cannot claim to be in grace[54] until their sins have again been cleansed, and through confession, remorse, and sorrow for their sins they return to true goodness.[55*, 56]

Therefore let those who are in grace boast of the grace of Christ;[57] let those who have sinned fear the wrath of God, for he punishes sin eternally. If God's goodness leads them to repentance,[58] let them diligently perform the deeds of repentance[59] so that they may receive mer-

---

49 Rv 13:6. [Original: *das heist den mund inn himell aufgeton.*—Trans.]

50 [The number of third-person singular male pronouns in this paragraph is confusing so the third-person plural is used.—Trans.]

51 2 Tm 2:26.

52 2 Cor 7:1.

53 1 Cor 6:11; Rv 1:5.

54 Rom 5:2; 6:14; 1 Jn 3:6.

55* Gloss: Such boasting of the truth is a credit to honest people.

56 1 Jn 1:9.

57 1 Cor 1:31.

58 Rom 2:4.

59 Mt 3:8; Lk 3:8.

cy.[60] If they receive mercy and grace, let them boast of Christ and not that they are sinners. But if they remain under the wrath and displeasure of God, let them confess themselves to be sinners and repent in the hope of receiving grace.[61] I do not refer here to the hardened, deliberate knaves who will neither be shamed, nor fear any sin or repent of any. I refer to two kinds of believers.

I mean, first of all, those who believe according to the law of malediction. They sin against God and his Christ; they know that Christ is the Saviour and that God is the avenger[62] and punisher of sin. Nevertheless, they hope that their sin will be forgiven through Christ, who will reconcile them with God his Father. Such individuals possess faith, but it is a faith under judgment, not under grace, until the time when Christ will pardon them. They are sinners under Christ who are not yet in the kingdom of Christ, that is, in the communion of saints, which is the sole fellowship of the body of Christ in the remission and forgiveness of sin. There alone, in the communion of saints, is the conscience cleansed of sin,[63] the heart vindicated[64] and made holy.[65] In that community there are no sinners, only those sanctified[66] through Christ, by faith in him. Those are acquitted, freed from sin, and bought through the blood of Christ.[67] The spirit of grace justifies them[68] to be heirs of

---

60 Rom 11:31.

61 [The preceding set of thoughts needs to be taken as a whole in order to grasp Marpeck's understanding of justification. It is God who leads the sinner to repentance, yet the sinner must perform the works of repentance. Yet there can be no boasting in these works, because it is Christ who makes them possible. Implied here is a criticism of the magisterial reformers, especially Luther, because the Anabaptists claimed that the reformers did not hold God's initiative and our response together.—Ed.]

62 1 Thes 4:6.

63 Heb 9:14.

64 Rom 1:17.

65 Original: *frum.* The meaning of this word depends on who the subject is. When used of a human being, the adjective means "devout"; when it refers to God, it means "holy." Here and following, the subject is God.

66 Original: *fromgemachte.*

67 Rv 5:9.

68 1 Tm 3:16.

Christ's eternal kingdom.[69] That is why there are no sinners in the kingdom of Christ and the communion of saints.

Those, however, who believe that they are damned by sin and that Christ might redeem them are under the judgment of Christ. As said earlier, these individuals repent and repent, and they do believe in Christ. Yet they are still sinners who do not belong in Christ's kingdom of grace, because they are stuck in sin and persist in it. My intention is to indicate the real differences between the true knowledge of Christ and the falsely acclaimed knowledge, and the differences between sinners and those justified in faith. Therefore whoever sins should acknowledge himself as a sinner, so that he may receive pardon.[70] Those who have been pardoned are not sinners—those who have been acquitted of sin are the redeemed. That is the peace, joy, and comfort of all believers.[71] Those whom the Son sets free are free indeed! [Jn 8 (36)]. How then can they be indentured prisoners of sin?[72]

There are three kinds of persons in the judgment and kingdom of Christ.

In the judgment of pardon, there are first of all sinners. "If we say we have no sin," says John, "we deceive ourselves, and the truth is not in us. If we confess our sins, he is faithful and just, and he will forgive our sins and cleanse us from all unrighteousness. If we say we have not sinned, we make him a liar and his Word is not in us" [1 Jn 1 (8–10)]. This text clearly shows that there are sinners and penitents under the judgment of grace. If someone has sinned and does not confess it, he makes God a liar, and his Word is not in a person like that. Nor does

---

69 Jas 2:5.

70 Jas 5:16.

71 Rom 14:17.

72 Jn 8:34; Rom 6:17–22; 7:14. [Marpeck claims that Christians are no longer sinners. The thoughts that follow explain what he means by this remarkable claim. It is that their identity is not that of sinners but of people set free: they are no longer under the dominion of sin. We see at various places in his writings that Marpeck acknowledges that the redeemed still commit acts of sin.

he desire any intercession to give him life again.[73] He thinks he lives. Really he is dead.[74*, 75]

But those who confess their sins, in the hope that Christ will cleanse them from all stain, are penitents and forsake sin. If Christ the Saviour cleanses such a person, he is pardoned and no longer a sinner; he is born anew of God. A part of that new birth is that he no longer sins. Therefore the judgment of grace is committed to the saints of God. Each should diligently test and judge[76] those who have been cleansed by grace and washed from sin in the blood of Christ.[77] They may eat of the bread of the Lord and drink from his cup[78] not as sinners but as those cleansed from all stain of sin.

That is the true communion of saints in Jesus Christ our Lord. Yes, the chosen people and royal priesthood [1 Pt 2 (9)], even the people of the being and nature[79] of God,[80] are born through the word of truth,[81] cleansed and washed from sin[82] in the blood of the Lord Jesus Christ[83] and also through the water of grace,[84] that is, baptism into the communion of saints. As co-witness with the Holy Spirit, baptism testifies that they are born of water and Spirit, that they are like newborn children[85] in the being and nature of the Lord Jesus Christ; filled with grace, love, faithfulness, truth, goodness, and righteousness. These are the fruits of the Holy Spirit [Gal 5 (22)], against which there is no law. These newborn children are not imprisoned but free children, peaceable and free in conscience and heart.

---

73 Jas 5:16.
74* Gloss: For such a one we are not to pray.
75 Rv 3:1.
76 1 Cor 11:28, 31; 2 Cor 13:5.
77 1 Cor 6:11; Rv 1:5.
78 1 Cor 11:28.
79 [Original: *art und natur Gotes.*—Trans.]
80 Acts 17:28; 2 Pt 1:4.
81 Jas 1:18.
82 1 Cor 6:11.
83 Rv 1:5.
84 [Original: *gnadenwasser.* The literal meaning of the text is that there is a washing through the blood of Christ and also through the water of grace.—Trans.]
85 Jn 3:5.

In Holy Scripture, all the prophets, David the psalmist, the evangelists, and the apostles witness to the kingdom, people, and generation of Christ.[86*] It is the highest and most noble lineage, and the virtues, treasures, riches, honour, and property have from ancient times belonged to this royal and most noble house[87] of Christ. These virtues, these priceless noble gems, are not worn externally on physical throats, arms, hands, or fingers; these gems are the power of the Holy Spirit in spirit and soul. The Father of lights, from whom all good gifts come,[88] gives and presents these gems to the most noble house of Christ. Through the Holy Spirit, they are given to the honour of the bridegroom Christ,[89] and they are to be worn on throats, arms, and hands in the real power of the virtue of the noble gems.

Those who have the Spirit do not need elemental gems. They only signify virtue but have no unchanging, eternally enduring power.[90*] In honour of its king, the royal family wears this power and virtue of the noblest, eternally enduring gem on their throats, arms, hands, and fingers. That is, they surrender all their powers and members to the power and effect of that noble gem given by the Father. With all diligence, they see to it that, before the Father and his Christ, the power and effect of this virtue remains unspotted in them. Particularly in the Revelation of John, the Holy Scripture says much about these noble gems [Rv 21 (19–21)], especially about their virtues, which only the nobility of Christ may wear.

The ornament of these precious gems and garments does not belong to those whose sin and whose wicked deceptiveness before God have made them into wretched peasants.[91*] Since the fall of Adam, all humans have been like that. To them, only the earth and earthly things

---

86* Note.

87 ["House" is used here in the sense of an aristocratic family (the house of Hapsburg, for example).—Trans.]

88 Jas 1:17.

89 Mt 9:15; Mk 2:19; Lk 5:34; Jn 3:29; Eph 5:25.

90* Gloss: Figuratively, the physical Israel wore the stone on hallowed garments.

91* Gloss: I do not speak here of the fleshly nobility or peasantry. In their fallen nature each asserts or raises itself, but before God neither one is better than the other.

have been given. They make their living with labour and the sweat of their brow. Since the fall of Adam they have not yet been ennobled by Christ,[92] for whose sake all things are, to rule and reign[93] over heaven and earth. Rather, because of sin, with the deceit of sin[94] and in all wickedness, they still build the cursed and not the blessed earth. Christ has not ennobled them to wear these gems and ornaments. Neither are they disciplined or instructed; they are coarse, knavish labourers, because of the original curse. Therefore they cannot handle the gems. The natural, earthly being knows and understands nothing about God.[95]

Therefore those who lay claim to natural nobility must be gifted with natural virtues, if they are to wear the elemental gems with justification, because they are only a sign of natural virtues. In the natural nobility, it is a scandal to wear much gold, chains, gems, and noble garments and to lack withal the natural honours and virtues. A nobility without virtue is like a sow bedecked with gold and gems.[96, 97*] She immediately drags it all through the dirt, rather than wearing it honourably. Now if one were to inscribe virtue on the coat of arms[98] of the fleshly nobility, one would find few true nobles. For their sake I would gladly be made a liar, and I readily grant them their natural honour.[99]

I write what I do, not because I am concerned with the comings and goings of the natural nobility or presume to scold them. I say it for this reason: an ancient, honourable, noble line does not gladly tolerate dishonourable persons who disgrace and dishonour their name and ancestry. How many hundreds of thousands times more should we, who claim to belong to the ancient, eternal name and lineage of

---

92 Gn 3:17–19.

93 Gn 1:26, 28; Rv 22:5.

94 Heb 3:13.

95 1 Cor 2:14.

96 Prv 11:22.

97* Note.

98 [Original: *die tugennth ans wappen schreiben.*—Trans.]

99 [Compare an interesting passage in the Reformation Sigismundi, in which the author, writing in 1439, states that a man is a noble only when he is also virtuous. See Heinrich Koller, ed., *Reformation Kaiser Siegmunds, Monumenta Germaniae historica 500–1500,* Staatsschriften des späteren Mittelalters 6 (Stuttgart: A. Hiersemann, 1964), 252.—Trans.]

the birth of the Lord Jesus Christ, who have been taken from the world and adorned with virtue and grace, gifted and pardoned by the Father of lights?[100] Should we not be concerned that there be no one among us who would dishonour and blaspheme the noble name and line of the most noble house of Jesus Christ!?[101]

Similarly, no one should be allowed to bear the noble name who is not legitimately born into this family, that is, born and conceived of the Holy Spirit and of the honourable bride of Christ. She conceives in her body children born to the Father of Jesus Christ;[102*] her body is the body of Christ, which is his holy church, and she raises them in her discipline. Christ and his church are one flesh.[103] She is espoused by Christ in the word of truth[104] and married with the ring of love which has no end.[105]

Through the water bath in the Word, which they believe for the remission of sins [Eph 5 (26)], she is the legitimate spouse who bears the children conceived by the Father.[106*] She nourishes and raises her children by the Father with her breasts filled with the pure milk of the Holy Spirit. According to the words of Peter, these children, born of God, are by nature eager to suck this milk for their own growth and increase.[107] For that is the nature of God. "Whoever is born of God"[108] "hears God's Word."[109] Whoever is not so born is not to be included in the house and lineage of Christ. And even if someone boasts of the Father and is not born of the legitimate mother, he is a bastard.[110] He

---

100 Jas 1:17.

101 Rom 2:24; Jas 2:7.

102* Gloss: No one should call anyone a Christian unless he is given testimony to birth from the Father and mother.

103 Eph 5:30–32.

104 2 Cor 6:7; Eph 1:13; Col 1:5; 2 Tm 2:25; Jas 1:18.

105 [In other writings Marpeck calls the church the mother of believers. Here he expands the image in a way that suggests she shares with Christ in the birth of believers. The gloss underscores this bold ecclesiological image.—Ed.]

106* Note.

107 1 Pt 2:2.

108 1 Jn 3:9; 5:18.

109 Jn 8:47.

110 Heb 12:8.

does not inherit, nor may he bear the name of the line, nor may he be included in the high nobility of Christ.

The first unfallen, creaturely Adam was the first bodily nobleman, created in the image of God, from whom all nobility and virtue derives.[111] He was the first earthly nobleman and ruler under heaven. His wife was created from his flesh and bone,[112] and of the same lineage, to help him;[113] they were to plant the garden of God without effort and work, not as peasants but as nobles, in obedience to their Creator. Functionally, they were lord and god to the creatures, for they had been thus appointed under heaven,[114] not to work in wretchedness as a peasant does by the sweat of his brow.[115]

If Adam and his wife had not sinned against their Creator, they and all their line, their descendants of earthly lords and nobility, would be without toil and labour.[116*] Nor would there be shame, disgrace, death, sickness, toil, or labour; nor would any suffering have come on them.[117] Rather, all other creatures would have obeyed them as their divinely appointed lords and nobles, and they, along with their descendants, would have been accepted as such by all creatures under heaven, until the appearance of the heavenly being,[118] also of Adam's line, Jesus Christ.

He ennobled Adam and his family even more, that is, in soul and spirit, and raised them into the heavenly realm. He established and made Adam a lord with the Lord Jesus Christ, who has all power in heaven and on earth.[119] Even the angels, who were subject to him and his obedient servants,[120] desired and were eager to see this ennobling of Adam.[121]

---

[111] Gn 1:27.

[112] Gn 2:23.

[113] Gn 2:18.

[114] Gn 1:28.

[115] Gn 3:19.

[116*] Note.

[117] Rom 5:12.

[118] [Original: *himlischen menschen.*—Trans.]

[119] Mt 28:18; etc.

[120] 1 Pt 3:22.

[121] 1 Pt 1:12.

For the whole human race Christ brought this freedom to become heavenly lords without tribulation, pain, death, and suffering with him.[122*] Through his own tribulation, suffering, and death, he brought it, to make heavenly human beings out of earthly ones, raised up with Christ through suffering with him into eternal liberty and glory.[123] Therefore, as Paul says, all creatures exist for our sake;[124] we exist for Christ's sake; and Christ exists for God's sake.[125] That is the true, highly gifted, and liberated noble ancient house which has its origin from eternity. We may boast that we belong to this noble house, that we may partake in such glory with Christ, and that we have the right to wear the golden chains with all the gems, necklaces, bracelets, and rings, as well as the elegant garments with which Christ honours his bride and wedding guests. As the legitimate and true nobility, we may use the glory and the liberty of the most precious gems and virtues that belong to Christians as the true nobility. Much could be written of these treasures, as Holy Scripture makes clear.

When, however, Adam and Eve despised the noble title given them by God, fell into shame and disgrace through the deceit of sin, and trespassed the command of their Lord and Creator, all their freedom and glory and their dominion over the other creatures was taken from them, and they were expelled from the garden of pleasure. The garden was closed along with the heavenly city, and the fiery sword of the wrath of God upon humankind was placed before it.[126*] Adam and his wife were made into peasants of the earth in the great village of this bleak world's wilderness, in order to make Adam's living by the sweat of his brow. With wretchedness and toil he and all his descendants were to make a living on it, and wives were to bear children in suffering.[127] There the primeval divine nobility and true human freedom with all its glory came to an end. The noble, divine house died off through death,

---

[122*] Note.

[123] Rom 8:17.

[124] [Original: *umbs menschen willen.*—Trans.]

[125] 1 Cor 3:21–23.

[126*] Note.

[127] Gn 3:1–24.

which came from sin,[128] and there were no heirs of humanity's glory. They all became wretched, coarse peasants and unfaithful labourers, working the earth in falsehood and deceit, in all wickedness, shame, and licentiousness, sold under sin[129] and made into coarse, undisciplined slaves of sin.[130]

That is the origin of that coarse generation of peasants which knows neither discipline nor virtuous custom before God. Since the time of Adam it has grown in coarseness, licentiousness, lack of discipline, and wickedness. The human race was raised up by the father of lies,[131] the enemy of all virtue and truth, and remained coarse, undisciplined peasants till the time of Christ. They have presumed to be noble, though like heathen, on the model of the pure nobility of creation mentioned above, but in their fallen nature they committed theft in the eyes of Christ and his noble virtue.[132*]

Therefore all who came before and lag behind Christ—but are not with him—are thieves and murderers [Jn 10 (8)]. They are not of the highborn lineage or nobility of Christ but a wild, undisciplined, coarse, bucolic lot, full of all vice, lacking goodness, loveless, unfriendly, wanton, proud, boastful, full of envy and hate, bloodthirsty, whoring, gluttonous, quaffers, greedy for vain honour, not desirous of the good, cunning and malicious, ready for all wickedness. The list is endless: they are also profiteers, liars, deceivers, miserly, thieving, murderous, unbelieving, idolatrous, sorcerers, contentious, quarrellers and brawlers, disobedient to parents, perjurers, faithless and deniers of the truth! [Rom 1 (28–32); 1 Tm 1 (9f.)].

In short, they do whatever they feel like, regardless of all natural honour, not to speak of any divine virtue. They are beastly people, like swine and dogs before whom precious pearls should not be cast;[133]

---

128 Rom 5:12.

129 Rom 7:14.

130 Jn 8:34; Rom 6:17f., 20.

131 Jn 8:44.

132* Gloss: Earthly emperors and rulers create nobles with shield, gems, and helmets. The virtues, however, which belong to nobility, they have no power to give. But those who are ennobled by Christ are also gifted with his virtues.

133 Mt 7:6.

rather, they should be kept and hidden from them. They are the coarsest of all people, to whom not even the earthly is commanded and entrusted, let alone the divine, any more than it would be given to beastly, unreasoning, raging animals which are inclined only to kill and destroy. All of that—one transgression after another—follows from the curse of sin.

Second, there are the legalistic, law and order[134] people who hold to a human respectability and piety for the sake of physical need and vain honour. It is rooted and written in their created nature. Thus they become a law unto themselves,[135] on the basis of which they love honesty and natural virtue, as the devout heathen have done, but know little or nothing about any God. They invent all manner of idolatry and shape it by their fallen reason, so that they learn to believe and love it.

For everything that is loved or feared above or besides God the Creator of heaven and earth is an idol, no matter what its appearance. Whatever is done with it is a rustic, earthly, coarse effort. Its essence is transitory and perishable; it is loved and feared only for earthly reasons. These are the coarse, earthly workers and peasants who as yet know nothing of the nobility and virtue of Christ. However, through the understanding and knowledge of Christ they may come to a mature faith in Christ and be gifted and ennobled with the virtue and goodness that comes through faith.

Third, there are people who are captive to the law of God, who believe and hold that all things are of God, who has made them and all creatures. But because of their rough, earthly, fallen, peasant ways, they cannot receive or follow the noble law of God. That is why they will endure condemnation and more heavy blows on their backs: they know the will of the Lord but do not do it. They proclaim it to be beyond their capacity and do not do it. Although they should do the good and inherit the blessing, they do evil and wickedness and inherit the malediction and the curse. Sin takes over in them against their own will

---

134 [Original: *Bolozeyische = polizeilich* (literally, "police" [adj. or adv.]). In the sixteenth century there were no police forces in the current sense; what is meant is civil authority.—Trans.]

135 Rom 2:14.

to such a degree[136] that they do not know where to turn to escape the stern anger of God. For regardless of what they try to cultivate in their earthly, fallen nature, only thistles and thorns grow. In spite of all their effort and work, the weeds[137]—that is sin—take over, and all their work leads only to tribulation and grief.[138]

But wherever sin thus takes over, grace can also take over.[139] If there is repentance in true remorse, and sorrow over sin, and a hearty dissatisfaction of self, then one can receive grace upon grace [Jn 1 (16f.)]. Even though one finds oneself condemned under the law given by Moses, which is good and given for humanity's salvation, one nevertheless receives grace and truth which comes from Christ,[140*] by which one is freed from sin and ennobled and graced with the virtues of faith in Christ.

Fourth, there are the hypocrites and dissemblers, who in all their coming and going seek to justify and hallow themselves—they regard themselves as devout and healthy. All the sects in the world are full of them! Even today they sit with the hypocrites in the temple, grandly thanking God that they are not like so-and-so [Lk 18 (11)]. Those who thus justify and heal themselves need no physician [Lk 5 (11)]. Their health remains an eternal illness and death; their sight, eternal blindness and darkness. Since they cannot produce anything to excuse their sin, it remains on them.

Here one also finds the opposite, namely, hypocritical sinners. These are they who in confessing that they are sinners imagine themselves to be better than the other hypocrites, even as those hypocrites think themselves better than the sinners! But they are all the same. These sinners in their villainy, wickedness, and sin presume to despise the righteous who are justified and sanctified by Christ through faith; they turn into hypocrisy the devotion and truth of Christ in those who are pardoned. They confess their knavery as better than the true devo-

---

136 Rom 5:20; 7:2–24.

137 Mt 13:7, 22; Mk 4:7, 18; Lk 8:7, 14.

138 2 Cor 7:10.

139 Rom 5:20.

140* Gloss: for them Christ hallows himself.

tion of Christ which comes from faith and not from the works[141] about which the hypocrite boasts. They presume by such confession of their sin to sanctify their wicked, sinful lives, and by doing so they make the faithful and devout appear to be hypocrites who expect to be justified by their works. They expect therefore to go from the temple justified[142] with all the sin and wickedness in which they lie (without any remorse and repentance or decision to forsake it). In so doing they slander the righteous and sanctified of Christ as dissemblers and hypocrites, although they themselves are the real mockers of Christ. They expect to sneak in under the parable of Christ and say with a false heart: "God be merciful to me a sinner."[143] But they have no intention, desire, or petition to abstain from sin. They are worse than any other dissemblers on earth.

Fifth and finally, there are those who have the appearance of faith in Christ but who seek their devoutness only in the hearts of other people. They accuse everyone of wickedness and sin, as though the sin of others were the reason for their own sin and wickedness, and as though they cannot get rid of their sin because of other people. They presume to judge and justify everyone. One is said to have done first this, then that. They seem to assume that they sin only because of the wickedness and sin of others. Otherwise they would be devout and upright. People like that usually go from one sect and error to another. The world is as full of them as the raging sea is full of terrible and marvellous beasts.[144*]

They run around to find the gospel and peace of Christ and never find it. All they have in themselves is a stone[145] and so they die of hunger, ever lacking the word of truth,[146] the true bread of God, because they do not look for it in that place where the Lord and his true nourishment alone is to be found, namely, in their own hearts. Whoever

---

141 Rom 3:28; 4:5.

142 Lk 18:14.

143 Lk 18:13.

144* Note.

145 Mt 7:9; Lk 11:1.

146 2 Cor 6:7; Eph 1:13; Col 1:5; 2 Tm 2:15; Jas 1:18.

does not find the Lord and his Word as soul food[147] there will find it in no other place eternally.

False prophets usually come to such people and say: "Come, I will show you Christ in our gathering, company, or congregation. You will find Christ there. You will see honest discipleship, grounded in Spirit and grace, and God dwelling in our hearts as his chamber[148] and temple. You will see the true light and salt[149] that belongs to the true food and with which it must be salted" [Mt 24 (5, 23)].[150] Therefore such people hear the falsely acclaimed Christians rather than those who truly know Christ. They are led into strange hearts unknown to Christ, away from their own hearts, in which alone they can and should find Christ. Thus they are imprisoned and deceived, evermore lost and undone in their consciences. They are clouds without water, that is, without the water of grace, driven by the whirlwind [Jude 1 (12)]; that is, by mere, inflated, vain, empty words, without the accompanying work of the Holy Spirit, who alone can bring it into the heart of the faithful.

May the Lord protect and preserve us from such prophets, about whom he himself warned us, as well as from all other evil and errors, that we might seek the goodness[151] of Christ in his Word and truth[152] in no other place than our own hearts. There he reveals himself to us, and with the Father dwells in us,[153] if we truly love and keep his commandments,[154] which are not difficult.[155]

That is the true sign by which each of us may judge whether Christ dwells in him [2 Cor 13 (5)]. Such a heart will soon find the true gathering and fellowship of his saints. For where the carcass is, the eagles will gather [Mt 24 (28)]. There also the gathering and true fellowship of the

---

147 Jn 6:27.

148 Mt 24:26.

149 Mt 5:13f.

150 [It sounds as if the author is quoting people whose ministry he knows and resents.—Ed.]

151 [This is an unusual case in which *fromkheit* is applied to Christ.—Ed.]

152 Jn 17:17.

153 Jn 14:23.

154 Jn 14:15.

155 1 Jn 5:3.

saints will soon be found. May he allow us to be found in his fellowship, which is his body. Amen.

The grace of our Lord Jesus Christ be with us all. Amen.[156]

My sister Anna[157] and I cordially thank you kindly for your gifts and contribution. This indication and proof of the spirit of your hearts is dearer to me in Christ than the gift, even if it were worth the whole world. I thank the Lord for you, even you. The congregation here, as well as I and my Anna, greet you fervently in the Lord. Brother Veit[158] himself writes his own greeting. Pray to the Lord faithfully for us, and we will, by God's grace, do the same.

Dated at Augsburg on December 9 in the year[159] 1547.

In the Lord Jesus Christ,
servant to you and all the faithful,
and comrade in the tribulation in Christ,[160]
Pilgram Marpeck

---

156 Phil 4:23; etc.

157 Marpeck's wife.

158 [This person is probably Veitenn Maurer. In no. 26 ("Concerning the Office of Peace"), Sigmund Bosch thanks Jörg Maler for sending Veit to him.—Trans.]

159 [Original: *anno.*—Trans.]

160 Rv 1:9.

39

An epistle of comfort compiled from Holy Scripture

Anonymous
1533

This plaintive testimony of perseverance under persecution is cut from the same cloth as other Kunstbuch texts, such as that of Hans Has von Hallstatt, "Concerning the Comfort of Christians under Persecution" (no. 23). It is taken from an anonymous *Trostbüchlein* ("little book of comfort"). Because of popular demand it was published twice in 1533, both in Augsburg and Nuremberg, and published again as part of a collection of writings by Valentin Ickelsamer and Caspar Schwenckfeld, renowned Spiritualist writers of the day. Scholars have identified both Ickelsamer and Schwenckfeld as the author of this pamphlet.[1]

Ickelsamer already has a place in this collection in Preface 2, "The Learned Ones; the Wrongheaded Ones." In that poem we see that Ickelsamer was not shy about putting forth his convictions. And on a decisive point, the outwardness of the church, he and Marpeck were on opposite sides. This was also the case with Schwenckfeld. He and Marpeck engaged in a long and passionate competition to set the direction of the Radical Reformation in their shared sphere of influence in South Germany. It is likely that Jörg Maler was aware of the pub-

---

Eine Trostepistel, aus heiliger Schrift zusammengezogen; 1533. Translation by Victor Thiessen and John D. Rempel.

1 BSOT, 610.

lishing history of the *Trostbüchlein.* By including a piece from it, was he taking sides in that debate? At the very least he was asserting that Spiritualist authors had insight and nurture to offer persecuted Anabaptists. At the same time Maler, or an earlier Anabaptist author, saw fit to alter the text. A polemic against infant baptism, and another polemic of special concern to Pilgramites, that of the redemption of Old Testament saints, have been added.

The theme of the epistle is the ways of God with humanity: is God absolutely trustworthy, in persecution and prosperity, in confusion and certainty, in life and death? Will I be put to shame if I follow Jesus' call and forsake everything? The author breaks through to a confident answer to these searing questions. It is not that Christians are spared suffering: "Yet how rich is my condition! God and Heaven are still mine own."[2]

The text is a stream of biblical quotations, flowing purposefully from one to the other by means of brief interpretive comments by the compiler. Often one scripture is used to interpret another one, with few additional remarks. The writer's purpose is to arm afflicted saints with "the sword and shield of the living Word of God and also Holy Scripture." Sayings from the synoptic Gospels have pride of place, followed by the Psalms, John, Hebrews, and the apocryphal book of Wisdom. Most of them lift up the will and foreknowledge of God: those who suffer remain secure in the care and purpose of God.

There are three sections, each called "a word of comfort," and a conclusion. The first word focuses on God's foreknowledge; the second, on an appointed time for suffering. The longer third word dwells on the necessity of suffering and also the power to bear it and even rejoice in it. Its most stunning image is that of the suffering church as a pregnant woman; she endures the pains of childbirth so that the earth might not be destroyed. The author shows his affinity for the promises to the suffering ones chosen of God, as found in the late post-exilic Judaic book of Wisdom; his reliance on these promises expands the sources of comfort available to the church.

---

2 From the first verse of Henry Lyte's hymn "Jesus, I my cross have taken" (1824; rev. 1833).

Woven into the text are warnings about—and occasionally declarations of—condemnation of the godless. When the wretched of the earth resort to such language, it has a different weight than such words have coming from those with earthly power and wealth.

In God's name. Amen.
A letter of comfort compiled from Holy Scripture. I hope that by grace it might be useful to all those who are sorrowful, sick, or imprisoned, so that in their fear, need, and horrible circumstances they might remember and be comforted through God's grace, remaining upright in the faith of God's Son unto the end, in God the Father, the Son, and the Holy Spirit, amen, together with all those who desire these things. Amen. Amen.

The Word of Christ in John 16 [33]:
You will have peace in me and fear in the world. But be encouraged, I have overcome the world.

1533

As soon as Jesus Christ our only Saviour[3] [Mt 1 (1–11)] was baptized by John in the Jordan,[4] he was attacked and tempted by Satan from that hour on.[5*] He rejected Satan and turned him away with Holy Scripture [Dt 6 (13, 16); 8 (3)]. Thus it is most necessary for all true believers and those marked by God, who have been sealed with the pledge of the Holy Spirit, and afflicted in these last dangerous days, in misery and taken captive, to be armed in their hearts with the armour of God [Eph 6 (13)], and Holy Scripture, given by God [2 Tm 3 (16)]. Then, wherever they are attacked or tempted by the devil [1 Pt 5 (8)] (who does not rejoice in this), the flesh and the raging world, such as through strange thoughts, doubts, cunning questions, prisons or harsh torture, they may protect themselves with the sword and shield of the living Word of God and

---

3 [Two titles, "*heilandt*" and "*seligmacher,*" are used here; both mean "Saviour" in English.—Trans.]

4 Mt 3:13–17.

5* Preface.

also Holy Scripture,[6] douse the fiery arrows, orient themselves toward God, gain strength, and persevere to the end.

That is what I wish to do, through grace, in this letter. It is composed on the basis of some texts, and set up in three writings of comfort, so that all distressed, believing hearts might know how to be comforted. Whoever seeks in earnestness finds; whoever asks in truth receives, and whoever knocks on the true door, to them it will be opened [Lk 11 (9f.)], so that they might find abundant pasture in their going out and coming in [Jn 10 (9)].

First, nothing will be thrown at believers that is not the will of God. Whatever happens to them, however, serves their good [Rom 8 (28)].

Second, God has placed a goal in the lives of believers, beyond which they may not go [Ps 39 (5)]. But the godless will not reach their goal.

Third comes suffering, which is in fact the way we must travel to eternal life. For Christ has prepared this way for us, and he and his servants have gone this way before us [Lk 9 (23); Mk 8 (34); Mt 10 (38)]. He will not prepare another way for anyone's sake. Thus we must take this road as well, or we will not reach the eternal gates of heaven and will travel the broad path that leads away into eternal punishment [Mt 7 (13)]. May God protect us all from that. Amen.

The first word of comfort

Nothing will be inflicted upon believers against the will of God, but whatever happens to them serves to bring them good in all ways [Rom 8 (28)].

Now follows the first word and testimonial: "Are not two sparrows sold for a penny? And one of them will not fall to the earth without your father [knowing]. The hairs of your head are all counted. So you should not fear. You are better than many sparrows" (Mt 10 [29f.]). If God counts the hairs on the heads of believers, without doubt he also numbers their pain, flesh and blood, and all their members.

"Are not five sparrows bought for two pennies? And not one of them is forgotten by God. All the hairs of your head are counted. Thus

---

6 [This distinction between an immediate and inward word of revelation and the Bible is a hallmark of Spiritualism.—Ed.]

you should not fear for yourself, for you are worth more than many sparrows" [Lk 12 (6f.)]. From this it follows that God will not forget the faithful in their need but will be with them in their sadness.

"You will be handed over by father, mother, brother, sister, friends, and some of you will be killed by them. You will be hated by everyone because of my name. But not one hair of your head will be lost. Through your patience you will retain your soul" [Lk 21 (16–19)]. Much less may your soul be lost, which is worth more than your hair.

Thus Paul comforts the seafarers in need [Acts 27 (33ff.)]. The comfort the seafarers received is also our comfort. God works all things according to the good council of his will [Eph 1 (5)]. Thus human counsels against God and his faithful must be routed (Gn 11 [7f.]; Ps 2 [1–5]).

"You may not make one hair black or white" [Mt 5 (36)]. No one can take counsel against a believer without God's will. "Who of you can add an elbow's length to your stature simply with your thoughts?" [Lk 12 (25)]. So no one can do anything to a believer without the will of God.

"The sinner looks upon the righteous one and seeks to kill him. But the Lord does not release him into his hands" [Ps 37 (32f.)]. The believer may believe that God has left him, but at that very time he is closer than ever.

"Had the Lord never stood by us—or rather, as Israel says, were the Lord not with us—as the peoples raged around us, they would have eaten us alive. As their anger let loose against us, they would have drowned us as with flood waters; yes, as with torrents they would have brought an end to us. The deep mud pits of pride would have sunk into our very souls. God be praised, that he did not give us as prey to their teeth. Like a bird, our life has escaped out of the poacher's nets. The ropes are torn, and we have escaped! Our help is in the name of the Lord who made heaven and earth" [Ps 124 (1–8)].

With this psalm (as follows) God should be praised and magnified daily by the faithful. "The Lord will not allow the sceptres of the godless to determine the fate of the pious, so that the pious will not extend their hands to do evil" [Ps 125 (3)].

"At the right time," Solomon says, "God will rescue and lead the faithful out of the hands of the godless" [Ws 4 (3:1)].

Joseph says to his brothers, "It was not your own counsel that led you to sell me to the Ishmaelites, but it happened that I was sent there by the will of God" [Gn 45 (8)]. Thus some will say that things go badly for them, but in fact they are of great benefit to them. The Day of the Lord will reveal it.

"Herod and Pontius Pilate, together with heathen and the people of Israel, came together in the city against your holy Son Jesus; you chose them to do the things your hands and wisdom had foreseen" [Acts 4 (27f.)]. Without the foreknowledge of God, Herod and Pilate would not have carried out anything against the faithful.

"The devils pleaded with Jesus, saying: 'If you drive us out of him, allow us to go into the herd of pigs.' And he said to them, 'Go ahead!'" [Mt 8 (31f.)]. The devils had no power to go into the pigs of the Gadarenes without the will of Christ. You are much more than pigs.

"Behold," said God to Satan, "Job is in your hands; only do not touch his soul" [Jb 1 (12); 2 (6); 5 (17–27)]. Just as the devil may not do damage to either the body or goods of Job without the will of God, so much less may he damage the soul of the faithful.

"Though Balak should give me his house filled with gold and silver, nonetheless I would not alter the Word of the Lord, my God, to diminish or add to it" [Nm 22 (18)]. Just as Balaam did not wish to curse the children of Israel against the will of God, the faithful may not be cursed or hurt by others unless it be the will of God.

James and John said to Jesus, "'Lord, will you allow us to request that fire come from heaven and consume the Samaritans?' Jesus turned to them and admonished them saying, 'Do you not recognize which spirit's children you are?'" [Lk 9 (54f.)]. If the disciples of Christ cannot bring fire from heaven without his will, no fire, sword, or water can ever harm the believers unless it be the will of God. "Since God is with us, who can be against us?" [Rom 8 (31)].

O God, you suffer no defect! We are glad to know this. Only strengthen our faith, so that no defect be found with us as well [Lk 17 (5)]. This is desperately needful [Mk 9 (29)]. Brother, writes Paul, we know that all things work together for good for those who love God (Rom 8 [28]). Thus the welts on St. Paul's cheeks, his chains, and his prison are of more use to God than his principality was to Ananias,[7] his kingdom was to Agripa,[8] and the entire Roman Empire was to Nero [Acts 23 (2); 25; 26 (29); 28 (20)].

The second word of comfort

God has already given the truly faithful a goal—indeed, for every day and hour of their lives—but the godless will not reach this goal [Ps 39 (5)].

The first writing and testimonial. Some said to Jesus, "Get out of here, for Herod will kill you. And he said to him, go and say to the fox, 'Take this to heart: I drive out the devil, I heal and restore to health today and tomorrow, and on the third day I will finish my work'" [Lk 13 (31f.)]. Christ taught the faithful that they will die not when the fox Herod wishes but when God wills it.

The disciples said to Jesus, "Rabbi, the Jews seek to stone you now, yet you are going there again. Jesus answered, 'Does not a day have twelve hours?'" [Jn 11 (8f.)]. By these words he gave comfort to all the faithful, that no one could kill them until the hours of their day had been completed. Thus they will die, even without that persecution, whether from a fever, plague, or illness, however God has ordained. How often did the Jews want to catch Jesus, Paul, and the other apostles, stone them, push them over a cliff, or kill them? [Jn 7 (1); 11 (8); Lk 4 (29); Acts 4 (3, 21); 9 (23f., 29); 2 Cor 11 (23–26, 32f.)]. But they were not allowed to harm them before the hour that God had seen fit. We belong to Christ in faith.

"Although I had been with you every day in the temple," said Christ to the Jews, "you did not stretch out your hands against me. But now is your hour and the hour of the powers of darkness" [Lk 22 (53)]. Prior to that darkness[9] the believer will not be killed.

---

7 Acts 23:2.

8 Acts 25:13ff.

9 [Original: *vor der Finsternuß*, but the reference to Ps 91 suggests the above translation.—Trans.]

"I will grant them fullness of days," God says to the believers [Ps 91 (16)]. Thus no one may shorten the day of the believers unless it be the will of God.

"Look, you have measured the length of my life, and my entire life is as nothing before you. Indeed, the entire human race is nothing but vanity" [Ps 39 (5)]. No one can diminish what God himself has measured out.

For "the bloodsuckers will not live out half their days" [Ps 55 (23)]. They will be measured with the measure they use, or God would otherwise not remain just. And that is far from his nature.[10]

"I will fulfil the number of your days," says God [Ex 23 (26)]. No one can diminish them.

"Lord, do not take me halfway through my days" [Ps 102 (24)]. The Lord takes and gives days according to his wishes.

O God, "the days of a mortal are short, and the number of his months is determined by you. You have set his limits; they may not be prolonged" [Jb 14 (5)]. Whoever considers these words in his heart will soon put an end to his pride.

"The cup that I shall drink," said Christ to the sons of Zebedee, "you will also drink" [Mt 20 (23)]. Here the faithful have been shown that the cross is already set before them and God has ordained the manner of their death, though they did not yet know the cross.

"Truly, I say to you," said Christ to Peter, "when you were young, you tied your own belt and went where you wanted. But when you have grown old, you will stretch out your hands and another will gird you and lead you where you do not want to go" [Jn 21 (18)]. Jesus said this to indicate the kind of death by which he would glorify God. This will be said to every one of the faithful who confesses with Peter that Jesus is the Christ, the Son of the living God [Mt 16 (16)].

"Upon my soul," says the rich man Nabal,[11] "you have collected many goods over many years. Rest, eat, drink, and live well!" At this point God said to him, "Fool, this night I will take your soul from you" [Lk 12 (19f.)]

---

10 Rom 9:14.

11 1 Sm 25:38.

From the scriptures it is made clear that God has already ordained the hour of death for each of the faithful, and also already decided what kind of death they would die. But he allows the evil ones to be master of their works. Yet they will not do this for long, but "as soon as they speak of peace and security, stormy weather and destruction will befall them, like the pain of a pregnant mother" [1 Thes 5 (3); Rv 3 (17)]. As a snare captures a bird, the Day of the Lord will surprise them as a thief in the night, "and they will not be able to flee" [Rv 3 (3); Lk 21 (35)].

The third word of comfort

Fear, need, poverty, misery, disgusting circumstances, persecution, prison, worry, wretchedness, and sorrow—indeed, suffering and the cross itself—is the way to salvation. Whoever does not want to pursue this path will not be saved, and no excuse will help.

The first text and testimony: "Whoever does not take up his cross," says Christ, "and follow me, is not worthy of me" [Mt 10 (38)]. Indeed, everyone wants to talk like a Christian but not carry a cross like one.[12] But this will not help them.

"If anyone wishes to follow me, he must deny himself and take up his cross daily and follow me." Take note: daily, daily, daily! "Whoever wishes to save his life will lose it. But whoever will lose his life for my sake will retain it" [Lk 9 (23f.)]. O God, how often we risk our life and body for the sake of idle honour, to please worldly lords and for temporal gain with great danger to our soul, but for the sake of Christ and his holy Word one does not risk the smallest finger.

"What good does it do a person who wins the whole world but loses himself and harms his soul?" [Mk 8 (36); Lk 9 (25)]. In the end, a person must let go of all the world.

"There is no continuing city here." Therefore one "should look to the future one" [Heb 13 (13f.); Col 3 (1f.)]. Indeed, "one should go" with Christ "outside the camp, outside the gate, and help him bear his shame."

---

12 [The play on words works better in German; Original: *Jaa, maulchristen, aber nit creutzchristen wolt man gern sein.*—Trans.]

"Everyone who confesses me before others, I will confess before my father who is in heaven. Whoever would deny me before others, however, I will deny before my father who is in heaven" [Mt 10 (32f.); 2 Tm 2 (12)]. People strive after the rewards of the world till they break their necks for it, but for the sake of Christ they won't so much as open their mouths.

"But blessed are they who mourn, for they shall be comforted." "Cursed are those who rejoice in the flesh, for they will have sadness and lament." "Blessed are those who are persecuted for the sake of righteousness, for theirs is the kingdom of heaven" [Mt 5 (4, 10); Lk 6 (21, 25)]. Justice has its persecutors as Abel had his brother Cain, David his Saul, and Christ his Annas and Caiaphas.

"Blessed are you when people speak ill of you for my sake and betray you and say all sorts of evil about you, lying. Rejoice and be glad, for your reward is great in heaven" [Mt 5 (11f.)]. Not only because of some evils, but all evil accusations, such as 'Samaritan,' 'heretic,' 'rebel,' 'Beelzebub,' and 'evildoer,' which will be made against all Christians [Jn 8 (48); 10 (20f., 33); Mt 12 (24)]. But this is nothing new, dear brothers, for all the prophets, Christ himself, and all his messengers and followers experienced this, and so it will go to the end of the world, as it happens even in the present day [Mt 23 (34, 37); Heb 10 (32f.); 11 (35–38)]. May the Lord Jesus Christ give us grace, that we might compose our souls with patience.[13] Amen.

"Christ had to suffer and then go to his glory." We are no greater than Christ[14] [Lk 24 (26)]. "For all who wish to live a godly life in Christ will suffer persecution" [2 Tm 3 (12)]. The one who says "all" does not exempt anyone. Truly, "we must enter into the kingdom of God through much suffering" [Mk 13 (19); Acts 14 (22)], not a life filled with squeals of delight.

"Where do war and disputes among you come from? Are they not from your selfish desires that do battle in your members? You are greedy and have nothing. You envy and hate and do not wish to overcome this. You battle and fight and have nothing, because you do not pray for it.

---

13 Lk 21:19.

14 Mt 10:24.

You pray and do not receive, because you do not ask properly, because you destroy it by your lusts. You adulterers, men and women, do you not know that friendship with the world is enmity with God? Whoever only wants to be a friend to this world will be God's enemy" [Jas 4 (1–4)]. Woe, woe to those who aggravate God so that they may remain friends of this world!

"Were I to seek to please people," says Paul, "I would not be a servant of Christ" [Gal 1 (10); 1 Thes 2 (4)]. A Christian must not carry two loads or serve two lords. There has to be only one [Mt 6 (24)], either day or night light or darkness, Christ or Belial [2 Cor 6 (14f.)].

"If the world hates you," says Christ, "you should know that they hated me before they hated you. Thus, if you were of the world, the world would have loved you as one of its own. However, you are not of the world, but I have chosen you from out of the world; that is why the world hates you. Keep in mind the words that I said to you: 'The servant is not greater than his master.' If they have persecuted me, they will also persecute you" [Jn 15 (18–20)]. If the Lord had to put on a bloody cloak, and in this manner pass into his glory and heavenly home, without doubt his servants will have to wear these colours on their sleeve, or they will not be members of the wedding party [Jn 12 (24–25); Lk 14 (27); Mt 22 (11)].[15]

"Keep in mind the days gone by," writes Paul, "in which you were enlightened, and suffered a great battle of tribulations. At times you were subjected to mockery[16] and abuse in rough times and tribulation, and became comrades of those who go through similar trials. For you have suffered with the captives, and have borne joyfully the robbery of your goods, and recognized in yourselves that you will receive a better and more permanent being. In accord with this, you should not depart from your hope—it will be greatly rewarded. You need patience, however, to fulfil the will of God and triumph over temptation.[17] For there is still a brief time in which will come to pass what must come to pass,

---

15 [This is a stunning image: the wedding garment is soaked in blood.—Ed.]

16 [Original: *ein fasnachtspil* (literally, a Shrove Tuesday play, which makes fun of people in authority).—Trans.]

17 [Original: *verheissung* ("promise," but the context suggests "temptation").—Trans.]

and it will not last long [1 Pt 4 (7); 1 Jn 2 (18, 28)]. But the just will live by faith. And should anyone withdraw, this would not please my soul. We are not children who slacken to the point of damnation but children of faith and perseverance to the preservation of our soul" [Heb 10 (32–39)]. Perseverance to the end brings salvation, but falling away brings eternal death [Mt 10 (22); 2 Thes 2 (3)]. May God preserve us.

"You brothers," Paul adds, "let us do away with all complaints and the sins connected with them, and let us go with patience into the battle that is set out before us. Let us look to Jesus, the prince[18] and teacher "of faith and its fulfiller, who after being presented with joy, patiently bore the cross with spite of shame and scandal, and now sits to the right of the throne of God. Consider those, then, who have withstood such opposition and resistance from sinners, so that you might not become tired and depressed in your spirit and fall away [2 Cor 4 (1)]. For in the battle against sin you have not yet resisted to the point of blood, and have forgotten the comfort that was given to you as children, saying: 'My son, you should not despise the discipline of the Lord, nor should you despair when you are punished by him. For the Lord will discipline those he loves' [Prv 3 (11f.)]. He also chastises each of the children he adopts. You should persevere in this testing; God expects it from you, as each of his children [Sir 2 (1)]. For where is there a son who is not tested by his father? But if you remain outside the discipline and testing in which all partake, you are bastards and not children." "Certainly, each test does not appear to bring joy when it occurs, but is a sad thing. Afterward, however, if it has been borne successfully, it brings inexpressible joy to all those who have passed through it. So, get up from your tired and sore knees, and walk boldly on your feet, so that you don't limp and go astray but are healed" [Heb 12 (1–8, 11–13)].

"Most dearly beloved," writes Paul, "you should not be surprised now and again at the momentary heat that is sent to you for a temptation, as though something new has come upon you, but be partners in the sufferings of Christ and rejoice in them, so that you receive joy and rejoice in the revelation of his glory" [1 Pt 4 (12–16)]. Briefly, suffering must be the daily bread of each Christian, as David says: "I eat ashes

---

18 [Original: *hertzogen* (literally, "duke").—Trans.]

as bread."[19] "I have become tired from sighing. I am awash in my bed at night, and soak my bed with my tears. My face is worn with mourning; I disappear among so many of my foes" [Ps 6 (6–7); 41 (43:3); 68 (69:3f.)].

Peter also writes: "Even if you suffer disgrace in the name of Christ, you will be blessed; the honour, glory, and power of God and his Spirit will rest upon you. But none of you will suffer like a murderer, or a thief, or a blasphemer, or one who envies another's goods. But those who suffer as Christians should not be ashamed but praise and honour God in the circumstances."

Paul says, "We have all sorts of tribulations, but we are not afraid! We are crushed, but we do not despair. We suffer persecution, but we are not forsaken. We are oppressed but have not be killed. At all times we bear the death of the Lord Jesus in our bodies, so that in our bodies the life of the Lord Jesus will also be revealed" [2 Cor 4 (8–10)].

Further, "And now, behold, I am bound by the Spirit to travel to Jerusalem. I do not know what will happen to me there, except that the Holy Spirit has told me all along that bondage and tribulation await me there. But I do not let this bother me at all. I do not count my life of any value to me. I await the end of my life with joy" [Acts 20 (22–24)]. "For Christ is my life, and death is my prize" [Phil 1 (21)].

Further: we are like those who have been sentenced to death and have become a spectacle before the world, the angels, and humanity. We are fools for the sake of Christ— weak, despised, hungry, thirsty, naked, and beaten with fists—and have no place that is home [Mt 8 (20); Lk 9 (58)]. We work and toil with our own hands. People curse us; we bless them. People persecute us; we bear it with patience. People tell lies about us; we plead earnestly. We are the refuse of the world and everyone's garbage" [1 Cor 4 (9-13)]. O God, help and save us, for you alone are our refuge.

Peter also writes: "It is time for judgment to begin at the house of God. Let it begin first of all with the true believers; but what kind of end will it be for those who do not believe in the gospel of God? And if the just shall barely be saved, imagine how it will go with the god-

---

19 Ps 102:9.

less and sinners. Thus those who suffer so much for God's sake should commend their souls with good deeds to their faithful Creator" [1 Pt 4 (17–19)]. After God has taken his own to himself, then he will begin to deal roughly with the godless and supposed Christians.

"I, Paul, rejoice in the sufferings I undergo for you, that in my flesh I fulfil those things that are lacking in the sufferings of Christ for his body, which is the church" [Col 1 (24)]. Whoever is not willing to suffer and does not fulfil the sufferings of Christ in his body is not a member of the body of Christ.

Thus Moses, the servant of God, chose "to suffer evil with the people of Israel rather than to have the satisfactions of temporal pleasures, and considered the shame of Christ to be greater riches than all the treasures of the Egyptians. For he looked to the reward. Through faith he forsook Egypt and did not fear the anger of the king. For he relied on the invisible, as though he had seen it, and was steadfast" [Heb 11 (25–27)].

"I say to you," so Christ teaches us, "you should not resist evil, but if one hits you on one cheek, offer him the other also. And whoever will dispute with you before judges and will take your cloak, leave him also your shirt. And whoever forces you to go with him for a thousand steps, go with him for two thousand" [Mt 5 (39–41)]. If people were as Christian as they claim they are, there would be very little war.

"This is the highest grace," says Peter, "if you suffer tribulation and sadness innocently for God's sake. For of what worth is it when you sin and then suffer a few stripes for it afterward? But if you suffer for the sake of having done good, this is true grace before God. That's what you are called to: Christ has suffered for us and obediently left us an example, so that we can follow in his footsteps" [1 Pt 2 (19–21]. Whoever walks in the footsteps of Christ cannot err.

"Who can harm you," says Peter, "if you are good disciples? If you suffer for the sake of righteousness, you are blessed. Do not fear fear itself, but you should make your hearts holy for the Lord Christ. But be prepared to answer everyone at all times who wants to know the basis for the hope that is in you, and do so in gentleness and fear. Have a good conscience, so that those who slander you as evildoers will be ashamed that they slandered and reviled your good conduct in Christ.

For it is better, as the will of God would have it, that you suffer for the sake of doing good than that you suffer for doing evil" [1 Pt 3 (13–17)]. A Christian fears "the one who has the power to kill and throw the soul into eternal fire" [Lk 12 (5)].

"Why are you so sad, my soul," says David, "and why are you distressed within me? Hope in God, for I will confess him still, O Saviour of my being, and my God" [Ps 43 (5)]. God hides himself for awhile,[20] so that he can test a person's true nature. But he does not remain absent for long; he shows himself in time of need."

"O Lord our God, you do all our work and are our wisdom. And although the powerful" of the earth, "who do not know you" or wish to know "you, would rule over us, grant us hope in you alone, and remember your name" and good deeds [Is 26 (12f.)]. "O Lord, you increase the people you visit with tribulation, but the fear that causes them to lament is only a trial you have sent to them. In the same way, a pregnant woman who, when she is about to give birth, becomes weak, screams, and suffers childbirth [Jn 16 (21)]. We are just like that, O Lord, before your face.[21*] We are pregnant; we suffer the pains of childbirth. With the aid of the Spirit, we give birth to salvation, so that the earth might not be destroyed and the residents of the globe might not be damned. But those who are dead in you, and those we have lost in death, have life and resurrection![22] Those lying in the earth awake and rejoice. For your dew is the dew of light and life. But the place of sacrilegious tyrants wastes away" [Is 26 (15–19)]. "And when they die they have neither life nor resurrection, for you, Lord, exterminate them and eliminate their memory" [Dn 12 (2, 13); Is 26 (14)]. "Go now, my people, into your chamber, close the door behind you, and suffer for only a moment [Mt 6 (6)]. For the Lord will leave his dwelling and punish the evil of those who dwell on earth. They will bleed the blood they have drunk; they will not be able to hide their wounded anymore" [Is 26 (20f.); 4 (2) Esd 15 (9); Jl 3 (4, 21)]. This is my advice, and that of Christ the Lord: whoever has laid a hand to the plow should not look back

---

20 Is 54:7f.

21* Gloss: Those who do not believe do not bear, but they die in birth; thus Christ also speaks of their woes (Mt 24 [19]).

22 [Original: *send im leben und urstende.*—Trans.]

again but remain patient; otherwise he will not be fit for the kingdom of God [Lk 9 (62)].

"There are three who give testimony in heaven: the Father, the Word, and the Holy Spirit, and the three serve as one. There are also three witnesses on earth: the Spirit, water, and blood.[23] And these three serve as one" [1 Jn 5 (7f.)]. The three are the true ancestors or godparents, who bear witness for a true Christian before God. It is not as the old and new popes have invented and established after the fact; they are enemies of the cross of Christ [Phil 3 (18)].

"Naked I came forth from the womb of my mother, and naked I will return. The Lord has given; the Lord has taken away" [Jb 1 (21); 2 (10)]. It has come to pass, as is pleasing to the Lord. "The name of the Lord be blessed." "If we have received good from the hand of the Lord, why are we not willing to suffer the evil?" Here Job teaches us the supreme surrender. Where this is present, God himself is present. Where this is absent, there is only unrest.

That is what the ancients did, "who died in faith"[24] "without having received the promise, but saw it from afar; they comforted themselves with the promise, clung to it, and confessed that they were guests and strangers on the earth [1 Pt 1 (1); 2 (11)]. For those who say such things show that they are searching for a homeland, a land of which they had thought, from which they had departed [Gn 12 (1ff.)], to which they would have returned, had they had time and opportunity to do so. But now they desire a better land. Therefore God is not ashamed to be called their God, for he had prepared a place for them"[25] [Heb 2 (11); Ps 17 (18:2); 21 (22:1f.)].

How much more is required of us for whom he has already prepared and finished a place—the very one for which they waited! Together we receive it every morning and will be perfected in it [Jn 14 (26); Heb 11 (40)]. To that end, may the Lord Jesus Christ, the Son of Man, assist us

---

23 This verse has been understood since the early church (including Anabaptism) to refer to the three kinds of baptism: Spirit (inner), water (outer), blood (martyrdom).

24 [Original: *die do "gstorben send nach dem glouben."*—Trans.]

25 This entire paragraph is a loose quotation of Heb. 11:13–16. There is a quotation mark at the end but not at the beginning.

so that we who are living today, together with those who lived in the past, count everything as loss for the surpassing value of knowing Jesus Christ. With Paul we despise everything else as garbage and dung, forgetting what lies behind and striving for the goal ahead of us [Phil 3 (8, 13f.); 1 Cor 9 (24–27], like Christ, who had nothing upon which to rest his head [Mt 8 (20)], that we might attain this treasure, this noble pearl [Mt 13 (45f.)], which is Christ himself, through grace. Amen.

"The hour is coming," says Christ, "when they will exclude you from their assembly" [Jn 16 (2, 4)]. As Ezra prophesied, those from the sodomistic sea (meaning 'the world') would reject (meaning 'persecute') its own fish [4 (2) Esd 5 (7)], "and everyone who kills you will claim to have done a good service for God." "These things I have foretold to you. Therefore the hour that you have awaited, about which I told you, is nearing." Those whom the world rejects, Christ accepts [Lk 6 (22)]. As long as one misses the world, I fear that Christ is not in him.

"The Spirit," writes Paul, "bears witness with our spirit that we are children of God. Since we are children, we are also heirs, heirs of God and fellow heirs with Christ. Indeed, as we suffer with him, we will also be made glorious with him. I certainly believe that the sufferings of this world are not at all worthy of the future glory that will be revealed in us" [Rom 8 (16–18)]. Whoever is not willing to suffer with Christ will also not rejoice with him,[26] just as the whole world backs away and flees, for it is not worthy [Heb 11 (38)].

"My son," the Spirit admonishes us, "if you wish to be of service to God, remain steadfast in righteousness and in fear, and prepare your soul for testing. Bring your heart under control and discipline yourself; turn your ear and receive the word of understanding. Do not rush into the time of tribulation. Patiently bear the tests of God, unite yourself with God, and humble yourself, so that in the end your path may go well. Accept everything that is sent your way, and bear up in pain, and persevere patiently in your misery.

"Gold and silver are tested in fire, but God will test in the oven of misery those people who accept him [Ws 3 (6); Ps 12 (6)]. Trust God; he will release you and direct your paths. Hope in him, hold him in

---

26 1 Pt 4:13.

fear, and remain true. You who fear God, look forward to his mercy and do not forsake him, that you do not fall away. You who fear God, trust him; then your reward will not be cancelled. You who fear God, love him; thus your hearts will be filled with light. Look upon the human race, you sons, and you will know that no one who has trusted in the Lord has come to shame.[27*] Who has remained true to his laws and then been forsaken, or who has called upon him and been ignored by him? For God is good and merciful; he forgives sin, helps in the day of tribulation, and is a protector of all those who desire him in truth.

"But woe to the doubting hearts, the shameful lips, the evil hands, and the sinner who tries to get in by another path! Woe to the straying hearts, who do not trust in God, and thus will not be protected by him. Woe to those who have lost their patience, who have left the true way and have turned to the ways of shame. Those who trust God, however, will not disbelieve his Word, and those who love him will guard his paths. Those who fear the Lord bear whatever pleases him, and those who love him will be filled with his law. Those who fear the Lord will prepare their hearts, and humble themselves before him. Those who fear God will keep his commandments patiently until they see him.

"For woe to us, should we fall into the hands of the Lord rather than into the hands of people (meaning, that we allow ourselves to depart from his Word) [2 Kgs 24; (2 Sm 24:14); Sus 1 (23)]. For although he is great and mighty, he is firm in his mercy toward those who let themselves by changed by his Word[28] and improve themselves by it [Is 66 (2)]. For whoever he finally takes hold of in his wrath will never escape: all those who remain unrepentant, those who sin and are arrogant toward the mercy of God" [Sir 2 (1–23)].

Closing comments

To all you most beloved brothers and sisters in the faith of the Lord Jesus Christ, together with all good-hearted, zealous searchers for God! Although many other testimonies from scripture could be inserted here to show that all those who wish to follow this path simply must push on through suffering and the cross, if we wish to follow Christ and

---

27* Note.

28 [Original: *so sich ab seinem wort entsetzen.*—Trans.]

in the end achieve eternal life, which God originally planned for us and called us to. We could also come to know this through the creatures, even though we had never read any scripture. God has ordained the creatures to be subject to us for our sojourn [Rom 8 (19–22)]; they must all come to their end in pain, so that we can use them.[29]

For whoever claims that he is a Christian (many now take the name but not the cross of Christ [Mt 24 (5)]), he must—to state it clearly—follow this path and walk where Christ has gone before us. Then he will arrive in the eternal fatherland. Otherwise it is in vain. Whoever does not walk or wish to walk in this way will be lost eternally [Jn 14 (6)]. Whoever walks another way is a thief and a murderer [Jn 10 (1)]. I believe these testimonies are sufficient for now. In them everyone who is serious may discover what is appropriate, since it is written in our hearts that all creatures (as stated above) must reach their end through suffering and pain [Heb 10 (32f.); 11 (4ff.)].[30]

For Adam, Abraham, Isaac, Jacob, Joseph, Moses, Joshua, Gideon, Job, Ezekiel, Josiah—indeed, the prophets, apostles, martyrs, and all servants and followers of God and Christ—have experienced the same thing. Nonetheless, this allows us to rejoice inexpressibly and gives us great comfort through the Holy Spirit, that we are certain and secure. The sores of Lazarus were of much greater use to the kingdom of God than was the rich man with his expensive woollen blankets, silk, and purple clothes.[31*] It happened that for all his goods he could not gain a drop of water [Lk 16 (19–31)].

Thus the patient and suffering Christian will find his persecution, hunger, thirst, frost, stench, martyrdom, ropes, bonds, prison, iron, and chains much more preferable, honourable, and glorious before God than the entire wealth of this world [2 Cor 11 (23–33); 1 Cor 4 (9–13)], yes, gold, silver, gold chains, rings, and precious metals.[32*] For

---

29 [This is a brief reference to the "gospel of all creatures," invoked occasionally by Marpeck but much more often by spiritualistically inclined Anabaptists, such as Hans Hut (no. 6, "A Beginning of a True Christian Life").—Ed.]

30 [Here it seems that humans share the same fate as the creatures, and must suffer as they do.—Ed.]

31* Parable.

32* Note.

all these instruments will bear witness for him on the Day of the Lord that he has been a true disciple of Christ to the death. Most especially, Christ Jesus shall provide an unceasing example and a memorial to the believer in all his sufferings [Is 53 (2–11)]. My Lord and Redeemer Christ has gone through the same ordeal! For my sake he was persecuted, hated, betrayed, sold, imprisoned, bound, beaten, pushed around, ridiculed, despised, scourged, crowned [with thorns], and martyred. He suffered as a criminal outside the gate and was crucified [Mt 27; Mk 15; Lk 22; Jn 19].

Therefore I am on the right path to the fatherland. I see Christ with his cross going before me! I will go with him outside the camp (meaning away from our own lusts and desires of the flesh and the world), and help him carry his shame [Heb 11 (14–16); 13 (13)]. I will remain on this path, which he himself has sprinkled, marked, and prepared with his rose-coloured blood. I'm on the right path! I'm on the right path! No one distracts me anymore; on this path I cannot get lost. For whoever remains on this path to the end will without doubt be crowned by God and draped in white robes [4 (2) Esd 2 (43–47)]; he will enter the great banquet with the Lamb.[33] Christ himself will spread the table lavishly and serve them. They will eat from the tree of life that is in the middle of paradise [Rv 2 (7)], and live with Christ eternally. For those who have kept the faith with Paul and all the elect, let there be praise, honour, and glory to God. May he help us win the battle, that we might embrace this treasure [2 Tm 4 (7f.)], even as we are embraced by him through grace. Amen.

"Then the holy ones will stand with great determination against those who pressure them and have attacked them in their work. When the attackers see this, what gruesome horror and amazement will come upon them at the quick and unexpected salvation! For they will groan in the fear of their being, and will reflect upon themselves, repentant and sighing for fear in their hearts: 'Those are the ones we earlier mocked as foolish, who became the target of our spite and evil talk. O how foolish we were, having thought their lives were senseless and

33 [Original: *abenntmahl* ("Lord's Supper").—Trans.]

their end without honour! Behold, how they are numbered among the children of God, and have their place among the holy ones.

"'We have departed far from the way of truth. The glow of their holiness did not enlighten us, and we did not comprehend the sun of their understanding. We have become weary in the ways of evil and destruction; we have traveled difficult paths; we knew nothing of the way of the Lord. What good has our arrogance brought us, or of what use has the glory of our wealth been for us? All these things have left like a shadow, like a rowboat that is left to float, like a ship that rides on the waves. No one sees where it is coming from or where it is going; its path on the water cannot be found. It is like a bird that flies through the air and no one can see where it has gone. All one hears is the beating of its wings, with which the air is moved and whipped around as the bird parts the air. With the beating of its wings, it creates a path that no one can see afterward.

"'Or it is like an arrow that parts the air in the direction of its goal. But the air folds back together as soon as it has passed, and no one can see where it came from.

"'It is the same with us. As soon as we are born we cease being[34] and show no sign of the virtue we have left behind. We die and are exposed in our villainy!'" Those who have sinned will speak these and similar words in hell. "For the hope of the godless is like dust that has been scattered by the wind,[35*] like a snowfall that is blown by a storm,[36*] like smoke that is dispersed by the wind,[37*] and like the memory of a guest who remains only for the night and then departs.[38*] The pious, however, will remain steadfast throughout eternity; their reward is with the Lord, and their memory with the Most High. Thus they will be part of a glorious kingdom and receive a beautiful crown from the hand of the Lord. With his right hand he will cover them, and with his arms he will protect them" [Ws 5 (1–17)].

---

34 [Original: *aufhörent sein.*—Trans.]
35* 1.
36* 2.
37* 3.
38* 4.

For "the souls of the pious are in the hand of God, and no pain of death may touch them. In the eyes of the unwise they are despised as they die, and their dying and death is seen as a waste. But they are in a secure resting place and at peace. And though they certainly suffer pain before others, nonetheless their hope is set on immortal things. They are disciplined with a little bit of suffering, but they will be paid back with many good things. For God tests and proves them, and discovers that they comply with him. Indeed, just as gold is tested in the blast furnace, so God has proved and clarified and accepted them as a burnt offering [Ps 12 (7)]; Sir 2 (5)]. In his time he will attend to them." "The godless, however, will be punished according to their own counsel[39]—those who despised the pious, and those who have departed from the Lord" [Ws 3 (1–7; 10); Sir 21 (18)]. It is a joy to the righteous to do what is right, but a fear to the evil doer. For the sinner has nothing to hope for, and the light of the godless will be extinguished [Prv 24 (20)].

In summary, as I said, I have put all this together in love as a co-witness to the truth, for comfort especially to all believers and seekers after God, and profitable to the honour of the Lord [Lk 19 (23)], that it may create and produce much fruit. May the Lord Jesus Christ give the growth and bounty and help to us all [1 Cor 3 (6f.)], who are of good will, in this dangerous time, that we might pursue all that is good with all our hearts, confess his holy truth and affirm it to the end. Amen.

Let us avoid, flee and cut ourselves off from whatever is evil and displeasing to God, so that he is and remains our God, Father and Lord, and that we remain his true children eternally, together with all those who join me in this desire. Amen.[40*]

God be with us all and preserve us according to Christ's intercession for us through his Holy Spirit. Amen. The Lord is the one to whom I give all honour; he knows me and calls me by name.

Be thankful in all ways, for that is the will of God
in Christ Jesus for you. (1 Thes 5 [18])

---

39 [Original: *nach iren ratschlegen.*—Trans.]

40* Gloss: Behold, the devil will throw some of you into prison, so that you will be tested, and your misery will last ten days. Fear none of the things that you may suffer. Remain faithful until death, and I will give you a crown of life (Rv 2 [10]).

40

Confession of faith according to Holy Scripture

1554

Jörg Maler

Jörg Maler was a passionate Christian whose faith had been refined in the fires of interrogation and imprisonment.[1] For his own safety, as well as the needs of the Pilgramite and Swiss Anabaptist communities, he lived and travelled extensively among them. On his return to Augsburg in 1550, Maler had been interrogated and professed faith in the teaching of Christ and the apostles, as well as the Twelve Articles of Faith (as the Apostles' Creed was called in the sixteenth century). This creed was the almost universally acknowledged sign of the true church. Many Anabaptists used it as the framework for setting out their beliefs, among them Leonhard Schiemer (no. 10, "The Twelve Articles of the Christian Faith"), Balthasar Hubmaier, and Peter Riedemann.[2]

In spite of the clarity of his profession, Maler was imprisoned again for two years. The text we have is probably a later elaboration on the statement Maler presented to the court; it has a personal and pastoral

---

Glaubensbekenntnis aufgrund der Heiligen Schrift; 1554. Translation by Victor Thiessen.

1 Maler's story is sketched in the introduction to this volume.

2 "The Twelve Articles in Prayer Form," in BH, 234–40; "The Apostles' Creed," *Peter Riedemann's Hutterite Confession of Faith,* ed. John Friesen (Scottdale, PA: Herald Press, 1999), 59–83.

tone, which suggests that it was intended to guide and encourage fellow believers.

That Maler had a profoundly personal faith, expressed according to the form of the ancient tradition, is unmistakable from his confession. In its passion, its christocentrism, and its surrender to the one it claims, the author's writing is representative of South German Anabaptist piety as a whole. But in its particulars, is it representative of the Marpeck Circle or of the Swiss Brethren? That question is more difficult to answer. On the one hand, Maler's unselfconscious and unguarded testimony emerges from his thirty years of spiritual formation in Anabaptist congregations: this is the faith he has come to through them. It is a tribute to this formation that Christians of every tradition in his day could have recognized their faith in his.

At the same time, Maler's editorial decisions suggest that he sought an intensity of faith and discipleship greater than what he had experienced in these circles. Scholars have speculated about why he took the manuscript of the Kunstbuch to Zurich for publication. Perhaps he judged that the Swiss would receive it more readily than the Pilgramites would.

Maler's confession is not an attempt to restate the Twelve Articles theologically. It is a meditation on its claims, an appropriation of the creed for his own life—and death. Especially striking about the first three articles is the author's staking his very existence on their truth. God the Father will never forsake him; God the Son has become his brother by taking captive death and hell; God the Spirit represents him before God "with unspeakable yearnings."

The article on the church clearly reflects the preeminence Anabaptism gave to an inaugurated eschatology in the life of the church, "without spot or wrinkle." But a marginal note—perhaps Maler's own expansion—cautions that only God can judge one's secrets. His affirmation that forgiveness of sins happens in the church gives his very personal piety a communal context. The choice of a Eucharistic image to carry his thoughts about eternal life is noteworthy. Surrender, patience, and comfort are his key concluding admonitions.

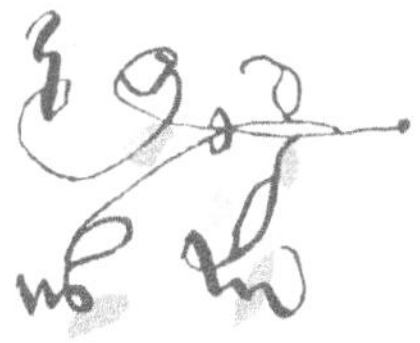

A confession of faith based on the Holy Scriptures, put together as follows:

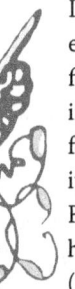

I believe in God, Father, almighty Creator of heaven and earth.[3*] In him alone I place all my comfort, hope, and confidence, and in his grace and mercy that alone can help me in all my fear and need and whatever might confront me, for the sake of his truth. No creature, no matter how holy it is, can do this [Hos 13 (4)]. And since he has become my Father through Christ, I believe firmly that he will gladly help me with all his heart, according to his promise [Ps 50 (15)]. He will stand beside me in all danger and never forsake me (as long as I do not forsake him), neither here nor there. And since he is the almighty Lord, I believe that he can protect and sustain me against all things that oppose me and wish to turn me away from him. For he alone is and will always be strong enough to oppose my enemies (be they visible or invisible), because of his omnipotence.

And since he is also the Creator of heaven and earth, I believe that he has all creatures in his hand and power, so that none of these can inflict a single wound upon me against his fatherly will [Rom 8 (38f.)]. Thus I am made worthy of all good things and eternal life by God, Father, and Creator. From him alone all things come, and whatever we require (out of necessity) is given by him. For he wants to give himself wholly and completely to me (if I offer myself to him), with all that he has with him in heaven and earth, together with all creatures, that they must serve me, be useful for me, and further my path to eternal

---

[3*] The Father.

life, which God has prepared for all those who love him[4] and obey his commands[5] [Rom 8 (28)]. To that end may he grant divine power and strength in faith.

I believe in Jesus Christ, his only begotten Son, our Lord,[6*] who was conceived by the Holy Spirit, born of the virgin Mary, suffered under Pontius Pilate, was crucified, died, and was buried, descended into hell, rose again from death on the third day, ascended to heaven, sitting at the right hand of God, almighty Father. From there he will judge the living and the dead.[7]

I believe from the heart that Jesus Christ, the Father's only begotten Son from eternity, took human form[8] upon himself for my sake; was conceived by means of the Holy Spirit (without a man's involvement), and was born of the pure virgin Mary (as from a proper, natural mother) [Rom 9 (5)]. And that this human being[9] was also truly God, as an eternal, inseparable person, both God and human being.[10] And that this Son of God and Mary, our Lord Jesus Christ, suffered for me, a poor sinner, was crucified for me, and died (according to the flesh) so that he could redeem me, a poor sinner, with his innocent blood from sin, death, and the eternal wrath of God. He himself suffered fear and death and experienced and overcame eternal hell so that I was reconciled to God (through him) and in him became lord over all my enemies through my faith in him [2 Cor 5 (15, 19); Heb 2 (18); Rv 1 (5)].

I believe that without the death of the Son, our Lord Jesus Christ, I could not have come to God's grace or salvation, either through works or merit [Gal 3 (5)]. I believe that Jesus Christ, my brother [Heb 2 (11)], is risen from the dead for the sake of my righteousness through him

---

4 1 Cor 2:9.

5 Dt 7:9; Neh 1:5; 1 Jn 5:2.

6* The Son.

7 [The second article of the Apostles' Creed.—Ed.]

8 [Original: *menscheit* ("humanity").—Trans.]

9 [Original: *mensch* ("person").—Trans.]

10 This language is borrowed, directly or indirectly, from the Chalcedonian Creed of 451, concerned with Christ's two natures.

[1 Cor 15 (4)], and has taken death and hell captive, so that they can never do harm again [Eph 4 (8)].

I confess that I should have died an eternal death, if Christ had not come to my help and taken upon himself my sins and well-earned guilt, damnation, and eternal death, and paid for it through his suffering (like an innocent lamb)[11] [2 Cor 5 (21); Is 53 (5)]. He was also condemned for my sake [Gal 3 (13)]. I believe that he still stands in my stead and represents me daily before the Father as a true, merciful mediator, Saviour, and sole, eternal high priest[12] [Jn 1 (1); Rom 8 (27)] and bishop of my soul [1 Pt 2 (25); 1 Tm 2 (5)].

I believe that Christ rules all things and fulfils all things together with God; that he has power over all things in heaven and earth [Eph 1 (20–22); Mt 28 (18)], a Lord above all lords, a king above all kings [1 Tm 6 (15)], and over all creatures in heaven, earth, and under the earth,[13] over death and life, over sin and righteousness. This same king and Lord will go before me in my suffering (in the world) and death; he will fight and do battle for me,[14] so that I can be lord together with him over all my enemies (of faith)[15] forever and eternally.

I believe that the crucified Christ (the Son of Man) will come in the future, at the last day, and judge and condemn all those (according to the words which he spoke) who did not believe in him [Lk 22 (69); Mt 12 (36), (41f.)], giving to each according to his works [Rom 2 (6); Rv 2 (23)], but preserve me, together with all the faithful and obedient, from the severe judgment of eternal damnation, and will say to us: "Come here, blessed of my Father: inherit the kingdom that has been prepared for you since the beginning of the world" (Mt 25 [34]).[16*]

I believe in the Holy Spirit, who together with the Father and the Son is truly one God and comes from and goes to the Father and the Son

---

11 1 Pt 1:19.

12 Heb 6:20.

13 Phil 2:10.

14 Dt 1:30.

15 [Maler, like other authors in this collection, tries to make it clear that military imagery is to be understood spiritually.—Ed.]

16* Whoever doesn't believe is damned (Mk 16 [16]; Heb 3 [19]).

eternally, but who is a distinct person in his divine being and nature [Jn 20 (22f.); Acts 2 (3f.); Jn 16 (7)].

I believe that I will be crowned with faith by the Holy Spirit—who is a living, eternal, divine gift and offering—freed from sin, raised from the dead, happy and comforted, made free and secure in conscience. For this is my defiance (but not in the flesh) of all attacks of the enemy, as long as I sense and carry in my conscience and heart that God will be my Father [Rom 8 (14); Gal 3 (26)], forgive my sins through Christ, and offer me eternal life through this Holy Spirit.

I believe that this Holy Spirit helps me bear my weakness and represents me with unspeakable yearnings and sighs [Rom 8 (26)], that he strengthens me and enlightens my heart to recognize the unfathomable riches of fatherly mercy, which he has given and presented to me through pure grace, without any merit and works of my own effort [Eph (2:7f.)], solely for the sake of Christ his beloved Son, through which the things of the Father are and will be offered to me.

The Holy Spirit alone has enabled me to know all this. The Spirit ignites my heart (with love) and enlightens me with the understanding and wisdom that such gifts come from above. Christ promised me, when he said, "'Whoever believes in me, as scripture says, streams of living water will flow from his body. This he said of the Spirit: all who believe in him shall receive him" [Jn 7 (38f.)]. From this faith the fruits of the Spirit arise and flow, as Paul proclaims: "Love, peace, joy, patience, friendliness, goodness, faithfulness, gentleness, power are of him" [Gal 5 (22)].

I believe in one holy Christian church, which is the communion[17] of saints, gathered through the Holy Spirit. I believe there is and will be one Christian church on earth, until he appears again at the end to hold judgment [Mt 24 (14); 1 Thes 4 (16f.)].[18*] That is the congregation and number or assembly of all Christians, in which there is one God, one Lord, one Spirit, one faith, one baptism (Eph 4 [4–6]). Of this church,

---

17 [Allusions to the Apostles' Creed are found throughout this section.—Ed.]

18* Gloss: Such a gathering does not consist of many persons (Mt 18 [20]).

our mother, Jesus Christ is the one partner and bridegroom. I believe that this church is the spiritual body, and Christ is its only head.

I believe that Christ is the Saviour of this, his body and church, "who gave himself for her (out of love), in order to make her holy and purify her through the water bath in the Word. Thus he has fashioned for himself a glorious congregation that has neither spot nor wrinkle nor anything of the sort" [Eph 5 (25–27); Ti 3 (5)]. That is, he punishes evil according to the Word, at least as much as has been revealed,[19*] "to make them holy and without blemish" (foremostly before the judgment seat), "a pillar and foundation of truth" and without contradiction ([1] Tm 3 [15]).

I believe that pardon and forgiveness of sins takes place in this Christian community where it is gathered in the Lord [Mt 18 (15–18)], for it is a kingdom of grace (in Christ) and of true indulgence for sin (not from Rome) [Mt 16 (19)]. Outside of this Christendom there is neither salvation nor forgiveness of sins. I believe that no one can be saved unless he is planted (through baptism) with good water (according to the order given through the Holy Spirit) [1 Pt 3 (21); Rom 6 (3f.); Rom 8 (4)] in this congregation and church as a living member in its body through personal faith. I believe that in this kingdom sins will be forgiven not just once but as often as one seeks and desires it from the heart [1 Jn 2 (1); Heb 5 (1)].[20*] For Christ is the true doctor, who cares for the sick and waits upon them, helps them, strengthens them, and makes them healthy. As Isaiah says: "A bruised reed he will not break, and a glowing wick he will not extinguish" (Is 42 [3]).

I believe in the resurrection of the flesh, that my body—which the worms eat, or which is taken away in another manner as God orders it—will rise again incorruptible [1 Cor 15 (42f.)]. This will happen in transfiguration[21] according to the intercession of Christ to the Father [Phil 3 (21); 2 Cor 3 (10f.)]. Christ will raise it up on the last day according to his promise [Jn 17 (9f.)], when he says: "This is the will of him

19* Gloss: No human, only God alone, can judge one's secrets.

20* Gloss: It would be better not to sin, for we cannot raise ourselves up.

21 [Original: *clarheit* (may be translated simply "clarity").—Trans.]

who sent me, that whoever sees the Son (meaning, with spiritual eyes) and believes in him will have eternal life. And I will raise him up on the last day." "And whoever eats of my flesh and drinks of my blood has eternal life, and I will raise him up on the last day" [Jn 6 (40, 54)].[22*]

I believe that after this life there will be an eternal life, that I shall live forever and eternally with Christ (and all those who belong to him and are known to him alone), according to the words of his promise, where he says: "Truly, truly, I say to you, whoever hears my words" (meaning with the inner ears), "and believes in him who sent me, has eternal life and will not face judgment, but he has already passed from death to life" [Jn 5 (24)]. And: "Truly, truly, I say to you, if one obeys my word, he will not see death eternally" [Jn 8 (51)]. "I am the living bread who has come from heaven," says Christ; "whoever eats of this bread will have eternal life" [Jn 6 (51)].[23*]

In summary and conclusion, here is my advice (out of love). Every God-fearing Christian who is surrendered to the truth should build on this most holy faith of Christ through the Holy Spirit [Jude 1 (20)] (who will live only in those who are not subject to sin [Ws 1 (5)]) and fight nobly (for no one will be crowned who does not fight well [2 Tm 2 (5)]). As a holy Christian he must be gallant in all patience through all trials and temptations, like a light in the world in the midst of this adulterous and perverted race [Phil 2 (15)]. There are no two ways about it: "Whoever will live a sanctified life in Christ must suffer persecution [2 Tm 3 (12)] and can enter into the kingdom of God only through much tribulation [Acts 14 (22)]. Truly, whoever refrains from evil is allowed the spoils [Is 59 (15)]. Therefore hold fast to the comforting promise of Christ your Saviour (who also took this path). Believe firmly in his word when he says: "I am the resurrection and the life; whoever believes in me will live, even though he die. And who ever lives and believes in me will not die eternally" [Jn 11 (25f.)]

[22*] Gloss: Apart from the new birth and renewal of the Holy Spirit no one can eat or drink of Christ.

[23*] Gloss: In the discipleship of Christ one eats of this food (through faith); this food is useless to someone who is still dead in sin and the old dough. Someone like that eats judgment upon himself (1 Cor 11 [29]).

Christ your Saviour will not forsake you. Be comforted by his words when he says: "In me you have joy; in the world, fear. But be comforted; I have overcome the world" [Jn 16 (33)]. Likewise, "This firm foundation of God stands and has this seal: The Lord knows his own" [2 Tm 2 (19)]. Whoever has the Spirit of Christ is his. "This same Spirit assures our spirit that we are God's children" [Rom 8 (9, 16)]. As Christ also says: "My sheep hear my voice, and I know them, and they follow me, and I give them eternal life, and no one will tear them out of my hand. The Father, who has given them to me, is greater than all, and no one can tear them out of my Father's hand. I and the Father are one" [Jn 10 (27–30)].

In a final summation, dear Christian, commend your soul—indeed, all your ways [Ps 31 (5); 37 (5)] and things—to your faithful God and Father, to whom you have entrusted and given yourself through faith and baptism (in Christ), according to his holy command. Speak with your heart as did your trustworthy brother Christ on the cross: "Father, into your hands I commend my spirit" [Ps 31 (5)] for all time. May the eternal Father help us (in grace) to true rest, and lead us through his good angels, that we may achieve a joyful resurrection (with Christ) at the last judgment. Amen. May he not let us be separated from his grace. Amen. But may his holy covenant (in Christ) be borne in mind at all times by us, the poor and needy, from now to eternity. Amen. Keep the faith! Hold fast to what is holy! In all you do and all you avoid, look to what is upright! Then in the end you will have peace with God in eternity [Ps 37 (11)].

In Christ the Lord,
Jörg Probst Rothenfelder, whom they call Maler[24]
1554

24 ["Painter."—Trans.]

Strasbourg, cathedral.

41

Concerning true godliness

[Christian Entfelder]
[Strasbourg, 1530]

This treatise brings Jörg Maler's original collection to a close.[1] It is included here as an anonymous text, but two of its four extant printings in the 1530s name Christian Entfelder as the author. The textual variants suggest that a now lost original copy of "Concerning True Godliness" was behind the 1530s printings.[2] Maler copied out a further edited version that included marginal glosses.

Little is known of Entfelder. In his seminal study of mysticism and early Anabaptism, Werner Packull writes that "Christian Entfelder was probably the most speculative mind associated with early Anabaptism."[3] He first appears in 1526 in Eibenschütz, Moravia (now Ivančice in the Czech Republic), an area of Anabaptist ferment, as a radical preacher influenced by Balthasar Hubmaier. During an outbreak of persecution of Anabaptists in 1528, Entfelder fled to Strasbourg. There he encoun-

[Christian Entfelder,] Von wahrer Gottseligkeit; [Straßburg, 1530]. Translation by Victor Thiessen and John D. Rempel.

1 After the final folio was filled, more pages were inserted to accommodate additional writings (Bern MS, no. 41, 1).

2 BSOT, 643–44.

3 MESG, 163; see also Geoffrey Dipple, *Just as in the Times of the Apostles* (Kitchener, ON: Pandora Press, 2005), 212–18.

tered clusters of radical dissenters, among them Pilgram Marpeck and Caspar Schwenckfeld. Out of the ferment among these and other radicals, Entfelder moved ever further from Anabaptism into Spiritualism. Written in 1530, "Concerning True Godliness" was Entfelder's first articulation of his mature position.

Characteristic of Entfelder's thought is his notion of human origins in a primeval unity with God. The gospel concerns the restoration of this lost oneness. Christ is, above all else, our guide in the seven stages of returning to God and experiencing the true Sabbath of rest in him. The author describes godliness as the peace the Spirit works in us through Christ, so that we might free ourselves from all creatures and ultimately from ourselves. Mary of Bethany and Mary the mother of Jesus exemplify the spiritual receptiveness needed if one is to undergo the process of liberation.

First, God offers his favour. Then we ask what we must do to receive it. Third, we are overtaken by fear of what God offers. Then we must wait for God's help. Fifth, we must surrender to God's purpose for us. Finally, this surrender becomes the way to oneness with God.[4] The rest of the treatise describes in piercing terms the way to God. Suffering is often the medium of our purification, but it should not become an idol. The end of the spiritual journey is the love of God, from which nothing can separate us.

A word about the theological context of "Concerning True Godliness" can help explain why Entfelder and Marpeck parted ways. Accompanying the mystical path set forth in the treatise was Entfelder's assumption that the unmediated experience of God transcends all mediated forms—Bible, church, and sacraments. For Entfelder the material world belongs entirely to the realm of the flesh. For that reason he could not understand why reformers of every stripe preoccupied themselves with the material forms of religion.

In an ironic twist, the very text that became the occasion for Marpeck's confrontation with Spiritualism was later given a place of honour in the writings cherished by the Marpeck Circle. By 1531

---

4 Packull describes Entfelder's thought as "a complex panentheistic process theology"; MESG, 166.

Marpeck had become convinced that what had begun as an invigorating corrective to Catholic and magisterial Protestant religiosity (as well as disputes about outward practices among the radicals) had gone dangerously wrong: a consistent spiritualizing of the gospel discarded New Testament teaching and trivialized the incarnation. To confront this challenge Marpeck attempted his initial formulation of a believers church ecclesiology and spirituality grounded in the incarnation.[5]

As is evident from their writings in this collection, Marpeck and his circle sought a single-minded following of Christ with an intensity like that of the Spiritualists. They agreed with the Spiritualists that the preoccupation with external conformity was the tragic flaw of Anabaptism. But Marpeck was convinced, already in 1531, that Spiritualism as an approach to the gospel, rather than a corrective to approaches preoccupied with externals, offered less than it claimed. Spiritualism was concerned with flowers, with bringing the striving of the believer to fruition. It gave no consideration to roots, trunks, and branches—the teachings, structures, and rituals that mediate the gospel from generation to generation. Its tragic flaw was that it tried to transcend our creatureliness, contrary to the teaching of the Gospel of John and the letter to the Hebrews.[6]

This text raises two questions of consequence for the nature and purpose of the whole Kunstbuch. First, what does the editor's selection of a text by an author Marpeck considered subversive say about Maler's own theology? Second, how did ordinary church members hear Entfelder?

First, we know that Maler was a deeply convicted yet enduringly restless Christian. His convictions were of an Anabaptist stripe but not dogmatically so. When he was arrested, he submitted to what the state church authorities demanded of him. This was clearly not because he lacked steadfastness but because he saw outer forms and formulations as secondary. The freedom with which he moved between strict Swiss Brethren and Pilgramite congregations illustrates the same stance.

---

5 "A Clear Refutation", WPM, 43–67; "A Clear and Useful Instruction," WPM, 69–106. See "A Clear and Useful Instruction" as a "point by point refutation of the arguments advanced by Entfelder" (MLDC, 141).

6 WPM, 76–86.

The case can be made that his decision to include "Concerning True Godliness" (as well as "War Ordinance of the Heavenly Emperor for His Officers," by the Lutheran Hartmut von Cronberg) was consistent with his ministry as a whole. Maler was dedicated to furthering a single-minded following of Christ. He saw Cronberg and Entfelder as inspired and reliable guides in this pursuit. Their piety, while not accounting for all that Anabaptists saw in the gospel, had an intensity and depth that made radical discipleship possible. The Anabaptist spirit, as it was articulated by the Swiss and the Dutch—Conrad Grebel, Michael Sattler, Menno Simons, and Dirk Philips—was cut from similar cloth ethically, but spiritually it lacked the mystical profundity that shaped the South Germans, and it took a legalistic turn when it came to the communal expression of discipleship. In this way of thinking, Maler thought he was furthering the radical cause by offering a spirituality of self-denial and rebirth that did not lose itself in legalism.

If Maler saw commonalities between elements of Marpeck's message—such as his quest for unity—and Entfelder's, did he also see conflicts between his and Marpeck's spiritual vision? Is that the—or at least a—reason leading him to leave out of his canon significant writings by Marpeck, such as his letter to Caspar Schwenckfeld and his letter to Helena Streicher? In both of these epistles Marpeck insists on the incompatibility of Anabaptism and Spiritualism, if the latter claims to be a complete articulation of the gospel in and of itself. Especially because of the egalitarian spirit of this kind of Anabaptism, we must also ask who established the canon. Was it Maler alone, or was there also a slow development of a canon of texts gathered over time by the communities we learn about in the Kunstbuch? If that is the case, does our collection of treatises suggest a broad theological continuum, with Hans Hut, Leonhard Schiemer, and Hans Schlaffer at the left end, and with Maler, Sigmund Bosch, Cornelius Veh, and Leupold Scharnschlager progressively to their right, and Marpeck at the right end? Is Maler and his spiritualistic Anabaptism therefore just as representative of the Pilgramite congregations as Marpeck was?

Let us turn to the second question. How did ordinary Anabaptist believers hear people such as Entfelder? From this collection and others we see that they welcomed with open arms this spirituality of self-denying participation in Christ. In so doing they were not discarding the letter of the Bible and life in community but animating them. In this way of thinking, Schlaffer and Entfelder were speaking as straightforwardly to and in behalf of church members as Scharnschlager and Marpeck were. To make a comparison in light of this argument, it is not surprising that "Concerning True Godliness" is included in a seventeenth-century Hutterite manuscript.[7] There too it was embraced as a guide for animating the practice of Christian community, not as a substitute for it. If you like, Marpeck's writing remains the larger context of the Spiritualist treatises we find in Hutterite manuscripts, the guardian of the roots, trunk, and branches from which the flower takes its life.

7 BSOT, 644.

Of true godliness;[8] how a person may come to it here in these days. A short, but very useful reflection, Rv 14 [7]. For godliness is beneficial in all things (1 Tm 4 [8]).

Since, as is commonly acknowledged, all honour, praise, and glory should go to the Lord God alone, I hope it will not offend any good person that this pamphlet on godliness is published without any other title or name, especially since a wise man places greater value on what is said than on who said it.[9*] And it is very much like someone who hungers after gold, who cares not at all who tells him[10] of a goldmine, as long as he tells him where it is.[11*] Thus someone who hungers after God does not idolize this or that person. It is irrelevant who shows him the noble pearl, as long as he is not deceived [Mt 13 (45f.)]. This writing (God willing) should not mislead anyone. Should it not prove edifying[12] (as I hope it will), it should nevertheless do no harm. Whoever cannot appreciate its wares will not be hurt thereby. Even if someone is unable to follow what is said, nevertheless we know how far we are from the truth, and whether one eagerly strives to come to the peace of God, indeed, to establish the true Sabbath here [Heb 3 (11, 18); 4 (1–11)]. For it is entirely certain that the God of hosts will put an end to all the unrest in this world once and for all, through the appearance of his Son from heaven. May he come directly to our aid with grace [2 Thes 1 (7)]. Amen.

---

8 [*Gotseligkeit* is translated as "godliness," to accord with the translation of this term in WPM, 309.—Trans.]

9* Preamble.

10 [To remain close to the original, gender-neutral language has not been used. Unfortunately, the word *Mensch* takes the masculine, but it can also be considered gender neutral. In English *der Mensch* can be rendered "man," but it can also be rendered "person," which is the term we have preferred.—Trans.]

11* Parable.

12 [Original: *Frumbts nit.*—Trans.]

Of divine godliness, at which everyone may arrive here in this life

Although there are those who have certainly written and cried out about godliness a good deal in these last years, against the ungodly, it is however to be feared that they damn themselves by that with which they judge others, as is apparent from the fruits. For many have spoken of a godly life, and yet have never experienced for themselves what true godliness is. Where they did know of it, however, they have nonetheless not lived by it. Unfortunately, we can clearly see this. But inasmuch as a Christian life ultimately rests upon godliness (which should be established here in the realm of faith), I will by means of God's grace offer a brief discourse on this topic according to my simple understanding and offer it to everyone's free judgment.

Furthermore, let it be known that true godliness is nothing other than a peacefulness that the Spirit of God works in someone through Christ, so that he might free himself from all creatures—indeed, even from himself. One can separate oneself from all his senses, heart, and thoughts (from the beautiful and desirous apple of this world). One can renounce father, mother, brother, wife, child, house, yard, field, property, goods, money, body, and life.[13] One can turn away from all outer things, and from then on one no longer makes use of the creaturely, except as much as utmost humility allows—and all this ultimately for the sake of God, to whom one turns completely and listens to what he says and offers. Such a person does not accept any of those things that all creatures normally strive to attain. What he has he treats as if he did not have it [4 (2) Esd 16 (42–45); 1 Cor 7 (29–31)]. If he has nothing, he acts contentedly, as if he had everything. He is indifferent to what he has or does not have, when it is not of God himself.

God alone is the one reality that a godly person considers necessary. God is the best part that he chooses. When he has that, he no longer asks about the affairs of the world. Whenever he has to deal with the world, he sees it as a cross. Thus the world loathes him. It wishes neither to hear nor see him. He must be its fool, idiot, and carnival clown[14]

---

13 Mt 19:29; Mk 10:29; Lk 14:26.

14 [Original: *fasnachtspil.*—Trans.]

[1 Cor 4 (9f., 13)]. For they count his life to be foolishness, insanity, and heresy. And though the world virtually screams, rants, and raves about such people, that they despise their business and disordered character and will no longer be like them, the blessed person nevertheless stands firm in his surrender,[15] remains silent, and allows his lover[16] to answer in his own time [1 Pt 4 (4); Rom 12 (2); Dn 12 (10); Is 30 (15)]. His lover will show him how to act (Ps 37 [5]).[17]

Christ defended Mary, who sat at his feet, heard his word, and allowed Martha to run restlessly hither and thither around the house. This bustle did not bother Mary; she acknowledged her own portion, that which was most precious to her [Lk 10 (39–42)]. It was he alone whose voice she listened to; and only what he said to her did she carry out. Her heart, will, and desire resided in this alone. All other things that were in the world were irrelevant to her (other than godliness): riches or poverty, poverty or riches; joy and sorrow, or sorrow and joy; life or death, death or life. She valued one over the other solely if she would become closer and more like him through it. And in this sense her poverty is her riches, pain her joy,[18] death her life and reward.[19] Through this she is brought to her original source, whom she desires as a deer desires a waterbrook.[20] Her bliss is complete.

However much such a person, because he is an earthen vessel[21] of flesh and blood, needs to use the elements of creation—like food, drink, clothing, wife, or money—nevertheless, he requires them for no more than his utmost humility allows.[22] (People call this "attitude,"[23] in the positive sense.) Such an attitude allows the person to choose what is necessary to the task, or what will assist one's neighbour, and at the

15 [Original: *gelassenheit.*—Trans.]

16 Christ.

17 Ps 73:25

18 2 Cor 6:10.

19 Phil 1:21.

20 Ps 42:1.

21 2 Cor 4:7.

22 Gloss: The Holy Spirit is in the new person (Eph 4 [24]).

23 [Original has both Latin (*mentem*) and German (*gmuet*).—Trans.]

same time not hinder the kingdom of God. So single-mindedly does the heart turn to God.

But reason (called *ratio*) roams ceaselessly here and there in external contradictions,[24*] which scarcely occurs without damage. Indeed, it is impossible, where the tools of the external senses such as seeing, hearing, smelling are not tamed and halted. For when Eve, Dinah, and David allowed their eyes to gaze upon external creatures, they fell into grievous traps, as the scripture relates.[25]

Now one may ask, however, how does it happen that a person finds such peace?[26*] Answer: at one time God (in Christ) allowed himself to be bodily conceived and born of a virgin, so that he could reveal this great secret (for our good) [2 Cor 5 (18f.)]. Thus, just as it happened bodily to Mary, all things must be brought to fruition in a spiritual manner and a person must be born again [Jn 3 (5)]. Otherwise he may not enter into the peace of God.

Initially God offered his grace to Mary through the angel Gabriel. He announced his greeting, favour, and goodwill, and his wish to be with her.[27*] She was disturbed by this, and considered what kind of greeting this might be. The messenger of God soon comforted her, and furthermore indicated to her that she would conceive and bear a son and call him Jesus. This amazed Mary all the more; indeed, she thought that it was impossible for her to do, because she had not known a man. She relied on external reason, which could not comprehend this. At this, the Lord (as one who gladly tolerates our weakness) discreetly explained to her and helped her understand that this would come to pass through the Holy Spirit in his almighty power.

In order to satisfy her external senses, he also showed her another work that was impossible to nature, that a barren woman should conceive—indeed, for the first time in old age.[28] As she heard this, she suppressed her own understanding, entrusted her reason to God's workings, and allowed the inner person to speak (which was created in the

---

24* Human reason.

25 Gn 3:6; 34:1f.; 2 Sm 11:2.

26* Question.

27* Greeting: "The Lord be with you" (Lk 1 [28ff.]).

28 [Elizabeth, mother of John the Baptist.—Ed.]

image of God, through which his almighty work can be done), and said: "Behold, the servant of the Lord (meaning, I will hold still before God). May his will come to pass within me according to his Word." Thus the power of God was able to make her his eternal resting place.

This needs to happen with everyone. First, out of pure grace and mercy, God the heavenly Father offers his favour and goodwill to each person, with whom he wishes to be.[29*] This takes place not only internally but also externally through his legates (but not those of Rome!).

Second, he explains to a person what he wants from him, what he should do, put aside, or suffer.[30*]

Third, a person will become fearful and worried regarding the matter at issue,[31*] as undoubtedly Mary also stood in great need and in danger of the hour of death, since she was pregnant before her betrothed took her into his house. For the penalty of the law was to stone her to death[32] with great shame, ignominy, and agony. This troubled the devout[33] Joseph.[34] Thus a person relies on outward understanding and realizes that if he should live in a manner that would please God, it would be impossible to remain in the world. Thus many holy people, some of them very much like Mary, fled to the mountains, wilderness, and forest.[35*] He may go where he will; nevertheless, he remains under the cross. Whatever he flees from in one place he encounters twice as much in another, as with Jonah.[36] There he sees before him both good and bad, death and life,[37] hell and heaven. According to external understanding he cannot reach the good life and heaven, or flee evil, death, and hell. Thus he is in fear and pain, like a mother giving birth [Jn 16 (21)].

29* 1.

30* 2.

31* 3.

32 Dt 22:21.

33 [Original: *frum*.—Trans.]

34 Mt 1:19f.

35* Note.

36 Jon 1:10.

37 Dt 30:15.

Fourth, God comes to the one who awaits him with longsuffering, helps him in his need with tenderness.[38*] In his goodwill, God makes it clear to him what is possible through the power God gives to him.[39*] God would not give it to him until he has been called to receive it—that is to say, until he accepts the affliction of God with his whole heart. God gave such desire to him so that he would have no complaint against him. May God not regret giving his gifts [Sir 15 (14)].[40]

Fifth, the believer willingly surrenders himself in order to become an instrument of God, to allow his powerful goodness to work in or through him whatever and however it wills,[41*] saying with a true heart (as is written in the title of the book), "Take note, I am coming; I want to do your will, O my God" (Ps 40 [8]).

Sixth, now the full power of God is here; it encompasses the believer, encircles him in the bonds of love,[42] and leads him where he does not want to go (Jn 21 [18]).[43*] Here God and a person come together in a single unity through the voluntary surrender[44] of the will, so that through the believer's willingness God may work everything he intends. In return, all things are possible for the believer in God. Indeed, without the help of flesh and blood a person can be conceived and born into the other world [Is 26 (17f.)], united with the firstborn, becoming one flesh and bone with him [Eph 5 (30f.)].

After these six steps, as after six days of hard work, the believer enters the Sabbath of divine rest. He has become one single unity, united with God in him and he in God through Christ in the Holy Spirit. Now the believer may take captive all his external senses, and make possible the inner being through the power of him who is in him. Not only does he begin to recognize the power that is in him to do all things, he also senses a hearty desire and pleasure to do and to bring to fruition all that God commands. Indeed, it would be hard for him to knowingly break

---

38* 4.

39* Gloss: [For] God is not impossible (Mt 19 [26]).

40 Rom 11:29.

41* 5. Gloss: Lord, what you wish, that I shall do (Acts 9 [6]).

42 Hos 11:4; Col 3:14.

43* Gloss: The medium is the human being Jesus Christ (1 Tm 2 [5]).

44 [Original: *freyer glassenheit.*—Trans.]

an iota of God's law. For when we are willing to say yes and receive the proffered Word of God with sincere assent,[45*] though it appears impossible as a truth someone can understand, it will happen according to his faith.[46] For the one who deals with him is true and faithful[47] and will let no one who trusts him come to shame.[48] As Mary says, "Behold, a servant of the Lord; let it be with me according to your will" (Lk 1 [38]).

God's faithfulness can be seen in two brief examples, among many from scripture.[49*] First, at one hundred years of age God promised Abraham a son from the unfruitful ninety-year-old Sarah.[50*] Had Abraham remained focused on the external, he would not in his lifetime have had a son promised by God. But since he quickly accepted the word, promise, and faithfulness of God,[51*] something that is humanly impossible happened to him.

Thus Peter had to shut his eyes to the sea and his ears to the wind; with his feet he stepped out onto the roiling water, as upon a rock and in the power of Christ, who said, "Come here!"[52*] To the degree that Peter returned to the external senses, he lacked faith. Had Peter not suspended the external senses at all, he would have been drowned. Since he was able to ignore them in part, but only in part, Christ allowed him to sink in part.

Take note, those who have eyes—what a great thing it is to hear the Word of God, and to believe it, that is, surrender oneself to it, rely on it completely, and suffer with Christ, who cooperates through his Spirit. Abraham said yes to the Word of God with his whole voice; thus his faith was great.[53*] Peter, however, responded with only half his voice;

45* Gloss: How one should and can keep God's commandments.

46 Mt 9:29.

47 Rv 3:14.

48 Is 49:23.

49* 2 examples.

50* 1.

51* The art of true faith.

52* From the power of God's Word (Heb 1 [3]).

53* Abraham.

thus his faith was small.[54][55*] Both received according to their faith.[56] In this the goodness and faithfulness of our holy God and Father reveals itself, who will honour one of little faith and keep him from drowning, though he may let him sink and flounder for a while.

It impresses me how one should not merely believe historically in God's Word but accept it entirely and lose oneself in it. Because a person does not wish to lose himself, he never comes to rest. He must simply be offered up [Rom 12 (1)], as is modelled in Christ; it is disgusting how we try to pay Christ off with words [rather than deeds]. How would you like it, O mortal, that a virgin promises to marry you but plays the whore with someone else again and again—and still makes it her express wish to inherit all your goods?[57*] Now we promise ourselves entirely to Christ in name but dwell with Belial,[58] for God's ways appear too narrow for us. We call out: "Lord, Lord," and do not do even the smallest thing that he requests of us.[59] If someone claims to dwell with Christ, I wish him luck; it is my plea and desire that he become one with Christ, as he hopes his betrothed will become.[60*] For if the betrothed of Christ does not hold himself upright, Christ would have every right to give him a letter of divorce.[61, 62*] The woman, however, who orients herself to her husband's will, follows, fears, obeys, and honours him, takes up the household concerns, is not stuck-up or flirtatious, will be preserved from much disadvantage.

In like manner: the less someone who wants to be a Christian allows his reason to wander among adulterers in the flesh but waits only for only his one betrothed, hears her voice, obeys it, and watches over the internal affairs of his house with care, so that he can also retain mastery over his external senses, the purer he remains. For if he allows his

---

54 Mt 14:31.

55* Peter.

56 Mt 9:29.

57* Parable.

58 2 Cor 6:15.

59 Mt 7:21f.; Lk 6:46.

60* Spiritual marriage (Eph 5 [23–27]).

61 Dt 24:1–3.

62* Parable.

eye to steal a single careless look, truly, it never returns to him as pure as when it left.[63*] If you see a chest painted on a wall, you want it and everything in it.

Therefore, if you speak a single wasted, useless word, you will pay for it, and with it you witness to the fact that an impurity that does not belong in a Christian marriage hides in your heart [Mt 12 (36)].[64] For whoever truly loves his betrothed, Christ, speaks no word, eats no bite of bread, drinks no glass of water, puts no thread on his body, and walks no step,[65] unless he first looks to his lover and ascertains whether it is against his will.[66*] The proper fear of God teaches us this, so that one becomes wise and understanding in God.

The believer knows, however, that nothing opposes his betrothed, Christ, more than to seek and think for himself and be fleshly oriented.[67*] When that is the case, even a good work may become evil.[68*] To preserve oneself unscathed by this terrible world,[69] and to look upon Christ in all we do and all we leave, is truly the sweet yoke and easy, light burden;[70] it is easily carried by the farmer in the field, the vintner in the vineyard, the artisan at his work, the fisherman on the water, the servant in service, the lord in his government, the woman at spinning, the servant girl at the stove in the kitchen.

Indeed, all may acknowledge their God and Creator with the works of their hands. So marvellously is the Lord revealed within his creatures,[71] when they are properly observed with the inner eye, when the goodness of God is recognized in them,[72] and why, to what end, by whom, and for whose good have they been created? Then, to some degree, people are at peace with the other creatures, to the extent that

---

63* Note.
64 Mt 12:34.
65 Col 3:17.
66* Note.
67* Gloss: To be self-centred and to seek oneself is contrary to Christ.
68* Note.
69 Jas 1:27.
70 Mt 11:30.
71 Ps 66:5.
72 Rom 1:20.

they have been drawn into the humility of God [Rom 1 (20)].[73*] Only then can humanity make proper use of them, for all creatures yearn and sigh over the vain purposes for which they must serve people, for whose sake they have been made subject [Rom 8 (22)].

No creature can ultimately find peace on earth unless it becomes one with humanity, to whom it has been subjected. None of them may become united with humankind in any way except that it suffers its will; in the same way, humankind will not find eternal rest until it becomes one with God. Then the true Sabbath day shall arrive with peace, joy, love, tenderness, comfort, and all delightfulness of the Holy Spirit[74] in this one unity.[75*] Such unity cannot come to pass, however, unless a person accepts the will of his God, which was demonstrated in Jesus Christ [1 Pt 2 (21)], the first of all creatures. Who he is was borne out in his deeds. As the image of God [Col 1 (15)], a person can dismantle all those pictures that are above in the heavens, here on earth, in the waters, and under the earth,[76] as stated above, and renounce everything he owns,[77] and take up his cross with Christ [Lk 9 (23) and 14 (27)]. Nothing can go forward without the cross, for the disciple is not above his master [Jn 15 (20)].[78] With Christ, he yields to a simple, poor, contemplative life that is dead to its old ways.[79]

And as each individual kernel of wheat dies in order to grow and become fruitful [Jn 12 (24)], thus also a true Christian—in true surrender—should allow himself to be threshed, winnowed, washed, run through a sieve, crushed, bagged, and baked.[80*] By holding still in all patience he will become true food for God the heavenly Father. His earthly and animalistic way will be eliminated[81] from him; he becomes

---

73* The surrender of the creatures.

74 Rom 14:7; 15:13; 2 Cor 6:6.

75* A Sabbath in Christ's kingdom.

76 Ex 20:4; Dt 5:8.

77 Mt 10:21; Lk 18:22.

78 Mt 10:24; Lk 6:40.

79 [For the author, relinquishing outward images of God is an inseparable part of giving up outward security for the "nakedness" of the cross.—Ed.]

80* Parable.

81 [Original: *verdeet* = *verdaut* ("digested").—Trans.]

one with his spirit; lives, works, and acts in longsuffering, just as he previously killed, destroyed, and strangled, which was unworthy before God.

For in this same way God became food for us through Christ,[82] who has always loved us. With his cross, cup, martyrdom, suffering, death, and indeed forgiveness, he made himself appealing[83] to us all, so that he could abide in us and we in him.[84] We live eternally from such food and are sustained by the bread of heaven, which has come to us from eternity [Jn 6 (31–33, 41, 50f., 54, 58)]; one may taste or experience its power and sweetness solely in true inner suffering.[85] When this happens the outer nature frequently joins with and furthers the inner. By this means the earthly taste for temporal lusts falls away from the person, and without any hindrance he turns to God in his united oneness [1 Pt 4 (2)]. Thus the heavenly food begins to be processed, to grow and increase in him,[86] cooked through the fires of tribulation. Its power proliferates, and the person senses the true sweetness, in which our flesh also takes on a pleasant taste similar to that of Christ's flesh. For as bad as it is to eat raw meat, so little will our raw nature (according to our first birth) be considered valuable in Christ.[87*]

But whoever turns from the Lord in suffering will carry his cross [Lk 9 (23)] with the criminal to Christ's left[88] and will find peace[89] neither here nor there. It is in such a poor, lonely inner life, despised by the world, as stated above, that one learns to know God. For the beginner who seeks God, he can become known to some degree through the foundations of wisdom[90] and through an understanding of the visible

---

82 Jn 6:55.

83 [Original: *behäglich.*—Trans.]

84 Jn 15:4.

85 It starts in the word of the cross.

86 2 Cor 9:10; 2 Thes 1:3; Eph 4:15f.

87* Parable.

88 Lk 23:39.

89 [Original: *zů rů kommen.*—Trans.]

90 Prv 1:7; 4:7; 9:10; etc. [Probably the wisdom literature of the Old Testament and Apocrypha.—Ed.]

creation, by which God's invisible greatness, righteousness, and goodness may be seen [Heb 11 (1)].[91]

But our loving Father, who loves us so deeply, will not truly become known except through the suffering of his Son in the Holy Spirit. There is no better way to learn the suffering of his Son than through participation in his suffering [Rom 8 (17)]. It is to be feared that whoever does not suffer with Christ knows neither the Father nor the Son.[92] To summarize, whoever wishes to know the Father and Son must bear all the articles of faith within himself through the power of the one and sevenfold Spirit. Through this he will become all powerful, for all things are possible for the believer [Mk 9 (23)]. The Son of God will be conceived within him, born, martyred, killed, and buried in the fulfilment of the complete sufferings of Christ within him [Col 1 (24)].[93*] Christ will also rise again in him through faith,[94] give him strength and power to walk in the newness of life.[95] This is called the first resurrection [Rv 20 (5f., 14)]. Thus the second death also has no power over him:[96] the new being[97] reigns with and in Christ over the flesh, sin, and gates of hell.[98] Whoever speaks of these things apart from this suffering and his own dying, which is the true experience of the resurrection in Christ and renewal of the Holy Spirit, speaks of these things as someone who is blind speaks of colour.

It should also be acknowledged that no one may make an idol out of his suffering, or boast of what he does not yet have.[99*] This happens when a person is pleased with himself and points to himself, and does not remain under the headship of Christ. God does not look, however, upon the suffering, but rather looks upon the yieldedness, steadfastness, surrender, and the yearning after the Spirit within the person for

---

91 Rom 1:20.

92 1 Jn 2:23.

93* Note.

94 Col 2:12; 3:1.

95 Rom 6:4.

96 [Rv 21:8.—Ed.]

97 Eph 2:15; 4:24.

98 Mt 16:18.

99* Note.

the sake of Christ. The believer has as little right to attribute such things to himself as the lost son has to the ring and income of the father! [Lk 15 (22)]. He should have admonished the son for his thankless evil and reminded him of the goodness of his pious father. For to that point the son had shamefully wasted his life in sin, and all his inheritance of godly gifts on worldly lusts. His high living lusts had to be driven out by hunger and misery among the pigs.

Nonetheless, the merciful father in Christ accepts him in such friendship, as though he had never done anything against him. Indeed, the father does not even reckon his son's misdeeds against him anymore, but runs to him, embraces him, kisses him, and gives back to him all his previous adornments! He also has a fatted calf slaughtered and celebrates with his whole household the return of the son who was once dead but now alive, once lost but now found.

In response the son finds such a burning, heartfelt love for his father that he pays attention to no one else. He fears and honours him; he keeps him before his eyes in all he does and refrains from doing. Indeed, he is ignited and burns in the love of the Father through Jesus Christ. In him he has rest, peace, salvation in abundance, so that he pays no further attention to the world. Without him he feels so poor that he could not be poorer though the whole world be his.[100] For there is nothing else but love—the love and the peace of Christ in the repose of the Holy Spirit,[101] wherein the now divinized mortal may shout in the joy of the free, princely spirit with Paul: "Who will separate us from the love of God; sorrow or fear, persecution, hunger, thirst, danger, or sword? I am certain that neither death nor life, angels, principalities or powers, neither the present nor the future, the heights or depths, nor any creature may separate us from the love of God which is in Christ Jesus our Lord" [Rom 8 (35, 38f.)].

That is the true godliness to which all those must come who wish to partake of and have communion with Christ, to which God the Father will help us with his grace. Amen.

---

100 Mt 16:26; Mk 8:36; Lk 9:25.

101 Rom 14:17.

Watch and pray! Be sober![102] For you do not know
the day or the hour.
(Mt 25 [13])

102 1 Pt 4:7.

Interlude 10

Rhyming maxims

These poetic aphorisms were preserved in various medieval collections.[1] It is noteworthy that an ancient secular philosopher (Seneca) and a medieval one (Hugo von Trimberg) were considered worthy of quotation in a radical community far removed from them. One possible explanation is that such quotations are often preserved in devotional books, including those with a mystical character.

Zwischentück 10: Sinnsprüche. Translation by Leonard Gross.

1 BSOT, 661.

If you want to be a fair-minded judge,
give equal weight to what each side is saying.
If at that point you still do not know how to proceed,
then consider well,
employing the council of those who are wiser,
and then judge with wisdom and reason.
In so doing, think of God's future.[2]
Respond to no one on the basis of affection or aversion.
Look not upon friendship, favour, or gifts.
God judges impartially.
Here the lord resides with the servant,
whereby each and every person perceives too late
who is lord and who is servant.
May each strive toward eternal rest;
Christ the Lord illumines our way there. Amen.[3*]

O mortal, you noble creature,
slay your evil nature!
If you want to become one with God,
then look upon the nobleness of your soul.[4*]

I have an advantage that is not mine.
Oh, God, what might it be?
It no longer remains in my power,
except to the degree that I desire and give, through God.[5*]

2 [The sense is: to whom you will have to give an account in the future.—Ed.]

3* The Sage.

4* Hugo.

5* Seneca.

42

Concerning the two golden calves (1 Kgs 12) and the two beasts (Rv 13)

Lienhart Schienherr

Before 1546 [1]

Most of what we know about the author of this lyrical, almost epic poem in rhyming couplets comes from the piece he has written. From it we learn that its composer is a master of the allegorical interpretation of scripture in relation to the events of his day. His argument is blunt, while his form is subtle. His text is accompanied by glosses that underscore and expand on what is said in the poem itself. For three reasons these glosses are probably Jörg Maler's work. For one thing, Maler included Lienhart Schienherr in the final stage of binding the manuscript of the Kunstbuch, when the binding process left empty pages at the end. For another, he tells us that Schienherr is his cousin. And most importantly, Schienherr's theology, a spiritualistic form of Anabaptism, is cut from the same cloth as Maler's. On the one side, the author plays a classic Anabaptist ace concerning church discipline; on the other side, he shows his spiritualistic hand by insisting that the outward assembly of Christians and their ceremonies have nothing to do with salvation.

Lienhart Schienherr, Von den zwei goldenen Kälbern (1. Kg. 12) und den zwei Tieren (Offb. 13). Translation by Walter Klaassen.

1 BSOT, 663.

Schienherr borrows his primary set of images from the story of Judah's king Rehoboam's unfaithfulness in 1 Kings 12. In order to set up places of worship that rival Jerusalem, he erects a shrine with a golden calf at both ends of Judah, in Bethel and in Dan. A secondary set of images is taken from Revelation 13. It describes two beasts, one that arises from the sea and another that arises from the earth. The first one blasphemes God; the second one deceives the inhabitants of the earth. The poet relates each calf to a beast. The calf at Bethel and the first beast refer to the pope, while the calf at Dan and the second beast refer to Martin Luther.

Among the many errors of the pope and Luther that are noted, the outstanding one concerns worship. Their worst sins are to fix worship in immutable forms and then to impose these forms on people by force.

To conclude this book there now follows [an account] of the two golden calves and the two beasts and their interpretations set in rhyme (3 [1] Kgs 12; Rv 13).

In the third book of Kings we read,
beginning in its chapter twelve,
when Rehoboam was the king
over the folk of Israel.
After the death of Solomon[1*]
who was his father, he destroyed
his peoples' peace with tyranny.
The people then refused his rule
and ten tribes fell away from him
when he became so harsh and grim.
They chose themselves another king
who was the man Jeroboam.[2*]
With him, the son of Nebat, then
all those ten tribes now cast their lot.
King Rehoboam, we are told,
retained the loyalty of two.
But Jeroboam was afraid
that when the people in their zeal
would go up to Jerusalem
and make their sacrifice to God,
as was the custom in those days,
they would forsake him as their king.
So he devised a cunning plan.
With pleasant words he told his folk,
"No longer will you need to walk
the long way to Jerusalem.
We will erect two golden calves,
each set in an especial place,
one to be located at Bethel,[3*]

1* Gloss: Solomon means king of peace.

2* Gloss: Jeroboam means a champion of the people.

3* Gloss: Bethel means house of God. Dan means judge.

the other at the site of Dan.
These are the gods," he said to them,
"that led you out of Egypt's land."
Whoredom they practised at these shrines
and did not worship the one God.

The king's name was Jeroboam.
His deeds illustrated his name.
He was a champion of the people
with cunning and with violence.

But now, take note:
he and his calves
are likenesses of the end-time
which John the Seer saw in visions
while he was on the isle of Patmos,
but in quite different images.
He writes: "I saw a beast arise
out of the sea with vehemence.[4*]
To it were given seven heads
and, pay attention, with ten horns.
The seven heads had seven crowns,
and on his head were written names
of blasphemy used at that time.
And lo, the beast was like a leopard,
with bears' feet
and a lion's mouth.
The dragon gave to him the might
and sovereignty of his kingdom.
And then I saw one of his heads,
which had received a fatal wound.
Immediately the wound was healed.
The people on the earth at once
prayed to that terrifying dragon

4* Gloss: This beast represents the pope; the ten horns, canon statutes and many laws; and the seven crowns, the many secular powers. The dragon is the devil.

who gave the beast authority.
They said: 'No one is like the beast!'
The beast was giv'n a mouth to speak
to say great things
and to blaspheme
God the Most High,
his dwelling place, his name,
and all who live in heaven.[5*]
The beast was given leave
on earth to fight
against the saints and win.
Moreover, he was given power
over all peoples; understand!
And all who lived upon the earth
prayed to the beast without delay.
Their names were not included
in the book of life
and of the Lamb
slain from the origin of the world."[6]

The calf at Bethel and this beast
mean the same thing, you understand.

The image of the other calf
set up at Dan at that same time
was seen by John by revelation.
A beast rose up out of the earth
which acted like the Lamb of God,
and had two horns upon its head.
But when it spoke 'twas like a dragon.
The power and might
of the first beast was wielded
by this second beast.

5* Gloss: The name of God is Christ. Those who live in heaven are the Christians. The dwelling of God is the flesh of Christ, and those on earth are the earthly minded. Christ is the book of life and the Lamb.

6 Rv 13:1–8.

The whole earth and those who lived there
prayed to the beast, whose fatal wound
was healed,[7] and who worked great miracles.
It caused fire to blast from heaven[8*]
on all who dwelt upon the earth,
and caused them all to fall away,
deceived by all the miracles
which it worked before the [first] beast.
It ordered all who live
on earth to make
an image of the beast, whose wound,
inflicted by the sword,
remained with it from hour to hour.[9*]
And to that beast the power was giv'n
to fill that image with the spirit
so that it had the pow'r to speak.
And it decreed that everyone
who did not worship the image
immediately be put to death.
Moreover, to all—
the small, the great, the poor, the rich,
the free, the slave—a sign
was giv'n on hand and forehead.[10]
These were accepted by the beast
and were allowed to buy and sell[11]
and practise usury and deceit,
provided they belonged to him.

Indeed, none of them could
go wrong by going

---

7 Rv 13:12.

8* Gloss: Fire from heaven represents the Holy Spirit which it claims to have.

9* Gloss: It is said that the image of the beast is Luther's teaching and ceremonies, and that whoever does not worship them, that is, hold them for the truth, is in danger for his life, as we can plainly see. The signs are Luther's sacraments.

10 Rv 13:16.

11 Rv 13:17.

to Bethel and to Dan
so long as when they arrived there[12*]
they had their golden worship fair.[13*]
And all this, even though the Lord
had promised long before that he
would gracious to that city be,
which was Jerusalem fair and free.[14*]
There and at no other place
but in the temp'l could they find grace.

Even today in mind and spirit
the whole world thinks:
it cannot be
that the two teachings,
the papal and the Lutheran,
are not true and are not from God.
Some, burdened low with sin, will say:
"Where can I find another way,
except among the sects and rebels?
But they're forbidden in the scriptures."

To this I say without delay:
"If it were true and could be proved
that this were certainly a sect,[15]
which some have ranted that it is."
Christ was defaméd and accused
by the order of Pharisees
of being a rebel and sectarian. Lk 23 (2, 5)
These liars in Jerusalem
were found among the educated,

12* Gloss: Whoever goes to the Lutherans' sacraments and believes their preaching cannot sin, even though he deceives the whole land.

13* Gloss: The world demands gilded worship, which has renown but without the cross.

14* Gloss: Jerusalem represents heaven; the temple, Christ. Outside of this temple and Jerusalem, God will be gracious to no one.

15 [This appears to be a reference to Anabaptists.—Ed.]

who were perverted before God.
The common man did not detect
what they intended, that their claim
that Christ deceived them was no lie,
And thus they shouted long and loud Mt 27 (23); Mk 15 (14)
that he should now be crucified
to end the life of the deceiver.

The world will have one form of worship
ev'n though God is not pleased with it.
The same thing happened to the Jews
when for a king they called, right now,
without God's counsel or his will. 1 Sm 8 (5); 10 (1)
I think their king showed them the truth.
The same thing happens to the world
with its own worship, as is clear
to everyone in our own time.
It's thought that everything is truth 2 Tm 4 (3f.)
that's said now by all the preachers,
no matter whether straight or bent.
They hold to them as God himself
who helps them in the hour of death.

Listen, the golden calf at Bethel
stands richly in the house of God.[16*]
It is the pope with all his members.
He valiantly promotes the world,
because that is where he came from.
He rose up from the sea. Please note:
the sea's the world with all its lust,
with all the coarseness of its vice.
The seven-headed ponderous beast
accurately depicts the pope

[16*] Gloss: The house of God in this time is the visible gathering of believers in which the pope took his seat and expects to teach them.

and with him all the heresy
of which he is the mastermind.

But since the first beast that appeared
with bears' feet and a lion's mouth,
so mighty and so powerful
with all his orders and his law,[17]
many finally understood
with hands and feet the whole deceit,
and that not all he said was true.
But still they had not lost all hope.
That's why in that same hour it took
from the great dragon a deadly wound.
That is Luther, the other calf,
to whom all peoples on the earth
together run, for they believe
that with him they will all be saved,
because that he condemned the pope,
destroyed the Mass, and more besides.
This is important! The pope received
from Martin Luther a mortal wound.
He could not heal it by himself,
so Luther fitted him with salve;
the mixture was the German Mass.[18, 19*]
The pope received it without scorn,
since nothing better could be had,
and let Luther trot beside him.[20*]

---

17 [The various monastic orders and church canon law.—Ed.]

18 [See the text of the German Mass in *Luther's Works,* vol. 53, *Liturgy and Hymns,* ed. U. S. Leupold (Philadelphia: Fortress Press, 1965), 51–90.—Ed.]

19* Gloss: At the same time the pope also partly suffers from the sacrament.

20* Gloss: The world argues that because the devil cannot be against himself, Luther's teaching must be the truth, since it is against the pope and others. But consider the Pharisees and Sadducees, the Jews and the Turks, four sects, none of whom has the truth, but among them have no unity. The Antichrist has seven heads, because he is not one with himself. But they unite to destroy Christ (Mt 22 [15, 23]; Lk 20 [19, 27]; Mk 10 [33]).

The golden calf at Dan fits well
for Martin Luther, as you see,
and with his groups, late and early.
Now note carefully what he does,
because he is adjudicator
of all the teachings of his time.
None can do it as well as he,[21*]
and whoso will not join with him
is damned without any recourse
and exiled from his land and home.
In his actions he's like the beast
that John saw rising from the earth.
This beast was given but two horns,
as is the case with every lamb.[22]
The horns are the two testaments,
but in their literal sense alone.
He asks not for the Spirit's sense
but sends it far away from him.
To the Trinity's dishonour
he now establishes instead
just watch, another trinity,
which folk can take into their hands.
First, he imprisons God in scripture,
then into poison turns the Word
and thence into idolatry.
In scripture one can find complete
eternal life and godliness.
From it people can now receive
faith, Spirit, and what else they need.
The first god now has been explained.
The other two, take careful note,
are his two holy sacraments.

21* Gloss: Luther came on the scene a better light than the pope. He had only two horns and wanted to be seen as a lamb, which is what happened.

22 Rv 13:11.

To put it briefly, in these three
he now desires his trinity
to be described with no difference.
All his writings are proof of this.
However, he adds "invisible,"[23*]
so he'll be left alone by those
who believe only when they see.
If one should ask him "How or when?"
He says: "You fool! You needn't see
or probe or peep too carefully.
So you don't know the how or where?
Simply believe that it is so,
and you'll be saved; just trust my words."
This is the sum of his three gods.

But listen now, his beast already
many wonderful signs has done.
It causes fire to fall on earth,
by which the people are deceived.[24]
This fire denotes the Holy Ghost
whom Martin Luther promises.
To those who will believe his preaching,
the Holy Spirit he will give.
As he says often in his writings,
he who believes the spoken word[25]
receives the gentle Holy Ghost
at once through the external word.[26*]

Without the Spirit, God can't give
knowledge of faith to anyone.
Luther persuades the folk with words
all up and down the German lands:

23* Gloss: here he cites Heb 11 [1]; 12 [11:27] at the beginning.

24 Rv 13:13f.

25 [Specifically, preaching.—Ed.]

26* Gloss: This is a perfect example of putting oneself in the place of God (Mt 24 [15]; Dn 9 [27]).

as soon as they have been baptized,
if they attend the Eucharist,
and then know the Apostles' Creed
then they are good Christians indeed.[27*]
They have, he says, the Holy Ghost
and are God's very own children,
without regard for life and works,
early and late, from day to day,
without conviction in the heart
and with a burdened conscience too.
The beast now speaks just like
the dragon, beside it standing here.[28*]
Luther is hardly different
from the pope and his teaching;
as he himself confesses,
he took over everything that was good,
like scripture and sacrament, from the pope,
Luther regards all this as true.[29*]
I can't describe it all to you.

[27*] Gloss: This means that those at Berea were also manic fanatics because they tested with scripture what Paul and Silas said (Acts 17 [11]).

[28*] Gloss: Both beasts serve the dragon, that is, Satan.

[29*] Gloss: Luther in his epistle about Anabaptism.
[The above gloss refers to a passage like the following one, from 1528:
"In the first place I hear and see that such rebaptism is undertaken by some in order to spite the pope and be free of any taint of the Antichrist. In the same way the foes of the sacrament want to believe only in bread and wine, in opposition to the pope. . . . It is indeed a shaky foundation on which they can build nothing good. On that basis we would have to disown the whole of scripture and the office of the ministry, which of course we have received from the papacy. We would also have to make a new Bible. . . . We on our part confess that there is much that is Christian and good under the papacy; indeed, everything that is Christian and good is to be found there and has come to us from this source. For instance, we confess that in the papal church there are the true Holy Scriptures, true baptism, the true sacrament of the altar, the true keys of the forgiveness of sins, the true office of the ministry, the true catechism in the form of the Lord's Prayer, the Ten Commandments, and the articles of

Those who've been taught by God will see
the situation as it is,
and also how it's all unfolding.

Behold! Pope, Luther: these two beasts
both have their hired sentries at
the tomb of Christ,[30] so that the Lord,
whom both of them have crucified
with their unclean and false teaching,
will never rise and punish them
in life and limb, and then cast down
their doctrine and their worshiping.
And soon he'll vindicate his own.

Both of the beasts control the world,
which considers both to be gods.
The pope holds emperor and kings
and other rulers in his power;
they uphold him with their sword,
and divide Christians from each other.[31*]
Likewise, Luther also has
half the empire as his own.
Saxony, Hesse, and many more,
who keep to him and his doctrine.
Whoever opposes either one
is forthwith forced to leave the land.
What a Christendom it is!
And its golden worship too!
Where they ride in covered wagons
and spend their time at writing desks,
and teachers are called "gracious Lord."
Where do they chastise sin and shame

---

the creed." *Church and Ministry* 2, edited by Conrad Dergendoff, in *Luther's Works*, vol. 40 (Philadelphia: Muhlenberg Press, 1958, 231–32.)—Ed.]

30 Mt 27:65f.

31* Gloss: Pharisees, Sadducees, Papists, and Lutherans can coexist and tolerate each other. Only [true] Christians are exposed to conflict.

with the use of the Christian ban,
as the apostles practised it?[32]

O yes! It almost slipped my mind:
there are some who presume to be
in no sense less—note what I say—
in their high place than the apostles.
But in their teaching and their life
they don't resemble them at all.
Read in the book of Acts and think,[33*]
and then, unless you are stone blind,
you'll see the contrast clear enough,
and be compelled so to confess.
Were the disciples together here,
O yes, they'd be ashamed of them.
The most important among us
could not aspire in his life
to be even like the least of
all the seventy disciples.

So if they find one of these least,[34]
no exertion is too much work.
These two beasts come before Pilate
and say: "Here is a heretic.
Kill him, for he deserves to die,
if you expect our loyalty."
They find names that are known to be
the worst that could be said of him,
as also did their ancestors.
Thus none would be led to believe
that they were spilling Christian blood

---

32 [Here Schienherr gives voice to a standard Anabaptist argument.—Ed.]

33* Gloss: The man who whored with his stepmother was better than our lechers, because he repented (2 Cor 2 [6f.]).

34 [BSOT, 672, fn 2, states that this is a reference to an unnamed group of Anabaptists that Schienherr rejected. This is misleading. These lines are the introduction to the condemnation of Jesus before Pilate.—Trans.]

to keep their program safe and sound.
But Christ who is both God and Lord
will rise triumphant in his pow'r,
although the Pharisees had giv'n
their permission to guard the tomb.
Thus does the pope and also Luther
with his grim Nestorian voice.[35*, 36]

God will show mercy on the poor
who've been misled, in his own time.
With power he will wrench his sheep
from the jaws of both these monsters.

Let every person be alert
never to follow in their way.
This warning is for everyone
who seeks to pass the test of God.
Never be part of a sect that's wrong.
Satan hides in many places
appearing as an angel bright[37]
to lead astray the Christian church.
Does it make sense to expect that
at every moment God will send
to us some teaching that is true?
God does not always send his aides![38*]
How did things go without Luther?
Were none that lived
before him saved?

35* Gloss: Nestorius, like Luther, divided Christ in suffering and birth. Note the Council of Ephesus in 4[31].

36 Nestorius (d. 451) taught that there were two persons in Christ, one divine and the other human. This teaching was condemned at the Council of Ephesus in 431.

37 2 Cor 11:14.

38* Gloss: How did the children of Israel manage 430 years in Egypt and 70 in Babylon? Were they condemned for it? They didn't even have open worship (Ps 126).

May God chastise whoever dares
with insolence to say such things.
What would happen to Christendom?
And where would be the article
that we confess in common faith:
"I believe that on earth there is[39*]
a Christian church." And I believe
that she has always been on earth
since Christ ascended into heaven.
I ask you: did they always have
a gathered church that's visible?
And did they have the sacraments
regularly given them on earth?
Or did they get them from others,
perhaps even from heretics?
They could have done without them too,
because Christ's Spirit was with them,
yes, Jesus Christ, invisibly.
They are not needed for salvation,[40*]
if one is forced not to observe them.
But when there's freedom to use them,
no Christian should absent himself.[41]
It must be done with honesty,
following Christ's command, I say.
But never in a way or form
of these two beasts, so often used
in false appearance. It will cause
them all to stumble and to fall.
Whoever dares to tell them so
will get the short end of the stick.

39* Gloss: Where two or three are gathered in my name, there am I in the midst (Mt 18 [20]). The same is true of one wherever in the world he may be.

40* Gloss: Luther destroyed the images of the pope and put others in place, namely, baptism and the Lord's Supper; horrible to see.

41 [This is the gist of Schienherr's view of the ceremonies, supported by Jörg Maler's glosses.—Ed.]

He'll be condemned from the pulpit,
as though he caused sorrow and murder.
Thus they give cause to governments
to find, arrest, and punish us
and force us to believe their lies.

O God in heaven, high above,
do thou for once look down on us!
To you we all commend ourselves
here in this harsh and troublous time.
Oh, be the victor in the strife
with these two terrible monsters.
Lead us with your Spirit holy
in this dark vale, morn and eve.
This is our prayer, through your grace.

For here your justice has no place; Is 59 [8]; 4 (2) Esd 15 [6]
many good people have suffered violence,
and I'm concerned it won't end soon.
For these two beasts direct their wrath
against pious Christians,
with their devious cunning,
as they are always wont to do,
pretending that they love the gospel.
They won't neglect in days to come
in every way to hate the pious
who will proclaim to them the truth.
So also had they done to Christ,
perverted and despised his Word
and everything he had taught them,
and set themselves against him then.
It is the same now as it was.
The Christian has to hide himself
and submit to these two monsters,
who wage a war against the saints.

John writes about it in his book,[42]
as we've described it in this poem.

Lord Jesus Christ, strong conqueror,
support us now in all we do
as freely we confess your Word.
Let us walk upon your pathway,
where you have left us an example.
Thus we'll not be disqualified,
O Lord, in our most holy faith
and so escape the second death. Rv 20 [14]; etc.

Lienhart Schienherr,
Jörg Maler's cousin

O mortal, love me as I love you!
That's all that I require of you.
And you'll be blessed eternally.[43*]

---

[42] Rv 13:7.
[43*] Christ.

Scripture index

OLD TESTAMENT APOCRYPHA AND PSEUDEPIGRAPHA

Mark

Index of proper names

Area and Places of
Marpeck's
Life and Work
Erfurt
Jena
Zwickau
Bayreuth
Germany
Frankfurt
Main
Mainz
Darmstadt
Hessen
Worms
Nürnberg
Neckar
Heidelberg
Speyer
Regensburg
Bavaria
the Rhine
Karlsruhe
Ingolstadt
Danube
Stuttgart
Baden
Württemberg
Strasbourg
Rottenburg
Horb
Ulm
Augsburg
Friedberg
Alsace
München
Colmar
Villingen
Freiburg
im Breisgau
Schleitheim
Ensisheim
Radolfzell
Schaffhausen
Mulhouse
Waldshut
Constance
Hall
Basel
Baden
St. Gallen
Innsbruck
Zürich
Zollikon
Appenzell
Küssnacht
Grüningen
Kappel
Einsiedeln
Schneeberg
Luzern
Bern
Schwyz
Chur
the Rhine
Inn
Swiss
Confederation
Brixen
(Bressanone)

Poland
Dresden
Gorlitz
Chemnitz
Karlovy Vary
Prague
(Praha)
Olmutz
(Olomouc)
Marianske Lazne
Pilsen
(Plzn)
Eibenschitz
(Ivančicè)
Brunn
(Brno)
Austerlitz
(Slavkov)
Auspitz
(Hustopeče)
Bohemia
Znajim
(Znojmo)
Nikolsburg
(Mikulov)
Moravia
Budwies
(CeskeBudejovice)
Morava
Krumau
(Česky Krumlov)
Kreuzenstein
Pressburg
(Bratislava)
Passau
Vienna
Danube
Inn
Linz
Danube
Eisenstadt
Wiener Neustadt
Neusiedlersee
Chiemsee
Austria
Salzburg
Hungary
Brück an
der Mür
Szombathely
Kitzbühel
Graz
Tirol
Badgastein
N
Klagenfurt
Villach
W
E
S
For easier reference, contemporary borders are shown.